Instructor's Manual to Accompany

MARKETING

FOURTH EDITION

William G. Zikmund
OKLAHOMA STATE UNIVERSITY

Michael d'Amico
UNIVERSITY OF AKRON

West Publishing Company
MINNEAPOLIS/ST. PAUL ■ NEW YORK ■ LOS ANGELES ■ SAN FRANCISCO

WEST'S COMMITMENT TO THE ENVIRONMENT

In 1906, West Publishing Company began recycling materials left over from the production of books. This began a tradition of efficient and responsible use of resources. Today, up to 95% of our legal books and 70% of our college texts are printed on recycled, acid-free stock. West also recycles nearly 22 million pounds of scrap paper annually—the equivalent of 181,717 trees. Since the 1960s, West has devised ways to capture and recycle waste inks, solvents, oils, and vapors created in the printing process. We also recycle plastics of all kinds, wood, glass, corrugated cardboard, and batteries, and have eliminated the use of styrofoam book packaging. We at West are proud of the longevity and the scope of our commitment to our environment.

Production, Prepress, Printing and Binding by West Publishing Company.

COPYRIGHT © 1993 by   WEST PUBLISHING CO.
                        610 Opperman Drive
                        P.O. Box 64526
                        St. Paul, MN 55164–0526

ISBN 0–314–01779–8

CONTENTS

Contents (continued)

Contents (continued)

Contents (continued)

Contents (continued)

PREFACE

This **Manual** in intended to complement *MARKETING*, Fourth Edition, by William Zikmund and Michael d'Amico. It incorporates features that will be of use both to Professors who are new to the text or course and to those who are academic veterans.

The **Manual** is part of an extensive teaching package that includes an annotated instructor's edition of the book, a verified test bank in computerized and printed forms, more than 250 full-color transparency acetates, more than 300 transparency masters, advanced instruction modules, supplemental lectures, Softcraft presenter software, multimedia guide, spreadsheet applications for marketing, instructor's course planning guide, the Marketing Plan Project manual, student earning guide, Microstudy version of the student learning guide, mass lecture section manual, computer exercises, and video cassettes and discs. The videos include video cases and Focus on Small Business videocases. In addition, discussion videos include the international series, the ethics series, the total quality management series, the company lecture support series, and the small business series. The text itself has been redesigned and includes much new material, as well as new cases, end-of-chapter questions, and ethics exercises in each chapter.

In this manual each chapter is presented in the following format.

1. A **Chapter Scan** begins each chapter. In a few paragraphs it recalls the focus of the chapter.
2. **Suggested Learning Objectives** associated with the chapter are listed.
3. A **Chapter Outline** lists the headings and sub-headings of the chapter, providing a quick view of the chapter.
4. The Chapter Outline concludes with a list of the **Key Terms** used in the chapter.
5. In a section titled **The Chapter Summarized**, the chapter is outlined in considerable detail. This follows the same format as the Chapter Outline mentioned above. In this section, key terms used for the first time in the text are in bold print.
6. Each Chapter Summarized concludes with a summary statement of the chapter, and a presentation of the chapter Learning Objectives as shown in the text. Each is followed, as in the text, with a summary statement of what was learned, showing that the Objective was achieved.
7. **Answer Guidelines** to the end-of-chapter **Questions for Discussion** are then provided.
8. The **Ethics Exercise** for the chapter is then presented, beginning with a summary of the short ethics case, then a discussion of the issues raised by the case.
9. The second portion of the Ethics Exercise, **Take A Stand Questions**, includes the questions raised in the text and responses to them.
10. There follows the **Guide to Cases**, in which each of the chapter's cases is summarized and discussed. The discussion includes responses to the case questions offered in the text.

We are certain that you will find this manual, and the rest of the materials that accompany *MARKETING* to be of use as you structure and teach your course. Thank you for considering *MARKETING*, edition four.

The authors wish their special appreciation to **Geoffrey P. Lantos**, whose thorough work on the Ethics Exercises adds much to this Manual.

The authors also thank **Faye Gilbert** who prepared answers for the Discussion Questions.

A special "thank you" to **Patricia Johnson**, who has done masses of word-processing through all four editions of Marketing.

1 THE NATURE OF MARKETING

CHAPTER SCAN

This chapter introduces marketing as a force in society and business. It defines marketing and the marketing mix and shows that marketing is an exchange process that is carried out in not-for-profit as well as business dealings. This exchange process is performed by organizations, such as industrial marketers, that may not be familiar to students. This chapter introduces the difference between consumer and organizational marketing.

Chapter 1 also describes the marketing concept as a business philosophy that, when properly applied, is the basis of all effective marketing. Accent is placed on the need for an integrated marketing effort. The management principle of Total Quality Management (TQM) is discussed.

The impact of external forces on the marketing organization is addressed, and the interplay between society's needs and those of the organization is acknowledged in a description of the societal marketing concept. Stress is placed on marketing's role as a creator of economic utility.

The chapter concludes with the reasons why the study of marketing is important to students, including non-marketing majors.

SUGGESTED LEARNING OBJECTIVES

The student who studies this chapter will be exposed to a broad introduction of marketing and will be able to:

1.   Understand how marketing affects our daily lives.

2.   Define marketing and discuss marketing in its "broadened" sense.

3.   Identify the elements of the marketing mix.

4.   Understand that marketers must contend with external environmental forces.

5.   Explain the marketing concept.

6.   Explain Total Quality Management.

7.   Recognize how marketing creates economic utility and understand the contribution of marketing to the economy and our way of life.

8.   Define the societal marketing concept.

CHAPTER OUTLINE

I.   INTRODUCTION

II.   MARKETING AFFECTS OUR DAILY LIVES

III. MARKETING: WHAT IS IT?

IV.   NOT-FOR-PROFIT ORGANIZATIONS ARE MARKETERS TOO

V.   A DEFINITION OF MARKETING

VI.   THE MARKETING MIX

    A.   The First Element: Product
    B.   The Second Element: Place
    C.   The Third Element: Price
    D.   The Fourth Element: Promotion
    E.   The Art of Blending the Elements

VII. THE MARKETING ENVIRONMENT: COPING WITH THE UNCONTROLLABLE

VIII. MODERN MARKETERS USE THE MARKETING CONCEPT

    A.   Production Orientation: "As Long as It's Black"
    B.   Sales Orientation: "Changing Their Minds"
    C.   The Marketing Concept: The Foundation of a Marketing Orientation

        1.   Consumer Orientation
        2.   Long-Term Profitability

    D.   Integrated Marketing Effort

IX.   TOTAL QUALITY MANAGEMENT (TQM)

X.   MARKETING AND SOCIETY

    A.   Economic Utility: Satisfying Consumer Needs
    B.   The Societal Marketing Concept

XI.   WHY STUDY MARKETING?

XII. SUMMARY

XIII. KEY TERMS

XIV. QUESTIONS FOR DISCUSSION (16)

XV.   ETHICS IN PRACTICE

XVI. CASES

    The following key terms are introduced and used in Chapter 1. They are defined in the text's Glossary.

Exchange process
Marketing
Market
Marketing mix
Four Ps of marketing
Controllable variables
Product
Place (distribution)
Industrial buyer
Channel of Distribution
Manufacturer
Wholesaler

Retailer
Ultimate consumer
Facilitator
Price
Promotion
Uncontrollable variables
Product orientation
Sales orientation
Marketing orientation
Marketing concept
Total quality management
Macromarketing
Economic utility
Form utility
Place utility
Time utility
Possession utility
Societal marketing concept

THE CHAPTER SUMMARIZED

I.   INTRODUCTION

The chapter opens with a discussion of The Body Shop, a British retailer now expanding in the U.S. market. The store stresses "natural" products and concern for the environment, e.g., shampoo bottles are returnable. The Body Shop is "ethical" and reflects the concerns of at least some of today's consumers.

II. MARKETING AFFECTS OUR DAILY LIVES

The discussion focuses on the pervasiveness of marketing in our lives and the importance of marketing institutions, even the less familiar organizations. Familiar and not-so-familiar corporate logos are shown in Exhibits 1-1 and 1-2.

III. MARKETING: WHAT IS IT?

Marketing may be defined in several ways.

.   In terms of "going to the market."

.   In terms of functions like selling or advertising.

More fully, marketing brings buyers and sellers together, consummates a sale, and satisfies a customer.

Marketing involves finding out what buyers want and developing products that fit those needs before other steps, such as production, are undertaken.

Example: Tyco produced the Incredible Crash Dummies (based on U.S. Department of Transportation advertisements, see Exhibit 1-3), a toy that illustrates the importance of wearing auto seat belts. After discussing the idea with adults and children, they realized that kids want fun and adults want lessons about safety to be taught. Each group has different needs. Result: A popular toy that attracts kids but also teaches a lesson.

IV. NOT-FOR-PROFIT ORGANIZATIONS ARE MARKETERS TOO

The Heart Association and other nonprofit groups, including police departments, antismoking groups, and churches, all engage in marketing activities. The characteristic common to all these situations is an exchange relationship.

The **exchange process** requires that two or more parties exchange or trade something of value.

This definition fits many, if not most, situations, permitting them to be viewed from a marketing perspective. (See Exhibit 1-4.)

V.   A DEFINITION OF MARKETING

The American Marketing Association defines marketing as follows.

Marketing is the process of planning and executing the conception, pricing, promotion, and distribution of ideas, goods, and services to create exchanges that will satisfy individual and organizational objectives.

Note that each party to the exchange gains something; revenues satisfy the marketer and products satisfy the buyer.

The American Marketing Association's definition of marketing embodies this principle.

The term "market" can be confusing since it is used in so many ways -- fish market, stock market, supermarket, Greater Houston Metropolitan Market. But each term suggests the presence of people or organizations with resources they are able and willing to exchange for something else.

A **market** is a group of potential customers for a particular product who are willing and able to spend money or exchange other resources to obtain the product.

VI. THE MARKETING MIX

The performance of marketing requires that many interdependent activities be performed. A wide choice of activities is usually available to the marketer, who must select which variables to include in the "marketing mix."

The **marketing mix** is the result of management's efforts to creatively combine interrelated and interdependent marketing activities to achieve organizational objectives.

The marketing manager must select and combine the "ingredients" (the **four Ps of marketing**) of the organization's marketing mix. The mix must be reformulated as environments change. The marketing mix of any organization is made up of four major parts or submixes as listed below. These are the marketing manager's **controllable variables.**

A.   The First Element: Product

The **product** is what the business or nonprofit organization offers to its prospective customers or clients. It may be a tangible good, a service, or an idea.

Buyers generally expect more of a product than just a "thing." Thus, a Xerox machine "includes" repair service, advice, and other customer services. This phenomenon is referred to by the term "total product." The Chairman of the Crayola Company has stated that Crayons are not "just Crayons" but are "fun products used to inspire creative self-expression."

Product strategy includes selecting brand names, packaging, warranties, service plans, etc.

Product-related marketing strategies must be consistent with the other elements of the marketing mix.

B.   The Second Element: Place

Place or **distribution** strategy focuses on how products get to customers, how quickly, and in what condition.

Transportation, storage, and the like are physical distribution or "P.D." activities.

Organizations may choose to specialize in production and/or promotion, or other activities, and leave distribution to "specialists" such as wholesalers and retailers. Most soft drink and beer makers do this. This is construction of a channel of distribution.

A **channel of distribution** is the complete sequence of marketing organizations involved in bringing a product from the producer to the consumer.

Its purpose is to make it possible to transfer ownership and/or possession of the product.

Example:

Manufacturer --> Wholesaler --> Retailer --> Consumer

The relationships between these channel members as each contributes to the satisfaction of a need is shown in Exhibit 1-5.

1.   Some definitions:

The **manufacturer** is the organization that recognizes a consumer need and produces a product from raw materials, component parts, or labor, to satisfy that need.

The **wholesaler** is an organization that serves as an intermediary between manufacturer and retailer to facilitate the transfer of products or the exchange of title to those products, or an organization that sells to manufacturers or institutions that use the product for ultimate resale (perhaps in another product form).

The **retailer** is an organization that sells products obtained from a manufacturer or wholesaler to the ultimate consumer.

The **ultimate consumer** is an individual who buys or uses the product for personal consumption.

The **industrial buyer** is an organization that purchases a product that it will use to produce another good or service that it will use in operating its business.

Note that some organizations perform more than one function, as when a local bakery produces products and retails them.

Some marketing organizations may assist the operation of a channel of distribution but not be a part of it. These are facilitating agents or **facilitators**: advertising agents, transportation companies, financial institutions, etc. They are not included in the definition of a channel of distribution.

C.   The Third Element: Price

The amount of money, or goods, or services, given in exchange for something is its **price**.

Just as a customer buys a product with money, so the producer "buys" the customer's money with the product.

Prices are always "on trial" in a marketplace. They are subject to change largely because price is usually the easiest aspect of the marketing mix (product, price, place, promotion) to change, though poorly planned changes can be disastrous.

In not-for-profit situations, price may be expressed as votes, donations, volunteer time, etc.

D.   The Fourth Element: Promotion

Promotion is communication, the means by which marketers "talk" to existing customers and potential buyers.

Promotion communicates information about the other elements of the marketing mix, such as uses for the product, prices charged, and/or places the product can be bought.

Advertising, personal selling, publicity, and sales promotion are all forms of promotion and are discussed in Chapters 17, 18, and 19. Individual organizations employ these tools differently in assembling their promotional mixes.

E.   The Art of Blending the Elements

The marketing manager's task has been compared with that of a chef. There is no "one best" marketing mix, just as there is no "one best" dinner. Both marketing manager and chef use their artistic and scientific abilities, along with information, to create a combination of ingredients to fit a given situation.

Marketing's ever-changing environment requires that marketing be "dynamic," constantly altering its approaches to the marketplace.

The many blending alternatives are illustrated by examples in Exhibit 1-6 in the text.

VII.   THE MARKETING ENVIRONMENT: COPING WITH THE UNCONTROLLABLE

All organizations operate within environments. Since managers cannot govern external forces, except in rare instances, they are termed **uncontrollable variables**. The influences of these variables are illustrated in Exhibit 1-7.

These variables are usually closely interrelated. For example, inflation may cause the Post Office to raise the price of stamps. This affects businesses that rely on mass mailings, the sale of products advertised in those mailings, and the number of Christmas cards the public is willing to buy after the stamp price increase.

Organizations may be viewed as surrounded by these uncontrollable variables. They have the four Ps (controllable, though influenced by the environment) as tools to achieve their objectives.

VIII. MODERN MARKETERS USE THE MARKETING CONCEPT

An organization's level of marketing sophistication is often reflected in the general principles underlying the way it conducts its activities. Is it marketing-oriented in its philosophy of business, or oriented towards production or sales?

A.   Production Orientation: "As Long as It's Black"

Some organizations have faced a sellers' market and could survive following a "production concept" rather than the marketing concept. This philosophy focuses on production and stresses technology. **Product orientation** is epitomized by Henry Ford's statement about the model Ts he offered, "You can have any color you want as long as it's black."

B.   Sales Orientation: Changing Their Minds

Many organizations stress pushy, hard-sell techniques in an effort to drum up business. Giveaways, contests, and other attempts to increase short-run sales characterize this approach. (It is found

especially in extremely bad economic times, e.g., the depths of the
Great Depression, 1929-1933.)

Sales orientation emphasizes short-run increases in sales volume of
existing products rather than long-term profits.

C.   The Marketing Concept: The Foundation of a Marketing Orientation

Many business people have come to understand that today's better-
educated, more sophisticated customers will not buy "almost anything"
(production era) or succumb to hard-sell gimmicks (sales era.) They
have a **marketing orientation**. This philosophy is the **marketing
concept**.

Exhibit 1-8 in the text illustrates these changes.

1.   Consumer Orientation

In the marketing era, the consumer is seen as the focus of all
an organization's activities. The answer to most questions
ranging from production to pricing and distribution becomes
"what the customer wants" rather than "what the organization
wants to do."

Though many organizations are true adopters of the marketing
concept, many are not or have failed to implement it properly.
In a sense, the consumerism movement represents a backlash
against firms that have not adopted the marketing concept. The
consumerism movement and the work of activists like Ralph Nader
serve as indicators that some firms have not developed a
consumer orientation.

2.   Long-Term Profitability

The marketing concept stresses customer satisfaction, but
within reason. Products cannot be given away, neither can the
organization "nail" customers with exorbitant prices. Both
steps would be inconsistent with the goal of the marketing
concept: long-range survival through achievement of long-term
profits.

Buyers would like to have Mercedes-Benz autos for $500, and
some customers might want to make a mess in a museum that would
have to be cleaned up. Catering to these desires would be
disastrous for the organizations' long-term profits.

D.   Integrated Marketing Effort

Marketing managers do not work in a vacuum. Anything they do affects
other parts of their organizations. The marketing concept's
prescription for success is an integrated effort among all to the
divisions of a customer-oriented organization.

Such an integrated effort may not be forthcoming because of
conflicts, e.g., the manufacturing division may desire to produce a
simple or inexpensive-to-make product while marketing is promising
buyers complex and/or high-quality products.

IX.   TOTAL QUALITY MANAGEMENT (TQM)

The management principle of **total quality management** (TMQ) involves
instilling the idea of consumer-driven quality throughout the organization
and managing all employees so that there will be continuous quality
improvement. Clearly this idea is much like the marketing concept itself.

Ford advertises that "Quality is Job 1." Production of good cars is
important here, but so are customer-satisfying marketing operations. TQM's
goals will be met if all the organization's systems work together to
achieve them.

X.   MARKETING AND SOCIETY

Marketing should be considered from the point of view of its role in society. The consideration of marketing as an aggregate or as a force in society is called **macromarketing**.

Marketing clearly affects our lives and society. In a sense, it "delivers a standard of living" to society.

Trade with other countries is a type of marketing. In some cases, the poverty of some lands may be blamed on their marketing systems' inability to "deliver" an improved quality of life.

A.   Economic Utility: Satisfying Consumer Needs

A profit or nonprofit organization performs its role in society (and survives) only if it provides economic utility for its customers.

Economic utility is the ability of a product to satisfy a want or need.

Some products satisfy more needs and wants than others.
Exhibit 1-9 portrays an array of products and their hypothetical relative economic utilities.

Greater Economic Utility:

. Water
. Pizza
. Beer
. Electricity

Lesser Economic Utility:

. Old bottle caps
. Old newspapers
. Parsnips
. Lawn trimmings

Economic utility is composed of several specific types of utilities.

1.   **Form Utility:** Transforming raw materials into finished goods that satisfy buyer needs creates form utility. Production and marketing work together to do this.

2.   **Place Utility:** Bringing a Pepsi-Cola from the bottling plant to the home refrigerator creates place utility.

3.   **Time Utility:** Storing turkeys to make them available at Thanksgiving and maintaining 24-hour banking machines create time utility.

4.   **Possession Utility:** For most, a house that can be owned now, via credit arrangements, is more useful than a house that will be available only after years of saving.

Note: Some authors also identify "information utility" to explain the place of promotion. Example: a good or service which is located due to an advertisement is more useful than a product that is never located because the potential buyer did not know where to obtain it.

Provision of these utilities is marketing's justification for existence in society.

B.   The Societal Marketing Concept

The recognition of marketing's important role in society has led some to refine the marketing concept, which stresses satisfying customer needs at a profit.

The **societal marketing concept** requires that marketers consider the collective needs of society as well as individual consumer's desires and the organization's need for profits.

The use of recycled products, the removal of chemicals from products, and the lowering of fat content in foods, are all examples of this. Note that the societal idea is not inconsistent with the "original" marketing concept.

XI.   WHY STUDY MARKETING?

One reason to study marketing is that the field offers many career opportunities. (At the end of the book there is a Career Opportunities appendix.) Even students not planning a career in marketing will work in an organization that does some kind of marketing, or will start their own businesses. In both cases, marketing knowledge is of real use. Indeed, in job hunting students have to "market" themselves to employers and others. Lastly, knowledge of how marketing works in our society and its importance globally is part of being an educated person.

XII. SUMMARY

In this chapter, we saw that the function of marketing is to bring buyers and sellers together and that marketing primarily involves an exchange process requiring that two or more parties trade things of value.

Learning Objective 1: Understand how marketing affects our daily lives.

Virtually everyone sees or hears advertisements, goes to stores, uses products manufactured thousands of miles away, and in other ways participates in activities influenced by the marketing process. Marketing makes these activities possible and allows us to consume products essential to our way of life.

Marketing brings buyers and sellers together by directing the flow of goods and services from producer to consumer. Marketing activities are basic to the operation of all organizations. They satisfy consumer needs.

Learning Objective 2: Define marketing and discuss marketing in its broadened sense.

Marketing is the process of planning and executing the conception, pricing, promotion, and distribution of ideas, goods, and services to create exchanges that satisfy individual and organizational objectives.

Effective marketing consists of a consumer-oriented mix of business activities planned and implemented by a marketer to facilitate an exchange so that both parties profit in some way. Consumers may exchange money, votes, blood, or something else to obtain the marketer's offering.

Learning Objective 3: Identify the elements of the marketing mix.

The marketing mix consists of four major elements: product, price, place (distribution,) and promotion. These are basic to any organization and are adjusted and combined by the marketing manager to achieve the organization's goals.

Learning Objective 4: Understand that marketers must contend with external environmental forces.

The marketing environment consists of uncontrollable forces that influence consumer behavior and provide both opportunities and constraints to an organization. The marketing manager's task is to adjust an organization's marketing mix to cope with the external environment. This involves anticipating the environmental changes that will affect the organization. Correct environmental assessment makes marketing decisions more successful.

Learning Objective 5:   Explain the marketing concept.

Scholars and businesspeople have developed the marketing concept as a philosophy of business and a set of objectives for organizations to pursue. According to this, organizations can succeed by focusing on consumers' wants and needs, long-term profitability, and an integrated marketing effort. Product orientation and sales orientation are less effective alternative philosophies.

Learning Objective 6:   Explain Total Quality Management (TQM).

Total quality management requires the instilling of the idea of customer-driven quality throughout the organization and managing all employees so that there will be a continuous quality improvement and that this improvement will be the top priority.

Learning Objective 7:   Recognize how marketing creates economic utility and understand the contribution of marketing to the economy and our way of life.

Marketing includes designing, distributing, storing, and scheduling the sale of products and informing buyers about them. It thus helps to create form utility, and creates place, time, and possession utility. By creating economic utility, marketing delivers a standard of living to society.

Learning Objective 8:   Define the societal marketing concept.

The societal marketing concept requires that marketers consider the collective needs of society as well as individual consumers' desires and the organization's need for profits.

XIII. KEY TERMS

XIV. QUESTIONS FOR DISCUSSION (16)

XV.   ETHICS IN PRACTICE

XVI.   CASES

ANSWER GUIDELINES FOR CHAPTER 1 QUESTIONS FOR DISCUSSION

1.   *Think about what you did this morning. In what ways did marketing affect your activities?*

ANSWER:

To stimulate discussion of the impact of marketing, students may be asked specific questions as they consider products they consumed or chose as apparel for the day; prices paid; promotion they have seen; or stores they visited or called. For example: How many of you patronized a fast-food restaurant for breakfast this morning? Was the packaging recyclable as a result of the marketing of "green" issues? How many of you are wearing a specific brand of athletic shoe? Was your choice influenced by the advertised image of the product? How many of you brushed your teeth today? Did you consider cavity prevention or whiter teeth in your choice of a toothpaste? Did you listen to the radio or watch a morning news program today? What advertisements do you recall? Will you write a check today for a purchase? How important was convenience in your selection of a bank for your checking account?

2.   *Define marketing in your own words.*

ANSWER:

Answers to this will, of course, vary. If the question is posed to students before the chapter is studied, the answers may stress marketing activities and functions: advertising, pricing, distribution, and so on. Such responses do serve, however, to help students focus on the vast array of marketing activities performed within the economy and lead to a better grasp of its importance.

A more desirable answer to this question would accent the role of marketing activities as these pertain to product development and the jobs to be accomplished as a product moves from producer to consumer. Such an answer better reflects a grasp of "marketing as exchange," though mention of interpreting consumer wants before products are developed and produced should be made.

The text states: "Effective marketing requires the conception and development of goods, services or ideas so they may be brought to market and purchased by buyers."

Relating this, or any other definition, is only a first step in understanding a concept. This, or any other definition, can be dissected. Subquestions are suggested:

(a)   What business activities?

(b)   Can marketing be done by someone who is not the "marketer" mentioned in the definition?

(c)   What kinds of things can be exchanged?

(d)   What is required for both parties to "profit in some way"?

In mid-1985 the American Marketing Association announced a new "official" definition of marketing:

> Marketing is the process of planning and executing the conception, pricing, promotion, and distribution of ideas, goods, and services to create exchanges that satisfy individual and organizational objectives.

This "official definition" can be analyzed to emphasize such terms as "conception" and "individual and organizational objectives."

3.   *If marketing activities involve exchange, what isn't a marketing activity?*

ANSWER:

This is a question that has been widely and inconclusively debated. The longer one looks at marketing, it seems, the more it appears that "everything" is marketing since virtually "everything" involves an exchange of some sort. Does, for example, exchange take place when a robber "exchanges" his victim's life for the victim's wallet?

Some possible factors that may eliminate, in some peoples' minds, certain activities from inclusion as marketing include:

.   The presence of force or absence of "free will," as in the robber example.

.   The intent of the "marketer" or even the "customer" to mislead or wrong the other party.

.   The absence of a true business relationship. Some authors claim that any nonbusiness "marketing" is not marketing at all.

.   The absence of an exchange of money.

.   The absence of a profit motive.

.   Love and affection. That is, an exchange of gifts with a friend may not be marketing.

It does seem that almost any situation can be made to appear a marketing transaction. At minimum, probably forcible "exchange," illegal activities, and intention to mislead an exchange partner would eliminate an activity from inclusion in a list of marketing activities.

The key criterion is "Did both parties benefit ... were they satisfied?"

4.   *Do lawyers, accountants, and doctors need marketing?*

ANSWER:

Despite their traditional avoidance of the appearance of "selling" their services, these professionals have always engaged in marketing of a sort.   In recent years they have become increasingly conscious of their need for effective marketing.

The "instant" medical care facilities, with names like "First Care," that have sprung up in recent years are perfect examples of a "breakthrough to marketing." Most newspapers include advertisements for these professionals.   A dentist in Akron, Ohio gives away certificates for restaurant dinners with each set of dentures purchased, and offers T-shirts to all new customers.   Most CPA partners will admit that the greatest part of their jobs is dealing with customers (marketing) while other accountants in the firm do the "real work" in the organization.   Still, the CPAs may not want to term themselves "salespeople" or "marketers."

Marketing for professionals goes beyond promotion, however.   Attention should be drawn to the other variables of the marketing mix.

Product	Quality of product offered, items in the product mix (some dentists do root canal work, others don't), and level of personal concern expressed for clients.
Price	Legal clinics are especially good at using the price variable to attract customers, such as free initial consultations and price discounts for certain services (simple wills, uncontested divorces).
Place	This variable is often the most difficult for students to grasp in this context. Some examples of its use will help: location of offices downtown or in malls, use of branch offices, willingness to visit clients at their own homes or offices, the hours services are available (being open on weekends or at night.) Some doctors do make house calls, some dentists drive vans equipped as mobile offices and visit their patients' homes to give treatment, and some barbers and beauticians go to hospitals and homes for the elderly.

5.   *Identify some goods, services, or ideas that are marketed by not-for-profit organizations or organizations that are not traditional businesses.*

ANSWER:

Students should be able to derive several examples.   As an aid in generating ideas, consider the following:

(a)   National Parks market their services and facilities in exchange for funds to improve the parks.

(b)   The local "Garden Club" markets beautification of the town as it promotes sales of flowers and landscape materials.

(c)   The local "food bank" must market its services both the people who need nutritional supplements and the donors of food items.

(d)   The Humane Society and local animal shelters must market unwanted pets for potential families, educational materials for humane treatment of all animals, and information to donors who provide funds to continue operations.

(e)   Colleges and universities market an image and set of classes for traditional students as well as nontraditional students.

(f)   Local churches create special functions for young singles, especially in college towns, to market religious involvement during the college years.

6.   *What are the elements of the marketing mix?*

ANSWER:

The term marketing mix describes the result of management's efforts to creatively combine many interrelated and interdependent activities which are meant to encourage exchanges. The four basic categories of elements in the marketing mix include: product, place (distribution), price, and promotion.

(a)   Product refers to a tangible or an intangible offering by a business for prospective customers or clients. The "total product" includes the basic good or service as well as extras such as courteous service, on-time performance and warranties.

(b)   Place, or distribution, decisions determine how goods get to the customer and includes physical distribution (transportation, storage, materials handling) as well as the selection of a channel of distribution (wholesalers, retailers or other intermediaries) to move goods and transfer of title from producers to consumers.

(c)   Price refers to the amount of money, or sometimes goods or services, given in exchange for something. In not-for-profit situations, price may be expressed in terms of volunteered time or effort, votes or donations.

(d)   Promotion is the means by which marketers "talk to" or communicate with existing customers and potential buyers. Promotion elements include advertising, personal selling, publicity and sales promotion.

7.   *Describe the marketing mix for (a) McDonald's, (b) your local zoo, (c) an antiair-pollution group, and (d) the Xerox Corporation.*

ANSWER:

The key here is to be sure students discuss all four "Ps" of marketing. It would be easy for a student to think, for example, that a zoo has an established location (place) and that there is nothing further to discuss on that point.

(a)   McDonald's

       Product: Food products for breakfast, lunch, supper, and snacks. Beef, chicken, fish, and egg products to cater to a variety of tastes. Also, drinks and desserts. Within bounds, these products are varied to fit customer tastes: "no pickle" or "no ketchup." The "total product" also includes such things as playgrounds in some locations, gift certificates, coloring books, souvenir glasses, birthday parties, balloons, etc.

       Place: Location of each outlet is important here, but so are such things as availability of parking, ease of entry, store hours, attractiveness, cleanliness of the building, and so on.

       Price: Prices are low at McDonald's, but vary to fit customer groups. Adults eat bigger food items, therefore, these items have higher prices than the hamburger or cheeseburger favored by small children. There is no tipping at McDonald's, a "price" factor. Parking, when available, is free. Coupons, though promotional in nature, are price-related.

       Promotion: Coupons, TV and other advertisements, appearances by Ronald McDonald or other "celebrities" at stores, signs, and the easily recognizable appearance of a McDonald's location.

       Mix: Attention should be drawn to how the marketing mix is varied to appeal to particular customer groups. Some TV ads are clearly aimed at children, others at adults. The same is true of prices, food items, even locations, e.g., providing bike racks as well as car parking spaces.

(b)   Local zoo

       Product: Entertainment, education, a way to pass time, a place to take children, a place to eat lunch or to picnic, the opportunity to feed or pet some animals, rides (such as a train that tours the zoo,) the park atmosphere (many zoos have carousels or other entertainments,) the chance to walk around out-of-doors, and the chance to "support a local institution of value."

Place: Location of main zoo, parking spaces, open hours, provision for parking of school or tour buses. Also, animals displayed at fairs, in schools, and in shopping centers. Some zoos "rent" animals, such as ponies, for children's parties.

Price: Admission charge and its variations such as "off-hour" reductions, "free days" to special groups, discounts to special groups, parking charges, donations, and tax dollars.

Promotion: Publicity in local media, advertising, T-shirts, "Adopt-an-Animal" plans, signs, maps, "talking displays" that describe the animals and their habits, special "days," e.g., mothers get free admission on Mother's Day.

Mix: As with McDonald's, the mix changes with the group appealed to.

Note: It would be interesting to explore the zoo's appeal to other target markets. For example, what does the zoo do for the high school students who may provide volunteer labor to the zoo?

(c)   An antiair-pollution group

Product: A belief that the issue is important: better health, a cleaner environment, proposed clean-air laws, better enforcement of existing laws, and probably, related environmental matters such as conservation of animals and flora. Such a group may also offer pamphlets speakers, buttons, T-shirts, and perhaps membership in a group and a monthly magazine or newsletter.

Place: Locations of meetings, provision of speakers, willingness to travel, use of mail or other means to spread the message, a booth at a shopping mall, a "reading room" or office to disseminate information.

Price: Membership dues, time of volunteer workers, variable dues charges (e.g., "Sustaining Member," "Charter Member," "Junior Member," etc.). Any fees associated with publications, speakers, etc.

Promotion: Signs and ad media messages, displays in malls, schools, and libraries, ads in the organization's own publication, T-shirts, special events like a "March for Cleaner Air," protest picketing of smokey factory locations.

Mix: Again, these variables are manipulated to fit given target markets, e.g., old supporters, new members, people who are worried about pollution vs. those who are not.

(d)   The Xerox Corporation

Product: For convenience sake, the discussion could be limited to Xerox's photocopier line. These products are quality items, come in a great number of models, and many models are "adjustable" by means of add-on features. Xerox's good reputation is certainly part of its product as is its sales force, repair services, auxiliary products like paper, the sense the buyer gets of having "the best," and the feeling that the Xerox Corporation will "be there" if something goes wrong with the machine.

Place: Xerox products are sold directly by the company. This is consistent with the quality of the product and the image the company wishes to maintain. In a sense, wholesalers and other distributors are not "good enough" to be trusted to deal with Xerox products, products that require great product knowledge and a high level of concern. Of course, a giant like Xerox can afford its own distribution system and this is an advantage in the competitive copier field.

Price: Xerox products are generally premium-priced. This fits the fine reputation for quality products. Yet the product line does, to a degree, offer something for "everybody." Further, billing arrangements, leasing agreements, and other such variables all have implications for the price variable.

Promotion: Advertising is heavily used to support the major element of the promotion mix, a high-quality personal sales force. Xerox's good reputation is also supported by generally good publicity. Xerox has traded on this in their ads showing that competitors sell their own products with the phrase "this is as good as a Xerox."

Mix: Xerox varies its marketing mix widely by customer type. Some customers are immense (e.g., the Federal Government); others are small (e.g., a dentist's office.) A good exercise would be to discuss how the marketing mix would vary among such disparate customer groups.

8.   *The marketing concept is profit-oriented. What kinds of profit does it stress? How does this apply to nonprofit organizations?*

ANSWER:

The marketing concept is not intended to be a charitable or "good guy" notion. It is based on the reality that profit, in some form, must be made if an organization is to be able to continue to provide the goods and/or services necessary to please its customers. BUT, the concept assumes that the organization is not "crooked" and intends to remain in operation. In this, the organization should seek long-term profits.

Some organizations may not seek this sort of profit. They may attempt to maximize short-term profits, as do fly-by-night home repair companies that "rip off" gullible homeowners and disappear from town. This is not marketing; this is essentially criminal activity.

Marketing concept-based organizations do not charge excessive prices in an attempt to maximize short-term profits. If they do, they run the risk of loss of customer loyalty, government action, and other undesirable results.

There may be times when customer interests can appear to be sacrificed to the notion of long-term profits, as when an auto maker drops a model of car that is achieving less-than-acceptable profit levels even though it is still popular with some buyers. The concept does not say that the car maker must keep every buyer happy at the risk of doing lasting damage to the finances of the organization.

These examples have counterparts in the not-for-profit field. Nonprofit marketers effect exchanges as do profit-seeking organizations, though price may not always be expressed in dollars. As in the profit-oriented examples above, the nonprofit organization cannot always provide its services "for free" (unpaid by the client, the government, a private donor, or someone else), or it will simply go broke and cease to exist. Like an auto maker, the nonprofit organization will find it hard to justify satisfying every possible client. While nonprofit marketers do often operate differently from profit-oriented organizations, their expenses must be met one way or another if they are to continue to exist and provide benefits to society.

A point may also be made that while profit-making organizations seek to increase their profits, nonprofits (usually) try to operate in a more bare-bones mode. For example, the offices of the local Goodwill Industries director are usually Spartan, even though the organization's budget can be tens of millions of dollars per year. Such organizations seek to save money or get more out of the money they spend as a sign that they are efficient and thus avoid giving the impression of spending donated money on frills.

The more they save the better they are doing. For a profit-oriented company the more they make the better they are doing. These are, in a sense, two sides of the same coin.

9.   *What organizations in your college town have not yet adopted the marketing era?*

ANSWER:

There are many possible answers to this and local examples may be particularly obvious to some students. They may wish to consider, however, whether a local "nonmarketer" is as bad as it may first appear to be. A nasty fellow who runs a local garage may be a pain to deal with but "he sure can fix cars ... and cheap, too." The fellow's marketing mix may need improvement but, it can be asked, is he as bad a marketer as it first appears?

Some possible organizations which have been slow to enter the marketing era are:

.   Banks, the telephone company, other utilities. The common point of reference here is their regulated or recently deregulated status.

.   Some professionals: lawyers, doctors, CPAs.

.   Many not-for-profit organizations.

.   Small, or even large, technically oriented firms. Some of Chrysler's pre-Iaccoca problems have been attributed to a concern with engineering rather than a concern with consumers. American car companies as a group have been accused of having been money oriented rather than consumer oriented, thereby falling prey to the Japanese car makers.

.   Firms with "captive markets," e.g., retailers in small college towns, the "official" campus bookstore, cable companies, and the food service in the dormitories.

10.   *How might a firm such as Pillsbury conduct its business as: (a) a production-oriented, (b) a sales-oriented, and (c) a marketing-oriented company?*

ANSWER:

While the answer to this question could be extrapolated from the text's examples and exhibits, the opportunity to introduce students to a classic marketing article is presented here. Robert Keith's "The Marketing Revolution" (*Journal of Marketing*, January, 1960, pp. 35-38) is cited in the text and in virtually every discussion of the marketing concept. In it, Keith traces Pillsbury's evolution from a (1) flour milling company to a (2) sales-oriented firm to a (3) marketing organization embodying the ideas expressed in the marketing concept. We recognize that it has become common to play down Keith's three eras as being too simplistic, but the article does contain a good deal of worth.

The Keith article is not too difficult for new students of marketing to read and it is both short and valuable. One of its values to students is as an example of a contribution to the "marketing literature" by a nonprofessor, that is, by a "real world" person. Also of interest is how such (to the modern eye) "obvious" ideas were once seen as "new." More recently, Keith's "three stages" have been under attack as not being truly representative of historical reality, however, they are still widely adhered to, and, in any event, do make a useful point.

11.   *Given the existence of the marketing concept, why do so many products fail? Why are consumer groups still displeased with many products and companies?*

ANSWER:

Some of the reasons that products fail and consumers are displeased are almost unrelated to the marketing concept. A firm like Procter & Gamble can spend fortunes on product development, marketing research, and hiring top marketing managers and still have product failures (or produce dangerous products) simply because marketing is not an exact science. The environment of marketing (consumer tastes, the economy, competition) shifts so rapidly that even the best planned marketing efforts can fail. The Edsel is perhaps the greatest historic example of this, New Coke is a more recent case, but smaller disasters occur with frequency, marketing concept or not.

The question suggests discussion of the fact that some firms do not follow the marketing concept -- they are production or sales oriented, or follow some other approach to business. In short, there are organizations that have not adopted the marketing concept. There are firms, too, that "don't care," or are attempting to make a fast buck. Marketing concept or not, such firms will produce poor, even dangerous, products. Lastly, some organizations claim to follow the marketing concept but do a bad job in living up to its goals. This may be due to a shortage of resources, simple lack of ability, or failure to work hard enough to succeed. The concept is a powerful one, but if it is not implemented properly it cannot, of itself, ensure product success and a happy public.

Peter Drucker, overstating for emphasis, once wrote that consumerism is the "shame" of the marketing concept. There is some truth to this, though there will always be unreasonable "nuts" who will never be satisfied. If every organization truly adopted the concept and if all were able to implement it fully, product failures and consumer complaints would be greatly diminished, if not eliminated. It is this author's opinion that in a dynamic environment "total success" can never be achieved.

12.   *How can an organization's management prove that it has adopted the marketing concept?*

ANSWER:

Various managements have tried to prove their adoption of the marketing concept by citing organization charts incorporating "marketing era" organizational principles, or pointing to higher profits, greater sales, more customers served, fewer letters of complaint, and so on.

These things may indicate that the company is trying to implement the marketing concept, or that it is pleasing its customers. They do not prove adoption of the concept. This is because the marketing concept is a way of thinking about businesses, it is a "school of thought" or a "philosophy." It is, in effect, a mental state. No evidence can prove the adoption of a philosophy or way of thinking. The "proofs" offered by some managers are, at best, helpful indicators, but not proof.

13.   *A zoo designer begins work by asking, "In what sort of landscape would I want to observe this animal?" Discuss this approach to design in terms of the marketing concept.*

ANSWER:

This question is based on a statement by Grant Jones, an architect invited by the City of Seattle to design a new gorilla house at the Woodland Park zoo. Instead of making a tour of other gorilla exhibits around the country, Jones consulted gorilla experts about how gorillas live in the wild. He determined that he would like to see gorillas in several aspects. "I would want to include mystery and discovery. I'd like to see the gorillas from a distance first, then up close. I'd like to be able to intrude on them and see what's going on without them knowing I'm there. I'd want to give them flight distance, a place to back off and feel secure. And I would want an experience that would take me back to a primordial depth myself. How did I spend my day some millions of years ago, living in proximity to this animal?"

Jones came up with a gorilla house like no other, with large trees (Seattle is in a temperate rain forest belt,) rocks, and other natural "decor." He hired rock climbers to try to "escape" from the area, though it developed that gorillas were able to escape the area because they had the motivation the rock climbers lacked.

The success of the gorilla house in Seattle has made it famous in zoo circles. Zoos have moved from a "bare cage" way of exhibiting animals to trying to let viewers see the animals as they really are. This is termed "landscape-immersion design". It intentionally breaks down the visitors' sense of security, reminding them that wild animals are really wild.

This story is told at length in "No Rms, Jungle Vu," by Melissa Greene, *Atlantic Monthly*, December 1987, pp. 62-78.

It would appear that whether or not the zoo designer in the question is following the tenets of the marketing concept is not a yes/no matter. Note that designer Jones consulted gorilla experts, not zoo-goer experts. He did no consumer research. In this case, this was all to the good as most zoo-goers would not be able to articulate (or even know) their desires in this area. The result was a wonderful gorilla house that is extremely popular with the public, even though the design was developed by an architect who started with the question, "How would I want to view gorillas?" What was actually meant, one imagines, was "How would people like to see these animals?" In this sense, the zoo designer did follow the tenets of the marketing concept.

14.   *Can a small business embrace the marketing concept philosophy as discussed in this chapter?*

ANSWER:

The answer is of course! The discussion may focus on different aspects of small business to encourage students to apply concepts to local establishments as well as international conglomerates.

For example, asking students to brainstorm examples of different levels of service and quality in local small businesses should result in a range of approaches to the marketing concept, from: a) embracing the concept and striving to satisfy consumer needs; to b) manipulating customers, seeking the fast buck or failing to care about the safety of their employees or customers. Students may also consider examples of production orientation or sales orientation exhibited by small businesses.

Some students may perceive that a small business "satisfies everyone" in town. While this may be true of a one-grocery-store town, given any competition students can usually be encouraged to supply a demographic description of the "target customers" for the store and an example of implementation of the marketing concept in the store's approach to this target. For example, in one town, mostly elderly consumers patronize the Piggly Wiggly where employees assist patrons to their automobiles; students buy from Kroger where employees hold groceries at the front so patrons can "drive-up" to load; and local economizers (and professors?) shop at the discount stores and load the groceries themselves.

Many small business owners operate without computers or access to data bases. Yet, when you talk to some of these owners about their customers, they can describe the needs of segments within the town. Some owners may track inventory by a daily visible inspection of the shelves rather than through written records or computerized re-ordering systems. Lack of sophistication may not mean they are ignoring the marketing concept.

Advisors with the Small Business Administration and the Small Business Development Center stress the critical importance for small businesses to understand their market, its environment, and changing customer needs. Since small businesses may be marginally staffed, marketing research or planning may be the most tempting task to neglect yet one of the most critical for long-term survival. Small businesses can and must implement the marketing concept through continuing education.

15.   *What role does marketing play in society?*

ANSWER:

The old statement that "marketing delivers a standard of living" is another way of stating that "marketing delivers the American way of life." While these statements sound a bit grandiose or best suited to a marketing pep rally or booster club meeting, they are true, as some reflection will show. Where did each of us get our food and clothing? Almost all of it from stores or some other marketing institution. Even if we make our own clothes, we probably got the cloth and needles from some supplier, that is, from some marketer. Chances are we bought our houses through real estate agents, our cars from car dealers, and our educations from "suppliers" who were paid tuition or were supported by our tax dollars.

In short, virtually all the material goods we possess, rent, or use are provided us by the marketing system. The text also makes the point that, to some degree, the standard of living in less-developed countries can be said to be delivered by their marketing systems. Some authors have gone so far as to state that good marketing could "cure" the economic woes of these poorer lands.

The current economic problems within Russia, the Ukraine and other countries of the former U.S.S.R. also emphasize the role of marketing in facilitating exchanges throughout a society in an efficient and effective manner.

16.   *What is the societal marketing concept?*

ANSWER:

As stated in the text, the societal marketing concept requires that marketers consider the collective needs of society as well as individual consumer desires and organizational profits. Organizations that subscribe to the societal marketing concept attempt to be socially responsible as they consider the ethical consequences of how their actions might affect the interests of others.

When firms take a long-term view of their business then socially responsible actions enhance customer satisfaction and are thus in harmony with the marketing concept. The Body Shop example at the beginning of the chapter emphasizes the donation of a part of the profits to environmental campaigns such as the Amazon rain forest. Balancing short-term oriented customer desires with long-term consequences to society requires businesses to reconcile conflicting goals.

ETHICS EXERCISE 1

CHAPTER 1 ETHICS IN PRACTICE

Overview

       Chapter 1 of the text has no "Ethics in Practice" questions since ethics are not discussed until Chapter 2. That each of the remaining chapters includes an Ethics in Practice section, each of these incorporating Take-A-Stand Questions and an Ethics Exercise is noted in the text. What follows is some additional background material on business ethics (some of which might be incorporated into lecture notes) as well as some suggestions on leading ethics discussions.

What are Ethics and Business Ethics?

       Ethics can be defined as the study of morality, i.e., standards that determine what is right and wrong, good and evil, helpful or harmful, acceptable or unacceptable. It is the name given to the attempt to think through the moral implications of human actions. Ethics is concerned with any situation where there is actual or potential harm to any individual or group from a particular course of action.

       Business ethics can be defined as the study of morality as it applies to business decisions. Business ethics aims at developing reasonable moral standards for business. Each functional area of business has its own ethical principles. For instance, marketing ethics is the study of the morality of marketing decisions and the determination of reasonable standards for those decisions.

       There are two types of ethical situations. Ethical lapses occur when there is a breach of common morality (moral common sense) which involves universal principles we can all agree on (e.g., deceptive advertising is a breach of honesty in advertising). More challenging to analyze are moral dilemmas which involve hard choices between alternative courses of action where the rightness or wrongness of the alternatives is not immediately obvious. They are not merely a simple choice between obvious right or wrong (e.g., is lying justified to save someone's life?).

Methods for Leading Discussions of Ethics[1]

Organizing Issues

It should always be kept in mind that the aim in discussions of ethical issues is to lead students to become more competent at resolving moral dilemmas. Several points should be kept in mind throughout:

1.   Interaction is best. Moral development occurs when students try to resolve issues and are challenged by peers and the professor.

2.   The professor shouldn't just lecture on ethics. Better to use a questioning strategy, i.e., the Socratic method.

3.   It is debatable whether or not the professor should introduce value judgements. Some people say the professor should not in order to better equip students to develop critical thinking skills. To reveal one's own ethics would constitute "indoctrination" and "proselytizing." The result may then be that students give answers just to please the professor.

The goal is to get students to think. Some people argue that such an approach encourages thinking but not morality because there is no closure. If the instructor can't see to it that the class draws some conclusions (leading them, if necessary) this subtly teaches that nothing is really right. Students must come away with at least a knowledge of good (although this doesn't necessitate a commitment to good, which must come from the heart as well as the head.)

Three Levels of Analysis

There are three levels of aggregation for analyzing the impact of ethical decisions. First is the systemic (macroenvironmental) level, i.e., the general environment. Concern is with the ethical rightness or wrongness of the system itself and the impact of ethical decisions on societal institutions (e.g., the law, societal values, the media, and especially questions of justice or equity within the social order). Examples of such value judgments would be statements such as "Government regulation stifles free markets" and "Comparative advertising provides consumers with useful information."

Second is the corporate level at which either the firm is the unit of analysis and/or the effects of the firm's decisions on other elements of its microenvironment/operating environment are studied. Within the organization, considerations include the impact of a decision on employees, labor unions, the salary structure and incentive systems, company policy, etc. In the operating environment, parties affected include suppliers, distributors, customers, competitors, and the local community.

Third is the individual level, at which the effects on individual persons must be considered. The individual reviews his own value system in trying to answer such questions as, "Should I blow the whistle on Joe for stealing tools from the company?" and "Should I pay a bribe?" The individual struggles in attempting to resolve the clash between individual values and corporate and/or societal values.

Most ethics cases require analysis at all three levels of aggregation since most ethical decisions have an impact at all three levels.

Who is Affected? Stakeholder Theory

A stakeholder (or the public) is defined as anyone affected by the firm's actions, including its ethical decisions, as well as anyone who can have an impact on the firm, e.g., the media, consumer advocacy groups, etc. These stakeholders exist at all three levels of analysis:

---

[1] The author of this section, Geoff Lantos, is indebted to Arthur Anderson & Co., S.C. for most of the ideas in this section.

1.   systemic stakeholders - the image of business, government, citizens, etc.

2.   corporate stakeholders - stockholders, employees, labor unions, suppliers, distributors, etc.

3.   individual stakeholders - superiors, subordinates, peers, family, etc.

In summary, the ethical analyst should first determine the levels of analysis to use (usually all three) and then figure out which stakeholders will be affected at each level of analysis.

Ethical Theories

Two Ethical World Views

There are two general approaches to ethics, i.e., two ethical philosophies or worldviews: relativism (a.k.a. situation ethics, some use the word "situational" or the term "speculative philosophy") and absolutism (a.k.a. moral idealism).

Relativism. Using relative standards, one denies that there are absolute answers to ethical quandaries which hold true in all instances. Rather, the correctness of a particular action depends on the situation. Morals are relative to the individual (e.g., "you must do what's right for you"), the situation (e.g., theft is justified if you cannot earn a living wage and meet your expenses), and society (e.g., community standards used in obscenity trials). In other words, "there are absolutely no absolutes" and "the only thing that is absolute is that nothing is absolute."

Absolutism. Absolutism, on the other hand, is concerned with the morality of the act itself or means, not with the consequences or other circumstantial factors. It judges the act on the basis of moral ideals or absolute universal standards ("traditional values") which hold true over time, place, and person. These permanent, immutable, rigid rules are to be followed regardless of the circumstances, i.e., there are certain behaviors that are plain right and wrong, good and evil. Moral law is as unchangeable as the law of gravity.

Analysis of relativism. Relativism has some advantages to recommend it. It provides pragmatic, expedient solutions to moral problems, not idealistic, unworkable platitudes. It leads to statements such as, "bribes are the only way to do business abroad." Another plus for relativism is its flexibility and ability to adapt to changing circumstances. Also, this approach is considered "nonjudgmental" or tolerant.

However, situation ethics has some serious shortcomings. It can lead to inconsistencies since analysis is done on a case-by-case basis. Thus, it can result in perceptions of decisions being unfair or arbitrary. Additionally, relativism often means no consensus; seldom will there be agreement among all concerned parties that you have made a morally correct decision. Because the different ethical approaches sometimes support different alternatives, the result can be moral anarchy. For instance, one person thinks puffery in advertising is okay but another does not. Who is to say which is correct? It is one opinion against another. The result is uncertainty.

Analysis of absolutism. Absolutism, on the other hand, offers much more certainty than relativism. The beauty of absolutes lies in their simplicity. We don't need fancy jargon, esoteric theories, complex formulae, and the like. Also, it is easier to judge actions than motives, net gain to society, and other relativistic yardsticks. Furthermore, moral absolutes have been time-tested and have been proven to consistently work. History teaches that societies crumble when they jettison traditional values (e.g., ancient Israel, Greece and Rome.) Additionally, absolutes tend to be impartial and thus just. Everyone's behavior, whether prince or pauper, is judged by the same standards.

However, there are some perceived and real problems with an absolute approach to ethics. Perhaps the greatest difficulty is the fact that gray areas still abound; reasonable people can differ on how to interpret a given principle.

Even devout Christians disagree on the morality of such issues as dancing, playing card games, drinking alcoholic beverages, listening to rock music, attending R- or even PG-rated movies, and the like. When faced with such less than clear-cut issues, the wise aphorism probably is "When in doubt, don't." Another objection to absolutes is that they are too rigid and inflexible. They do not bend or adapt to extenuating circumstances. Closely related is the charge that holding only to traditional values is "narrow-minded." Then there is the taunt that traditional values are "Neanderthal" -- out of tune with the times. Absolutists respond that some things in life are not to be manipulated or adjusted. This is understood in mathematics, science, and other intellectual disciplines, yet it is often denied regarding standards for human behavior.

A final (and probably the most important) sticking point with absolutes is disagreement on the source of the standards. Who is the ultimate authority? Some might turn to the law. However, some laws are immoral or at least controversial (e.g., abortion, capital punishment, legalized prostitution and gambling). The law merely provides a floor or moral minimum for business conduct. Laws are sometimes inconsistent, both over time (e.g., abortion laws) and place (e.g., state and local laws vary greatly).

Cultural relativists suggest relying on societal standards. Cultures vary widely, and what is moral depends on the culture. . However, cultural diversity does not necessarily mean that both parties are right, because logically we cannot have conflicting truths.

Natural law provides another basis for absolute standards - an act is morally wrong if it is incompatible with human nature. For instance, this would forbid drunkenness (leads to sickness, vile behavior, etc.) and "casual sex" (sexually transmitted diseases are not "casual" things).

Other possible sources of values include parental standards, the educational system, and the workplace. Whereas these are all manmade value systems, another source of values is found in traditional religion. (Of course, one could raise the question "Whose religion?") Fortunately, there are common moral values in all religious traditions which most members of society share. Dostoyevsky said that if there is no God then all is permissible. Right and wrong become matters of personal preference.

Five Ethical Theories

Work in the field of normative ethics in this century has evolved from three basic kinds of moral theories. Each approach uses different kinds of criteria to evaluate the ethics of human behavior. They are utilitarian theory, the theory of rights, and the theory of justice or fairness. There will also be discussions on the more simplistic approaches of ethical egoism and intuitionism. By and large, these approaches are all relativistic in nature (except when rights and justice approaches adhere to absolute standards of rights and justice.) Egoism and utilitarianism use teleological frameworks, i.e., they look at the consequences of a particular act. Rights and justice theories use teleological frameworks, i.e., they focus on duties, rights, and justice.

Intuitionism. The intuitionist judges the actor's motives or intentions. The decision is correct if the individual's conscience says that it is right. As long as one feels that one's motives are good (i.e., "sincere") and one does not intend to harm anyone, then all is well. It is the "what's right for me" value system.

Although intuitionism is simple to implement, often experience-based, and presumably allows one to sleep at night, there are some problems. First, a person can be well-meaning but misguided, sincere but sincerely wrong. ("The road to hell is paved with good intentions.") Second, this approach does not incorporate others' views. Third, it is difficult to justify intuitive decisions. Scientific, analytical decision making is preferred to relying on slippery, squishy feelings, especially in business. Finally, it is difficult to judge another person's motives.

Ethical egoism. This approach says that people should promote their own self interests, seeking the most good (consequences) for themselves. An act is right if it gives one more pleasure than pain. The only advantage to egoism is that it benefits the individual. Problems are that it is hedonistic and selfish, ignores other stakeholders, and therefore invites regulation.

Utilitarian theory.   Utilitarianism looks at the consequences of an act to determine its moral worth. The idea is to act so as to produce the greatest good for the greatest number (rather than just the good of the individual or of the firm). If the consequences of an action result in a net increase in society's well-being or welfare (or at least not a decrease), then an act is considered to be morally right. For instance, at the systemic level, squandering of societal resources would be considered bad, since it is an inefficient means. At the corporate level, it would be unethical to sell Product A to a customer if Product B gives greater utility per dollar spent.

The procedure utilitarian decision makers are required to use is: (1) identify relevant stakeholders; (2) identify alternative strategies; (3) estimate costs and benefits of each alternative for each stakeholder; and (4) select the best option (i.e., the one that produces the greatest good for the greatest number).

There are several advantages to the utilitarian approach. Most people end up satisfied and better off; it uses rational, objective analysis (vs. intuition) and yields quantifiable results; it is goal-oriented (therefore managers feel comfortable using it and it is easy to justify to others); and it encourages efficiency and productivity.

However, there are some serious shortcomings to the utilitarian model. First, there is a tendency to neglect long-run outcomes and measure only short-term consequences. Thus, unintended, unanticipated long-run consequences are not accounted for. For instance, marketing cigarettes or junk food can yield ultimate negative results. Second, minorities often suffer the "tyranny of the majority," i.e., someone or some group gets stung when the majority rules, resulting in an unjust allocation of resources and/or in individuals being deprived of their rights. For example, in the "bad old days" many marketing efforts were targeted toward WASPs while largely ignoring ethnic minorities. Third, using utilitarianism can be a calculative nightmare. It can take much time and effort to make calculations and forecasts for many different stakeholders. Although it is usually a pretty straightforward matter to measure costs since these are tangible items, intangible benefits are more problematic to quantify and measure. Fourth, a desirable end might be caused by an unjust means or a bad motive. In effect, utilitarianism is akin to saying that the ends justify the means. For instance, if the student's end is to get good grades so as to land a good job and the means is to cheat ... fine.

Theory of Rights. The theory of rights mandates that any individual has the right to be treated in ways that ensure the dignity, respect, and autonomy of that individual. The focus is on fundamental human/personal rights, given as birthrights, such as freedom, health, privacy, safety, property, etc. It is respect for these rights which should guide decision making. The rights of individuals take precedence over the rights of organizations and institutions. The theory is duty-based; we judge the actor's fulfillment of duties/obligations to other individuals in the exchange process. The arguments for rights are twofold: (1) it is necessary for individuals to have self-respect and (2) rights support freedom and well-being.

One variation on rights theory is the Golden Rule model, with its foundation in the Bible. This states that one should choose the action which treats others with the same dignity and respect that one would want for oneself (costs or consequences are only of secondary importance). Thus, an action is morally appropriate if it treats all stakeholders with the same respect and dignity one would expect from others.

Two basic categories of rights can be identified. Liberty rights suggest that people should be free from restriction or control. An individual should have the right to act, believe, or express herself/himself. Basic liberty rights include privacy, free speech, freedom of conscience, and free consent. Second are welfare rights, which include health, happiness, and general well-being, which assert a right to a minimum standard of living. Specifically, welfare rights include employment, food, housing, and education.

Today, more businesses, acting as "good corporate citizens," are paying more attention to these and are helping to meet some community needs (e.g., McDonald's Ronald McDonald houses). The concept of duties or obligations means that for every right that someone has, there is a duty of someone else to respect that right. Regarding liberty rights, the duty is simply not to interfere. With respect to welfare rights, the duty is to provide what is needed (e.g., employment).

The procedure that rights theorists are required to use is: (1) identify all relevant stakeholders; (2) determine all of each stakeholder's rights; (3) figure out management's duties to the various stakeholders; and (4) prioritize the duties.

Rights theory has certain advantages. It is relatively simple; acts are rejected when they victimize just one person (vs. making utilitarian calculations involving many people); it assures minimal levels of satisfaction for all individuals (vs. some suffering the tyranny of the majority); and it can lead to certainty if absolute rules/principles are followed in determining rights.

However, rights theory is not without problems. There might arise conflicts among rights of competing individuals or groups (e.g., to balance the rights of smokers to smoke against the rights of nonsmokers to breathe clean air?). Consequently, there is the sometimes difficult task of prioritizing duties. Another problem is that rights theory can encourage individualistic, selfish behavior when people scream about "my rights." Finally, rights theory can lead to suboptimal consequences if personal prerogatives set an obstacle to productivity and efficiency.

Theory of justice. The theory of justice or fairness holds that equity, fairness, and impartiality should guide decision making. Justice arises from fairness in the distribution of benefits and burdens in society. Individuals who are similar in the relevant respects should be treated similarly, and persons who differ in a relevant respect should be treated differently in proportion to the differences between them. For instance, if Jack and Jill each hold the same job, have the same skills, equal experience, etc., and Jack is paid twice as much as Jill, this is an unjust situation if gender is an irrelevant characteristic. Bribery can be considered unjust in that it unfairly favors the bribe payer. Relevant attributes and characteristics on which differential treatment is based must have a clear relationship to goals and tasks. For instance, price discrimination is illegal except where price differences to different buyers are cost-justified. Large industrial accounts receive quantity discounts which small firms do not get.

Thus, an action is morally correct if it treats all stakeholders the same except where there are sound reasons for giving different treatment to different individuals. Fair administration should occur both within the organization (e.g., a bonus plan for the sales force should be available to all salespeople) and outside the organization (e.g., performance-based discounts should be equally available to all distributors). Norms of compensation/restitution exist for injuries or harm. Individuals should be compensated for their losses by the party responsible for those losses. Examples include monetary compensation for damage done and media make-goods for advertisements which do not run as scheduled.

In general, the advantages of fairness approaches to ethics include the fact that it ensures that a "fair" allocation of resources (however one defines "fair") is democratic in that it does not allow a society to become status- or class-conscious, and protects interests of minorities.

However, it is difficult to apply justice criteria (e.g., determining the criteria upon which differential treatment is based). Justice can encourage a sense of entitlement that reduces risk/innovation/productivity as well as diminished incentives to produce goods and services. It can result in curtailing some peoples' rights to achieve canons of justice. Affirmative action, for instance, has been labeled by some as "reverse discrimination." Also, conflicts arise among different claims of justice (e.g., seniority vs. merit; market values vs. other criteria in determining compensation).

Implementation Issues

Two problems arise in trying to apply the various theoretical moral philosophies. One is lack of information by the decision maker (e.g. intangible consequences for utilitarian decision making.) The second is the decision maker's lack of ability to employ the criteria (e.g., if not permitted to or is pressured by supervisors.)

Seven-Step Model

A seven-step model has been developed by ethicists working in conjunction with Arthur Anderson & Co., S.C. It can be used by a person confronted with an ethical dilemma and in analyzing cases using the case method. It consists of seven questions:

1. What are the relevant facts? The decision maker must be able to clarify/distinguish facts and assumptions in the situation.

2. What are the ethical issues? Critical ethical issues, i.e., possible violations of moral standards, need to be defined at all three levels of analysis.

3. Who are the primary stakeholders? Rather than coming up with an exhaustive list of individuals or groups which might be affected by a decision, key persons and groups should be identified.

4. What are the possible alternatives? The possible courses of action should be creatively identified without regard to their ethical impact.

5. What are the ethics of the alternatives? The three theories should be applied to determine how each alternative affects all stakeholders and which alternatives offer an acceptable moral solution.

6. What are the practical constraints? Factors which might limit the decision maker's ability to implement an alternative, such as ignorance or lack of ability, should be identified.

7. What actions should be taken? This includes selection and implementation of an alternative, along with justification.

GUIDE TO CASES

VIDEO CASE 1-1   FEDERAL EXPRESS (A)

FEDERAL EXPRESS - SETTING THE PACE FOR THE 1990s

SUBJECT MATTER: Marketing Concept, Marketing Mix, Environment

Please see the Guide to Video Cases for video length and other information.

AT-A-GLANCE OVERVIEW

Every night of the workweek, more than a million overnight packages arrive at Federal Express' hub in Memphis, Tennessee, and then depart on jet airplanes to locations throughout the world.

The idea for the Federal Express operation (Fed Ex) began as a term paper at Yale University. Frederick W. Smith formulated and developed the idea for an overnight package-delivery service to receive credit for an assigned paper in an economics course. Smith's paper discussed the idea of a hub-and-spoke system for package delivery. Eventually, Smith founded Federal Express based on the idea in his term paper. (The story has it that he received a passing grade on the paper only because the professor admired his creativity. The professor thought the idea itself would not work.) After a few years, the company revolutionized overnight package delivery. One reason for the company's rapid growth in the

1970s was its focus on customer satisfaction. It recognized that fast reliable service was extremely important to anyone who was receiving a package or document. Its television advertising with the slogan "When it absolutely, positively, has to be there overnight" creatively expressed the notion that with Federal Express customers could be confident their packages would "be there" by 10:30 in the morning.

As time passed, U.P.S., the U.S. Postal Service, DHL, and other Federal Express competitors began offering similar services, often at lower prices than Federal Express. Furthermore, in the 1980s and 1990s, competition from facsimile machines (FAX) arose as faxing became a common activity in many businesses.

This video tape describes the innovative nature of the Federal Express company. It explains the nature of the service Federal Express offers and discusses how Fed Ex has "changed the way America does business." This video is extremely useful to illustrate a complete marketing mix (especially when used in conjunction with the segment showing many of FedEx's television commercials from 1979 to 1989.)

This tape provides the professor with the opportunity to discuss the marketing concept and marketing myopia.

DISCUSSION QUESTIONS

1.   *What do customers get in exchange for the money they pay Federal Express?*

Federal Express offers a delivery service. However, Fed Ex clearly provides more than this. It might be said that Federal Express's product consists of a group of airplanes and a group of dedicated pilots that fly in the dark of night, penetrating weather systems and maintaining flight schedules to deliver packages. However, what Federal Express really sells in on-time reliability. It markets risk reduction and provides the confidence that people shipping packages will be "Absolutely, positively, certain their packages will be there by 10:30 in the morning."

Notice the material near the end of the video. The video shows examples of how Federal Express sells much more than reliable delivery. Federal Express designs tracking and inventory management systems for many large companies. In other words, its customers buy more than just delivery service. They buy a solution to their distribution problems. In another example, a warehouse designed and operated by Federal Express is part of the distribution center for a very large computer firm. In other organizations, customers can place an order for inventory as late as midnight and the marketer, because of Federal Express's help, can guarantee delivery by the next morning. Federal Express has positioned itself in the thick of today's distribution revolution as a company that solves its customers' problems. In the video, it is mentioned that Fed Ex is setting a pace for the 1990s and bringing the power of Federal Express to serve business in ways never dreamed. These people are not myopic about the nature of their business.

Federal Express's product is the service it provides. It is also its guarantee, its brand name, the packaging it offers for customer use, the delivery and check-in personnel's uniforms, etc.

People are part of its service/product. One important ingredient is the public's image of a group of dedicated pilots. Their mission, flown in the dark of night, penetrating weather systems and maintaining flight schedules calculated to the second, would place unprecedented demands on these men and women who serve Federal Express customers. To ensure the highest standards of safety and on-time reliability Federal Express created its own flight training center. These pilots had to be proficient, able to utilize the advanced avionic systems aboard the Federal Express all-weather aircraft. Equally as important as the flight operation was a unique ground-support network.

To specifically answer the question "What do customers get in exchange for the money they pay Federal Express?" the video allows the instructor to point to two specific customers shown in the video and indicate that they got solutions to

their problems. It can be shown that marketing produces customer satisfaction.
The customers attest to this.

Customer: In the mail-order business, overnight delivery has become the
rule, not the exception and Federal Express has become a
valuable partner in our operations. They installed this
computerized shipping station - all the power of the COSMOS
computer system right here on my desk. It's our direct link to
the Federal Express network where I can track the location of
any package that's just left and tomorrow morning find out the
name of the person who signed for it - even what time they
received it. Really unbelievable.

Customer: In the fashion industry, competition couldn't be tougher and
the old routing of ordering inventory six months in advance
just doesn't cut it any more. Time is everything in this
business. That's why we closed a lot of our warehouses. Now
we can ship from our overseas manufacturers to this central
warehouse and on to our retailers in just 72 hours. They might
call it a tracking system - I call it an inventory management
system.

2.   *Based on what you know about Federal Express, describe the elements of its
marketing mix.*

Product

This question overlaps with the question about what is exchanged. The answer is
discussed above.

Distribution

This is an interesting matter. Federal Express uses a channel of distribution
that is direct. In other words, they sell their service direct to their
customers. There are no wholesalers or retailers. For other companies, that is,
Fed Ex customers, Federal Express is a facilitator. Federal Express is not a
member of its customer's channel of distribution.

A concept that is now familiar to many students who fly into commercial airline
hub cities is hub-and-spoke marketing. In Federal Express's operation, as with a
wheel, there is a hub or center and all the spokes (routes) go to the hub. The
hub-and-spoke transportation system pioneered by Federal Express uses Memphis,
Tennessee. The video says it is being copied by every air express company.
Federal Express engineers designed and built their own special airline terminal
called "The Super Hub." It serves as the nerve center of this highly innovative
network, where shipments from around the world come to be sorted and sent to
their destination cities. Unlike the nation's passenger terminals that transfer
only 150,000 passengers in an entire day, Federal Express transfers more than one
million packages between connecting flights in less than three hours every
evening. Fed Ex has expanded this network to stretch around the globe which
includes international hub centers in Los Angeles, Chicago, Indianapolis, London,
Brussels and the Far East.

The video explains that everyone was enthusiastic with the super hub when it
first opened. It operated just as planned. But one of the company's system
analysts was curious about increasing the efficiency of operation even further.
So he took a look at the docking sequence, the order in which nearly 100 planes
taxi in and out of these gates every night. He took the initiative and built a
computer model of the hub operation. After running a computer simulation
hundreds of times, fellow employees were all surprised to find out that by simply
changing the launch order on three gates, the company was able to speed up the
departure of out-bound flights by 23 seconds.

Price

The answer to this question is not highlighted in the video tape. However, the
professor can ask students whether they think Federal Express charges a premium
over their competitors. Though competitors are imitating the hub-and-spoke

system, Federal Express remains highly competitive (although priced slightly above many other competitors).

Promotion

Federal Express uses a sales force and telephone "order takers" who perform many selling functions. The Federal Express video shows that the Federal Express name (and logo) is on its trucks, its airplanes, its packaging, its employee uniforms and almost everywhere a customer comes into contact with the company. The Federal Express name is placed prominently on all letterhead and other company communications.

The Federal Express commercials are often highly creative. However, when Fed Ex first started out, its price was low, and this was the theme of their advertising.

Most Federal Express ads are creative and innovative. The message that the advertising communicates is the importance of reliable shipping to its business customers.

3.   *Has Federal Express adopted the marketing concept?*

The answer to this question is clearly yes. As mentioned in the case, one reason for the company's rapid growth in the 1970s was its focus on customer satisfaction. It recognized that fast, reliable service was extremely important to anyone who was receiving a package or document. Its television advertising with the slogan "When it absolutely, positively, has to be there overnight" creatively expressed the notion that with Federal Express customers could be confident their packages would "be there" by 10:30 in the morning.

4.   *What environmental factors influence Federal Express? How can a marketing-oriented organization adapt to change?*

The two major factors illustrated in the video are technology and the weather. Federal Express has pioneered many new applications of computer technology to refine their own service. For example, even though the company has a customer call volume that surpasses many of today's airlines, vital information from all reaches of its distribution network can be accessed in seconds through the Federal Express computer system called COSMOS. Federal Express technicians monitor the COSMOS system around the clock. The top priority is to maintain full customer service without a moment's interruption.

At the Federal Express weather command center, meteorologists monitor live satellite pictures of weather systems all around the world. Their early warning alerts provide critical information to flight systems control. They have the option of scrambling "hot spares" - the emergency fleet of back-up aircraft. These hot spares, strategically stationed throughout the world, stand at the ready during all flight operations and can be launched on a moments notice whenever, wherever assistance is needed. Federal Express pilots are trained to use the most advanced avionics possible (simulator). Space age instruments allow them to electronically see a runway in the most limited visibility permitted by the FAA. The task of maintaining this sophisticated fleet of aircraft is entrusted to the company's own highly trained aircraft mechanics, and with a vast reserve of spare parts kept at critical points of this world-wide operation, these skilled mechanics ensure the highest level of dependability and safety for hundreds of flights each day.

Throughout the Federal Express network, people are constantly exploring new applications of technology to improve all levels of operation.

The Fed Ex fleet of courier vans is equipped with the latest in data transfer terminals - computers that talk to other computers. It is faster than a two-way radio system where drivers have to write down what the dispatcher said. The enhanced system allows Federal Express to track every customer's package anywhere within the system. Routing codes for each shipment (information) are entered with a hand-held "super-tracker" at every pick-up and delivery and automatically relayed to main center. This allows the company to know exact load volume, the number of packages that require special handling, and how many couriers it will take to deliver all this the next morning.

VIDEO CASE 1-2 TEXAS DEPARTMENT OF TRANSPORTATION

"DON'T MESS WITH TEXAS"

SUBJECT MATTER: Exchange, Marketing Concept, Not-for-Profit Marketing

Please see the Guide to Video Cases for video length and other information.

AT-A-GLANCE OVERVIEW

In the 1960s, 1970s, and 1980s, the population of Texas grew at unprecedented rates. And with the population growth, the state's highways and cities' problems with litter grew. The careless disposal of beverage containers became a particular problem. By 1985, the cost of litter along the state's highways amounted to more than 20 million dollars.

The Texas Department of Transportation determined that a marketing effort to educate the people of Texas concerning the detrimental effects of littering was in order. It believed that every citizen needed to be reminded or persuaded not to litter. Furthermore, it wanted to be proactive and encourage citizens to become active in the antilitter effort. In 1985, it was decided that a full-blown public education program should be established. It was decided that researching public opinions about litter, sponsoring antilitter and cleanup programs, creating antilitter materials, and advertising in the mass media were among the many possibilities facing the Department.

The video tape shows several television commercials from the "Don't Mess with Texas" promotional campaign.

DISCUSSION QUESTIONS

1.   *Can a state agency such as the Texas Department of Transportation implement the marketing concept? Who are its consumers? What benefits do they seek?*

Effective marketing requires the conception and development of goods, services, or ideas so they may be brought to market and purchased by buyers. Pricing, promotion, and distribution of these goods, services, or ideas facilitates the basic function of bringing marketers (suppliers) together with consumers (buyers). Each party must gain something -- revenues satisfy the marketer's objectives, products satisfy the consumers' needs.

Scholars and businesspeople have developed the marketing concept as a philosophy of business and a set of objectives for organizations to pursue. According to this, organizations can succeed by focusing on consumers' wants and needs, long-term profitability, and an integrated marketing effort. Product orientation and sales orientation are less effective alternative philosophies.

Organizations, which have adopted the marketing concept, realize that the organization must see itself not as producing goods and services but as "buying customers, as doing the things that will make people want to do business with it." The organization must be consumer-oriented.

In the case of the Texas Department of Transportation, the citizens of Texas are its consumers. They support the government because it does the things that a government is supposed to do. Citizens expect government to help maintain and improve their quality of life. In exchange they pay taxes, volunteer their time, and vote. However, low taxes is a major benefit that most citizens desire. Being consumer-oriented means satisfying the public's desire for a clean environment without excessive taxation.

The for-profit organization concerns itself with long-run profitability. In the case of the government, the organization seeks efficiency. Between 1979 and 1985 the cost of picking up highway trash had increased by 15 to 20 percent annually. By 1985 annual pick-up cost exceeded $24 million. The Texas Department of Transportation's focus on efficiency was also an attempt to implement the marketing concept.

2.   *What is the product being marketed by the Texas Department of*
        Transportation? What is exchanged between the Department and its
        consumers?

Marketing creates exchanges that will satisfy individual and organizational
objectives. Effective marketing consists of a consumer-oriented mix of business
activities planned and implemented by a marketer to facilitate the exchange or
transfer of goods, services, or ideas so that both parties profit in some way.

The term "product" refers to what the business or nonprofit organization offers
to its prospective customers without regard to whether the offering is a tangible
good such as a car, a service such as an airline trip, or an intangible idea such
as the importance of litter-free highways.

The Texas Department of Transportation determined that a marketing effort to
educate the people of Texas concerning the detrimental effects of littering was
in order. Broadly speaking, education and social action were the Transportation
Department's product. Citizens exchange taxes, volunteer time, and votes to
help maintain and improve their quality of life. In other words, the public's
desire for a clean environment when driving on the highway was exchanged for
taxation.

However, as discussed below, the Transportation Department wants the public to
help keep the highways clean. In exchange, the citizen will get a sense of
public pride or pride in Texas.

3.   *What type of antilitter and clean up programs should the Department*
        develop?

The Texas Department of Transportation implemented several programs.

        The Adopt-A-Highway was initiated in Texas. It called for private citizens
        and local groups to "adopt" two-mile sections of highway which they agreed
        to clean at least four times a year.

        The Great Texas Trash-Off was a one-day statewide cleanup encouraging
        thousands of volunteers to get the trash off the highway in time for the
        spring wildflower season.

        The Great Texas Cleanup-Green Up was a volunteer program to clean up litter
        and plant wildflower seeds.

        Spread the Word, Not the Waste was an educational program for schools. It
        included a 4 1/2 minute video program, a teacher's activity book, posters,
        and reply and evaluation cards for teachers.

        A Girl Scout Patch program was developed by the Transportation Department
        in conjunction with the Lone Star Girl Scout Council to reward anti-litter
        and waste disposal activity.

        The "Don't Mess with Texas" promotional program was initiated. It
        included advertising, litter bags, bumper stickers, decals and other items.
        See question 4.

4.   *Identify and evaluate each element of the Texas Department of*
        Transportation's marketing mix. In particular, what promotional efforts
        would you expect from the Department?

We have discussed the general nature of the product in questions 1 and 3. Price
refers to what is exchanged: taxes, volunteer time, and antilittering behavior.
Distribution varies with the program. For example, the "Spread the Word"
materials had to be distributed to the schools. Advertising is a major
promotional element. And, publicity and public service announcements (PSAs) are
especially important sources of promotion for not-for-profit organizations.

Marketing research had indicated that slogans like "Pitch In" has no effect on
habitual litterers, mainly men 18 to 34. (Note this fact is not mentioned in the
case because most students will be familiar with this type of campaign. When the
students suggest this solution, the instructor can present the class with this

fact.) The primary promotional theme was "Don't Mess with Texas." A slogan appealing to men 18-34 that evoked civic pride, and made littering appear to be "anti-Texas" and, not incidently, "anti-macho."

The video shows several commercials featuring celebrities (e.g., Willie Nelson, The Fabulous Thunderbirds).

2 MARKETING MANAGEMENT: STRATEGY AND ETHICAL BEHAVIOR

CHAPTER SCAN

The chapter introduces the concepts of planning, strategies, and tactics as they apply to marketing management at the corporate level, the strategic business unit level, and the operational level of management.

The chapter discusses the concepts of organizational mission, competitive advantage, total quality management (TQM), the product/market matrix, and positioning. It also relates how managers determine marketing objectives and establish a marketing plan.

The chapter further explains the nature of marketing ethics and social responsibility.

In short, the chapter illustrates marketing strategy and its components.

SUGGESTED LEARNING OBJECTIVES

The student who studies this chapter will see that marketing executives are managers who plan, execute, and control the organization's marketing activities. Among other things, the student will be able to:

1. Differentiate between marketing strategies and marketing tactics.

2. Discuss the role of marketing planning at the corporate level, strategic business-unit level, and the operational levels of management.

3. Understand the concept of an organizational mission.

4. Understand the nature of a competitive advantage.

5. Understand the importance of Total Quality Assurance strategies in the Total Quality Management process.

6. Explain the market/product matrix.

7.   Understand how managers determine marketing objectives and establish a marketing plan.

8.   Identify the stages in the strategic marketing process.

9.   Explain what positioning involves.

10. Understand the nature of marketing ethics and social responsibility.

CHAPTER OUTLINE

I.   INTRODUCTION

II.   MARKETING MANAGEMENT

III. WHAT IS A MARKETING STRATEGY?

IV.   PLANNING - DESIGNING A FRAMEWORK FOR THE FUTURE

A.   Planning is a Forward-Thinking Activity
B.   Planning Occurs at Various Levels in the Organization

V.   TOP MANAGEMENT MAKES CORPORATE STRATEGIC PLANS

A.   Defining the Organizational Mission
B.   Establishing Strategic Business Units

VI.   MIDDLE MANAGERS PLAN STRATEGIES FOR SBUs

A.   Business-Unit Strategies for Competitive Advantage

1. Total Quality

B.   Planning Business-Unit Growth Strategies

1.   Market-Related Strategies for Existing Products
2.   Market-Related Strategies for New Products

VII. THE STRATEGIC MARKETING PROCESS

A.   Identifying and Evaluating Opportunities

1.   Matching Opportunities to the Organization
2.   Managers Need Information to Evaluate Opportunities

B.   Analyzing Market Segments and Selecting Target Markets
C.   Planning a Market Position and Developing a Marketing Mix Strategy
D.   Preparing a Formal Marketing Plan
E.   Executing the Plan
F.   Controlling Efforts and Evaluating Results

VIII. PLANNING, EXECUTION, AND CONTROL ARE INTERRELATED

IX.   MANAGERIAL ETHICS AND SOCIALLY RESPONSIBLE BEHAVIOR

A.   Ethical Dimensions of Marketing Strategy

X.   SUMMARY

XI.   KEY TERMS

XII. QUESTIONS FOR DISCUSSION (17)

XIII. ETHICS IN PRACTICE

XIV.   CASES

The following key terms are introduced and used in Chapter 2.   They are
defined in the text's Glossary.

Marketing management
Marketing strategy
Tactics
Strategic planning
Operational planning
Corporate strategic planning
Strategic corporate goals
Organizational mission
Marketing myopia
Strategic business unit
Competitive advantage
Differentiation strategy
Total quality management
Total quality assurance
Market/product matrix
Market penetration
Market development
Product development
Product diversification
Strategic marketing process
Marketing opportunity analysis
SWOT
Strategic gap
Organizational opportunities
Strategic window of opportunity
Consumer market
Organizational or business market
Market segment
Market segmentation
Target market
Positioning
Market position or competitive position
Marketing plan
Marketing objective
Annual marketing plan
Execution
Control
Marketing audit
Social responsibility
Marketing ethics
Moral behavior
Norms
Ethical dilemma
Code of conduct

THE CHAPTER SUMMARIZED

I.   INTRODUCTION

LensCrafters' approach to selling eye wear is based on researching customer
wants and responding to those desires, primarily for quality products
conveniently obtained.   Hence, LensCrafters staffs heavily to reduce
waiting time and makes glasses on-the-spot and within one hour while
customers shop other retailers in the mall, or watch the technician
actually make their glasses ... a "personal touch."

II.   MARKETING MANAGEMENT

All organizations need managers to develop rules, principles, and ways of
thinking and acting to achieve the organization's objectives.   Corporate
managers work on long-term plans.   Marketing managers work at the

organization's middle level, and, because they deal with change, the management process is a continuous one, developing appropriate strategies.

Marketing management is the process of planning, executing, and controlling marketing activities to attain marketing goals and objectives effectively and efficiently.

II.   WHAT IS A MARKETING STRATEGY?

Marketing strategies, like military strategies, are focused on obtaining objectives. Thus a number of military terms have been adopted by marketers as they have by football coaches.

A **marketing strategy** consists of a plan identifying what basic goals and objectives will be pursued and how they will be achieved in the time available.

The military sees **tactics** as "what lieutenants do" and **strategy** as "what generals do." Thus, tactics are specific actions intended to implement strategy, and are associated with the execution of plans, e.g., McDonald's "family restaurant" strategy is implemented by the tactic of of fering Happy Meals for children at reasonable prices, and explaining that "your fork" is the only thing that's not nutritious in a McDonald salad. These tactics show that McDonald's offers "quality, cleanliness, service, and value."

IV.   PLANNING - DESIGNING A FRAMEWORK FOR THE FUTURE

Planning is the process of envisioning the future, establishing goals and objectives, and designing organizational and marketing strategies and tactics to be implemented in the future.

Careful planning can pay off in any effort. In business, anticipating the future and designing a strategy for future actions is crucial.

A.   Planning is a Forward-Thinking Activity

The purpose of planning is to go beyond diagnosis of the present and attempt to predict the future, devising means to adjust to an ever-changing environment before problems develop. Planning allows the manager to "act" rather than "react."

Planning involves deciding in advance.

B.   Planning Occurs at Various Levels in the Organization

There are many marketing functions within an organization, performed by different levels of administration.

For simplicity's sake, we speak of three levels of responsibility: top, middle management, and operational or first-line management. These are shown in Exhibit 2-1.

Each level is important, though as we move downward in the organization, planning and strategy become less important, while tactics and execution become more important.

Middle managers plan marketing mix strategy and supervise operational managers concerned with day-to-day execution of marketing activities. At the operational management level, **operational planning** (day-to-day functional activities) become most important. This is illustrated in Exhibit 2-2.

V.   TOP MANAGEMENT MAKES CORPORATE STRATEGIC PLANS

Corporate strategic planning is the responsibility of top management, and pertains to long-term planning for the whole organization. It is the process of determining the organization's primary goals, and creating the organizational framework for accomplishing them.

Strategic corporate goals are broad statements about what the organization wants to accomplish in its long-term future.

A. Defining the Organizational Mission

A decision that influences all others is the defining of the **organizational** or **corporate mission,** the statement of company purpose, explaining why the organization exists and what it hopes to accomplish, thus providing direction for the entire organization.

The text provides a seven-point statement of mission from The Limited.

The definition of the mission should be consumer-oriented and not short-sighted or narrow-minded. Thus, railroads can be defined as "transportation" and movies as "entertainment." Failing to take this wide view has been termed **marketing myopia.**

B. Establishing Strategic Business Units

Mission statements and corporate goals serve as guidelines for determining what organizational structure is most appropriate to the organization's marketing efforts. Many organizations are diverse and individual strategic business units within them can be identified.

A **strategic business unit (SBU)** is a distinct unit, such as a company division, department, or product line, of the overall parent organization with a specific market focus and a manager who has the authority and responsibility for managing all unit functions.

Thus, Time-Warner can compare the performances magazines, book publishing units, and mail order divisions against similar competing units, not against the performance of entire organizations that happen to compete with it.

IV. MIDDLE MANAGERS PLAN STRATEGIES FOR SBUs

Top managers are responsible for the entire organization and assign responsibilities to middle managers, strongly influencing the marketing planning activities of these managers. (See Exhibit 2-3.)

A. Business-Unit Strategies for Competitive Advantage

A common strategic goal is to establish and maintain a **competitive advantage,** to be superior to or different from competitors in a way important to potential customers.

Here are two basic marketing strategies that seek to establish competitive advantages.

The price leadership or low cost/low price strategy emphasizes a standardized product, low unit cost, and underpricing all competitors. Hyundai, Samsung and other Asian firms have successfully entered the U.S. market using this strategy.

The **differentiation strategy** emphasizes a distinctive product and a marketing mix that accents that distinctiveness. Ho-Lee-Chow Oriental fast food and Zubaz provide good examples of strategic plans that emphasize differentiation.

1. Total Quality

Making quality assurance a top priority is one of the most common differentiation strategies for both goods and services. For many years, U.S. businesses did not make top quality an absolute goal. The marketing concept requires that the definition of "quality" be that of the consumer, not of the company.

Total quality management is the process of implementing and adjusting the marketing strategy to assure customers' satisfaction with the product's quality.

Total quality assurance programs are not exclusively marketing's domain, but they are key to customer satisfaction.

B.   Planning Business-Unit Growth Strategies

Managers responsible for SBUs typically focus on opportunities for business growth. The **market/product matrix** helps categorize alternative opportunities. (See Exhibit 2-4.)

MARKETS

	OLD/EXISTING	NEW
PRODUCTS		
OLD PRODUCTS	Market Penetration	Market Development
NEW PRODUCTS	Product Development	Product Diversification

1.   Market-Related Strategies for Existing Products

There are two paths available to expand sales of existing products. **Market penetration** refers to growth of an established product's sales by increasing sales among existing customers. Baking soda is offered as a deodorizer for refrigerators. Cereals are often touted for nonbreakfast purposes such as snacking or baking.

Market development means attempting to draw new customers to existing products. Currently, Eastern Europe is thought to be "opening up" for trade with the West and presents an opportunity for market development.

The desire to expand demand for an existing product may come from a belief that an existing market is shrinking or from the fact that the organization has resources (capacities) that are not being used to the fullest. Restaurants try to bring in customers during "slow" hours in an attempt to sell more of the same basic products they offer.

2.   Market-Related Strategies for New Products

A restaurant's management may seek to enlarge its customer base by offering new products. McDonald's has added many "new" menu items over the years. This is **product development**, the marketing of new or "improved" products to existing markets.

Marketing new products to a new set of customers is called **product diversification**. For example, Mr. Coffee has introduced the Iced Tea Pot.

Diversification may be implemented by developing new products internally or by "buying" new products from other companies via merger or acquisition.

VII. THE STRATEGIC MARKETING PROCESS

Marketing managers engage in many diverse activities, from formulating new strategies to evaluating old strategies. All this must be done with the customers' needs in mind. This is the key lesson of the marketing concept.

There are six general steps in the development of marketing strategy (below,) though the timing and sequence of the steps varies from situation to situation.

A.   Identifying and Evaluating Opportunities

Marketing faces a dynamic environment in which marketers must "read" and translate what is perceived into marketing opportunities.

Marketing opportunity analysis is the diagnostic activity of inter-preting environmental attributes and change in light of the organization's ability to capitalize on potential opportunities.

This analysis serves as both a warning system and an appraisal system. It provides a foundation for planning and strategy development.

Marketing opportunity analysis also requires an inward look at the organization.   Internal strengths and weakness are evaluated in relation to the external environment.   The acronym SWOT helps us remember to evaluate the internal and the external environment -- Strengths and Weaknesses, Opportunities and Threats.

Exhibit 2-6 shows how threats and opportunities, strengths and weaknesses, are related.   Usually, where a company wants to be is different from where it is.   The difference may be called the **strategic gap.**

1.   Matching Opportunities to the Organization

The world is full of opportunities, but, given the strengths and weaknesses of an organization, not all **environmental opportunities** are **organizational opportunities.**

.   Procter & Gamble is a very rich company but does not use that money to enter the nuclear power business.

.   Budweiser has good distribution in bars and beer and wine stores, thus, Eagle Snacks.

To help match environmental opportunities to the organization, many organizations have developed guidelines based on strengths, weaknesses, goals, or special abilities. (This is a good example of how advanced planning can be used to "make decisions" about new products or market opportunities.)

.   What competitive advantages will we have to aid our entry into this market?

.   Do we have some special abilities to bring to this opportunity?

.   Do we have any weaknesses that will hurt us?

.   Does the opportunity meet our organizational requirements? (e.g., a company may focus on leisure goods.)

These questions must also take into consideration the strengths and weaknesses of competitors (even possible new competitors) and competitors actions and responses to the actions of others.

Analysis of opportunities might reveal a **window of opportunity**, the time in which an organization's capabilities may provide it with an advantage over competitors. BUT the firm must move within that time frame. Many companies have failed to take advantages of their strengths.

2.   Managers Need Information to Evaluate Opportunities

Managers need information about their environment. Chapter 3 discusses broad trends in the external environment. Marketing research and information management are discussed in Chapter 4.

B.   Analyzing Market Segments and Selecting Target Markets

A **market** is a group of possible customers for a product.

Markets are of two major types. If a product is bought to satisfy a personal use, it is a **consumer product** sold in the **consumer market**. If a product is purchased to help operate a business or other organization, or to be resold as by a wholesaler, it is an **organizational product** or **business product** sold in the **organizational** or **business market**.

A **market segment** is a portion of a larger market.

African Americans constitute a market segment, African Americans aged 30 to 40 are a smaller segment, female African Americans of that age group are a smaller segment, and so on.

Market segmentation is the dividing of a heterogeneous mass market into a number of (smaller, more specific) segments.

Segments seen as containing potential customers for the organization's product (and which become the focus of an organization's marketing activities) are its **target markets**.

Market segmentation and targeting makes good sense ... "you can't be all things to all people." (It is treated fully in Chapter 8.)

Evaluation of marketing opportunities must be followed by decisions as to where marketing efforts will be directed (segmenting and targeting) before the third and final step (planning and developing the marketing mix) can be undertaken.

C.   Planning a Market Position and Developing a Marketing Mix Strategy

After a target market has been selected, marketing managers position their brands in the market and develop a marketing mix that will establish that positioning objective.

Positioning refers to the way consumers think about competitors in a market.

Market position, or **competitive position**, refers to the way consumers perceive a brand relative to its competition.

Brands and products have "position" relative to other brands or products in the minds of consumers. Thus, it is in the marketer's interest to plan the **market position**. *Business Week*, for example, gives a weekly "thought out" view of business news, while the *Wall Street Journal* gives daily and "newer" news. Positioning, like segmentation, is discussed more fully in Chapter 8.

The marketing mix (4 Ps) is the means by which a marketing manager achieves goals. Some combination of product, price, distribution, and promotion is always necessary in solving marketing problems. Much of the text, specifically Chapters 10-21, deal with the creation of the marketing mix.

D.   Preparing a Formal Marketing Plan

The preparation of the formal marketing plan is the final planning stage of the strategic marketing process.

A formal **marketing plan** is a written statement of the marketing objectives and strategies to be followed and the specific courses of action to be taken when (or if) certain future events occur.

The plan outlines who is responsible for managing specific activities and provides a timetable for performance of those activities.

Marketing managers must determine where they want to be in the future and how to get there. A **marketing objective** is a statement about the level of performance to be achieved by the organization, SBU, or other operating unit.

Objectives define results in measurable terms and include a time frame such as "growth of sales by 15% by the end of next year."

Marketing plans may be categorized by duration -- long-term (5 or more years), moderate in length (2 to 5 years), and short-term (one year or less). An annual marketing plan is most common since marketing activity must be coordinated with annual financial plans.

E.   Executing the Plan

Plans are "made to be executed." (The word means "carried out.") **Execution** involves organizing and coordinating people, resources, and activities, staffing, directing, developing and leading subordinates. Marketing "mistakes" can also be labeled "bad execution." There are many examples of good ideas poorly executed. (Text offers anecdotes of easily recognizable errors in execution.)

F.   Controlling Efforts and Evaluating Results

The purpose of **control** is to ensure that planned activities are completed and properly executed. It involves three major steps:

.   Establishment of performance standards
.   Investigation to assure task was done
.   Assessment of actual performance

These provide feedback to managers ... were plans matched "in the field?" Corrective action might be needed.

Related closely to this is the formal marketing audit. The audit is discussed more fully Chapter 22 but is defined here as follows.

The **marketing audit** is a comprehensive review and appraisal of the total marketing operation. It requires a systematic and impartial review of an organization's operations and its marketing environment.

VIII. PLANNING, EXECUTION, AND CONTROL ARE INTERRELATED

The topics discussed in this chapter are closely interrelated. Consideration of the environment can lead to development of plans which then must be executed and controlled. Each has ethical dimensions.

The interrelationships, the flow of these steps, is shown in the text's Exhibit 2-7.

IX.   MANAGERIAL ETHICS AND SOCIALLY RESPONSIBLE BEHAVIOR

Stories of organizations,and individuals in organizations acting in unethical fashion can be found in the news almost daily. Some marketers respond to environmental threats, for example, by reformulating their

products.   Marketers are expected to obey the law, but some recognize a
responsibility that goes beyond legal responsibility.

Social responsibility refers to the ethical consequences of a person's or
organization's acts as they might affect the interests of others.

Ethics involve values about right or wrong conduct. **Marketing ethics**
involves the principles that guide an organization's conduct and the values
it expects to express in certain situations. **Moral behavior** in the
marketing context reflects how well an individual's or organization's
marketing activity actively exhibits those ethical values. **Norms** suggest
what ought to be done under given circumstances.

An **ethical dilemma**, in a marketing context, is a predicament in which a
marketer must resolve whether an action, although it benefits the
organization, the individual decision maker, or both, may be considered
unethical.

Problems arise particularly in situations where others do not share the
marketers beliefs, e.g., in many countries bribery is standard business
practice.

J.F. Kennedy's "four basic consumer rights" (to safety, to be informed, to
choose, and to be heard) provide some guidance, though other rights can be
mentioned. It can also be argued that certain groups require more
protection than others, e.g., children. Many companies, trade associations,
and others have developed **codes of conduct**. The American Marketing
Associations Code of Conduct is shown in Exhibit 2-8.

A.   Ethical Dimensions of Marketing Strategy

       Ethical values can influence all aspects of marketing strategy.
       Exhibit 2-9 presents ethical questions applicable to all portions of
       the marketing mix.

X.   SUMMARY

This chapter discussed marketing strategy and tactics and how marketing
managers must plan, execute, and control the organization's marketing mix.

       Learning Objective 1: **Differentiate between marketing strategy and
       tactics.**

A strategy is a long-range plan to determine what basic goals and
objectives will be pursued and how they will be achieved in the time
available. A strategy entails a commitment to certain courses of action
and allocation of the resources necessary to achieve the identified goals.
Tactics are specific actions to implement strategy.

       Learning Objective 2: **Discuss the role of marketing planning at the
       corporate level, at the strategic business unit level, and at the
       operational level of management.**

Planning occurs at the corporate level, strategic business unit level, and
the operational level of an organization. Top management engages in
strategic planning to determine long-term goals for the entire
organization. Managers at the strategic business unit level plan
strategies for the business unit and for individual products, while
operational managers are concerned with planning and executing the day-to-
day activities of the organization.

       Learning Objective 3: **Understand the concept of the organizational
       mission.**

An organizational mission is a statement of a company's purpose. It
explains why an organization exists and what it hopes to accomplish.

Learning Objective 4:   Understand the nature of a competitive advantage.

A business or product that is superior to or different from its competitors in a way that is important to the market, offers a competitive advantage. It may offer lower cost for the same quality or some unique feature.

Learning Objective 5:   Understand the importance of Total Quality Assurance strategies in the Total Quality Management process.

Total Quality Assurance makes market-driven quality a top priority. Total Quality Management is the process of implementing and adjusting the marketing strategy to assure customers' satisfaction with the product's quality.

Learning Objective 6:   Explain the market/product matrix.

The market/product matrix broadly categorizes strategic business unit opportunities in terms of strategies for growth. The four strategies are market penetration, market development, product development, and product diversification.

Learning Objective 7:   Understand how managers determine marketing objectives and define the marketing plan.

A marketing objective is a statement about the level of performance the strategic business unit or operating unit intends to achieve. A marketing plan is a written statement of the marketing objectives and strategies to be followed and the specific courses of action to be taken when or if future events occur.

Learning Objective 8:   Identify the stages in the strategic marketing process.

The six stages of the strategic marketing process are: (1) identifying and evaluating opportunities, (2) analyzing market segments and selecting target markets, (3) planning a market position and developing a marketing mix, (4) preparing a formal marketing plan, (5) executing the plan, and (6) controlling and evaluating results.

Learning Objective 9:   Explain what positioning involves.

Each product occupies a position relative to competitors in the consumer's mind. A key marketing objective is to determine what position the company wishes to occupy. Positioning is accomplished with the development and implementation of a marketing mix.

Learning Objective 10:   Understand the nature of marketing ethics and socially responsible behavior.

Social responsibility refers to the ethical consequences of a person's or an organization's acts as they might affect the interests of others. Ethics involves values about right and wrong conduct. Marketing ethics involves the principles that guide an organization's conduct and the values it expects to express in certain situations. Marketers' moral behavior reflects how well marketing activity exhibits these ethical values. Ethical principles reflect the cultural values and norms of a society. Marketing decisions often have ethical dimensions and may involve ethical dilemmas.

XI.   KEY TERMS

XII.   QUESTIONS FOR DISCUSSION (18)

XIII. ETHICS IN PRACTICE

XIV.   CASES

ANSWER GUIDELINES FOR CHAPTER 2 QUESTIONS FOR DISCUSSION

1.   *What are the three major tasks of marketing management?*

ANSWER:

Management's three major tasks are planning, execution, and control. The text identifies the three major tasks of marketing management as: planning, execution, and control, a set of operating activities that help the firm achieve its goals.

Simple restatement of this triad of activities may be an inadequate response to a "discussion question." Perhaps students should be assigned a familiar product and asked to speculate on what steps were taken in planning, executing and controlling the marketing activities associated with that product.

An alternative approach to this attempt at explaining marketing management might be the "diagramming" of a marketing decision, again using a familiar product. The goal would be to show the flow of events and inter-relationships present in the simple phrase "planning, execution and control."

Almost any of the text's cases could be assigned as an exercise in identifying and explaining the functions of planning, execution, and control.

2.   *Distinguish between a strategy and a tactic.*

ANSWER:

A strategy is a general, long-range framework formulated to accomplish a specific brand, organizational or divisional goal, while tactics are specific actions intended to implement strategy.

Many examples are in the text and obvious from casual observation. The military view that strategy is what generals do ("Bring peace to Iraq and Kuwait" or "Preserve Bosnia") and tactics is what lieutenants do ("Hold this building against attacks") is useful. Similarly, vice-presidents of marketing generally devote most of their time to planning while salespeople implement the plans. At the university or college, the president and Board of Trustees handle the strategy, the professors spend more of their own time on tactical matters.

McDonald's strategy is to be a family-type restaurant and almost everything McDonald's does serves to help implement this strategy. That, of course, is the purpose of all properly executed tactics. Examples:

.   No pinball machines or electronic games.
.   No pay phones.
.   Accessible bathrooms (a necessity for kids).
.   No cigarette machines.
.   "Friendly" employees (many of them young, and many of retirement age, which holds down personnel costs and, thus, prices).
.   Array of food offerings, including fish, salads, and chicken.
.   Playgrounds.
.   "Happy Meals."
.   Kid-oriented advertisements supported by adult-oriented ads.
.   Nutritional chart showing McDonald's food is good food.
.   Kid-oriented premiums (coloring books, items tied into currently popular movies).
.   Birthday parties.
.   Few sharp edges on furnishings.
.   Quick service.
.   High chairs, booster seats, easy-wipe surfaces.

3.   *What is Pepsi Cola's strategy?*

ANSWER:

Students will find it somewhat difficult to discuss strategies without also discussing tactics.

Strategies are to be developed in a systematic way.

Stage 1:   Identify and Evaluate Opportunities

    a)   Consider Organization's Strengths and Weaknesses
    b)   Match Opportunities to the Organization

Stage 2:   Analyze Market Segments and Select Target Markets

Stage 3:   Plan and Develop an Appropriate Marketing Mix.

These steps or stages, or some other framework, should be used by the students in responding to this question. That is, they should not be allowed to simply name or describe a strategy. Rather they should be asked to defend their selected strategies, telling "where they came from."

While Pepsi Cola may be best known by students as a soft drink, Pepsico also has divisions of other food products (Pizza Hut and Taco Bell, for example).

Stage 1: Pepsico has strengths in its size and diversity allowing it to take advantage of opportunities in disparate areas. The company has searched for opportunities in food-oriented lines which match the skills of the organizational team. Relative to Coca-Cola, Pepsi Cola's weakness is in its relatively smaller number of distributors.

Stage 2: The target markets served by Pepsico vary slightly by division but also reflect a relatively younger segment of consumers. Slogans for various divisions help isolate Pepsico's strategic thrust. For example, Pepsi Cola's slogan has evolved from: "The choice of a new generation" to "You got the right one baby, uh-huh." Advertisements for Taco Bell feature a "Run for the Border" sung in a contemporary style.

Stage 3: The marketing mix developed to attract a younger target market matches the theme of advertisements to the atmospherics of its restaurants. Pizza Hut, for example, spent several years developing its "pan pizza" and all divisions consistently search for new products to meet the demand for novelty and difference in younger-aged segments.

4.   *Why are marketing planning activities important?*

ANSWER:

Marketing planning activities fall into two categories: operational planning and strategic planning. In both instances, the importance of planning remains more or less the same, even though various points of difference and varying emphases may be noted.

The overall importance of planning marketing activities may be described by means of this progression:

.   Marketing planning involves the establishment of marketing goals and the design of marketing programs likely to be implemented in the future.

.   Without goals, the organization cannot know "where it is going." Without some idea of what marketing programs are likely to be implemented in the future, the organization cannot begin to accumulate the resources that might be required. The organization could, in many ways, be totally unprepared to move when opportunities or threats appear.

.   Without goals and plans, the organization confronts every happening without guidelines for action. As is shown in the chapter, the world is full of opportunities. Should the organization, for example, decide to add a newly invented product to its line of goods? If the product is incompatible with the organization's goals and plans, the answer would seem to be no. We do not wish to make it appear that goals and plans make the marketing manager's decision but it is so that the more carefully and properly goals and plans are drawn, the more useful they are as helps in evaluating situations of both threat and opportunity.

Planning, in short, helps an organization "shape its own destiny" by anticipating changes in the marketplace.

5.   *Identify several corporations, or not-for-profit organizations (perhaps Toshiba Corporation, Walt Disney Productions, Eastman Kodak, and Ford Motor Company), and describe your interpretation of their corporate missions.*

ANSWER:

The term "mission" strikes some students as unnecessarily grandiose, so it may be necessary to point out that, no matter what you call it, all organizations need some understanding of what is to be accomplished.

This is clearly the starting point for developing goals and plans. As such, the mission is generally stated (and it should be stated, not just "understood") in broad terms. This broadness of statement increases the "life" of the mission, e.g., the March of Dimes once had the mission of helping wipe out polio. This accomplished, its mission was changed to helping to overcome the problem of birth defects. A broader mission at the start, such as "Service to the health of the society," would not have had to be changed, though it is arguable that such a statement of mission is too broad. The March of Dimes example shows, by the way, that missions are not forever. They can be changed. Students may have to be made aware of that.

The question asks for comments on the likely missions of three organizations, thus speculation is required. Here are some suggestions.

.   Toshiba Corporation. To be an industry leader within its markets and to achieve this by producing quality products at reasonable prices. (Note: such a statement of mission might not be as market-oriented as it could be.)

.   Walt Disney Productions. Disney has long been an "entertainment company," not just a cartoon, film, toy or amusement park company. The accent has always been on "family" entertainment. Disney has been a technology leader, mixing cartoons and live actors, introducing animated figures at its amusement parks, and pioneering in film use of computer graphics. A simple mission statement like "entertainment" does include all these things but does not begin to describe what Disney has done over the last 60+ years.

.   Eastman Kodak. Eastman Kodak has a record of product development and of competing on virtually every level of the "picture market": black and white, color, and "self-developing" consumer cameras, movies and similar consumer goods, industrial products, microfilm, etc. Kodak's mission may closely match the broad type recommended by Theodore Levitt in "Marketing Myopia." (*H.B.R.*, July-August, 1960)

.   Ford Motor Company. Ford has relied on slogans and advertisements built around the concept of product quality. This tradition goes back to the Model T, though the slogan "Have you driven a Ford lately?" suggests that Ford may be trying to overcome an image problem uncovered by its marketing research: a perception of "sturdy but unexciting," perhaps. The slogan "Quality is Job 1" suggests that the company perceives a need to offset a perception that Fords are inferior to Japanese cars in matters of quality.

It might be a good idea to ask students to suggest other organizations, including nonprofit or foreign outfits, with which they are familiar. This obviously broadens the topic under discussion.

Perhaps a student's family-owned business, or other employer or volunteer group, has a mission that the class might evaluate. If it has none, a discussion of what the mission could be and how the firm has managed without a formally stated mission could be pursued.

6.   *Several corporate slogans are listed below. Discuss how each reflects a corporate mission.*

    (a)   Federal Express - "When it absolutely, positively has to be there overnight."
    (b)   Panasonic - "Just slightly ahead of our time."
    (c)   Smith Corona - "Tomorrow's technology at your touch."
    (d)   The Equitable Financial Companies - "We have great plans for you."
    (e)   Raytheon - "Where quality starts with fundamentals."

ANSWER:

Slogans serve to communicate something of the corporate mission to consumers. They are not statements of missions.

(a)   Federal Express - "When it absolutely, positively has to be there overnight."

Federal Express's mission appears to be that of (profiting by) being an assured and rapid deliverer of letters, packets and packages. The slogan communicates parts of this mission in the words "absolutely positively" which tell the customer that Federal Express can be trusted. One Federal Express advertising campaign reenforced this with the question, "Why fool around with anybody else?" The slogan also communicates rapid delivery with the word "overnight." It also answers the customer's wonderings about when his or her package will arrive -- "Tomorrow!"

(b)   Panasonic - "Just slightly ahead of our time."

The mission statement appears clear in this slogan. Panasonic's mission is to be and remain at the forefront of the electronics market. This long-term intent is suggested by the choice of words. Panasonic is not "working on the 21st Century" or some other fixed time, but is "always" going to be "slightly ahead of our time," no matter when our time is.

The slogan also suggests that Panasonic can solve today's problems ("just slightly ahead") and is not concerned particularly with pie-in-the-sky ideas. That the firm is customer-oriented is suggested in the words "our time" which could be yours and mine. The "our" also links Panasonic with "the rest of us."

(c)   Smith Corona - "Tomorrow's technology at your touch."

Smith Corona is a very old company. Its name is almost synonymous with typewriters. However, typewriters are very much on the way out. In 1993 only two companies in the world still made manual typewriters, and not many more manufacture electrics. Smith Corona is an organization that seeks to survive and flourish in the future ("Tomorrow") and to succeed with products very different from its old standby typewriters. In telling us that they have "tomorrow's technology" management is suggesting that the company is ahead of its time and that they will be around for some time to come. Further, the use of the word "technology" suggests "hi-tech" products, a notion not associated with the old-time typewriter maker. The phrase "at your touch" does provide some linkage to the typewriter image, an image of a long record of turning out trustworthy machines, known for generations as good products. The slogan brings to mind, therefore, both the old and the new, and suggests Smith Corona's intention to build on a proud past while moving forward quickly to new, technologically advanced products.

(d)   The Equitable Financial Companies - "We have great plans for you."

Equitable has been known as an insurance company and, like almost all large insurance companies, now offers a range of investments, annuities, retirement plans, IRAs, SEP plans, funds, and so on. Equitable's total product includes advice on which mix of insurance and investments is best for "you." The company can develop a mix of programs that, supposedly, can meet the individual customer's goals -- protect the family, save for retirement, invest in growth funds, utilize tax shelters, etc. Thus, the company is offering plans in the sense of insurance and investment plans, and plans in the sense of "big picture, long-range" plans.

Equitable means to suggest that it has an array of wonderful plans. And, the "for you" can be read two ways. The customer who believes he or she is knowledgeable about finances can read it to say that Equitable has plans to offer for consideration. The person who is not knowledgeable and feels the need for investment advice can read the slogan to mean that the company can plan things for the customer. The word "plans" is somewhat vague. What plans? Plans about everything financial. This is consistent with the company's mission of offering a total package of insurance/ financial advice/investment to its customers.

(e)   Raytheon - "Where quality starts with fundamentals."

Raytheon, like Smith Corona discussed earlier, has been around for many years. People who don't know much about the company at least recognize the name. "The company has lasted a long time, so it must make good products," thinks the consumer. Thus, the word "quality" is in the slogan, as is the word "fundamentals." Surely an old company has mastered the "fundamentals." This is a good image to have. In everything from high finance to baseball, we all know, it's the "fundamentals" that count.

The slogan, therefore, suggests that Raytheon produces quality products that are somehow based on hard work, basic science, and getting all the little things right. Who can argue with that? Get the fundamentals down and the rest will follow, right? There is also a suggestion that the company does the whole job, beginning to end, starting with the fundamentals.

7.   *What is a strategic business unit? What are the basic growth strategies for SBUs?*

ANSWER:

An SBU is a distinct unit, such as a division, department, or product line, of the overall parent organization with a specific market focus and a manager who has the authority and responsibility for managing all unit functions.

The market/product matrix identifies four basic strategies for business unit growth.

(a)   Strategies for existing products include:

(1)   market penetration where SBUs increase sales to existing customers. For example, Arm & Hammer promotes use of baking soda for teeth, refrigerator or food odors, kitty litter, and as a drains or carpet freshener.

(2)   market development involves the SBU attempting to attract new customers to its existing products. For example Eastern Europe and the former U.S.S.R. represent opportunities for U.S. firms to sell existing products in new markets.

(b)   Strategies for new products include:

(3)   product development where innovative or "new and improved" products are sold in existing markets. For example, Hardees now sells fried chicken as other fast-food restaurants also add new products to retain interest.

(4)   product diversification involves new products and new markets as, for example, Mr. Coffee developed its Iced Tea Pot and recently introduced a potato cooker.

8.   *What is total quality management and how do total quality assurance strategies affect TQM?*

ANSWER:

Total quality management is the process of implementing and adjusting the marketing strategy to assure customers' satisfaction with the product's quality.

Total quality assurance programs are not exclusively marketing's domain, but they are key to customer satisfaction. Making quality assurance a top priority is one of the most common differentiation strategies for both goods and services. For many years, U.S. businesses did not make top quality an absolute goal. The marketing concept requires that the definition of "quality" be that of the consumer, not of the company.

If a firm is to practice TQM it must have in place the strategies that will make this occur. The TQM philosophy should be expressed in some form or another, from the organization's mission statement on down to its personnel policies. To pledge high quality and not provide high quality is among the biggest blunders a firm can make. A minimum goal is "at least" customer satisfaction, and a relentless quest to better that minimum is what appears to be required in the Nasty Nineties.

9.   *What is competitive advantage? Suppose you were the marketing manager for Saturn automobiles. What marketing strategies would you develop to compete with imports?*

ANSWER:

A competitive advantage is an attempt to be superior or to be favorably different from competitors in a way that is important to the market.

Consumers appear to believe that imports have higher quality than U.S. cars, thus one aspect of Saturn's strategy must address quality assurance. Given a slow, or recessionary economy, Saturn may also position its automobile as American-made with comparable quality to combat the perception of superiority by imports. Bothered from the start by recalls, Saturn may find this to be tough going.

10.   *Is it possible for two competing companies to have the same goal but to use different strategies to reach the goal?*

ANSWER:

One expression used to refer to the fact that different organizations seem to seek similar goals using various strategies (and tactics) is "That's what makes it a horse race." This means that as in a race, each horse has some chance of winning, and bettors seem willing to bet on any horse if the potential payoff is large enough.

As in any fair race, there are no guarantees in marketing. The basic idea of the marketing mix is that there is no one best way to "do marketing," no "best" product, price, distribution system, and promotion.

This is evident in most industries. One familiar example is radio. Each station on the dial wants to attract listeners in large numbers and, thereby, attract advertisers willing to pay well for air time. In this, most stations share the same overall goal. Each station in a given market programs different music, or news, or talk-show formats. Some stations rely on "personalities" (disk jockeys or talk show hosts) while others brag that they have no disk jockeys at all. Some stations program "elevator music" by soupy-sounding orchestras, while others feature "light favorites," "light rock," "top forty," or classical music. The variations in programming are many and sometimes difficult to distinguish. Students might be asked to discern and describe the strategies used by local radio stations to achieve their overall goals.

In summary, very few things are certain in marketing. As the text points out, strategies are something like roads on a map. Many roads can be taken to go from St. Louis to Baltimore ... the quickest route, the scenic route, the route that permits a visit to Washington, D.C., and so on. Just as the traveler may pick the road that best suits him or her, the marketer must pick the strategy (and tactics) that he or she believes will lead to the goal in a way the organization can afford.

11.   *Describe the stages in the strategic marketing process.*

ANSWER:

The stages of the strategic marketing process consist of planning, executing and controlling activities.

Planning includes 4 stages which include:

(1)   Identifying and evaluating opportunities (in light of organizational strengths and weaknesses);

(2)   Analyzing market segments and selecting target markets;

(3)   Planning a market position and developing a marketing mix strategy;

(4)   Preparing a formal marketing plan.

Executing the plan is the fifth stage and includes organizing and coordinating: (a) staffing, leading and training people; (b) allocating resources; and (c) coordinating and following schedules as activities are enacted.

Controlling efforts and evaluating results comprise the sixth stage which involves: (a) defining plans and objectives based on the company's goal; (b) establishing performance standards; (c) investigating activities and determining why deviations occur; and (d) evaluating and correcting deviations from standards.

12.   *What is positioning? How is Dr. Pepper positioned relative to Coke and Pepsi?*

ANSWER:

Positioning refers to consumer perceptions of a product or service in comparison to competitive offerings. Asking students to position familiar products reinforces the idea of distinct features and approaches for differing market offerings. Since students may become confused if they try to consider relative positions for Classic Coke/New Coke, or for Sugar or Caffeine free products, it may be helpful to limit the discussion to Classic Coke, Pepsi Cola and Dr. Pepper.

While answers and "perceptions" may differ, the first positioning difference may be the age group of the target market. Pepsi obviously targets younger consumers while Classic Coke appeals to Baby Boomers, more middle aged. From its advertisements ("So give me a Dr. Pepper, it's what the doctor ordered" or "Be a Pepper, drink Dr. Pepper") Dr. Pepper seems to target ages in between Pepsi and Coke. Another dimension for positioning differences may be taste, where Pepsi is considered to be similar to Classic Coke (though sweeter) while Dr. Pepper is a completely different sensation.

13.   *Identify a retail store or a manufacturing company operation in your local area that has a sound marketing plan but poorly executes the plan.*

ANSWER:

This question may seem unanswerable. Do students know what organizations have good plans? They do, either directly or by guessing. For example:

.   Sears must have some good plans, yet when I go to my local Sears I often find the help to be unknowledgeable about the stock: poor execution at a key point in Sears' marketing process.

.   J.C. Penney uses computerized ticket readers designed to relay information to some control point, speeding up the billing process. Yet somehow incorrect totals are read, credits are recorded as debits, etc. Thus two goals of the system are not met; consumers don't get accurate bills and, because of mistakes, collections are not made more quickly.

. Scandinavian Health Spas appear to be successful. It is said, however, that its largest group of employees is in sales and the second largest group in collections. What this means in terms of the company's marketing plan is a good topic for speculation.

Other examples may be known to a class member or to the professor who has knowledge of the workings of particular firms. The potential for this question to generate student comments is great. Within reason, a "bull session" about things that go wrong is not a bad idea. Things run more smoothly in marketing texts than they do in the real world.

14.   *Identify some typical execution errors.*

ANSWER:

Students may be assigned to check today's newspapers for "bloopers" or to recount those heard on radio or TV.

Typos, inverted words, mispronunciations, timing errors, mechanical failures, bad choices of prices, payment plans for salespeople, choices of locations for stores, use of a "frustrating" delivery system, etc. are all possibilities.

Some examples:

. An autobody shop (in Akron, Ohio) advertised a "rebate plan" whereby if the shop got your accident business, it would "rebate" several hundred dollars to you. This, in fact, was a rip-off of insurance companies. Besides being unethical or illegal, the plan should never have been advertised -- the ads attracted the ire of citizens, especially that of the insurance companies.

. The December, 1980 *Mechanix Illustrated* ran an ad headlined "Relieves the Pain and Itching of Hemorrhoids" but mistakenly ran a picture of pliers and wire-cutters with the words, "There's never a dull moment with these babies on the job."

. Chrysler and other auto makers have, from time to time, run rebate deals. Local used car dealers wanted to get in on the act. One local dealer placed a large sign in his showroom window that announced "REBAITS!"

. Small businesses often attempt to increase sales with huge signs proclaiming: "ON SELL!" OR "WE SALE FOR LESS."

Care might be taken to include failures of execution relating to all 4 Ps.

15.   *What are marketing ethics?*

ANSWER:

Ethics involve values about right and wrong conduct in our society. Marketing Ethics involve the principles that guide an organization's conduct and the values it expects to express. In a multicultural sense, marketing ethics reflect the values of culture and society. For example, marketing ethics and laws in some countries encourage the development and sale of products which are patented by another firm. Thus, within these societies, it is acceptable to copy, or "steal" a brand name. Or, in other cultures, marketing ethics condone bribes for government officials as a natural part of doing business. These values change within the U.S.

As another example of varying marketing ethics, consider the use of sex appeal by firms in the U.S. or Europe as compared to the Saudi Arabian ban on such promotions in that country.

16.   *What are some examples of socially responsible behavior and socially irresponsible behavior?*

ANSWER:

With a little encouragement, students should get involved in a discussion of variations in perceptions of responsible and irresponsible behaviors by companies. As a few examples, consider:

.   Tylenol is considered to be socially responsible from its reaction to the cyanide poisoning in its capsules. The company quickly addressed the issue, withdrew and redesigned its capsules and kept consumers informed of all developments.

.   Dentists who do not autoclave (heat sterilize) their instruments between each patient (as opposed to simply wiping the drill with a disinfectant) may be considered socially irresponsible given the threat of transmission of AIDS through contaminated instruments. Further, government agencies which refused for some time to change the standards for instrument cleanliness or to warn consumers may also be considered socially irresponsible.

.   In 1992, Sears gave millions of dollars in $ 50 merchandise certificates to customers who claimed they had been "ripped off" (in fact, most of them had) by Sears Auto Center repair shops. Admittedly, this was as much public relations as social responsibility.

17.   *How do codes of conduct help marketers make strategic decisions?*

ANSWER:

A code of conduct establishes a company's or a professional organization's guidelines with regard to its ethical principles and what behavior it considers proper. Since strategic decisions require a firm to evaluate opportunities based upon organization strengths, a code of conduct helps eliminate the obviously unacceptable alternatives. Based upon the AMA's Code of Ethics (Exhibit 2-8) for example, Tyco would reject a new toy which would be unsafe for children. Even though the toy might represent a financial opportunity, it would not match the code of conduct if this were established for the firm.

Codes of conduct also help decision makers by clearly specifying the standards and expectations of the firm. In the absence of a code of conduct, managers apply their own moral standards which may be divergent from the image desired by the firm.

ETHICS EXERCISE 2

CHAPTER 2 ETHICS IN PRACTICE

Overview

     This case deals with an organization named Legatus, founded by Domino's Pizza founder Tom Monaghan. The organization's members are corporate chief executive who are Catholics, and is intended to "apply the teaching of the Church to the business world." It raises several highly controversial but fundamental issues regarding ethics in business, and is therefore a good case with which to begin the semester. The salient issues are: the morality of the marketing concept; the morality of the profit motive; the relationship between religion, Judaeo-Christian values, and ethics; and the role of top management in ethical decision making.

1.   *Is this business organization compatible with the philosophy of the marketing concept?*

The first question is, "Is the marketing concept moral?" The first pillar of the marketing concept calls upon all organization members to be consumer-oriented in all activities. Marketing would appear to have a very moral purpose: to satisfy human needs and wants and to assist customers through the exchange process. Good marketing helps to identify deficiencies of current marketplace offerings and to present to the consumer an alternative to correct the deficiency. In effect, the marketing concept is one of anticipatory service to our fellow human beings, as reflected in adages such as, "The consumer is king (or queen)," "Find a need and fill it," and "Love the customer, not the product."

Critics of the marketing concept have argued that if people want what isn't good for them or in society's long-run best interests, then giving people what they want (e.g., unhealthy foods, environmentally unsafe products, and the proverbial "sex, drugs, and rock n' roll") isn't necessarily moral. Enter the societal marketing concept, which tempers the marketing concept with the idea that long-term collective societal needs must be considered in addition to individual short-term desires. The idea is to minimize social costs and enhance the quality of life. The focus is not only on the customer's interest and the organization's self-interest, but also on the general good/public interest.

The controversy arises in trying to define what is in society's best long-run interest and in trading off/balancing the interests of the organization, customers, and society. As in all ethical dilemmas, norms and values can come into conflict here, and others might not share the marketer's principles or values which guide her actions. The philosophical objection to the societal marketing concept is that businesspeople substitute their judgement and perception of what is in the social good for consumers' and/or elected policy-making officials' views. The pragmatic objection is that marketing managers have no special expertise in defining and acting in the public interest. Marketers might not be able to foresee the unintended negative consequences of their "socially responsible" actions.

For instance, it has been argued that McDonald's response to pressures from environmentalists might have actually had adverse consequences for the company and society. The argument is that they responded to a small but very vocal group of noncustomers who protest the waste of disposable containers, label the McFare "junk food," and accuse the company of clogging American arteries and hyping high blood pressure. Now, McDonald's is becoming too dictatorial in concluding that everyone must avoid salt and cholesterol, and treats the customer who has no health problems as the exception rather than the rule. No one consulted the customer about tasteless fries with less salt, the McLean Deluxe burger (made from seaweed, which could soon turn out to be the McEdsel burger!) and abandoning foam containers, which keep food hot, for coated paper, which allows food to cool more quickly and is not recyclable. Woe to the business which ignores the very specific preferences of its customers!

As another criticism of "social engineering," Milton Friedmann and other conservative economists have argued that a firm's goal should simply be to maximize profits and hence shareholder wealth; to do otherwise is to go beyond fulfilling management's mandate and a waste of stockholder's money (i.e., economic values are the only values which should be considered.) Businesses are established for economic purposes, not beneficent reasons; business should pursue profit, productivity, and efficiency, not goodness and kindness. In *Capitalism and Freedom* Friedman said "[In] a free economy ... there is one and only one social responsibility of business - to use its resources and engage in activities designed to increase its profits so long as it stays within the rules of the game, which is to say, engages in open and free competition without deception or fraud." (p. 136)

However, to Friedman one could reply that studies consistently demonstrate that companies which practice the societal marketing concept and ethical behavior prosper in the long run. As the adage says, "Good ethics is good business"; doing good and doing well aren't mutually exclusive; there is a return on integrity. In the long run, due to the self-regulating nature of the free enterprise system, the businessperson who eyeballs only profit position and cuts ethical corners, while perhaps prospering in the short run, destroys his firm's image and tarnishes his profession's image in the long run. After all, the firm's assets have little value without customer goodwill. Companies which look to the long-term value of doing business based on common moral standards, not just bottom-line reasoning, attract customers, honest employees, suppliers, and distributors. The trick is to balance economic and ethical performance. Instead of profit alone, perhaps reasonable and responsible profit should be the goal of the marketer with enlightened self-interest.

The second pillar of the marketing concept is a stress on long-term profitability. Historically (as well as currently) the morality of the profit

motive has been seriously questioned. There is an entrenched stereotype of
"robber baron" capitalists as being greedy, exploitative, and manipulative. The
profit motive (concern for financial reward) is viewed as less than virtuous
because it emphasizes self interest. Socialists argue that significant business
decisions need to be made in the public domain in order to ensure the public
good.

Proponents of capitalism and free markets would reply that we need the profit
motive because humans are basically selfish and lazy. The profit motive is
necessary if society is to maximize productivity and efficiently allocate its
resources. The profit motive ensures the production of those goods and services
that society desires the most at the lowest possible cost (i.e., that use the
least amount of resources). Competition is the reason why capitalism produces a
more prosperous society than socialism. The profit motive assures that resources
aren't systematically wasted (as under socialism) and that innovation and hard
work are rewarded. A reasonable profit rewards a firm for its contribution to
the public good, recognizing the degree of risk undertaken by the firm. A free
market is a moral achievement; it is the product of discipline and of the
postponement of present satisfaction for future (long-term) goals. Capitalism
rewards and reinforces service to others; competition forces people to act as if
they care about others.

The third pillar underlying the marketing concept is integration and coordination
of the marketing function with other corporate functions. If one buys into the
marketing concept as a moral ideal, this should pose few problems. Simply
stated, marketing is everyone's business; it is a philosophy of business which
should permeate the organization. The marketing department's job is to preach
the marketing gospel: to drive everyone to think in terms of long-term profits
achieved through customer satisfaction.

The objection comes from those in other functional areas who have their own goals
and agendas to pursue. Most managers and workers, at least in large companies,
are too far removed from the customer. Departments tend to have a parochial
perspective, act independently, and too often work at cross-purposes with one
another (see the text for examples). For many nonmarketing majors the concept of
a market-driven firm will be a tough sell. (It is in practice too! Marketing
training workshops and regular cross-functional meetings to discuss customer
needs are typical tools used to instill a marketing culture.)

The next question is, "Is an organization of Catholic senior managers who want to
apply the Church's moral teachings to the business world and to their personal
lives consistent with the marketing concept?" Assuming that students are
convinced that, at least in theory, marketing is a moral discipline, it can be
argued that Christianity and the marketing concept are perfectly compatible. In
fact, the marketing concept is based upon the biblical philosophy of life. This
is because the marketing concept doesn't put money first (this would be idolatry,
according to biblical teaching), it puts people first ("Love thy neighbor as
thyself") and says that the money will follow. The Christian life is one of
service to and love for others (as is also true of Judaism, the religion which
gave birth to Christianity.) As we have seen, the marketing concept mandates
that we serve others, caring about their needs and wants, which is what a servant
lives to do.

An objection could be raised that ultimately the marketing concept is concerned
with making money, and that the Bible says that "money is the root of all evil."
However, actually it says that "the love of money is the root of all evil."
Money is simply a tool, a servant - a medium of exchange and a store of value.
But if the marketer is out to make a buck, isn't he or she being materialistic,
which is incompatible with Christianity? That's perhaps true, but the Sermon on
the Mount didn't teach that material things are evil, but rather that they must
not be sought as ends in themselves. Rewards for service (both temporal and
eternal) are promised in the Bible.

Another objection might be that marketing is such a sleazy profession (visions of
fast-talking, conniving hucksters, cheats and frauds) that it is incompatible
with Christianity, a religion of brotherly love. The image of the unethical,
Machiavellian marketer persists, and while it has some basis in truth, it is more
the exception than the rule. Every discipline has its share of bad apples who
substitute a bag of tricks for the tools of the trade, and marketing is no

exception. The problem is not with the marketing practice but with the practitioners; responsibility for abuse lies with the people, not the process. Society needs people who can build better quality products and services, price them attractively and fairly, distribute them conveniently, and clearly communicate their superiority to the marketplace. This is good productive work, which is something else the Bible extols.

Some students might object to the notion of a group of religious people foisting their views about morality into the marketplace. While this might cause students discomfort, it should be pointed out that in a free enterprise system they certainly have the right to run their business according to what they believe to be true moral principles, so long as they don't conflict with the law (which Christian principles rarely do). They are not forcing their views on others, and as consumers we are free to take our business elsewhere if we object to their Christian or Catholic orientation. Throughout history, societies' moral values have been rooted and grounded in religious beliefs. You might want to challenge your students to think through what their own worldview is and the source of authority for the moral principles they hold.

2.   *Should nonCatholics be included in this group?*

One could argue that the members of this group have freedom of association, and so if they feel that non-Catholics have different values, they are justified in excluding them from the group. Christianity, Judaism, Islam, and many other faiths, teach the dangers of compromising with the world, and so these executives might be rightly wary of letting non-Catholics in.

On the other hand, Protestantism and Judaism, while having some theological differences with Catholicism, in essence share the same set of absolute moral values (honesty, courage, fidelity to family and friends, kindness and compassion, individual responsibility, self-discipline, thrift, etc.) and so it could be argued that members of these religious persuasions who take their faith seriously should be admitted.

Or, it could be argued, Monaghan and company should admit any senior executives who subscribe to their code of morality. After all, there are many agnostics and atheists who live an upright life and who have valuable ideas to share. They just don't believe that God is the ultimate source of those values.

3.   *Should managers who are not at the top of their organizations be included in this group?*

Again, this would seem to be a matter of the personal preferences of the organization's members. Certainly CEOs and senior executives who meet whatever criteria are established in question 2 above should be encouraged to join, for it is well known that corporate consciousness comes from the top. One of the most important factors in the literature on moral corporate cultures is the influence of the leaders in an organization. Their behavior serves as a model and a message-sender to all employees. Ideally, they lead by example (there should not be different standards of ethics at different levels in the organization) by written policy statements on the moral dimensions of business which are made clear in a public forum, by holding periodic management meetings to discuss the moral dimensions of business, and by hiring what they perceive to be ethical people.

It might make sense to include middle and even operating managers in the group, since they are closer to the daily implementation of the ethical guidelines. They might have valuable feedback to provide and would probably be more committed if, through participating in this type of organization, they felt more of a sense of ownership in the policies on business ethics.

CHAPTER 2 TAKE A STAND QUESTIONS

1.   *It's been said that Wendy's should stop wrapping its products in packages that just end up littering the neighborhood. Do you agree?*

The question would seem to be, "Whose responsibility is the littering?" If Wendy's is to blame, as economist George Stigler once noted, then we can blame waiters in restaurants for obesity. One should recognize the concept of individual responsibility.

On the other hand, if a viable, inexpensive option to these packages can be found, Wendy's would be practicing the societal marketing concept in choosing it. However, for fast food to go, it's not clear what that option would be. Perhaps Wendy's could take partial responsibility for the problem of litter by tagging their TV commercial spots with public service messages on the importance of keeping America beautiful, putting reminders on the packaging itself, placing notices on trash bins to "pitch in," etc.

2.   *Do you think that tobacco companies should be put out of business because their products promote cancer, other health problems, and also annoy a large percentage of the population that does smoke?*

Some people classify tobacco products in any form (along with alcoholic beverages, war toys, etc.) as "sin products" which promote immorality and, by various means, harm others (e.g., second-hand smoke, drunken drivers, violent children, etc.) One obvious problem with shutting down producers of such products is that it would throw a lot of people out of work, at least in the short run. However, in the long run, resources (including labor) will be reallocated to other industries. Another problem is that it would deprive people of freedom of choice. Of course, it could also be argued that we shouldn't have the choice to indulge in products which can potentially be harmful to others or even to ourselves.

A thornier problem is which businesses will be shut down. If we ban tobacco, shouldn't we also ban alcoholic beverages, since its abusers cause significant safety hazards? However, it is well known that Prohibition was a miserable failure and was hence repealed. Beef is high in cholesterol and fat - should we ban it? What about sugared products and products high in salt? Where does one draw the line in defining which products pose "significant health hazards"?

And, wouldn't it be cruel to deprive moderate users of such products of their right to enjoy these products? What about the pain and suffering that would be visited upon people who are addicted to such products?

A more moderate solution than an outright ban on tobacco products would be more responsible marketing by tobacco companies and more responsible usage by consumers. For instance, the Joe Camel Cool Character has been found to have high recognition appeal with kids, perhaps sending the message that it's okay to smoke. While it is debatable whether advertising is a powerful enough force to get kids started smoking (peer pressure is a much more potent force), nevertheless the advertising is putting a moral stamp of approval on smoking and making it appear appealing to at least some children. Similarly, lifestyle appeals (beautiful people enjoying nature, athletic activities, and smoking all the while) perhaps unnecessarily glamorize the activity. Also, consumers need to be sensitive to the effects of second-hand smoke on others, limiting their smoking to certain times and places.

Some argue for a ban on advertising tobacco products in all media (they are, of course, no longer advertised on TV or radio) although this might be seen as infringing on advertisers' rights to free commercial speech. Others have argued for limitations on the style of promotion (e.g., only allow "tombstone ads," which are restricted to basic information.) But again, the problem becomes one of where we draw the line. If Congress outlaws tobacco ads, what about ads for sugar, salt, caffeine-laden products, automobiles, bicycles, and bunk beds? Do we want the taste police deciding what advertising is and is not in good taste? These are subjective judgement calls, and not everyone will agree with the verdicts.

3.   *Government could do more to control television programs viewed by some to be offensive (like Eddie Murphy comedy shows) or recordings judged by some to be obscene (like those sung by Public Enemy). Take a stand.*

This is dealing with the regulation of taste. What is in good taste? Good taste is something that you and I, but very few other people have, i.e., it is very subjective. This is a very soft issue (vs. the hard issue of truth and accuracy). Taste is a function of the culture and the audience. In a free society, many people would find the regulation of taste to be dangerous; what will our moral monitors in government find next to be in bad taste? If you want free speech you usually have to tolerate some bad speech.

Taste is probably best left to the marketplace where consumers choose and vote with their dollars. According to economic theory, TV shows and other media that offend too many people will fail to capture large enough audiences to make them financially lucrative.

However, it might be argued that public morals and children need to be protected. Industry trade associations can adopt codes on taste. Also, individual consumers and consumer advocacy groups need to take responsibility. Consumers who are offended by a given activity can write a letter of complaint to the sponsoring company; if the firm receives a bagful of negative mail, the activity will soon stop. They can also write to the participating media vehicle. And, consumer boycotts are an effective means of shutting down an undesirable operation.

In a free society, consumers have the right to speak out against certain products and not buy them. An example would be the American Family Association, which has successfully promoted boycotts against sponsors of television shows their members find offensive (due to excessive sex, violence, profanity, and negative stereotyping of Christians) has convinced thousands of stores to stop selling pornographic magazines, and has convinced many theaters and video stores to stop distributing movies with the new NC-13 (formerly "X") rating, among other activities.

GUIDE TO CASES

VIDEO CASE 2-1   ANCHOR BREWING COMPANY

SUBJECT MATTER: Organizational Mission, Strategic Marketing, Marketing Concept

                        Please see the Guide to Video Cases for video length and other information.

AT-A-GLANCE OVERVIEW

The case describes the efforts of Fritz Maytag, heir to part of the Maytag fortune, to recreate the beer he drank in college, Anchor Steam, the high-quality product of a small, venerable (1896) brewery in San Francisco. He took the company over in 1966, pushed money into such areas as equipment and "quality," worked on developing a strong and involved group of employees, and operates "the cleanest delivery trucks in the U.S." By 1975 the company was on a strong footing, sending beer in bottles to 30 states, and selling it alongside expensive imports (over $ 7 per six-pack). The brewery is still small. Its annual production is exceeded by the big brewers in single production runs.

Anchor's marketing mix includes support of a woodwind ensemble rather than of a sports team, special, low-volume products sold at Christmas-time and other occasions during the year, and the like. Mr. Maytag does almost no marketing research, however. One "effort" included simply placing questionnaire post cards in six-packs, though it must be admitted that the survey results supported his efforts. Maytag claims he operates on "feelings." So far he's doing pretty well.

DISCUSSION QUESTIONS

1.   **Outline Anchor Steam's marketing mix.**

Anchor Brewing's marketing mix may be somewhat different from that of the major brewers, which, as the text notes, brew in minutes an amount equal to Anchor's annual output. Anchor's marketing mix does resemble that of many small businesses that compete with large firms by specializing in satisfying small market segments.

Product

Anchor Steam's main product is Anchor Steam Beer, a top quality beer that
competes with top-of-the-line beers, most of them imported. The beer is
distinctively packaged, and quality of the product is carefully monitored. The
company also produces a special "Christmas" beer, Ale, Porter, and Old Foghorn.

The product element of the marketing mix includes auxiliary dimensions more fully
discussed in Chapter 9. Among these is the distinctiveness of Anchor Steam, a
"dark, foamy brew." The beer, and the secondary beers, ale, and porter, are
"special," are "different." These characteristics are supported by the packaging
and the brand names, names which conjure up nautical images and/or San Francisco
images, that city being one with a sea port tradition and famous fog.

Place

Maytag has tried to make the physical elements of his distribution mix match the
quality of the products he makes. In the stores that carry Anchor, the product
is displayed with the expensive foreign beers. This implies that the products
are not available in every dumpy little store but offered only in places whose
clientele buys expensive and exclusive beers.

Anchor products are delivered in "the cleanest delivery trucks in the U.S." And,
while it is true that distribution is limited because production is limited,
limited distribution is suggestive of fine product quality. That there is a
backlog of would-be distributors also suggests exclusivity. The fact that the
beer, once a draft beer available only in San Francisco, is now available in
thirty states because it is bottled, demonstrates the interrelatedness of the
elements of the marketing mix.

Price

At the time this case was written, Anchor Steam was selling for $ 7 per six pack
outside its hometown. At the same time, Budweiser and Michelob, domestic good
quality beers, sold for slightly more than half Anchor's price. Anchor's price
is virtually equal to all but the most expensive imported beers. This is
consistent with product quality and image, as well as with the realities of the
market -- limited supply and high demand.

Promotion

As Coors was once able to do, Anchor sells well with limited promotion because of
its exclusive image. Limited advertising, in some ways, helps to preserve the
high-quality image of Anchor's products. If "everybody" knows about Anchor, it
becomes a "mass market" product and "just like all the other beers." That Maytag
can sell out his Christmas beer with "a couple of local print ads" shows that
Anchor is almost operating in a classic seller's market. Sponsoring a woodwind
ensemble rather than baseball broadcasts accents the quality image and narrowly
targets Anchor's promotional efforts on the "quality people" who drink this
"exclusive" beer.

Should Maytag decide to increase his promotional efforts he will, it seems,
continue to focus his promotions carefully. His mention of radio suggests this
-- classical music stations and NPR station support fit the quality and
exclusivity criteria. Certain magazines also fit them.

2.   *Has the company adopted the marketing concept?*

It is impossible to "prove" that a company has adopted the marketing concept.
Improved sales, a great image, customers beating down the doors, a backlog of
would-be distributors -- none of these can "prove" the adoption of the marketing
concept. This is because the concept is a philosophy of business, a way of
looking at things, and a system of values. The marketing concept is essentially
a mental process, the adoption of which cannot truly be proved.

Having noted this, it can be said that Anchor seems to have adopted the marketing
concept, at least intuitively. Maytag set out to recreate the beer of his youth,
to make a quality beer. In this, his plan seems to have been to make a quality
product that he personally liked. Obviously, millionaire or not, he knew he

Chapter 2: Marketing Management: Strategy and Ethical Behavior   59

would have to sell the beer to stay in business. It appears that he assumed
there were others like himself seeking a quality "dark, foamy brew." Yet his
marketing research appears to have been nil at the start and, even to the time of
this case, to have consisted, in toto, of a little questionnaire distributed in
six-packs of his own beer. Not very "scientific."

In short, Maytag started out to please himself and assumed that there were other
people who agreed with his views. This is not unusual in businesses, though many
businesses based on similar thinking fail. Many retailers fail because they are
interested in models of ships, for example, and assume that other people are too.
They open a store and no one shows up. In some respects, Maytag appears to have
"lucked out," assuming a market which, in fact, proved to exist.

Note, however, that Maytag is no longer dreaming of the beer of his college days.
He knows what sort of market he faces and considers what his customers want and
are willing to pay for. He seems to have an understanding of his market and how
to reach it. He has assembled a very effective marketing mix, focused on a
specific target market. Maytag admits he finds it hard to develop a marketing
plan, but he obviously has one "in his head" if not on paper. In sum, it appears
that Anchor has adopted the marketing concept.

3.   *Prepare a written statement of Anchor Brewing Company's organizational
      mission. Include a definition of its business domain.*

The students' statements of Anchor's mission will probably be based on the
information given in the case. Most students not living in the San Francisco
area will not be familiar with this product. It can be expected that a statement
of mission would include all or most of the following terms and expressions found
in the case.

.   High product quality
.   Word of mouth promotion
.   Expansion of market area consistent with quality maintenance
.   Appeal to beer "aficionados"
.   Relatively low production levels
.   Emphasis on brewers' workmanship
.   "Special Edition" beer production
.   Emphasis on exclusivity and "specialness"

A reasonable statement of mission, based on the case, might be:

      To produce a product line which suits the tastes and lifestyles of
      our target customer group by stressing quality in production, limited
      expansion consistent with quality goals, and marketing efforts aimed
      at maintaining customer loyalty.

Some facts not presented in the case may be of use in evaluating the ideas of
Anchor's mission developed by students.

.   Anchor was founded in 1896 and is still a very small brewer. Before
      Maytag's expansion of production, however limited, it was a "micro" brewer.
      There are perhaps 10 to 15 brewers in the U.S. (producing bottled/canned
      beers) as small as Anchor.

.   Maytag plans to continue expansion, but at no more than 10 percent per
      year. His feeling is that even small expansion (including what he has
      planned) may be dangerous given his quality goals.

A statement of Anchor's business domain should include mention of the market
segment to which Anchor caters: that portion of the market for beer that seeks a
high-quality product, not a mass-market product, reflective of their developed
tastes, their desire for the unique, and their willingness to go out of their
way, and pay a premium, to satisfy their tastes.

4.   *Identify some of the marketing strategies used to market Anchor Steam Beer.*

Students may argue that Maytag's seeming seat-of-the-pants methods mean that
there are no marketing strategies involved in Anchor's success. Many can be
identified, however, even if they are not formally spelled out.

.   Market segmentation
.   Target marketing
.   Controlled growth
.   Product quality emphasis
.   Status/exclusive imaging
.   Status pricing
.   Limited geographic distribution
.   Selective distribution
.   Positioning (equivalent to imports)
.   Developing and maintaining "mystique"
.   Careful dealings with distributors ("cleanest trucks in the U.S.")
.   Supporting of the major brand with other special brews

The instructor may want to list these and similar efforts, then ask students to discuss how each one "fits in" with the others. They all tie together.

5.   *Identify some of the tactics used to market Anchor Steam beer.*

Tactics are used to implement strategy. The "cleanest trucks in the U.S." practice is a tactic used within Anchor's distribution strategy. It is a tool that helps distribution to be handled in a way consistent with Anchor's image as an exclusive, high-quality product. The strategy of positioning Anchor as the equal to expensive imported brands is supported by the tactic of charging a price equal to that of those beers.

The sponsorship of a wind ensemble bearing the product's name is a tactic within the promotional strategy of maintaining a quality, high-class image.

This is a good case for class discussion rather than a written assignment because the class, having listed "n" strategies, can then be asked to list tactics that support each strategy. Also, students have a traditional association with beer.

VIDEO CASE 2-2   HEIDI'S FAMILY RESTAURANT[1]
FOCUS ON SMALL BUSINESS

SUBJECT MATTER: Organizational Mission, Marketing Plan, Demand Fluctuation

> Please see the Guide to Video Cases for video length and other information.

AT-A-GLANCE OVERVIEW

Heidi's Family Restaurant operates three restaurants and a bread store. In 1986, the company opened its first Heidi's Family Restaurant in Carson City, followed by restaurants in Minden (1988) and Reno (1990.) Heidi's "The Bread Store" opened in 1990.

Heidi's restaurants are located on sites where bankrupt or closed businesses were previously located. The challenges inherent in taking over a closed or bankrupt businesses included a nonexistent or demoralized work force, a negative public image and a lack of customers. Additionally, because of their locations, Heidi's Family Restaurants are forced to compete in a highly price-sensitive market against hotels and casinos that offer rock-bottom prices to attract gambling patrons. Another challenge is the seasonal nature of business in a resort area, where sales between the second and fourth weeks of December can increase 200-500 percent.

---

[1] Case and Video materials based on *Strengthening America's Competitiveness*, pp. 52-53, copyright 1991 by Connecticut Mutual Life Insurance Company.

To build and rejuvenate the work force, the company hired employees who enjoy working in the restaurant business. It educated the new staff about the corporate culture and expectations of Heidi's Family Restaurant and let them know they were now part of a winning team. As the restaurants grow, the company raises employee wages.

The video segment illustrates Heidi's situation, then indicates the results of Heidi's plan.

The Results

Due to its efforts, the company has experienced significant success with its restaurants. The Carson City Heidi's Family Restaurant has experienced at least 20 percent sales growth in each year of operation. In calendar year 1990, net profit has grown and now regularly equals the company's initial investment. Profits have helped fund the company's expansion. The Minden restaurant has shown a significant return on investment in its second year of operation.

Heidi's in Reno has shown the highest gross sales of each of the newer restaurants, and has been profitable since its first day of business. And The Bread Store experienced an 18 percent growth in sales in its first two months of operation. The company has expanded an existing client base of 30 wholesale businesses with eight new clients.

DISCUSSION QUESTIONS

1.   *Outline a marketing plan for Heidi's.*

Heidi's Family Restaurant marketing plan initially focused on turning several bankrupt or closed businesses into highly successful enterprises. It has been successful because of hard work, perseverance and an innovative business strategy.

In order to build a customer base, the company purchases high-quality products and ingredients, and makes sure that guests perceive the improved quality of the food through use of recognized, quality brand-name products. The "Heidi" theme is reinforced indoors through attractive decor and uniforms, and outdoors through flower-beds and planters.

Heidi's Family Restaurants maintains active involvement in the community, which boosts its local image. It is involved in a number of service projects, such as a Christmas gift tree for needy children and donating food to homeless shelters. Public awareness of the company's efforts in this area also led to increased sales. As other ways of gaining local acceptance, the company actively solicits small (6-30) business meeting groups, service club committees and office parties that are too small for the hotels/casinos, and members of Heidi's management serve on the boards of local organizations.

2.   *How important is friendly service in Heidi's marketing mix?*

As a way to address its second challenge, competing in a price-sensitive market, Heidi's uses a marketing mix that recognizes the importance of price, but does not emphasize price. Heidi's offers quality, upscale meals, personalized and efficient service and a pleasant ambiance. By delivering in these areas, it is able to overcome price resistance. Its bakery products are made fresh each morning by Heidi's, which distinguishes the company's product from the competition's.

3.   *What can Heidi's do to manage seasonal sales fluctuations?*

The company's approach to its third challenge, seasonal sales fluctuations, is to build a flexible production and service staff. It has positive relationships with several colleges with respected hotel/restaurant management schools. Students travel across the country to Nevada for working vacations during the winter holiday and summer seasons. Seasonal sales fluctuations also are reduced through strong marketing efforts.

3 THE EXTERNAL ENVIRONMENT

CHAPTER SCAN

This chapter shows marketing as operating within a multifaceted, ever-changing environment, both restricting the actions of marketing managers and presenting them with new opportunities. This environment incorporates domestic and international elements, social values and beliefs, demographic trends, economic institutions and practices, shortages of products, laws and governmental agencies, and competitors and their actions.

The chapter also describes the interrelationships that exist among these forces and the reactions of marketers to environmental changes.

SUGGESTED LEARNING OBJECTIVES

The student who studies this chapter will be exposed to a discussion of the environment of marketing in all its aspects and its effects on marketing managers as a source of both constraints and opportunities, and will be able to:

1. Describe marketing's domestic and foreign environments and their effects on organizations.

2. Understand that social values and beliefs are important environmental forces.

3. Explain how demographic trends influence marketers.

4. Explain the various ways in which economic conditions, institutions, and practices influence marketers.

5. Identify the various types of competitors and understand how marketers anticipate and react to competitors' strategies.

6. Define "demarketing."

7.   Understand the three levels of U. S. law and the growing need to understand the laws of other nations.

8.   Explain how the various elements of the marketing environment interact.

CHAPTER OUTLINE

I.   INTRODUCTION

II.   A WORLD PERSPECTIVE

III.   THE PHYSICAL ENVIRONMENT

IV.   THE CULTURAL ENVIRONMENT

V.   SOCIAL VALUES AND BELIEFS

    A.   Social Values and Beliefs in Other Cultures

VI.   DEMOGRAPHICS

    A.   The U.S. Population

        1.   Migration
        2.   Urbanization
        3.   Growth in the Sunbelt
        4.   Age
        5.   Profile of the "Average American Consumer"
        6.   A Multicultural Population

    B.   World Population

VII.   ECONOMIC AND COMPETITIVE FORCES

    A.   Competitive Market Structures
    B.   Economic Conditions
    C.   Economic Institutions

        1.   Suppliers
        2.   Marketing Intermediaries
        3.   Competitors
            a.   Product Class
            b.   Product Category
            c.   Brand

VIII.   SCIENCE AND TECHNOLOGY

IX.   POLITICS AND LAWS

    A.   Three Levels of U.S. Law

        1.   The Federal Level
        2.   The State Level
        3.   The Local Level

    B.   International Laws

X.   ENVIRONMENTAL INTERACTIONS

XI.   SUMMARY

XII.   KEY TERMS

XIII.   QUESTIONS FOR DISCUSSION (11)

XIV.   ETHICS IN PRACTICE

XV. CASES

The following key terms are introduced and used in Chapter 3. They are defined in the text's Glossary.

Domestic environment
Foreign environment
Physical environment
Green marketing
Culture
Cultural environment
Social value
Belief
Demography
Economic system
Pure competition
Monopolistic competition
Oligopoly
Monopoly
Gross domestic product (GDP)
Gross national product (GNP)
Business cycle
Suppliers
Demarketing
Product class
Product category
Brand
Science
Technology
Political environment
Legal environment
Antitrust legislation
Federal Trade Commission (FTC)
Multinational marketing group

THE CHAPTER SUMMARIZED

I. INTRODUCTION

The chapter opens with a brief discussion of how McDonald's demonstrates its corporate concern for the environment. Of special concern is beef grown in formerly rainforested areas. McDonald's claim is that nowhere in the world does it use beef from rainforest (or recently deforested rainforest) land. McDonald's demands that all suppliers adhere to this and, if they depart from the policy or cannot prove they are following the policy, they are "discontinued" as suppliers.

This stand demonstrates McDonald's recognition of the increasing public concern for the environment. If an organization is to be successful, its marketing managers must adapt to environmental changes.

II. A WORLD PERSPECTIVE

You may use a (French) Bic pen, and fuel your (German) Mercedes with Venezuelan or Nigerian oil. Improved communications and transportation tools have made multinational marketing a force of great importance in the world. The world is getting smaller.

Some companies market their products only in their home countries and are influenced only by their home environments, but most organizations today, both large and small, must monitor environmental opportunities and threats in the domestic AND foreign environments. (See Exhibit 3-1.)

An environment may be seen as having two parts: physical and the cultural aspects. This is illustrated in Exhibit 3-2.

III.   THE PHYSICAL ENVIRONMENT

The **physical environment** includes: natural resources, climate, the human population, and other aspects of nature, such as changes in the ecological system.

The influence of the physical (or "natural") environment is often quite obvious. Countries with petroleum resources produce products that can be made from petroleum. More umbrellas are sold in Seattle than Tucson, more food products are sold in New York City than in Enid, Oklahoma.

The physical environment includes the presence (or absence) of substances harmful (or helpful) to the Earth's ecology. Smog, acid rain, the safety of animal life, and so on, have led to a phenomenon known as **green marketing**. This is the marketing of ecologically safe products and making efforts to help preserve or revitalize the physical environment.

IV.   THE CULTURAL ENVIRONMENT

Marketing operates within societies and every society has a culture. **Culture** can be defined as "everything we are not born with." We are born with a need for food, but what foods we eat and how we prepare them is "cultural."

The **cultural environment** is the part of the environment shaped by humankind. It is that complex whole which includes social values and beliefs, economic conditions, institutions and practices, scientific and technical knowledge, and political and legal factors.

V.   SOCIAL VALUES AND BELIEFS

Changing social values affect virtually every organization. For example, more women working means fewer volunteer workers for charities.

A **social value** embodies the goals society views as important and expresses preferred ways of acting.

These are reflective of ideas about what is good and bad, right and wrong, e.g., that it is wrong to steal. Among the beliefs held by a majority of Americans are:

 .   **Freedom** of the individual to act as he or she pleases (within the law)
 .   **Achievement and Success** through honest efforts
 .   **Work Ethic** to work on a regular basis and not be "lazy"
 .   **Equality**, especially of opportunity
 .   **Patriotism** or pride in living in the "best country in the world"
 .   **Individual Responsibility and Self-Fulfillment** or, as in the Army's slogan, "Be all that you can be."

A **belief** is a statement concerning the existence and characteristics of physical and social phenomena. Smoking is "believed" to cause health problems.

Note the effects of these even if they are not true. Smoking may not really cause health problems, but many people behave as if this were an absolute certainty, e.g., no-smoking sections in restaurants.

It is the marketer's job to "read" the social environment and reflect the surrounding culture's values and beliefs in a marketing strategy.

A.   Social Values in Other Cultures

Social values vary widely around the world. Effective marketers seeking to operate within these other cultures adjust their marketing mixes to reflect this fact. A chicken dinner in Japan is valued far more highly than such a dinner in North America.

Thus, Kentucky Fried Chicken operations in Japan differ from those in the U.S. and Canada.

In a similar way, buyers and government workers behave differently in different cultures. Taking one's time is seen in some lands as creating a friendly atmosphere, but Americans may see this as "delaying action." What some view as "gifts" or "tips" we often perceive as simple "bribes."

The Japanese **keiretsu** (corporate family) binds some companies to one another, keeping out, for example, competing suppliers of goods. To us this appears to be unfair "locking out" of competition.

VI.   DEMOGRAPHICS

Demography is the study of the size, composition, and distribution of the human population ("demos" = "people" in Greek) in relation to social factors such as geographic boundaries.

A wealth of demographic information is to be found in the *Statistical Abstract of the United States.*

A.   The U.S. Population

The U.S. population is constantly changing, but Census data is believed to be fairly accurate. The Census indicates:

- About 254 million people living in the U.S.
- Birth rate of 16.0 per thousand
- Death rate of 8.6 per thousand
- 51.2 percent females, 48.8 percent males
- Population of 268 million by the year 2000

1.   Migration

U.S. migration within the country has continued since earliest times. The 1790 Census shows the center of population east of Baltimore, Maryland. The 1990 Census shows this point to be in Crawford County in southwestern Missouri. The point traditionally moves to the south and west.

2.   Urbanization

The U.S. and the world have become increasingly urbanized since the 1880s. Growth of suburbs has created merged urbanized areas like the Northeast Corridor extending from north of Boston to south of Washington, D.C.

The 1990 Census shows that half the population of the U.S. live in just 39 metropolitan areas. Seventy-six percent live in one of the 284 metropolitan areas, up from 56 percent in 1950.

Core city populations have fallen, but suburban growth means areas actually grow. Chicago's city population declines, Chicago area population has grown. The most dramatic growth of population 1980 to 1990 was in suburban areas. Mesa, Arizona, and Plano, Texas, have become cities.

3.   Growth in the Sunbelt

Text's Exhibit 3-3 shows rates of change in states' population. Since 1985, 80.5 percent of U.S. population gain has been in the South and West.

The growth of the Sunbelt is much discussed. It should be noted that the greatest population and economic growth has occurred in Texas, Florida and California. When these three are removed from the figure citing Sunbelt growth, the growth of other Sunbelt states is put into a different light.

4.   Age

In 1790, the median age in the U.S. was 16 years, today it is
32.6. The aging of the "baby boomers" has driven up the age of
the U.S. population. (See Exhibit 3-4.)

A consumer's "age cohort" has a great influence upon buying
behaviors. Many products are more heavily purchased by one age
group than by another. Seniors spend a lot on medicine, but
also on vacation travel.

In recent years there has been a "baby boomlet" with strong
implications for demand for child-oriented products, including
elementary school education. This group represents a resource
in that, in some twenty years, they will be forming households
and families of their own.

Birth rates, death rates, life expectancy, average age, etc.
have major importance for marketers.

5.   Profile of the "Average American Consumer"

In fact, there is no "Average American Consumer" because of the
many variables inherent in our population. Interesting
statistics, however, include:

- There are more females than males.
- Median age is about 32.6 years.
- Median years of schooling is 12.7.
- Average household size is 2.62 persons.
- Half of households have no children under 18 living at
  home.
- 20.8 percent of households include just one child.
- Only 9.8 percent of households include 3 or more
  children.
- Median family income in 1990 was $35,353.
- Inflation has been such that the average family's
  purchasing power increased by less than ten percent in
  the years 1970-1990.

Presence of more career-minded singles, more divorced people,
more widowed people contribute to these figures. Though U.S.
population is rising, the number of households is rising much
more quickly.

6.   A Multicultural Population

- One of every four Americans is Black, Hispanic, Asian or
  a member of another minority.
- Blacks are about 12.5 percent of the population,
  Hispanics 9 percent, Asians about 3 percent.
- There are about 31 million Blacks, 21 million Hispanics,
  and 7 million Asians.
- Hispanics are the fastest growing group but will not
  overtake the black population until at least 2010.
- Only a small percentage of immigrants are of European
  heritage. In 1960, 9 of 10 Americans was white, in 1990
  about 3 of 4 are white.

Exhibit 3-5 contrasts the growth of various groups.

B.   World Population

World population exceeds five and a half billion. While this
provides opportunities for marketing, it also poses grave problems
for the planet as a whole. Marketers cannot ignore these.

World population is estimated to grow at a rate of 16,000 per hour. World population is expected to grow by at least 140 million per year.

Exhibit 3-6 shows the growth and distribution of world population.

Though the chapter addresses demographic matters primarily at the national level, it is important to note that marketers must also know what is going on with "the rest of the world."

VII. ECONOMIC AND COMPETITIVE FORCES

Economic and competitive forces are elements of the cultural environment and strongly influence all levels of marketing activities.

Each society's economic system determines how it will allocate scarce resources. In the Western world the economic system can be classified as "modified capitalism." Under this system the forces of competition, foreign and domestic, influence supply and demand. There are several models of competition.

A. Competitive Market Structures

The market structure in which an organization operates strongly influences its pricing practices, and other business practices.

Pure competition exists when there are no barriers to competition. Price is not controlled by buyers or sellers. There are many small competing firms and products are homogeneous. The markets for basic food commodities approach this situation.

Monopolistic Competition. Typified by product differentiation. Sellers offering similar products that are different to some degree, e.g., McDonald's and Burger King. The difference is enough to permit some influence over prices.

Oligopoly. A few large companies, each with strong influences within the industry's market, e.g., aircraft manufacturers. Each company has a strong influence on the industry and on pricing and other business practices. A would-be new competitor faces significant barriers to entry.

Monopoly. No suitable substitute products, one supplier, e.g., local electric company. U.S. law strictly limits monopoly situations.

B. Economic Conditions

GNP (Gross National Product) and **GDP (Gross Domestic Product)** are good measures of the health of an economy. GNP refers to the value of all goods and services produced by U.S. residents and corporations regardless of where they are located in the world. GDP refers to the goods and services produced by labor and capital in the U.S.

Business cycle refers to recurrent fluctuations in general economic activity.

The four phases of the business cycle are: prosperity, recession, depression, recovery.

Prosperity. The phase in which the economy is operating at or near full employment, both consumer spending and business output are high.

Recession. The downward phase, in which production, spending, and employment are decreasing.

Depression. The low phase of the cycle. Unemployment is high, spending is low, output has declined drastically.

Recovery. Upward phase, when employment, spending, and output are rising.

The business cycle is difficult to forecast but marketing strategies must be altered to fit periods of prosperity and those of recession or depression.

C.   Economic Institutions

Within each market structure are many economic institutions, e.g., distribution system members.

1.   Suppliers

Most marketers obtain some goods and services from **suppliers** (or vendors.) Most deal, directly or indirectly, with overseas suppliers. The ability to locate suppliers who fulfill their commitments can greatly affect marketing activities, especially pricing strategies.

a.   Supply Problems and Demarketing

Only recently have American marketers, as a group, worried about supply. Raw materials, for example, were "givens." Recent events have changed that. Where we once were concerned with finding buyers for our products, now we may find it necessary to discourage buyers.

Demarketing is a term used to describe activities that intentionally discourage all or some customers from buying or consuming a product either on a temporary or permanent basis.

Demarketing is aimed at diminishing or controlling demand in such a way that customers can be kept over the long run. It is the application of the marketing concept in an undesirable situation.

The text includes several examples, e.g., Budweiser advertised "We're brewing more as slow as we can" when shortages occurred in some areas. The ads were consistent with Bud's quality image.

2.   Marketing Intermediaries

The available distribution system is a major factor influencing marketing managers' decisions. The U.S. and Canada, compared to Angola and Peru, can easily distribute most products. Japan's high retail prices are blamed, in part, on a system that uses many more middlemen than are necessary to distribute products.

3.   Competitors

In some industries competition is intense and changeable. Competitors' strategies may be the most important factors in determining the organization's success or failure. Competition often leads to lowering of prices. VCRs cost $1500 when first introduced but competition had cut the price to $200-250 within a few years. The video cassettes themselves, and, more recently, cellular phones have gone the same route -- cheaper AND better.

Competition comes from the substitutability that is possible among many goods and services. A bus trip is substitutable for a train trip, but a fur coat is also substitutable for a car when a consumer is thinking about how to spend his or her money.

Product strategies cannot be planned without consideration of the competition. The following three terms are used to describe competition:

a.   Product Class

A **product class** is a group of items that may differ from each other while performing more or less the same function, e.g., household cleaner product class includes all sorts of powders, liquids and sprays.

b.   Product Category

Product categories are subsets of product types contained within a product class, e.g., the household cleaner product class includes liquid, powder and spray categories. Regular beer, light beer, dark beer, etc. are similar categories.

c.   Brand

A **product brand** identifies and distinguishes one marketer's product from its competitors, e.g., the liquid category of the household cleaner product class includes Top Job, Lysol, or the various brands of light beers.

Who is the competition? In a sense, members of the same product class compete against each other, but the realities of the market suggest that the narrower categories include the "true" competitors (e.g., Lysol vs. Top Job rather than Top Job vs. Spic and Span.)

VIII. SCIENCE AND TECHNOLOGY

Though the two words are often used interchangeably, they are different in meaning.

Science is the accumulation of knowledge about human beings and the environment.

Technology is the application of knowledge to practical purposes.

The impact of both on marketing activities is very clear: the knowledge that saccharin causes cancer, the application of space technology to consumer products, the microchip, the development of super conductivity, the *New England Journal of Medicine*'s report that oat bran did not greatly reduce cholesterol that reduced demand for oat bran by half within a few months of publication, the space program's development of Tang, the application of space technology to such earthly jobs as fire fighting.

Science and technology are part of the environment of marketing. Marketers must monitor change just as they do in the cases of changes of other aspects of marketing's environment.

X.   POLITICS AND LAWS

The **political environment** is the practices and policies of governments.

The **legal environment** consists of laws and interpretations of regulations.

These may:

- Limit activities (antitrust laws)
- Require activities (listing contents of food products)
- Prohibit activities (sale of illegal drugs)
- Control exports (sale of high-technology products to the Libya or Iraq)
- Have international impacts as did the Soviet Union's attempt at perestroika (economic restructuring) and glasnost (increased candor about political and public events) and as did the Chinese government's violent response to student demonstrations in Tiananmen Square.

A.   Three Levels of Law

The three levels of law in the U.S. mean a vast array of regulations and regulatory agencies. One study suggests that a marketing organization might confront nearly 100,000 sets of rules and regulations.

1.   Federal Level

Many federal laws can be named: Sherman Act, Clayton Act, the Public Health Smoking Act, etc. Text mentions many such acts. Exhibit 3-10 summarizes some of these.

The F.T.C. Act is more important than many because of its effects on virtually all marketers on a day-to-day basis.

2.   State Level

Most states have laws and agencies which parallel those at the federal level. All states have laws that affect the marketing mixes of organizations operating in those states.

- Liquor laws
- Tax laws
- Banking laws
- Laws barring certain materials

3.   Local Level

Local ordinances, licensing regulations, tax laws and regulatory boards affect marketing. Green River Ordinances are good examples.

B.   International Laws

Laws governing marketing activities vary widely from country to country. In some, misleading advertising is punishable by heavy fines and stiff prison sentences.

Further, some countries have joined to form **multinational marketing groups** (unified markets) that can have their own legal restrictions.

X.   ENVIRONMENTAL INTERACTIONS

It is a difficult task, but marketers must consider the whole of the environment in which they operate, not just its parts.

The complexity of the marketer's task in dealing with the environment is made greater by interactions within that environment. A volcanic explosion may increase the interest in "disaster" movies, improved medical abilities may lead to fewer childhood deaths which may lead to couples having fewer children which may affect many industries, which affects jobs, etc.

VIII. SUMMARY

This chapter describes the dynamic environment in which marketing managers operate and the demographic, psychological, social, legal and ethical aspects of that environment.

Learning Objective 1: Describe the domestic and foreign environments in which marketers operate and their effects on the organization.

Marketing managers must adjust an organization's marketing mix to cope with the domestic environment and often foreign environments as well. In both cases, the marketing environment consists of uncontrollable forces that provide both opportunities and constraints to an organization. The physical environment includes all natural phenomena, such as natural resources and climate. The cultural environment includes demography, economics, science and technology, social values and beliefs, and politics and laws. Correct environmental assessment makes marketing decisions more successful.

Learning Objective 2: Understand that social values and beliefs are important environmental forces.

A social value embodies the goals a society views as important and expresses a culture's shared ideas of preferred ways of acting. A belief is a conviction concerning something's existence or characteristics. It is the marketers's job to "read" the social environment and reflect the surrounding culture's values and beliefs in a marketing strategy.

Learning Objective 3: Explain how demographic trends influence modern marketers.

Important demographic trends include the aging of the population, a general trend toward having fewer children, and an increasing number of households. These and other demographic factors not only affect the demand for goods and services but also lead to variations in pricing, distribution, and promotion.

Learning Objective 4: Explain the various ways that economic conditions, institutions, and practices influence marketing organizations.

The business cycle, the competitive market structure, and the economic institutions have a strong influence on marketing activity. Suppliers and competitors have a direct impact on marketing strategy.

Learning Objective 5: Be able to identify the various types of competitors and understand how marketers anticipate and react to their strategies.

Product class, product category, and brand are terms used to identify an organization's potential competitors. A competitive analysis of each competitor's strengths and weaknesses may point to a window of opportunity for an organization.

Learning Objective 6: Define demarketing.

Demarketing occurs when environmental changes create shortages of certain products. It is a marketing strategy intended to diminish demand while maintaining adequate consumer satisfaction during the shortage period.

Learning Objective 7: Understand the three levels of United States law and the growing need to understand international law.

Federal laws control many business activities such as pricing and advertising by manufacturers, wholesalers, and retailers. The FTC, in particular, affects almost all marketers. State laws deal with many areas including foods, manufactured goods, lending, real estate, banking and insurance. Local laws affect zoning and licensing, among other things. Laws that govern the marketing of products in foreign countries and in multinational marketing groups are subject to tremendous variation and will affect any organization that engages in international marketing.

Learning Objective 8: Explain how the various elements of the marketing environment interact.

Changes in any aspect of the environment usually bring about changes elsewhere in the environment. Several environmental forces may combine to encourage changes in consumer behavior or marketing mixes.

XII. **KEY TERMS**

XIII. **QUESTIONS FOR DISCUSSION (11)**

XIV. **ETHICS IN PRACTICE**

XV. **CASES**

ANSWER GUIDELINES FOR CHAPTER 3 QUESTIONS FOR DISCUSSION

1. *What environmental factors might have the greatest influence on: (a) General Motors, (b) McDonald's, (c) Morton Thiokol, producer of engines for the U.S. space shuttle?*

ANSWER:

A major difficulty some students will face in dealing with this question is where to stop. It would be possible to cite hundreds of examples of influences on G.M., McDonald's, and Morton Thiokol. Thus, the matter really becomes one of demonstrating a grasp of the types of factors that may have an effect, and of expressing an understanding of their importance while mentioning the interrelationships to be found among them.

A workable response format can be built around the major topics of Chapter Three: physical environment, cultural environment, economic environment, scientific and technological environment, social environment, and political-legal environment.

Some examples are:

(a) General Motors

The consumer auto market is considered here, though the truck, bus, or train markets may prove more challenging.

Physical: Locations of population, climatic extremes, terrain ruggedness, sand or dust, density of population (fewer people = fewer gas stations = need for bigger tanks on cars), availability of fuel (gas guzzlers may sell better in Saudi Arabia than in Belgium.) Disasters like 1992's Hurricane Andrew may destroy many cars in certain areas, causing a rise in demand for cars to replace them.

Cultural: Preference for big cars or small cars, firm-riding or soft-riding, cheap or gaudy and expensive, and other variants, may be part of the given cultural tradition.

Economic: Bad times may mean demand for cheaper cars and/or more readily available G.M.A.C. credit plans, or desire for fuel efficiency, or for cars the owner can repair.

Scientific and Technological: Cars might be made to run on alcohol, methane gas, or some other alternative. Road-building technology led to our Interstate Highway System and the faster speeds these permitted, plus the development of auto air conditioning contributed to lessened preferences for convertibles.

Social: Changes in society (more divorces, more singles, more freedom granted to teenagers) have played a part in raising demand for relatively

inexpensive cars. So have fuel prices, demonstrating the relationships
among these environmental factors. The trend toward fewer children could
mean more money for sportier cars.

Political-Legal: Government regulations on pollution and safety equipment.
Import-export laws and quotas. Nature of relationship with Japan. The
mandated 55 m.p.h. and 65 m.p.h. speed limits.

(b)   McDonald's

Physical: Concentrations of population are a key factor in the McDonald's
site selection process. Terrain and climate are important in building
design and the decision to have an outdoor playground.

Cultural: Americans like hamburgers, fries, coke, etc., while people in
other countries may not like the McDonald's menu. Most people want ketchup
and/or mustard on their hamburgers. North American cultural values favor
fast service, but this is not true in Spain, Italy, and other countries,
(though these people are "learning" our ways). People in New England like
vinegar on french fries, and call "milk shakes" by the names "velvets" and
"cabinets."

Economic: Economic bad times may mean more moonlighting and more spouses
working, which leads to the demand for inexpensive restaurant foods and
precooked foods from supermarkets. Bad times could lessen customer desires
to drive to a McDonald's just for a snack, and could raise demand for
cheaper items while dropping demand for more expensive menu items. In some
depressed parts of the country, McDonald's has lowered the prices of
several menu items. Increased competition has led to new menu items.

Scientific and Technological: The McNugget is made of processed chicken --
a "technological breakthrough." Scientific knowledge may develop that
shows pickles cause stomach cancer -- "Hold the pickle!" New packaging
materials and cooking and food storage methods could affect McDonald's
greatly. The knowledge that salt and fat can be bad for you has caused
McDonald's to change some recipes and create new items like its McLean.

Social: There is a social trend toward better health and fitness. Cutting
salt and fat content of the products offered may follow. Reflecting this,
McDonald's has installed posters that list contents of Big Macs, etc.,
along with vitamin content to show the products are nutritious and provides
health information pamphlets.

Political-Legal: Antilitter ordinances. Concern with taxing. Businesses
that generate great amounts of trash. Local health ordinances. Zoning
laws. Parking regulations. Decisions to alter auto traffic patterns.

(c)   Morton Thiokol, producer of engines for the U.S. space shuttle

For a company dealing with the federal government on a project of such
significance as the shuttle, many problems can be overcome simply by asking
for more money. The frequent stories about super-overpriced toilet seats,
rubber washers, and hammers attest to that.

Before mentioning a few environmental influences on Morton Thiokol, it
should be noted that this company, maker of the engine on the ill-fated
shuttle that killed seven astronauts, continued to build and test engines
for about two years. Problems kept surfacing and, worse, so did news
stories about the company. In 1988, the government opened bidding for the
shuttle engine project and Morton Thiokol did not bid, removing itself from
the shuttle business entirely. It can be surmised that bad publicity at
the time of the disaster, continued scrutiny in the press, subsequent
engine tests that failed (all reported in the press), law suits, "whistle
blowing" employees, and so on, led management to the belief that it might
as well cut its losses and "get out of the kitchen."

Cultural: The free press tradition of the United States, the placing of
the shuttle program in the spotlight (something that would not have

occurred in the U.S.S.R.), the decision to include two civilians (including a teacher and mother from New Hampshire) on the shuttle, and other culturally biased decisions, contributed to Morton Thiokol's difficult position.

Economic: As mentioned, economics is not as major an issue as might be expected. The government, after all, is legally permitted to tax, borrow, or print money at will. However, economics can influence the shuttle, and other programs, over the longer run if the federal deficit, costs of space programs, and the recognition that for the price of the shuttle program some other program(s) could be completed, cause legislators and the public to question the project's worth and, thereby, affect companies involved with the project. We are seeing this in 1992-1993.

Scientific-Technical: The story of the shuttle failure is familiar enough. We might recall, however, that the faulty O-rings that caused the famous disaster were suspect. Some engineers had warned that the weather at the time of launch was too cold and that the frozen rings might fail.

Social: In the case of Morton Thiokol, social changes and influences are of minor importance unless one wishes to discuss here the concern for human life touched on under the "cultural" heading.

Political-Legal: The company was sued by families of the dead astronauts. It was the target of what must have been an excruciating congressional investigation, including televised hearings. Also, our political system encourages each member of government to "jump on the bandwagon" in an effort to gain publicity for him-herself. Some critics argued that the shuttle would not have been launched in the too-cold weather had not the Space Administration "needed" a successful launch to regain public attention and support for the program. Political changes on the international level affect Thiokol -- no threat from the Soviet Union means less of a drive to be "first in space."

2.   *What impact would the development of efficient solar energy have on each of the following industries: (a) the housing industry, (b) the automobile industry, (c) another industry of interest to you?*

ANSWER:

This question is relatively specific and answers could be buttressed with library research fairly easily.

(a)   The housing industry

Students should distinguish between effects on market segments within the housing industry: new housing, the "retrofit" market, apartments.

Effects might include less reliance on fossil fuels, but housing costs might rise because of the expense of solar energy equipment. Houses might change radically in design. This is true, also, of existing houses modified to accept solar power. These changes would have to be culturally and socially "acceptable."

The role of government tax incentives might be mentioned. Population shifts might occur as people move to sunnier climates to lower their fuel bills. Existing houses might be moved to better utilize the new technology. The phrase "lovely wooded lot" might disappear from real estate advertising.

It is important that students answer this question from the perspective of the housing industry, not the consumer only. "Reduced energy costs" is a benefit to the consumer but ignores the housing industry.

(b)   The automobile industry

Autos themselves would have to be drastically redesigned. Additional equipment might be necessary for full use of cars, e.g., a solar battery at the home garage to be charged during the day then used to refuel the car at night.

There might be fewer gas stations, although solar cars might have gasoline engines for back-up use on cloudy days. Fewer gas stations means, however, fewer spots to sell auto-related products. New distribution outlets for these may be required. Mechanics would have to be retrained, and, to a lesser degree, auto salespeople.

Advertising would have to be made credible enough to convince people that this new breakthrough actually would work. Auto prices might have to be lowered to lessen the risks involved in buying a nontraditional car. Marketing mixes would have to be varied geographically by climate zones. Perhaps the "old" cars would be sold in cloudy and cold parts of the country, the "new" cars in the Sunbelt.

As in part (a) of the question, the discussion should focus on the marketing problems and opportunities of the industry in question.

(c)   Another industry of interest to you

Some possible industries to consider: utility companies, coal, oil and gas, steel, nuclear power, government, glass, road construction, trucking, airlines. (Would you fly in a solar airplane?)

3.   *Evaluate society's continuing concern for physical fitness from the point view of each of the following: (a) a manufacturer of packaged foods, (b) a leasing agent for an office building, and (c) a manufacturer of athletic shoes and clothing.*

ANSWER:

As was the situation in Question 2, the student should be reminded that the task at hand is to focus on the marketer under scrutiny, not just the consumer of the products mentioned.

(a)   A manufacturer of packaged foods

Some suggestions:

.   The fitness-minded crowd seems to want less sugar and salt, fewer calories, fewer preservatives, a "less full" feeling after eating, less caffeine, more fiber, and so on. Yet good taste cannot be sacrificed too greatly, nor can ease of storage and preservation. Packaging and advertising will have to reflect these concerns.

.   There is probably considerable overlap between taking the time to be fit and not having time, not every day at least, for preparing meals. Thus "healthy but convenient" food would seem to be desired.

(b)   A leasing agent for an office building

The agent, we are assuming here, is trying to lease existing buildings rather than attract customers to buildings yet to be constructed. Similar ideas might apply in either case, however. The agent might:

.   Locate buildings that have fitness facilities in them or have space for activities, e.g., a roof suitable for jogging.

.   Price the office offering as including free access to a fitness facility.

.   Promote the office facility as including a fitness facility or as being near such a facility, or near a park for jogging.

.   Attempt to interest the operator of a fitness facility to move into the building.

.   Include a free Nautilus machine or electric treadmill with every five-year lease.

The effect of the trend on the agent is, then, to create the need to change his or her marketing mix to reflect that trend.

(c)   A manufacturer of athletic shoes and clothing

The fitness trend bodes well for this marketer, but also presents some concerns.

.   The "boom" has created many competitors, whether this "marketer" is a manufacturer or a retailer.

.   The "boom" in running has created many market segments necessitating an array of marketing mixes: competition runner, runner who exercises for health, pavement runner, outdoor track runner, indoor track runner, older person, good-weather runner, all-weather runner, and so on. Add to this list of runner types the fact that they vary widely in skill, income, location, and so on, and a great number of marketing challenges are presented.

.   The "boom" has created, besides runners, tennis players, racquet ball players, squash players, basketball amateurs, flag football enthusiasts, softball players, bicyclists, etc. Each, supposedly, has specific shoe and attire needs, as well as price, distribution, and promotion-related peculiarities.

.   The "boom" has led to the development of a variety of media aimed at fitness buffs. The marketer has some work to do in evaluating these for effectiveness. The same problem is faced in marketing distribution decisions.

4.   *World population has risen much more quickly than the U.S. population. What opportunities does this present to American marketers? What constraints?*

ANSWER:

It would probably be best to select specific products to be discussed. The opportunities facing marketers of wines are obviously different from those facing marketers of bulldozers. Also, opportunities vary by market. (This question could be turned into a library project. Present a matrix, products listed on one side, countries on the other, and have students or groups identify the opportunities and constraints presented by each "cell" or combination in the matrix.)

In general, overseas markets with rising populations tend to be less developed countries. Many of these are populous, but wealth, particularly per capita GNP, is not impressive. Thus, for many goods we consider basic, demand may be high and the products purchasable. Food products, appliances (likely modified to fit the needs of the populace), clothing, construction machines, modular housing, technical assistance (e.g., medicine and sanitation) come to mind. Similarly, in wealthier countries, U.S. marketers may be able to offer specialty food items, California wines, major machinery, and stylish clothing.

In addition to the economic constraints involved, particularly in the case of the poorer countries, such matters as legal constraints, the existence of economic communities that we have difficulty "cracking," our own limitations on exporting high-tech or other "sensitive" goods, and restrictive trade practices such as those of Japan, all have effects.

In the case of the less-developed countries in particular, a major restraint on marketing activities might be termed "public relations." Sometimes rightly, and sometimes wrongly, U.S. firms have been accused of trying to "take over" entire economies, even governments. Some products marketed overseas have proved to be public relations horror shows -- infant formula that is not as healthful as "mother's milk," apple juice that is actually a concoction of sugared water, tobacco products that are failing here because of the link to cancer but are sold overseas. Notice that in many cases the American marketer is facing (sometimes fai ling) ethical tests.

5.   *Minority groups are often served by small companies such as makers of specialty foods. Why might a large firm such as Procter & Gamble, Toyota, or Stroh's Brewing Company avoid marketing to these groups?*

ANSWER:

Immigrant groups and other minorities are frequently provided for by small firms dealing in, for example, specialty food products, traditional clothing, and religious goods. Obviously, larger firms are not attracted to these market segments until their membership becomes large enough and/or rich enough to gain their attention. When the market gets big or attractive enough, the P&Gs of the world will move in on it.

Consider the Asian-American market, a small but growing market segment. Asian-American families have an average family income that is 25 percent larger than the average U.S. family income. Big business has learned to adjust its marketing to fit this segment. Here are some examples.

- Research showed that a top priority in Asian-American families is the security and education of children. Ads for Metropolitan Life show Asian couples holding babies and children. The copy reads, "You protect your baby, who protects you?"

- Metropolitan also has developed a personal sales presentation especially targeted toward Asian-Americans. It stresses the fact that the company is a venerable 120-year-old firm, which appeals to the traditionally conservative Chinese. Other ads for Met feature Charlie Brown and Snoopy, but Chinese consumers are not about to buy insurance from a dog. They want to deal face-to-face on such personal matters.

- Remy Martin cognac discovered that the Chinese consider red to be a good luck color, and feature Johnnie Walker Red Label Scotch at important celebrations such as New Year's or college graduations. The cognac company developed a series of ads depicting Orientals celebrating with cognac rather than Scotch.

- Safeway and McDonald's run television commercials aimed at Orientals (in English, but including subtitles) in parts of the country where the Oriental population is high. An example of this is San Francisco, whose Oriental community is large enough to justify the existence of an Asian-American TV station.

- The Los Angeles area has many Asian-Americans. Grand Chevrolet, a large dealership, employs a sales force that speaks a total of fifty Asian languages, and sells cars in ways that are common in other lands. In the Philippines, for example, cars are sold through catalogs, so Grand stocks many brochures, keeping them handy for customer browsing.

- If your students live in or near major cities they surely have seen billboards aimed at minority language groups, or listened briefly to foreign language radio stations. These stations (often Spanish) advertise nationally known products, the names of which are detectable even by speakers of English only.

6.   *What businesses would be influenced if a fire destroyed a telephone switching station and it took two weeks to get local service working?*

ANSWER:

This question was suggested by the situation that affected major Chicago suburbs when just such a fire occurred in 1987. A similar event occurred in New York City some years earlier.

The telephone, like electricity and water, is something you don't think about until it's not there. Even when we know the electricity is out or the phone doesn't work, we, by habit, continue to "turn lights on" as we enter rooms and to pick up the phone to "call" somebody.

Of course, virtually every businesses was affected in the Chicago situation. Some simply closed down for the duration, others took inventive steps or "recycled" old, pre-telephone methods of doing business.

Doctors, for example, began calling on the homes of their regular patients, especially those with possibly serious conditions. Other service providers such as dentists and veterinarians spent longer hours at their offices in case clients, who could not call in for appointments, took a chance and "dropped in." At least a few such professionals took up overnight residence at their offices so as to be available to their clients. Food wholesalers, and other suppliers, looked to their records to gather and deliver "typical" orders to their regular customers when daily communication had become impossible.

In short, "everybody" is affected by events of this sort. It is amazing how resourceful marketers can be when required.

7.   *What U.S. states seem to be bellwether states - that is, states predicting future environmental trends throughout the rest of the country?*

ANSWER:

This is a very tricky question. It is our opinion that a student who lists the obvious possibilities - New York, California, or some such - is missing the point. There is no bellwether identifiable unless it is decided what is under discussion. Is it clothes? Then maybe New York and California are reasonable answers if it is recognized that not all styles popular in these places spread across the country. In fact, many citizens of other locations see New York and California as "nut houses" whose styles and manners are to be avoided.

If the topic is "green" issues, perhaps the answer is Oregon. If it is medical care for the elderly, perhaps Florida.

Despite the brief success of the "urban cowboy" dress code, and a general belief that people should be able to wear what they want, a ten-gallon hat worn in Baltimore or Newark, N.J., draws stares and snickers. Outfits that are common in New York or Los Angeles might generate a lynch mob in Wyoming. Seventy-three percent of the adults in Dallas buy canned chili; in Boston, the figure is six percent. People in Newark, Ohio, may leave their doors unlocked, but hardly anyone in Newark, New Jersey, does that.

Any so-called bellwether locations should be observed by marketers. They can be significant helps in the forecasting process. But the U.S. market is too vast, too varied, and too dynamic to analyze in terms of mechanical progressions of trends or slavish imitation of "bellwether locations."

9.   *Demarketing is often discussed in terms of major shortages of fuel or raw materials. Are commonplace goods like coffee or paper towels ever demarketed?*

ANSWER:

Examples include:

.   Gillette's Aapri facial scrub was quickly sold out when it was introduced. Gillette ran ads declaring it "sold out by popular demand."

.   Budweiser was in short supply in some markets. Advertisements announced "We're brewing more for you as slow as we can."

.   The Washington (D.C.) Metro raises rates during rush hours; the Cleveland Zoo gives free admission to folks who arrive before 11 a.m.

.   Bad agricultural situations have led, from time to time, to quantum leaps in retail food prices. This leads retailers to limit sales ("One to a customer") as a form of rationing. In extreme cases, retailers have been known to sell some goods at cost or at a loss to avoid the ire (unjustifiably) directed at the retailer by consumers.

. During the 1970s, Johnny Carson set off a national panic when he mentioned a supposed shortage of toilet paper and other paper products. The next day, householders streamed into stores buying rolls of paper products for hoarding purposes. Retailers had to restrain sales of these goods by limiting the number of rolls sold to each customer.

. Anchor Steam Beer is popular but produced in small quantities. It is distributed by means of a selective distribution system, and at high prices. Coors, in its heyday as a "cult" beer did much the same thing.

Local examples are easy to find. Many downtown restaurants charge lower prices for dinner than for lunch, while restaurants located away from work sites may do the opposite. The phone company raises rates during peak hours, electric companies try to reduce peak hour demand.

Any form of seasonal discount or dated coupon might exemplify an attempt to increase off-season or off-hour demand but also be an attempt to lessen peak demands. An "early bird special" has the same intent.

10.   *What laws are unique to your state?*

ANSWER:

Certain industries, such as banking, are traditionally tightly regulated. These regulations vary widely from state to state, with the number of branches permitted being a commonly encountered law. Most states regulate the sale and pricing of alcoholic beverages, with some (Ohio and Pennsylvania, for example) making the sale of bottled liquor a state monopoly. Most states also regulate "drinks by the glass" (bars), locations of liquor stores in relation to schools and churches, numbers of liquor licenses issued, sale of tobacco to persons under a given age, and so on.

Students may uncover less common legal variations, such as regulations controlling the playing of sporting events on Sundays, "blue laws," and legal holidays unique to their state (e.g., "Statehood Day"). Tax laws commonly vary widely. In Ohio, for example, residents get a state income tax break for making certain home improvements.

Many states have laws on their books that are never enforced (minimum mark-up laws are commonly ignored.) However, it is well to know what these laws are since, from time to time, an overly zealous prosecuting attorney might seek to enforce these laws in an effort to gain attention from the press.

11.   *How much can marketers control political and legal influences on the marketing mix?*

ANSWER:

Most authors term political and legal influences on marketing "uncontrollable variables." This is due to the simple fact that such matters are rarely controllable or easily influenced by any one marketer acting alone. Exceptions exist, of course. Lee Iacocca, a man of personal charm and having the Chrysler organization behind him, was able to influence Congress to bail out his firm when it suffered serious financial problems. And the president of DuPont has more influence than the president of the Ponca City Beauty Supply Company. But it remains that, even for the presidents of DuPont or G.M., influence over our legal system, not control, is the most that can be claimed.

Marketers with less than Iacocca's clout can band together to lobby for or against specific legislation, or can perhaps see to it that certain potential laws or ordinances are given consideration by legal authorities. Nonetheless, except in the extreme case of bribing a dishonest official, legal matters remain largely "uncontrollable," to be taken usually as "givens" or constraints, as the marketing manager develops the marketing mix. In 1985, however, Philip Kotler suggested that marketing's 4 Ps be replaced with 6 Ps, one of which was intended to reflect that organizations can influence their environments by means of public relations and public awareness campaigns.

Interestingly, the lobbying effort is itself a marketing job, and one that hinges ultimately on the needs and wants of consumers. The influence of any lobbyist is limited by what legislators, or other officials, believe to be in the best interests of the citizenry, and (through the election process) of themselves. Again, the efforts of the marketer-lobbyist can be stymied if it cannot be shown that the legal steps he or she seeks to have taken are consistent with the wishes of that other "uncontrollable variable," the consumer.

ETHICS EXERCISE 3

CHAPTER 3 ETHICS IN PRACTICE

Overview

This case deals with an increasingly critical and yet debated aspect of the marketing environment - the impact of marketing activities on the physical environment. An emerging social value in the U.S. and abroad is environmentalism - concern for the cleanliness and healthiness of our environment. Consumers are increasingly bothered by the fact that we live in a throw-away society which creates an unfortunate avalanche of waste. The United States alone puts about three-quarters of the 100 million tons of solid waste it generates into landfills, more than half of which will be filled by the mid-1990s.

Perhaps the area of the marketing mix which has been most affected by the concern for our deteriorating environment has been packaging. Because of the growing concern for solid waste disposal, recyclable material, reusable packages, and biodegradable package materials, companies are spending more resources on developing environmentally friendly ("green") packaging. Yet, some critics have responded that too much of the activity here is simply a marketing ploy to gain more favorable public perceptions. Nonetheless, more companies are involved in green marketing, whereby marketers consider the environmental ramifications of their activities for society.

1.   *Why did McDonald's switch from polystyrene foam to paper?*

During the 1980s McDonald's was given kudos for introducing plastic-foam box packaging for its burgers because the boxes kept food piping hot until opened. However, in the late 1980s environmentalists and media commentators began to clamor that McDonald's should give up the boxes in favor of recyclable or biodegradable paper packaging. While the public perception was that the foam boxes would forever sit in landfills, McDonald's countered that they were at least theoretically recyclable. Although McDonald's sales and profits held steady, the environmentalists' message was being widely proclaimed in high-profile television and magazine stories that claimed McDonald's management was more interested in the bottom line than in environmental responsibility.

A McDonald's spokesman announced in late 1990 that "Mickey Dees" would stop using styrofoam containers since paper wrappers are better for the environment. Beginning in 1991 they would wrap such favorites as Big Macs and McDLTs in biodegradable paper, while the firm searched for packaging that can ultimately be made recyclable.

There are several possible motives underlying McDonald's switch, one or more of which could have been operative. As in the rain forest example in the chapter, it could have been a reaction to McDonald's recognition of the growing public concern for protecting the environment. McDonald's, practicing the societal marketing concept, recognized that in order to be successful, it must react and adapt to environmental changes by making socially responsible decisions about marketing efforts, including marketing ecologically safe products and services. Although it recognized that, from an environmental perspective, there are pros and cons to using foam and to using paper packaging, from a cost/benefit perspective (utilitarianism) they figured paper is preferable to foam.

Another possibility is that McDonald's was acting in its own self-interest in making the switch. Some firms use package compatibility with a safe, clean, resource conserving environment as a tool to segment and serve markets. McDonald's may have noted that in public opinion polls, the percentage of the population that makes purchase decisions based on environmental factors has rapidly grown, and decided that this was a lucrative segment to pursue. It could even be the case that McDonald's did not believe that it was doing the environmentally correct thing but merely the politically correct thing. Some evidence suggesting this will be presented below. In other words, public perceptions (beliefs) were that foam is bad for the environment relative to paper, and McDonald's simply pandered to the perception while ignoring the possible reality that the opposite might be true.

A third, and perhaps related, possibility is that McDonald's was reacting to threats from members of the highly visible and vocal environmental groups who have protested the waste of disposable containers. McDonald's has reacted to other concerns of this movement by prominently posting information on the nutritional value of its products (which many customers ignore), replacing attractively designed bags (which appealed to the younger set) with plain brown bags made from recycled paper.

Although consumers were in one sense given additional choice via new products (e.g., McLean Deluxe, carrot sticks), in another sense their choice was restricted because some former products which consumers enjoyed (e.g., french fries fried in beef tallow to add flavor) were reformulated in "new and improved" versions. Anyway, it is worthwhile to speculate that McDonald's regulars, long content to dutifully carry their foam containers to the trash receptacles, would have probably just as willingly submitted them to the firm's planned recycling efforts.

2.   *What should McDonald's have done?*

The matter of recycling and what to do about waste has been wide open for debate in the media. According to the information presented in the case, there is a case to be made for both polystyrene foam and paper packaging.

The case suggests that the advantages of paper packaging are that:

. Trees are a renewable resource, whereas polystyrene foam is made with oil and gas, which are essentially nonrenewable

. Paper is biodegradable, whereas foam isn't.

. The production process for paper does not create ozone pollution, whereas the pentane used to blow the beads used to make foam does create ozone pollution.

The case suggests certain advantages of foam packaging:

. It uses less energy in the production process than paper, energy which is essentially derived from petroleum.

. It uses fewer polluting inorganic chemicals in the production process than does paper.

. Degrading paper produces carbon dioxide and methane, both so-called "greenhouse gases."

So, based on the information in the case (which doesn't include relative costs, health hazards, and the like of factors such as ozone pollution and greenhouse gases) the decision between the two appears roughly to be a wash, lending credence to the suspicion that perhaps McDonald's decision was made mainly with public relations instead of the environmental good in mind.

3.   *Which is better - paper or foam?*

Some additional information has been recently published in the media on the relative merits of foam vs. paper. Some salient points in favor of foam:

.   In landfills, foam is completely inert and creates no post-disposal problems.

.   Polystyrene is one of the most recoverable of packaging materials. In clean, energy-producing incinerators, it can be converted to electricity in place of fossil fuels.

.   The manufacture of recycled products (such as paper packaging) often creates more pollution and consumes more resources than the manufacture of new products. This is because recycling programs use more resources than does landfilling waste. They require more trucks, which means more fuel consumption and more air pollution.

.   The paper wrappers contain plastic and aren't biodegradable, unlike plain paper.

Some additional arguments in favor of paper:

.   Paper can be recycled.

.   Recycling will help cut down on the trash glut and address the fact that every year there is less "environmentally safe" landfill space.

So, there are solid arguments on both sides of the table. Anyway, you will probably find that for some of your students this is a high involvement issue and that they are mostly familiar with the arguments trumpeted in the media against foam and in favor of biodegradable paper and recycling.

CHAPTER 3 TAKE A STAND QUESTIONS

1.   *Do you agree that products containing chlorofluorocarbons (CFCs) should not be sold in the United States?*

Chlorofluorocarbons (CFCs), powerful greenhouse gases, have been alleged to diffuse into the atmosphere and have been linked by some scientists to global warming and destruction of the ozone layer. Products containing CFCs include windshield washer fluid, hair styling gel, furniture polish, room air freshener, nail polish remover, tile cleaner, gasoline, natural gas, and many other products, including those made of plastic.

The levels of greenhouse gases in the atmosphere have increased dramatically since preindustrial times. This is the most solid, unambiguous result in the science surrounding global warming, one over which there is little controversy. (Betty Hileman, "Web of Interactions Makes It Difficult to Untangle Global Warming Data," *Chemical & Engineering News*, April 27, 1992.) These greenhouse gases include carbon dioxide (from our cars, factories, and power plants), methane, nitrous oxide, ozone, and the CFCs and other halocarbons from refrigerants, solvents or spray cans.

Some scientists believe that these greenhouse gases trap heat in the atmosphere, which will heat the earth's surface and its waters, creating the so-called greenhouse effect. Some of these scientists disagree how soon that will happen and how serious it will be. Some foresee radically fluctuating weather patterns, turning the Farm Belt and other agricultural regions into giant deserts; melting of polar ice caps, causing flooding of coastal cities; transformation of northern climates into tropical climates; mighty lakes and rivers turning into giant mud flats; and creation of a new generation of super hurricanes.

Also, some scientists believe that such chemicals contribute to destruction of the ozone layer, which is the earth's protective sun visor that filters out ultraviolet rays. Less protection means more exposure to ultraviolet rays, which cause skin cancer and eye cataracts, injure the human immune system, and harm crops, animals and marine life.

If these scientists are correct, and the media generally paint the picture that they are, then clearly some action should be taken by the manufacturers of these products, not just in the United States, but in all industrial nations of the world. Although in the short-run it might not be feasible to ban some of these products, since they are near-necessities, it would behoove companies to gear up their research and development departments to begin to search for feasible alternatives for producing these products (e.g., one environmentally safer alternative for some of the ozone eaters has been discovered to be citric acid – the stuff that makes lemonade tart).

However, what is unknown to many people is that global warming and ozone depletion (not to mention acid rain, endangered species, and other environmental issues) are complicated issues on which scientific consensus has not yet emerged. For instance, it was suggested by some scientists in 1992 that the global warming caused by CFCs is approximately canceled by cooling from the stratospheric ozone depletion they induce. (*C&EN*, 4/27/92) During the past few years researchers have raised a number of issues that have called into question some aspects of the science of global warming and ozone depletion.

It has been noted that the belief that the end of the world is upon us unless we turn from our materialist way of life is a human constant; Malthusians, either ignoring or looking at one-sided evidence, have always claimed that humanity would shortly bring about its own demise. However, time and again warnings of impending doomsday have been wrong. For instance, earlier warnings about acid rain, asbestos, radon, and alar in apples have turned out to be only a fraction of the problem they were originally cracked up to be. (Acid rain has not wreaked the havoc on lakes, forests and crop yields that were predicted; asbestos, it turns out, is harmless if left alone but deadly if ripped out; 99% of people never encounter radon; alar contained only minute traces of a carcinogen, but the apple panic wrecked the apple industry for a year and denied millions of people the healthful benefits of eating apples. (P.J. Wingate, "Let's Not Panic Over Ozone Layer Threat," *USA Today*, 4/19/91, p. 6.A)

In the mid-70s, it was predicted that pollution would lead to lethal worldwide global cooling, and the Club of Rome predicted global starvation by the 1980s. (William A. Rusher, "Needed: A Coalition for Environmental Sanity," *Human Events*, 12/8/90, p. 9)

Environmental Protection Agency-supported theories of global warming and global ozone depletion are simply not backed up by sufficient evidence. Regarding global warming, the doomsday models have failed to predict even short-run temperature changes. Studies indicate that there has been no net warming since 1938 when the controversial CO_2 buildup began, and that the Northern Hemisphere has actually cooled during most of the period. (Patrick Cox, "USA Mustn't Fall for Global-Warming Fright," *USA Today*, 11/15/89, p. 12A) As for ozone depletion, the "'ozone hole' isn't a hole at all but a harmless, short-term lessening of the amount of ozone over the poles. It occurs a few weeks every year, then snaps back to 'normal.' It's directly related to natural fluctuations in solar radiation, not chlorofluorocarbons." ("Ozone depletion is a Myth," R.H. Holzknecht, *USA Today*, 2/14/92, p. 6A)

The lesson would appear to be that we should treat apocalyptic warnings by "scientific experts" with caution. Quite often we have legislators passing environmental laws based not on scientific evidence but on fashionable theories.

The media then promote the sensationalist doomsday scenarios, thereby justifying draconian government action. (Cliff Kincaid, "Scientists Protest 'Political Correctness,'" *Human Events*, 6/1/91, p. 7)

Given the uncertainty associated with global warming and ozone depletion, it would seem wise for companies to continue R&D efforts on alternatives to halocarbons without abandoning current products. Government could fund some of this R&D. But to pass legislation banning products made of halocarbons would appear to be premature.

2.   *Should products containing high sodium levels, such as fast food hamburgers and breakfast sausage, be advertised on children's television?*

An even larger issue here is whether or not advertising should be targeted to children, and if so, should limitations (content, types of products, media) be placed upon it? This is probably the most controversial and emotionally charged issue in advertising. Although the issue in this question regards the types of products to be advertised, it would be instructive to review some of the major arguments for and against advertising directed towards children.

Arguments against advertising to children include:

. Children lack the cognitive/perceptual defenses of adults. They (especially those under seven or eight) are unable to discriminate programming from commercials, are less aware of advertising's persuasive intent, are more trusting than adults, lack alternative information sources, and pay more attention to and have more favorable attitudes toward commercials.

. Advertising disrupts family harmony; kids incessantly yammer for products pitched at them. Parents make the ultimate buying decisions, so they should be the ones who see advertising for products in which children have an interest.

. Advertising encourages excessive materialism.

Points made by proponents of advertising for children include:

. Advertising gives children additional information they might not otherwise have. The only way children can become better consumers is to view commercials and then discuss them with their parents.

. Restrictions on such advertising violate advertisers' right to free commercial speech.

. Restrictions on such advertising will result in fewer and lower quality programs for kids.

. Advertising to children is already the most heavily regulated area of advertising, with all kinds of restrictions on content, use of endorsers, use of disclaimers (e.g., "batteries not included"), number of commercial minutes per hour, and the like.

. Parents have a responsibility to monitor their children's TV viewing habits and to discuss what they see with their kids. If they don't like the shows or commercials, they can turn the darned thing off or else substitute videos and PBS shows ("Sesame Street" et al.) instead.

. Advertising influences the socialization process, being a means whereby children learn the value system and norms of the society they are entering.

. Advertising is not the most influential determinant of children's purchase and request behavior - personal factors such as peer pressure and parental preferences are.

If one rejects advertising to children per se, then the issue of advertising food products with potential health hazards becomes moot. However, many of the objections to advertisements aimed at kids are really objections to some of the products advertised rather than to the concept of child-targeted advertisements. These include "war toys" (e.g., G.I. Joe), toys patterned after TV show heroes (and vice versa, e.g., Teenage Mutant Ninja Turtles,) over-the-counter drugs and vitamins (e.g., Flintstones vitamins,) candy and other assorted "junk food," and sugared cereal (sugar appeal for kids seems to be the counterpart to sex appeal for adults.) The arguments against products containing high levels of sodium (and fat, cholesterol, etc.) parallel those made against other "unhealthy" foods. The basic arguments here are:

. Advertisers shouldn't promote dangerous products, especially to our most vulnerable citizens.

. Such ads might increase consumption, thereby harming children's health.

. Purchase decisions, especially for products such as fast-food hamburgers and sausages, are made by parents, and thus advertising for such goods should be targeted at adults.

. When family dietary habits are poor, food advertising is more likely to harm children.

Points in favor of advertising such food products are:

- Children are heavy influencers and occasionally deciders, and so should have the right to see advertisements for them.

- Advertising doesn't affect the amount of consumption of such products (those decisions are based on environmental factors such as peer pressure, parental upbringing and the like as well as children's individual tastes and preferences) but rather merely results in brand choices within the given product categories (e.g., choosing Jimmy Dean sausages instead of Parks sausages).

- Limitations could be placed on such advertising (such as special disclaimers on health hazards).

3.   *Should English be made the national language? Should all products have labels in English only?*

In recent years there has been a running debate as to whether English should be made the official language of the U.S. A nonprofit group known as U.S. English has been pushing for an amendment to the U.S. Constitution making English the USA's official language. The group also advocates repealing laws mandating multilingual ballots and voting materials and restricting government funding for bilingual education programs (which require that children from nonEnglish-speaking backgrounds be taught in their native languages, sometimes for several years, while they learn English) to short-term funding only. About 14 states have passed laws or amended their constitutions to make English their official language. Meanwhile, various ethnic (especially Hispanic) leaders and some members of Congress have been vigorously battling this movement.

Reasons for favoring English as our official language include:

- Laws requiring that ballots be printed in languages other than English and bilingual education programs might serve as a disincentive for immigrants to learn English, keeping such people functioning outside the mainstream of our English-speaking society, thereby harming the very people they intend to help. Mastering English is the key to becoming successful and prosperous.

- Earlier in this century, immigrants were required to know the rudiments of English as a condition for naturalization; no bilingual ballots were printed at public expense, and the public schools were unabashedly used as instruments for the assimilation of immigrant children. The result was that immigrants were effectively acculturated into our society. We should want immigrants to assimilate, integrate, and participate in our society. This will benefit both the individuals involved as well as society.

- The effect of bilingual education and ballots has been that Hispanics have a growing attachment to the Spanish language as well as a shortchanging of students and adults not proficient in English by teaching them their native language and culture rather than English and mathematics. There is a higher dropout rate and more academic failures among those subjected to bilingual education.

- Maintenance of foreign languages and cultures is not a government responsibility. Rather, it is the immigrant's duty to learn the language and culture of his or her adopted country.

- Without English as our national language, national unity will be weakened. Many Hispanic political and academic leaders publicly admit or imply that their goal is bilingualism and biculturalism, with two official languages and cultures. Probably nothing separates peoples more deeply than differences in languages (witness the tensions and even occasional violence in Canada where French-speaking citizens have called for secession and in Sri Lanka and Belgium where people slaughter each other over language differences.) And once bilingualism takes root, there is no turning back; it is irreversible. A common language is the glue that holds a country together.

- Bilingual policies require government to "help" only a few privileged languages; some immigrants' heritages are slighted while they pay taxes to print languages in their neighbors' equally foreign language.

- Making English the official U.S. language would not affect the languages spoken in homes, churches, or businesses; it would not restrict individual freedoms.

Reasons for opposing English as our official language include the following:

- English is already our national language anyway; we don't need a law and all of the efforts necessary to pass a law to declare this. Without English-only laws, generations of immigrants have assimilated just fine.

- Immigrants can be encouraged to learn the English language without laws and without needing to abandon their native tongues.

- New citizens already have an incentive to learn English without laws, for they know that if they want to continue successfully living and working here, they must learn English. In fact, in most cases their incentive to learn English is the same incentive that brought them to our shores - economic, educational, and social opportunities.

- Most minorities do not refuse to learn the English language.

- Making English the official language would put an undue burden, especially on older, nonEnglish-speaking people; it's very hard to learn a new language later in life.

- Bilingual programs are needed to celebrate ethnic pride and to make the transition into U.S. society.

- The Supreme Court has struck down English-only laws, ruling that "Protection of the Constitution extends to all; to those who speak other languages sa well as to those born with English on the tongue." The constitutional rights to free speech and to vote are such cherished right in the U.S. that bilingual ballots are mandated by federal law.

- Those who advocate English as our official language are racists and bigots. They are attempting to block individuals from participating in public life and the political process. Such laws would only serve to divide us by encouraging mistrust and bigotry.

- Studies show that bilingual education students outperform immersion students in reading, language, arts, and mathematics.

- Lack of bilingual ballots would block minorities' participation in the political process.

- A new law will not change the fact that we are a multi-ethnic, multicultural society; the melting pot is a myth, and ancestral cultures should not be betrayed.

Many of the arguments for or against having labels in English only parallel those above for or against making English the national language. Additionally, one should think in terms of the marketing concept and the societal marketing concept. The marketing concept suggests that if there is an ethnic segment of consumers who prefer labels in their native language, then those consumers should be provided such labels. This would apply primarily to either products consumed virtually only by Hispanics (e.g., canned chili peppers, Inca Kola) or to products consumed by both natives and non-natives (e.g., salsa, certain Mexican beers). For the former, distribution would likely be confined to stores in ethnic neighborhoods, while for the latter products, with Spanish labels would be targeted toward ethnic stores, and products with English labels would be distributed in mainstream stores. Additionally, some Hispanic products distributed primarily in Hispanic stores have bilingual labels.

The societal marketing concept should also be considered. Would nonEnglish labels be helpful or harmful to the ethnic groups? (Many of the points in the discussion above apply here.)

4.   *Tokyo-based Ito-Yokado owns a 70 percent share of the 7-Eleven convenience store chain. Should this fact be stated on a decal on store windows?*

On balance this would appear to be an unusual and unnecessary tactic.

Arguments in its favor include:

.   The consumer has a right to know. There is currently a strong buy-American sentiment which should be catered to.

.   To withhold such information might in a sense be misleading, since 7-Eleven has sort of an all-American image (sort of like Chevrolet and Coca-Cola.)

.   Foreigners are taking over the American business landscape. Any effort to discourage this should be taken.

Arguments against posting the decal include:

.   Most products sold in the stores are produced domestically.

.   It would put 7-Eleven at an unfair competitive situation, given the strong buy-American feelings.

.   Slippery slope - where do you draw the line? Should we put decals on cars that have components and parts made by foreigners? What if a store was under only 50% foreign ownership? 30%? What about VCRs, TVs, cameras and other electronics products made in Japan?

.   This would stir up racist feelings among nonJapanese (especially in light of the current Japanese-bashing) and would put Japanese-Americans on the defensive.

GUIDE TO CASES

VIDEO CASE 3-1   BANC ONE CORP

SUBJECT MATTER: Environment of Marketing, Marketing Concept, Customer Orientation

                            Please see the Guide to Video Cases for video length and other information.

AT-A-GLANCE OVERVIEW

Banc One Corporation is a $48.7 billion bank holding company with 17,800 employees. Banc One operates 57 affiliate banking organizations in Illinois, Indiana, Kentucky, Michigan, Ohio, Texas and Wisconsin. Expansion plans include Colorado and Missouri. Banc One's strategy is to acquire retail and middle market banks that need a turnaround. It injects financial strength and operating expertise from outside to improve earnings.

Banc One has been very innovative in its marketing approach to attract customers for its savings, checking, and loan services. Banc One attempts to keep at the forefront of banking by keeping consumer satisfaction at the cornerstone of it business.

DISCUSSION QUESTIONS

1.   *What environmental factors are most likely to influence a bank's operations and the marketing of its services to its customers?*

Banks, especially the interest rates they charge and offer, are strongly influenced by the government and the general state of the economy. Specific actions by governmental agencies, in particular the Federal Reserve Bank, but also such governmental units as the Department of the Treasury, Ginnie Mae, Fannie Mae, the Agriculture Department, the Department of Housing and Urban Development, and at times, the Defense Department. Congress also affects banks, not only by legislation, but also by permitting increases in the national debt. Many of these same influences of government are encountered at the state level, though on a smaller scale.

Demographic factors strongly influence banking. Ask your students how many of them are actively engaged in saving and how many have loans. In general, young people borrow and older people save. This demographic influence helps explain the program in Richmond, Indiana, where the Banc One affiliate bank has a senior citizen program called Senior Champs. It requires that eligible customers maintain a certain balance and in return the bank provides many special services for its members. Although the product offered has value to the senior customer, the program's real focus is on establishing relationships. Banc One of Richmond provides educational seminars, fashion shows, and other social and travel events.

Cultural factors also influence banking. See the video and answer to the next question. Psychological factors influence banking too. Fear of bank failure, or doubts that the government will back particular banks, leads to "runs" on banks from time to time.

Obviously, almost any environmental factor will have some effect on banks, including the weather (hurricanes and earthquakes, etc.). A good question might be "Can you name an environmental element that does not affect banking?" It would be hard to do since banks are at the heart of most people's economic concerns.

2.   *Is it a good idea to have a bank inside a supermarket? What environmental factors might influence this strategy?*

In the last several decades, the traditional roles of sole breadwinner and housewife have changed to roles involving both partners working. This has reduced the amount of time for shopping and banking. For example, in Worthington, Ohio, a bank is located inside a Big Bear supermarket. It has both Saturday and Sunday hours. Employees include both tellers and account service personnel who process the opening of accounts and perform traditional bank functions. Banks in supermarkets are no longer a novel concept. They seem to have proved themselves in the marketplace and, thus, seem to be a "good idea." This change in banking can be directly attributed to changes in the environment.

And though we mentioned government influences in part (a), it can be noted here that a general perception that our money is safe in a bank (thanks to supposed government protection) "permits" banks to operate in a supermarket. A few decades back, banks were built like fortresses, had bars on "cages," and were formal places indeed. Loans were hard to get, and banking was treated very seriously indeed. In these more informal times, and in times when people probably feel "protected" by government agencies put into place during the Depression, a bank in a supermarket seems "no big deal."

3.   *Who are a bank's customers? What problems do consumers have with banks? How can a marketing orientation improve the bank marketing process?*

As suggested in part (b), banking has changed over the past fifty years. Students can still find old-fashioned bank buildings with walls six feet thick, statues, heavy marble floors, and a general sense of physical safety for deposits entrusted to the bank. One reason banks are less imposing today is the aforementioned sense of security that government protection plans lend to the industry. Another reason is that the customer base has changed since those olden times. Now banks reach out to every one, granting credit via charge cards, loaning money to "regular folks," permitting these same "regular folks" to mortgage their homes, get car loans, and the like. Students would have to ask their grandfathers (at least) to discover this was not always the case. Banks at one time catered mostly to the wealthy or at least middle class, securely employed types. Getting a loan was a major accomplishment in those days, and the old movie image of the customer nervously beseeching the loan officer, then being tossed out on his backside, come close to describing the reality of those times.

Today, the bank's customers are "everyone," except for a few old-line banks that deal only with major financial players. A bank like Banc One deals with college students, young people, old people, and people of every economic status, trying, in fact, to steal these folks away from other banks with premiums like toasters.

What do these customers want from their bank? Almost certainly the first concern is safety for one's money. Again, government regulations, rightly or wrongly, lead the average bank customer to feel that his or her money is probably equally safe in most, if not every one of, the nation's banks. Then the key point is not safety but, depending on the customer, some combination of the following bank services: reasonable interest rates, various "customized" checking and savings plans, bank-by-mail, convenient location, convenient hours, nice personnel, loan availability, credit cards, check-cashing cards (for use at retail outlets), drive-up service, good parking, access to transportation in cities where driving and parking are difficult, financial advice, pleasant surroundings, and on and on.

A marketing orientation can improve the bank marketing program immensely. Banks came to marketing late, but have embraced it fiercely. Unlike the banks of yore, they welcome business. In the old days, when they made dealing with financial matters very difficult, they were clearly in a "production era" ... offering services only to those who "rated" with them, and booting out or intimidating those who did not. Banks now pay careful attention to the services customers want, how customers perceive the bank and its employees, and how "atmospherics" affect their beliefs. For example, new bank buildings are not built like forts, but many are built in a colonial "Williamsburg" style to suggest both tradition and permanence.

CASE 3-2   JAMAICA'S ECONOMIC DEVELOPMENT AGENCY

SUBJECT MATTER: Service Products, Environment of Marketing, Factors
                                Encouraging International Marketing Activities

AT-A-GLANCE OVERVIEW

This long case deals with Jamaica's Economic Development Agency, whose purpose is to stimulate business growth and investment in Jamaica. A part of the work is to advertise and provide information about the country. A few years ago the government deregulated and privatized the economy, and the country has enjoyed a boom in exports: raw materials (primarily bauxite), clothing, agricultural products, and information services. Tourism remains important. Over one million tourists per year spend something like $800 million per year. This business is handled in a professional manner, and what was once a playground for the rich is now offered as a playground for the world.

Yet inflation is high (about 60%), currency value is sinking, and the people are subject to "shifting moods." In short, the transition to a market economy is underway, but it hurts. Currency controls were dropped in 1991. Agricultural subsidies are being phased out. Government-held land is being sold, though slowly. Services run by the government's National Investment Bank of Jamaica, including Air Jamaica, the Government Printing Office, hotels, and many services, are being "taken to market." Jamaica is said to rank first in the world in terms of state-owned enterprises for sale.

Jamaica's business community, often through its Private Sector Organization of Jamaica, is keeping the pressure on the government to continue down the path of privatization.

DISCUSSION QUESTIONS

1.   *What is the Jamaican Economic Development Agency's product? To whom is the
        product marketed?*

The Agency's purpose is to stimulate business growth and investment in Jamaica. Thus, it could be said that its product is the effort it puts forth to accomplish this objective. But it is clear that advertisements and "sales jobs" to potential investors are not the products the Agency's managers are supposed to be producing. They are supposed to be producing results. That is, when an outside company moves to Jamaica, buys Jamaican exports, or otherwise contributes to Jamaica's economic health, then the Agency's "product" has been produced.

In a larger sense, the product of the Agency is not just the creation of new business or development. Its product is the health of the country's economy. This is a "big picture" goal of the Agency. In many ways, the future of the country depends on efforts like those made by the Agency.

Most immediately, the Agency's product is Jamaica itself -- its resources, climate, natural resources, stable government, and hard-working people. This "total product" is marketed to outside economic interests who can help, rather than exploit, the country.

2.   *What aspects of the physical environment and cultural environment would influence an organization's decision to locate or operate in Jamaica? What environmental factors are likely to discourage business in Jamaica?*

This question can be addressed in terms of the text's Exhibits listing aspects of the environment.

Among the physical aspects would be climate, raw materials, soil conditions for growing various food products, population to provide the labor force, the fact that the country is an island, and location. (Near what other countries is Jamaica?)

Cultural factors are, by definition, man-made. For example, the fact that the population of Jamaica is about 2,250,000 is, though influenced by cultural matters such as availability of and attitude toward birth control, essentially a physical environment factor. However, such matters as level of education, traditional work values, language, attitude toward females in the workplace, deference to authority, friendliness to outsiders, etc. are all cultural. The state of the economy, its development level, the support among the people for the privatization efforts, the stability of the government, etc. are also cultural. Laws are also cultural, and visitors tell us that "partying" in Jamaica is more prevalent than in the U.S., and that these include open use of substances that are controlled in the U.S.

Which types of environmental factors are likely to discourage business in Jamaica? Its island location might make it less than ideal in terms of distribution of some products. At the risk of sounding ethnocentric we might mention the country's long history as a controlled economy, first as a colony, then under strong central rule. Though things seem to be changing, the case mentions that this "hurts." How far will the program of privatization go? Will the people, or some government or military faction, think it has gone far enough? The location of the country, in an area that has not proven to be politically stable, might scare off some investors. The "party image" of the island might be good for tourists, but is it good for my data processing business? Further, some of the attraction of the place is due to lower wage rates than are found in other countries. Ironically, the more successful Jamaica gets at attracting business the more likely it is to become like "everywhere else."

Though the case contains a good deal of information about Jamaica, a useful assignment might be to do some library research on just how appealing Jamaica might be to manufacturers of light industry goods like clothing or baseball gloves, high-tech firms, and restaurant chains.

3.   *How important is tourism to Jamaica? What environmental factors influence this aspect of the Jamaican economy?*

Very. Jamaica was, thirty years or more ago, a "playground for the rich" exclusively. It has democratized this image in recent years. Jamaica pulls in over 1.2 million tourists a year and is a most popular spot for tour ships. Factors influencing this include physical setting, climate, facilities for tourists, attitude of the people toward tourists, laws (e.g., it must be admitted, drug laws,) proximity to the U.S., at least as far as Americans are concerned, and "bargains" created by currency differences or duty free arrangements.

Tourism is one of Jamaica's top two industries, and, the text says, tourists are taken seriously and treated professionally. The case mentions Jamaica's problems with an unstable currency. Those outside dollars (from the U.S. and Europe) are important in such a situation. Jamaica, says the case, has something for everyone. Unlike some countries, Jamaica seems willing to capitalize on it. Aren't all countries? Not Cuba (from 1960 to 1990) and Cuba could have used those outside currencies.

4 INFORMATION MANAGEMENT

CHAPTER SCAN

The chapter deals with the place of information in effective marketing, specifically with the development of useful data and its management through the Marketing Information System (MIS.)

No organization can make use of the information it has gathered unless it has meaningful form and can be presented in a useful format. This is the purpose of the MIS.

Marketing research tools and techniques are shown to be many and varied. A purpose of this chapter is to describe how the researcher selects from among these, assuring that they are appropriate to the marketing problem being addressed by management.

Though marketing research efforts must be altered to fit particular situations, in general, these studies follow a progression of seven major steps. These steps and some of the choices made as the research process unfolds, are the focus of much of this chapter.

Sales forecasting tools, methods, and time frames are treated in the final portion of the chapter. A review of the purpose and value of research concludes the chapter.

SUGGESTED LEARNING OBJECTIVES

The student who studies this chapter will be exposed to a broad discussion of the place of information in the marketing decision-making process and will be able to:

1. Explain why information is essential to effective marketing decision making.

2. Describe a successful Marketing Information System.

3.   Describe a data collection system and a decision support system.

4.   Analyze the contribution of marketing research to effective decision making.

5.   Describe the stages in the marketing research process.

6.   Show how exploratory research relates to particular marketing problems.

7.   Tell why secondary data are valuable sources of information.

8.   Outline the advantages and possible uses of observation, surveys, and experiments.

9.   Demonstrate knowledge of the purposes and procedures involved in sales forecasting.

10.   Evaluate the advantages and disadvantages of the various forecasting methods.

CHAPTER OUTLINE

I.   INTRODUCTION

II.   INFORMATION: THE BASIS OF EFFECTIVE MARKETING

III.   MARKETING INFORMATION SYSTEMS

A.   Data Collection Systems: Generating Input
B.   Decision Support Systems: Storing and Analyzing Information
C.   The Successful MIS

IV.   WHAT IS MARKETING RESEARCH?

V.   THE STAGES IN THE RESEARCH PROCESS

A.   Stage One: Defining the Problem

1.   Problems Can Be Opportunities
2.   Don't Confuse Symptoms with the Real Problem
3.   Exploratory Research
4.   What Is a "Good" Research Objective?

B.   Stage Two: Planning the Research Design

1.   Research Designs - Secondary Data
2.   Research Designs - Primary Data

a.   Observation
b.   Surveys
c.   Experiments

C.   Stage Three: Selecting a Sample

1.   Probability Sampling
2.   Nonprobability Sampling

D.   Stage Four: Collecting Data
E.   Stage Five: Analyzing Data

1.   Editing
2.   Coding
3.   Analyzing

F.   Stage Six: Drawing Conclusions and Preparing the Report
G.   Stage Seven: Following Up

VI.   SALES FORECASTING: RESEARCH ABOUT THE FUTURE

     A.   Break-Down and Build-Up Forecasting
     B.   The Three Levels of Forecasting
     C.   Conditional Forecasting - "What If?"
     D.   Forecasting by Time Periods
     E.   Forecasting Options

          1.   Executive Opinion
          2.   Sales Force Composite
          3.   Survey of Customers
          4.   Projection of Trends
          5.   Analysis of Market Factors

     F.   Some Practical Considerations

VII. SUMMARY

VIII. KEY TERMS

IX.   QUESTIONS FOR DISCUSSION (17)

X.   ETHICS IN PRACTICE

XI.   CASES

    The following key terms are introduced and used in Chapter 4.   They are defined in the text's Glossary.

Marketing information system (MIS)
Data
Information
Primary data
Secondary data
Data collection system
Internal records and reports system
Marketing intelligence system
Decision support system
User interaction system
Database
Analytical models system
Marketing research
Problem definition
Exploratory research
Focus group interview
Hypothesis
Research design
Scientific observation
Survey
Systematic bias
Experiment
Laboratory experiment
Sampling
Sample
Population
Census
Target population
Probability sample
Nonprobability sample
Simple random sample
Random sampling error
Stratified sample
Cluster sample
Convenience sample
Judgment sample
Quota Sample
Pretesting
Editing

Coding
Data analysis
Sales forecasting
Break-down method
Build-up method
Market potential
Sales potential
Sales forecast
Market factor
Market factor index (or) market index

THE CHAPTER SUMMARIZED

I.   INTRODUCTION

The chapter is introduced with a description of how Fisher-Price tests toys
in its "Play Laboratory." Toy designers and marketing researchers observe
children through two-way mirrors. One goal is to identify how much "play
value" can be associated with each toy, that is, how much time is spent
with each toy vis-a-vis its price. Parents want their money's worth,
especially from expensive toys. Also, some toys include features that kids
won't use but parents insist upon, such as a "slow" speed on an electric
(riding) car. Fisher-Price is trying to take some of the guesswork out of
the business of designing and marketing fun.

II.   INFORMATION: THE BASIS OF EFFECTIVE MARKETING

Whether or not it is obtained through formal means, information is a
valuable management tool, reducing uncertainty and risk. All 4 Ps may be
affected.

Examples are provided to show that systematically gathered information
reduces uncertainty and improves the quality of the decision-making
process.

   .   After a 200 point drop in the Dow-Jones averages (October, 1989)
        Fidelity Investments of Boston phoned mutual fund investors across
        the country to determine if they had lost confidence in the stock
        market and the economy. Most had not. Fidelity could make good use
        of this information, BUT...

   .   The American Animal Trap Company of Lititz, Pennsylvania, made the
        mistake of researching the home trap market only after its "new
        improved trap" had been rejected by the marketplace in favor of the
        old stand-by wooden model.

Information can come from internal records, government data, surveys, trade
association figures, test markets, or any other source. Systematically
gathered information reduces uncertainty and improves the quality of the
decision-making process.

III. MARKETING INFORMATION SYSTEMS

Information may be encountered as regularly supplied data, periodically
supplied data (as from a survey), or informally gathered data such as news
reports or even rumors. Managers need some way to select from and manage
the data they have. They need to manage information just as they manage
their other responsibilities, though they sometimes do not do so because
they are busy "putting out fires."

A **marketing information system (MIS)** is an organized set of procedures and
methods by which pertinent, timely, and accurate information is continually
gathered, sorted, analyzed, evaluated, stored and distributed for use by
marketing decision makers.

Note that this definition emphasizes an ongoing process designed to help
managers make decisions by providing a continual flow of information. The
two major subsystems of an MIS are illustrated in Exhibit 4-1.

A.   Data Collection Systems: Generating Input

Data is simply facts; information is a body of facts in a format suitable for use in making a decision.

Primary data are gathered specifically for the project at hand.

Secondary data are data previously collected and assembled for some purpose other than the project at hand.

The **data collection system** is comprised of three major subsystems, each generating a different type of output.

- The **internal records and reports system** includes such activities as gathering sales figures and other reports in an orderly way.

- The **marketing research system** emphasizes the gathering of new data.

Definitions of marketing research stress that it is focused on solving specific problems as does a survey or research experiment.

- Marketing intelligence may be defined as follows:

A **marketing intelligence system** consists of a network of diverse sources that collects both primary and secondary data about changes in the marketing environment.

Sources of such information include members of the sales force, customers, trade magazines, and organizations specializing in gathering industry information.

B.   Decision Support System: Storing and Analyzing Information

The **decision support system** is a computer system that stores data and transforms it into accessible information.

Using computers, decision makers can confront problems through direct access to databases.

A **database** is a collection of information arranged in a logical manner and organized in a form that can be stored and processed by a computer.

The **analytical models system** uses modern electronics to convert endless columns of numbers into color charts, graphs, and maps, all of use to the decision maker.   Via **interactive** systems, managers can use computer terminals to request and retrieve data and generate "tailor made" formats suitable for evaluation of alternatives and consequences.

SUMMARY: A database is a collection of information arranged in a logical way in a form that can be stored and processed by a computer. The analytical models system contains the software that manages the database.   For example, a customer list may be broken down in terms of customer size, characteristics of various types, cost-related information, and so on.

C.   The Successful MIS

In a successful MIS, a flow of relevant information is available to decision makers and information not "in the pipeline" can be made available as needed, all in a format that satisfies management's information requirements.

IV.   WHAT IS MARKETING RESEARCH?

Marketing research is the systematic and objective process of generating information for aid in making marketing decisions. This process includes specifying what information is required, designing the method for collecting information, managing and implementing the collection of data, analyzing the results, and communicating the findings and their implications.

This suggests that marketing research involves special effort, not casual or accidental information gathering.

Marketing "research," like statistics, can be used to "prove" anything. Improperly done research is really no research at all.

Marketing research includes far more than surveys and can be used to develop information about prices, promotion and distribution as well as about products.

Marketing research does not give the manager "the answer" but simply broadens his or her viewpoint, providing insights or information. It does not replace managerial judgments.

Manager and researcher must work together. The researcher must present information in a usable format. The manager should, if necessary, explain how the information might better be presented.

V.   THE STAGES IN THE RESEARCH PROCESS

Marketing is not an "exact science," but it can be approached in a scientific manner. Systematic steps to gaining knowledge can be used.

Seven steps in the marketing research process can be identified, though they are closely interrelated and may not occur "in order." The seven steps are shown in Exhibit 4-2.

There is no "best" way to do research. The "best" way is the way that yields the information that suits the problem at hand.

A.   Stage One: Defining The Problem

Research is likely to begin when symptoms suggest that some problem exists. A clear definition of a problem should be had before other steps, e.g., collecting data, are begun.

This stage is likely to begin with the realization that some problem exists because symptoms have been noted. If there is uncertainty as to what the problem is, managers should ensure that research is not begun without adequate understanding of exactly what information needs to be collected.

"A problem well-defined is a problem half-solved."

1.   Problems Can Be Opportunities

Problems are not always "bad." The "problem" might be to discover which group of anxious-to-buy customers is most anxious-to-buy.

2.   Don't Confuse Symptoms with the Real Problem

Pain is the symptom of a medical problem, it is not the problem itself. Similarly, "no customers" is not a marketing problem but a symptom of a problem, such as a shift in the competitive environment. Exhibit 4-3 shows that problem definition should begin the research process.

3.   Exploratory Research

What some see as problems, e.g., "no customers," are often symptoms of problems. Exploratory research investigates and clarifies problem areas so managers can "get a handle" on a situation. Providing conclusions is not the purpose of exploratory research.

Generally, it is a mistake to begin to make changes in a marketing mix or even to run off and "do a survey" without using exploratory research to add clarity to the situation.

A **focus group** of ten or twelve people might help identify problem areas ("looks like it breaks easily") or opportunities (the sale of baking soda as a refrigerator deodorizer came out of focus group sessions).

4.   What Is a "Good" Research Objective?

The best way to **express a research objective is as a testable** hypothesis.

A **hypothesis** is an unproven proposition or possible solution to a problem, a statement that can be supported or refuted by empirical data.

Once testable hypotheses have been developed, researchers are ready to select a research design.

B.   Stage Two: Planning the Research Design

The **research design** is a master plan which specifically identifies the tools and procedures that will be used to collect and analyze information relevant to the research problem.

The design must be consistent with monetary, resource, and time constraints.

1.   Research Designs - Secondary Data

Marketing research does not always involve generation of new data. Previously gathered information (secondary data) may do the job. Exhibit 4-4 shows some examples of various secondary data.

The primary advantages of secondary data are that they can be gathered quickly and, almost always, more cheaply than primary data. Weaknesses include the age of the data, the problem of finding exactly the information sought, and the possibility that the data found is inaccurate.

2.   Research Designs - Primary Data

It may be necessary to gather new information, specifically for the project at hand.

a.   Observation

Some customer actions are easily observed and recorded, e.g., which bus route carries the most people. **Observation research** is the systematic recording of behavior, or facts, or events, as they are witnessed.

Observation's biggest strength is that it involves actual recording of the situation of interest. Its biggest weakness is that it does not tell the researcher why an action occurred.

The A.C. Nielsen Company's "peoplemeter" provides an electronic means of observing television viewing.

b.   Surveys

A **survey** is any research effort in which information is gathered from a sample of people by means of a questionnaire.

There are four general forms (mail, mall interviewing, personal, telephone) compared in Exhibit 4-5.

When properly planned, surveys can be:

.   quick
.   efficient
.   accurate
.   flexible

How better to follow the marketing concept than to ask people what they want?

The text's Exhibit 4-5 summarizes the strengths and weaknesses associated with personal, mail, and telephone surveying techniques.

Surveys are frequently taken and used improperly. In essence, the category **systematic bias** includes all errors other than sampling errors. (poorly worded questions, misinterpretation of responses, etc.) also called "nonsampling errors."

Wording the survey is a skill that can be learned. The goal is avoidance of complexity and use of simple, accurate language that does not confuse or bias the respondent.

Rating scales are commonly used. Examples:

.   A **Likert scale** employs a statement and "choices" like "strongly agree, agree, undecided, disagree, strongly disagree."
.   Semantic Differential uses a scale which respondent checks, e.g.,

Nike Tennis Shoes

Expensive __: __: __: __: __: __: __: Inexpensive

c.   Experiments

Control of experimental elements is not as easily accomplished by marketing researchers as it is by biologists working with mice, yet marketing researchers do use experimental techniques, manipulating variables and observing the effects of the changes in other variables.

Examples: taste tests, test markets (e.g., of pizza at McDonald's), "laboratory settings" where new TV shows might be shown to test audiences. As with other forms of research, care in planning and execution are required, but marketing experiments can yield valuable information.

C.   Stage Three: Selecting a Sample

A **sample** is a portion or subset of a larger **population**.

A survey of all members of a group is a **census**.

Care must be taken in answering sampling questions.

.   Who is to be in the sample? Identifying the relevant target
     population is important.

.   How big should the sample be? The answer must be "big enough
     to properly **represent the target market**," though sampling
     techniques, degree of accuracy required, etc., can greatly
     affect the total necessary size.

.   Who should be included in the sample?

Many sampling methods are available. Examples are shown below.

1.   Probability Sampling

      A **probability sample** is one in which every member of the
      population has a known, nonzero probability of selection. A
      sample selected in any other way (by judgment or for
      convenience sake) is **a nonprobability sample**.

      Variations include:

      .   **Simple random** sample, whereby choice of an individual
           from a list is determined by chance selection.

      .   **Stratified** sample, whereby the researcher divides the
           population into groups or strata. A random sample of
           each stratum is then taken.

      .   **Cluster** sample, whereby areas or clusters are selected
           and individuals within those areas sampled, e.g., a study
           of behaviors of Midwesterners might focus on Chicago,
           Cleveland, and St. Louis.

2.   Nonprobability Sampling

      There are three sorts of nonprobability sampling.

      .   **Convenience** sample, e.g., customers of a nearby mall or
           members of a church group chosen as a sample because it
           is convenient for the researcher.

      .   **Judgment** sample, e.g., a sales manager decides to sample
           "typical customers."

      .   **Quota** sample, e.g., researcher instructs surveyors to be
           sure that ten percent of all respondents have family
           incomes over $80,000. Surveyors are expected to meet
           that "quota."

D.   Stage Four: Collecting Data

A key point is minimization of errors, making sure interviewers
conduct themselves properly, that responses are not misinterpreted,
etc.

Pretesting of the method of data collection is one way to accomplish
this. Redesigning the study may be shown to be necessary, or
questions may have to be rephrased.

E.   Stage Five: Analyzing Data

Data gathered must be manipulated and processed so that it is in a form that will answer the marketing manager's questions.

1.   Editing

Omissions, obvious errors, correctable errors, are sought out. "Unusable responses" are discarded.

2.   Coding

Data is set up in ways that make it easier to process, e.g., 1 = male, 2 = female.

3.   Analyzing

Analyzing can be qualitative, quantitative, or both. Statistics can range from simple percentages or totals to the extremely complex.   In all, the needs of the manager who is to use the data should be paramount.

F.   Stage Six: Drawing Conclusions and Preparing the Report

Generally, managers want information upon which they can act, not detailed treatments of how the information was generated.

Graphs, charts, summaries, etc. all serve this goal, and help assure that the researcher's findings will be read and probably used.

G.   Stage Seven: Following Up

Follow-up is necessary to discover how management used the report and/or how the report could have been more useful.

Management, for its part, should let researchers know this information.

VI.   SALES FORECASTING: RESEARCH ABOUT THE FUTURE

Sales forecasting is the process of predicting sales totals over some specific future period of time.

An accurate sales forecast is one of the most valuable pieces of information since it affects planning and performance in all areas including production, distribution, pricing, inventory, etc.

The sales forecast also performs a control function in that it provides a standard against which performance can be measured.

A.   Break-Down and Build-Up Forecasting

Forecasting efforts can be aimed at estimating general economic conditions, the size of a market, market share, and so forth.

Some use the **break-down method**, as when a local bank uses the Wharton forecast of the American economy, then breaks down the data to reflect local conditions and prospects.

The **build-up method** starts at the level of the individual purchaser and builds to a larger forecast, as when the tool needs of one carpenter are multiplied by the number of carpenters in an area to estimate a total demand.

B.   The Three Levels of Forecasting

For the organization, three levels of forecasts are most important:

- **Market potential**, which refers to the upper limits of industry demand or the expected sales volume of all brands of a particular product for a particular time frame. (Example: How many cars in all will be sold in the U. S. next year?)

- **Sales potential**, which refers to an estimate of an individual company's maximum share of the market or the company's maximum sales volume for a given time period. (Example: How many Fords could be sold next year?)

- **Sales forecast**, which refers to the expected actual sales volume for a given period. (Example: How many Fords will we actually sell next year?)

Note that the sales forecast could be equal to the sales potential or even to the market potential in a monopoly circumstance. Still, in general, the forecasts as shown above are in order of declining size.

C.   Conditional Forecasting: "What If?"

A common approach to forecasting is to assume that the future time period will be much like the past. (Note: If followed blindly, this is called the "naive" approach.) A refinement is to assume three sets of circumstances: the worst, the best or most optimistic, and most likely. These three sets of assumptions of conditions lead to three forecasts.

D.   Forecasting by Time Periods

A good forecast includes a mention of a time frame in which the forecast will be met. Otherwise "forever" is implied as the time available to achieve the goal.

Traditionally, three terms are used as follows:

- **Short term:** one year or less.
- **Long term:** five to ten years.
- **Intermediate term:** from one to five years.

These terms can vary in meaning from industry to industry. What is "long term" to the Pet Rock business is very short term to the electric generating business.

Uncertainty and risk increase dramatically as the length of time used in the forecasts is enlarged. This is illustrated in Exhibit 4-6.

E.   Forecasting Options

There is no one best way to forecast sales. The available time, resources, expertise, and other factors affect "which is best." In general, using several methods is recommended as this approach provides several projections which can then be evaluated.

1.   Executive Opinion

A survey of executive opinion is a quick and inexpensive way to estimate future sales. It is based on the knowledge of people supposed to be experts, but it is subjective.

2.   Sales Force Composite

Asking each salesperson to predict sales for his or her territory and combining these into a total forecast constitutes this approach.   Like the survey of executives, this method is

very subjective, though the underlying logic, that the
salesperson knows the territory, is attractive.

3.   Survey of Customers

The basis of this approach is simply to ask customers what they
intend to buy. This works well when the product is established
and familiar, permitting a reasonable estimate. If the product
is brand new or unfamiliar, the method is difficult to defend.

4.   Projection of Trends

Extrapolating past data into the future is the basis of trend
projection.

Statistical methods from very plain to very complex are used.
If it is reasonable to believe that future trends will be
somewhat like past trends, it will often yield good forecasts.
If the marketplace is very dynamic, their worth is
questionable.

5.   Analysis of Market Factors

There may exist some association between sales and another
market factor. Such an association can be used to forecast
sales. More food market sales are made in New York than in
Connecticut because there are more people in New York. If
several factors can be used, they are referred to as a **market
factor index** or a **market index.**

An index, developed by *Sales and Marketing Management* magazine
utilizes three factors (income, retail sales, and population)
which are weighted (5,3, and 2) to arrive at an index number
that can be used to compare the buying powers found in various
cities, counties, etc. This is called the **Sales Management
Buying Power Index.** A similar index of industrial buying is
also available.

F.   Some Practical Considerations

Most organizations use several forecasting methods, not all of them
sophisticated. In some situations, such as there being a short time
available, a method such as a survey of executives may be used even
if it is not "the best." In all cases, it should be recalled that
the forecast techniques are aids to management, not ends in
themselves.

VII.   SUMMARY

Effective marketing management relies on accurate, pertinent, and timely
information, supplied in appropriate form by a well-designed marketing
information system.

**Learning Objective 1: Explain why information is essential to
effective marketing decision making.**

The marketing manager needs timely information about the organization's
customers, environment, and marketing activities to implement the marketing
concept. Without systematically gathered information, the marketing
manager has no accurate basis on which to decide courses of action.

**Learning Objective 2: Describe a successful Marketing Information
System.**

A marketing information system (MIS) is an organized set of procedures and
methods by which pertinent, timely, and accurate information is continually
gathered, sorted, analyzed, and distributed for use by marketing managers.

Learning Objective 3: **Describe a data collection system and a decision support system.**

The data collection system includes: the internal records and support systems that stores the data generated within the organization; (2) the marketing research system, a formal system for gathering new data; and (3) the marketing intelligence system, an informal network that provides data about the external environment. The decision support system includes: (1) databases that provide logically organized data; (2) the analytical models system, a set of software systems for analysis of data; and (3) the interactive system, which allows managers to retrieve data and perform analytical operations.

Learning Objective 4: **Analyze the contribution of marketing research to effective decision making.**

Marketing research is intended to provide objective information about marketing phenomena to reduce uncertainty and lead to more rational and effective decisions. It can employ a vast array of techniques to achieve this goal.

Learning Objective 5: **Describe the stages of the marketing research process.**

Marketing research studies generally follow seven major steps: (1) defining the problem, (2) planning the research design, (3) selecting the sample, (4) collecting data, (5) analyzing data, (6) drawing conclusions and preparing the report, and (7) following up.

Learning Objective 6: **Show how exploratory research relates to specific marketing management problems.**

Exploratory research clarifies the nature of problems that are not clearly understood so that further research can be conducted.

Learning Objective 7: **Understand why secondary data are valuable sources of information.**

Secondary data have been previously collected and assembled. They are inexpensive and may be obtained quickly.

Learning Objective 8: **Outline the advantages and possible uses of observation, surveys, and experiments.**

Primary data are collected by observation, surveys, and experiments. Observation is used to record actual behavior, but does not reveal the cause of that behavior. Surveys are used to study large groups of subjects by mail, telephone, or personal interview. Experiments are tightly controlled research designs that manipulate an experimental variable and measure its effect under controlled conditions.

Learning Objective 9: **Demonstrate knowledge of the purposes and procedures involved in sales forecasting.**

Sales forecasting is the predicting of an organization's anticipated sales over a specific time period. The forecast is used to plan such activities as production schedules, distribution, and promotion and to measure the success of these and other activities. Good forecasting improves planning and control.

Learning Objective 10: **Evaluate the advantages and disadvantages of the various forecasting methods.**

Forecasting methods such as executive opinion, sales force composites, and surveys of customers use the opinions of experienced individuals. Personal biases or lack of knowledge may, however, affect the results. Trend analysis is appropriate in some situations but assumes that the future will be like the past. Market factor analysis and published indices are useful where sales are affected by certain external variables.

VIII. **KEY TERMS**

IX.   **QUESTIONS FOR DISCUSSION (17)**

X.   **ETHICS IN PRACTICE**

XI.   **CASES**

ANSWER GUIDELINES FOR CHAPTER 4 QUESTIONS FOR DISCUSSION

1.   *What role does marketing research play in the development of marketing
      strategies and the implementation of the marketing concept?*

ANSWER:

The costs and risks involved in the performance of most marketing activities
usually make it well worthwhile to systematically gather information that can
contribute to the reduction of risk. Marketing research can be seen as a
risk-reducing investment, just as insurance is viewed by many businesspeople.
Yet many businesspeople do not see marketing research in that way, in part
because they often think that they know what's "good for sales" without doing "a
lot of research that's going to tell us what we already know."

Yet the marketing concept tells us to attempt to achieve certain goals, and that
the greatest among them is "customer satisfaction." It is the key to long-range
profitability and all the rest. If "all" activities are to focus on consumer
needs, the marketer must know what those needs are, how they affect the
perception of an appealing marketing mix (all 4 Ps), what aspects of the mix can
be changed to improve the appeal of the mix, and so on.

There is a story that says the most dangerous saying in marketing is "My wife
says ..." Sensitive instructors may care to change that to "I think ...." In any
case, the moral is that research among customers and potential customers, not
among family members or golf buddies, is what effective marketing requires.

If the instructor wishes to move beyond consideration of "the customer" and talk
about, for example, market segments, marketing research's role in identifying,
measuring, and analyzing segments of markets may also be discussed here.

Marketing research contributes information that aids in the selection and
development of marketing strategies, and the subsequent evaluation of the success
or failure of those strategies. As the text suggests in summary, the marketing
concept tells us to do what the customer wants. How better to approach that task
than by asking the customer what he or she does, in fact, want?

2.   *Some marketing managers seem unable to manage information as well as they
      perform their other duties. Why is that?*

ANSWER:

All managers actually manage several things: their assignments, the people
around them, the planning process, and so on. Because information is a key to
their successes, it too should be managed with care. Even though "everybody
knows" this to be the case, it is true that many managers do not manage
information well, or at all.

There are several major reasons for this. The text makes the point that in most
task environments, but especially in marketing, there always seems to be many
"fires to put out." Handling problems as they come up consumes a great deal of
time, leaving little time for managing information and/or providing the excuse
for not taking the time to organize information.

Too, managing information is easily put off until "tomorrow." Not only is there
the press of daily events just mentioned, but there is also the simple truth that
many marketing tasks can be handled without marketing research or formal handling
of information being involved. For this reason it is easy for the manager to
postpone dealing with information management until he or she "has time to get to that.

Additionally, as was mentioned in the answer to question 1, many managers feel
that they have the know-how and experience to handle whatever difficulties arise
without having to manage their information in the way that both common sense and
the marketing management literature say they should.

Lastly, and this is more of an excuse than a reason, some managers face vast
amounts of information that may be pertinent to their tasks. It is tempting to
shirk the responsibility of organizing and managing such mountains of
information.

Of course, the very reasons *for not managing* information are, in fact, reasons
for managing information -- that there is a lot of information is a reason to
attempt to manage it, not an excuse not to manage it.

3.   *Describe the information category known as "marketing intelligence."*

ANSWER:

The definition of marketing intelligence system employed in the book is:

> A marketing intelligence system is a network of diverse sources that
> collects both primary and secondary data about changes in the
> marketing environment.

Thus, marketing intelligence is "everyday information" about changes in the
organization's external environment.

Other definitions put a bit more emphasis on the competitive situation, including
such matters as the activities of competing organizations. In a sense,
therefore, the idea of "marketing intelligence" can be linked to the concept of
"military intelligence," knowing what the other guy is up to, and, in a limited
and legal way, "spying."

Marketing intelligence can be gathered in many ways. The text provides an
example of the Corningware coffeepot which was withdrawn from the marketplace
after the company, by means of letters sent to purchasers, discovered that the
handles of the pots had an unacceptable number of separations from the pots. The
payoff to Corning Glass Company was that it was able to "do right" by its
customers and make an attempt to keep their good will. Here is a case of
marketing intelligence gathered in an orderly way from customers.

Other opportunities for gathering intelligence are available. Most companies
admit that their major source of information about the marketplace is the trade
press. To the degree that marketers make a conscious effort to monitor trade
magazines and newspapers, this is a "set of regular procedures" that provide
information.

Many firms require their sales forces to report the goings-on in the marketplace
in a formal way. This may be done in writing in the form of regularly scheduled
reports, via electronic means such as computers linked to the home office, or
face-to-face in regular meetings or teleconferences. Other reporting means are
certainly available.

The major strength of marketing intelligence is its specific focus on the
competitive environment. Further, the category includes a broad range of
information taken from a wide variety of sources. Also, it is not special-
project-oriented. It operates "constantly."

One weakness should be noted. Marketing intelligence is gathered from and by
sources which may not always be accurate. Mistakes frequently appear in the
trade press, salespersons' reports can include wrong, misunderstood, or even
"planted" information, or can be unintentionally biased by the salespeople
themselves.

4.   *Define or describe, in your own words, the following: a. Marketing
      research system b. Database c. Analytical models system d. Marketing
      research e. Marketing information system.*

ANSWER:

(a)   Marketing research system

Marketing research yields information that joins other bits of information to form the "sum of knowledge" upon which marketing managers base their decisions. The marketing research system is the means whereby that information is gathered. Aspects of the marketing research system include the methods of gathering secondary data (from government, trade, and other sources), and methods of gathering primary data (including surveys, test markets, and other research projects).

As definitions of marketing research generally note, marketing research emphasizes specific projects intended to gather new data (or data which shows that existing beliefs are correct or no longer correct). The greatest number of marketing research projects are not on-going. Even if they are, it is possible to view them as individual, specific projects in themselves.

In short, when a research project or program is conducted to generate information about a specific problem, the data is generated by the marketing research system.

(b)   Database

A database is a collection of information that is arranged in a logical manner and organized in a form that can be stored and processed by a computer, e.g., population and income data by zip code or county.

Note that the database includes data, but not totally "raw" data. The facts and figures have been organized in a way that permits further manipulation and analysis. Database information is not analyzed data. The researcher will use it to perform analysis, typically using a computer. (Though the text stresses use of a computer it is, of course, possible to analyze databases without using a computer. This would be an arduous task, however.)

Databases may be generated by the organization itself or by outside organizations, both governmental and private. Many companies gather and sell databases, making them available in various ways, including on-line. The library carries several directories of such services. These include descriptions of the data provided, up-date information, costs, and so on.

It should be noted that some databases can be used for purposes not intended by the gatherers of the information. For example, the Department of Education is a source of many databases pertaining to education, children, teachers, health problems of children, etc. These typically include data gathered from literally millions of children/families/teachers. This data may prove of great use to toy makers, food marketers, or textbook publishers.

(c)   Analytical models system

The analytical models system contains the database management software that provides access to the data stored in the computer's memory. It includes statistical software systems, spreadsheet software, and decision model banks that combine and restructure data from the database, diagnose relationships among variables, make estimates, and perform other analysis.

A large department store might have collected great amounts of data about its credit card customers. The software the store uses may permit analysts to identify customers spending more than $1,000 per year at the store, or to identify those who shop heavily in the Christmas or back-to-school seasons, or to discover which areas of the market served contain the major customers, perhaps presenting this broken down by ZIP codes. The store's management can then employ this analysis in evaluating such promotional efforts as direct mailings, billboard placement, and telephone selling.

The analytical models system can further assist management by presenting information like that mentioned above in tabular, graphic, or map forms (among others), that help management grasp and use the information presented.

(d)   Marketing research

As was mentioned in part (a) of this question, marketing research definitions stress that marketing research involves specific efforts aimed at providing information that will be of use in solving particular problems. It is not, therefore, learning some fact "by accident" nor is it casually discovering some piece of information in a trade magazine.

Marketing research is defined in the text as:

> The systematic and objective process of generating information for use in making marketing decisions.

The text goes on to state (that) this process includes defining the problem and identifying what information is required to solve the problem; designing the method for collecting information; managing and implementing the collecting of data; analyzing the results; and communicating their findings and implications. (It might also be mentioned, and is later in the text, that the process should include a follow-up to see if and how management used the report, how it could have been made more useful, etc.)

Again, when the student defines marketing research in his/her own words, some emphasis must be placed on the specificity of marketing research to particular problems.

(e)   Marketing information system

The text defines the MIS as:

> An organized set of procedures and methods by which pertinent, timely, and accurate information is continually gathered, sorted, analyzed, evaluated, stored, and distributed for use by marketing decision makers.

This may be phrased in more humble terms. Marketing managers are confronted with mountains of information coming from many sources including marketing intelligence, marketing research, and just plain casually encountered information and rumors. All this information should somehow be organized in a way that the manager can "get at it" when it is needed, that is, it should be categorized, grouped, and otherwise arranged so that relevant information can be found as necessary.

It is for this reason that some definitions refer to the MIS as a "framework" for information. Because the job of organizing information and making it available in usable form is so immense, computerization of the effort is a virtual necessity. However, it is our contention that an MIS can be operated without sophisticated computers. Our argument for this is: every marketing manager has an MIS of a sort. It may be in his or her head, it may involve some ledger books and a hand-held calculator, it may include a shoe box full of papers, but it is this manager's system. It follows, that since there is a system, why not work on it a bit to make it do a better job?

5.   *What does marketing research do for the manager? What does it not do?*

ANSWER:

The purpose of this question is to draw the student's attention to the fact that marketing research is not some panacea, not a crutch which managers can use to somehow excuse themselves of managerial responsibilities and the need to make judgments.

Marketing research can do the following:

- Provide information managers can use to arrive at decisions.
- Present additional dimensions of a problem.
- Help to uncover and identify problems or issues that management might address.
- Monitor marketing operations.
- Evaluate the success or failure of marketing programs.

In short, marketing research ideally gives the manager more information, better information, and better organized information than he or she would have had without the help of research.

Marketing research does not do the following:

. Replace the manager's judgment.
. Give the manager "the answer."
. Tell the manager what to do.
. Show that the manager was "wrong" in what he or she was doing.

In short, marketing research does not claim to give managers the answers to their marketing problems. Care is always taken to stress that research cannot replace judgment. As sophisticated and advanced as modern marketing research is, it would be foolish to claim that the paths it suggests should be blindly followed regardless of what experienced managers think should be done.

It might be mentioned that one reason why researchers have historically accented that they are not telling the manager what to do is the natural and traditional fear of managers that they will be "replaced by a computer." This fear is thought by many to be a major cause of old-line managers' ignoring marketing research findings. Thus, researchers are careful to avoid saying, in effect, "our figures show that you have been doing your job incorrectly for the past thirty years." Now that younger, more quantitatively trained managers are in high places, "fear" of research has probably dissipated. Now, ironically, managers have to remind themselves that facts, figures, and computers are tools to be used, not blindly followed as a means to escape exercising judgment.

6.   What is exploratory research? Give an example of its proper application.

ANSWER:

The overriding purpose of exploratory research is to clarify and explain the nature of a marketing problem. It may be needed as a first step in a process that will lead to more specific research efforts. For example, the manager of a theater may believe that attendance has been steadily declining and discover that his records bear this out. A symptom has been noted. The problem is not the declining attendance. The problem is why this is happening. Exploratory research, aimed at identifying the problem, and perhaps discovering its dimensions, is in order. The manager might interview individual patrons or groups of patrons, or locate and interview former patrons, or try to find out if this situation is common in other area theaters, and so on.

The purpose of exploratory research is to "explore" and clarify a problem rather than to find "an answer." It is used when a problem area is not fully understood and uses methods that are general in nature, yielding information upon which to build a more detailed research program.

7.   What are the stages in a formal research project? Which is the most
      important?

ANSWER:

The stages in a formal marketing research project include: (1) defining the problem, (2) planning the research design, (3) selecting a sample, (4) collecting data, (5) analyzing data, (6) drawing conclusions and preparing a report, and (7) following up.

The stages of a research project overlap and affect one another. As the text indicates, research objectives will affect sample selection and data collection. The target sample will also affect questionnaire wording. However as Albert Einstein noted, "the formulation of a problem is often more essential than its solution." If managers rush to plan the research design or select a sample, they may fail to ask the right question and miss providing information to help solve the marketer's dilemma.

8.   *Why would a marketing manager choose to investigate secondary data rather than primary data?*

ANSWER:

The advantages of secondary data stem almost entirely from its accessibility and relative ease of use.   Secondary data may be adequate to begin a formal research effort and may be less expensive than primary data as well as being faster to obtain.

But data gathered by others should be closely scrutinized.   Questions like the following may be posed:

.   How old is this data?
.   Who gathered it?
.   How was the work done?   What was the methodology?   What was the sample size and was it appropriate?
.   Is the data compatible with our needs?   Does the study cover, for example, the same geographic area we wish to cover?
.   Did the researcher want to "prove" something in doing this "research"?
.   Is this data consistent with what we think to be correct, or is it "off the wall"?

It is easy to find reasons why secondary data might be, at the least, imperfect. In general, the inherent disadvantage of secondary data is it may not specifically meet the researcher's needs.   The instructor might ask the class if the "wrong" answer to questions like this mean the data should not be used? Except in the case of suspected dishonesty of the researcher, the answer is, at minimum, a resounding "Maybe."   Old data is not necessarily bad data, nor is data drawn from a small sample.   The data should be evaluated on its own terms and in terms of how much the time and resources would be necessary to collect "new" data.

9.   *What are the strengths and weaknesses of the following marketing research methods?   a. Mail and telephone surveys   b. Observation studies   c. Experiments*

ANSWER:

(a)   Mail and telephone surveys

These are contrasted, along with personal surveys, in the text.   Though the advantages and disadvantages vary with the situation and the availability of time and resources, a general comparison can be drawn.

ADVANTAGES - MAIL

Appropriate for surveying large numbers of respondents.   Appropriate when subject matter is confidential or when answers would have to be "looked up," e.g., "How do this year's net sales compare to those of 1970?"   Cost can be low if used properly.   More questions can be posed than on phone.   No immediate influence of human questioner involved.   "Gift" to encourage response can be enclosed.

DISADVANTAGES - MAIL

Cost can be high for response since response rates are often low.   No interviewer present to explain difficult questions or to observe respondent's race, sex, house, etc.   Person responding may not be the person addressed.   Self-selection (respondent "chooses" himself by responding or not).   Slow means of getting data compared to phone.   Easy for respondent to give incorrect information.

ADVANTAGES - PHONE

Quick response -- once you've hung up, you've got the answer.   Can phone people when they are doing what you are interested in, e.g., watching T.V. during the 8 to 9 p.m. time slot.   Well-designed, brief survey may get high response rate and, thus, low cost per response.   Interviewers can make many calls as opposed to time a personal interview would take.   Provides a "personal touch" though some respondents resent being called.

DISADVANTAGES - PHONE

Must be short. Can be expensive though WATS lines, etc. can reduce this. People called may be suspicious of caller, e.g., really trying to sell something. Problem reaching "no answers," unlisted numbers. Certain people, e.g., wealthier people, tend to be at home less than population in general. Could reach "wrong" person in household. Easy for respondent to give false information.

(b)   Observation studies

Observation involves actually watching consumer behavior in action. As such, it is not suited to studies involving great lengths of time, e.g., waiting for a selected individual to go out and buy a car or new house. Observation is used where events of interest occur quite rapidly (customers making purchases at a supermarket) or in controlled situations where an action or reaction can be observed. Some organizations set up experimental stores and give subjects an amount of money, like $10 or $20, and direct them to "get in there and shop."

Some situations in which observation could be used include:

.   Observe which car people in an auto show are clustering about.

.   Observe how parents and children behave when buying cereal.

.   Observe how many riders get on a bus or subway at given stops.

.   Observe how carefully an industrial purchasing agent compares model A with model B.

.   Observe if shoppers seem to select items from particular shelves, e.g., eye-level shelves.

Again, the technique of observation is very useful but there is no certain way to "observe" why a given action took place. Subjects of observation may be surveyed or simply asked why they took a certain action, or the researcher might infer a reason for behavior.

(c)   Experiments

In an experiment, a researcher attempts to hold other variables steady while varying the experimental variable in an effort to determine the effect of that variable. This is comparatively "easy" in certain situations, as when rats or minerals are subjected to experiments to determine the effects of variables upon them. It is far more difficult to utilize experiments in marketing (and other social sciences) because the experimenter is dealing with thinking human beings, not rocks or chemicals.

A well-run marketing research experiment has these things to recommend it. It permits the researcher to observe closely the subjects (buyers or whomever) in a controlled environment. It also permits the experimenter to alter the circumstances in which the subjects are operating and to infer from their behaviors how they are affected by the variables involved. Ideally, the researcher can also make some judgments as to how the subjects would behave in a real-world setting.

The weaknesses of experiments are all too obvious. To begin with, the experiment is an artificial situation and there may be reason to believe the subjects do not behave similarly in artificial and real-world settings. Even if the researcher is satisfied that experimental subjects behaved reasonably in the experiment, there is no guarantee that they will behave the same at home.

Further, the real-world environment may change quickly, meaning that actions noted in an experimental situation may never occur in the changing environment to which the participants return.

Perhaps most importantly, human experimental subjects may "figure out" what the experiment is all about. They might then react to the experimental variable (new product, price, ad, etc.) differently than they would have in the real world. At the least, they are more aware of the product, ad, etc. Also, they might "tell you what they think you want to know," e.g., that the new ad really moves them, or they might resolve to confound the experiment by refusing to change or even to give their opinions.

Self-selection, maturation, panel mortality, and many other problems abound in experiments. Describe a marketing research experiment to the class and let them "pick it apart."

10.   *What are the primary considerations in the selection of a sample?*

ANSWER:

A sample is simply a portion or subset of a larger population. Sampling involves answering the following three questions:

(1)   Who is to be sampled?

This involves a specification of the target group of interest or the target population and obtaining a list from which the sample will be taken.

(2)   How big should the sample be?

The sample must be of a sufficient size to represent the target population given cost constraints. If appropriate techniques are utilized, a small proportion of the total population will give a reliable measure of the whole.

(3)   How should the sample be selected?

The sampling procedure is a major determinant of the accuracy of the project and includes two major methods: probability sampling and nonprobability sampling. Alternative probability sampling techniques include: a simple random sample, a stratified sample or a cluster sample. Examples of nonprobability samples include convenience, judgment or quota.

11.   *Give some examples of population lists from which samples may be drawn.*

ANSWER:

This question encourages students to first consider the target population and to then derive a sampling frame, or accurate list from which to draw the sample. Students can be quite creative in relating the concept once they understand the concept. A few examples include the following:

Target Population	Potential List
Physicians	American Medical Association Directory
College students	Registrar's list of enrolled students
Voters	List of registered voters, or active voters in recent years
Home owners	Tax rolls
Town residents	Telephone directory

12.   *What is the difference between market potential, sales potential, and the sales forecast?*

ANSWER:

The basic difference between these three types of forecasts is the level of aggregation. Specifically, each may be defined as follows:

Market potential is the upper limit of industry demand, the expected sales volume for all brands of a particular product during a given period.

Sales potential is the maximum share of the market any individual organization could expect during a given period (under perfect conditions).

Sales forecast is the actual sales volume an organization (realistically) expects during a given period.

13.   *What market factors might help predict market potential for the following products? a. Forklift trucks b. Chain saws c. Soft drinks d. Playground equipment*

ANSWER:

This question challenges students to consider basic factors associated with demand for various products. As such, there should be flexibility in encouraging "brainstorming," or allowing the class to generate lists from which to choose the perceived "best" factors.

(a)   Sales of forklift trucks may be related to:

Number of wholesalers
Number of manufacturers
Number of discount retailers

(b)   Chain saw market factors may include:

Number of Forestry Service units
Number of lumberjacks
Utility company trimming frequency
Number of do-it-yourself-type landowners

(c)   Soft drink market factors could involve:

Population
Teenage population
Teenage employment rate

(d)   Playground equipment:

Number of children
Number of playgrounds per square mile
Birth rate and/or family formation rate
Passage of taxes for community improvement

14.   *Why is it necessary to forecast market potential as well as individual company sales?*

ANSWER:

Market potential sets an upper limit to industry demand for all brands during a given period. Thus, it reflects the market's ability to absorb a type of product. Since marketing is implemented in a dynamic environment, assumptions must be accurate if the sales forecast is to direct efforts effectively. Factors such as the length of time the product has been on the market, the arrival of new competitors or other environmental changes may not be noticed if market potential is not estimated. Further, the market potential forecast allows the firm to compare its performance to the industry potential over time.

15.   *What forecasting method would be best for the following products? a. Cigars b. The Sony Watchman miniature portable television set c. Baseball attendance at your university*

ANSWER:

In answering these questions, the instructor should emphasize that several forecasting methods are generally used by companies as an aid in checking accuracy. Issues which alter the usefulness of various techniques include the length of time the product has been on the market and the level of stability in sales.

(a)   Cigars

Since this product has been available for a long period of time, companies have a wealth of past data to use for a projection of trends. Time series data is appropriate for this mature market if no dynamic changes are anticipated with greater emphasis placed on more recent sales figures. However, given the emphasis on reductions in smoking, this historical data may also be supplemented with executive opinion, or a survey of retail customers.

(b)   The Sony Watchman miniature portable television set.

Once this was a new product with no past sales history, so Sony was unable to project trends. Thus, sales force composite, survey of retail customers, executive opinion, and/or analysis of market factors would be more appropriate.

Now the product has been around for some years, so market factors may be usable, as might certain facts about the market for this product that may have become clear since its introduction. These include numbers of people in age groups and/or income groups that are important to this product's success, the (possible) greater popularity of the product in some parts of the country rather than others, the "wear-out-rate," Sony's understanding of whether or not people replace their sets with new ones when new features are introduced, and so on.

Integrative questions to reinforce issues within this chapter could include asking students where to obtain a list of retailers who sell this type of product and what factors they would expect to affect sales.

(c)   Baseball attendance at your university.

Assuming the baseball program has been in operation for some period of time, a projection of trends could be used to generate average levels of attendance for a season. However, in this case attendance at any one game may be expected to fluctuate based on the opponent faced, the pitcher scheduled to pitch, the return of an injured star, a player's individual performance (e.g., nearing a Conference record for home runs), competing leisure activities, number of home games, won-lost record, or the weather. Thus, to refine the forecast for a particular game, executive opinion, is also suggested.

16.   *Why is trend extrapolation dangerous?*

ANSWER:

Forecasters often assume that future time periods will remain similar to the past. However, the marketing environment is dynamic and may change rapidly. Further, the danger of extrapolation increases with the time frame of the forecast. Short-term, long-term and intermediate-term extrapolations will vary in safety by products. For example, consider the potential problems of forecasting demand for cigarettes a decade from now based on sales in the 1980s.

17.   *What do the executive opinion and sales force composite methods have in common?*

ANSWER:

Both methods use experts who have experience in the industry. Executives are knowledgeable of broad market factors and sales representatives are familiar with local market areas. Both methods also may suffer from the subjective nature of the process because people are biased and may be overly optimistic or pessimistic.   Further, executives may overlook local market changes while sales representatives may be unaware of broad market trends.

ETHICS EXERCISE 4

CHAPTER 4 ETHICS IN PRACTICE

Overview

Recently the major television networks have agreed to voluntarily withhold information from exit polls until the polls close on the West Coast.   This was apparently a reaction to the negative press they had been receiving from West Coast residents and political commentators across the country about the influence of exit polls on voting behavior.   There is some evidence that learning the results from exit polls does influence people's voting behavior; it especially has the effect of lowering voting participation rates, especially in elections where there appears to be a clear winner.   People then reason that the decision has been made and their vote won't matter anyway.

1.   *Are early election projections an ethical practice?*

This issue only affects election pollsters and those involved in political candidate marketing and news broadcasting.   Hence, the issue is not dealt with in either the American Marketing Association's Marketing Research Code of Ethics nor in the Code of Ethics of the Marketing Research Association, Inc.   None of the issues covered in these documents (e.g., selling under the guise of research, confidentiality of client information, etc.) would seem to have applications to this issue.   However, a number of textbooks on marketing research have identified some issues regarding the rights of the public and the corresponding duties of researchers which would appear to be relevant.   The underlying idea is that a research professional operating in the public arena has a duty to focus on the needs of society.

One item here is incomplete reporting of information.   Exit polls are based on incomplete information, since all voters have not yet gone to the polls, and voters on the West Coast, or those who otherwise vote later in the day, might differ in key ways (demographically, psychographically, etc.) from the general public; hence to exclude their votes would be to use an unrepresentative sample.

Another possible problem is misleading reporting.   First, to some extent, exit polls deal in self-selected samples since some people refuse to divulge personal information to pollsters.   As a result, there can be a serious sample bias.   Second, there is some evidence that people are often unwilling to give truthful information about their voting behavior (i.e., they lie to pollsters..)   This social desirability bias was recently discovered when it was found that voters lie to pollsters when blacks run against whites.   This apparently explains why black candidates such as Mayor David Dinkens in New York City and Governor Douglas Wilder in Virginia won by much narrower margins than polls predicted.   People who intend to vote against the black candidate, for whatever reason, are reluctant to admit it to pollsters for fear of being labeled a bigot or racist, so they lie.

And, the biggest problem is that turnout rates are adversely affected when voters who haven't voted learn of the results of election projections.   This could be viewed as an indirect threat to our constitutional right to vote.   People assume that their vote doesn't count, and yet, given the threats to the validity of such polling (nonrepresentative samples, false reporting) perhaps the results of some elections aren't as skewed as they appear to be and late voters can have an influence.   It is also argued that if a national race is one-sided, some voters will stay home, and turnout will be reduced in local races on the same ballot.

Also, there is some evidence that people sitting on the fence or those poorly informed and/or without an opinion on whom to vote for are heavily influenced by exit polls (a kind of a bandwagon effect).   In effect, there is no longer a level playing field across the country.

Proponents of releasing results of early election polling would argue that the public has a right to know. However, the threats to the validity of the results weakens this argument. They would also argue that the press' rights to free speech would be threatened if a law were passed prohibiting releases of exit polls. However, they would not lose their right to release information, only the timing would be delayed. The pollsters also say that if voters decide not to turn out that is their own free choice, and there is nothing in democratic theory that holds local elections should be decided by voters whose only reason for coming out to the polls is interest in the national race. Also, early poll results are just one kind of information that can change the way people vote. If some voters want to go along with the majority - or with the underdog - that is their privilege.

It would seem that the strongest consideration is the fact that exit polls distort the democratic election process. Although a law could be passed setting limits on election polls, a more desirable course of action seems to be the voluntary limitations the TV networks have placed on themselves.

CHAPTER 4 TAKE A STAND QUESTIONS

1.   *A retailer asks customers for their phone numbers which are then entered (via the cash register system) into a computer file. The retailer then sells its customer list, which includes both names and phone numbers, to other marketers. Is this ethical?*

The ethical issue here is the consumer's right to privacy, which is the right of individuals to decide for themselves how much of their thoughts, feelings, and the facts of their personal lives they will share with others. Polls have discovered that a vast majority of Americans believe that collecting and giving out personal information without their knowledge is a serious violation of their privacy. This might reflect a concern about having personal data placed in a computer bank as well as a decrease in trust in both business and government. (Laczniak and Murphy, *Marketing Ethics: Guidelines for Managers*, p. 62)

It seems that to sell a consumer's personal data without his or her consent is a violation of the faith or trust the customer has placed in the marketer. Although a consumer could reasonably expect to receive follow-up direct marketing efforts from the retailer collecting the data (after all, why else would they bother to collect it?) many consumers would likely withhold personal data if they knew it would result in an avalanche of direct mail and a deluge of telemarketing phone calls. A more reasonable approach, often used by direct marketers, is to offer customers an "opt out" provision whereby they can express their willingness to keep information about themselves from being shared with other marketers.

Unfortunately, database managers are able to secure all kinds of personal data about us. How would you like to give total strangers information about your income, the value of your home, your net worth, or your personal habits, including everything from gambling to catalog shopping? Well, don't worry about giving this information to strangers - they already have it. Every time you apply for a credit card, license a car, have a child, or call an 800 number, you're giving somebody valuable data about yourself which will be sold to marketers. However, just because this is common practice doesn't make it right. The Direct Marketing Association's guidelines for ethical business practice state that if you gather information and rent your customers' names, it is incumbent upon you to let them know and to give them an opportunity for it not to happen. The ethical marketer will strengthen customer relations by touting the fact that such information is not for sale.

2.   *Should an individual's answers to a survey be confidential?*

Confidentiality of answers means that the research company knows the respondent's identity but that this is otherwise protected from dissemination. Anonymity means the identity of the respondent is never known to anyone. The research firm will collect personal demographic data but will only use this data to give more information on differences in responses to survey questions between demographic groups. Most surveys conclude with a section in which demographic data is collected, with instructions stating something like "The following data will be used for statistical purposes only." This puts the respondent at ease in sharing personal information that he might otherwise be reluctant to divulge. The result should be that respondents will be wiling to answer more questions and to answer them honestly.

The Code of Ethics of the American Marketing Association explicitly states that, "If respondents have been led to believe, directly or indirectly, that they are participating in a marketing research survey and their anonymity will be protected, their names shall not be made known to anyone outside the research organization or research department, or used for other than research purposes." It also says that "Research assignments and materials received, as well as information obtained from respondents, shall be held in confidence by the interviewer and revealed to no one except the research organization conducting the marketing study." The Code of Ethics of the Marketing Research Association, Inc., says that researchers should "protect the anonymity of respondents and hold all information concerning an individual respondent privileged, such that this information is used only within the context of a particular study."

If a researcher plans on sharing the respondent's name and other personal data, the respondent should be informed before the interview begins. This is consistent with the respondent's right to know how she might be affected by the results of a survey as well as her right to choose whether or not to participate in such a study. It should also be noted that the Federal Trade Commission has indicated that it would take appropriate action if it discovers that research firms have obtained information under the guise of anonymity but in fact actually coded questionnaires with invisible ink so they can identify the respondents. The FTC considers this to be an unfair and deceptive trade practice.

However, some would argue that individual respondents must decide how much of their lives to share with others. As long as a researcher obtains the respondent's informed consent to interview them, the research does not invade the respondent's privacy rights. This would appear to be a minority position, however.

3.   *Is telephoning calling someone at 8:30 p.m. and asking them to participate in a survey ethical?*

The issue here is again one of privacy rights. The dilemma lies in deciding where the rights of the individual end and those of society to obtain better information on consumer preferences kick in. A common standard of courtesy among research firms is not to interview late in the evening and at other inconvenient times. Where one draws the line on this would depend on the target audience. It would seem safe to say that a significant number of people (especially those with young children who might be awakened by a phone call) do not wish to be disturbed after 8 or 8:30. On the other hand, if the target market is college students living away from home, calling even at 11 p.m. at night is probably no problem.

A minority position is that to limit the times when researchers can call restricts their right to gather data. After all, most people aren't home during the day and no one likes to be interrupted by telephone calls during the dinner hour. People have the right to answer their phone and/or to hang up if they don't want to be bothered. However, if researchers bother a significant number of people by phone calls, this will result in more refusals to participate and harm the image of marketing research and possibly of the research firms and/or sponsoring companies.

4.   *In its telephone solicitation for cemetery plots, a company begins the call by saying it is conducting a survey. Is this ethical?*

Virtually everyone agrees that this is morally wrong. The practice is known as sugging - selling under the guise of marketing research. When used by fund raisers to sugarcoat appeals for contributions it is known as frugging - fund raising under the guise of marketing research. This is a major concern of legitimate researchers. Both telephone and personal interviews have been used for sales solicitations, especially by marketers of unsought goods such as cemetery plots, encyclopedias, magazines, and home improvement services. (Answer a few questions and suddenly you find yourself eligible to buy a product or service.) Also, some mail surveys have served to generate sales leads or mailing lists. This, of course, alienates the general public and is deceptive to those who are unable to tell the difference between legitimate marketing research and selling efforts. Those consumers who catch on to the marketer's motives can turn the tables on the "researcher" by either providing a few choice words and hanging up or by playing along, pretending to be interested, and then terminating just when the marketer thinks she's closed the sale. Thus, this unethical practice can boomerang on the marketer.

The AMA Code's first ethical principle says that "No individual or organization will undertake any activity which is directly or indirectly represented to be marketing research, but which has as its real purpose the attempted sale of merchandise or services to some or all of the respondents interviewed in the course of the research." The FTC has indicated that it is illegal to use any plan, scheme, or ruse that misrepresents the true status of the person making the call as a door-opener to gain admission to a prospect's home, office, or other establishment, and it has issued cease and desist orders in such cases. In short, this sales ploy is considered unethical as well as illegal, and it erodes the public's trust.

There are several things a researcher can do to avoid the appearance of such an impropriety. First, he can assure the respondent in an introduction or cover letter that he will not attempt to sell the respondent anything at this time nor will he use information obtained in the course of the research at hand for unethical purposes in the future. Then he can do as promised.

GUIDE TO CASES

CASE 4-1   SPACE WHEYFERS

SUBJECT MATTER: Marketing Research for New Products, Problem Identification, Need for Information, Sales Forecasting

AT-A-GLANCE OVERVIEW

Space Wheyfers are spacecraft-shaped crispy snacks made from whey, a product left over when cheese is produced and often dumped by cheese manufacturers. Space Wheyfers have fewer calories and less fat that other snacks, like potato chips and pretzels. They have much more protein since they are made, in effect, from milk. Star Wars and other popular space-related movies suggest to management that a space theme is a good one for their product.

Blue Lake Cheese Company developed this product, a "natural" for the company. The product helped the environment since dumping whey into streams and rivers pollutes the water and encourages algae growth. The snack food is healthier than most and can be flavored and colored in any manner desired. The flavor and texture of the Wheyfers needs to be investigated in a taste test.

QUESTIONS FOR DISCUSSION

1.   *What is the marketing problem facing management at Blue Lake Cheese Company?*

A major problem facing the company is the lack of information. Although there is some information - a feel for the market, a general knowledge of "space awareness," knowledge that some people would favor a product that was healthy and "green" in the bargain - the information at hand is not exactly what is required. It certainly would be helpful to have proper information, since what is now available, mostly hunches, "general knowledge," feelings, etc., does not always work. There is less risk when actual facts are available.

Another problem is the way the development of the product seems to have been approached. The Blue Lake Company seems to have developed the new product because it had a waste product that could be used and because technology permitted manufacture of this product. This is understandable, after all the product "is a natural for the company." No mention is made of it being a "natural for the consumer." There are, however, some reasons to think it might be, but we don't know for sure, or even "partly for sure." The item seems to be based on a product-oriented view of things. The company would be better served by using a marketing orientation as the marketing concept prescribes.

2.   *Do you agree that the taste test should be the very first marketing
      research project?*

Although taste is very important, it is not appropriate to make the taste test
the very first marketing research project. Basically, the company has a product
in search of a market, and there have been assumptions made about who comprises
that market. While assumptions can be correct, the company should confirm its
hunches. It appears that Blue Lake has not devised a systematic approach for
gathering information, but is, instead, charging off to get information relevant
to each problem as it arises.

3.   *What additional information would be useful to help in the marketing of
      this product?*

Within reason, as much relevant information as possible would be helpful.
However, the most critical information concerns the market itself. The
popularity of space and galactic themes may be short-lived. If not exactly a
fad, interest in space certainly appears to wax and wane. Indeed, any interest
there might be in space at any given time may be gone before the product can be
brought to market. What age groups are most interested in space? The targeted
age group, or perhaps a younger one? Who knows at this point? Missiles and
flying saucers might appeal in the short run, but how about investigating other,
less faddish, shapes? Other target markets may thus be approached, perhaps with
great success.

4.   *How can the company forecast sales?*

When making a forecast, the company should consider several time frames. This is
especially true if the space theme is used. Especially in an area as risky as
snack food, a market full of fickle and short-term customers, there is no one
best way to forecast sales. Management should use several methods and
combinations and see if there is any "general agreement" among the results
produced. The company's executives have experience in the market, so try
"executive opinion." The salespeople have experience calling on groceries and
may have some "junk food" insights of value -- for example, how are space-related
items doing? How about focus group studies to discover if there is any interest
in the product? Another possibility is to utilize some form of experimentation.
Place the product in a limited number of stores and monitor sales, projecting
them for the total market.

VIDEO CASE 4-2 NANCY ROTH

SUBJECT MATTER: Marketing Research, Surveys, Contribution of Surveys/Research
to Consumers

Please see the Guide to Video Cases for video length and
other information.

AT-A-GLANCE OVERVIEW

Nancy Roth just finished her junior year at Coe College in Iowa. After taking
her first course in marketing, she knew a career in marketing research was going
to be her goal. Nancy was young, healthy, athletic, and outgoing. She thought
being an interviewer would be the ideal summer job. However, before applying for
a job with a Minneapolis marketing research company, she reviewed some materials
supplied by the Marketing Research Association, and she anticipated several
questions that might be asked during a job interview.

DISCUSSION QUESTIONS

1.   *If Nancy is asked "What benefits does marketing research provide to the
      consumer?" how should she respond?*

First, let us agree that the marketing research firm in question is a legitimate
one, not a front for some manner of sales scheme. Clearly, a shady operation's
managers would not want the marketing concept-based answer Nancy would give.

Nancy, as a marketing major, should be familiar with the marketing concept and its consumer-based philosophy. One approach would be to discuss briefly the importance of marketing itself in society, both in the for-profit and not-for-profit arenas. Having said that, she could mention that the marketing concept (or some variant of it) is the basic philosophy of a successful organization and that the concept tells managers to find out what the customer wants and give that "mix" to the customer if possible while still meeting organizational goals. Also, it tells the manager to view the product offered from the customer's perspective. Now, how can these things be done if the manager doesn't know what the customer wants or how the customer sees the product and the other elements of the marketing mix? Providing this sort of information is what marketing research is all about. In fact, it is not too much to say that marketing research (sophisticated or not-so-sophisticated) is a pillar of the marketing-era organization.

Ergo, marketing research serves the customer (almost) as much as it serves the marketing organization. The customer wants satisfying products (surrounded by a good marketing mix, whether or not he/she knows that) and "tells" organizations through several means -- a major one of which is marketing research -- what to produce, what the price should be, where it should be distributed, and how it should be promoted.

2.   *If Nancy is asked "Do you understand that there are different types of surveys and that the interviewing required for each of them may differ?" how should she respond?*

This question would give Nancy a chance to show off her knowledge about marketing research. Rather than mumbling something along the lines of "Yes, I do," she might do well to mention that she well realizes that the interviewing could vary depending on what kind of setting is involved and what sorts of information is being sought. There is, for example, quite a difference between a non-structured, focus group sort of setting and a mall-intercept study. Also, the information being sought is probably very different. The focus group setting seeks wideranging discussion that may reveal some "surprises," while the mall-intercept is almost certain to involve simple, yes/no or multiple-choice questions.

We might note that Nancy is walking something of a tightrope here. She should not recite a textbook or appear too much a know-it-all. This is a summer job, after all, and she is there to learn as well as to work. On the other hand, she should show a fair amount of knowledge. Some employers interpret a lack of knowledge as indicative of a lack of interest in the field being discussed, and that, in turn, to mean the applicant is just looking for "any old job."

3.   *What are the stages involved in conducting a survey? What does an interviewer contribute to accuracy in marketing research surveys?*

The survey is a part of the total marketing research project. Such project involve these general steps: define the problem, plan the research design, select the sample, collect data, analyze, draw conclusions and prepare the report, and follow up. Clearly all the steps are important and interrelated. Nancy's job as a data collector is key. Just as a salesperson in a store can mess up the entire plan of a great marketing company, so can a bad interviewer mess up a research study. Oftentimes interviewers must select the person to be interviewed (as in a mall study), approach the person, gain their cooperation, elicit truthful answers, keep the interview going if the subject seems impatient to quit, conduct the interviews in more or less the same way over time, try to keep personal feelings, including simple tiredness, out of the process, and record data accurately.

People who have served as interviewers may be in the class. If they are honest, they will admit that the temptation to avoid certain potential interviewees and concentrate on attractive young women/men is strong, as is the temptation to complete or even fill in a few surveys when things are going slowly. At the least, they will admit they did a better job at the start of a several-hour interview period than at the end.

If the interviewer falls prey to any of these difficulties, the effect of the interviewer on the accuracy of the findings is obviously great.   On the other hand, being a good (and careful) interviewer leads to good effects in the process.

5 CONSUMER BEHAVIOR: UNDERSTANDING DECISION MAKING PROCESSES

CHAPTER SCAN

This chapter describes the psychological and situational factors that influence consumer decision making, a five-stage process that includes problem recognition, search, evaluation, purchase decision, and postpurchase evaluation.

An understanding of the reaction of consumers to stimuli is fundamental to an understanding of the individual buyer and the consumer decision-making process. Motivations, cognition, learning, attitudes, personality, self-concept and their effects on decision making are discussed.

SUGGESTED BEHAVIORAL OBJECTIVES

The student who studies this chapter will become familiar with the psychological influences that affect consumer behavior and will be able to:

1. Understand the basic model of consumer behavior.

2. Describe the Consumer Information Processing (CIP) approach to the study of consumer behavior.

3. Analyze the consumer decision-making process and understand factors, such as consumer involvement, that influence it.

4. Appreciate the importance of perceived risk, choice criteria, purchase satisfaction, and cognitive dissonance.

5. Develop a comprehensive grasp of motivation theory.

6. Gain insight into such cognitive activities as perception, learning, and attitude change.

7. Recognize the influence of individual differences, such as personality, on consumer behavior.

CHAPTER OUTLINE

I.   INTRODUCTION

II.   WHAT IS CONSUMER BEHAVIOR?

III.   A SIMPLE START: SOME BEHAVIORAL FUNDAMENTALS

IV.   THE DECISION-MAKING PROCESS

        A.   Step 1: Problem Recognition
        B.   Step 2: Search for Alternative Solutions and Information

                1.   Internal Search
                2.   External Search

        C.   Step 3: Evaluation of Alternatives
        D.   Step 4: Choice: Purchase Decisions and the Act of Buying
        E.   Step 5: Postpurchase Consumption and Evaluation
        F.   Situational Influences on the Decision-Making Process

V.   INDIVIDUAL FACTORS SHAPE THE DECISION-MAKING PROCESS

        A.   Motivation and Needs Defined
        B.   Classifying Needs and Motives
        C.   Maslow's Hierarchy of Needs
        D.   Motivation and Emotion

VI.   COGNITIVE PROCESSES

        A.   Perception

                1.   Selective Perception?
                2.   The Screening Process
                3.   Perception and Brand Image Marketing
                4.   Subliminal Perception

        B.   Learning

                1.   How Learning Occurs
                2.   Learning Theories and Marketing

        C.   Attitudes

                1.   A Tripartite Theory of Attitudes
                2.   Modern Attitude Theory
                3.   How Attitudes Influence Buying Behavior

VII.   PERSONALITY AND SELF-CONCEPT

        A.   Personality Theories
        B.   Self-Concept: How We See Ourselves
        C.   Personality Theory Evaluated

VIII.   SUMMARY

IX.   KEY TERMS

X.   QUESTIONS FOR DISCUSSION (10)

XI.   ETHICS IN PRACTICE

XII.   CASE

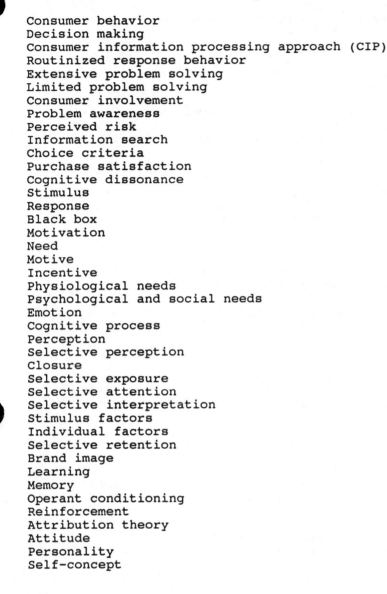

The following key terms are introduced and used in Chapter 5. They are
defined in the text's Glossary.

Consumer behavior
Decision making
Consumer information processing approach (CIP)
Routinized response behavior
Extensive problem solving
Limited problem solving
Consumer involvement
Problem awareness
Perceived risk
Information search
Choice criteria
Purchase satisfaction
Cognitive dissonance
Stimulus
Response
Black box
Motivation
Need
Motive
Incentive
Physiological needs
Psychological and social needs
Emotion
Cognitive process
Perception
Selective perception
Closure
Selective exposure
Selective attention
Selective interpretation
Stimulus factors
Individual factors
Selective retention
Brand image
Learning
Memory
Operant conditioning
Reinforcement
Attribution theory
Attitude
Personality
Self-concept

THE CHAPTER SUMMARIZED

I.   INTRODUCTION

      Mazda's popular Miata is designed to fit consumers' perceptions of what a
      sporty car should be, right down to the sound of the exhaust. A major
      catalog retailer discovered that the return rate for its boys' slacks was
      greater than for its other products. Mothers returning the slacks reported
      that they did not fit. The problem was not with the size-selection
      instructions in the catalogs. The slacks actually fit perfectly. The
      problem was that mothers ordered several pairs of slacks in the hope that
      their teenagers would find one pair they would be willing to wear. The
      rest were returned. The mothers were "uncomfortable" about this, but were
      reluctant to "confess" the real reason for making returns and gave "poor
      fit" as the cause. Consumer behavior is interesting, but can be baffling.

II. WHAT IS CONSUMER BEHAVIOR?

It is simply more productive to find out what customers want and offer it to them than to offer a product and hope to convince customers that they need it. This is the basic logic of the marketing concept.

The study of consumer behavior, also called buyer behavior, is an emerging science. It can give marketers a way to organize their thinking and a means to predict future behaviors.

Consumer behavior consists of the activities that people engage in when selecting, purchasing, and using products and services so as to satisfy needs and desires. Such activities involve mental and emotional processes in addition to physical actions.

III. A SIMPLE START: SOME BEHAVIORAL FUNDAMENTALS

Consumer behavior is a subset of human behavior. Behavior is a function of the interaction between the person and the environment.

> Stated as a formula: $B = f(P,E)$

Unfortunately, the forces that influence behavior are often difficult to observe and understand, and the behaviors themselves are complex.

The basic formula $B = f(P,E)$ is expanded in Exhibit 5-1, showing that many factors in the environment and in the individual affect the purchase decision.

IV. THE DECISION MAKING PROCESS

The **Consumer Information Processing (CIP)** approach to decision making portrays consumers as problem solvers weighing alternatives, seeking and processing information.

Decision making is a set of cognitive processes, such as memory, thinking, and information processing, aimed at the making of a valuative judgment.

Routinized response behavior is the least complex. **Extensive problem solving** may take months to complete. **Limited problem solving** is an intermediate level of decision making.

Both the "routine snap-judgment" and the extensive analysis involved in buying a house or computer are decision making. Both fit the simple model shown in Exhibit 5-2.

A. Step 1: Problem Recognition

Problem awareness is a result of stimuli: a flat tire, a friend's comment, noticing that the refrigerator is empty.

The problem may be so familiar that the decision maker moves quickly to action. If the problem is less familiar, he or she will "search."

B. Step 2: Search for Alternative Solutions and Information

Once a problem is recognized, the decision maker will search, long or briefly, for solutions. If **perceived risk** (of money, of social standing, etc.) is high, the **information search** will be longer and more detailed. For example, bringing spouse or friends when shopping for clothes is an attempt at risk reduction. Exhibit 5-3 identifies several types of risks.

The search gives marketers many opportunities, e.g., to supply information, to lower prices, to offer a guarantee. These steps assist in the search process and serve to reduce risks.

1. Internal Search

   Internal search is retrieval of information from memory. After problem recognition, the individual scans the memory to see if there is enough experience/information to know what to do. This internal search may or may not be enough to solve the problem.

2. External Search

   External search involves sources other than memory. It is most likely to occur in high-involvement situations and to be limited in low-involvement situations. (Factors likely to influence external search are shown in Exhibit 5-4.) In such instances consumers are willing to consider more complex promotional messages, information, and discussions of product features.

C. Step 3: Evaluation of Alternatives

   Alternatives, once identified, must be evaluated. Often this too is with an eye toward reducing risks. Evaluations rely on **choice criteria**, the critical attributes used to evaluate a product or brand, e.g., safety, price, social acceptability, convenience. For consumers, these criteria are less likely to be the "rational" ones used by organizational buyers.

   Situational factors may affect choices made. If the car is running very low on gas, the importance of convenience of location is more important than if the tank is half full.

   There is evidence that most consumers do not want detailed information, but desire to simplify complex decisions. Honda's slogan "We make it simple" reflects this.

D. Step 4: Choice: Purchase Decisions and the Act of Buying

   Eventually, the decision maker/purchaser must make a decision. It may be not to buy, but unless the problem that began the process has disappeared, the process is likely to begin again.

   If a "buy" choice is made, some purchase-related decisions must be made, e.g., cash or credit?

E. Step 5: Postpurchase Consumption and Evaluation

   If the decision was made to buy, the decision maker must decide whether or not satisfaction has been achieved. The approval of self and friends plays a big part in this.

   Dissatisfaction could occur. The theory of cognitive dissonance, which says that people do not like to hold conflicting ideas or beliefs at one time, tells us that buyers seek information to support the thought that the right decision was made.

   Example: people who just bought a Ford do not want information telling them they've made a mistake; they want to hear how good Fords are. They want to avoid psychic tension or postpurchase dissonance.

   Cognitive dissonance is a psychologically uncomfortable postpurchase feeling. It refers to the negative feelings that can occur after a commitment to purchase has been made.

   Some marketers capitalize on this. Real estate agents may contact buyers after a purchase to congratulate them on making a great buy.

F. Situational Influences on the Decision-Making Process

As situations change, so will behavior, no matter how well we think we understand behavior. Financial problems, time constraints, and many other factors could be considered by marketers and addressed by their marketing strategies.

V. INDIVIDUAL FACTORS SHAPE THE DECISION-MAKING PROCESS

Here we explore some of the psychological variables that affect the decision-making process.

A. Motivation and Needs Defined

The term **motivation** refers to a state which causes consumers to initiate behavior. Humans have needs (a **need** is an innate desire basic to humans, like the need to eat), but the needs are not always activated. A feeling of hunger "activates" the need to eat. Such stimulated needs are **motives**. The food or other object that the individual believes will satisfy the motive is termed an **incentive**.

An unfilled motive serves as an internal stimulus or **drive**. It energizes behavior.

An external stimulus, like an advertisement, may also arouse motives to be acted on. Some psychologists describe the motive as creating a "tension" that the person acts to relieve, e.g., hunger leads to steps to alleviate that hunger.

Exhibit 5-6 illustrates the pattern: (1) **stimulus** acts upon need creating motive, (2) motive causes search for satisfaction resulting in response behavior, (3) response behavior yields satisfaction (stop) or dissatisfaction (continue search for satisfaction).

B. Classifying Needs and Motives

Needs and motives have been classified in many ways, but in general, two basic groups are discussed.

. **Physiological needs** stemming from our natural biological mechanisms.

. **Psychological** or **social** needs resulting from our interaction with the social environment.

C. Maslow's Hierarchy of Needs

Abraham Maslow's scheme of human needs, ranging from the "lowest" to the "highest," is shown in Exhibit 5-7. From lowest to highest, they are:

. Physiological needs (food, water, air, sex, control of body temperature - also called "visceral needs")

. Safety needs (protection, security from threats)

. Love and social needs (affection and feelings of belonging)

. Self-esteem needs (feelings of self-worth, achievement, prestige, respect)

. Self-actualization needs (self-fulfillment, becoming what one is capable of becoming)

The theory also states that:

. Individuals try to fill the most basic needs first, moving on to the others.

. A well-satisfied need is no longer a motivator.

It has been noted that:

. A "low" need can motivate behavior even though normally satisfied, e.g., hot day at the beach drives thirsty bathers to buy virtually any drink.

. Importance of needs can vary, e.g., heightened concern with crime leads to buying guns, alarms, etc. This reflects the safety need, a "lower need" suddenly has increased importance.

D.   Motivation and Emotion

Emotion plays a complex role in motivation, a role that is hard to measure. People may go shopping simply because they are bored. The experiential perspective on consumer behavior suggests that consumers buy certain products just to have "fun."

Distinctions are difficult to draw, but motives have been divided into two groups:

. Rational
. Emotional (The terms "irrational" and "psychological" are also used.)

Though this view is incorrect, the dichotomy serves to remind marketers that consumers are not strictly "rational." They want a car that "looks good" as well as one that is mechanically sound, properly constructed, etc.

Industrial buyers usually analyze the purchase carefully; consumers go by appearance, friends' opinions, etc. There are many exceptions, however, even in the case of organizational buyers.

VI.   COGNITIVE PROCESSES

Arousal of a motive sets off a broad range of mental activities so that the state of "tension" may be reduced. This **cognitive process** (interpreting stimuli and organizing thoughts and ideas) is often so rapid that we are unaware of it. We can sometimes note the process "in action," however. The decision of what to order at a hot dog stand is made quickly, but that decision at an unfamiliar restaurant with a wide array of choices lets us better see the "steps" involved in making a choice.

Three major aspects of the cognitive process are:

. Perception
. Learning
. Attitudes

A.   Perception

There is, in fact, no one "reality" in the sense that we all see things differently.

A used car is different things to the dealer, the teenager who wants it, the parents involved, and the teenager's little brother.

Perception is the process of interpreting sensations and giving meaning to stimuli.

Perception is an ongoing process that occurs because people constantly try to "make sense" of their world and to relate new bits of information to others.

1.   Selective Perception

The ability to experience a stimulus, the individual's
personality, the context in which the stimulus was encountered,
the person's intelligence, thought processes, and moods combine
to create the mental phenomenon of selective perception.

Selective perception is the individual tendency to screen out
certain stimuli and to color or interpret other stimuli with
meanings drawn from personal backgrounds.

This phenomenon is easily observed. Two people at the same
political speech may have totally different interpretations.

Everything is influenced by selective perception. We can't
escape past experiences, prejudices or other limitations. In
marketing, the phenomenon is significant.

One interesting perception-related matter is **closure**, our
tendency to "finish things off." (Example in Exhibit 5-8.)
Some ads do not show a product, or show only its shadow, yet we
"see" the product. Some say this involvement makes the ad more
effective. A risk, though, is that a viewer may not be able to
complete the picture and become frustrated and annoyed.

2.   The Screening Process

Perception is affected by what has been described as a series
of screens or sieves.

.   **Selective exposure:** the person did not see the
     advertisement on T.V.

Information that gets past selective exposure is subject to:

.   **Selective attention:** the person may or may not have paid
     attention to the ad.

Information that gets past selective attention is subject to:

.   **Selective interpretation:** the person interprets the
     information in light of experience, current situation,
     etc.

Information, now quite well "processed," goes into the "bank"
of:

.   Retained internalized stimuli.

As Exhibit 5-9 shows, stimuli can be "discarded" at each of
these stages. Some **stimulus factors** are believed to increase
the chances of successful passage through the screening
process, e.g., use of color in ads. However, **individual
factors** must also be considered, e.g., a small, unattractive ad
promising "quick weight loss" may get a great deal of attention
from its target audience.

3.   Perception and Brand Image Marketing

The "perception of quality" is more important to the individual
than "true reality" (if that is definable at all).

The consumer's perception of the product offered for sale is
more important to the consumer than is the "real" product.

This fact is the basis of **brand image** (a complex of symbols and
meanings associated with a brand) and the basis of the success
of products like Pepsi and Coors even though tests show that

consumers cannot tell the difference between brands of products once labels are removed.

4.   Subliminal Perception

Since the 1950s, there has been some debate over the existence of "perception without awareness." Exhibit 5-10 illustrates a supposedly "subliminal" message. Current belief is that messages are not perceived at an unconscious level. That is, if one sees the "message" it is not "subliminal."

B.   Learning

Name a brand of light bulb. G.E.? You and 86 percent of Americans have learned to be loyal to G.E. light bulbs.

1.   How Learning Occurs

Learning is any change in behavior or cognitions, such as attitudes, as a result of experience.

As a child learns through experience, so does a consumer. Satisfactory results from a product "teach" the consumer that the product is acceptable.

Bases of learning theories are identified:

- Learning can come from observation of the learning episodes of others. Buyers often purchase products recommended by others who have used those products. This is **social learning**.

- Exhibit 5-11 illustrates **operant conditioning**. A new product (stimulus) results in a purchase (response). If the product is satisfactory, the buyer gets a "payoff" (**reinforcement**). Learning takes place as this process is completed over and over.

  The reward may be functional (truly clean clothes) or symbolic (sense of pride in using the "best" detergent).

- The **attribution theory** of learning stresses that the reward obtained must be attributed by the learner to the action taken. A clean wash attributed to a new washing machine or water softener and not to Tide does not lead to learning that Tide cleans clothes well.

2.   Learning Theories and Marketing

Most learning theories are compatible with marketing activities and the marketing concept. They stress rewards that lead to repeated behaviors.

C.   Attitudes

Attitudes are seldom, if ever, 100% positive or negative. Most likely a person has both sorts of attitudes about another person or a product, with positive or negative attitudes happening to be dominant.

An **attitude** is a learned predisposition to respond in a consistently favorable or unfavorable way with respect to a given object.

Note these aspects of the definition:

- Attitudes are learned. (It may be possible to change them via good marketing.)

.   Attitudes are generally enduring. In this, for good or bad, they help people to organize mental processes. (They contribute to development of a "core" market.)

.   Attitudes are directed toward some object. For marketers, this object is a product, service, person, or idea. (Altering the object might alter the attitude.)

1.   A Tripartite Theory of Attitudes

Attitudes are thought to have these parts.

.   Affective - The emotional component, reflecting feelings. Is the brand good or bad?

.   Cognitive - The beliefs, knowledge and thoughts about the object. Is the product durable? Is it suitable?

.   Behavioral - The actual behavior to want the object. The predisposition to act (to buy).

Examples in the text illustrate these factors, noting that their relative "weights" vary from situation to situation.

2.   Modern Attitude Theory

Attitude is now thought of as based on cognitive beliefs. Exhibit 5-12 illustrates this view. Beliefs and attitude shape the individual's predisposition towards purchase.

3.   How Attitudes Influence Buying Behavior

Attitudes are not the only influences but do affect answers to such uncertainties as:

.   Which brands to consider
.   Which brand to choose

Note that favorable attitudes, e.g. toward Rolls Royce, do not mean purchase will occur. But attitudes are important if the other purchase variables, such as money, are in place.

Negative attitudes can account for nonpurchase.

VII.   PERSONALITY AND SELF-CONCEPT

Many individual differences in human behavior are related to personality.

A.   Personality Theories

Personality is the fundamental dispositions of individuals, and the distinctive patterns of thought, emotion, and behavior, that characterize each individual's response to the situations of his or her life.

Exhibit 5-13 identifies five personality traits common to most theories. These are found repeatedly in studies around the globe.

B.   Self-Concept: How We See Ourselves

The term **self-concept** refers to the individual's perception and appraisal of himself or herself. It is the person's "picture" of who he or she is, and who the person is in the process of becoming.

There are two basic elements:

.   The internal or private "picture" -- how we see ourselves.

. The external "picture" -- what others think.

The two don't always match up, e.g., the fellow who dresses in an "individualistic" way (to him) may be seen by others as a slob.

Self-concept is important to most purchase decisions:

- Buy a "polo player shirt" to appear "preppy" to others (or to yourself).

- Buy a cheap economy car, even though you are well off, to show others that you don't care about material things.

C.   Personality Theory Evaluated

Experience indicates that marketers can make scant use of personality in predicting specific consumer behavior. More appropriate is a consideration of demographics and other factors, not personality studied apart from these factors.

In short, personality theory focuses on the person as a person; consumer behavior theory focuses on the person as a consumer.

XI.   SUMMARY

Understanding consumer behavior helps the effective marketer bring about satisfying exchanges in the marketplace.

Learning Objective 1: Understand the basic model of consumer behavior.

Consumer behavior results from the interaction of person and environment. Consumer behavior theorists have expanded and explained this basic model with many theories.

Learning Objective 2: Describe the Consumer Information Processing (CIP) approach to the study of consumer behavior.

The CIP approach treats consumers as problem solvers, making choices among various alternatives, and actively acquiring the knowledge they need to make optimal choices. It expects problem-solving behavior to vary depending on how routine the consumer perceives the situation to be.

Learning Objective 3: Analyze the consumer decision-making process and understand factors, such as consumer involvement, that influence it.

In multistep consumer decision-making, consumers (1) recognize the problem, (2) search for alternative solutions, (3) evaluate those alternatives, (4) decide whether to buy, and (5) if a purchase is made, evaluate the product purchased. Many internal and environmental factors affect this process, including consumer involvement and situational influences such as physical settings, social circumstances, and economic conditions.

Learning Objective 4: Appreciate the importance of such concepts as perceived risk, choice criteria, purchase satisfaction, and cognitive dissonance.

Perceived risk is the consumer's uncertainty about whether a product will do what it is intended to do. Choice criteria are those critical attributes the customer uses to evaluate a product alternative. Cognitive dissonance is the sense of tension the consumer might feel after deciding to make a purchase. Marketers must address all these issues if satisfactory exchanges are to take place.

Learning Objective 5: Develop a comprehensive grasp of motivation theory.

Motivation theory attempts to explain the causes of goal-directed behavior in terms of needs, motives, incentives, and drives. Needs can be classified in many ways. Maslow's needs hierarchy ranks human needs from the most basic (physiological) to the highest (self-actualization.) The theory suggests that as the lower needs are satisfied, the higher needs become more important to the individual.

Learning Objective 6: **Gain insight into such cognitive activities as perception, learning, and attitude change.**

Cognitive activities include a broad range of mental activities. People organize sensations according to their backgrounds, moods, knowledge, personality, and other attributes. Each person's perceptions differ at least slightly from everyone else's. Selective perception is the process of screening out or interpreting stimuli.

Learning theory is important to marketing because consumers learn to favor certain products and brands and to find others less satisfying.

Modern theory stresses the affective nature of attitudes. However, attitudes are formed on the basis of cognitive beliefs.

Learning Objective 7: **Recognize the influence of individual differences, such as personality, on consumer behavior.**

Personality reflects the individual's consistent ways of responding to his or her environment. It is generally agreed that the influence of personality on consumer behavior should be studied along with other factors, such as attitudes and demographic characteristics, to predict specific behaviors.

IX.   KEY TERMS

X.   QUESTIONS FOR DISCUSSION (10)

XI.   ETHICS IN PRACTICE

XII.   CASE

ANSWER GUIDELINES FOR CHAPTER 5 QUESTIONS FOR DISCUSSION

1.   *Use the consumer behavior model shown in Exhibit 5-2 to explain how an individual might arrive at a decision to: a. Buy a package of Doublemint chewing gum, b. Not buy an Alfa-Romeo sports car, c. Buy a new house, d. Not take a group of three children to the Ice Capades.*

ANSWER:

Exhibit 5-2 shows that a purchase decision is reached (or a decision not to buy is reached) after a series of steps has been completed. Among these are (working backwards from the decision): evaluation of alternatives, information search, and problem recognition. After the purchase, postpurchase evaluation occurs.

The process is influenced by social and environmental factors (culture, class, etc.), individual factors (attitudes, personality, information processing, etc.), situational factors surrounding the decision-making process, and the marketing activities themselves.

(a)   Buy a package of Doublemint chewing gum

For the habitual, hard-core gum-chewer, the recognition that one wants a piece of gum but has none is more jarring than for the occasional users. Nonetheless, each will recognize a problem (wanting gum but not having any). This sets off an information search. (Where to buy gum? Which gums are available?) An evaluation of alternatives follows. (Which store to buy from? Which brand to choose?) Then, the purchase decision to buy.

In the case of a product like gum, the stages are passed through so quickly as to appear not to have been encountered at all. Yet, even though the purchase is virtually habitual and automatic, the consumer did (however fleetingly) consider the various sources of gum. (Where is the nearest store or vending machine?) Then the consumer glanced at the array of brands available. The point may be made that the process is more easily noted in unfamiliar situations (as when we carefully consider the menu at a new restaurant), but the steps are the same.

"Behind" this process of buying gum are such things as personal preferences (mint rather than fruit flavor), experience (the buyer likes Doublemint), or learning, and other factors, as well as situational and marketing factors. For example, this could have been the customer's first purchase of Doublemint, brought about by an ad for the product that inspired the buyer to give it a try.

Old buyer or new, a favorable postpurchase evaluation will encourage a re-buy, a negative one will inhibit further purchases.

(b)   Not buy an Alfa-Romeo sports car

The buying process often is the "not buying" process. For a purchase such as this, social/environmental factors can have strong influence. A given social class may never consider an Alfa and be only vaguely aware of what it is. Family influences ("Don't throw that much money away on a car!"), group influences ("Are you trying to show off?"), and so on, have obvious effects.

Individual factors may have led to the consideration of buying an Alfa. The individual has learned that Alfas are driven by major figures in the sports car world and by important movie stars and billionaires. The individual thinks he or she has what it takes to be equal to those hot shots. The person is motivated to show the world what a "cool" person he or she is.

Information search, evaluation of alternatives ... and then the decision NOT to buy. What happened? Perhaps the individual discovered he or she could not afford the car, or couldn't qualify for a loan on such an expensive car, or could pay for the car but not the insurance, or decided that the worry about somebody stealing it or crashing into it was too much to bear.

(c)   Buy a new house

The decision to buy a new house is likely to be triggered by such "problems" as arrival of a new baby, the last child leaving home, a feeling that friends have nicer homes than "we" do, a mother-in-law moving in, or some other situation requiring a solution.

Recognition of the problem leads to a search for information: looking through the newspaper, driving around looking at neighborhoods, talking to friends and co-workers, calling a few realtors. Examining houses, rejecting some, liking others "except for the living room," then finally making the decision to purchase, all follow along.

Satisfaction may result ("I just LOVE my new house.") or some form of dissatisfaction ("That guy should have told me I'd need a new $2,000 air conditioner.").

The process was influenced by various motives (to better ourselves, get the kids in a better school system, move to a house with air conditioning), and obvious social forces (to impress in-laws and friends, fulfill the American dream of a big house and a two-car garage). Situational factors played a part (raise in pay, big bonus this year, barking dogs next door to the old house), and marketing activity (realtor pointed out all the neat features of the place and found a buyer for the old one).

(d)   Not take a group of three children to the Ice Capades

The problem was recognized: need to take the kids somewhere on a rainy day or to let them experience entertainment they would enjoy. Information search (the newspaper or radio ads) yielded information on various entertainments currently in the area. Evaluation of alternatives led to discovering that the Ice Capades are cheaper than some of the other alternatives and is indoors so there will be little discomfort. Yet the decision was made not to go. Why?

Situational factors might include parental fatigue, car troubles, snow covered roads, and "one of the kids is coming down with something."

Marketing activity might have included a newspaper coupon for "family rates" at a theater just down the street that is playing *Bambi*.

Individual factors (Dad imagines most male ice skaters are "strange") and social factors (Dad's friends all think male ice skaters are "strange") are easy to link to the decision not to go to the Ice Capades.

2.   *One way to study consumer behavior is to use the consumer information processing (CIP) approach. Explain, in your own words, what CIP entails.*

ANSWER:

Consumer information processing (CIP) is a popular explanation of the way consumers respond to stimuli such as advertisements, friends' comments, and other stimuli. These stimuli are "processed" by the consumer. CIP takes the point of view that buyers are problem solvers and see their consumption problems as choosing among various alternatives. Buyers are further viewed as actively involved in acquiring and processing information and other inputs to help them make the proper choice from among the alternatives they face.

Information processing can also be termed thinking, reasoning, problem solving, or decision making. But, regardless of what it is called, it ends up with an output that is readily observable. A choice (or decision not to choose) is made.

Recognition of consumers as information processors is an acknowledgement that many things affect behavior: memory, thinking, judging, and so on. It also recognizes that consumers will vary in how they process information and that this process will vary situationally. Consumers vary, too, in intelligence, backgrounds, and experiences.

Acknowledging this complexity is a step forward in the study of consumer behavior. Earlier efforts focused on the "eventual" development of a "model" or formulation that would "explain" and even "predict" consumer behavior. CIP may appear to the student to be a disappointment in that it seems to say that "everything" is important and varies greatly from case to case. In fact, it is more accurately reflective of reality than are proposals purporting to "predict" buyer behavior.

3.   *Using examples from your own experience, explain how the following have affected your purchasing behavior. a. Extensive problem solving, b. Perceived risk, c. Choice criteria, d. Cognitive dissonance.*

ANSWER:

Answers will vary, but this question serves the purpose of showing that the "theoretical stuff" in the book actually has application in the real world.

(a)   Extensive problem solving

Extensive problem solving is most commonly found in the purchasing of a major item like a house or a car. In the case of a house purchase, the family is likely to put some effort into deciding how many bedrooms are necessary, how much "play space," what kind of yard, what neighborhood, and what price range will be considered. The family may spend days, weeks, or months touring houses, making banking arrangements, and so on. Purchasing a car can involve a similar process. So can selecting a college, university, or graduate school.

It should be noted that extensive problem solving can be found in the purchase of other, less grand products, too. We all know a man or woman who spends great amounts of time "looking good." These people expend great effort in deciding if they need a new suit, what color looks best, where to buy suits, etc.

(b)   Perceived risk

The goal is to insure that students consider all five types of risk as they analyze their perceptions of a purchase situation. Since many students delay consideration of starting career positions, one stimulus for discussion could be risks associated with the purchase of a suit for interviews (or risks associated with selecting companies as target firms for employment). In relation to business suits, performance risk may relate to uncertainty over appropriate materials or colors and if it will resist wrinkles or wear well over time. Financial risk is seen in the cost of such purchases and the uncertainty over finding similar products at a lower price. Social risk relates to the reactions of others as well as the interviewer's perception, and time-loss risk may be seen in alteration requirements as well as time to find the best fit. While physical risk may not be a factor, students may consider the health implications of various materials or chemicals on the cloth.

(c)   Choice criteria

Choice criteria are those critical attributes used to evaluate a brand or product. Which criteria are used depends on the individual and the situation in which the individual is operating. They may be "rational" or "emotional/irrational."

Among the products commonly purchased where the influence of choice criteria is clear are automobiles. Almost anyone can come up with a few brand names when asked the question, "What car would you buy if you were buying a car today?" The next question, in class or in real life, is "Why?" The answer suggests the choice criteria important to that person. They may include "looks good," "cheap," "trouble-free operation," and "I need a van to carry my drum set."

As in the previous portion of this question, choice criteria may be discussed in terms of selecting a college or graduate school. "What company (or kind of company) would you want to work for?" also engenders a discussion of choice criteria.

(d)   Cognitive dissonance

Cognitive dissonance theory "cuts two ways." It suggests that we: (1) seek to avoid the state of "psychic tension," but also (2) that once in such a state, we will seek to escape it.

How might this affect our purchasing behavior? We might really want to have a Jaguar automobile and actually have the money to afford it, BUT we have heard that Jags have a terrible record for mechanical troubles ("They look great in your driveway but they don't run"). So, even though we love the way the Jaguar looks and would love to have it, we know that we will hate it. We don't buy the car; we avoid psychic tension.

In many cases, cognitive dissonance follows a purchase, often when the product doesn't live up to expectations. It doesn't work well, doesn't do what we hoped it would, or for some other reason, causes psychic tension. A student who wanted to have her ears pierced, gets her ears pierced, and then wonders if this was such a good idea, provides us with an example.

Cognitive dissonance theory suggests that once in a state of psychic tension the individual will take steps to get out of it. The person who enthusiastically buys a Volvo and finds out it's a lemon takes the relatively "easy" step of trying to get the dealer to fix it. If the dealer cannot, the buyer gets rid of it and takes something of a financial bath. The consumer may even go so far as to further relieve the psychic tension by telling everyone how bad the Volvo and the Volvo dealer really are.

4.   *Tell how the last purchase you made can be linked to perceived risk and information search behavior.*

ANSWER:

The key element in this answer is linkage of the extent of information search behavior with the perception of risk involved in the purchase.

Some examples:

.   I needed a nice leather notebook for business interviews or meetings. While the financial risk was relatively small for a product under $20, the social risk prompted me to compare products at several stores.

.   Bungee jumping is a relatively new "sport." It commands a high dollar price for each jump as well as extensive physical risk. However, the social risk of not jumping in front of friends prompted one individual to complete the task rather than risk disapproval. In this case, information search consisted of reports from friends.

.   I was required to bring potato chips to the company picnic. I searched memory for a chip which tasted good and performed well with dips and selected a remembered brand.

.   My feet hurt because my sneakers were all ripped up on the inside. I was getting blisters. Since my internal knowledge of current athletic shoe brands was limited, I visited several stores and talked with sales representatives about the attributes of various brands. I also watched others engaging in sports to assess preferred brands. The risk of a wrong decision included performance, financial, physical harm, social and time-loss, thus I spent time considering the alternatives before purchasing a new pair.

5.   *Name the five levels in Maslow's need hierarchy. Which group of needs is the most powerful?*

ANSWER:

The five classes of needs, according to Maslow, are:

    a.   Physiological (food, water, air, sex, control of body temperature)

    b.   Safety (protection, security from threats)

    c.   Love and social (affection, feeling of belonging)

    d.   Self-esteem (self-worth, achievement, respect, prestige)

    e.   Self-actualization (self-fulfillment, becoming what one is capable of being)

The question of which is the most powerful of these needs must be answered by first asking in what context the question is posed. It is arguable that the most powerful needs are physiological in that we need food and air every day.

Within our society, for most people, these lower needs are satisfied regularly and cease, as Maslow noted, to be major concerns. Food, for most of us, is not constantly on our minds as it is for many in Ethiopia and other troubled lands. The second need, safety, is also a less powerful influence on most Americans than it is for Amazon Indians surrounded by wild animals and enemy tribes. Yet when we drive, we wear seat belts (or at least think we should), and news stories about rapists inspire us to buy home security systems. Thus we see that the lower levels of needs become important in certain circumstances. In these circumstances, they are the "most powerful."

For a person heavily involved in exercise programs or marathon running, self-esteem and self-actualization may come into play as "most important." The person might begin running to lose weight and build-up some muscles, that is, to get

into shape and look good again. This is a matter of self-esteem. After some
effort, the person begins to find that he or she is a good runner, enters local
races, then regional marathons, then the Boston and New York marathons. This is
self-actualization -- being all you can be -- coming to the fore.

Thus, the "most powerful" needs level is the one that is most powerful in a
particular context. Like much in marketing, the strength of the need is
situational.

6.   *What is selective perception? How does it influence behavior?*

ANSWER:

Selective perception is the name given to the phenomenon of "screening out"
certain kinds of stimuli and interpreting other stimuli in light of past
experiences or current beliefs.

Some examples:

.   A voter might "screen out" messages from Bill Clinton because he doesn't
     like him. Even Clinton's good ideas will be ignored by this voter.

.   A person who has just bought a Chevy pickup is not likely to visit Dodge or
     Ford showrooms or to read literature which would "go against" his choice.

Since the connection is not made specifically in the text, it might be
interesting to ask students to link the concept of selective perception to that
of cognitive dissonance, i.e., selective perception is a means to avoid cognitive
dissonance by "keeping blinders on."

7.   *Use learning theory to explain why products are repurchased.*

ANSWER:

Most modern learning theories are variations on stimulus-response models. In
this they depend ultimately on reinforcement. There are other theories. One is
that children learn because their minds are comparatively "blank." Thus, says
the theory, virtually all that they encounter "registers."

Reinforcement is the basis of operant conditioning, as it is of the attribution
theory of learning. Both stress that reward is necessary to learning, though
this is cloaked a bit in attribution theory by the emphasis on the learner's need
to know to what to attribute the reward received. (Was it the new washing
machine or the new detergent that made the clothes whiter?)

Of the theories mentioned in the text, only the theory focusing on repetition
alone is not enough to encourage meaningful learning. Most of us can remember
telephone numbers from radio or T.V. ads, especially jingles, but this of itself
does not sell products. In a 1984-like totalitarian setting, a victim can
"learn" through repetition of some doctrine or slogan, but even then some reward,
such as being permitted to leave, can be identified.

Addressing the question directly, we may state that each trial of a product is a
learning experience. Faced with a question like what to do about scuffed shoes,
we try various solutions: using crayons, shoe polish (paste, liquid), having the
shoemaker polish them, going to a shoe shine stand, etc. If we find that one of
those product-solutions works, we have attained a reward and have learned to
re-buy that good or service. Then, each time we buy the product, we in effect
re-test the product, learning that it still works or that we should try something
else.

Experiencing a reward is the key to repurchase behavior as it is to other forms
of learning. The marketing concept, with its stress on long-term satisfaction of
customer wants, acknowledges the learning process.

It should be recalled that the "rewards" involved could be:

- Functional: car really runs better.
- Symbolic: pride in owning a well-cared-for car.
- Both (some combination of the "real" and the symbolic).

8.   *Do unfavorable attitudes lead to behaviors that are undesirable?*

ANSWER:

Unfavorable attitudes occur when the negative beliefs about an object or person outweigh the positive ones. Unfavorable attitudes can certainly lead to undesirable behaviors. We observe this frequently in the world at large, e.g., the problem of race relations. Other examples include:

- People in any city develop attitudes towards that city's newspapers, radio stations, and TV evening news teams. They may perceive the newspaper as a no-class "rag," think the "elevator music" on many stations is for "old folks," and think the anchor man on Channel 2 is a "jerk." Effective marketing managers must be aware of these attitudes and, if appropriate, take steps to correct the situation.

- Newcomers to a town may be debating what church to join. If their attitude towards one denomination is that only "stuffed shirts" are members, or that another denomination is too liberal or too conservative, their choice of a church will be very strongly affected. Effective marketing can be and in some cases is, used by churches to project an attractive image or to offer services which appeal to a broad range of "customers."

In the purchasing context, the same phenomena is easy to observe. In fact, negative attitudes might be so strong as to totally eliminate a product or supplier from a potential buyer's consideration.

Purchasers of Firestone 500 tires (during the 1970s) found that the tires almost always failed in use, often with dangerous consequences. Consumer attitudes obviously were affected. Some were willing to buy other Firestone models but some refused to buy any Firestone tires. The company countered these negative attitudes with a recall program, repayment to some customers, and ads for other tire models featuring actor Jimmy Stewart, a down-to-earth, honest spokesperson. Negative attitudes have also been addressed in commercials by Lee Iacocca (arguing that Chrysler quality is as good as the Japanese car's), by the president of Sears (defending Sears' auto repair services and apologizing for any aberrations in Sears' totally honest efforts to serve drivers), and by any number of politicians (Dan Quayle defending himself against media stories that he is a bumbler).

Students can certainly mention nonproduct-related instances. A negative attitude toward an unfriendly salesperson can prejudice buyer feelings against the products offered and/or the place of sale. All of us have thought, from time to time, "I'll never shop there again."

This question can be "reversed" to discuss how unfavorable attitudes might lead to undesirable behavior on the parts of sellers. Industrial salespeople, after failing to make a sale for a time, may become distressed enough that their negative attitudes towards "all" customers ruin future prospects. A retail salesperson may let his or her racial or ethnic prejudices affect interactions with customers.

9.   *What purchases might be particularly influenced by the buyer's personality and self-image? Name some products and explain your choices.*

ANSWER:

Personality is defined in the text as:

> The fundamental disposition of individuals and the distinctive patterns of thought, emotion, and behavior that characterize each individual's response to situations in his or her life.

A listing of "personality types" appears in the text. While an individual's "personality" is so all-encompassing as to influence virtually every action, it is possible to identify some particular influences on buyer behavior. This discussion can be related to various personality types. Some examples:

.   The reserved personality might be less inclined to purchase "in" or popular items than would the outgoing personality. Such an individual may feel like "doing my own thing," or expressing independence by not following the crowd. The outgoing person, seeking friends and other personal contacts, may attempt to keep up-to-date, be one of the crowd, be popular.

.   The trusting personality may be easily influenced by salespeople, magazine articles, advertisements, etc. Purchases may be made on the recommendation of friends. The suspicious personality, on the other hand, might need "hands on" experience with a product, demand close inspection of the item, require assurances that there is a money-back guarantee, etc.

While all of these connections between personality type and purchasing behaviors would appear to be meaningful and "obvious," the text notes that one should not rely on personality as a predictor of behavior. Like other influences, it must be viewed within a context that encompasses many other factors. These other factors include demographics, finances, the purchase situation, and so on.

The notion of self-concept, the appraisal of the individual by him or herself, is also an influencer of buyer behavior, but one that must be considered in a context of many other factors. A portion of the total self-concept is how others see us and/or how we think others see us.

Self-concept and personality would seem to be considerably influential in the purchase of such products as:

.   Beer: drinking beer is "manly," makes you "one of the guys," and the brand chosen provides some indicator of how the beer drinker sees himself and would have others see him.

.   Cigarettes: the advertising for Marlboro, Salem, Newport, and most other brands suggest these are for macho men, or for people seeking "refreshment," etc. The link between personality/self-concept is made clear by the line, "Are you man enough to smoke a Virginia Slim?"

.   Automobiles: also reflect personality/self-concept. Buying a Mercedes or BMW or Rolls Royce has got more to do with image than with money.

.   Houses: also reflect personality/self-concept. For example, the executive who has made it to vice-president may buy a bigger house because his or her self-concept, or concern for how others see him or her, helps make the decision to move.

Again, no single factor can, in virtually any case, be portrayed as the sole influencer of purchase behavior. However, it is not difficult to link personality and self-concept to certain purchases of products and brands of products. Notice that when we do so we are assuming all the other necessary influences as well: money, availability of product, credit worthiness, and so on.

10.   *What might a marketer do to reduce cognitive dissonance in the following situations?* a. A consumer purchases an automobile, b. A wholesaler agrees to carry an industrial product line, c. A parent purchases an expensive video game for her children, d. A man purchases a magazine subscription on a "to be billed later" basis.

ANSWER:

Cognitive dissonance can be associated with any purchase, but the magnitude of certain purchases (car or house) or the perceived risk involved (car - money risk, new jacket - social risk) can heighten the importance of dissonance to both buyer and seller. It is in the interest of the seller to reduce this dissonance risk in an effort to increase customer satisfaction.

(a)   A consumer purchases an automobile

Sellers can head off some dissonance "in advance" by making it clear that good
service will be provided by the best mechanics, or by offering something that is
sure to be collected after the purchase. Two hundred and fifty gallons of free
gas would be a possibility. Some car dealers offer trips to a resort.

Guarantees suggest a quality product and repair if needed, also heading off
dissonance. Some other tools that have been used include:

.   Phone call or letter to buyer congratulating him or her on a good purchase.

.   Guarantee to make up the price difference if a better buy is found in six
     weeks time.

.   Pick up car for the first "free" checkup.

.   Special effort to involve spouse in decision to buy in an attempt to
     eliminate complaints from that source.

(b)   A wholesaler taking on an industrial product line

The organizational buyer is more "rational" than the consumer. Attempts to
reduce dissonance here must be more nuts-and-bolts or bottom-line oriented. Some
commonly used tools:

.   Consignment selling is not usually attractive to sellers but does nearly
     eliminate risk to buyers.

.   Literature showing that product is "sweeping the country," a fast riser,
     etc.

.   "Hot line" or other means to order and/or get product information.

.   "Factory training," not only improves wholesaler's ability to sell the
     product but also makes him or her feel like "part of the family."

.   Computerized or other assistance in keeping inventory stocked at adequate
     but not too high levels to control wholesaler's size of investment.

.   Sales support, e.g., pamphlets, displays, sales instruction and help.

.   Sales promotions, e.g., advertising assistance, prizes for high sales,
     trips to Las Vegas for the dealer's convention.

(c)   Purchase of an expensive video game

The store and/or manufacturer might try to reduce dissonance by:

.   Guarantees of product.

.   Offering inexpensive repair contract.

.   Sending out "newsletters" detailing new games, popularity of this game
     system over others, or quality advantages.

.   Offering "bargain rates" on games or new components to those who own the
     basic game.

.   Atari did this: advertise on T.V. after the big Christmas sale period to
     thank and congratulate all those people who bought or got an Atari for
     Christmas.

(d)   Magazine subscription, subscriber to be billed

The situation here is that the subscriber has mailed in a card, called a
toll-free number, or been solicited on the phone or by an in-person canvasser.

- See that the person gets the magazine. (Frequently they do not. Ever.)

- Get the magazine to them quickly or send a pamphlet describing the "Adventure soon to be yours in XYZ Magazine."

- Permit buyer to discontinue if not satisfied.

- Provide change of address instructions in each issue to minimize missed issues.

- Put change of address requests through quickly.

- Give a free book or special magazine edition with subscription.

- Assure subscribers that they will get bargain rates forever.

- Point out that subscription price is half the newsstand price.

ETHICS EXERCISE 5

CHAPTER 5 ETHICS IN PRACTICE

Overview

This exercise deals with one of the most fundamental debates regarding the power of marketing - the ability of marketers to manipulate demand and cause us to buy things we neither want nor need. The exercise contrasts the comments of marketing expert Theodore Levitt who defends marketing and advertising as creating images and symbols that "bring out possibilities that we cannot see before our eyes and screen out the stark reality in which we must live," with those of the late actor/author Sterling Hayden who claims that all a man really needs is the bare minimum, but that "we are brainwashed by our economic system until we end up in a tomb buried beneath a pyramid" of payments and unnecessary gadgetry. It relates to several concepts discussed in the chapter: problem recognition, and motivation and needs. The underlying issue is whether marketers can mold demand, creating dissatisfaction and "false" needs. Or, are consumers sovereign, being beyond the manipulation of the Machiavellian marketer?

1.   *What would each author say about the others' viewpoint?*

These two authors are clearly at opposite ends of the spectrum on this issue. Sterling Hayden represents the traditional consumerist critique of marketing activity - that advertising and promotion make us dissatisfied with current goods (i.e., marketers create problem awareness) and create demand for new, unnecessary goods. Marketers accustom us to constant change rather than stability; they make us believe that the grass is greener elsewhere. Liberal economists claim that advertising has turned such once-luxuries as microwave ovens, VCRs, and personal computers into necessities, i.e., it has created "false needs." Too many marketers are hucksters, sly shysters, and snake oil salesmen. Theodore Levitt represents the traditional apologist for marketing. What consumers buy are benefits or satisfactions, not merely product features. These benefits can be broadly construed to encompass psychological benefits such as self-confidence, status, and self-image, as well as more basic physical benefits such as fulfillment of hunger and thirst needs, provision of comfortable shelter, and protection from the elements. Marketers simply create want satisfiers, rather than the wants per se. The marketing concept says that we succeed by giving the people what they want. If we try to do otherwise we will fail, for consumers are sovereign.

2.   *Does advertising create needs?*

In other words, is Hayden correct? First, recall the distinction between needs and wants. A need is a state of felt deprivation of physiological requirements necessary for optimal life conditions. It is a requirement for something essential that is lacking. Necessities (e.g., food, clothing, shelter) satisfy needs. A want is a requirement for something desirable (but not essential) that is lacking. It is the form that needs take as determined by culture and society. Luxuries (the definition of which differs from individual to individual and society to society) satisfy wants. In many, if not most countries, autos, washing machines, and other products most of us take for granted are considered luxuries by most people.

An obvious problem is where do you draw the line between needs, wants, and even whims? This can open up a very interesting philosophical debate as to what people need beyond the necessities for survival. Do we really need all of these new goods and services? Fashion sunglasses? People to organize our closets for us? Who is to say? Some folks - a good many - thought we didn't need the automobile. Jet travel? Who needed to get to London in six hours? Computers? Just toys. However, if only needs were satisfied, we'd live in tents, not houses; we'd drive a horse and buggy, not a car; we'd wear animal skins, not high-fashion clothing. All we really need is a piece of meat and possibly a fire. In fact, probably porridge would do. People don't really need art, music, literature, etc. Right?

The problem, then, is to determine what represents the basic requirements of life at a given point in time, for a given society. Who are the elitists who will make these determinations - the liberal economists? No, rather in a free marketplace the sovereign consumer decides.

So, the question is: do marketers create needs? Clearly not, for needs are biologically determined. Needs preexist marketers. The more difficult question is: do marketers create wants? It is certainly true that society creates wants, and marketing is a part of society, but it does not necessarily follow that marketing creates wants per se. Wants are a function of individual psychological influences as well as sociological factors such as family, friends, religious and educational institutions, and the mass media (in which most marketing communications appear). In a rapidly progressing capitalistic society, what were once luxuries soon become necessities.

Marketers don't create new wants or demand, only demand satisfiers. New wants have always been "created" by the appearance of new products (such as the first bow and arrow, first painting, first perfume, etc.), However, the wants for such products preexist the products themselves. Sometimes business goes so far as to persuade you that you have a need for something you haven't thought of yet. This is what had to be done for electric light, cars, safety razors, and even frozen orange juice, so even this can't be all bad.

Marketers don't manipulate people like marionettes, they discover latent needs and dormant desires, and then develop and market new goods and services to satisfy those wish lists. Marketers can make us aware of new possibilities and act as catalysts, but not determinants, of wants and desires. Marketers convert generic needs into product- and brand-specific wants.

Classical economic theory holds that corporations are accountable to the marketplace where consumers are deemed to be sovereign. (They have a free will and are in control of their actions.) They buy products of their choice and in so doing reward the good companies and penalize the poor ones. As John Stuart Mill said, "Over himself, over his own body and mind, the individual is sovereign." Man is not a deterministic machine subject to manipulation and control by environmental stimuli. Consumers use selective perceptual barriers to deal with discrepant and unwanted information. Today's consumers are better educated, better informed, more discerning, more skeptical, and more demanding. In a perfectly competitive marketplace, consumers (with exceptions such as children) are sovereign. The forces of competition force each seller to satisfy customers, who can always take their business to another seller. One problem with this argument, however, is that often we are dealing with imperfect competition; monopoly power and deception would be two important exceptions.

If your students agree with you on this (most business students do), then play devil's advocate and ask them if they ever bought something they didn't really need or want. Did a salesperson ever buffalo them into buying something? Doesn't advertising sometimes create problems by saying something like "The dirt you can't see," which leads to guilt, which is an invented problem solved by the advertised good? What about Dash detergent's suds in the closet? "Housetosis?"

"Ring around the collar?" The answer is that these appeals must have been to latent needs. The needs were activated (becoming motives) via marketing communication. But if you haven't at least subconsciously noticed that your pooch has "dog breath," no amount of advertising will convince you otherwise. In short, marketing activities can make us more aware of problems and of dissatisfaction with our actual state of affairs. It is easier to fill an existing want or need, no matter how dimly perceived it might be, than to create a new want or need. As the old proverb said, "It is useless to tell a river to stop running; the best thing to do is to learn how to sail in the direction it is flowing."

The bottom line is that marketers can't manipulate needs, although they can certainly influence our behavior. Marketers do have the power to stimulate trial purchases, build brand loyalty, and get people to buy styles, quantities, and at times that they otherwise might not have. But when we say marketers put a gun to our heads and force us to buy, we are merely passing the buck, making marketers the scapegoats and whipping boys for behaviors for which we do not wish to take individual responsibility.

3.   *Which of these two views is ethically correct?*

One could argue this both ways. Hayden has a point where the marketplace breaks down. If consumers are snookered into buying things via deception (i.e., where people are led to believe their needs and wants will be adequately met when the marketer knows that they won't be), this is clearly wrong. To lie is to violate a basic standard of common morality. But to say that we are "brainwashed" by the economic system is to say that we are sheep, just pawns capable of being manipulated about the great chess board of life.

If Levitt is right, the fault for "bad" purchases lies with the consumers. Is it right to buy an expensive perfume or aftershave lotion because we think the image it will help us project will ensure that we entrap that desired member of the opposite sex? Are we now manipulating them? Or did the marketer manipulate us? We will buy such goods only if the expected benefits meet or exceed the expected costs. If such products give us emotional satisfaction which we deem worth the price paid, then the marketer has helped us to be better off (even if, from an outsider's perspective, what we are buying appears to be "crazy"). As long as no physical or psychological harm comes to either us or to others from our purchase and consumption of the product, all would seem to be well.

CHAPTER 5 TAKE A STAND QUESTIONS

1.   *After a winter storm, your car is covered with ice. There is an old can of deicer in the basement. You read the ingredients and discover that it contains fluorocarbons. Do you use the spray?*

These nonreactive organic compounds containing carbon and fluorine were once used as aerosol propellants (for hair sprays, deodorants, air fresheners, insecticides, paints, waxes, household cleaners, etc.) as well as refrigerants, solvents, and lubricants in making plastics and resins. The use of fluorocarbons as aerosol propellants has sharply dropped since 1973 because of the harm caused by these gases in degrading the ozone layer - a thin sphere of ozone in the stratosphere that protects the earth by filtering harmful radiation from the sun. A government ban in 1978 in the U.S. affects about 97 to 98 percent of all aerosols using fluorocarbons as propellants.

As noted in the Chapter 3 Take a Stand Question number 1, the impact of such compounds on the ozone layer is subject to debate among scientists. The fact that aerosols containing fluorocarbons are illegal would clearly make their manufacture and marketing unethical. Their use by consumers, however, is a grayer issue. The answer depends, in part, on to what extent one is convinced that they are harmful to the environment. (See the discussion for Chapter 3 Take a Stand Question number 1.)

A useful way to analyze this issue is to use Immanuel Kant's categorical imperative. This philosophy of ethical decision making basically says that if everyone were to behave as you do and the result is chaos, then your behavior is immoral. (If everyone lied, language would be meaningless and we'd have social chaos.) Using this line of reasoning, if you believe that your use of the old deicer would have a minuscule adverse impact on the environment, but that if enough people used such old products containing fluorocarbons the results could contribute to the eating away of the ozone layer, then use of the product would be wrong. However, the fact that most people don't in fact have access to such products might cause you to rationalize your use of the product. After all, if you can't quickly deice your car, you won't be able to get to where you want to go on time. The urgency of your need to get out of the house could enter into utilitarian calculations as to whether or not you'll use the product. Nevertheless, it would seem to be more socially responsible to take the time and trouble to let the car warm up and naturally deice, and then spend the money to get a new can of deicer. (But what about the pollution caused by driving to get a new deicer? And won't the old deicer end up in the environment anyway, sooner or later, when the cans rusts out?)

2.   *You purchased a new copy of Lotus 1-2-3 at a computer store. Several weeks later a friend says he would like to have a copy of Lotus 1-2-3 and asks you to transfer your copy to his computer. Do you let him?*

The issue is piracy of copyrighted materials. Such software comes with written notification that copying is limited to a given number of backup copies, and such backups may be used only by the original purchaser. The owner must make reasonable efforts to protect the software from unauthorized use, production, distribution, or publication. Lending or transferring the software or copies of it is prohibited without prior written authorization.

Although, ethically, this is a fairly black and white matter (i.e., to engage in the behavior in question would be an ethical lapse), it is a common area of abuse. For instance, if one has two personal computers (at work and at home), one is not supposed to load the software program into both computers. Yet, people do this all the time. Because of the high cost of software, many people let friends and relatives borrow the software to load onto their own hard disk drives. Sometimes people rationalize that, "Well, I can't afford to buy the program anyway, so it hurts no one if I borrow it since the software manufacturer would not have gotten my sale anyway (no harm, no foul). It will make me more productive, thus benefiting society" (a utilitarian calculation). Plus, I could argue that the Lotus company knows this copying goes on and "builds this into the price."

However, to copy the software or to allow someone to do so violates the copyright owner's intellectual property rights. In short, it is theft and is hence wrong according to common sense morality. The fact that "everyone is doing it" doesn't make it right.

3.   *Is using embedded stimuli in advertisements immoral? Is using symbolism in advertisements immoral?*

Embedded stimuli in advertisements (i.e., hidden words or pictures, often of a sexual nature such as breasts in ice cubes, the letters S-E-X airbrushed in peoples' hair and beards, and reproductive organs airbrushed into package graphics) have been strongly debated in the popular press and fairly widely researched in the academic (marketing and psychology) literature. The thinking is that their presence is not consciously known to the consumer, but that subconsciously they register, triggering drives, creating positive attitudes, and ultimately achieving behavioral change such as the purchase of a product.

Most research suggests that "embeds" cannot trigger the desired effects. At best, they might induce a weak emotional response, but not a behavioral response. The reason gets back to consumer sovereignty: one cannot get a person to purchase a product the purchase of which is against their will. (See the discussion above in Ethics Exercise 5.) Stimuli, of whatever nature, are only effective when they are consistent with existing predispositions (wants, needs, values, expectations, etc.) So we need not fear being turned into mindless automatons or quivering globs of compliance at the marketer's mercy.

Are embedded stimuli actually used by advertisers? There is some evidence to suggest that they are, although probably not to the extent that critics such as

Wilson Bryan Key (author of four books on the subject and lecturer on the college campus circuit) suggests. It is probably fair to say that many of the so-called embeds are simply a figment of the viewer's imagination. (All of us "see" all sorts of things from time to time in clouds, trees, and mountaintops.) The American Association of Advertising Agencies (a trade group for the advertising agency business) has claimed in a series of ads that subliminal embeds are just a figment of overactive imaginations. Even advertisers have mocked the concept in some of their ads (e.g., John Cleese for Schweppes, Seagram's Extra Dry gin's easily spotted "hidden" figures in ice cubes, and Miller Light's use of Kevin Nealon, the "subliminal man" from "Saturday Night Live.") Yet it is quite possible that some art people and perhaps others are including embeds in ads for "kicks" or because they truly believe they are effective.

If the latter is the case, it is clearly immoral. Trying to get people to buy through such sneaky means violates the consumer's right to know. The Bureau of Alcohol, Tobacco and Firearms has ruled that the use of such techniques would constitute deceptive advertising. The only fair or just way to sell products is to do so in an aboveboard manner. Whether or not embeds "work," the motives behind their use are clearly devious and hence wrong.

Using symbolism in advertisements is a horse of a different color. Symbolism is based on the notion that people buy products not only for their functional value, but also for their symbolic meaning. For instance, brand image can result in psychological value added from product use. If users feel more self assured because they sprayed their armpits in the morning with Sure deodorant, or if a woman feels more glamorous because she uses a certain brand of perfume which has been endowed with a certain image she wishes to convey, then they have derived meaningful utility from the product and are willing to pay a higher price to get this utility.

Intangible attributes are often more important to consumers than tangible characteristics, and they can satisfy customers and help them solve their problems. Only the elitist critics allege that the consumer is getting ripped off and is getting nothing in return. Symbolic consumer behavior is a reality, and the marketer who ignores it will be at a major competitive disadvantage in the marketplace. For the consumer, perception becomes reality.

GUIDE TO CASE

CASE 5-1 THE McGEES BUY THREE BICYCLES

SUBJECT MATTER: Consumer Decision-Making Process, Individual Differences in
Buying Behavior, Store-Choice Decisions, Choice Criteria

AT-A-GLANCE OVERVIEW

The McGee family lives in Riverside, California, west of Los Angeles. Terry, the father, is a physics professor at U. C.-Riverside, mother Cheryl works 10 hours a week as a volunteer, children Judy and Mark are 10 and 8.

Cheryl's mother sent $50 to buy Judy a full-size bike for her birthday. Both Cheryl and Judy felt Judy would not get much use out of a bike so they decided to buy the cheapest full-size bike they could find. Judy didn't know or care much about bikes and had only one preference -- blue color. Phoning stores listed in the phone book, Cheryl found that the local department store had the lowest prices. Mother and daughter went to the store, found a blue bike, and bought it, but found that within six months the chrome was peeling and the tires had to be replaced.

A year later, another $50 arrived from the grandparents, this time for a bike for Mark. By now the McGees had learned not to buy the cheapest bike, and, anyhow, Mark wanted a red, ten-speed imported bike with lights, special pedals, etc. Mark was very active and somewhat careless and his parents were afraid he would not maintain such a bike properly. Having seen an ad for Montgomery Ward, the parents took Mark there and found row upon row of red ten-speeds of a type the parents thought would be right for Mark. After chasing away what he felt was a pushy salesperson, Terry (the father) and Cheryl (the mother) helped Mark decide

he wanted one of the red ten-speeds. A wire basket was enough to satisfy the
boys's desire for accessories.

Soon Terry decided he would like a bike for himself. Once quite a bike fan,
riding 50 miles at a time, he had not owned a bike for 15 years. He read a copy
of *Touring* and *Consumer Reports*, which helped him decide that he wanted a Serrato
-- lightweight and durable -- but he could not find a shop that carried the
brand, so he decided he really didn't need a bike, having done without one for so
long.

One day he noticed a small bike shop. It was run-down and messy, and the owner
was a young, grease-covered man. He told the younger man about the Serrato, but
the shop owner told him that brand was not very reliable. He suggested a Ross,
and showed Terry what he had in stock. Terry thought $400 was too much for a
bike, but the owner got him to test-ride it, with the owner along, on a ride
through the country. The owner, some of his friends, and Terry went on a 60-mile
tour, and Terry really enjoyed it. It reminded him of his college days. So,
Terry bought the bike.

DISCUSSION QUESTIONS

1.   *Outline the decision-making process for each of the McGees' purchases.*

Basically, the decision-making process is the same for all purchases. The
process specifics vary, as do the circumstances surrounding each step, but the
process always involves five steps. These are: 1) problem recognition, 2) search
for alternative solutions and information (internal and external searches), 3)
evaluation of alternatives, 4) choice, 5) postpurchase consumption and
evaluation.

The three purchases discussed in the case are interesting in part because they
are sequential, and each one was made under conditions of increasing amounts of
information being available. The first bike was bought with only one thing in
mind: price. The second involved other concerns, but the parents had learned
that "cheap" had several meanings. In the case of the third purchase, Terry
actually read up on bikes, talked with a (supposed) expert, and took a good long
test ride.

Problem Recognition

In the case of the bikes for the children, problem recognition occurred when
grandmother sent $50 to be used to purchase the bikes. Even when the daughter
did not really want a bike there was still the problem of what to tell grandma.
In short, a bike "had to" be purchased. A similar event kicked off the decision
process for son Mark's bike, even though he seemed more interested in having a
bike than did his sister. Terry's purchase process was begun by the recognition,
brought on by trying the kid's bike, that he had enjoyed biking in the past,
seemed to still enjoy it, and felt he might like to get back into it and,
therefore, should consider getting a bike.

Search for Alternative Solutions

In the case of the first bike, the search was based strictly on price
considerations. The "internal search" led the family to conclude that it wanted
the cheapest possible bike based on the daughter's lack of interest in having a
bike. The external search involved the phone book and calls to many stores. It
seems that the price tag was the major information input at that point, except
for the fact that the bike was blue, the desired color. This incident, of
course, may have taught Terry a little something about salespeople, and other
sources of information, since the bike he bought turned out to be a piece of
junk.

In the case of the second bike, there was more internal search than in the case
of the first. Son Mark actually wanted a bike and had given some thought to what
he wanted: red, ten-speed, some gadgetry, etc. The parents knew the boy would
not take the best care of the bike, and that influenced the search for
alternatives. While they did visit the store in person, the father "ran off" the
salesperson he believed was "pushy." Apparently Terry felt he knew something

about bikes and that his internal sources of information were better, at least, than this particular external source.

In the case of the third bike, Terry spent much more time searching for alternatives and information. He thought about bikes he had in the past and how he used them (long rides.) He read up on bikes, made a decision as to what he wanted, and was disappointed that he couldn't find the brand he wanted. He went without the bike for a time, probably still mulling it over. He visited a bike shop, and talked, not to a salesman (he thought) but to an expert with the grease stains to prove it. (This guy's no salesman, he's a mechanic, and he knows what he's talking about!)

Evaluation of Alternatives

In the case of the first bike, evaluation was based on price, with color also playing a role. The alternatives considered were, it seems, other cheap bikes, but they were not evaluated closely as the family looked only at the cheapest bike in town. In the case of the second bike, evaluation was more involved. Considerations other than price were considered. Mark had preferences that Judy did not. The parents eliminated some alternatives because they thought the boy would treat the bike roughly and carelessly. In the case of the third bike, Terry looked through literature that compared bikes. Though he didn't buy at that time, he did consider alternatives by means of *Consumer Reports*. Later, he talked with a bike expert. And, he took a long ride on the recommended bike.

Purchase Decision

In all cases, the decision was, eventually, to buy. In the case of the first bike, this was a quick and easy decision. (We have to have some kind of bike to tell grandma about; it has to be cheap, it has to be red, here's one, here's the money, we are outta here.) In the case of the second bike, there was more effort and time devoted to the purchase decision, more criteria to consider, and maybe more money involved since there is no indication in the case that this is a cheap bike. In the case of the third bike, the decision to buy was a decision not to buy. But the "problem" remained. Terry still was thinking about bikes when he went to that bike shop. It took awhile, but his "problem" was eventually solved when the decision to buy was made.

Postpurchase Evaluation

The first bike satisfied very little. The chrome peeled, the tires split; it was a piece of junk. It satisfied one thing, however. The family could tell grandma what a nice blue bike "she" bought for Judy. However, buying new tires and watching the thing peel must have led to considerable dissatisfaction, dissatisfaction that found expression in the purchase procedures used for the other bikes. As far as we know, the bike for Mark (being more carefully thought out) suited the boy just fine. We know of no complaints. Ditto Terry's bike. The long ride gave him adequate chance to check out the bike; he bought it from a shop that can repair it for him; he felt he had the help of experts in buying the bike; the shop owner (not a salesman, remember!) is now his bike-riding buddy -- in short, he's probably very happy with that Ross bike.

2.   *Compare the different purchase processes for the three bicycle purchases. What stimulated each of the purchases? What were the factors considered in making the store-choice decisions and the purchase decisions?*

Much of this answer was covered in the discussion above. To be more brief, we might mention the following points.

Purchase Stimulation

Bike 1:   the present (money) from grandma.
Bike 2:   the present from grandma plus Mark's personal desire for a ten-speed, red bike.
Bike 3:   Terry tried out the son's bike and found he still enjoyed bikes as he had in the days of his youth.

Store-Choices Purchase Decisions

Bike 1:   Cheryl called around town and found the cheapest price, and that was
           the major store-choice criterion. Other things probably played
           lesser roles, e.g., the store was known to Cheryl, probably had a
           decent reputation, and was probably not too inconveniently located.
           They found a cheap blue bike at the store and they took it.

Bike 2:   The family saw an ad for a bike sale and probably had learned not to
           go to the store where they bought bike number one. Montgomery Ward
           is a "safe" place to buy things, appropriate for the purchase of a
           kid's bike (i.e., it's not an expensive specialty shop). The store
           has a decent, if unexciting, reputation, probably a reasonably good
           location, and it had rows of the bike type Mark wanted available.
           They had considered the kind of bike that would be appropriate, found
           it at the store, modified it with a wire basket, and that was that.

Bike 3:   Terry had not been able to find the bike he wanted, but "lucked into"
           a shop operated by (not a salesman!) a bike expert. If you are going
           to spend a lot of money on a bike (and the case says this is what
           Terry thinks about $400), you feel more comfortable dealing with an
           expert/mechanic/bike-riding chum. Bike 3 provides a good example of
           the salesperson as information source. This was the biggest
           influence on the purchase decision. Of course, the bike had to be
           fairly good and appropriate to Terry's needs since he is not a
           neophyte rider.

3.   *How do the choice criteria vary for each decision?*

As we have seen, the first bike purchase involved very low-level criteria. Judy
didn't even particularly want a bike (or so it is said). They had the money,
they had to spend it on a bike, and it had to be blue. That's it -- so might as
well buy the cheapest.

For bike two, there were more criteria involved. The wishes and criteria of the
boy were important, but so were the wishes and criteria of the parents. They had
learned that quality should be considered, since the cheapest bike proved to be a
problem, maybe not for Judy, who didn't want a bike anyway, but for her parents,
and the cheap way out would have meant problems for Mark since he was actually
going to use the bike and, it seems, was expected to be rough on it.

For bike three, the criteria seem to be cost, quality, and something else --
nostalgia? Recapturing one's college days? Keeping in shape? These must be
among the most important criteria. Why do we say that? Well, first the price
seemed too high, but Terry "came around" on that issue. And Terry didn't like to
deal with salespeople, but he was willing to deal with a salesman disguised as a
mechanic. And he postponed the sale. In fact, he thought he canceled it, until
he found just the right bike, in just the right store, sold by just the right
guy. Then it all clicked together, and he was "hooked" on the Ross. It reminded
him of his college days.

6 Consumer Behavior: Social Influences

CHAPTER SCAN

This chapter considers the consumer or buyer as a member of many groups. Within each group, the buyer plays a role, holds a status, and shares values and norms that he or she cannot easily disregard. Culture, subcultures, class and various social institutions strongly affect our behavior.

The chapter discusses demography and the importance of that study to marketers. Important changes that have occurred in American households and families are addressed. The roles of individuals in the buying/decision-making process are also considered. Again, the stress in this chapter is on the buyer as a group member. The more individual, or psychological, factors affecting behavior were discussed in Chapter 6.

SUGGESTED LEARNING OBJECTIVES

The student who studies this chapter will be exposed to a view of the consumer or buyer as a group member in both the family and the entire culture in which he or she operates. Among other things, the student will be able to:

1. Provide a sociological perspective on consumer behavior.

2. Explain the nature of culture.

3. Discuss social institutions in terms of values, norms, and roles.

4. Define subculture.

5. Provide some examples of demographic categories and explain their importance to marketers.

6. Characterize social class in the United States.

7. Know how to analyze the influence of groups on individual buyers.

8.   Identify changes that have occurred in the American family.

9.   Examine the significance of each role in the joint decision-making process.

CHAPTER OUTLINE

I.   INTRODUCTION

II.   SOCIAL FORCES

III.   CULTURE

A.   Cultural Symbols

IV.   SOCIAL INSTITUTIONS

A.   Values and Norms
B.   Roles

V.   SUBCULTURES, DEMOGRAPHIC CATEGORIES, AND SOCIAL CLASSES

A.   Subcultures: Cultures within Cultures
B.   Demographic Categories
C.   Social Class

VI.   GROUPS

A.   Reference Groups
B.   Group or Opinion Leaders

VII.   FAMILY

A.   The Changing American Household

1.   Single-Person and Single-Parent Households
2.   Working Women
3.   Family Income

VIII. JOINT DECISION MAKING

IX.   SOCIAL SITUATIONS AND ROLES

X.   SUMMARY

XI.   KEY TERMS

XII.   QUESTIONS FOR DISCUSSION (11)

XIII. ETHICS IN PRACTICE

XIV.   CASES

The following key terms are introduced and used in Chapter 6. They are defined in the text's Glossary.

Sociology
Social institution
Role
Prestige
Subculture
Demographic category
Social class
Conspicuous consumption
Primary group
Secondary group
Reference group
Membership group

Voluntary membership group
Aspirational group
Opinion leader
Family
Socialization process
Joint decision making
Syncratic decision
Autonomic decisions
Influencer
Gatekeeper

THE CHAPTER SUMMARIZED

I.   INTRODUCTION

      Pawnbrokers are shaking their image as the last source of income for drunks
      and others down on their luck. The industry is trying to reposition itself
      as a lending institution for the working poor. In recent years pawnbrokers
      have lent out just under $2 billion annually, mostly in $50 increments.
      The founder of Cash America, a chain of pawn shops, stresses the same
      marketing ideas that have worked for convenience stores: location first
      among them.

      Changing the image of pawnbrokers involves changing people's perceptions of
      the shops, how people feel about others knowing that they use pawnshops,
      attitudes, and many social forces.

II.   SOCIAL FORCES

      It is impossible to conceive of a person acting alone with no interaction
      with others in the social environment. Because consumers deal with other
      people and with various forces within the government, they are subject to
      myriad influences. Sociology is one field that studies such influences.

      Sociology is a discipline that investigates human behavior through the
      study of social institutions and their interrelationships.

      A buying event can be thought of as the top of a pyramid supported by a
      wide range of social influences. Exhibit 6-1 portrays this.

III. CULTURE

      Culture is the sum total of all institutions, values, beliefs, and
      customary behaviors learned and shared by the members of a particular
      society. (See Chapter 3.)

      The text shows that "culture" is difficult to define perfectly, but a
      common thread among definitions is that culture is man-made rather than
      innate. (We are born with a need for food, but what foods, when eaten, how
      prepared, etc. are all cultural matters.) Cultures obviously vary around
      the globe and affect marketing's activities.

      What "works" in one culture may not in another.

      .   Brazilian homemakers seem to be reluctant to buy canned soups, but
            view "soup starters" as acceptable because they add their own
            ingredients to them.

      .   In Japan, soup is regarded as a breakfast item.

      .   The imagery of slogans, e.g., "Come alive with Pepsi," often
            mistranslates in other cultures, for example, appearing to claim that
            Pepsi brings one back from the grave.

      A.   Cultural Symbols

            Mainstream and variant cultural values must be considered by
            marketers. Colors and symbols communicate, perhaps silently or

subconsciously, messages to those who view them.   These values, like the rest of marketing's environment, can change.   Some ads (Aunt Jemima, Uncle Ben) once widely accepted are now seen as racist.

IV.   SOCIAL INSTITUTIONS

Even primitive societies develop ways to deal with recurring problems in their societies.   These are social institutions.

A **social institution** consists of a stable cluster of values, norms, roles, and other means that have developed over time to fulfill the institution's central purpose.

Examples of institutions given in the text include: the family, religion, the political system, and the legal system.   Exhibit 6-2 illustrates how certain social institutions fill their purposes.

A.   Values and Norms

Values are goals that society views as important.   Norms are rules of conduct to be followed in particular circumstances.   (Defined in Chapter 3.)

For example, a "free economy" is a value of a capitalistic society. Salvation is a goal of many religious societies.   It is a value.

Norms are situation-specific.   Thus crowding and jostling others at a parade is generally accepted by Americans while like behavior in other circumstances would not be tolerated.

Norms and values vary by culture and are subject to change.   Example: it has become increasingly "the norm" not to smoke in certain public places.

B.   Roles

Any social organization creates and defines roles for its members.   A **role** is essentially a cluster of behavior patterns, defined largely in terms of other roles.

Examples: student role and teacher role, son role and father role, company president role and employee role.

Roles, like norms, "tell us what to do," and have influence on marketing.

.   The KMart clerk behaves differently than the salesperson at an exclusive fur salon.

.   The shopper behaves differently in a jewelry store than in a 7-Eleven.

The idea of "higher" or "lower" is a matter of **prestige**, the assignment of value judgments about a status or role.   Society grants more prestige to the president of duPont than the president of Jim's Supermarket.

Role, status, and prestige define customary patterns for behaviors in marketing and other endeavors.

V.   SUBCULTURES, DEMOGRAPHIC CATEGORIES, AND SOCIAL CLASS

Distinct subunits can be identified within most societies.

A.   Subcultures: Cultures within Cultures

Within society there is a dominant culture, but many cultural differences exist within it.   Language groups are good examples of this. Regional differences in food preferences demonstrate subcultural differences.

A **subculture** is a group within a dominant culture that is distinct because it differs from the dominant culture in some way.

B.   Demographic Categories

Demography is the study of the size, composition, and distribution of human populations. A **demographic category** is a group related to these characteristics, e.g., an age group or an income group. A longer discussion of these matters is presented in Chapter 8.

Gender

In most cultures, the roles assigned to the sexes differ, influencing occupation choices, income, and other matters. Despite changing views, many of the roles and characteristics of the two sexes remain "in force" to some degree. (See Exhibit 6-3.) Many products remain aimed at one or the other sex.

C.   Social Class

A **social class** is a group of people with similar levels of prestige, power, and wealth who also share a set of related beliefs, attitudes, and values in their thinking and behavior.

Exhibit 6-4 summarizes one view of social classes in the U.S.

That class is important to marketers is easily seen.

   .   Who shops at Neiman-Marcus? Who at KMart?

   .   Who buys Gucci loafers? Who gets shoes at Shoe City?

   .   Who takes a cruise? Who takes the bus?

People live in neighborhoods with people of their own class, and seem to know which stores and products are "for them" and which are not.

Thornstein Veblen, American economist, coined the term **conspicuous consumption** to satirize those who seek to "show off" by means of what they buy. This behavior is most associated with the nouveaux riches.

Social Class Structure Varies Around the World

Class structure in the U.S. reflects our economic development and our culture. In other countries (India, for example), class distinctions are far more powerful. Marketers seeking business in those countries should be aware of how wealth and power are distributed.

VI.   GROUPS

Each individual person belongs to many groups. These can be divided into two categories.

   .   **Primary groups** such as family or close friends where close contact endures over time.

   .   **Secondary groups** are larger, more impersonal groups, such as age groups, racial groups, and neighborhoods.

The influence of each is clear. People tend to have the same political, religious, and purchasing beliefs and practices as their parents. "Regular people" go to Sears rather than to Neiman-Marcus.

A.   Reference Groups

A **reference group** is a group that influences an individual because the individual is a member of that group or aspires to be a member of it.

Reference groups have influences on individuals. Older brothers or neighborhood kids might be the reference group for a younger child; members of the Armed Forces might be the reference group for an R.O.T.C. cadet.

The individual being influenced by a **voluntary membership group** is actually a member of that group. Members of an Army company, fraternity, or club are influenced by other members, largely via peer pressure.

Some membership groups are voluntary. We choose to join them: fraternities, political parties. Some are involuntary in that we have no choice: age group, race. The individual influenced by an aspirational group behaves like the members of a group he or she hopes to join. The young person in business might "dress for success."

Note: A negative aspirational group is one that a person avoids imitating. The "junior executive" does not dress like a janitor.

Reference Groups Influence Some Products more than Others

Some branded product usages, especially when the products are used in public, are heavily subject to reference group pressure. Cigarettes (Marlboro vs. Virginia Slims), beer (Budweiser vs. Generic). In these cases, the brand is the key element.

Some brand choices are hardly affected by reference group influences: Libby vs. Del Monte canned peaches. In these cases, brand is essentially irrelevant to reference groups.

Some product classes are affected by reference group influence: instant coffee vs. regular coffee, especially at a fancy dinner party.

These can vary by situation, as in the case of use of instant coffee.

B.   Group or Opinion Leaders

Groups frequently include one or more **group leaders** or **opinion leaders**. Fraternity members may admire the chapter president. African Americans may look to Rev. Jesse Jackson for leadership.

The role of group leader may alternate among individuals. The fraternity president may influence operations of the fraternity except for parties, which are run by another fraternity member known for being a wild party guy. Jesse Jackson may be a political leader, but may have little influence over his follower's choice of cigarette brand.

In many cases, word-of-mouth advertising is "best" because "the man who owns one" is seen as the expert in the product area under consideration.

VII.   FAMILY

The family is both an important social institution and an important reference group. The family is responsible for the **socialization process** -- passing down the cultural values and norms of society or group to the children.

One of the things passed down is the buying role.

A.   The Changing American Household

The composition of households and families has changed drastically from what was once "traditional."

.   About one-quarter of U.S. families fit the tradition of a few kids, a mother, and a father.

.   Single-parent households and unmarried individuals-as-households have proliferated.

.   Average household membership was 3.1 persons in 1970, 2.6 in 1990.

1.   Single-Person and Single-Parent Households

Single-person households (people living alone) account for 25 percent of U.S. households. A greater proportion than ever of the population has never been married; many young people are staying single longer; women live longer than men making widows a meaningful market segment; and there are nearly 11 million households headed by single women.

2.   Working Women

The advent of the careen woman is a major change in U.S. society. By the year 2000 the labor force will be between 137 and 144 million people and women will account for about two-thirds of the growth. In more than 60 percent of married households both spouses work.

Facts like these lead to changes in marketing. Take-out food, microwave meals, soap operas aired at night, convenience foods, etc. all are reflections of these changes.   Remember, however, that there are still many "traditional" families whose needs must be met.

3.   Family Income

In 1990, median annual household income in the U.S was $35,225. For couples with one spouse working, the number was about $24,000, for couples with both working it was nearly $43,000. There are about 10 million two-income families earning over $50,000. Working wives contribute about 40 percent of family income.

VIII. JOINT DECISION MAKING

Some consumer decisions are made by groups of two or more people. Houses and cars are often bought in this way. This is **joint decision making**.

Frequently, the decision involves some group member taking a dominant role. Stereotypically, but true, the husband or son dominates when cars are the subject, the wife dominates when furniture is to be bought, and so on.

When a decision is truly made by two or more people, together and equally, it is termed a **syncratic decision**. Choice of entertainment, or of a vacation spot may be made this way. In situations where repeat buying occurs, different family members make individual decisions on different occasions. (Example: buying gasoline.) These may be termed **autonomic decisions.**

There are five roles played in any buying decision.

.   The **buyer** who actually purchases the item.

.   The **user** who actually uses the product.

.   The **decision maker** who decides what product or brand to buy.

.   The **gatekeeper** who controls the flow of information.

.   The **influencer** who expresses an opinion to the decision-maker.

A purchase of baby food might involve five people: the teenager sent to the store to buy, the baby who eats, the mother who decides which brand is best, the grandmother whose opinion influences the mother, and the neighbor who gives the mother a magazine article on baby food quality. The purchase of gum or cigarettes might involve just one or two persons.

Given the three roles, which should be the focus of the marketer's attention? The person who has the real "say" in the matter -- the decision maker.

IX.   SOCIAL SITUATIONS AND ROLES

Lastly, the buying event may be defined by the social situation and the roles played within it. Friends may shop together just for fun, a Mother's Day gift may be selected on the basis of what amount spent would be appropriate. One brand may be bought in one situation, another in a different situation.

IX.   SUMMARY

Consumer behavior is affected by a variety of social factors. These influence the decision-making process and must be taken into account by marketers.

> **Learning Objective 1**: **Provide a sociological perspective on consumer behavior.**

Consumers interact with other members of society thus their behavior is influenced by sociological factors such as culture, subculture, social class, reference groups, family, and role. By studying these pervasive and powerful influences marketers gain insight into the buyer's decision-making process.

> **Learning Objective 2**: **Explain the nature of culture.**

Marketers look at culture as the institutions, values, beliefs, and customary behaviors learned and shared by the members of a society. Language and symbols are important aspects of culture. Insofar as consumers in a society share a culture, they will think and act in similar ways.

> **Learning Objective 3**: **Discuss social institutions in terms of values, norms, and roles.**

Social institutions develop values, norms, and roles to deal with recurrent social problems. Values are the goals that society deems important. Norm's are society's rules or standards for appropriate behavior. Roles define the behaviors expected of various members of a social institution. Judgments about role value determine social ranking and prestige.

> **Learning Objective 4**: **Define subculture.**

A subculture is a group within a dominant culture that has distinctive characteristics and values or beliefs not shared with the larger culture.

> **Learning Objective 5**: **Provide some examples of demographic categories and explain their importance to marketers.**

Age, gender, educational levels, and income level are demographic categories. Such variables are of interest to marketers because individuals often identify with and behave like others in these categories.

Learning Objective 6: **Characterize social class in the United States.**

A social class is a group of people with similar levels of prestige, power, and wealth. According to one view, U.S. society may be roughly divided among five social classes determined by education, occupation, and other measures of prestige. Social classes differ in lifestyle, purchase preferences, and shopping and consumption patterns.

Learning Objective 7: **Analyze the influence of groups on individual buyers.**

Groups strongly influence individuals' behavior. Primary groups, such as the family, pass on cultural values through socialization. Many other membership and aspirational reference groups provide points of comparison by which the individual evaluates his or her social position. These groups have many direct and indirect influences on purchasing behaviors.

Learning Objective 8: **Identify changes that have occurred in the American family.**

Increases in the numbers of working women and single parent households has changed the nature of the typical American family. Nevertheless, the family remains a major social institution with a strong influence on consumer behavior.

Learning Objective 9: **Examine the significance of each role in the joint decision-making process.**

The joint decision-making process includes the roles of buyer, user, influencer, gatekeeper, and decision-maker.

XI.   KEY TERMS

XII.   QUESTIONS FOR DISCUSSION (11)

XIII.   ETHICS IN PRACTICE

XIV.   CASES

ANSWER GUIDELINES FOR CHAPTER 6 QUESTIONS FOR DISCUSSION

1.   *What are some cultural symbols used by marketers?*

ANSWER:

"Culture is everything we are not born with," and was defined earlier in the text as all the institutions, values, beliefs, and customary behaviors learned and shared by the members of a particular society.

Most definitions reflect this common thread. They employ such terms as "acquired by man," "learned," "man-made," and "acquired knowledge." Thus, we are born with needs to eat and to drink liquids. These are innate to humans. But "everything else" about eating and drinking is cultural. Do we drink water or tea? Do we know or care about the risks of drinking unclean water? Do we like hot drinks in the winter or, as some societies do, in the summer? Do we want our beer cold or at room temperature? All these, and "everything else," are cultural matters.

A cultural symbol represents and expresses a common meaning to members of a society and may be verbal or nonverbal. Cultural symbols reflect the values of a society and thus vary among and within countries. Where possible, students benefit from comparing symbols from various cultures to reinforce international awareness.

A few examples of cultural symbols to generate additional discussion from students may include, but should not be limited to, the following ideas:

Cultural Value	U.S.	Potential Meaning Other cultures
Colors		
White	purity	death (Orient)
Blue	male	female (Holland)
Animals		
Bull	strength	sacred (parts of India)
Eagle	freedom	lower form of life (Thailand)

Further, students may consider a broader perspective for cultural symbols. For example, consider the following examples:

.   Buying a big car in a culture that seems to prize big cars and providing proper roads for them is symbolic of wealth or luxury. European cultures, including fuel costs as a part of the culture, favor small cars and tend to have smaller roads.

.   Buying a pair of jeans. Has anyone except the very poor ever bought a pair of jeans just to keep warm? We have laws requiring clothes in most situations, customary ways of dressing, senses of what looks good and what does not, etc. Marketers use symbols on the jeans and in selling the jeans which reflect cultural values.

.   Food purchases. Though some cultures value sheep eyes as delicacies, most of us would not knowingly buy and eat sheep eyes. If we did, or found out later, we would experience a sense of revulsion, a culturally induced reaction.

The influence of culture on our behaviors is not readily apparent. It is so much a part of us from the moment of birth that we seldom think about it. How often do we dwell on the slippery workings of our tongues, for example? Occasionally, our subcultural influences occur to us as "different," such as always eating fish on Fridays, going to church on Wednesday nights, etc. But even at this, we seldom dwell upon them. A discussion of culture, symbols in society which communicate values, and situations wherein its influence is recognized essentially confirms the nearly absolute effect of culture on all we do.

2.   *How might a social institution such as the military influence consumer values?*

ANSWER:

A social institution is a stable cluster of values, norms, roles and other means developed over time to fulfill a central purpose. As outlined in Exhibit 6-2, the military fulfills a social need for aggression or defense against enemies of the state. This social institution values discipline and includes norms for following orders and for recognizing rank differentials.

Since social institutions are a culture's means for dealing with recurrent problems and demands, the military both reflects and changes consumer values. For example, veterans influence their family members and social groups as they transfer military values into their civilian lives. Thousands of civilians who work for the military or contractors who supply equipment also interact with this social institution which may influence values. Further, supposedly successful military operations, such as Kuwait, may influence consumer values for patriotism, strength, or fairness. In contrast, military failures may cause a shift toward ethnocentrism or compromise.

3.   *Distinguish between norms and values.*

ANSWER:

Values reflect the goals a society views as important, while norms establish rules of conduct based on these defined goals. Values reflect the moral order of a society, while norms are situation-specific in defining behavior appropriate for varying circumstances.

For example, U.S. citizens value freedom and independence. A common norm is for pedestrians to avoid touching each other with apologies expected for jostling or bumping into another person. However, norms are situation-specific with the same jostling behavior considered acceptable during a parade.

4.   *How might the marketers of McDonald's be influenced by cultural forces in U.S. marketing? In international marketing?*

ANSWER:

As we have seen, the influence of cultural factors is so great within the domestic market (and even more obvious when the cultures of several nations are compared), that a plethora of examples answering this question are to be found.

Domestic Marketing

.   Ronald McDonald is a clown, and yet a spokesman for a large company. We do not equate "clown" with "fool."

.   Playgrounds for children are accepted since we seek to entertain kids and do not view all meals as serious, sit-down family gatherings. Further, we are "rich enough" to play when we eat.

.   Menu items reflect our cultural preferences (hamburgers rather than bat-burgers, potatoes rather than spinach-sticks) and our subcultural forces: hamburgers are acceptable to some Jews, while cheeseburgers are not, and some people still eat fish on Fridays and order fish fillets.

     NOTE: A few years ago McDonald's had to do some scrambling to show that no kangaroo meat shipped to them from Australia had actually made it to the serving counters.

.   Individual wrapping of items reflects our desire for warm foods and cleanliness.

.   Ketchup on hamburgers is "automatic." Customers must ask for no ketchup. McDonald's prices are not all the same in the U.S. They reflect costs and the state of the local economy, even within individual states.

International Marketing

.   Varying menu items. In some countries, the two burger patties on a Big Mac are seen as a ridiculous waste. Totally different (from U.S.) menu items are also encountered.

.   Drink items on menus are also varied to allow for preferences for teas or juices instead of soda and coffee.

.   Space problems in many countries mean smaller restaurants and few or no parking lots.

.   Decor varies. In many European countries, the desire for lower prices, plus limits on space, make "eating bars" at which customers stand rather than sit, far more common than in the U.S. In Japan, on the other hand, it is "bad taste" to eat while standing.

.   In some countries going out for dinner is a leisure activity. Most people would not go to McDonald's for the evening meal so the restaurants must stress "quick lunches."

.   Care is taken in transporting ads and promotions to other countries. "McDonald's and you" may be far too familiar a usage in Germany or Japan.

.   Prices must be in line with local ability to pay and with the local value system's determination of what a given product is worth.

In addition, McDonald's domestic and international operations have been affected by the increased cultural emphasis on the environment. For example, the firm refuses to buy rain forest beef and has altered its packaging, a clear indication of cultural forces influencing the firm's strategic decisions.

5.   *How likely is it that the following people would purchase a ticket to the ballet, to a professional baseball game, and to Disneyland? (a) 34-year-old steel worker who graduated from high school, (b) 44-year-old college professor, (c) 21-year-old executive secretary, and (d) 21-year-old counter helper at Burger King.*

ANSWER:

This question is intended to engender discussion of the matters of social class, education, etc. Students can always find plenty of exceptions to everything, but speaking in generalities, we might find the following:

LIKELY TO BUY A TICKET TO:

	A Ballet	Baseball Game	Disneyland
34-year-old steel worker	NO	YES	YES
44-year-old professor	YES	MAYBE	YES
21-year-old executive secretary	MAYBE	MAYBE	NO
21-year-old counter helper at Burger King	NO	MAYBE	NO

This matrix is obviously based on nearly stereotypical perceptions. Some exceptions could be easily found. Noting the dangers of using stereotype judgments instead of proper research, our choices were selected as follows.

(a)   34-year-old steel worker

1.   Ballet. Stereotype says "No," exceptions are possible. His (or her?) buddies better not find out.

2.   Baseball. Baseball is most popular with the "working class" and an employed steel worker probably can afford to go.

3.   Disneyland. Our answer was "YES" based on the assumptions that the worker was employed and that he has kids to take.

(b)   44-year-old professor

1.   Ballet. Of these, the professor is most likely to go to a ballet. This is "accepted behavior" in his or her circles. Even if the professor hates ballet, he or she might "fake" an interest.

2.   Baseball. Going to a game is probably a simple matter of liking baseball, taking the kids, or going with "the gang."

3.   Disneyland. Assuming the professor has kids, the answer is likely to be "YES."

(c) 21-year-old executive secretary

1. **Ballet.** Debatable response. Does he or she like ballet? Did he or she go
to college and hang around with a group that approves of "the arts." The
young age of the "executive secretary" could flag a high school background
with four or five years work. The answer here would then tend to be
negative, hence the "MAYBE."

2. **Baseball.** Again, does the person like baseball? Does the person's spouse
or boy-girl friend like baseball? If the secretary is employed, money
should not be a big problem.

3. **Disneyland.** The "NO" is based on the assumption that the 21-year old has
no children old enough to enjoy it.

(d) 21-year old counter helper at Burger King

1. **Ballet.** The "NO" answer flows from the stereotype. If the counter helper
is a college student, perhaps even a dance major, the picture changes.

2. **Baseball.** The stereotype would suggest a "YES" answer since baseball's
followers are generally less educated, blue collar types. Other matters
(Does he or she like baseball?) come up.

3. **Disneyland.** The "NO" flows from the age, twenty-one, which suggests being
too old to be very much interested and too young to have children of the
appropriate age. However, it is arguable that the Burger King worker may
have no "high aspiration," no need to impress anyone, and would be likely
to go to Disneyland just for fun.

6. *Is social class useful in marketing planning? Name three products whose
purchase might be influenced by the buyer's social class.*

ANSWER:

Yes, in the marketing of certain items. It has been said that a rich man is not
just a poor man with money. Tastes, interests, and pastimes vary widely across
classes, as does willingness to spend money on selected items (e.g., imported
mustard at $15 a jar). These variables affect all 4 Ps:

. Products desired and their quality.
. Prices payable, values set on products.
. Place where products will be sought, e.g., "carriage trade" shops.
. Promotion possibilities, e.g., media chosen and emphasis on a personal
approach.

Though there is much overlap among groupings, the consumption of certain products
can be closely linked to class. Some examples:

. Upper Class: Yachts, large estates, cultural events, charitable
organizations, plus many of the products linked to the upper-middle class.

. Upper-Middle Class: Legal (tax) and investment services, trust funds,
horses, large boats, expensive vacations, "good education" for children
(Harvard), expensive houses, wines, etc., classical music records,
concerts, maid service.

. Lower-Middle Class: Education for children at respected colleges (below
Harvard level), vacations, smaller boat, cabin or vacation bungalow, lawn
mower and like equipment for personal use, insurance to build up estate
"for the kids," health services.

. Working Class: Clothing appropriate to working environment, autos of the
Ford and Plymouth type, advice on savings plans, limited vacations (tend to
go to established spots like Disneyland, or to visit family), at-home
entertainment, beer.

. Lower Class: Income and employment is limited thus day-to-day food and
housing problems are the focus. Little interest in education, "cultural

       matters," savings, health services, insurance.

7.   *Is a reference group likely to influence the purchase of the following*
       brands or products? (a) laundry soap, (b) shampoo, (c) Polo sports shirt,
       (d) wristwatch, (e) athletic club membership, and (f) milk.

ANSWER:

The influences of reference groups vary considerably. They are
situation-specific. The situational variables mentioned here are two: brands
and products. If we assume "everything else is equal" we face four possible
combinations of these variables:

    .   Strong product influence, strong brand influence.
    .   Strong product influence, weak brand influence.
    .   Weak product influence, strong brand influence.
    .   Weak product influence, weak brand influence.

Students might, thus, be asked to place products a-f into the proper "box."

                      INFLUENCE ON PRODUCT

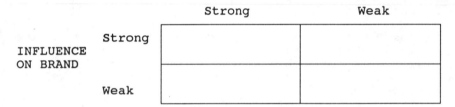

Our opinions, given our own experiences, are as follows:

(a)   Laundry soap

This product is common. It is assumed that "everybody" uses it. Thus, there
would be little reference group influence on product class. Also, it is used in
a private way. There is low visibility. Thus reference group influence on brand
choice is low. An exception: a mother seeking a gentle soap for diapers may be
influenced to use Ivory Flakes.

(b)   Shampoo

Like laundry detergents, shampoo is used by "everybody" and used out of the sight
of others. Apart from the situation wherein a shampoo is recommended by a
friend, brand and product choice should be weakly influenced by others. An
exception would be the case where a person has particularly frizzy hair, oily
hair, or dandruff. Even here, however, it is the hair that is the object of
reference group approval or disapproval, not the shampoo. Thus, if dandruff can
be diminished by use of a shampoo that no one else has heard of, it will be used
without reference group approval of the shampoo itself.

(c)   Polo sports shirt

Polo is a well-known (and trendy) style of shirt and brand name. Thus, in proper
circumstances, its purchase is heavily influenced by reference groups. The
symbolism used on such shirts (alligators, polo ponies, etc.) is too obvious to
be ignored, though it appears that a "reverse snobbery" is entering the market.
Izod now makes a good proportion of its shirts without the alligator. Trivia
Question: is the Polo player right or left handed? Answer: Right.

(d)   Wristwatch

This product class is influenced by reference groups given the right
circumstances. A "young executive" would be expected to have a wristwatch and it
would be expected to be a good one. Having no watch, or a $3 "throw away" would
surprise his or her fellow "executives." Particular brand selection would
probably be unimportant as long as the brand were a good one or, at least, the
watch looked good.

In some situations, however, other influences would prevail. A person doing factory work or climbing telephone poles might find that having a watch or not makes no difference to fellow workers, but that wearing a very expensive watch is seen as "stupid" or "showing off."

(e)   Athletic club membership

In certain situations, certain types (young, upwardly mobile types) may be expected to be members of some athletic club or even of a particular club. In other cases, the choice of clubs may be made strictly on the variable of convenience though going to a club could have been influenced by a friend's or boss' comment that "You're getting way out of shape."

Aspirational reference groups is a good topic to bring up here since, of the products mentioned in this question, this one is most germane to aspirations. Some people join clubs to be seen with the right people or on the chance they may get to befriend the president of their company, who happens to go to the same club.

(f)   Milk

Like laundry soap, milk is consumed privately. Further, the effects of milk would be very difficult to detect. Thus, the influence of reference groups on choice of milk brands is likely small. Also, milk quality is standardized and controlled by law. Only if one brand were found to have been contaminated (even once) might reference group influence make it a nonacceptable brand.

Whether or not one uses milk as a product may be situationally influenced. A health-oriented reference group might influence a person to buy 2% or skimmed milk rather than whole milk. At a dinner party the host, who usually puts milk in his coffee, may serve cream instead.

8.   *How much husband-wife joint decision making would you expect for the following purchases? (a) life insurance, (b) steam iron, (c) trip to Europe, and (d) box of candy.*

ANSWER:

Many studies have shown that the focus of decision-making authority shifts as the product considered changes. Often the decision-making power shifts stereotypically: Dad "handles" cars, Mom "handles" furniture and redecorating. Obviously, this is changing as more women become employed outside the home, become C.P.A.s, etc.

Some decisions are of the "joint" type where a group of two or more persons considers a purchase, though often a group leader emerges because of real or assumed expertise, seniority, earning power, or some other factor.

In the following four comments, it is assumed we are discussing a family with two spouses. Obviously, a single career-woman's insurance decision differs from that of a married woman.

(a)   Life insurance

Insurance decisions are likely to be joint in nature, though men have traditionally been the "group leaders." The effects of insurance, both the cost and the payoff, fall on the family as a unit. The decisions as to who needs the most coverage, how much payoff would be needed to keep the family together, etc. all call for joint input, especially in "modern times" where both spouses are working or where women have a bigger "say" in general, in these matters.

(b)   Steam iron

The decision to purchase a steam iron will probably be made by the person who will use the iron. Little joint decision making would take place, though a husband and wife happening to be shopping together might talk over the "benefits" of one model versus another.

(c)   Trip to Europe

A trip to Europe should involve much joint decision making. If it is a family trip, each family member will, in one way or another, have to invest time, interests, money, etc. Each will have preferences as to itinerary, time of year to go, length of stay, mode of travel, places to stay (camping vs. hotel,) etc.

Because of these concerns and the need to reach compromises, all members of the concerned group are likely to be involved in the decisions made.

(d)   Box of candy

The candy will be selected by the purchaser in most cases, though the preferences of others (e.g., "Mom's favorite") may play a role.

Not much joint decision making will be likely unless there are two or more purchasers, for example, two children buying a present for a parent. Even here, the preferences of the parent, if known and followed, lessen the likelihood of there being much joint decision making.

9.   *What is a household? What do you predict will be the nature of households in the year 2010?*

ANSWER:

A household is a dwelling unit occupied by a group of related people, a single person, or several unrelated people who share living quarters. A family, in contrast, is a group of two or more persons related by birth, marriage, or adoption residing together.

The text includes a good deal of demographic and lifestyle data that can be used to answer this question. Since the year 2010 is drawing near, such predictions shouldbe close to the mark. However, the danger of assuming trends to be absolutely predictive should be mentioned.

Assuming the demographic and lifestyle information at hand to be projectable, we may decide that:

.   Families will have fewer children than has been "traditional" to this point. Medical advances and career opportunities for women should see to that. Households will then be smaller than has traditionally been the case.

.   There will be more households than ever before, but the "families" in them will be more likely to consist of single people, single parents with children, widows, and to a lesser degree, widowers and divorced people.

.   There will be a higher than ever proportion of senior citizens. Even the "baby boomers" will then be sixty or thereabouts.

.   The family will probably have given even more "power" to women because their incomes should be more equal to men's than today and more households will be headed by women.

.   If current trends continue, the average household income should be higher than it is currently, assuming the proportion of two-income households continues to rise.

10.   *In a family consisting of a father, a mother, and an 11-year-old daughter, what roles might be played, and by whom, in the purchase of a new home?*

ANSWER:

In the purchase of a new home, all family members play some sort of role. At the least, the parents consider the children when calculating the number of rooms preferred, the number of bathrooms desired, the need for "play space," and so on.

The roles the question asks us to consider are these:

- The buyer: the person who actually buys the product.

- The user: the person who will actually use the product.

- The decision maker: the person who actually decides which brand or product to buy.

- The influencer: persons who **express** opinions that influence or persuade the decision maker.

- The gatekeeper: the person who has control over flows of information.

The purchase of a house best fits the model of joint decision making (or household decision making) wherein families make a decision together. Thus, the roles played could be played jointly. The user role is an obvious case, since all family members will live in the house.

It just so happens that one of your faithful authors had an 11-year-old daughter, a wife, and had just bought a new house. He will herein describe the roles played in this decision. The experiences of others may have been different.

The buyer role was performed jointly by the father and mother. This is true in a formal, legal sense in that both signed the mortgage agreement, both names appear on the deed, and both names appear on related paperwork such as property tax forms, water bills, etc. The role was played jointly in the economic sense in that both spouses work and make about the same salaries. In situations where the wife doesn't work outside the home, it could be argued that the husband alone bought the house. He would be foolish, indeed, to advance such an opinion to the wife.

As stated above, the user role was/will be played jointly by all three persons (unless the situation changes, such as when the daughter goes to college). Certain parts of the house are used to a greater or lesser extent by individuals, e.g., the parents make more use of the bar than does the 11-year-old girl.

The decision-maker role was played by the wife. However, insofar as the husband acquiesced to the deal, it could be argued that the husband played a joint role in the decision to buy.

The role of influencer was played by several persons. The 11-year-old influenced the decision, though never saw the house until it had been purchased. The influences she had can be seen in the parent's decision to buy not too far from the daughter's school, to buy a house wherein the daughter could have her own room and a bathroom separate from that of the parents, to buy a house with a large, finished basement where the daughter can play with her possessions, and (rue the day) hang out with friends.

The role of influencer was also played by parents living thousands of miles away. Having a house that pleased "mom" was one of the goals the wife wanted to achieve. Also, insofar as the house is "bigger and better," the wife's friends, (all of whom seem to have big houses) played their roles as influencers.

The gatekeeper function was played by several persons within and without the family unit. For example, the real estate agent directed the couple not to every available house, but to houses the agent chose. To a degree, a gatekeeper function was also played by the wife. She gathered information on houses available and dealt with the real estate agent. The husband, busy with preparing a textbook, encouraged the wife to play this gatekeeper role.

11. *Think of a recent purchase. Identify all the social forces that may have influenced your purchase.*

ANSWER:

This question may serve as a review of the chapter's material as all factors may play a role in varying purchase situations. Transparency 6-1, and Exhibit 6-1 in the text portrays the pyramid of options which may have affected a specific buying event.

As an example, consider the potential social influences for the purchase of an automobile by a graduating senior.

Culture influences desired colors, size and perh aps country-of-origin.

Subcultural norms and social class may affect preferences for styles, options, or purchase of a truck or van as opposed to a car.

Reference groups may now include aspirations within business which may affect the decision. For example, some firms require sales representatives to drive specific types of cars; or, current reference groups in college may influence the selection of a sportier model.

Family may not be a consideration for a new college graduate unless married and/or with children. However, parents and siblings may co-sign a loan or influence the decision.

Role and social situation is similar to reference group considerations but can also involve other influences. For example, a graduate who will receive a company car in the career role may spend less for a personal vehicle than a new graduate who must use a personal car for business purposes.

ETHICS EXERCISE 6

CHAPTER 6 ETHICS IN PRACTICE

Overview

This case concerns a seven-year-old boy who pestered his father to take him to McDonald's to play the "Dick Tracy" game in progress at the time. The father, a lawyer, sued McDonald's, asserting that the game had turned his son into a gambling addict in just one week, and that the game constituted an illegal lottery. He also sued Disney Studios, maker of the film. He asked for double the $35 he had spent at McDonald's during the game and that McDonald's drop the game itself.

Working through the questions for this case will help the student to see that even what appears to be fairly routine consumer behavior is influenced by a multitude of sociological factors. It also shows how ethical values are influenced by society. Finally, the case brings up the issue of filing consumer lawsuits - an increasingly common behavior in American society.

1.   *What sociological factors influenced the father's willingness to take the boy to McDonald's?*

Although at first glance this would seem to be a fairly straightforward situation - the son kept badgering the father, so finally he gave in to have some peace and quiet - there are several important yet somewhat subtle sociological forces at work here.

As the chapter discusses, the family is one of the major social institutions influencing consumer behavior. Part of the socialization process is that many of our attitudes towards products, brands, stores, etc. are formed early in life through family influences. We swear by (at) certain products because our parents swore by (at) them. For instance, there is a strong similarity of brand preferences of adults and their children. This is especially so regarding food preferences (e.g., "Kool Aid. You loved it as a kid. You trust it as a mother"). Ask your students how many of them brush with the same toothpaste they grew up on, drink the same sodas they drank as children, etc.

Thus, it is quite possible that the father, the lawyer of the case, was influenced by the environment in which he grew up to become a Big Mac biter and Egg McMuffin muncher. He was taught that McDonald's was always willing to see that you could have any number of menu items, and could ask for certain variations (no pickle -- the American cultural value -- freedom of choice.)

Thus, Mickey Dees seemed like the logical place to take his child and perhaps recapture a few childhood memories. (As the old adage says, "Like father, like son.") In fact, McDonald's has always positioned itself as a fun family-oriented place (what with Ronald McDonald and friends, play lands, kids' meals, etc.)

Another major social institution (not found in Exhibit 6-2) influencing the dad's marketplace behavior is entertainment. Eating out is a major leisure time activity for most Americans. However, families with kids often find it a major hassle to eat at traditional sit-down restaurants (even if they are positioned as "family restaurants") because the little ones get itchy-twitchy waiting for the food. So, fast food (even to go) is viewed as a desirable alternative, even though ambience, and sometimes quality, are sacrificed in the process. And, McDonald's does provide entertainment for the kiddies (play lands, special kids' meals, promotional appearances by the McDonald's Land characters.)

The chapter notes that culture tends to homogenize behavior. You probably couldn't think of a better example than McDonald's - the all-American eating venue providing the all-American meal: a hamburger, fries, Coke, and hot apple pie. Sometimes, it seems that the U.S is nothing more than a bland glob of humans tied together by TV, WATS lines, and McDonald's outlets (although the presence of subcultures negates this notion). McDonald's is an institution promoting cultural uniformity as opposed to the currently trendy cultural diversity. Hamburger eaters of every race, creed, color, and income level find McDonald's fare to be convenient, appetizing, safe, and reasonably nutritious (especially with a new menu whose healthiness has been beefed up [pun intended]).

A trip to McDonald's fulfills certain cultural values. These would include promptness (fast food), cleanliness (McDonald's toilet bowls are kept clean, and the company hires clean-cut youths to man the counters), individualism (there is still a sense of "have it your way," even if the slogan is Burger King's), and informality (grazing, i.e., eating on the run, has taken off big time in recent years).

Societal norms also influenced this father to take this excursion with his son. For instance, fathers should spend "quality time" (preferably also quantity time) with their children. The family is a normative reference group, and family norms include things like what is appropriate to eat, when, and where.

Fathers are important role models for their sons, and so are expected to take them places and do things with them. Traditionally, the father's role regarding consumer behavior is to be more involved with long-range decisions, finances, and the like, whereas children take a more active role in decisions for recreational and play activities as well as for some foods (such as a visit to a fast food outlet).

Social class, however, would appear not to be an influence on this purchase decision. McDonald's casts a broad net, going after all social strata. Note that the father's occupation is lawyer, suggesting that he is at least upper-middle class. Although many retail outlets position themselves along social class lines (e.g., upscale Neiman Marcus and down-scale Price Club), McDonald's goes broad scale, like mass merchandisers such as Sears, KMart, and Wal-Mart.

It is also possible that reference groups influenced this visit to the home of the Big Mac (to paraphrase a competitor's slogan). Perhaps close personal friends of the son influenced him to want to go to McD's to play the "awesome" new Dick Tracy game. Or, maybe friends of the father took their kids and gave a positive word-of-mouth endorsement.

Finally, another societal factor is the fact that, in general, children are becoming more influential in family purchase decisions; consumer kid power is on the upswing. Children have changed from penny candy purchasers to designer brand buyers; from followers of parental purchase patterns to pace-setters for family consumption behavior. The reasons are many: rising affluence, more single-parent households (due to high divorce rates), more working moms (and hence more independent children), smaller family sizes (hence more proportionate influence per child), more educated children, and more time spent with the media (especially TV, a powerful socialization agent). Hence, more and more, kids are calling the shots, as this son seems to be doing.

2.   *Was filing the lawsuit the right thing to do?*

There seem to be two ethical issues here. First is the ethics of filing what
would appear to be frivolous lawsuits. Second is the issue of McDonald's running
what some might view to be an illegal, addictive lottery.

First is the issue of consumers' right to sue. Most commonly this crops up in
product liability suits. Product liability is based on the legal obligation of
sellers to pay damages to individuals who are injured by defective products or
unsafely designed products. Today, the purchaser can sue not only the
manufacturer or dealer but also the service provider for physical/bodily injury
and allegedly economic and emotional damages. Punitive damages (above and beyond
actual damages) are awarded in civil lawsuits to punish corporations and to deter
irresponsible corporate behavior.

One viewpoint is that consumers' ability to easily file and win lawsuits against
corporations has kept the firms on their proverbial toes, forcing them to think
safety (both physical and mental) first. Supposedly the threat of suits and
mega-judgments forces firms to churn out safer products. For instance, today
automobiles have air bags, roll bars, and explosive-resistant fuel tanks, all
thanks to product liability lawsuits. The thinking is that consumers have a
right to a safe environment, including good health, protection from injury,
monetary harm, or other afflictions. Hence, the seller has a correlative
obligation to preserve this safe environment in the manufacturing and marketing
of products. This includes a duty to adequately warn consumers of possible
hazards and to instruct them on how to avoid them.

Sometimes the problem is that a product is targeted to the wrong user (e.g.,
alcohol ads aimed at youth, or smokers with lung cancer suing tobacco companies
for advertising to them). This could be a problem in the McDonald's case. Many
would agree that gambling-like games shouldn't be promoted to children. Hence,
the father would be justified in suing to halt a game which could seemingly harm
the psychological well-being of his son and other children (not to mention
threaten his own sanity due to the child's incessant badgering).

Another viewpoint is that we live in an increasingly litigious society where
lawyers sue at the drop of a willfully negligent hat. Sue happiness is a disease
that has become an epidemic, and lawyers are the carriers of the disease. The
roles of buyers and sellers have changed dramatically: the buyer is now the
favored party, and, if he is incredibly lucky, he could win a punitive damage
award of lottery-size proportions. Especially in product liability suits the
"deep-pocketed" companies (including manufacturers' insurance companies) are
pursued.

Some view this as class-struggle economics which pits "rich" producers against
"poor" consumers in an effort to redistribute wealth. Where this is the motive,
the real problem would seem to lie in a society where the first question asked
is: "Who can I sue?" Envy, greed, and selfishness can be powerful motivators,
but the "soak the rich" concept does not promote economic justice. The result
has often been higher product prices for consumers, discontinued products,
delayed or never-introduced new products, plant closings and loss of jobs,
reduced ability of American firms to compete in an international marketplace, and
in some instances higher-priced commercial insurance policies or even
unattainable insurance (undesirable from a utilitarian perspective). However, in
this case, the father is only suing for double the $35 he spent on purchases and
petitioned the court to stop the game. It appears that his motives were pure:
to stop the sale of something he deemed harmful to youth.

According to some observers, a related issue in many product liability suits is
an unwillingness of many people to take personal responsibility for possible
negative consequences of risks incurred. Denial of individual responsibility is
pervasive in our society today (whereas once this was an American cultural
value). Yet many products and services have inherent risks which a reasonable
buyer could foresee (e.g., the possibility of falling off of a ladder; yet
ladders have warnings plastered all over them since manufacturers get sued so
much. If you ever read all the warnings, you'd never climb another ladder
again).

A 100 per cent risk-free environment is unattainable, yet utopians demand unattainable perfection through compulsion of the law. Hence, it could be argued that this father should take individual responsibility for dealing with his son's (perhaps unreasonable) demands. He should exert his authority and "just say no." In fact, it was the father's acquiescing to his son's whims which promoted the "gambling fever." He has no one to blame but himself.

The second issue is the morality of running a game of chance. The father's argument was that it was an illegal lottery which was addictive to kids. However, legally, this is not lottery, for a lottery requires a purchase. Sweepstakes (where winners are selected based on chance) and games (where one must make repeat visits to the dealer to keep playing and getting things which may or may not help him to win a prize) do not require product purchase in order to keep them from qualifying as an illegal lottery in most states. There is plenty of precedent for firms running these sweepstakes and games, even when targeted at children (e.g., McDonald's popularized corporate-sponsored games in 1981 with their Build a Big Mac game. Later they introduced a Monopoly game: collect three pieces to complete a monopoly board).

Although it would seem that legally the father did not have much of a case, morally he might have. It could be argued that McDonald's should promote the main product (i.e., the restaurant) rather than the game (an analogue is selling products to kids on the basis of the premiums offered). However, it could also be said that if the game offers utility to children, this is fair. Also, it might be suggested that McDonald's is disrupting family harmony. (This argument was dealt with in Chapter 3's Take a Stand, question 2.)

Finally, it could be alleged that McDonald's is promoting a potentially dangerous and addictive product to children, an especially vulnerable group. This could be the start of a lifelong addiction to gambling for at least a small minority of the children, an activity which has "been the ruin of many a poor man." On the other hand, it could be argued that since no consideration is given, this isn't gambling. Also, if a person has a propensity to get addicted to gambling, they will indulge in the real thing soon enough anyway.

3.   *What sociological factors influenced the father's initiation of the lawsuit?*

His profession was probably the largest influence. One reason why there are so many lawyer jokes is probably the real or imagined notion that so many of them are ambulance chasers out to "sue the b*&$#@!" This would relate to the values, norms, and roles of lawyers. It could also be due to the increasing refusal in society to accept individual responsibility for one's actions. Also, perhaps there was a certain amount of prestige in his going up against a high-profile company like McDonald's (obviously the lawsuit garnered some publicity).

CHAPTER 6 TAKE A STAND QUESTIONS

1.   *When you pick up a friend, she is wearing a fur coat. Do you tell her she shouldn't wear the coat because of animal rights?*

There are two general issues involved here. First, is it moral to wear a fur coat? Second, if we assume it is immoral, how do we treat a friend who is wearing a fur coat?

The morality of wearing fur is an issue which has been hotly debated. There are some good arguments on both sides of the table; thus this becomes an issue of balancing your personal values with potentially differing values of others.

Arguments against wearing fur put forth by animal rights activists (e.g., People for the Ethical treatment of Animals) include:

.   Animals are terrorized, trapped, or deprived of all their natural instincts on fur farms.

.   It is immoral to support this activity by buying and/or wearing fur products. We should care about the suffering animals.

- Although the fur industry claims that trapping helps to manage the wildlife population, it should not appoint itself God and try to balance nature. Nature was balancing itself millions of years before the greedy fur industry came along.

- People have a right to wear fur if they want to, but their choice should be an educated one. Our job is to expose the bloody underside of the fur trade.

Arguments for wearing fur put forth by the American Fur Industry include:

- Nature is cruel. Animals in the wild do not live in idyllic conditions, frolicking through fields of wild flowers all their lives until they die of old age. Animals that aren't caught in traps die of overpopulation, starvation when they grow too old to forage (a most unpleasant demise), or predation.

- Minks, which account for over 75% of the fur coats produced in this country, are raised humanely on fur farms and killed painlessly. (Don Feder, "Animal Rights Agenda: Tan the Human Hide," *Human Events*, 1/20/90, p. 14) Over 90% of the mink produced in the U.S. comes from farms that are certified, meaning they are under the care of veterinarians who will be sure that these farms take care of the animals in the best possible way, so that they are free from stress and have the proper lighting and food. ("Fur Coats: A Fashion Choice or Cruelty to Animals?" *USA Today*, 21/23/91, p. 13A)

- The fossil fuels used to produce acrylic fabrics, which are recommended as a substitute for fur, are a source of pollution. (Feder)

- If we reject wearing fur, consistency demands that we reject consumption of animal flesh (steak, chops, etc.) as well as leather and wool garments (many animal rights activists are vegetarians and admit they are opposed to leather and wool products). We must also reject other uses of animals, such as zoos, circuses, and medical research (which many animal rights activists do reject).

- Wearing fur is a very personal choice issue. Most people reject some or all of the animal rights agenda.

Note that both sides agree that a basic human right is to decide whether or not to wear fur. It would be quite arrogant for you to tell your friend not to wear the fur because of animal rights. It is not an illegal product, and so she should have freedom of choice. However, if you agree with the animal rights activists, you should diplomatically (tactfully) use the educational approach to try to sway her to share your convictions.

2.   *After 76 years in the Southwest Athletic Conference, the University of Arkansas switched to the Southwest Conference to obtain higher television revenues. Did the University violate any norms?*

Norms are situation-specific rules of conduct. In the business world, loyalties are often broken (e.g., switching advertising agencies or suppliers) in order to increase profitability. Professional sports teams also often break loyalties with their fans when they relocate to different cities. Of course the fans claim this is unfair, but the teams remind them that they are a business and need to go where the grass is greener.

On the other hand, academic teams should have other goals in mind, so some say. Since they are nonprofit institutions, and state schools (such as the University of Arkansas) are supported by taxpayers, they should not be engaged in the business of profit maximization. Furthermore, their players are not even being paid. Some would thus claim that schools should not jump ship and abandon old loyalties to leagues and fans by switching leagues.

Others would argue that, in fact, academic sports teams from major universities are businesses. The teams serve as the universities' cash cows, allowing money to be invested in other worthwhile ventures. Thus, cross-subsidization of other worthwhile university activities is said to be a worthy ends served by a means

that might not please everyone. Penn State used this justification a few years
ago when it joined the Big Ten.

In some cases, it might be argued that money-making teams reduce the tax burden
on the state's people.

The critics reply that sports should not be used to pay the bills for other
school activities. Why can't other areas of the schools be self supporting?

3.   *This chapter began by indicating that pawn shops are now marketing
     themselves as "lending institutions for the working poor." Does this
     service raise any ethical issues?*

Some people are disturbed that pawn shops cater to the working poor. They argue
that these outlets are taking advantage of a group which is ignorant about how to
manage their finances (for instance, many don't use banks and pay high fees to
have checks cashed). They would also say that pawn shops "rip off" their
customers, paying less for the hocked items than they are really worth.

Others, however, would say that pawn shop proprietors are providing a valuable
and needed service for their clientele. They have practiced the marketing
concept, finding a need (for ready cash) and filling it (lending it, usually in
$50 increments). Presumably, without the pawn shops, some people would be
strapped for cash. The money earned by pawn shops is simply a fee for services
rendered. If the proprietors were earning abnormal profits, they would be
"competed away" in a free marketplace.

Critics would reply that what is needed is education. Pawn shop customers should
be taught (presumably by government or nonprofit groups) how to manage their
money (and perhaps their lives) so they don't find themselves in dire straits.

GUIDE TO CASES

VIDEO CASE 6-1   MALL OF AMERICA[1]

SUBJECT MATTER: Environmental Factors,   Trends in Retailing,   Cultural
                            Effects on Marketing

                            Please see the Guide to Video Cases for video
                            length and other information.

AT-A-GLANCE OVERVIEW

Mall of America in Bloomington, Minnesota, is the world's second largest shopping
center. It is four stories tall and includes 4.2 million square feet. That's 34
times bigger than the average shopping center. Developers hope to lure 40
million people a year, over 110,000 daily, and a billion in up-front investment
is on the line. They predict hundreds of thousands of visitors from Japan alone.
The Mall employs 60 people just to help customers find their way around the Mall.
Knott's Camp Snoopy, a four-story miniature golf "mountain," Bloomingdale's,
Macy's, Sears, Nordstrom, six huge night clubs, hotels, a plethora of public rest
rooms, and many specialty stores are in the center. There will be an Underwater
World aquarium, 14 movie theaters, and more than 270 shops. But many respected
economic observers predict, if not failure, difficulty in making money on the
project. They note that the country may well be over-built with shopping
centers. There is, they point out, at this writing, 19 square feet of center
space for every U.S. resident.

Just before Mall of America opened in Bloomington, Minnesota, many others
wondered if the huge project would be a success.

---

[1] Excerpts reprinted from Can Koeppel, "Mall of America: The Malls,:
Adweek's Marketing Week, June 22, 1992, pp. 20-24.

DISCUSSION QUESTIONS

1.   *What environmental trends favor Mall of America? Which trends may be
      detrimental to its success?*

Mall of America promotes itself as being in the geographical center of North
America. The first environmental factor of concern in Bloomingdale
(Minneapolis), Minnesota, is the weather. The weather is quite cold in the
winter. (Cars are equipped with electric heaters that you plug in when you park,
and leaving a car outdoors overnight is viewed as something to be avoided.) On
the other hand, it can be quite warm during the summer months. This
environmental factor has had an impact on the building of a major enclosed mall
like Mall of America. The only other mall of its type in Edmonton, Canada, is
also in a very cold climate. The shopper, visitor, and traveler can spend an
entire vacation under one roof. Thus, winter weather is not a factor as long as
the visitor can get to the mall, and this should not be a major problem since in
that part of the country the equipment needed to clear the roads of snow is
available. People in that area seldom let winter weather interfere with their
plans.

Mall of America is located at the intersection of two interstate highway systems.
Americans drive to the places where they shop. The suburban lifestyle in the
1950s created the shopping centers. The automobile still has an impact on
shopping. The Minneapolis area has, besides the interstates, a good road
network. However, when the Mall opened, the traffic was so great that the roads
approaching the Mall will have to be reconfigured. This process is being planned
now (late 1992). Obviously, this should be done as quickly as possible if
customer satisfaction is to be maintained.

The trend toward air travel rather than driving places for a vacation is also
another positive fact. Many visitors from the Mall of America were expected to
be from Japan. Arguably, this is an "international mall." The Mall of America
being conveniently located near the airport in Minneapolis successfully
complements this idea.

Another positive trend is the trend towards leisure. The Mall of America
confines the drawing power of a regional shopping mall with the excitement of an
entertainment center. Knotts's Camp Snoopy is at the heart of the mall.
Visiting theme parks is another environmental trend.

The trend toward airline travel on vacations also influences the hotels near
entertainment sources. For example there are many hotels near Disney World. In
Mall of America, there are hotels in the mall so that shoppers and visitors can
take advantage of the amusement park activities. We should note that at the time
of the Mall's opening, the airlines were involved in a "price war" and all manner
of travellers were using the airlines. It is possible that the airlines might
stop this kind of price competition (and may have by the time you are analyzing
this case) thereby lessening the Mall's appeal to distant consumers.

Income trends, as the video explains, are also positive for Mall of America.

High technology is reflected in Mall of America. The people mover is an example.

What environmental trends may be detrimental to Mall of America's success?

As mentioned, shifts in air fares could hurt the mall. Also, major increases in
gasoline prices are possible, especially if certain plans to more heavily tax gas
are put into place.

Mall of America was originally intended to be larger than the West Edmonton mall
in Canada. However, in 1988, the retail industry had problems due to the
publicity surrounding over-leveraged junk bond deals and a general down turn in
consumer spending. In fact, during 1991, '92, and '93, retail failure rates were
quite high, due largely to a trend to cut back on purchases at full-price
specialty shops and to patronize, instead, places like Wal-Mart.

Another detrimental trend is the fact that retailing already has a large supply
of shopping outlets including major shopping centers and specialty stores not
only in Minnesota but in the rest of the United States.

In the retail industry, during tough economic times, stores like Wal-Mart and other discounters generally do better than department stores and specialty stores that dominate a place like Mall of America. (The case mentions that Daytons, the major department store in Minneapolis, refused to go into the Mall.)

2.   *What place does the shopping center play in American culture? How does the Mall of America reflect American culture?*

The cultural goal of suburban life and movement away from the city is reflected in the Mall of America which is located in suburban Bloomington, Minnesota. The shopping center has taken the place of the old downtown. Today shopping centers serve as meeting places for teenagers and the place for events such as charity activities. Indeed, in many urban shopping centers the Halloween ritual, Christmas "parades," and Easter egg hunts, take place in the shopping center rather than in the neighborhoods.

The Mall of America reflects America in many ways. For example, eating outside the home is a part of American culture. The food court reflects this aspect of American culture. Self-indulgence is another mark of much of American life. Treating children, and other folks, as people who should be coddled is reflected in Mall of America with the miniature golf courses, theaters, and other amusements that indulge. The Imagination Center which incudes 60 large-scale Lego models, appeals to this cultural value, and it is (vaguely) educational. The night clubs, restaurants, and hotels reflect both indulgence and the movement of these sorts of institutions away from their traditional locations in the city.

Regional cultures are also reflected in Mall of America. For example, Paul Bunyon and Babe the Blue Ox are part of Camp Snoopy. And the shopping avenues, such as East Broadway, reflect aspects of American culture.

3.   *What norms and roles are commonplace in shopping behavior?*

The two most prominent roles in consumer behavior are shopper and store clerk. Clearly the shopper expects certain courtesies and deferential behavior from store clerks. Children learn the shopper role very early in life. For example, a mother may give a five-dollar bill to the child who in turn is to give it to the clerk. Children are often asked to pick something out for themselves. Consumers are socialized into the shopper role. The role of parent as teacher and provider can be seen, as can the role of child as obeying (??!!) the instructions of the parent.

The basic norms of the shopper are to be honest and courteous. Another norm when there is a crowd is that the shopper is expected to wait for a certain period but not too long. In the theme park business, park workers are expected to be even more friendly to families on their vacations. This is true in restaurants and hotels too.

4.   *Will Mall of America be a success? Why or Why not?*

On the day the Mall opened, the crowds were enormous. The Mall opened earlier in the day than had been intended because of the crush of people. During the first week Mall of America was open one million visitors visited the mall. This kind of attention continued through the first five months of operation. Furthermore, the mall opened in August and the tourism department booked 1,200 bus tours between August 15th and the end of the year. So at the outset the Mall of America was clearly a success. The question is whether the success is sustainable in the long run. For example, the expectation that 200,000 Japanese will patronize the Mall annually is either a stroke of genius or a pipe-dream. By the time you are analyzing this case, the answer may be common knowledge.

Indoor mall or not, travel can be rough in many months in the old Northwest Territory. The Mall advertises itself as in the geographic center of North America, but look at the map. Minneapolis is at the center alright, but there's a lot of empty space between Minneapolis and Seattle, and virtually nothing but thinly populated plains and tundra and ice on up to the top of North America. Off to the southwest the population's pretty thin too, until you get to Los Angeles. This idea of being at the center of the continent would appear to be more a slogan than anything meaningful.

On the other hand, the huge mall in Edmonton, Alberta, seems to survive, and it is located in a part of Canada that is relatively sparsely populated.

In short, it is hard to imagine that the planners of this huge project, and all the retailers who moved in, are totally wrong in their expectations. We find it hard to believe that the Mall will be a complete failure. However, we imagine that the changes wrought in the economy right about the time that the Mall opened made the Mall's supporters "sweat" some.

Students considering this case in class will have more information than is available to us at this writing. An assignment might be to check the *Business Periodical Index* for stories relating to the Mall's current status, with an eye to determining causes for its success (or failure).

CASE 6-2   ORE-BEST FARMS

SUBJECT MATTER: Consumer Behavior, Marketing Concept, Cultural
                                   Environment, Class, Reference Groups

AT-A-GLANCE OVERVIEW

Ore-Ida Best Farms is a rabbit processing plant that markets vacuum-packed rabbit fryers. The packaging includes recipes for preparing the "tender, country-raised" rabbit. The advertising stresses taste and nutrition, but keeps carefully away from anything suggestive of cute bunnies. The company plans to market ground rabbit, cutlets, fillets, etc. as have the chicken and turkey growers. The taste of the all-white meat is similar to veal. The company can sell nonedible parts of the rabbits (like the fur) to other firms. Foreign countries have expressed interest in Ore-Best rabbit growing and packaging processes.

Statistics show that rabbit is high in protein and low in cholesterol, fat, and calories. The price of rabbit is very competitive with other meats. Yet, rabbit meat is not a staple in the American diet, and accounts for about one-half cent of each dollar spent on meat. In Europe this figure is 15 cents. There rabbit is a dietary staple.

The case explores the cultural aspects of eating rabbit.

DISCUSSION QUESTIONS

1.   *What cultural factors will help the marketing of Ore-Best Farms rabbit meat product? Which will hinder the marketing of their rabbit meat products?*

Since "culture" consists of everything we are not born with, that is, everything other than our most basic innate needs, it is possible to link an almost infinite number of cultural aspects to everything we do.

While students will certainly come up with more connections between culture and the eating of rabbit meat than we can here, we list the following points, intending them to help get discussion started. We are sure no definitive answer for this question exists.

Factors Helping the Marketing of Rabbit Meat

.   The meat is nutritionally sound. It is the lowest of all meats in
       cholesterol, fat, and calories, and the highest in protein. While some
       will refuse to eat rabbit despite these facts, the facts do fit in
       perfectly with our current concerns over heart trouble, calories, and
       general good health.

.   The packaging is similar to bacon packages. We are all familiar with this
       packaging so there will be no culture shock in that department. Further,
       the packaging will diminish the perception that this is "a bunny." A whole
       rabbit might prove less appealing than one packaged like bacon.

.   Rabbit meat tastes and looks like chicken or veal. It can be cooked much
       like chicken too. This fits in with the lifestyles of most North

Americans. Chicken and veal are not everyone's favorites but most people like these meats occasionally or at least accept them.

- People who like veal are constantly reminded of the conditions under which veal calves are raised. No such problem with rabbit.

- We cook our meats in this culture. Ore-Best is providing recipes to help us get used to rabbit cooking.

- Rabbit meat is popular in Europe. This has more cultural appeal in the U.S. and Canada than does making the claim that rabbit meat is popular in Ethiopia or Pago Pago.

- Cutting rabbit meat into "cutlets, fillets, ground meat, pates, sausages" etc. further disguises the loveable bunny.

- There already are many people in the U.S. who eat rabbit meat at least on occasion. These include hunters, those who raise and/or trap some of their own food, and certain ethnic groups.

- Our cultural attachment to rabbit's feet as good luck charms, the fact that we use fur products, and other cultural characteristics, play into Ore-Best's plans to make profit on the entire rabbit -- meat, feet, fur, etc.

Factors Hindering the Marketing of Rabbit Meat

- We think rabbits are cute and cuddly. We use the rabbit as a holiday symbol at Easter. We have such famous rabbits as Bugs Bunny to think about. These are cultural elements that don't seem to bother European rabbit eaters as they might U.S. citizens and Canadians.

- When it comes to food, we are often reluctant to try new items, even if they are highly recommended to us. Many people still won't "eat their vegetables" despite years of prodding. How many Americans have tried or regularly eat snake meat, exotic animals, "strange" vegetables, bugs, snails, frogs' legs, or even certain fish products?

- Though some of us may be willing to try rabbit, we may be reluctant because of the cultural hang-ups of others: our children who think we killed the Easter Bunny, the friends who think the whole idea is "gross," and so on.

- Our cultural "prohibition" against eating rabbit will, of itself, delay acceptance. Many consumers may feel that they don't know how to prepare rabbit, or can't tell a good rabbit from a bad one, etc. Of course, Ore-Best is seeking to diminish the effect of this cultural inertia by providing consumers with recipes and a new kind of packaging and promotion.

- The fact that the product tastes more like veal than anything else is something of a cultural hinderance. Veal is not as commonly eaten by Americans and Canadians as is, say, hamburger and chicken. To some people veal has a "foreign" Italian/French connotation.

2. *Will social class be a consideration? Will the product be most appealing to one particular class?*

The case points out that U.S. consumers spend one-half cent of their "meat dollar" on rabbit compared with 15 cents in Europe. Thus, very little rabbit is consumed in the U.S. This is a small sample on which to base any judgment; however, it is possible to imagine that class will have some effect on rabbit sales.

Note that rabbit is comparable in price to beef, not the cheaper chicken it seems to resemble. Thus, it is not an inexpensive meat. This suggests that lower classes might not buy it. However, it is also true that rural people already keep rabbits for consumption. They also hunt rabbits for food. It is likely then that some people who might be judged as "poor" or lower class are likely to be customers.

At the same time, it is likely that upper classes might be likely rabbit meat adopters. The appeal of dining as do Europeans and the willingness to experiment with new foods and recipes that characterize this group make them adopter candidates. This group also manifests concern for healthy foods and lifestyles.

Often the middle classes are the most conservative in these matters -- less likely to "kill the Easter Bunny and eat him" than the upper classes trying to appear suave or adventurous, and the lower classes trying to stretch the food budget.

It is interesting to note that Ore-Brands is starting out on the West Coast. This is understandable given that the plant is in Oregon, but it may be that the matter of class is less important than the simple matter of location. California was in the first market area served, and Ore-Brand's second plant was planned for Southern California. This may be because of "lifestyle" considerations.

By the time this case is in use in classrooms, stories will have appeared in the business press detailing the success or failure of this venture. A good assignment would be to have students try to find out what parts of the country have accepted the product and which have not, and whether class, economics, or other factors have played major roles.

3.   *Will reference groups be influential in the consumer's decision to purchase rabbit meat?*

A good approach to this matter would be to have students list the various reference groups shown in the text and then discourse upon their likely effects on the decision to purchase the product.

It appears that the effect of the groups will be situational.

.   A person with small children will have to consider the children's reaction to eating "bunny."

.   Another situational variable would be the occasion of use. One could try rabbit meat in the privacy of the home but be reluctant to serve it to company. Or one might be willing to serve it to adventurous friends but not to grandmother.

.   If some "in" restaurant begins serving rabbit to an enthusiastic celebrity clientele, eating rabbit might become the fashionable thing to do.

.   Certain buyers may be inspired by their European aspirational or membership groups to try the product. Others may shy away from an "unAmerican" dinner meat.

.   Since reference groups influence almost all purchases in some way, it is likely that their effects will be strong in this case involving acceptance of a food that is new to many and colored with our perceptions.

At this writing, by the way, Ore-Best is planning new processing plants and getting together with the few U.S. producers of rabbit meat to develop a cooperative promotional effort to encourage primary demand for rabbit meat products. This cooperation is possible because the total industry (rabbit meat) is still so small that competition has yet to heat up. Also, at the time of this writing, Ore-Best is processing many more rabbits per year than it did the year before. So, it seems, sales are hopping right along.

7 BUSINESS MARKETS AND ORGANIZATIONAL BUYING

CHAPTER SCAN

The text as a whole gives considerable attention to industrial/ organizational marketing, but the importance of this topic requires that special attention be focused on it. Industrial or organizational markets include all sorts of buyers and products (except consumers and consumer products) bought in straight rebuy, modified rebuy, and new task purchase situations. Thus, manufacturers, churches, governmental units, etc. are included in this market. The concept of the buying center helps explain their purchasing behavior.

Industrial/organizational products rely on derived demand for their sale. Buying motives surrounding them may differ from those surrounding consumer goods. Thus, certain marketing tools (such as the SIC system) and techniques are especially applicable to this area of marketing.

SUGGESTED LEARNING OBJECTIVES

The student who studies this chapter will be exposed to a review of the industrial/organizational marketplace and will be able to:

1. Identify the types of organizations that make up the business or organizational market.

2. Know the steps involved in an organizational buyer decision.

3. Characterize the three basic organizational buying situations: the straight rebuy, the modified rebuy, and the new task purchase.

4. Explain why the buying center concept is important to business-to-business marketing.

5. Appreciate the needs of organizational buyers and explain how marketers can react to those needs.

6. Describe the nature of industrial demand.

7.   Describe the SIC system and analyze its usefulness to marketers.

CHAPTER 7 OUTLINE

I.   INTRODUCTION

II.   ORGANIZATIONAL BUYING BEHAVIOR

III.   CHARACTERISTICS OF THE BUSINESS MARKET

IV.   THREE KINDS OF BUYING

V.   THE BUYING CENTER

    A.   How One Buying Center Worked
    B.   Roles in the Buying Center

VI.   WHY DO ORGANIZATIONS BUY?

    A.   Product Quality
    B.   Related Services
    C.   Prices
    D.   Reliable Delivery and Inventory Management
    E.   The Bottom Line

VII.   THE NATURE OF INDUSTRIAL DEMAND

    A.   Derived Demand
    B.   Price Inelasticity
    C.   Fluctuating Demand

VIII. THE SIC SYSTEM: CLASSIFYING BUSINESS MARKETS

IX.   SUMMARY

X.   KEY TERMS

XI.   QUESTIONS FOR DISCUSSION (8)

XII.   ETHICS IN PRACTICE

XIII. CASE

The following key terms are introduced in Chapter 7.   They are defined in the text's Glossary.

Business-to-business marketing transaction
Organizational buying behavior
Strategic alliance
Buy phase
Straight rebuy
Modified rebuy
New task buying
Buying center
User
Buyer
Gatekeeper
Decider
Influencer
Single sourcing
Derived demand
Acceleration principle
Standard Industrial Classification (SIC) system

THE CHAPTER SUMMARIZED

I.   INTRODUCTION

During the 1980s, Xerox had a problem. Service calls were up as were complaints of unreliability. But service people were reporting that the calls they were making usually were unnecessary. Xerox taped members of their own staff using photocopiers at Xerox. It was found that Xerox's own people had trouble using the "idiot proof" machines engineering had produced. The machines in the field weren't really broken. People just had trouble figuring out how to use them. Making the machines easier to use solved this buyer/supplier problem in the business marketplace.

II.   ORGANIZATIONAL BUYING BEHAVIOR

A **business marketing transaction** takes place whenever a good or service is sold for any use other than personal consumption.

Thus, the marketing process is **business-to-business,** and is termed **business-to-business marketing.**

Is a given product a consumer or an organizational product? Ask two questions.

   .   Who bought it?
   .   Why did they buy it?

Notice that what the product is is basically not important here.

Manufacturers require raw materials, component parts, supplies and services to produce both consumer and industrial products. Producers of non-manufactured goods, such as farmers, buy and use industrial goods. So do wholesalers, retailers, hospitals, nonprofit organizations, federal, state, and local government units. (The federal government is the largest single buyer of industrial products.)

All these sales are made to organizations, so the term **organizational buying behavior** may be substituted for the word "industrial" when we speak of industrial marketing or industrial buyer behavior.

The purchase of industrial, or organizational, goods and services can be a complex matter. Need must be determined, information sought, evaluations of alternatives performed, and negotiations with supplying organizations completed. This requires internal and external communication, establishment of financial relationships, and knowledgeable and rational individuals. The buying process is generally not simple, and may be spelled out in corporate manuals in a step-by-step manner.

Exhibit 7-1 illustrates some business buying behaviors.

III. CHARACTERISTICS OF THE BUSINESS MARKET

Though types of industrial buyers are all quite different from one another, they share certain characteristics, especially when compared to consumer goods buyers.

   .   Fewer in number (only a few firms make tires, for example).

   .   More geographically concentrated.

   .   Preference for direct purchase, in part, due to a desire to buy in
          large amounts (perhaps to earn larger quantity discounts) and, in
          part, because many industrial products are of a technical sort and/or
          made-to-order.

   .   A tendency to repeat transactions, that is, to buy over and over
          again from the same supplier. This has led to a focus on the series
          of exchanges rather than the single purchase. The phrase
          relationship marketing refers to the developing of strong working-

together relationships that serve the interest of buyer and seller. Some informal partnerships, called **strategic alliances**, have been formed that permit such things as Sherwin-Williams permitting Sears executives to help select the Sherwin-Williams sales people who would service the Sears account.

. Comparative expertise in buying, a tendency to buy in a "scientific" way, basing purchases on close analyses of products and alternatives.

All of these suggest marketing responses. Geographic concentration of a few well-informed customers suggest having an organization's own sales force of well-trained people calling directly on buyers.

IV.   THREE KINDS OF BUYING

The industrial buyer goes through a decision-making process similar to, but more complex than, that of a consumer (as discussed in Chapters 5 and 6). Exhibit 7-2 illustrates the buy phases or steps in the multi-phased organizational buying decision. Industrial buyer behavior phases are shown in Exhibit 7-2. Other models exist.

The amount of time and effort spent in completing each stage is likely to vary with the situation. There are three basic situations.

. The **straight rebuy** wherein an organization is buying goods or services from a regular supplier. The process is "automatic." Everything can be bought in this manner, if the buyer is satisfied with the seller's product and performance.

. The **modified rebuy** applies when the buyer thinks it may be of value to "shop around."

. The **new task** buying situation exists when the organization has a need it has not faced before. It is not aware of what products or suppliers will best fill its needs. If the purchase is expected to be an expensive one, the sense of uncertainty is heightened.

Exhibit 7-3 describes the characteristics of these three buying situations. Each situation suggests a different marketing goal and marketing mix. These are presented briefly in Exhibit 7-4.

V.   THE BUYING CENTER

Many individuals are involved in an organization's buying process.

The **buying center** idea encompasses these as an informal, cross-departmental decision unit in which the primary objective is the acquisition, impartation, and processing of relevant purchasing-related information.

The buying center includes all people and groups that have a role in the decision-making process of purchasing. They share the goals and risks involved. The size of the buying center may vary from decision to decision and during a single decision-making process. It may range in size from a few people to perhaps 20. It is not on the organization chart. Membership is essentially informal so no "announcement" of who is in and who is out is made.

A.   How One Buying Center Worked

Buying centers have been studied in a formal way. What people at a hospital might participate in the purchase decisions related to an expensive piece of equipment? At least these: doctors, nurses, hospital administrators, engineers, purchasing department. How the importance of their roles would vary as the decision process unfolds is shown in Exhibit 7-5.

B.   Roles in the Buying Center

These roles are to be played in the buying center: users,
gatekeepers, influencers, deciders, buyers. (These are the same
roles as were identified in Chapter 6 in connection with consumer
buying decisions). Their importance can vary widely from
circumstance to circumstance, but the seller's big job is to figure
out who really must be dealt with.

An example is the purchasing agent who may simply be filling out
forms and have "nothing to say" about a given purchase. It is worth
the effort to study the ramifications of the buying center in
particular marketing situations.

Five generalized buying roles are identified.

   .   Users - those who actually use the product. They may have
        little influence on the actual decision to buy.

   .   Gatekeepers - those who influence purchases by controlling the
        flow of information (perform the gatekeeper function) as might
        a person assigned to collect literature from potential
        suppliers.

   .   Deciders - those who make the actual purchase decision.

   .   Influencers - those who affect the purchase by supplying advice
        or information.

   .   Buyers - those who formally purchase the product, e.g., the
        purchasing agent.

It is certainly in the marketer's interests to devote time and
interest in investigating the effects of the buying center in the
marketing situation at hand.

VI.   WHY DO ORGANIZATIONS BUY?

There is some debate whether or not rational buying motives always dominate
emotional buying motives in an industrial buying situation. Some suggest
that dominance virtually excludes the so-called "irrational" buying
motives. Yet pride in having "the best" seems to play a part on occasion,
as does the salesperson's or ad's persuasiveness. It is the text's
position that emotional buying motives can be seen, in almost every case,
as incidental to the buying process. No buyer, is the contention, would
endanger his or her job by buying a product just because the salesperson
gave out good theater tickets.

This discussion focuses on a few of the most influential purchasing
criteria with the caveat that each of these generally comes down to a
"bottom line" criterion.

A.   Product Quality

Few industrial buyers fail to closely analyze the product purchased,
though the scrutiny is less than painstaking for such products as
thumbtacks, unless they are somehow defective. Many products,
including services, are made to the buyer's specifications,
indicating close consideration of exactly what is required.

Total Quality Management (TQM) programs have become so important to
certain buyers that they will not buy from suppliers who have not
adopted TQM programs of their own.

B.   Related Services

Services are particularly important to industrial buyers. Lack of
supplies, parts, repair, etc. causes "downtime." Marketing

strategies to achieve high service quality are discussed in Chapter 13.

C.   Prices

Demand for industrial goods may be price inelastic, but this doesn't mean buyers don't pay close attention to price levels. Industrial marketers frequently face strong competition from producers of the same or substitutable products. A bidding system may be employed and industrial buyers can be expected to "know prices" far better than do consumers. Further, their expert product knowledge allows them to closely evaluate value.

D.   Reliable Delivery and Inventory Management

The term **single sourcing** refers to buying from a single vendor. Close cooperation can lead to delivery of required items just as the buyer's supplies are becoming depleted. This topic is dealt with more fully in Chapter 16.

E.   The Bottom Line

Companies need products to make their own products. Good service may be extremely important. No buying motive stands alone. They all interplay in the buyer's mind. Yet the bottom line is always the same. It's summed up in this statement on General Motors' truck and coach business: "GM customers don't buy these vehicles because they like them - they need them to make money."

VIII. THE NATURE OF INDUSTRIAL DEMAND

The demand for industrial goods differs significantly from the demand for consumer goods as the following three sections suggest.

A.   Derived Demand

As we saw earlier in the text, the demand for certain products is strongly linked to the demand for other products (the demand for windows and doors is linked to the demand for houses). This is **derived demand.**

All demand for organizational products is derived from consumer demand for ultimate products. Ford Motor Company would not buy so much as a pencil unless it thought that pencil could be used to "help sell cars" to consumers. Government purchase of cars can be traced to consumer demand, though of the grudging sort, for government services involving cars. In fact, the suppliers who sell Ford parts, tools and cleaning services rely, ultimately, on consumers' direct and indirect demand for Ford cars. This reliance on derived demand is suggestive of the immense effect a cessation of consumer demand for any product would have on many organizations. For example, consider how many firms would be "hurt" if consumers stopped drinking beer in cans. The phrase **acceleration principle** has been coined to describe how a small increase or decrease in demand for a product at the consumer end of the channel would "whip lash" through the economy.

1.   The Significance of Derived Demand

The workings of derived demand are such that some producers of products can attempt to stimulate a primary demand in the hope that its effects will "work back" to them. Example: ads encouraging consumers to buy milk in plastic jugs are usually sponsored not by producers of milk or plastic jugs, but by producers of machines that make plastic jugs or by oil companies whose products are used to make plastics. Thus, steps can be taken to use derived demand to increase the sales of an industrial product though the "distance" from the true source of demand may make it hard to focus on.

B.   Price Inelasticity

Most industrial buyers are not particularly sensitive to price for at least two reasons:

- They are in a position to "pass along" price increases to their own customers (assuming demand is healthy).

- Most industrial products represent a small proportion of the price of the final products they go to produce. If the demand for Chrysler mini-vans is firm, a rise in the price of sheet metal will have little effect on that demand since the increase "gets lost" in the price of the finished van.

There are exceptions, especially in the short-run. (Example: a buyer faced with a price cut might not buy in hopes that there will be further cuts) but demand for organizational products is, in general, price inelastic.

C.   Fluctuating Demand

When compared to the demand for most consumer goods, the demand for industrial/organizational goods fluctuates widely. Some reasons are:

- As the economy moves up and down, so does the demand for most industrial goods.

- Many industrial goods are "postponable purchases."

- Many machines can be fixed rather than replaced.

- Many industrial products (e.g., boilers) have long lives.

- Many buyers "stock up" on purchases such as parts or raw materials.

VIII. THE SIC SYSTEM: CLASSIFYING BUSINESS MARKETS

Knowing what kinds, how many, and other facts about what customers are "out there" would obviously be a big help to an industrial marketer. Fortunately, there is a great deal of data available, most of it classified using the **Standard Industrial Classification (SIC)** system which was developed by the federal government.

The SIC system is based on code numbers. The longer the code number, the more detailed the description. The "primary divisions" are shown in an exhibit in the text. The system is widely used in government and non-government publications. In fact, users of the system often refer to an "industry" meaning, not as others might, the farming industry, for example, but meaning a 4-digit product code in the SIC system.

Example:

26	=	manufacturers of paper and allied products
264	=	converted paper and paper board products excluding containers and boxes
2648	=	stationery products
26482	=	tablets and related products

An example of usage of SIC codes to calculate a geographic market potential is given in the text.

IX. SUMMARY

This chapter explores the industrial or organizational marketplace along with buying practices and marketing efforts appropriate to this special market. The behavior of industrial/organizational buyers often differ significantly from that of ultimate consumers.

Learning Objective 1: Identify the types of organizations that make up the business or organizational market.

The business or organizational market is composed of all businesses, nonprofit groups, charitable and religious organizations, governmental units, and other nonconsumers. Thus, a marketer's organizational customers may include manufacturers, farmers, churches, schools, and a host of others.

Learning Objective 2: Know the steps followed in an organizational buying decision.

Organizational buying takes place over time, involves communications among several organizational members, and demands financial relationships with suppliers. An organizational buying decision is the result of a multistage process that includes: (1) anticipating or recognizing a problem, (2) determining the characteristics and quantity of product needed, (3) describing product specifications and critical needs, (4) searching for and qualifying potential sources, (5) acquiring and analyzing proposals, (6) evaluating proposals and selecting suppliers, (7) selecting an order routine, and (8) using feedback to evaluate performance.

Learning Objective 3: Characterize the three basic organizational buying situations: the straight rebuy; the modified rebuy; and the new task purchase.

The straight rebuy requires no review of products or suppliers; materials are ordered automatically when the need arises. The modified rebuy occurs when buyers are discontented with present products or supplier performance and investigate alternative sources. The new task purchase involves an evaluating product specifications and reviewing possible vendors in a purchase situation new to the organization.

Learning Objective 4: Explain why the buying center concept is important to business-to-business marketing.

The buying center is an informal network of persons with various roles in the purchasing-decision process. The people and their roles vary over time. Roles including users gatekeepers, influencers, deciders, and buyers can be identified in the process. Marketers must identify members of the buying center and evaluate their importance to the buying process at various stages in the process.

Learning Objective 5: Appreciate the needs of organizational buyers and explain how marketers can react to those needs.

Buyers of organizational products may seek certain product attributes such as quality, efficiency, long life, or reliability. They may seek low price, favorable credit terms, assured delivery, or information, repair service, and supplies from the seller. These needs must be determined by the marketer so that the marketing mix can be altered to meet them.

Learning Objective 6: Describe the nature of organizational demand.

Consumer buying decisions can affect many organizations because demand for products in the organizational marketplace ultimately depends on consumer demand, even when a particular purchasing decision is quite removed from consumers. Organizational demand is price inelastic in that the amounts of products demanded by buyers are not likely to change significantly as the prices for the products rise and fall. Finally, for a number of reasons, the demand for industrial goods fluctuates widely.

Learning Objective 7: Describe the SIC system and analyze its usefulness to marketers.

The SIC system, a coding method used to classify many organizations, can be used to identify products, individual manufacturers, purchasers of various products, and other useful facts. Government, trade associations, and other sources use these codes to categorize information. Marketers who understand the system have access to vast amounts of published data and can use the codes to determine market potentials and gain other insights into the structure of markets.

X. KEY TERMS

XI. QUESTIONS FOR DISCUSSION (8)

XII. ETHICS IN PRACTICE

XIII. CASE

ANSWER GUIDELINES FOR CHAPTER 7 QUESTIONS FOR DISCUSSION

1. *In what ways does organizational marketing differ from consumer marketing?*

ANSWER:

This is a very "large" question, but a traditional approach to the discussion of organizational marketing has been to compare it to consumer goods marketing.

Students, especially if this question is handled as a classroom discussion item, can name many differences. They might then be asked to group them according to the four Ps or some other classification system.

The following fifteen items are just some of the many points that could be mentioned, and are intended only as a means to start the answering process, not to provide a definitive list.

Organizational marketing differs from consumer marketing in that:

. There are fewer customers.
. Customers are more geographically concentrated.
. Customers are more "rational" in their buying and patronage motives.
. Customers are better informed about products and options and often prefer to buy directly from makers.
. Customers frequently draw up product specifications.
. Leasing and trade-ins are more common.
. Selling through catalogs and trade shows is more common.
. Derived demand is of utmost importance.
. Buyers may make decisions via a committee approach.
. Salespeople must be more knowledgeable (in a scientific sense).
. Reciprocity is far more commonly found.
. Advertising is far more narrowly focused, e.g., using specialized trade magazines.
. The role of the buying center (and those of its members) has been used to help explain organizational buyer behavior.
. Demand is more price inelastic.
. Buyers are better able to analyze price.
. Guaranteed distribution and uniform quality of product are generally more important.

2. *Compare and contrast the consumer decision-making process and the organization's decision-making process.*

ANSWER:

The chapter makes much of the organizational buying center concept. This could be described as somewhat similar to a consumer household's decision-making process for jointly used items. Whether in a family or organization, buying

center participants perform similar functions. Both processes involve a rather
rational approach to purchase decisions but differ in degree.

The consumer decision-making process was outlined suggesting that these steps be
followed. (Oversimplification admitted, to be sure.)

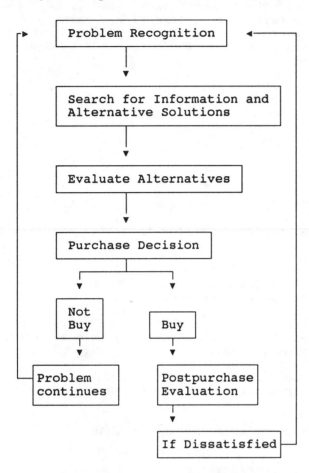

There are many very complicated models to describe the organizational buying
process. The treatment in Chapter 7 of this text suggests this series of steps
in an organizational buying decision (based on Exhibit 7-2).

Anticipation or Recognition of a Problem (need)
▼
Determination of the characteristics of the
product and the quantity needed
▼
Description of precise product specification
and critical needs
▼
Search for and qualification of potential sources
▼
Acquisition and analysis of proposals
▼
Evaluation of proposals and selection of suppliers
▼
Selection of an order routine
▼
Performance feedback and evaluation

This sequence of events would be significantly speeded up and/or modified
depending on the buying situation. In general, a new task buying situation would
involve "all" steps, while a straight rebuy situation would move from step one
("out of paper clips" = "recognize need") to buy from the selected (regular)

suppliers. The modified rebuy situation would mean that the full process might not be completed, but the focus would rest (depending on why the process was being modified) on particular steps. While the processes are similar to one another, since both reflect a logical approach to a problem situation, they differ in detail and in the lengths of time they would typically take to complete. Further, the comparative potency of irrational/emotional and rational motives would vary. We suggest, therefore, that class discussion might be aided by the use of the list of characteristics of organizational marketing developed in response to the previous question.

3.   *For the following products, indicate whether the buying task will be a straight rebuy, modified rebuy, or a new buying task: (a) lawn maintenance service for the Mercedes-Benz regional headquarters building in suburban New Jersey, (b) roller bearings as a component part for Snapper lawn mowers, (c) an industrial robot to perform a function currently done manually, and (d) personal computers for top-level managers.*

ANSWER:

Situations vary, but, given certain assumptions, these buying tasks might be categorized as follows.

(a)   Lawn maintenance service

The mention of "headquarters" without the adjective "new" suggests an established corporate headquarters. This indicates that the situation is a modified rebuy case since we assume that there is an existing lawn and that somehow it has been taken care of to this point, but that the service has been somehow unsatisfactory.

Some corporations do move to nearby H.Q.s and use the same satisfactory lawn service used at the old location. This would be a straight rebuy. Some corporations move from no-lawn city locations to suburban locations with lawns. Such a situation would be a new task buying case.

(b)   Roller bearings as a component part

Chances are this is a straight rebuy, unless, of course, no bearings of this type had ever been bought before because no product using bearings was produced (new task), or the current supplier has been unsatisfactory in some way (modified rebuy).

(c)   Industrial robot to perform a production function currently done manually

The key phrase here is "currently done manually." This means the organization is shifting away from a traditional means of accomplishing a task to a modern or, at least, new to the organization, method. Thus, the situation is a new task buying situation.

(d)   Personal computers for top-level managers

The question suggests that this purchase could be of replacement computers or new computers. Thus, this could be a new buying task or a modified rebuy.

It might be noted, however, that certain models may be more familiar than others, and executives may have preferences or, possibly, a favorite model or two at home.

Thus, the new buying task paradigm might apply but not without some softening influences. A PC is not the same "new buy" as a nuclear weapons system.

Given the expense involved in buying even small computers, and the range of products available, it is virtually impossible to argue for a situation wherein this could be a straight rebuy situation.

4.   *What difficulties for sellers are suggested by the buying center concept?*

ANSWER:

The concept of the buying center offers marketers useful insights into the organizational buying process but also suggests many of the difficulties associated in dealing with that market.

The buying center is defined as "an informal, cross-departmental decision unit in which the primary objective is the acquisition, impartation, and processing of relevant purchasing-related information." The center includes "all the people and groups that have a role in the decision-making processes of purchasing."

"All the people" is suggestive of complications, as is "all the groups." Words like "informal" and "cross-departmental" also suggest problems. The buying center is not identified on any organization charts. It is up to the seller to determine who is in the buying center. Further, persons and groups come and go as the purchasing process advances and as particular problem areas develop. The make-up of the buying center is also situation-specific, as when engineers are needed to help make decisions about technical matters but are not needed to make decisions about simple products like inter-office envelopes.

Furthermore, the importance of the members of the buying center changes as the purchasing process continues, but there are no announcements of who has been dropped or added, or who has more or less influence at any given stage in the process.

The roles of various members of a hospital's staff in a purchase decision are illustrated in the text. The roles are: users, gatekeepers, influencers, deciders, and buyers.

Again, the buying center is a useful and important concept but, like many other things, the more it is studied the more complex it appears.

5.   *What variables might be used to estimate demand for the following products? (a) paper clips, (b) staplers, (c) lubricants for industrial quality drill presses, and (d) forklift trucks.*

ANSWER:

Products (a) and (b) could be used by consumers but the focus of the question is on organizational users.

(a)   Paper clips

Paper clips are a product that falls into the "operating supplies" category of organizational goods. They constitute a staple good of sorts (sorry about that) and their usage rate is, in the aggregate, likely to be relatively constant. Further, the number of users of paper clips is "easy" to determine since almost every business is a user of these common items.

All of this suggests that the demand for paper clips is best predicted from past data. Paper clip sales totals can be obtained from U.S. Government data and from office supply trade associations. Further, on the local level, these sales can be related to such data as number of persons employed, number of businesses in operation, and so on. Few products lend themselves to such mechanical demand estimation, but among the best in this regard are staple items like paper clips.

It should be noted that as electronic storage of information has increased, demand for paper clips has slipped somewhat. In the "long run," paper clip demand may fall drastically.

(b)   Staplers

Staplers do not fall into any one category of organizational goods. There are too many kinds of staplers.

The demand for the common office stapler (operating supply) might be estimated in the straightforward ways suggested for paper clips. The same warning, that electronic storage of data could ultimately doom use of staples, can be made.

More specialized staplers are quite another story. It would be first appropriate to discover what sorts of industries use staplers (printers, builders, publishers, upholsterers, furniture makers, etc.) then determine what sorts of staplers are used. It is likely that trade association data would be of help.

SIC numbers could be used, as is shown in the text, to help estimate sales. Stapler users could be located and linked to output of those (SIC) industries. Knowing that a furniture producer which employs X workers, or produces Y units, or Z dollars worth of furniture each year buys N staplers annually permits a good estimate of demand as long as care is taken to allow for turndowns in the economy or for possible stocking-up on staplers during the year from which data was taken.

(c)   Lubricants for industrial quality drill presses

This product is, depending on your perspective, either an operating supply or a process good. It essentially doesn't matter which, since, in either case, mechanical estimation methods would apply.

Use of the product can be linked to two variables: having the drills and, more importantly, using the drills. Use of the oil can thus be linked to the output of those organizations which use drill presses. The same SIC-based approach used in (b) can be used, e.g., what companies buy and use drill presses and how much oil do they use, that is, what is oil use per dollar (or other measure) of output? Since many types of outfits use drill presses, this could be a long process. However, the data can be found to make the process ultimately quite an exact one.

(d)   Forklift trucks

Again, the SIC-based approach mentioned above could be used (production-generated vs. forklifts used/bought). However, forklifts are not so neatly linked to output as is oil. Forklifts are pieces of accessory equipment, and fairly expensive ones at that. They have reasonably long lives and they are repairable. Thus, the state of the industry must be taken into consideration. The worse it is, the more likely that existing forklifts will be repaired and new purchases postponed. Also, the "current inventory of goods" phenomenon is important. If forklifts now in use have an average age of three years, this bodes ill for the forklift marketer. If the average age is fifteen years, it bodes well. Thus, customers might be evaluated (on a local level) in terms of the state of their particular industry and the age of their particular forklifts.

6.   *Define derived demand and give an example of its effect on the sale of packaging materials.*

ANSWER:

The demand for all organizational products is derived demand. No organization will buy a single paper clip unless it "thinks" that product will help it to sell its own products. Thus, demand for the organizational good "derives" from the demand for the product the organization produces and/or sells.

For a classroom example closer to home, consider that the accounting major may not want to take a principles of marketing course but does so because he or she wants to get an accounting degree and must take a marketing course as part of the curriculum. Demand for the marketing course derives from demand for the accounting degree.

The influence of derived demand on packaging materials is clear. Consider milk cartons. If consumers do not buy milk in treated paper cartons, bottlers of milk will not buy the treated paper cartons from the makers of those cartons. It is possible, for example, that consumers come to prefer milk in plastic jugs to milk in cartons. This would wipe out a large portion of the carton producers' business and cause injury to those businesses that sell to the carton producers (ink suppliers, paper suppliers, even paper clip suppliers). See the discussion of the "acceleration principle" in the text.

The importance of derived demand is recognized by producers of packaging. We, as consumers, often see advertisements telling us that "beer tastes better in bottles" or that "unbreakable, recyclable cans" are what we should buy. Producers of treated cardboard milk cartons may promote the fact that their cartons are more biodegradable than plastic jugs while the plastic jug producers tout the easy to hold handle on the jugs. Note that such ads are generally not from the milk companies but from the packaging producers. Some of these ads are from the firms that supply the packaging producers, as when makers of bottle-making machinery tell us that "glass is best for taste."

7.   *Explain, in your own words, why the demand for organizational products is generally inelastic with respect to price.*

ANSWER:

As a general rule, demand for organizational products is price inelastic. Some exceptions can be found (as when price falls), but buyers hold off buying to see if it will fall further, or they will choose to "stock up" in the belief that it will not. Both of these are individual psychological situations, as is the case where prices rise and the buyer purchases more product in fear that the price will rise still further. Some energy companies, notably natural gas firms, are now suffering consumer scrutiny because, in a perceived period of shortage in the 1970s, they bought rights to "expensive gas." Now that there is greater availability of gas, these companies are selling expensive gas to consumers at high prices even though far cheaper gas may be available to buyers in other locations.

In the following situations, and in combinations of them, demand for an organizational product would be price inelastic.

.   The buyer, as a rational businessperson, has determined a need for two boilers. A "sale price" on the third and fourth boilers would not lead to additional purchases (except for "gray market" resale) if two boilers were the carefully determined need.

.   The buyer faces a strong enough demand for the product ultimately produced that a rise in the price of an organizational product can simply be "passed on down the line."

.   The product purchased makes up such a small part of the total of the finished product that a price rise affects that finished product price very little. E.g., any part of a finished locomotive is a fairly small proportion of the price of the locomotive.

It should be recalled that price inelasticity of demand for organizational goods is an industry-wide phenomenon. It does not mean that an individual firm's demand is price inelastic. Thus, exceptions to the rule, like those mentioned earlier in this answer guideline, suit individual organizations but not "all" or "most" as does the general rule of price inelasticity.

8.   *Is a business-to-business marketer more likely to stress personal selling or advertising in promoting a product? Why?*

ANSWER:

While it is possible to mention organizational products for which advertising is important (e.g., operating supplies), even for these, personal selling is also important. For many organizational goods, advertising is nonexistent, or at best, produced as an aid to personal salespeople (e.g., by attempting to develop recognition of the company name).

The characteristics of the business-to-business market all suggest that personal selling rather than advertising must bear the greatest portion of the marketing (sales) effort.

- Organizational markets are more geographically concentrated than consumer markets.

- Organizational markets contain far fewer customers than do consumer markets.

- Organizational buyers demonstrate a preference for buying directly from producers, seeking price savings, technical information, assured delivery, or any number of other benefits that may be associated with buying direct.

- Organizational buyers are, comparatively, expert buyers, buying in a "scientific" way, carefully weighing product, delivery, pricing, and other matters. They need to deal with "expert" salespeople.

These four major characteristics of the business-to-business marketplace all suggest employment of a direct selling force rather than the use of advertising. Strength of competition, the possible need to have a field force to keep up with developments in a rapidly changing market, and other situation-specific matters, may be mentioned.

Again, all this is not to say that there is no place for advertising in the business-to-business market, but advertising is a supplement to personal selling in almost every instance.

ETHICS EXERCISE 7

CHAPTER 7 ETHICS IN PRACTICE

Overview

This case recounts a situation wherein a group of American businessmen entertained a group of Japanese businessmen. To assure that the Japanese would not feel "uncomfortable," it was decided that businesswomen and wives of executives would "stay home." This addresses two fundamental ethical issues. First, is cultural relativism: when doing business with Romans, should one do as the Romans do, even if it is considered wrong in our society? Second, is the whole matter of discrimination against women in the workplace.

1.   *If you were in charge of a social function for Japanese businessmen, would you invite women?*

This seems to be a "damned if you do and damned if you don't" situation (a Hobson's choice involving two undesirable alternatives). It's a no-win situation because if you practice the marketing concept and try to please your clients, you end up alienating the wives of men invited to the business party and the women executives who weren't invited. On the other hand, if you invite the wives and women executives, you alienate your clients. And, when competing on a global scale one cultivates such clients carefully and tirelessly, aware that one's rivals in London, Paris, and Sydney are doing likewise. If the client you're wining and dining isn't at ease doing business with women, wouldn't it be foolish, with so much at stake for your career and company and maybe even your country, to handicap yourself by including women at the courting party? Not only do you have an ethical dilemma, you have a strategic dilemma.

From a purely pragmatic perspective, it's not clear what your best option is. You would need information on the likelihood and extent to which the Japanese businessmen would be offended and how this would negatively affect your business relationships with them. You'd also need to consider how the wives and women executives would react if not invited and how this would affect the work performance of husbands (e.g., marital stress hurting concentration at work) and working women (e.g., negative attitude toward the company harming productivity). In other words, economic utilitarian calculations could be made to decide which course of action will cause the least expected harm to the company's bottom line. However, it would seem that such calculations would be extremely subjective. The experiences of others could help, to some extent.

However, moral judgments should also come into play here. Cultural relativism is the idea that morality is relative to a particular culture, society, or community; being ethical is doing whatever society accepts. This suggests that we can't judge the morality of a particular culture, that we should just try to understand it. One problem with this concept, from an absolutist position, is that it's impossible to have conflicting truths. (One society advocates slavery and another doesn't. Can they both be right?) Another problem is the question of whether one society has the right to impose its morals on members of another society when they are working together (or otherwise associating) in one of the two societies. For instance, people in the United States are straightforward and open in their business dealings, even if such behavior does sometimes hurt others' feelings. While most of us believe that such behavior is ethical, in Latin American cultures people avoid saying things that would make others uncomfortable. Should one or both of the parties bend their behavior when dealing with the others? Can they both be right?

In this case, the question is whether the Japanese should have a right to expect that their values will be respected by their hosts. For one thing, this would seem to violate the cultural truism, "When in Rome, do as the Romans do." After all, in this case it is the Japanese who are "in Rome" and should, perhaps, do things our way. On the other hand, would you want to lose business by insisting that they do things our way? Also, it would seem that what we are dealing with are not so much moral values as social customs, i.e., norms and expectations about the way people do things in a specific country. (For example, in France, men wear more than twice the number of cosmetics that women do.) A nation's values, on the other hand, reflect the religious or moral values of its people (e.g., McDonald's and other hamburger restaurants wouldn't have a chance in India, where the cow is considered sacred.)

It doesn't seem that the Japanese would argue that it is morally wrong to invite women to a business gathering. Rather, they would just prefer that women not be invited. It would not seem unreasonable to explain to the Japanese that in our culture wives and businesswomen are customarily invited to such functions, and that to do otherwise would be deeply offensive to them. Also, you could explain that when we are in Japan, we will be willing to restrict attendance at social gatherings to invited guests, whomever they may be.

In discussion of this item, and of the following one (2), the question could be raised whether or not discriminating against women in some areas of the firm's operation might not actually be pro-women overall. Example: playing along with the Japanese and Arabs might bring in business which then serves to put more women to work in the firm as a whole.

2.   *Should women be part of an international sales team?*

From a purely pragmatic perspective the answer is that in many countries you wouldn't want to have women sales executives because it goes against the society's customs and expectations. For example, in many Middle Eastern nations women are usually mothers and housewives, but seldom businesspeople. Although women executives have been successful in Arab and other countries where the presence of women in business goes against the cultural grain, success has not come without great difficulty.

It could be argued from a moral perspective that this constitutes discrimination against women in the workplace. From a rights perspective, such discrimination is improper since it violates women's right to employment, treating them as inferior to males. From a justice perspective it is also wrong, since arbitrarily giving some individuals less of an opportunity to compete for jobs than others is unfair. However, in an international context, hiring only men can be justified since gender is relevant to the tasks they can perform and the results they will get in that society. Also, from a utilitarian perspective, society's productivity will be optimized since, even though women might be more competent than men at the sales task, they will be less successful due to societal norms against saleswomen. From a cultural relativist's position, discrimination against women is justified on the basis of cultural norms and values.

"Middle Eastern companies may refuse to negotiate with saleswomen at all or may take an unfavorable view of foreign organizations that employ saleswomen. The ethical issue in such cases is whether foreign businesses should respect Middle Eastern values and send only men to negotiate sales transactions, denying women employees the opportunity to further their careers and contribute to organizational objectives. The alternative would be to try to maintain their own ideas of social equality, knowing that women sales representatives will probably be unsuccessful because of cultural norms in these societies." (O.C. Ferrell and John Fraedrich, *Business Ethics: Ethical Decision Making and Cases*, Boston: Houghton Mifflin Company, 1991, p. 157)

3.   *Is there a conflict between equal opportunity law and foreign business customs?*

Title VII of the Civil Rights Act, passed in 1964, prohibits American businesses from discriminating on the basis of race, color, sex, religion, or handicap in their hiring, firing, and promotion decisions. It also created the Equal Employment Opportunity Commission (EEOC) to enforce the provisions of Title VII. In the United States it is clearly illegal to discriminate against women who are equally qualified as men for a given job. However, if your sales force is employed by a foreign subsidiary, it is perfectly legal to hire only men in those countries; there is no Equal Employment Opportunity Commission to deal with. Discrimination is often a fact of life overseas. However, the ethics of this remain questionable, at best.

CHAPTER 7 TAKE A STAND QUESTIONS

1.   *A purchasing agent likes to work with company A whose prices are rarely the lowest. The purchasing agent solicits competitive bids from Company A and two other companies that are known for exceedingly high quality and extremely high prices. Two other companies whose quality meets the organization's specifications and whose prices are generally the lowest in the industry are not invited to solicit bids. Company A, whose product quality meets minimum specifications, wins the contract. Is this ethical?*

The issue here is one of effective stewardship, of an agent's responsibility to his master, perhaps the most ancient of management problems. Many a biblical parable is framed in terms of this relationship, and modern political scientists and economists have tried to make it their own under the rubric of "agency theory."

This scenario is useful for illustrating the "law of agency," which specifies the duties of persons ("agents") who agree to act on behalf of another party and are authorized by the agreement to act. A manager or employee is expected to act as a loyal agent of the employer and has a duty to serve the employer as the employer would want to be served (it is considered the employer's right to expect this). The employee's major obligation to the firm is to work toward the firm's goals and to engage in no activity which would harm those goals. To deviate from these goals and to serve instead one's own self interest would be unethical, a breach of your implied contract.

In this scenario, there is a so-called "agency problem," which arises whenever the goals and/or values of the employee diverge from those of the employer. This leads to a tension between the desire to serve the employer loyally and the desire to act in one's own best self-interest. In other words, there is a conflict of interest here between the purchasing agent's self-interest (dealing with a supplier he enjoys working with) and the best interests of the firm (purchasing from a supplier who offers the best value [ratio of quality, performance, benefits, etc.] to price). By buying from competitor A, which has a suboptimal offering, the purchasing agent is not fulfilling his fiduciary responsibility to the firm, and in this sense his behavior is unethical. He is not fulfilling his duty to the firm, and is, therefore, abridging the firm's rights. Also, justice is not being served to the two companies excluded from the bidding process. They are being denied the right to fairly compete. This is unjust, for they are being treated differently than competing firms, where the differential treatment cannot be justified for business reasons.

2.   *A purchasing agent attends a lewd party sponsored by a company that wants to do business with the agent's company. Should the purchasing agent have attended?*

Notice that this question does not specify the sex of the purchasing agent. If the students discuss the matter using a male (or female) example, ask they if their opinion changes once you "change" the sex of the purchasing agent.

This is a good example of a conflict between personal values and corporate values. The purchasing agent finds himself/herself in a compromising situation; he or she is asked to compromise his/her own moral standards for the sake of the company getting some additional business. Also, if the purchasing agent is a women she might feel even more uncomfortable at the party than might a male. It would be clearly unethical for any supervisor to place the agent in such a compromising situation (a violation of "The Golden Rule").

However, in this question we are viewing the situation from the purchasing agent's perspective: what are the alternatives if he or she is asked to go to a party that is morally offensive? One extreme would be to grit the teeth and go, rationalizing that it is a "cost of doing business." If the agent feels a lack of control in the sense that he or she can't persuade the employer to grant an excuse from attending and fears some sort of reprisal if fuss is raised, this alternative would make some sense. Ethicists would say that in this situation the agent is not morally responsible. However, he or she faces possible problems if he or she does go, such as guilt, mental contamination, negative effects on a relationship with God, etc.

At the other extreme, the agent could refuse to go in a diplomatic fashion, explaining that attending the party would violate personal moral standards. At worst, this could result in getting fired and at best getting excused from going.

Or, the purchasing agent could try some sort of compromise solution; for instance, agree to just pop in briefly on the party, agree to meet with company personnel in an alternative social setting, or get the company to host a social event to which personnel in the other company are invited, etc. In all cases, diplomacy is called for. The purchasing agent probably doesn't want to give the other company's employees the reason for refusing to attend their party for fear of alienating them (unless the agent has the courage of his or her convictions and feels the most important thing to do is to speak out against evil, regardless of the ramifications for his or her career).

3.   *A company policy gives preferential treatment to raw materials suppliers who are minority owned. Is this a good policy?*

This question deals with the difficult issue of job discrimination, which can be defined as making an adverse decision (or set of decisions) against employees (or prospective employees) based upon their membership in a certain class, usually either a racial or ethnic minority (blacks, Hispanics, Asian Americans, etc.), or a sexually defined group (women and homosexuals). Discrimination is unjust because it involves differential treatment of individuals based on characteristics that are irrelevant to job performance. It causes harm to those against whom it is practiced, benefit to those chosen, and harm to society. From a utilitarian perspective, discrimination harms society because insofar as jobs are assigned to individuals on the basis of criteria unrelated to competency, productivity declines. Discrimination is also improper from a rights perspective because it does not treat each individual as a free person equal to any other person; discrimination is based on the belief that one group is inferior to other groups. From a justice perspective, discrimination is unjustifiable because it arbitrarily gives some individuals less of an opportunity to compete for jobs than others.

However, the issue gets sticky because, historically, blacks and other minorities were discriminated against in the workplace. In order to rectify the effects of past discrimination, many employers have instituted affirmative action programs whose goal is to achieve a more representative distribution of minorities and women within the firm by giving preference to women and minorities. (These programs are now required of all firms that hold a government contract.) The firm makes an effort to ascertain whether there are fewer women or minorities in a particular job classification than would reasonably be expected by their

availability in the area from which the firm recruits. If there is such a
disparity, the firm tries to remedy it via preferential hiring, i.e., hiring one
person rather than another, on the basis of some nonjob-related characteristic
such as sex, race, or ethnicity.

Is preferential hiring (the so-called class or group approach) ethical? Many
people would agree that it is not right if people from the previously
discriminated-against groups were chosen in favor of more qualified white males.
This constitutes "reverse discrimination" against the white males and has the
same adverse consequences that discrimination always has: it harms some
individuals to favor others, it hurts the firm's competitiveness, and it results
in a decline in society's productivity.

However, some would say that although such reverse discrimination doesn't use a
just procedure (unfair means it violates the principle of equal treatment for
equal skills), it does produce a just outcome (a good end, "social justice").
This is called compensatory justice: we need a just way of compensating people
for what they lost when harmed by others via past discrimination. Thus,
preferential treatment programs attempt to remedy past injustices against groups.
The problem is that, traditionally, compensatory justice meant that individuals
have an obligation to compensate other individuals whom they have harmed.
However, here we are dealing with compensation coming from members of a group
(white males) who were not individually responsible for the past discrimination.
They will rightly claim that they are not guilty of discrimination, and that it
is unjust to punish sons for the sins of the fathers.

It would appear that the class approach to discrimination and compensatory
justice itself involves discrimination, produces harm to innocent parties that
did not cause it, does not solve the social problems (bigotry, racial prejudice,
etc.) underlying discrimination, and is immoral because to use hiring criteria
other than those stated or that are obviously job-related is to mislead, deceive,
raise false hopes, and violate an implied practice governing hiring. (Richard T.
DeGeorge, *Business Ethics*, third edition, New York: MacMillan Publishing
Company, 1990, p. 369) Even if an ad were to state up front that preference is
given to minorities, this is still discrimination. (Consider the reverse
situation where an ad says "Preference will be given to white males" - that would
certainly be discriminatory.) (DeGeorge, p. 370)

In addition to compensatory goals, however, preferential hiring can also have
social goals. The argument is that the public welfare will be served if the
position of groups impoverished by prior discrimination is improved by giving
them special employment (and educational) opportunities. However, this can also
backfire in that affirmative action programs imply that women and minorities are
so inferior to white males that they need special help to compete. Also,
preferential hiring could breed resentment in those who are the objects of
reverse discrimination, turning us into a more racially and sexually conscious
nation.

In the situation where minorities are equally as qualified as white males,
preferential hiring is more easily justified. Given that two individuals are
equally qualified on every job-related criterion, using ethnicity or other such
criteria could be justified as serving the two goals discussed above: 1)
compensation for past injuries, and 2) advancing public welfare, i.e., helping to
level the playing field between previously discriminated-against groups and
others. For these reasons, it could be argued that, all else equal, race and sex
become relevant hiring criteria.

GUIDE TO CASE

VIDEO CASE 7-1 A. SCHULMAN

SUBJECT MATTER: Organizational Buying, Organizational Marketing Strategy,
                         Marketing Concept in Organizational Marketing

                              Please see the Guide to Video Cases for video
                              length and other information.

AT-A-GLANCE OVERVIEW

A. Schulman has been in the rubber and plastic industry since 1928. The firm's
specialty plastics go into everything from pens and candy wrappers to lawn
furniture. The company is an international marketer that has a solid commitment
to quality. It uses statistical process quality control to meet customer
satisfactions. Its management works with customers to design the plastics they
need. The general concept is that bigger firms cannot fill special orders like
Schulman does and make any money. Schulman can, and focuses on developing long-
term relationships with its customers. It goes so far as to stop jobs in
progress, work on weekends to fill special orders, then return to the stopped
job. The firm conducts many tests to assure overall quality of their engineered
plastics. Schulman also focus on outstanding service. Doing it right on time.
One quote: "We don't talk price. We talk quality."

This video illustrates the nature of a successful marketer of organizational
products in the business-to-business market.

DISCUSSION QUESTIONS

1.   *Identify what type of organizational buying situation faces most of
       Schulman's customers.*

Schulman is a leading supplier of performance compounds. In many situations it
faces a new buying task. That is why the company stresses quality control in
manufacturing. The company works with its customer to design innovative
engineered plastics. However, after the products have been designed to be the
raw material for other products, much of the business is the straight rebuy, or
in the case of product modification, modified rebuy. Another aspect of many
buying situations the company faces is the "emergency" aspect. Firms using
materials cannot afford to run out of them lest they have to close down their
production. As the case notes, Schulman will figure out ways to meet those
emergency demands. Obviously the buyers to whom they sell pay for this kind of
service.

The video illustrates the many products made from Schulman's plastics.

2.   *How would you characterize Schulman's overall marketing strategy?*

Schulman, first, is consumer-oriented. The firm has clearly adopted the marketing
concept. Second, it employs a market segmentation strategy that emphasizes
customization. This is very common with many business-to-business marketers.
Finally, Schulman chooses to position itself as a high-tech, quality marketer of
engineered plastics that believes in providing great service. It fills special
orders quickly.

The quote stating "We don't talk price. We talk quality." extends to service as
well as product. Quality service, like quality product, justifies a higher
price. As the case notes, coming through with what its customers need, even when
overtime is involved, means good relationships with loyal buyers.

3.   *Is Scuhman a marketing-concept oriented company? How important is the
       integration of the marketing function with other aspects of the business?*

As mentioned above, Schulman is the epitome of a marketing concept oriented
company. It goes far out of its way to satisfy customers, especially those who
its larger competitors ignore. Schulman integrates its engineering and
manufacturing with the marketing strategy of positioning itself as a producer of
innovative quality products.

In short, marketing alone does not do the job. Schulman has excellent engineering and production, but doesn't rely on that. It offers the customer a total (call it integrated, if you will) package that includes science and technology, production, and knock-ourselves-out service.

8 MARKET SEGMENTATION AND POSITIONING STRATEGIES

CHAPTER SCAN

This chapter defines what is meant by a market and discusses market segmentation, one of the most powerful concepts in marketing. It also describes the related tool of target marketing and describes the development of effective marketing mixes that will satisfy those targets.

The chapter also distinguishes between undifferentiated, concentrated, differentiated, and custom marketing strategies. The 80/20 rule and majority fallacy are also discussed. The chapter outlines the many variables that can be used by a marketing manager to effectively identify, analyze, and target marketing opportunities.

It also discusses the concept of positioning a product or brand so that the product or brand may be differentiated from its competitors.

SUGGESTED LEARNING OBJECTIVES

The student who studies this chapter will be exposed to a thorough discussion of market segmentation and the concepts related to it. The student will be able to:

1. Define the term "market."

2. Explain the concept of market segmentation.

3. Relate the identification of meaningful target markets to the development of effective marketing mixes.

4. Distinguish among undifferentiated, concentrated, differentiated, and custom marketing strategies.

5. Demonstrate the effect of the 80/20 rule and the majority fallacy on marketing strategy.

6. List the market segmentation variables available to marketing managers and explain how marketers identify which ones are appropriate.

7. Explain what a positioning strategy does.

CHAPTER OUTLINE

I.   INTRODUCTION

II.   WHAT IS A MARKET? WHAT IS MARKET SEGMENTATION?

    A.   Choosing Meaningful Market Segments
    B.   The Market Segment Cross-Classification Matrix
    C.   Matching the Mix to the Target Market

III.   FOUR STRATEGIES FOR TARGET MARKETING

    A.   Undifferentiated Marketing: When Everyone is a Customer
    B.   Concentrated Marketing: Zeroing in on a Single Target
    C.   Differentiated Marketing: Different Buyers, Different Strategies
    D.   Custom Marketing: To Each His Own

IV.   IDENTIFYING MARKET DIFFERENCES

    A.   Geographic Bases of Segmentation
    B.   Demographic Bases of Segmentation

        1.   Age
        2.   Family Life Cycle

    C.   Socioeconomic Bases of Segmentation
    D.   Lifestyle and Psychographic Segmentation
    E.   Behavior Pattern Segmentation
    F.   Consumption Pattern Segmentation
    G.   Consumer Predisposition Segmentation
    H.   Geodemographic and Zip Code Segmentation

V.   SEGMENTING BUSINESS MARKETS

VI.   FINDING THE "BEST" SEGMENTATION VARIABLE

VII.   POSITIONING: THE BASIC FOCUS FOR THE MARKETING MIX

VIII. SUMMARY

IX.   QUESTIONS FOR DISCUSSION (13)

X.   KEY TERMS

XI.   ETHICS IN PRACTICE

XII.   CASES

    The following key terms are introduced in Chapter 8. They are defined in the text's Glossary.

Disaggregated market
Cross-classification matrix
Undifferentiated marketing
Concentrated marketing
80/20 principle
Majority fallacy
Differentiated marketing
Multiple market segmentation
Custom marketing
Multinational, or international, marketing
Family life cycle
Psychographics
VALS-2
Benefit Segmentation
Geodemographic segmentation
Head-to-head competition
Repositioning

THE CHAPTER SUMMARIZED

I.   INTRODUCTION

The chapter opens with a discussion of Mattell's "Barbie" doll, a thirty-plus-year-old product so popular in the U.S. that 90 percent of all girls ages 3 to 11 have one, and the average owner has five. (Mattell is now introducing the doll in Eastern Europe under the name "Friendship Barbie.") Mattell has concentrated on what it knows best, selling the doll and its multiple accessories to younger girls while offering Barbie sunglasses, stationery, backpacks, and other items to "older" girls (7 to 11) who still enjoy Barbie but are sensitive about having others notice they still play with dolls. Mattell is practicing market segmentation.

II.   WHAT IS A MARKET? WHAT IS MARKET SEGMENTATION?

A market is a group of actual or potential customers for a particular product. But three additional criteria must be met. The people or organizations who may want the product must also:

.   have the necessary purchasing power,

.   be willing to spend money or exchange other resources to get the product, and

.   have the authority to make such expenditures.

Nonmarketing texts, especially economics books, often discuss "consumers" or "the market" as if all customers are the same. Experience tells us that this is not the case. Marketers see many demand curves, not one "market" demand curve as economists do. They practice market segmentation. The logic is this:

.   Not all buyers are the same.

.   Subgroups within markets may be identified.

.   The subgroups will be smaller and more homogeneous than the group as a whole.

.   It should be "easier" to deal with smaller groups of similar customers than with large groups of dissimilar customers. (Concentrating efforts in a given market segment should mean a more precise program satisfying specific market needs.)

In some markets, e.g., certain industrial markets, each product must be "made to order." In effect:

Number of Prospects = Number of Segments

This is a **disaggregated market**. No groups seem to be present. Usually, however, clusters of customers with similar demands can be found. For example, the computer software market can be divided into the domestic and foreign markets, the domestic market can be divided into business users and at-home users, the at-home segment can be divided into sophisticated computer users and "game players," and so on.

The marketer will probably not pursue all the segments identified but focus on the part or parts of the market he or she can best serve. The segment selected is the target market.

An example of "breaking down" a market into segments is shown in the text (Exhibit 8-3). The total market is "broken down" into its parts and the customers are regrouped into segments whose members have characteristics in common.

A.   Choosing Meaningful Market Segments

These five things make a market segment meaningful:

.   It has one or more characteristics which distinguish it from
the overall market. The characteristic(s) should be stable
over time.

.   It has a market potential of significant size. (It is large
enough to be profitable.)

.   It is accessible (e.g., via distribution methods or promotional
methods).

.   It is likely to respond favorably to a mix tailored to its
specialized needs.

.   Its potential is measurable, permitting the marketer to
identify and quantify purchasing power.

The determination of meaningfulness is shown in the text's Exhibit 8-4.

In general, attaining profitability depends on how well marketers use
criteria to identify target markets. A segment that exists but is
hard to identify is of little use, as is one that is too small to
support the marketing effort.

B.   The Market Segment Cross-Classification Matrix

Effective marketers segment the markets they address and select
attractive target markets. Almost any factor (e.g., corner chosen by
a boy selling newspapers) "segments" the market. But proper
segmenting and target market selection requires serious effort.

One approach is the **cross-classification matrix**, a grid used to show
variables can be considered for their effect on markets being
studied. Exhibits 8-5 and 8-6 in the text show how managers of a
tennis shop in New York City might employ the matrix.

C.   Matching the Mix to the Target Market

The marketing mix should be formulated to match the target market's
needs. All four P's should be evaluated in terms of those needs.
(What brands to stock, how to advertise, etc.)
This is "easier said than done" but the segmenting process by which a
target market is selected simplifies some of the choices to be made.

III.   FOUR STRATEGIES FOR TARGET MARKETING

Segmenting and target marketing has been compared to using a rifle to aim
at a specific target rather than a shotgun that has a far wider dispersion
of effort.

A.   Undifferentiated Marketing: When Everyone is a Customer

Sometimes the "shotgun" approach is appropriate if the segmenting
approach is not worth the effort. Marketers of garbage cans for
consumer use may face such a situation. "Everybody" who wants
garbage cans is a possible customer, so one well-constructed
marketing mix may be sufficient. This is illustrated in Exhibit 8-7.

One Well-Prepared
Marketing Mix

```
Marketing                    . Product        Target
Organization -->             . Price    -->    Market
                             . Place          ("Every-
                             . Promotion      body")
```

However, close consideration may reveal segments, even within markets
for mundane products, if primary and secondary desires of consumers
are considered, such as consumers who prefer facial tissues in a
standard package vs. tissues in a Little Mermaid pack.

Undifferentiated marketing can succeed, as when a small grocery store
in a small, isolated town, serves "all" the people in that town. The
store must, however, offer a well-prepared marketing mix that please
"all" (or at least most) of the customers.

B.   Concentrated Marketing: Zeroing in on a Single Target

If a market is seen to contain a number of segments and the marketer
chooses to concentrate on one of them, that marketer is practicing
concentrated marketing. This is illustrated in Exhibit 8-8.

```
                    One-Well Prepared     Market for
                    Marketing Mix         Chain Saws

Marketing               . Product         Target Market -
Organization -->        . Price     -->   Home users of
                        . Place           light-weight
                        . Promotion       chain saws

                                          . Farm users of
           Segments           ┌─────        medium-weight
           Not       -------  │            saws
           Targeted          │           . Professional
                             │             users of
                             │             heavy-duty
                             └─────        saws, etc.
```

Concentrating on one segment is often appropriate when a company
believes that it has some particular competitive advantage. Examples
include jewelers who cater only to the very wealthy, radio stations
that play only one sort of music, advertising agencies that service
only a small circle of clients.

But concentrated marketing involves some risks. The organization is
"putting all its eggs in one basket." The chosen market may prove to
be too narrow. The chosen market on which the organization depends
may change, e.g., suddenly become price-conscious. The organization
may become so identified with one segment that it cannot attract
other potential customers when it wants to.

1.   80/20 Principle

      The **80/20 principle** (though the actual numbers may vary) is
      often found to apply in marketing. Specifically, it often
      happens that a small percentage of the customers (e.g., 20%)
      accounts for a large percentage of sales (e.g., 80%). A great
      portion of beer sales is accounted for by the "heavy users"
      group, the fellows who drink a six-pack or two a day and more
      on weekends. Thus, most beer ads stress situations in which a
      lot of beer will be consumed.

      A marketer might be tempted to "go after" a segment of the
      market because it is particularly attractive, e.g., heavy users
      of beer. To do so blindly is to fall for the **majority fallacy**.

"Everybody" knows which segments are the heaviest users of a
product, or the most wealthy, or the most populous.   All
competitors are probably going after that same attractive
segment.   The segmentation process identified other segments,
e.g., light users.   Perhaps an organization should consider
"going after" one of these.

C.   Differentiated Marketing: Different Buyers, Different Strategies

An organization might target its efforts toward more than one market
segment.   This would necessitate preparing different marketing mixes
for each segment, and is called **differentiated marketing** or **multiple
market segmentation**.   The approach is widely used.   Marriot
Corporation operates five types of hotels targeted at various groups
of potential guests.   But it should be recalled that as the process
becomes more elaborate, the costs associated with the process go up.
Exhibit 8-9 illustrates differentiated marketing.

	Three Well-Prepared Marketing Mixes	Market Segments
	--> P P P P -->	Target Market #1
Marketing Organization	--> P P P P -->	Target Market #2
	--> P P P P -->	Target Market #3

D.   Custom Marketing: To Each His Own

It could happen that a market is so diverse that no meaningful
segments can be identified.   The market is disaggregated.   There is,
in effect, complete segmentation.   Then each customer will require a
unique marketing mix to satisfy its unique needs.   This is **custom
marketing** and is not at all uncommon, especially in the industrial
setting.   It is illustrated in Exhibit 8-10.

	Custom Marketing Mixes	Disaggregated Market
	--> P P P P -->	Customer A
	--> P P P P -->	Customer B
Marketing Organization	--> P P P P -->	Customer C
	--> P P P P -->	Customer D
	--> P P P P -->	Customer E
	etc.	etc.

Architects, tailors, lawyers, and makers of specialized equipment are
likely practitioners of custom marketing.

Exhibit 8-11 summarizes the four basic market segmentation
strategies.

IV.   IDENTIFYING MARKET DIFFERENCES

Marketing is a creative activity and many of its successes rest on creative
identification of market segments with unfulfilled needs.

For example:

- No-tears baby shampoo pleases children and parents who would prefer to avoid crying and fussing.

- Dog foods can be formulated for puppies, grown dogs, old dogs, fat dogs, and "gourmet" dogs.

- Pepsi is aimed at the youth market.

Almost any variable could be used in the process of market segmentation. Two facts simplify this prospect.

- The variables can be grouped into categories for "easier handling" as shown in Exhibit 8-12.

- A relatively small number of variables are, in fact, most commonly used. In fact, just two or three in any given situation might prove to be the major variables worthy of close attention.

A.   Geographic Bases of Segmentation

Simple geography may lie behind demand for a product.

Some examples:

- Certain products sell best in certain locations, e.g., snowmobiles in the northern states, suntan lotion in Miami.

- Some products sell best in certain areas for ethnic or other reasons (chili in Texas and ginger ale on the East Coast). There are underlying reasons for these phenomena but "geography" is easier to employ as a segmenting variable than are those underlying causes of buyer behavior.

Population boundaries crossing political boundaries are often more useful than political boundaries: "Chicagoland," "Greater New York," "The Dallas/Fort Worth Metroplex."

Recognizing this, the Bureau of the Census developed the Metropolitan Statistical Areas system which "assembles" market areas and information on those areas. There are three metropolitan categories.

- Metropolitan Statistical Areas (MSAs) are relatively free-standing, surrounded by nonmetropolitan counties. Fargo, Syracuse, and Omaha are such areas.

- Primary Metropolitan Statistical Areas (PMSAs) are markets within larger metropolitan markets. Gary, Indiana is such a market, sizable itself but part of the larger Chicago Area. Pasadena (Los Angeles market) and Jersey City (New York market) are PMSAs.

- Consolidated Metropolitan Statistical Areas (CMSAs) are large "mega-markets" like the Los Angeles CMSA which includes Anaheim, Riverside, etc., as well as Los Angeles proper.

Marketers selling their products outside their own countries are practicing **multinational** or **international marketing**, a form of geographic market segmentation, and probably are creating specific marketing mixes to meet the needs of people in each market area.

B.   Demographic Bases of Segmentation

Demographic information describes people (age, sex, race, family size, etc.) Demography provides a common basis of market segmentation because:

- It has obvious use. (Families with children buy more toys than families without children.)

- Data is relatively easy to come by. Census figures, for example, can be found in any library.

- It's relatively easy to generate. ("How many Oriental people came to this restaurant for lunch?" is easier to answer than "How many carefree people were here for lunch?")

1.   Age

The impact of age on marketing is clear (aging population, fewer children, decline in the 13-24 age group the heaviest users of soft drinks, an "adult boom" instead of a "baby boom.") In 1900 one in twenty-five was over age 65, in a few years that will be one in five. Many marketers' appeals reflect this fact, e.g., appliances featuring bigger, easier-to-see knobs and lettering.

2.   Family Life Cycle

The **family life cycle** shown in the text (Exhibit 8-14) portrays a series of stages through which most people pass, though they do so at varying rates of speed.

The worth of the family life cycle is that it reflects lifestyle and purchases better than age would alone, e.g., married people with children under six buy different products than married people whose children have grown up and left home. Yet it is possible for a person of 42 to be in either situation.

C.   Socioeconomic Bases of Segmentation

Socioeconomic variables reflect a person's social position and/or economic standing within a society. Some possibilities:

ECONOMIC STANDING

		High	Low
	High	Famous Heart Surgeon	College Professor
SOCIAL STANDING			
	Low	Garbage Removal Worker	Dishwasher in a Diner

These variables can be related to purchase activities, e.g., shotgun shells, expensive sports cars, concert tickets, large charitable donations, etc. Exhibit 8-15 shows a socioeconomic profile of heavy users of shotgun ammunition.

1.   Social Class

Social class is clearly related to purchases.

- Who is most likely to go to a posh restaurant, a doctor or a street sweeper?

- Who is more likely to buy classical music records or to hold tickets to the Metropolitan Opera?

D.   Lifestyle and Psychographic Segmentation

A **lifestyle** is a pattern in an individual's pursuit of life's goals, indicating how a person spends his or her time and money.

Psychographics represents an attempt to "get inside the customer's head," to examine beliefs and lifestyle. Two young married women, each with two children and equal family incomes, may live two different lifestyles which affect their particular buying patterns.

Psychographics are far more difficult to use than demographic or socio-economic variables. However psychographics have real use.

One popular psychographic classification scheme is **VALS-2** (<u>V</u>alues, <u>A</u>ttitudes, <u>L</u>ifestyles -- second version). It identifies eight lifestyle types: actualizers, fulfilleds, believers, achievers, strivers, experiencers, makers, and strugglers, and associates certain products with each. Thus, American Express's Gold Card speaks to achievers by advertising that it is the card to use in meeting challenges and attaining goals.

Exhibit 8-16 illustrates the famous shotgun shell user psychographic study, illustrative of the "outdoors" lifestyle person.

Because psychographics are more difficult to deal with than the simpler demographic variables, marketers often use them in combination with demographics. Example, the "self-indulgent" lifestyle might be "translated" into 20-45 year-old male, college-educated, annual earnings over $85,000.

E.   Behavior Pattern Segmentation

Consumers demonstrate behavior patterns worthy of the marketer's attention.

.   Customers behave in such a way that 40 percent of soft drink sales are accounted for by vending machines and fast food outlets. Seven-Up has been trying to get its product into more of these outlets.

.   Customers behave in this way -- on hot days they "grab a cold drink." Some 7-Elevens and other convenience stores put cans of soda in ice buckets near check-out counters during the hottest months.

F.   Consumption Pattern Segmentation

Basically, consumption patterns are the focus of marketing. Marketers want people who consume their products to continue to do so and those who do not consume the products are the focus of efforts to get them to change their consumption patterns.

.   Heavy consumers of baseball games or of operas can get season tickets to these spectacles.

.   Some customers choose to "consume" banking services at just one bank. This led to the "Full Service Bank" slogan.

Of course, the consumption pattern of major concern (e.g., purchase of hotel accommodations) may be linked to the purchase occasion of travel. A previous consumption pattern may influence a current one, e.g., a few people buy new furnaces if they have not bought (or decided to buy) a house.

G.   Consumer Predisposition Segmentation

Consumers vary widely with respect to knowledge, beliefs, reasoning, attitudes, etc. and these variables affect their purchasing behavior.

.   Audio buffs buy component systems at audio specialty shops
while novices buy "assembled" sets at department stores.

Closely related is seeking to identify consumers by the benefits they
seek, **benefit segmentation**.

.   People in the Crest toothpaste segment want fewer cavities.
Buyers of Ultra-Brite want white teeth. Close-Up buyers expect
a clean breath benefit.

.   Some buy Miller Lite beer because it tastes great, some because
it's less filling.

H.   Geodemographic and Zip Code Segmentation

Direct marketers can base segmentation on ZIP codes. People living
in the same ZIP code tend to be similar demographically and
socioeconomically.

Geodemographic segmentation refers to the combination of demographic
variables with a geographic variable, such as zip codes, to
characterize clusters of like individuals.

The PRIZM system (Claritas Corp.) breaks down the 36,000 U.S. code
areas, classifying them with colorful names such as "Gray Power" for
retirement communities. Some of these are illustrated in Exhibit 8-
17.

V.   SEGMENTING BUSINESS MARKETS

Exhibit 8-18 shows that business markets may be segmented on the basis of
geography, organizational characteristics, purchase behavior, usage
patterns, and predispositions. Segmenting of the business market is
similar to segmenting the consumer market.

VI.   FINDING THE "BEST" SEGMENTATION VARIABLE

The "best" is the one that leads to the identification of a meaningful
target market segment. A combination of variables may be "best." The
"best" variables are the ones that lead the marketer to the identification
of a meaningful target market.

VII.   POSITIONING: THE BASIC FOCUS FOR THE MARKETING MIX

Brands appealing to a given market will attain a "position" in the
consumer's mind. After selecting a target market, managers plan the
position the brand will occupy in that market. The market position or
competitive position is the way consumers perceive the brand relative to
the competition. In general, marketers identify their brand's competitive
advantages and stress these to differentiate their brands from the
competition's brands. Ben-Gay, once a pain reliever for arthritis
sufferers, is now positioned as a "warm-up cream" for amateur athletes.
Positioning may be directly against the competition (**head-to-head** or "me
too" competition), or away from competitors, if that is where it is
believed the competitive advantage lies.

Marketing research can be used to identify how consumers perceive various
products. These perceptions can be plotted on a "map" as in Exhibit 8-19.
This "map" (8-19) shows that the Porsche is seen as expensive and
expressive, while Buick, Olds, and Cadillac are seen as very similar to one
another. The maps may also show a position not yet filled by a competitor,
a "product space" that may be a good opportunity awaiting marketing action.

Many products have been **repositioned**. That is, they have been "moved" from
one position to another. For example, Jello has been advertising that its
product can be made into "Jigglers," snack items that can be eaten with the
hands. This is a clear repositioning from dessert item to snack.

VIII. SUMMARY

Market segmentation is one of marketing's most powerful tools. Whatever variables they use, effective marketers try to identify meaningful target segments so they can develop customer-satisfying marketing mixes.

Learning Objective 1: Define the term "market."

A market is composed of individuals or organizations with the ability, willingness, and authority to exchange their purchasing power for the product offered.

Learning Objective 2: Explain the concept of market segmentation.

In order to identify homogeneous segments (subgroups) of heterogeneous markets, marketing managers research an entire market, disaggregate it into its parts, and regroup the parts into market segments according to one or more characteristics, such as geography, buying patterns, demography, and psychographic variables.

Learning Objective 3: Relate the identification of meaningful target markets to the development of effective marketing mixes.

Marketing mixes are effective only if they satisfy the needs of meaningful target markets. A meaningful target market has a significant (and, ideally, measurable) market potential, is distinguishable from the overall market, responsive, and accessible through distribution or promotional efforts.

Learning Objective 4: Distinguish among undifferentiated, concentrated, differentiated, and custom marketing strategies.

The undifferentiated marketing strategy is used when no meaningful segment is identified. If one meaningful segment is the target of an organization's marketing mix, the concentrated marketing strategy is used. If several market segments are targeted, the differentiated marketing strategy is employed. When markets are so disaggregated that each customer requires a special marketing mix, the custom marketing strategy is appropriate.

Learning Objective 5: Demonstrate the effect of the 80/20 rule and the majority fallacy on marketing strategy.

According to the 80/20 principle, the majority of a product's sales are accounted for by a small percentage of the product's market; however competitors also target this market. Failure to take this into account is the majority fallacy. One purpose of market segmentation is to identify segments which may have gone undetected by competitors.

Learning Objective 6: List the market segmentation variables available to marketing managers and explain how marketers identify which ones are appropriate.

In consumer markets, segmentation variables include geographic, demographic, socioeconomic, and psychographic variables, as well as behavior and consumption patterns, consumer predispositions, and geodemographic variables. In business markets, geographical areas, organizational characteristics, purchase behavior, usage patterns, and organizational policies are used as segmentation variables. The appropriateness of any one variable or combination of variables varies considerably from case to case. The marketing manager must determine which variables will isolate a meaningful target market.

Learning Objective 7: Explain what a positioning strategy does.

Each brand appealing to a given market segment has a position in the consumer's mind. The gist of a positioning strategy is to identify a product's or brand's competitive advantage and to stress salient product characteristics or consumer benefits that differentiate the product or brand from those of competitors.

IX.   KEY TERMS

X.   QUESTIONS FOR DISCUSSION (13)

XI.   ETHICS IN PRACTICE

XII.   CASES

ANSWER GUIDELINES FOR CHAPTER 8 QUESTIONS FOR DISCUSSION

1.   *Why do organizations practice market segmentation?*

ANSWER:

Most, if not all, organizations practice some type of market segmentation, sometimes in its extreme form of "custom marketing" wherein each potential customer must be approached using a unique, specially constructed marketing mix. Even when such a common product as table salt is considered, we can find segmentation being practiced. There are flavored salts, salt in different sized containers, salt with and without iodine, etc.

Market segmentation may seem to be less common for organizational goods than for consumer goods because some organizational goods are homogeneous products like raw materials or because there are simply fewer organizational customers than there are consumers. But it is easy to discover situations in which an industrial goods producer alters product, price, distribution systems, and/or promotion to appeal to a given market segment. Selling a computer to a state government is quite different from selling a computer to a small, local business.

An example of segmentation in organizational goods: Jonbil, a Virginia-based maker of jeans, sells Long Haul Jeans, "the most comfortable jeans in the world," to truck drivers. Its research shows that the jeans, made for people "too big for your britches" appeal to other blue collar workers aged 35 to 49 who are into outdoor and home improvement work. These were found to be accessible by, and responsive to, direct mail ads. Jonbil is now reaching more potential buyers by placing posters on long-haul trucks. Trucks of this type are believed to "create" three million visual impressions. Who sees trucks? Target market members (truckers and other workers) among other people. If some of the "other people" buy Long Haul Jeans too, so much the better.

Lawyers, doctors, food services, and janitors are among the many providers of services to organizations who alter the product (and other aspects of the marketing mix) from customer to customer.

The common reasoning behind all segmentation is that it should be easier to develop a marketing mix that suits a smaller and more homogeneous group than it is to develop a mix that will please "everybody." Also, it is undeniable that certain groups within a market have needs that other groups do not have. Further, by segmenting a market, an organization might find a potentially attractive segment that is currently being underserved, not served at all, or one that matches up with what the organization has to offer.

Market segmentation makes so much good sense that it is one of a comparatively few marketing tools or concepts that is agreed by "all" to be appropriate in virtually every situation. Also, since almost everything a firm does will affect its appeal to particular market segments (e.g., stay open all night long and get a different type of customer than the one who shops during the day), it makes sense to pay attention to market segmentation and try to control its effects.

2.   *Think of some creative ways the following organizations might segment the market: (a) a rent-a-car company, (b) a zoo, (c) a personal computer manufacturer, and (d) a science magazine.*

ANSWER:

Here are some possible ways to segment these markets.

(a)   A rent-a-car company

Car rental companies rely on business users for a great portion of their sales, thus they are primarily industrial suppliers. Since no particular company is mentioned in the question, students might focus on any company from Hertz to Rent-A-Wreck (which rents used cars cheaply).

The rental companies' slogans and/or names usually tell "who they are after." Hertz is "Number 1." In this, the company seems to be targeting frequent car renters who want the best, who don't want to "mess around" with lesser companies, and who feel that there are advantages to working through Hertz (e.g., more locations mean less chance of being "stuck" somewhere; better image suggests cars are in better shape). Budget Rent-A-Car takes another, more customer-oriented track with its "You're Number One" approach, an obvious suggestion that Hertz ("Number One") doesn't care about "you" but only about itself and its "Number 1" position." The name "Budget" suggests savings, but the slogan tells the target segment that the savings do not necessitate giving up good service. Avis has been trying harder for years. The message is much like Budget's: Avis is going to do its best to win your business.

Other segments are identifiable in these ways:

.   Airport locations for the travel segment.

.   Product line (cars) for the luxury or budget-minded.

.   Services like baggage pick-up, one-way rentals, and credit card acceptance.

.   Speed of service, as stressed by Hertz, for people in a hurry.

Similar discussion can revolve around the various "consumer" segments. The infrequent renter who needs a car only for special occasions, the vacationer, the person who would rather lease than own. The frequent renter, perhaps a city dweller who rents cars for weekend trips with some regularity.

Students may also consider entirely new approaches or product lines in transportation as rental services. Consider:

.   stretch limousines targeted for proms with licensed drivers to reduce DUI problems;

.   recreational vehicles or vans for rent could be targeted toward families to travel on vacations less expensively than by other means of transportation;

.   medical helicopter rentals might allow several communities to maintain air emergency service.

(b)   A zoo

Zoos do approach their various market segments in different ways. The San Diego Zoo is a good example of a zoo that has identified several likely segments. The San Diego Zoo seeks to appeal to local residents of Southern California, nearby Mexico (a wide geographic area), and the great flow of tourists into the area. Locally it offers attractions for young and old, plays up its educational value and its beautiful park-like appearance. To show how successful this program has been, ask any group to name three good U.S. Zoos.

We think the San Diego Zoo, with its wide exposure on T.V., etc., will be at the top of the list.

Zoo "segments" include: parents, grandparents, conservation-minded people, animal/bird lovers, educators and students, vacationers, picnickers, and people wanting to schedule a "day" (e.g., birthday party for kids).

(c)   A personal computer manufacturer

Possible segmentation variables may begin with domestic or international and may then continue with:

Organizational User	Home User
Size of business	Uses (games or nongame)
Jobs to be accomplished	Need for programs
Knowledge of computers	Need for instruction
Money amount investable	Computer hobby use
Place of use (e.g., schools vs. work location)	Place of use (e.g., need portability)
Some use for personal purposes	Some use for business purposes

(d)   A science magazine

A magazine dealing with "popular" treatments of scientific topics can be aimed at several possible market targets. Possible segments are: children who use it as a learning device, adults (mostly men?) who are not scientists but are interested in scientific matters, entire family units who want to "learn together," gift-givers (e.g., grandparents) who want "educational" gifts for youngsters, professional scientists who want a quick way to keep up with happenings outside their immediate specialties.

Consider this example.

> Time, Inc., utilized market segmentation to enter the science field with its magazine, *Discover*. Though this publication competes with *Scientific American*, *Popular Science*, and *Science Digest*, Time's marketing people felt that there was a market niche, or market segment, worthy of becoming the target market for a "news magazine of the sciences."

> Time's executives apparently saw an unserved market that differed from (1) *Scientific American*'s (scientists and sophisticated science buffs) and (2) *Science Digest*'s (nonscientist interested in factual feature material). *Discover* would be more "news oriented."

> All this implies that Time's marketing managers felt that the target market was there and of great enough size to be useful, that it was accessible, and that it could respond to Time's marketing efforts and support the new magazine.

3.   *What are some unusual ways markets have been segmented?*

ANSWER:

"Unusual" is of debatable meaning. Students who come up with nontext examples, examples drawn from reading newspapers or magazines, or examples not familiar to ordinary consumers should probably be rewarded even if the examples are not "unusual" to the instructor.

Some possibilities include:

.   Segmentation by type of market, e.g., B.F. Goodrich has abandoned the original equipment (O.E.) market made up of car manufacturers to concentrate on the replacement (or "aftermarket") business and the distribution system serving it.

. Segmentation by occupation. "Long Haul Jeans" for truckers were mentioned in Answer number 2. Many magazines are aimed at occupational segments. Some include *Sludge*, a magazine for sewer engineers, and *Doctor's Wife*, *The Michigan Bar Owner*, and *Policeman*.

. A "field trip" to a well-stocked newsstand reveals vast arrays of unfamiliar market segments. Balaun's, in Akron, Ohio, stocks the *Miami Herald* and other Florida-based publications for sale in a well-off area of town to people with property and/or relatives in Florida. Other "unusual" products it carries include such segment-oriented magazines as *Used Airplane Buyer* and *Chess*. A review of the "dirty magazines" (not quite pornography) carried by newsstands reveals magazines that focus on particular activities, sexes, and parts of the body. An amazing array of "girlie magazines" exists: girls and cars, girls and motorcycles, girls in bathtubs, etc. There is a magazine called *Feet* for people with "special interests" in that part of the body.

. In one city of which the author is aware, furniture sales are segmented by religious affiliation with Baptist, Catholic, Jewish and Methodist members each shopping in different stores.

. The working woman market has several segments now served by, for example, *Working Woman* magazine. There is also a *Working Mother* magazine, and a *New York Working Woman*.

. Religion is used by some food processors, e.g., all-beef hot dogs are aimed at Jewish buyers as are kosher foods. There are hundreds of newspapers and magazines catering to various religious groups. An organization called CORPUS publishes a newsletter for ex-priests.

4. *Identify and evaluate the target market for the following: (a) Wall Street Journal, (b) the Chicago Cubs, (c) Air Jordan shoes, (d) Perrier bottled water, and (e) "New Age" music.*

ANSWER:

Obviously the question could be asked about any product. It might be useful to pose additional questions about related products. For example, if the student discusses the target market for the Chicago Cubs, he or she might then be asked to tell how this differs from the target market of the Chicago White Sox.

Evaluation can be limited, if desired, to the characteristics of a "meaningful" market segment: possessing distinguishing characteristic(s), significant size, accessibility, and likely to respond to a marketing mix tailored to its needs.

(a) *Wall Street Journal*

In the grossest sense the target market for the *Wall Street Journal* is anyone interested in business. However, the readership of the *Journal* is looking for something different from that of the readers of *Barron's*, *Forbes*, and other business publications. For one thing, they are looking for daily rather than weekly or monthly news. They are looking for general business news rather than, for example, strictly financial news. They are also readers of the Journal because they feel that they have to be. That is, there is a psychological payoff sought in being up-to-date, in being able to converse on matters covered in the Journal, and even in sitting on the train reading the *Journal* like a "good businessperson" should. There is also some "risk" in business to admit to someone that you do not read the *Journal*.

There are certainly several distinguishable groups within this gross segment (established businesspeople, people who hope to get rich, stock market hobbyists, yuppies, etc.). The *Journal* attempts to cater to these by means of its marketing mix. For example, in certain parts of the country the *Journal* is not readily available on newsstands (small towns). The *Journal* is available via mail for these readers and others who want to miss not a single copy of the paper. On the other hand, it is available on newsstands for early birds headed for the train and for persons who are only occasional readers. The paper itself is fairly heavy on financial news but also offers a smattering of standard news fare and even a daily "funny" story and a cartoon. While some press analysts claim that this "nonbusiness" content has watered down the *Journal* and made it less appealing to its major target market, the fact is that the *Journal* is (along with *U.S.A.*) the most widely circulated daily newspaper by far.

As students evaluate the *Journal*'s target market they are tempted to focus on some general "wealthy businessman market." They should be asked to break this down into subsegments like the ones mentioned above and then to evaluate these in terms of age, race, sex, income, education, dwelling place, etc. Surprising differences can be easily identified.

(b)   Chicago Cubs

The target market is, in general, baseball fans located mainly in the Chicago area, but submarkets appear to be of some significance.

.   National League fans.

.   North-Side people vs. South Siders who are often White Sox Fans. There is
       a racial side, and a class side to this, by the way. When the Sox do well,
       and begin attracting Cubs fans, regular Sox fans hold up signs at the
       ballpark that say things like "Yuppy Cubs fans go back to Wrigley (and
       worse).

.   People in other parts of the country who have moved from Chicago or who
       have come to know the Cubs via wide-ranging cable T.V.

The main target market is sizable due to "Chicagoland's" great physical size, and population size and density.

The market is loyal, fiercely so, given that the home stadium, until 1988, had no lights for night games and that the club has won only one championship of any kind in some thirty years.

The market is accessible, via all sorts of media, and seems responsive, though it would respond more to a winning team.

The "total product" of the Cubs should be considered: games, radio and T.V. games, memorabilia sold at the stadium and in stores, great announcers, etc.

(c)   Air Jordan shoes

Given the fact that most people with any interest in basketball believe that Michael Jordan is almost certainly the most talented player ever to play the game, his name would appeal to many market segments.

We might start by dividing the market into playing and nonplaying people, then look for smaller segments within those groupings.

Some who actually play basketball will want Air Jordan shoes because they will "help them play better," others will want them to "show off," others will want them to have "the best, or at least the shoes Michael says are the best," others will harbor secret notions about their "star performances" while wearing the shoes -- sort of like playing "air guitar" and pretending to be a rock star. There will, of course, be nonplayers who want the shoes for reasons of identification with Michael Jordan (a popular, personable fellow), or because the shoes are "cool," or because others in the purchaser's peer group have the shoes. It is also likely that some people will buy the shoes because they believe they are good shoes. For one thing, the chances that the great Michael Jordan would allow his name to be associated with a BAD shoe would appear to be slim. Also, the shoes are fairly expensive and certainly well-advertised, both things that people associate with quality. Plus, there's that little, secret hope in most of us that somehow these shoes will make us ten times better than we are at whatever sports we try.

(d)   Perrier bottled water

Perrier appeals to a health and weight-conscious market that is, or tries to be, "sophisticated." A risk is that such people are often trendy to the degree that they might quickly drop today's "in" drink for tomorrow's. The introduction of sparking waters with fruit flavors inspired Perrier to do likewise in 1988, but there is plenty of competition from U.S. and Canadian products. Perrier drinkers are upscale, educated, and interested in "good living."

As it happens, during the Nasty Nineties this market appears to be in decline, as formerly spendthrift yuppies begin to wonder about buying water in fancy bottles. At this writing, late 1992, the beverage industry trade press carries many stories about the decline of the Perrier-type bottled water market.

The size of the target market segment is probably still more than adequate, however, especially with increasingly bad publicity given to alcoholic drinks, the accent on safe driving, and increasing public distaste for drunkenness and, especially, drunk driving. The market is accessible via proper media: trendy magazines, selected T.V. programs ("Tennis from Wimbledon"). It is also important to access this market by having the product available in upscale restaurants and watering places. Even though the market for Perrier-style drinks might be declining, Perrier is still a top name in the field and can trade on that fact. As the market for waters declines, it may be necessary for Perrier to narrow its focus, perhaps concentrating on the "special occasion segment" as several beer producers (Lowenbrau) and whiskey makers (Johnny Walker Black) do.

(e)   "New Age" music

While the inventors of "New Age" music may not have had a specific target market in mind as they noodled out their tunes, the promoters of the music quickly learned of its appeal for Baby Boomers-grown-older or former "yuppies." People in this age group (late 20s, early 40s) grew up with rock and roll. Now, having achieved a certain age and a certain success (and perhaps a certain stress level in their lives), they feel that perhaps they are too old for the crash and bang of rock and roll. Perhaps they even catch themselves quoting their own parents to the effect that "today's music is too loud and I can't understand the words and it all sounds the same to me."

Casting about for something else to listen to, they are attracted to "New Age," a sort of mixture of jazz, light rock, and just a touch of classical music. These former rock fans are generally not knowledgeable about classical music or jazz, so they can't move on (grow up) to those forms. They can understand the watered down, soothing tones of "New Age."

In short, they know they are too old for heavy metal thunder, but can't bring themselves to listen to what their parents did, or to "beautiful music" stations. "New Age" music, in some places broadcast as "The Wave," provides them with another, easy-to-take option.

By the way, "The Wave" programming was introduced in Washington, D.C. on station WBMW. That tells something of the target market sought in the late 1980s.

5.   *What questions should be asked to determine if a market segment is meaningful?*

ANSWER:

The text suggests four points to be mentioned in answering this question.

.   Does the segment have distinguishing characteristics to set it apart from the overall market?

.   Does it represent a market potential of significant size, that is, large enough to be profitable?

.   Is the segment accessible via distribution and promotional methods?

.   Does the segment have a unique need, and is it likely to respond favorably to a marketing mix tailored to this specialized need?

.   Is the segment's market potential measurable, preferably in a fairly easy manner?

Some other questions can be posed.

.   How does our marketing mix stack up in light of products and mixes already in use?

.   Can the segment's responses be measured?

.   Is this segment, and/or any characteristics of it, likely to change in the future? How will these changes affect us?

.   What will competitors do if we go after this segment?

6.   *Think of examples of companies that use (a) undifferentiated marketing, (b) concentrated marketing, (c) differentiated marketing, and (d) custom marketing. Why is the strategy appropriate in each instance?*

ANSWER:

Before suggesting examples of utilization of different strategies, the basic answer to the "why is it appropriate" querie can be mentioned. The answer is always, at base, the same: "Because it suits the market." A buyer of a car is not the same as a buyer of a can of pepper even when the person doing the purchasing is one and the same.

(a)   Undifferentiated marketing

Producers of many food products (meat, cheese, and eggs in their from-the-farm state at least), nails, many construction materials, many industrial goods. These are (usually) commodity goods, standardized, and far from glamorous. Though buyers might be distinguishable by size of purchase, and while each customer deserves some special considerations according to the marketing concept, these sorts of products fit undifferentiated marketing.

(b)   Concentrated marketing

Any marketer who concentrates on one market segment, e.g., publisher of one magazine, operator of a "Music of Your Life" radio station, producer of T.V. programs or toys for kids age 5-12, a veterinarian who runs an "emergency clinic" open only from 6 p.m. to 1 a.m., a barber who "sells" haircuts and shaves to hospital patients. Maternity shops. Big and Tall shops. These marketers are focused on one market segment, practicing forms of concentrated marketing. As long as the segment served does not decline, concentrated marketing can be very successful and represent a means to use resources most efficiently by "specializing."

(c)   Differentiated marketing

Any marketer who offers more than one marketing mix, each aimed at a particular segment, e.g., Procter and Gamble, Colgate-Palmolive, Beatrice Foods (the largest U.S. foods producer, but "unknown" to many since its marketing mixes include different names for its products, e.g., Sumner's Butter). For the most part, auto makers fit this category. Differentiated marketing provides a means to appeal to different segments and do it (usually) while making effective use of resources. For example, the cereal companies make many types of cereals from many market segments from kids to old folks, but the products are, in general, similarly produced, packaged, distributed, etc. In other words, why not appeal to many segments when you can do so utilizing essentially the same resources and talents?

(d)   Custom marketing

Any marketer who, in effect, fashions a "new" marketing mix for each buyer, e.g., many industrial goods sellers must offer made-to-order goods. Large computer installations are designed to meet the needs of specific buyers. Seamstresses often custom design clothing for each patron. The strategy is appropriate because the customer demands it. While other segmenting strategies are also customer-based, custom marketing most clearly demonstrates the customer-driven nature of market segmentation.

7.   *Should firms always aim at the largest market segment?*

ANSWER:

No marketer should always do anything (except satisfy customers).

This question obviously calls for mention of the majority fallacy which points out that the temptation to blindly go after the largest, richest, heavy-user or other attractive segment should be avoided since competitors may also be aiming at that target making for high levels of less-than-profitable competition. Firms should consider making an ultimately more profitable appeal to a smaller, "less attractive" segment.

The beer industry tends to focus on reaching the "heavy user," but some brewers produce six and seven ounce bottles of beer aimed at "light users" (thought primarily to be women). Other brewers are too small to go after heavy users, especially on a wide geographic basis. Instead, they make a high quality beer with "mystique." Lienenkugel in the Chicago area is a good example; Anchor Steam in San Francisco is another.

The majority fallacy reminds us of the very essence of the segmenting process. Its purpose is to find market segments which are then evaluated for their "meaningfulness." Its purpose is not to find the one segment that is the obvious target for all firms in an industry.

8.   *What is benefit segmentation?*

ANSWER:

Students should focus on the consumer here, not the product. A benefit is something "you" receive as distinguished from a product feature or characteristic.

Benefit segmentation focuses on the benefits sought by the buyer when he or she buys the product offered. Toothpaste is the common example: "you receive" better checkups, clean breath, white teeth, good taste, etc. Different brands of toothpaste stress these in their ads. Other examples:

.   Mouthwash - good taste vs. mediciney germ killer vs. plaque fighter

.   Light Beer - less fattening than regular beer

.   Diet Soda - less fattening than standard sodas

.   No-Caffeine Soda, Coffee, Tea - health advantage

.   Low-Salt Ketchup - health advantage

9.   *How might Levi's segment the men's clothing market? How might Anheuser-Busch segment the market for beer?*

ANSWER:

Levi's can segment the men's clothing market in many ways. Among the variables it has employed, or might employ are:

.   Age
.   Weight
.   Benefits sought (long wear vs. appearance)
.   Occasion of use (need a hammer loop or not?)
.   Geography (Western-style stitching or not?)
.   Lifestyle (may need reinforcement because of athletic use)
.   Income (willingness to buy expensive models)
.   Self-image (some Levi's are a "scosh bigger" even though you still buy "your same old size")

Combinations of these and other factors are possible. For example, the person who wants his jeans "a scosh" bigger has a certain self-image, is probably over thirty, a bit out-of-shape (or more than a bit), probably has enough money to buy "noncheap" jeans, leads a life (or thinks he does) appropriate to wearing jeans, etc.

This having been said, it might be appropriate to note that Levi's researchers believe they have identified five psychographic segments in the men's clothing market.

1)   The Utilitarian Customer. Wears jeans for work and play, doesn't care much about clothing.

2)   The Trendy-Casual. High fashion awareness, loves to be noticed, young, fad consumer.

3)   The Price Shopper. Concerned mostly with price. Shops discount stores, department stores, and wherever bargains are best.

4)   The Mainstream Traditionalist. Levi's best customers for the slacks and accessories line. Married men, 45 and over, shop with their wives, value wives' opinions. Conservative in tastes and politics. Shop mostly at standard department stores.

5)   The Classic Independent. A "clothes horse." Spends more on clothes than the other segments. Buys nearly half of all wool sports jackets and suits. Looking good is very important. They shop alone and "know what they like," shop in specialty stores, dress with a conservative look, believe alterations and tailoring are important, and don't want to feel "mass-produced."

The class might discuss these segments and how Levi's marketing mixes do or do not reflect this research.

Anheuser-Busch segments the market for beer in some obvious and not-so-obvious ways.

The company brews several brands of beer, each with a slightly different image. Michelob is a super-premium, high-quality beer, intended for use on special occasions and times of relaxation (like weekends). Busch is for the younger, more athletic crowd. Its advertisements often feature sports or outdoor activities like fishing trips and "heading to the mountains." Budweiser is a premium beer, with good quality and a long tradition. Now each of these comes in a "light" version. Michelob is not-so-light, but does contain somewhat fewer calories than the regular beer. Bud Light (notice the nick-name "Bud") is more than a low-calorie version of Budweiser. It's for a younger crowd, it's "fun" as attested to by the Spuds MacKenzie ads, the Bud Bowl, etc. Busch also has a light. (Bud Dry is a newer product with a different taste. It has some connotation of lightness and trendy appeal. Its track record, at this time, is spotty. Many buyers use it as a "change of pace" rather than a "regular.")

Beyond all this, Michelob comes in a dark version, for those who want a quality dark beer with a European association, who feel they "know good beer" and don't want to hear about calories.

The beers come in cans or bottles. Each package has its fans as attested to by the fact that both are available at your supermarket. However, in some areas, almost all beer is sold in cans and little in bottles. In those areas Anheuser-Busch distributes mostly cans.

Some beer drinkers want a small can or bottle. These are made available. Some want quart bottles and those can be found, too. Some want a six-pack, some a twelve-pack, and some 24-bottle or 24-can cases. They can find all of these.

Thus, Anheuser-Busch segments its market by brand preference, quality sought, "image," calorie-consciousness, amount purchased, occasion when product will be consumed, and to a degree, by price preference, as well as other variables.

10.   *What variable do you think is best for segmenting a market?*

ANSWER:

This is a question that can elicit almost any response depending on the product or market in question. The "answer," of course, is always "the variable(s) that lead to identification of a meaningful market segment."

Students should be asked to consider their responses in terms of practical considerations. There is, in fact, a "family man" segment. If variables are chosen that set this segment up as the meaningful one, questions follow as to how such a segment can be identified, measured, located, appealed to, distributed to, etc.

The text makes the point that demographic variables are often most useful as segmentation bases. They are relatively easy to understand, use, find data on, are often predictable, etc. They cannot, of course, be defended as "best" unless situations are such that other bases are, for whatever reason, eliminated from consideration.

11.   *What variables might a business-to-business marketer use to segment a market?*

ANSWER:

Selected bases for segmenting organization markets are shown in the text. Briefly, such bases include:

Geographic: Political boundaries such as cities or states, or domestic/ international boundaries. Physical boundaries, like mountains and rivers could be important too, as might characteristics of the land and weather. (Not all farm equipment is suited to all locations.)

Organizational Characteristics: Industry types; organizational size; technology used.

Purchase Behavior and Usage Patterns: Order size or heavy/light usage; single- vs. multiple-sourcing; centralized/decentralized purchasing; type of purchase as straight rebuy to new task.

Organizational Predisposition or Policy: Product knowledge; benefits; organizational problems; single- vs. multiple-supplier policy.

As long as free enterprise exists, there will be other examples of potential segmentation variables which could work for given situations. For example, sellers of canned music for organizations might segment markets based on the average age of employees, or music listening preferences within geographic areas as well as characteristics such as size.

12.   *What is positioning? Provide some examples.*

ANSWER:

A market position, or competitive position, represents the way consumers perceive a brand relative to its competition. A typical positioning strategy attempts to identify a product's competitive advantage and to stress salient characteristics or benefits that are differentiable from those of competitors. When a competitor positions its product directly against another, it is referred to as head-to-head competition and the goal is to occupy the same position as opposed to differentiation.

Students typically enjoy positioning local businesses and bars (as well as beers and cars) on preference maps, both as a break from lecture and a reinforcement of concepts. Should you be so inclined, consider local restaurants, using price (high or low) and ambiance (subdued or lively). To reinforce research concepts, you may even ask students to generate questions, scale responses, and collect data from their friends before quantitatively estimating the relative positions.

As an example to stimulate thought:

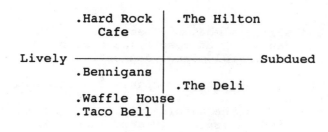

```
                        High Price

            .Hard Rock     | .The Hilton
               Cafe        |
                           |
    Lively ────────────────┼──────────────── Subdued
                           |
            .Bennigans     |
                           | .The Deli
            .Waffle House  |
            .Taco Bell     |

                        Low Price
```

13.   *Identify the positioning strategy for the following brands: (a) 7-Up; (b)*
       American Airlines; (c) American Telephone and Telegraph.

ANSWER:

To stimulate discussion, ask students to first identify the features or benefits
of each business which differentiate it from the competition. Ask students how
consumers evaluate competitive products; which characteristics are most
important in choice; how the brands compare on the important characteristics. It
may be helpful to draw a positioning map, label the axes, and place each product
as well as a few of its competitors in their approximate positions. Drawing maps
and estimated positions reinforces the logic of identifying differentiable
features of products and business organizations.

(a)   7-Up

This product has, at various times, positioned itself as a healthier, lighter,
"clear" alternative to Coca-Cola and Pepsi. ("Caffeine? Never had it, never
will." and "The Un-Cola.") Relevant characteristics students may consider to
differentiate alternative offerings could include: color (light/dark); caffeine
(high/low); taste (strong/weak) (refreshing/flat).

(b)   American Airlines

American Airlines (something special in the air) is positioned as a leader in the
market, aggressive in such areas as lower pricing or frequent flier miles. As
students consider relevant characteristics, ask them to focus on specific market
segments within the airline industry. For example, dimensions such as price may
vary in description by business or vacation markets. A competitive edge in
frequent flier mile policies may be more important to the former while the latter
might be more interested in multiple person discounts or special weekend rates.
Students may recognize a pertinent issue as business/family image for specific
airlines, especially if a local airport has commuter flights or smaller
companies. Characteristics for consideration in constructing a map might
include: dominant market (business/family); scope (domestic/international);
price (low/high); image (prestigious/bargain); climate (friendly/cold).

This question may have to be adjusted by the professor given the volatile nature
of the airline business at the time the text and this manual were being written.
Airlines have been very hard hit in the late 80s and early 90s.

(c)   American Telephone and Telegraph (AT&T)

In the settlement for the 1981 antitrust suit against AT&T, the company divested
itself of regional telephone operating companies and retained control of
interstate networks, manufacturing (Western Electric), research (Bell
Laboratories), and information (data processing). It may be easiest for students
to compare the relative positions of interstate telephone networks (AT&T, Sprint,
MCI) than to analyze the other major AT&T markets. AT&T is positioned as the
leader in its market with, by far, the largest market share and the longest track
record. Students should recognize that AT&T may not offer the lowest price. The
firm's image is built on the superior quality, service (credit for misdialed
numbers), and efficient business packages rather than price. Characteristics
which may help stimulate discussion include: price (low/high); service

(strong/weak); discount packages or plans (frequent/infrequent); quality or clarity of phone service (high/low); billing accuracy (always/never).

A late-comer to marketing, AT&T has done well given that in the space of a few years it went from an all-controlling monopoly with "no marketing," to a floundering company forced to operate in an unfamiliar market-driven environment, to the successful competitor it has become. Students may have to be informed as to how powerful "Mother Bell" was before the break-up and how it ran the show with little real regard for the marketplace.

ETHICS EXERCISE 8

CHAPTER 8 ETHICS IN PRACTICE

Overview

The marketing of Uptown cigarettes, targeted at African-Americans, was a highly controversial plan which got a lot of coverage in the media, especially in the business press. Late in 1989, R.J. Reynolds (RJR) Tobacco Company proclaimed that it planned to test a new menthol cigarette targeted specifically at African-Americans the following February in Philadelphia. According to a company spokesperson, the firm's intent was to market a cigarette among smokers who currently purchased competitive products.

The spokesperson explained that research showed that African-American consumers prefer a lighter menthol cigarette, and Uptown was designed to satisfy this need, delivering a lighter menthol taste than the firm's Salem brand. Uptown was carefully researched and designed: everything from the name to its packaging was tailored to the tastes of the African-American consumer.

What made Uptown unique was that it was the first brand to be specifically pitched to African-Americans. Although tobacco companies had marketed to African-Americans in the past, this was the first time that a company had openly declared that a cigarette was targeted to a minority group. For example, menthol brands had been promoted in Black publications, on billboards in African-American neighborhoods, and by sponsoring Black-oriented special events. As cigarette consumption has fallen in the U.S., tobacco companies have increasingly directed their marketing efforts to niche groups, such as Blacks, Hispanics, and certain segments of women (e.g., Uptown cigarettes in question 1 below) who are heavier consumers of the products.

What immediately ensued upon RJR's announcement was an outcry from critics such as the American Cancer Society and other antismoking groups, Black community leaders, the Junior League, and the U.S. Secretary of Health & Human services, Louis Sullivan (a Black man,) who said that "Uptown's message is more disease, more suffering, and more death for a group already bearing more than its share of smoking-related illness and mortality." RJR replied that in announcing the marketing plan for Uptown it was simply being upfront about its intentions.

As a result of the uproar, in early 1990, RJR announced its decision to cancel plans to test market Uptown, claiming it could not get accurate results from the test market under the cloud of controversy. Some observers believe that the Uptown affair will make it more difficult for tobacco and liquor companies to target their brands to minorities, women, and youth. And, the concern continues to grow that big corporations have targeted minority communities as lucrative markets for "unhealthy" products such as tobacco, alcoholic beverages, and even candy.

1.   *Is it ethical to segment a market based on race?*

Race is a demographic base for segmentation, and it appears in many standard lists of market segmentation variables. A person's race is based on their skin color (white, black, yellow, brown, and red). A person's nationality is based on country of origin, e.g., Asian Americans (Japanese, Chinese, Vietnamese, etc.) and Hispanics (Mexicans, Puerto Ricans, Cubans, etc.)

There is nothing inherently unethical in marketing to a given racial or ethnic group.   These are usually viewed as subcultural groups with unique wants and needs, tastes and preferences, values, norms, and other characteristics.   Hence, according to the theory of market segmentation, such groups should be considered as viable market segments for certain products.

The question is: are there any products for which using racial or ethnic groups as target markets would be unethical?   The answer given by some is that it is unfair to target such groups for unhealthy or "sin" products, especially alcohol and tobacco products.   The idea is that these groups are more vulnerable or manipulable (perhaps due to their disadvantaged backgrounds stemming from a history of racial discrimination).   For example, statistics from the U.S. Public Health Service show that African-American men have a 58 percent higher incidence of lung cancer than white men and lose twice as many years of life as do whites because of smoking-related diseases.   One could argue that justice is not being served by the cold-blooded singling out of a particularly vulnerable group for purchase of a product potentially hazardous to its members' health.

On the other hand, RJR in effect argued that it was simply practicing the marketing concept, designing a product to appeal to a particular market segment. They and some media commentators claimed that it was unfair for Secretary Sullivan and "a small coalition of anti-smoking zealots" to single out RJR for targeting Black customers when others do it as well, albeit less openly.   The company believed that Black smokers should be given the freedom of choice to select a product designed with their needs in mind and that Uptown's withdrawal represented an erosion of the free enterprise system.   *Advertising Age* magazine opined in an editorial that RJR shouldn't be effectively barred by the government from marketing such a cigarette as long as cigarettes are legal.

Also, some African-Americans, such as civil rights activist Benjamin Hooks, saw the opposition as a form of paternalism.   He said that the reasoning underlying the protest is that Blacks are not capable of making their own free decisions. It has been argued that ignoring minority communities would be insulting, and disallowing these marketing efforts is a form of censorship.

CHAPTER 8 TAKE A STAND QUESTIONS

1.   *Is the marketing of sugar-coated cereals on Saturday morning television good for society?*

The argument against this practice is similar to that against marketing cigarettes to blacks and women: we are marketing a potentially dangerous product to a vulnerable group.   If one believes cigarettes shouldn't be marketed to African-Americans, to be consistent one should also argue that sugared cereal (as well as candy and other "junk foods") shouldn't be marketed to children since they are an even more vulnerable group: less educated, less able to deal rationally with persuasive messages, etc.

The arguments against and for such advertising aimed at the younger set were detailed in Chapter 3 Take A Stand question 2.   The basic matter is whether this is a fair (just) practice, given children's special weakness for sweet treats. Do children eat high-calorie junk foods because of the many commercials for such products and because TV-watching has become a traditional snack time for children?   The jury is still out.

2.   *Is segmentation based on race discrimination ethical?*

As seen in Chapter 7 Take A Stand question 3, discrimination involves treating different groups in different ways based on irrelevant characteristics. Discriminatory action awards benefits or imposes burdens on a basis not related to relevant characteristics or needs, and this is deemed to be unfair.

As seen above, it could be argued in the case of cigarettes and other unhealthy products that such treatment is unfair in that the groups are more vulnerable and are already heavy consumers of such products.   However, for other goods and services, such discrimination is not inherently ethical.

"Discrimination" is an emotionally loaded word, but the fact is that market segmentation is simply applied discrimination.   The characteristics upon which it is based are relevant to the marketing efforts in that different consumer clusters have different needs, wants, desires, etc. If the targeted groups are more satisfied as a result, and no other groups are harmed (how could they be?), society's welfare is increased.

3.   *Dakota cigarettes were designed to be marketed to active working class women. Is this right?*

The issue is basically the same one as above: should a possibly vulnerable group be targeted with a potentially hazardous product? Dakota cigarettes were supposed to be test marketed by RJR in April 1990 in Houston. An antismoking group somehow got their hands on RJR's marketing plan for Dakota. The plan apparently revealed that Dakota was to be targeted to young, "virile," white, blue-collar women under 21, with no education beyond high school. Psychographically this group was interested in "cruising," "partying," and participating in various activities with their boyfriends such as "hot rod shows," "tractor pulls," drag races, carnivals, and wrestling matches, and their favorite TV program was "Roseanne."

The critics argued that such consumers are the least informed about the dangers of smoking and the easiest to attract to cigarettes. When asked to comment on the proposed marketing plan Secretary Sullivan said, "It is especially reprehensible to lure young people into smoking and potential lifelong nicotine addiction."

The cigarette companies in response put forth the arguments in the Uptown case above. Regarding cigarette advertising, their claim is that they do not cause people to smoke; rather they simply shift brand preferences. Generic consumption patterns are due to more fundamental factors such as peer and parental influences (see the discussion for Chapter 2 Take A Stand question 2). Also, they claim that those under 18 who are legally prohibited from purchasing cigarettes are not included in the target market.

GUIDE TO CASES

VIDEO CASE 8-1 GOOD HOUSEKEEPING

SUBJECT MATTER: Market Segmentation, Positioning, Women Values

Please see the Guide to Video Cases for video length and other information.

AT-A-GLANCE OVERVIEW

The Hearst Corporation, an conglomerate communications organization with interests in newspapers, broadcasting, and publications, publishes *Good Housekeeping* magazine. It acquired *Good Housekeeping* in 1911.

Good Housekeeping began in 1885 when Clark W. Bryant thought housewives, who worked long and hard cooking, sewing, and cleaning, deserved a magazine of their own. Although housewives' lives had not changed much in decades, Mr. Bryant believed a magazine could help improve the situation. One way to do this, among many others, was to protect housewives against misleading advertisements and dangerous products.

For example, at the turn of the century, advertisers could say anything they wanted to and make outlandish claims for their goods. Cough syrups with 40 percent alcohol, and sometimes laced with morphine, were advertised as healthy cures. In 1902, to help its readers avoid confusion about problems like this, *Good Housekeeping* guaranteed the truth of any ad placed in the magazine. In 1910, continuing its battle for quality standards, it created its Good Housekeeping Seal of Approval. The Good Housekeeping Institute rated products and only those products rated acceptable by its institute could receive the seal and be advertised in the magazine.

Over the years *Good Housekeeping* has changed with the times. For instance, in the 1910s, it supported women's suffrage. During the Great Depression (1929 -

1933), the magazine contained articles on how to economize and maintain good nutrition in the home. During World War II, its articles focused on helping women cope while husband or boyfriend was away at war.

During the '50s, '60s, '70s, and early '80s, *Good Housekeeping* was known as one of the Seven Sisters women's magazines: *Good Housekeeping, Ladies' Home Journal, Family Circle, Redbook, McCall's, Woman's Day,* and *Better Homes & Gardens.* In 1966, *Good Housekeeping* became the leader in the general women's magazine field.

Today, however, the women's market is becoming increasingly diverse. All areas of magazine publishing are increasingly competitive, but women's magazines are especially, even ferociously, competitive.

Some industry members say the "Seven Sisters" label is no longer appropriate in an era of specialization. Being general is considered a negative, so many women's magazines are associating themselves with a segment within the mass market. In the 1990s, the *Good Housekeeping* focus is on the "New Traditional" woman.

DISCUSSION QUESTIONS

1.   *How have women's roles and values changed since Good Housekeeping beginnings?*

There have been dramatic changes in the role of women since the turn of the century. The video dramatically illustrates this. In the previous century, things did not change much. Woman's work was drudgery. Also, marketing has changed along with women.

Over the years *Good Housekeeping* has shown its publisher's ability to change with the times. For instance, in the 1910s it supported women's suffrage. During the Depression (1929-1933), the magazine contained articles about how to economize and maintain good nutrition in the home. During World War II, its articles focused on helping women cope with the wartime situation.

In the 1950s, there was a baby boom and a movement to the suburbs. Women were more affluent and more mobile. In the late 1960s and early 1970s, feminism became more popular. There was a new generation of women with different values, women who were willing to protest and try to change the status quo. In the late '70s and early '80s, more and more women continued to work outside the home after marriage and childbirth. The 1980s were known as a decade of materialism.

According to the video, the 1990s are a decade of decency. Women are voicing concern for society through their pocketbooks. They are concerned with about the environment. Leisure time and free time have become increasingly valued. Women, feeing harried, are seeking "time" and are willing to pay for it.

Women in *Good Housekeeping*'s target segment believe their homes to be their haven. They indulge themselves somewhat. Women are individualists.
According the video, the new traditionalist's brand loyalty can be established by providing information and good value in products.

2.   *What segments exist in the market for women's magazines?*

One segment which *Good Housekeeping* targets is the general women's magazine segment. Historically this segment was known as the "Seven Sisters." Today, however, many of these general magazines stress their individuality because the general women's market is so competitive. Today, in an era of specialization, to be general is considered a negative, and that is why many of the old Seven Sisters have repositioned themselves to a niche within the mass market. *Redbook* redesigned its look and positions itself with the tag line "The Juicy Red Book." *McCall's* has taken fashion as its definition. Increasingly, with the aging of the population, some magazines cater to the older woman segment, an idea that would have been anathema a decade or two ago. Race and social class are the basis of appeal of several women's magazines.

"Tabloid," fashion, sport, health, fitness, leisure, and gardening are among the most common segments for women's magazines. There are also special magazines for teen and pre-teenage girls. Furthermore, the presence of various hobby segments and special interest segments make a clear cut definition difficult.

3.   *What is Good Housekeeping's niche in the market. Why would Good Housekeeping choose a strategy to position itself as a magazine for "new traditional" woman?*

Good Housekeeping promotes traditional values. In the terms of the 1992 presidential campaign, it represents "family values." It also targets women who are concerned with value in products, and, as the title of the magazine suggests, has done so from the beginning. The Good Housekeeping Institute and Seal of Approval symbolically reflect this concern with economic value and wise home economics. In the 1990s, value means not only products that have proven their worth over time, but value to society. For example, environmental awareness is at an all-time high among women, and advertisers are adopting strategies that address these consumer concerns.

"New traditional" is a tricky phrase. It clearly attempts to say "We're modern, but we retain the good old stuff too." Some compromise like this is probably necessary. Is a totally "new" woman going to buy an old standby magazine like *Good Housekeeping*? Is a woman who is basically old-fashioned going to admit it? Don't most people want to be "with it"? So, this positioning lets *Good Housekeeping* (try, at least) to have things both ways.

VIDEO CASE 8-2   FOCUS ON SMALL BUSINESS
THE OLYMPIAD[1]

SUBJECT MATTER: Competitive environment, positioning

Please see the Guide to Video Cases for video length and other information.

AT-A-GLANCE OVERVIEW

The Olympiad is a Burlington, Vermont, health club offering squash, racquetball, and aerobic and cardiovascular exercise. Founded in 1982, the firm has 63 employees.

In the Spring of 1988, when a competing health club opened across the street, the Olympiad's business survival was at serious risk. Along with offering a larger space and additional facilities, the new club began an aggressive marketing campaign specifically aimed at the Olympiad's members.

DISCUSSION QUESTIONS

1.   *What is marketing opportunity analysis? How can it help to evaluate the competitive situation facing the Olympiad?*

The marketing environment consists of uncontrollable forces that provide both opportunities and constraints to an organization. Some organizations, even those marketing products and services only in their home countries, are influenced by opportunities and threats presented by forces in both the domestic environment and foreign environments.

In the case of the Olympiad, and most service retailers, competition is primarily domestic. Marketing opportunity analysis looks at threats and opportunities in the external environment and also analyzes internal strengths and weaknesses. The Olympiad is in clear need of this. After all, the new competitor, bigger (better?) and aggressive, is right across the street.

---

[1]Excerpts reprinted from *Strengthening America's Competitiveness*, p. 121, copyright 1991 by Connecticut Mutual Life Insurance Company.

2.   *How should the Olympiad position itself in the Burlington, Vermont,
        marketplace?*

There are a number of options. For example, a body building position is taken at
some "gyms." The Olympiad chose to position itself as the health club with
personal services. It stressed the personal relationship between clients and
employees. It also focused on health improvement.

3.   *How should the Olympiad respond to its new competitor?*

In general, the company should carefully study its situation before taking any
drastic moves. Assuming this was done, the next step is to reformulate the
marketing mix, if necessary, in an attempt to garner a market position that is
defensible against this new competitor. To some degree the Olympiad is operating
from a position of strength. It is established and apparently doing well,
suggesting that it has many satisfied customers. A health club's members are
fairly loyal customers. They tend to think of the place as "my club" and welcome
the chance to see familiar people, both workers and other members. (This
suggests that a problem the Olympiad should address is the "stealing" of its more
popular employees by the competition.)

Also, customers may be "tied" to the club, at least for a period of time, by
membership dues. This, however, is a price issue, and price is the most easily
matched element of the marketing mix, at least over the short run. The
competitor might, for example, encourage club switching by simply honoring the
Olympiad member's paid up time at the new establishment.

All aspects of the marketing mix should be evaluated, including "place."
(Should off-site training be considered?) Adding features to the total product
should be contemplated.

In the case at hand, here's what happened. The Olympiad was able to fend off its
competition and increase its customer base by altering its marketing efforts. In
response to the competitive challenge, the Olympiad introduced a number of
personalized fitness services and launched a new television advertising campaign
accenting its health-oriented approach. In addition to providing annual
cardiovascular evaluations, instructors began to develop individualized training
programs and intensified their efforts to know the club's clientele. Fortifying
this theme in its ad campaign, the Olympiad's marketing message reinforced its
personalized fitness aims.

As a result of these efforts, the firm's sales have increased 10 percent annually
since 1988 and membership retention is considerably higher than the national
average. Buoyed by this success, The Olympiad is now pursuing expansion plans of
its own.

9

GLOBAL COMPETITION AND INTERNATIONAL MARKETING

CHAPTER SCAN

This text makes frequent mention of international marketing. However, the topic is of such importance that specific attention to it is required.

This chapter takes two main approaches to the topic. One is to consider the impact of international marketing on our economy and provide examples of marketing successes and failures on the international level. The second is to address international marketing from the viewpoint of an American organization seeking to develop nondomestic markets, and discuss the steps necessary in such ventures. The intent here is to show both the opportunities and the complexities found in international marketing.

SUGGESTED LEARNING OBJECTIVES

The student who studies this chapter will be exposed to an overview of international marketing and will be able to:

1. Describe the impact of international marketing on our domestic economy and on the economies of our trading partners.

2. Outline the steps a domestic marketer must complete in analyzing and developing foreign markets.

3. Explain the theory of comparative advantage.

4. Understand how the nature of foreign environments influence the decision about which markets to enter.

5. Identify the different levels of involvement in multinational marketing.

6. Discuss the adaptation of domestic strategies and marketing mixes to foreign markets.

CHAPTER OUTLINE

I.   INTRODUCTION

II.   GLOBAL COMPETITION

III.   THE IMPORTANCE OF MULTINATIONAL MARKETING

IV.   GETTING INVOLVED IN MULTINATIONAL MARKETING

      A.   Decision 1: Do We Get Involved in International Marketing?

           1.   Factors Encouraging International Marketing
           2.   Factors Discouraging International Marketing

      B.   Decision 2: Which International Markets?

           1.   The Cultural Environment
           2.   The Political Environment
           3.   The Economic Environment
           4.   The Demographic Environment

      C.   Decision 3: How Much Commitment in Each Market?

           1.   Exporting
           2.   Joint Venturing
           3.   Direct Foreign Investment

      D.   Decision 4: How Should We Organize for International Marketing?

           1.   Export Department or International Division?
           2.   The Multinational Company versus the International Company

      E.   Decision 5: How Much Should We Change Our Domestic-Based Marketing?

           1.   International Marketing Research
           2.   Product Planning
           3.   Other Marketing Mix Decisions

V.   SUMMARY

VI.   KEY TERMS

VII.   QUESTIONS FOR DISCUSSION (10)

VIII. ETHICS IN PRACTICE

IX.   CASES

     The following key terms are introduced and used in Chapter 9. They are defined in the text's Glossary.

Comparative advantage
European Community (EC), or Common Market
General Agreements on Tariffs and Trade (GATT)
Tariff
Import quota
Embargo
Boycott
Exchange rate
Devaluation
Ethnocentrism
Dumping
Undeveloped countries
Less-developed countries
Developing countries
Developed countries
Countertrade

Exporting
Indirect exporting
Buyer for export
Export management company
Direct exporting
Joint venturing
Licensing
International franchising
Contract manufacturing
Joint ownership venture
Direct foreign investment
Export department
International department
Globalization strategy
Customization strategy

THE CHAPTER SUMMARIZED

I.   INTRODUCTION

    Eastern Europeans are fascinated by Western advertising. It opens their
    eyes to all the West has, but makes them resent the bleakness of their own
    lives. J. Walter Thompson, Inc., has found Eastern Europeans to be
    educated and sophisticated, but not when it comes to consumer behavior.
    Thompson recommends ads that describe quality and workmanship, factors
    missing in the products with which these people are familiar. Certain
    situations in Western advertisements (e.g. "excessive" friendliness)
    Russians and others find unbelievable. They find actors younger than 50 to
    be less than credible spokespersons. Western marketers have to alter their
    approach, their marketing mixes, when dealing with other cultures.

II.   GLOBAL COMPETITION

    Political boundaries between countries are still in place, but flows of
    financial and industrial activities show little respect for those
    boundaries. Coca-Cola is sold worldwide, Honda makes lawn mowers in North
    Carolina, Sony is known the world around.

    The U.S., and the world, has passed from being domestically oriented to
    being globally oriented. Competition is not just domestic competition, but
    competition from other countries. The future of marketing is global.

    Though some distinctions may be drawn, the terms "international" and
    "multinational" are commonly used interchangeably.

    An organization selling its products beyond its home nation is a
    multinational marketer engaged in international marketing.

    Multinational or international marketing involves the adoption of a
    marketing strategy that views the world market rather than a domestic
    market as the basis for geographic market segmentation.

III. THE IMPORTANCE OF MULTINATIONAL MARKETING

    Gillette, Coca-Cola, and Johnson & Johnson are among many large U.S.
    multinational firms. The U.S. government encourages firms to enlarge their
    overseas efforts. Though the volume of U.S. exports is large, U.S. exports
    amount to a bit less than 7 percent of GNP. Japan's rate is 13, West
    Germany's 27, Britain's 20.5, and Canada's 29 percent of GNP. (For some
    countries, the percentages are much higher: Taiwan's is more than 50
    percent, South Korea's more than 40 percent.)

    World trade provides what domestic economies cannot: oil for the U.S.,
    food for other lands, and "imported luxuries" where these are in demand and
    affordable. It can also stimulate domestic competition (as when U.S. auto
    makers decide to do something to combat Japanese imports). In short,
    international trade can raise the standard of living of many countries and
    contribute to economic growth.

Trouble can result, too. "Culture shock" and concerns over "decadent Western influences" are examples. It must be admitted that international trade can lead to unwanted effects.

Balance of trade difficulties are another possible result and can contribute to inflation, tariffs, taxes and other problems as governments attempt to solve their trade deficits.

IV.   GETTING INVOLVED IN MULTINATIONAL MARKETING

Not all organizations have to engage in international trade to be successful. But many foreign markets promise higher market potential than does the U.S. By the year 2000, India's population will approach a billion, Brazil 205 million, Indonesia 223 million, and Nigeria 154 million. Of course, population alone is not a good indicator of market potential. The population's willingness and ability to purchase must be considered. Disposable diapers will sell far better where per capita income is high than where it is extremely low.

U.S. students are likely to base their view of international marketing on the American perspective. The text approaches the area in the same way in terms of the following five questions.

A.   Decision 1: Do We Get Involved in International Marketing?

Despite the seeming attractiveness of a "worldwide" market and the success of some international firms, the answer to this question is not always an easy "yes." Many domestic companies have neither the monetary not managerial resources to handle such a task. The U.S. Government has not been (traditionally) export oriented.

Economics tells us that, according to the theory of **comparative advantage**, trade between two countries should benefit each. Each should specialize in the products it can best produce efficiently. If unrestricted world trade existed, global efficiency should thus be increased. Japan's trade is a good example. Japan imports vast percentages of required raw materials yet has a very healthy economy because it "specializes" in activities other than producing raw materials. In the world in general, however, nationalism and politics stand in the way of the comparative advantage theory holding sway.

1.   Factors Encouraging International Marketing

Why might a company get involved in multinational marketing? (Exhibit 9-2 gives a brief summary of pros and cons.)

Some reasons:

.   Domestic market saturation, lack of new markets.

.   Technological obsolescence of products that may better fit less-developed markets.

.   Domestic climate (such as government or social policies encouraging business to "look elsewhere").

.   Foreign opportunities (rather than domestic problems).

In short, many companies see opportunities in international business and wish to take advantage of them. Formation of economic communities, such as the **European Community**, also known as the **Common Market**, makes it easier for member countries to trade with each other and for outsiders to trade with member nations.

Membership in the E.C. is listed in Exhibit 9-3. The year 1992 was to be the year for creation of a "borderless" economy among those member nations. This market will have more than 323 million people and be the largest single market in the world. A similar system, with 350 million people, involving the U.S., Canada, and Mexico is being planned.

GATT (General Agreements on Tariffs and Trade) are a series of accords reached by member nations not geographically concentrated but seeking to encourage international trade. Again, the goal is to reduce tariffs and trade restrictions.

2.   Factors Discouraging International Marketing

Such factors include:

- **Tariffs** -- taxes imposed by a nation on products brought into that nation. The effect is to make those goods more expensive. The usual goal is to protect a domestic industry producing competing products.

- **Import quotas** -- limits on amounts of products importable. Sometimes these limits are set in absolute numbers (such as tons of oranges) or by means of a very high tariff that becomes effective once a given level of imports is reached.

- **Embargoes** and **boycotts** -- provisions against importing any goods of a specified type from a given country.

The U.S. is as "guilty" as most countries in using these methods to restrict trade.

Another complicating factor is the **exchange rate**, which indicates the value of one country's currency compared with the currency of another country. **Devaluation** is a government act that decreases the value of a the domestic currency relative to a foreign currency, **revaluation** raises the value. Thus, Japanese tourists like revaluation of the yen (versus the U.S. dollar) because this makes a trip to Hawaii or San Francisco more affordable. This de- and re- evaluation makes the pricing of products sold in foreign countries even more complex.

B.   Decision 2: Which International Markets?

If the decision (#1) to become involved in international marketing is "yes," target markets (countries) must be identified. Note that the steps involved in the process are really no different from those involved in investigating any potential market.

- Estimate existing potential market.

- Forecast future potential market.

- Forecast expected sales.

- Forecast costs and profits involved.

- Estimate rate of return on investment.

Among not-so-typical concerns are degrees of economic development, political stability, existing market mechanisms, and political regulations.

1.   The Cultural Environment

Culture consists basically of the values, beliefs, patterns of living and social institutions shared by members of a society. Cultural differences exist among nations and even among the parts of the U.S. and Canada. One author has proposed that North America could be redivided into nine culturally homogeneous "nations."

Failure to understand these differences can lead to surprising marketing developments. For example, McDonald's found that duplicating the national emblem of Mexico on placemats in the country infuriated Mexican customers.

One cause of failure to grasp cultural differences is **ethnocentrism,** our tendency to think our way of doing things is "natural" and "right." This is also termed the **self-reference criterion.**

Ethnocentrism violates the marketing concept's prescription for success -- being consumer oriented. Several examples appear in the text, such as the U.S. attempting to sell unmodified American cars in Japan where people drive on the left side of the road, or Budweiser offering its beer in Germany as a "premium priced" beer and suffering rejection.

Nuances in language are difficulty to deal with. Foreigners may use expressions incorrectly, misunderstand native speakers, or mistranslate words, e.g. "tomato paste" is not the same as "tomato glue."

2.   The Political Environment

The attitude of a country's government toward international trade is a key political concern. Some set up many restrictions, others almost none at all. For example, some countries virtually ban importation of products that domestic companies are capable of producing, others mandate joint ownership of ventures with high percentages of ownership being "local," or they require that some minimum percentage of employees be "local" citizens, or prohibit trade altogether for political reasons.

Governments may control prices. A marketer seeking to unload excess inventory at a low price may be accused of **dumping,** the practice of pricing products sold in foreign markets at less than their comparable fair market value in the domestic market.

Another political concern has been stability of government. Investors shy away from many South American countries, for example, putting their money in the more stable nations of the world.

3.   The Economic Environment

Many countries lack what we see as the most basic of marketing/distribution systems. Literacy, technological development, distribution structure, and many other factors can be related to these stages of economic development.

- **Undeveloped countries:** economy based on agriculture. Countries, as a whole, possess relatively little purchasing power.

- **Less-developed countries:** economy includes small manufacturing, mining or other limited technology industries. Marketing mechanisms likely primitive or nonexistent.

- **Developing countries:** evidence of social change, increasing market activity and of emerging business-based middle class.

- **Developed countries:** exhibit specialization within the economy, full-scale marketing structure, large markets for a wide array of products (Canada, the U.S., and Germany are examples).

These are summarized in Exhibit 9-4.

Another aspect of economic development is the presence of a currency for trade. Many countries do not have a "hard" currency. Trade may have to be conducted on a barter basis because the currency of a given country is not acceptable outside that country's borders. International barter on a large scale is called **countertrade**.

An important economic health indicator, and thus an index of attractiveness to international marketers, is gross domestic product (GDP) and, more importantly, the GDP per capita. It should be noted that in some countries, especially developing countries, these figures may not be accurate.

4.   The Demographic Environment

World population exceeds five billion and is concentrated in certain areas, not evenly distributed. Population size, growth patterns, family size, etc. are all important considerations both in terms of market size and the future. For example: population growth might outrun resource capabilities holding down development of the economy.

Exhibit 9-5 shows population, area, and population density for selected countries.

C.   Decision 3: How Much Commitment in Each Market?

There are three major forms of involvement, each requiring increasing levels of commitment. Market potential and other variables influence the decision of which to chose. Different approaches may be used in different markets.

1.   Exporting

Exporting involves selling products in foreign markets. Such sales may be accomplished directly or by using a merchant or agent middleman. Exporting is usually seen as the "lowest level" of commitment a company can make to international marketing. America's top export customers are shown in Exhibit 9-6.

Indirect exporting can make use of a buyer for export, a type of merchant intermediary who exports a mix of products for sale in foreign markets. The manufacturing or producing firm typically treats such buyers as "just another customer."

Export management companies are intermediaries that specialize in buying from sellers in one country and marketing the products in other countries. Since they typically take title to the goods, they reduce risk for the exporting company.

Indirect exporting involves dealing with overseas customers, not using independent middlemen. This approach is used when the exporter wants greater control over foreign sales of its product. Since direct exporting involves overseas business dealings, many firms set up overseas offices. Others send representatives to other countries periodically. The occasional visitor would seem less likely to be able to succeed than the full-time export office, branch or division.

2.   Joint Venturing

The second level of involvement is **joint venturing**, the joining of home and host country companies to set up production and/or marketing facilities in an overseas market. There are several forms of joint venturing.

- **Licensing** -- an agreement permitting the licensee (foreign firm) to use the production methods, name, etc. or the licensor (home company) in exchange for a fee or royalty.

- **International franchising** -- where franchise agreements are set up much as they are in the home country.

- **Contract manufacturing** -- a home company permits the foreign company to produce a product for consumption in the home country. For example: U.S. firms may provide product specifications to a firm in Haiti and import the produced items into the U.S.

- **Joint Ownership Venture** -- the domestic and foreign partners both invest capital and share ownership and control of a partnership in agreed-upon amounts. Such agreements are often required by host countries, and the joint ownership is not always equal. Sharing risks and investment may also be attractive to the domestic (U.S.-based) company.

3.   Direct Foreign Investment

If a foreign market's potential is great (and the local government permits it), the domestic company might invest directly in manufacturing and marketing facilities in the host country. This is called **direct foreign investment**. Even when such investment occurs, the possibility of nationalization always exists. (Exhibit 9-7 contrasts five basic multinational strategies.)

D.   Decision 4:   How Should We Organize for International Marketing?

A would-be international marketer must decide what organizational structure will best match its commitment to those markets.

1.   Export Department or International Division?

An **export department** deals directly or indirectly (through intermediaries) with overseas customers. If a larger commitment has been made, an **international department** or division might be needed. These divisions are usually organized around geographic territories, product groupings, or customer types.

2.   The Multinational Company versus the International Company

Many businesspeople use the term "international company" to refer to a firm based in a home country that deals in foreign or different countries. These businesspeople see the true multinational organization as one which has no home orientation and pursues opportunities wherever they may occur in the world. Exhibit 9-8 lists some of the largest multinational companies in the world.

E.   Decision 5:   How Much Should We Change Our Domestic-Based Marketing?

A decision as to how much the organization should change its domestic-based marketing mix must be made by the would-be international marketer. In the interest of maintaining an identity, many firms seem to develop a unifying worldwide strategy, a **globalization strategy**, which is adjusted tactically to fit local markets. Obviously, a unified approach that inhibits local adjustments would carry the idea of unity too far, but the costs of adjustments must be weighed against estimates of sales potentials.

A **customization strategy** adapts the marketing strategy to each country where the good or service is marketed.

1.   International Marketing Research

All marketing begins with marketing research. Unfortunately, U.S. marketers are accustomed to easy access to vast amounts of research data. Such data is not available in many countries. People may view researchers with suspicion, census figures may be nonexistent, in some places streets are not named nor are houses numbered, telephone and other directories may be absent.

Yet research should be attempted to avoid the disaster of making avoidable mistakes with products, brand names, prices, etc., that are "unacceptable" to other cultures.

2.   Product Planning

Three general product-related strategies exist:

.   Sell the same product, unadjusted, overseas.

.   Sell the same product, adapted to overseas markets.

.   Sell a new product "invented" for overseas markets.

The answer to which approach to take rests in how sensitive to local conditions a product is. As a rule, for example, industrial products are far less sensitive to local conditions than are consumer goods.

The "new" product for sale in a foreign market may be what has been called a **backward invention**, a product that is obsolete in the U.S. but suited to overseas conditions. Foot-powered sewing machines may be antiques in the U.S. and Canada, but perfect for use in villages in Bolivia. **Forward invention**, creating a new product for the new market conditions, is costly and risky, but the potential for rewards is also great.

3.   Other Marketing Mix Decisions

All elements of the marketing mix are subject to local conditions. As in the domestic market, segments in the international market may differ, and the marketing mixes aimed at them may have to differ.

V.   SUMMARY

International marketing often requires significant adaptation of the marketing mix. The marketer must be aware of cultural differences.

Learning Objective 1: Describe the impact of international marketing on our domestic economy and on the economies of our trading partners.

Multinational marketing is growing in importance as communication and transportation technologies improve. Trade between nations is complicated by differences in language, cultures, currencies, trade barriers, and governmental regulations. World trade may help a nation's economy grow but it may also lead to undesirable cultural change and trade deficits.

Learning Objective 2: Outline the steps a domestic marketer must complete in analyzing and developing foreign markets.

A domestic company first decides to get involved in international marketing, then decides which markets to enter, what commitment to make, how to organize its efforts, and finally, how to adjust its marketing for foreign markets.

Learning Objective 3:   Explain the theory of comparative advantage.

The theory of comparative advantage holds that nations become involved in international trade to take advantage of their specializations and to fill needs with the specialized outputs of other nations.

Learning Objective 4:   Understand how the nature of foreign environments influence the decision about which markets to enter.

In investigating the markets to enter, a firm must consider such factors as the cultural environment, the political environment, the economic environment, including the level of economic development, and the demographic environment.

Learning Objective 5:   Identify the different levels of involvement in multinational marketing.

A firm may choose to become involved in a foreign market on various levels including export, joint venturing (such as licensing, franchising, contract manufacturing, or joint ownership venture) and direct foreign investment.

To begin its involvement in overseas operations, the international company may establish an export department or an international department or division.   Truly multinational organizations view the whole world as a potential market.   They do not have a domestic versus foreign perspective.

Learning Objective 6:   Discuss the adaptation of domestic strategies and marketing mixes to overseas markets.

Marketing planning in multinational operations must be modified to fit various markets.   Marketing research in many other nations is difficult because of the lack of data and the poor status of research in general. The marketing mix is often based on a global strategic approach with local adjustments in tactics.   A product may be extended intact into other nations, adapted somewhat, or created new.

VI.   KEY TERMS

VII.   QUESTIONS FOR DISCUSSION (10)

VIII.   ETHICS IN PRACTICE

IX.   CASES

ANSWERS TO CHAPTER 9 QUESTIONS FOR DISCUSSION

1.   *What five decisions must a firm make before it decides to engage in international marketing?*

ANSWER:

Each of the five decisions are discussed in the chapter.   A summary of the major decisions and discussion points follows.

Decision 1:   Do we get involved in International Marketing?

In addition to a large U.S. market and the theory of comparative advantage, Exhibit 9-2 summarizes factors which encourage international marketing.   Factors which may prevent a firm from international involvement discussed in this section include: tariffs, import quotas, restrictive controls, inflation, and exchange rates.

Decision 2:   Which international markets?

To answer this question, companies must identify likely target markets using a quantification process similar for any potential market.   A five-step process described in the text encourages companies to: 1) estimate the existing potential market; 2) forecast the future potential market; 3) forecast the sales to be expected; 4) forecast the costs and profits involved; and, 5) estimate the rate of return on investment. In addition, companies must also describe the environmental forces which may affect operations. The discussion in the text emphasizes culture, ethnocentricism, symbols, trends, gestures, political-legal issues, economic development, and demographics as information needed to select appropriate international targets.

Decision 3: How much commitment in each market?

To answer this question, managers must decide the level of organization ownership and management involvement in international markets. The choices discussed in the text are exporting, licensing, international franchising, contract manufacturing, joint ventures and direct investment. The basic multinational strategies are summarized in Exhibit 9-7.

Decision 4: How should we organize for international marketing?

The organizational structure should match a firm's desired level of commitment with options including export departments, international departments, and multinational companies.

Decision 5: How much should we change our domestic-based marketing?

The answer to this question requires marketers to determine whether a globalization or customization strategy is most appropriate for the product offering. Globalization strategies standardize the product and promotion mix for various countries throughout the world. Soft drinks and the Marlboro Man are examples of products which achieve a level of standardization worldwide. Customization strategies adapt marketing mix elements to each country where the good or service is offered.

2.   *What factors encourage and discourage international marketing?*

ANSWER:

Factors which many encourage international marketing are summarized in Exhibit 9-2 and include the following:

(a)   Domestic problems encourage firms to seek international business. Examples include saturated domestic markets, lack of new markets, or technological obsolescence of a domestic product where firms seek to extend the life in international markets. Further, the domestic government or business climate may be antibusiness, such as prolabor cycles or periods of increased legislation.

(b)   International opportunities also compel firms to target new and untapped demand within growing market segments. Firms also find production opportunities to lower the cost of labor, raw materials and transportation or to increase the productivity of labor or facilities.

(c)   Governments also encourage international business through laws and the formation of ties with other countries. Economic communities, trade acts between countries to stimulate business exchange, the General Agreement on Tariffs and Trade (GATT) as a series of agreements by member nations to reduce restrictions, all serve to encourage international marketing.

Factors which may discourage international marketing include tariffs, import quotas, restrictive controls, inflation, and exchange rates. Tariffs are taxes imposed on imported goods while quotas limit the number or types of imported goods. Restrictive controls may range from requirements to use a central ministry for all international trade to boycotts or other barriers to restrict product imports. In periods of high inflation as in Brazil or Russia, firms lose the ability to control margins and retail prices charged by middlemen as prices vary from market to market. Major fluctuations in the exchange rate values for a country's currency also increase the risk involved in international business.

Further, answers to the remaining decision areas for international marketing may also discourage involvement. For example, the market potential may be too small;

the culture may not value the benefits provided by the product, and it may be too costly to customize; the climate may be too harsh or volatile to justify a major developmental commitment; the firm may not have the resources to take advantage of identified opportunities; the forecasted return on investment may not meet company objectives; the level of economic development may be insufficient to warrant attempted sales.

3.   *What makes the multinational firms in Japan effective marketers?*

ANSWER:

Answers to this question may vary, but students should be encouraged to consider the major topics in this chapter as they consider what may cause any multinational firm to be effective.

Multinational firms in Japan are effective in international marketing research and use information to develop customized strategies for varying cultural targets. These firms have also selected the multinational company as an organizational option representing a high commitment to international ventures. This is seen in their frequent use of direct foreign investment to maximize control and involvement in host countries. The political environment in Japan is very stable and favorable for its domestic companies.

What makes the multinational firm effective? Perhaps it is the ability to identify and use information, resources, government aids, or contacts to successfully identify and satisfy needs of people from different cultural backgrounds.

4.   *What economic factors determine the marketing decision to export to certain countries?*

ANSWER:

The focus of this answer should reflect varying stages of economic development as they relate to an organization's product.

(a)   Stage of economic development: undeveloped countries engage in barter with little specialization, marketing activity or international trade; less-developed countries have small-scale cottage industry and limited entrepreneurial activity; developing countries have specialization but limited marketing activities; while developed countries have mass distribution systems and a market orientation.

        For example, IBM may not be interested in exporting major computer systems to an undeveloped country, but Whirlpool may find opportunities for its nonelectric, wringer washing machines (obsolete in the U.S.) within developing countries.

        There are also several other economic factors which may affect whether a firm will export to certain countries.

(b)   Exchange rates and inflation may present unattractive risks for organizations.

(c)   Economic communities or agreements may encourage a firm to export or to seek joint ventures as well.

(d)   The basic level of demand for the product may inhibit or compel a firm's export decision.

5.   *What is a joint ownership venture? Find some examples.*

ANSWER:

A joint ownership venture is a joint venture in which domestic and foreign partners invest capital and share ownership and control. Joint venturing is an arrangement between a domestic company and a foreign host company to set up production and marketing facilities in a foreign market. The investment of capital and shared ownership distinguish the joint ownership venture.

Once rare, examples of joint ownership ventures are becoming easier to find. A few examples are provided to initiate student discussion.

- Bell South Corporations's paging unit and SWATCH, the Swiss watchmaker to produce and market a wristwatch pager.

- Celestial Seasonings and Perrier to produce and market a line of ready-to-drink teas.

- AT&T, PTT Telecom of the Netherlands, and the Ukraine's State Committee of Communications to modernize phone service in the Ukraine.

- John Deere and Hitachi to produce machines.

- Michael Foods of Minneapolis and SKW Trostberg, AG, of Germany to produce and market SimplyEggs, a real egg product with 80% less cholesterol than the natural good.

6.   *Pick three foreign markets, perhaps Greece, Brazil, and Hong Kong, and try to find out what the customs and courtesies for greetings are in these countries.*

ANSWER:

International students may also be encouraged to describe customs and courtesies for greetings in their own countries. It may also be helpful to ask students how they would approach finding the answer to this question as well. To provide insight for the three markets mentioned above, various encyclopedias provide a basic description of the country but do not offer specific greetings. Language texts typically describe common courtesies exhibited in forms for expression.

Greece

The ethnic composition, language, and heritage of Greece is Greek, a country influenced by its crossroads position for Europe, Africa and the East. The Church of Greece (Greek Orthodox Church) is the dominant religion.

According to S. A. Sofroniou, author of texts on the Greek language, Greek possesses variable words which change inflection and endings based on their usage. Avoiding an attempt to phonetically transcribe the words of greeting, the verbs and nouns change to denote person and number. Articles which precede nouns are divided into masculine (ó), feminine (ñ), and neuter (τό). Thus, to greet a potential business partner would require not only knowledge of the words, but also the correct article to precede the greeting.

Brazil

In Brazil, the dominant language is Portuguese, but there are four major sub-cultural groups within the country: indigenous Indians, Portuguese, Africans, and immigrants of European and Oriental descent. Portuguese culture and customs dominate with 90% of the population members of the Roman Catholic church. The spoken language has changed from that in Portugal due to Indian and immigrant influences incorporated into the language, but there is an almost universal use of "tchau" from the Italian "ciao" for farewell.

According to the text *Portuguese*, by Carlo Rossik, a simple "hello" for friends is "aló," however there are courtesy differentiations which are expected. For example "tu" means "you" in English but is used only with friends or family. "Good afternoon _____" would be "Boa tarde, Senhor, Senhora, or Senhorita," for greeting men, women, or young ladies, respectively.

Hong Kong

As Hong Kong was a British colony for many years, English is used for all legal or governmental matters and is an official language of Hong Kong, in addition to Chinese. Thus, a simple "Good Morning" would probably be understood. Cantonese is the common spoken language with a variety of ethnic dialects used for smaller groups.

According to John DeFrancis in *Beginning Chinese*, the Chinese language differentiates courtesies when greeting or communicating with others.   Thus, in one Chinese dialect, "How are you?" is spelled phonetically in Chinese as follows: Nì-hào (singular); Nìn-hào? (polite); Nìmen-hào? (plural).

7.   *The brand name of a popular Japanese cigarette is Hope.   Would this be an appropriate name for an American cigarette?*

ANSWER:

Names acquire meaning for people within a cultural context.   Given the current environment in the U.S., Hope would not be appropriate.   Negative publicity would surely result.   Antismoking activists could also easily mock the name (e.g., Hope?   To die?   To have a stroke?).

8.   *What social mistakes might a business person make when visiting a foreign country?*

ANSWER:

With an ethnocentric viewpoint, an infinite number of social mistakes could be made in foreign countries.   Several examples are provided of social blunders U.S. business people have made in foreign countries.

. "Meishi" involves the exchange of business cards in Japan and is a very important social aspect of business encounters.   U.S. executives would err if they attended social functions without their cards.

. In France, addressing a business associate with the informal "tu" (you) rather than the formal "vous" (also you) is a social mistake.

. As highlighted in the competitive strategy box in the text, flashing the classic American okay sign with the thumb and forefinger in a circle would be a social error in Rio where the gesture is obscene.

. When invited to dinner in Germany, it is a social error to arrive without flowers or wine as a gift for the hostess.

. Handing an Arab business executive any object with the left hand is considered rude as this hand is reserved for the bathroom.

. In many countries around the world, the American style of immediately acting friendly toward strangers is considered rather aggressive.

9.   *Japan is now manufacturing automobiles in the United States.   What impact has this had on the world automobile market?*

ANSWER:

Opinions and answers to the question may vary.   The question provides a good opportunity for students to consider the major topics of the chapter as they relate Japanese international business practices and their impact on world markets.

Establishing production facilities in countries with high potential enables companies to avoid import restrictions such as tariffs or quotas.   Manufacturing facilities in host countries also may lower shipping expenses and the cultural or political pressures associated with buying "foreign" goods in countries such as the U.S.

For example, an ad for Honda lawn mowers at the beginning of the chapter in the text emphasizes the North Carolina manufacturing facility used by this Japanese firm.   In lawn mowers as well as automobiles, top Japanese firms seem to follow a rigorous path of research, increasing commitment and involvement in target countries leading to direct foreign investment.   In stable countries with favorable long-term trends, direct investment justifies the long-term commitment required.

Has the Japanese practice stimulated a wealth of other joint ownership ventures in the worldwide automobile market? U.S. manufacturers purchase parts from other countries where lower labor costs result in lower prices. International firms are also building new manufacturing facilities in the U.S. Will the long-term impact reflect the true globalization of business practices?

This question could also provide a research opportunity. Students could be asked to quantify global sales of automobiles before Japanese firms began manufacturing automobiles in the U.S. and afterward.

10. *For the following marketers, indicate whether a standardization or customization strategy would work best and explain why. (a) McDonald's (b) Guess jeans (c) Komatsu welding equipment (d) American Express cards (e) Hilton Hotels (f) American Airlines.*

ANSWER:

Answering the question correctly may not be as important as the discussion of reasons why one approach over another may be correct. Several assumptions must also be made. For example, Hilton Hotels may not be a viable product at the present time for undeveloped countries. The suggestion that a hotel service can be standardized assumes a relevant range of suitable markets as opposed to every single country on the globe.

Students may find it easier to locate the relative position of these firms on a continuum. We have tried to position the firms and provided a rationale for each placement while recognizing that opinions may vary.

```
Standardization         Some adaptation              Customization

|----------------------------------------------------------------------|
|            |              |           |             |          |
-Komatsu     -American    -McDonald's  -Hilton      -American   -Guess
welding      Airlines                   Hotels      Express     jeans
equipment                                           card
```

(a)   McDonald's

The temptation is to suggest a standardization strategy for McDonald's based on minor variations to the basic menu items. In Europe and Moscow, this strategy appears to be viable. As reported by Masato Ishizawa (*World Press Review*, May 1992, p. 43), McDonald's uses an adaptation strategy in Japan. The latest innovation is McChao, a fried-rice dish. With 870 outlets developed over 20 years of operating in Tokyo, its menu is adapted to local tastes and the changing preferences of Japanese consumers for variety in take-out foods. Perhaps the strategy could be described as adapted, which is partially standardized yet somewhat customized to local markets.

(b)   Guess jeans

Granted, an argument could be made that jeans are universal clothes which should not change globally. However, sizes differ in countries using a metric system so labels will not transfer, and common sizes will also vary greatly suggesting potential cost efficiencies in tailoring manufacturing for specific areas (e.g. Oriental, European, Russian). Further, promotion of jeans involves cultural symbols requiring customized representation of social norms and values. For example, not only could Guess not show Arabic women in advertisements, but the product would also need to be completely new to appeal to this target. Distribution could range from outdoor markets in developing countries to government controlled outlets in still others. In Italy, as well as other countries, the Guess label may be licensed to an Italian company, preventing the original Guess manufacturer from selling the product with its own name in that country.

(c)   The placement of Komatsu welding equipment on the standardized end of the continuum reflects the assumption that many industrial products may be used

in much the same way in all markets in the world.   While safety
requirements or laws concerning tank sizes may cause minor product
modifications, welding seems a rather universal task suggesting the company
can sell the same product, largely unadjusted, in a global market.

(d)   American Express cards

Our admitted guess is that American Express would have to customize its
contracts, agreements, and applications for customers.   The card itself might not
change much, but local language needs would have to be met.   Also, some countries
might require that information, such as interest rates, be printed on the card.
The firm could face divergent cultural attitudes toward credit usage as well as
payment.   Further, the company would have to start from near zero in attracting
business customers willing to accept the card from consumers.   Given legal
approval, we could see a standardized approach for England or developed countries
based on a number of multinational concerns willing to accept the card worldwide.

(e)   Hilton Hotels

While the diversity of local hotels in foreign cities tempts one to place Hilton
on the customization end of the continuum, consider Hilton's global appeal for
business travelers.   If the objective is to appeal to multinational business
executives, then the Hotel may have to adapt to local laws, ordinances, food or
linen purchases, but would seek to offer the same image on a global scale.

(f)   American Airlines

International flights seem to require a rather standardized approach to air
travel.   Laws and procedures simply must be the same, or very similar, in the
interest of safety.   While promotions targeted toward business versus vacation
travelers may vary as well as language or uniforms, the air transportation
service seems to suggest the possibility of a rather standardized approach.

ETHICS EXERCISE 9

CHAPTER 9 ETHICS IN PRACTICE

Overview

In the U.S., any good meant to be ingested by consumers must have Food and Drug
Administration approval before it can be sold.   A multinational firm has
developed an over-the-counter drug which has not received F.D.A. approval, so it
plans to sell the drug in several Asian countries where approval of this sort is
not required.   The firm has tested the product and believes it to be safe.

Business decisions that seem to be rational, straightforward, and ethically
justified in a domestic context often become complex and extremely gray in an
international environment.   This is a common principle underlying the ethics
questions for this chapter.

The marketing of over-the-counter drugs unapproved by the Food and Drug
Administration (FDA) for the U.S. by multinational companies going abroad has
been a frequent occurrence.   The control of drugs in the U.S. is probably more
stringent than in any other nation in the world.   The FDA mandates strict testing
standards; any drug to be sold in the U.S. must pass long and comprehensive
testing.

Several questions are suggested by the situation described.

First, is it socially responsible for a pharmaceutical manufacturer to market in
Asian countries a drug it has tested but which has not received FDA approval if
those countries do not require government approval?

The argument in favor of FDA testing is that there are risks to health and life
when one takes a drug.   If a drug is discovered to have certain dangerous side
effects, it should be sold only under certain conditions, and under a doctor's
care.   If the drug is known to cause serious or even fatal illness, such as

cancer, it should not be sold at all, or else only under very rigidly controlled circumstances.

However, American drug companies and critics of the FDA feel that often FDA standards are needlessly stringent. For instance, we've witnessed the denial of proven treatments to people dying of hepatitis and heart disease because of relatively minor side effects. The AIDS epidemic seems to pit FDA against protesting groups and persons on every nightly news broadcast.

It is argued that the testing process is expensive, which raises the price of drugs, sometimes putting them out of reach of the poor. The testing process is too cumbersome and long, often delaying the introduction of important new drugs. Government interference in individual medicine-buying decisions encroaches on the most intimate and critical decisions we make.

In the international arena, critics contend that it is inappropriate to impose U.S. standards on the operation of U.S. companies in other countries. They argue that the standards might be appropriate for Americans but not necessarily for people in some other countries due to those nations' unique conditions.

Whether or not the drug should be sold in this scenario depends on several things. First, why has the drug not been given FDA approval? If it is due to the slow approval process and the firm's testing has found the drug to be safe, then marketing it abroad might be morally justifiable. If the drug has not been approved due to dangerous side effects, its marketing is morally questionable. The FDA does allow some drugs which have possibly harmful side effects to be sold. The rationale is that the side effects are usually less severe than the illness that is being treated; the risks involved are worth taking so long as the patient and doctor know about them and decide to take the risks, exercising due caution.

Second, will buyers be informed about possible harmful side effects? If not, the drug's sale can't be morally justified. The principle here is informed consent: the buyer must be given plainly stated full disclosure of all possible adverse consequences of taking the drug.

If sufficient information is given, if there is no alternative drug, and if the risk is reasonable (from a utilitarian perspective), the sale of the drug is justifiable, whether or not the FDA permits its sale in the U.S. However, if there is a similar or better product available, which does not cause the side effects of this drug, the former should not be marketed at all, neither in the U.S. nor abroad. (Richard T. DeGeorge, *Business Ethics*, third edition, New York: MacMillan Publishing Company, 1990, p. 412)

CHAPTER 9 TAKE A STAND QUESTIONS

1. *A multinational food company markets powdered milk around the world. Critics say many third-world mothers do not comprehend that mixing the product with impure water is unsafe. Because many mothers are incapable of using the products properly, they should only be distributed through physicians.*

Many students will recognize this scenario as being reminiscent of the well-known Nestle infant formula case. During the 1970s, Nestle and several other U.S. manufacturers marketed powdered infant formula in some of the developing nations. This product is used in the supplemental feeding of infants and has been tested as safe when properly used; it is wholesome, delicious, and in some cases life-saving. Thus, there seemed to be a good social justification for introducing this product into African countries as an alternative to breast feeding.

Most formula firms used direct consumer advertising via mass media as well as personal selling efforts. A few firms targeted health-care professionals as their "gatekeepers" and salespeople. In either case, the firms came under the attack of critics who alleged that the promotional efforts got new mothers "hooked" on formula feeding without giving breast feeding, the internationally preferred method for infant feeding, a fair chance. The critics charged that formula makers were coercing vulnerable consumers who couldn't resist free samples given to doctors and maternity wards, sophisticated and extensive

mass-media advertising which implied that they'd have healthy babies if they used
the product, and the "medical advice" of health professionals who were also
company salespeople. Company representatives, called "milk nurses," explained
and promoted formula feeding to new mothers, sometimes by disparaging breast
feeding as primitive. Medical personnel were awarded gifts of equipment, trips,
and conferences.

Formula companies responded that malnutrition and disease together create a high
mortality rate for infants and young children in many developing countries. They
pointed out that infant formula provided a rational means of fighting these
problems, and that they were supported in this by the governments of many
developing countries.

However, Nestle and other companies were soon attacked by many individuals and
groups who claimed that their aggressive promotions were actually causing
dramatically rising infant mortality rates.   Investigators discovered that,
because of high illiteracy rates, many mothers were unable to follow instructions
for correctly using the formula. Additionally, water used to mix with the
formula was unsafe, and poor mothers often diluted the formula to save money,
which reduced the nutritional value of the feeding.

Nestle and the other firms seemed to pay little attention to the fact that proper
use of the formula required sanitary conditions and a fairly high literacy rate.
They responded at first with classic free-market rationales that emphasize
consumer choice and product quality.

Nevertheless, the controversy heated up, and by 1977 an organization called the
Infant Formula Action Coalition (INFACT) attempted to create public awareness and
economic pressure through a nationwide boycott of all Nestle products. Nestle
was singled out since it was the dominant firm in the industry. As the boycott
began to take its toll on the company, firms banded together to work toward
development of an international code of marketing ethics under the sponsorship of
the World Health Organization, and the Code was adopted by the U.N. in 1983.
Compliance with the Code is strictly voluntary, although all major formula
manufacturers are complying. The result has been that the firms have stopped
promoting infant formula and have revised product labeling and educational
materials to clearly state the importance of using infant formulas correctly and
the preferability of breast feeding.

It would seem that, in view of the unintended consequences of the infant formula
marketing, the firms' rationalizations aren't justifiable. It appears that
compliance with the Code is the ethical (as well as strategically smart) thing to
do, for its essence is full disclosure. Note that simply distributing the
product through physicians was not a solution to the original problem since, at
times, the doctors' self-interest overrode ethical concerns.

2.   *The French government insists that attractions, such as "Fantasyland" and
      "Pirates of the Caribbean" in the recently completed EuroDisneyland
      translate their names into French. Disney officials refuse to do so. Who
      has the right to decide?*

The French are amazingly adamant about the purity of the French language.
Indeed, the French government supports a panel of scholars who decide what will
and will not be considered an "official" word or term in the language. It also
promotes language purity by holding an annual, very difficult, spelling contest
for adults from around the world. American words such as "hamburger" and "disco"
have been found by marketers to cause consternation among French customers, and
the French government fights hard against "Franglais," French "corrupted" by the
English language. There is a bureau in the French government that actually
monitors usage of foreign words and prevails upon companies to use French words
instead.

Clearly a private company such as Disney, operating on private property, has the
legal right to use its trademarks and language as it wishes, as long as it is in
good taste as defined by community standards. Disney's property rights include
its trademarks, which it may use subject to any legal restrictions France might
impose. The problem is that, in this context, use of such names borders on being
morally offensive to some people. Deliberately insulting or offending people
cannot be morally defended. Pragmatically, from a public relations perspective,

offending one's target market is unwise. Disney would probably be smart to drop the English names, even though in so doing they risk losing some of the brand equity in those names (i.e., the names are familiar and liked, especially by travelers from overseas.)

3. *Is "American-style advertising" good for third world countries, countries in which most of the citizens are poor and could not purchase the goods that are attractively advertised?*

This question is analogous to the oft-asked question, "Does advertising for luxury goods cause consternation among the poor who see ads for the goods but can only dream of owning them?" No doubt it does, and under an ideal market segmentation scheme, this problem would be eliminated. However, audience sheltering (avoiding exposing nontargeted people to your communications) is not usually practical, unless the campaign is restricted to highly targeted media such as direct mail and neighborhood billboards. Otherwise, there will always be some advertising for goods beyond the means of the poor which will nevertheless reach them. (As Scripture says, "The poor you will always have with you.")

The real issue is: "What effect does advertising for luxuries which reaches the poor have on them?" It is often alleged that advertising:

.   Creates needs rather than simply showing how a product satisfies needs;

.   Surrounds consumers with images of the good life and suggests that the acquisition of material goods leads to contentment and happiness, adding to the joy of living;

.   Suggests that material possessions are symbols of status, success and accomplishment and/or will lead to greater social acceptance, popularity, etc.

The question is to what extent advertising actually creates desires for the unattainable goods and surrounds them with an aura of status, contentment etc. It is difficult to prove the extent to which advertising contributes to materialistic values as opposed to simply mirroring the values and desires that are already there. In *The Mirror Makers*, Stephen Fox suggested that advertisers "are just producing an especially visible manifestation, good or bad, of the American way of life" (p 330). While it is probably unrealistic to hold advertising as solely accountable for materialistic desires, it is probably reasonable to conclude that it does play a contributing role.

Given this, the marketer of luxuries, be it in the U.S. or in third world countries (where a small minority of the population would be in the target market), probably should try to minimize or offset negative effects of advertising seen by the poor. Blatant appeals to power, status, and the like should probably be toned done if not altogether avoided. Media vehicles which will be least likely to be seen by the poor (e.g., upscale magazines, direct mail) should be used. And, perhaps some kind of charitable work in inner-city ghettos or contributions to philanthropic organizations serving the poor would be in order. This would obviously also be good from a public relations standpoint.

GUIDE TO CASES

VIDEO CASE 9-1   INTERNATIONAL INFORMATION SERVICES

SUBJECT MATTER: International Marketing and Marketing Research

Please see the Guide to Video Cases for video length and other information.

AT-A-GLANCE OVERVIEW

International Information Services is a marketing research company specializing in analyzing markets outside the U.S., providing the latest statistics about population trends, political conditions, etc. Each year since its founding, its consulting revenues have increased by more than 15 percent.

A recent project is to provide a client with information about Pacific Rim countries. Executives of the client company believe exporting to Japan might be the best way to crack the Asian market, but are not certain of this. The client asked IIS to provide information on Japan, but also on Taiwan, Hong Kong, and South Korea.

DISCUSSION QUESTIONS

1.   *What essential facts about Japan should be included in International Information Service's report?*

The first thing students should find are basics statistics about the country.[1]

JAPAN - GENERAL PROFILE

Area	143,760 sq mi
Population 1988	122,626,000
Population Growth	0.46 %
Population Density	853 /sq mi
GNP 1988 (millions)	$1,977,419
GNP per Capita	$16,289
Capital City	TOKYO

Basic demographic information is also important:

JAPAN - DEMOGRAPHICS

Population 1975	111,573,000
Population 1988	122,626,000
Population 1989	123,190,000
Population 1990	123,757,000
Population 2000	129,569,000
Population Growth	0.46 %
Population Density	853 /sq mi
Population Doubling Time	151 years
Literacy Rate	99 %
Urbanization	75.7 %

However, knowledge of the Japanese market requires a knowledge of the culture and how to do business in Japan.[2] In the video, Yue-Sai Kan suggests:

> If your company is considering doing business with Japan but has not yet begun, establish initial contracts before your trip. Do not go to Japan "cold." If you can't make contacts directly in Japan, consider an approach through the branch office of a Japanese company in the United States. Middlemen play an important function in business relations in Japan: don't hesitate to use them.
>
> A good strategy might be to time your visit for a trade show, allowing a week after the show to follow up and develop contacts you make at the show. Whenever possible, make use of introductions from Japanese in the industry you want to do business with: find ways and take time to build up credibility. If you want to sell to Japan, consider the possibility of first becoming a customer in related products or services. Work your way into the network in whatever way

---

[1] The demographic and economic information is from *PCGlobe*.

[2] This material is adapted with permission from Northwest Airlines "Doing Business In Japan."

possible: remember the importance of the network to successful
Japanese companies and use it in the same way.

In addition to name cards, take along any samples, catalogs, and
brochures of your company. If it is possible, have them translated
into Japanese. The Japanese want to be assured of the size,
stability, and continued existence of the people with whom they do
business.

When approaching the Japanese market, think of other cities besides
Tokyo. Don't neglect Osaka and Nagoya, important business centers in
their own right. Many foreign companies have found them more
flexible than bureaucratic and hugely expensive Tokyo.

Some cardinal rules that Coca-Cola uses for doing business in Japan:

1.   Japan is the second largest market in the world and there are profits to
      be made, but Japan is also difficult: either get in for the long run or
      don't get in at all.

2.   Ally yourself with a strong Japanese company: make it in your Japanese
      partner's best interests to have your business succeed.

3.   Quality is paramount: have a good product to begin with, and keep making
      it better.

In the video, Yue-Sai Kan's also offers "five Ps" to help businesses succeed in
the Japanese market:

   "Patience: Don't expect decisions to be made overnight."

   "Presence: Do let your counterparts get to know you. 'Face to Face'
   is so important in Japan."

   "Preparation: Do your homework before you come. Know the market,
   know your competition and know why you're here."

   "Product: Have a high quality product and believe in it."

   "Protocol: Be sensitive to local customs and proper etiquette."

An important part of doing business requires knowing the cultural aspects of
negotiating with the japanese. Here are some tips.

   "Don't put the people you negotiate with into a corner where they can only
   say yes or no. Always leave enough room to maneuver." (Fred Langhammer)
   While this is true for business in every country, it is particularly
   applicable in Japan. Most rules of business conduct are appropriate
   everywhere, including sensitivity to the other party's culture; so much
   emphasis is placed on business style and conduct in Japan because the
   Japanese themselves have to fit into specific hierarchical roles.

   Play the game: they have to fit into a rigid business structure, so do
   you.

   Take the time: budget extra leeway into time for meetings, trips, projects
   - much more time than you would expect to have to give in the USA.

   Know the hierarchy or learn it fast: giving face to the man on top is
   vital. He may not be the chief negotiator, but give him respect. Titles
   denote rank - key in to them.

   Use apologies liberally: form matters in Japan; content is sometimes
   secondary.

   Be alert to signals of hesitation: body language is as important as words.

   Do not engage in "wishful hearing": get it in writing.

Consult and use an intermediary if problems arise.

Do your homework: have all the facts and figures in hand, and use them.

Be precise: impress the other side and pin down spoken innuendos with fact.

Give appropriate gifts: a good Scotch is always appreciated, as are French and Italian name-brand items. One businessperson finds that a case of fine American wine is a very welcome gift.

Present name cards and presents formally, with two hands: ritual is alive in Japan.

Allow for silence: Silence is an indication of productive thought in Japan. You may encounter long pauses in discussions - don't feel obliged to fill them in.

ECONOMIC BACKGROUND

Knowing the economic situation is also important. Students should be able to present data such as that found below:

JAPAN - GROSS NATIONAL PRODUCT (GNP)

GNP 1987 (millions)	$1,924,296
GNP 1988 (millions)	$1,997,419
GNP 1989 (millions)	$2,073,321
Annual GNP Growth	3.8 %
GNP per Capita	$16,289
Percentage GNP for Agriculture	3 %
Percentage GNP for Industry	41 %
Percentage GNP for Services	56 %
Percentage GNP for Defense	0.9 %

JAPAN - IMPORTS & EXPORTS

Major Imports	Crude Oil
	Metal Ores
	Raw Materials
	Foodstuffs
	Machinery
Major Exports	Machinery
	Vehicles
	Iron & Steel
	Electronics
	Semiconductors
Balance of Trade	$87,010,000,000 (1987)

LABOR FORCE:

When the video was produced, Japan had a labor force of 60 million people, over half of whom (53%) are now involved in services and trade. Around one-third are employed in manufacturing and construction.

A major change in the labor force in recent years has been the entry of part-time and full-time female workers. Although they are paid far less than men, women now account for 40% of the total labor force. Compared internationally, the rate of Japanese female employment is below that of the U.S. but above that of the U.K., France and West Germany. A large number of highly educated Japanese women are underutilized in Japanese society - these women form a talented labor pool which Western companies should be aware of. IBM has been a particularly notable employer of Japanese women.

UNEMPLOYMENT:

Unemployment in Japan is low - it runs between 2 and 2.5%, although the figures are calculated differently in the U.S.A. and are not directly comparable.

BUSINESS STRUCTURE:

Smaller business establishments account for the vast majority of all Japanese companies, including 50% of all manufacturing, 60% of wholesale business and 80% of retail business. These companies generally have fewer than 100 employees, who are not granted the guarantee of lifetime employment (another myth about the Japanese market): lifetime employment was a fact only in the largest companies, and even in them, it is now breaking down fast. NOTE: As a result of the dichotomy in business structure, Japan is said to have a dual economy - very large corporations subcontract business to smaller entities, which can be cut off quickly when business slows down.

CURRENCY:

After the Plaza Agreement of September 22, 1985, the yen began to rise rapidly against the dollar, going from 242 to the dollar to 154 a year later. This was a long-overdue reflection of the strength of Japan's economy. Since then, it has traded at between 120 and 160 to the dollar. The yen finances only around 2% of world trade, compared with 50% for the dollar. As a foreign exchange market, Tokyo ranks only fifth.

INFLATION RATE:

Japan has traditionally enjoyed a low rate of inflation, which has varied from below 1% to less than 3% for the past several years.

INVESTMENT:

Since the Foreign Exchange and Foreign Trade Control Law was modified in 1980, Japan's government is no longer the primary influence on direct foreign investment in Japan. Factors such as competition and the cost of doing business are more important in explaining the relatively low level of direct investment.

BANKS:

The six largest banks in the world, in terms of capitalization, are owned by the Japanese. Starting in the 1950s, in order to rebuild the country after the war, Japanese banks began lending on an asset base that is smaller than that allowed by regulations in the U.S. The practice has continued and the effect has been to allow easy financing for expansion of business. Inflated values of land and stocks have given banks even greater paper assets on which to lend.

FINANCIAL MARKETS:

Financial deregulation has been proceeding slowly over the last decade. Until 1980, restrictions on moving money out of the country prevented private Japanese from investing abroad. In December 1980, the Bank of Japan and the Ministry of Finance liberalized foreign capital outflow.

By 1990, the capital outflow reached US$ 130 billion per year. Japan has become the world's largest capital creditor nation.

There are eight stock exchanges in Japan, but most trading is conducted on the Tokyo exchange. Around 25 foreign firms have been granted membership rights on the Tokyo Stock Exchange; over 90 foreign companies are listed on the Exchange.

Note on NTT: NTT (Nippon Telephone and Telegraph) is the biggest company in the world. With a market capitalization of around US$ 110 billion, it is almost twice as big as IBM at US$ 60 billion. Capitalization of NTT constitutes almost 4% of the Tokyo Stock Market.

2.   *Gather information about Hong Kong, South Korea, and Taiwan.*

This assignment will vary according to the professor's desires. The appropriate "Doing Business in Asia" video tape should provide adequate information. Some basic information is provided below[3]:

```
--------------------------------------------------------------------
                    HONG KONG - GENERAL PROFILE
--------------------------------------------------------------------
     Area                              402 sq mi
     Population 1988             5,651,000
     Population Growth                1.05 %
     Population Density             14,073 /sq mi
     GNP 1988 (millions)          $50,615
     GNP per Capita                $8,957
     Capital City                  VICTORIA
--------------------------------------------------------------------


                    HONG KONG - DEMOGRAPHICS
--------------------------------------------------------------------
     Population 1975             4,396,000
     Population 1988             5,651,000
     Population 1989             5,710,000
     Population 1990             5,770,000
     Population 2000             6,405,000
     Population Growth                1.05 %
     Population Density             14,073 /sq mi
     Population Doubling Time          66 years


            HONG KONG - LANGUAGES, ETHNIC GROUPS & RELIGIONS
--------------------------------------------------------------------
     Languages                 Cantonese
                               English

     Ethnic Groups             Chinese          98 %
                               Other             2 %

     Religions                 Traditional      90 %
                               Christian        10 %
--------------------------------------------------------------------
```

SOUTH KOREA

```
--------------------------------------------------------------------
                    SOUTH KOREA - GENERAL PROFILE
--------------------------------------------------------------------
     Area                           38,031 sq mi
     Population 1988            42,773,000
     Population Growth                1.33 %
     Population Density              1,125 /sq mi
     GNP 1988 (millions)         $124,687
     GNP per Capita                $2,915
     Capital City                  SEOUL
--------------------------------------------------------------------


                    SOUTH KOREA - DEMOGRAPHICS
--------------------------------------------------------------------
     Population 1975            35,281,000
     Population 1988            42,773,000
     Population 1989            43,342,000
     Population 1990            43,918,000
     Population 2000            50,121,000
     Population Growth                1.33 %
     Population Density              1,125 /sq mi
     Population Doubling Time          52 years
```

---

[3] The demographic and economic data are from *PCGlobe.*

```
------------------------------------------------------------------------
              SOUTH KOREA - LANGUAGES, ETHNIC GROUPS & RELIGIONS
------------------------------------------------------------------------
    Languages              Korean
                           English

    Ethnic Groups          Korean                   99 %
                           Other                     1 %

    Religions              Buddhist & Confuc.        72 %
                           Christian                 28 %
------------------------------------------------------------------------
```

```
------------------------------------------------------------------------
              SOUTH KOREA - GROSS NATIONAL PRODUCT (GNP)
------------------------------------------------------------------------
    GNP 1987 (millions)              $113,249
    GNP 1988 (millions)              $124,687
    GNP 1989 (millions)              $137,281
    Annual GNP Growth                   10.1 %
    GNP per Capita                    $2,915
    Percentage GNP for Agriculture      11 %
    Percentage GNP for Industry         43 %
    Percentage GNP for Services         46 %
    Percentage GNP for Defense         4.8 %
------------------------------------------------------------------------
```

TAIWAN

```
------------------------------------------------------------------------
                    TAIWAN - GENERAL PROFILE
------------------------------------------------------------------------
    Area                        13,892 sq mi
    Population 1988         20,004,000
    Population Growth             1.14 %
    Population Density            1,440 /sq mi
    GNP 1988 (millions)        $82,814
    GNP per Capita              $4,140
    Capital City                TAIPEI
------------------------------------------------------------------------
                    TAIWAN - DEMOGRAPHICS
------------------------------------------------------------------------
    Population 1975         17,263,000
    Population 1988         20,004,000
    Population 1989         20,232,000
    Population 1990         20,463,000
    Population 2000         22,919,000
    Population Growth             1.14 %
    Population Density            1,440 /sq mi
    Population Doubling Time         61 years


------------------------------------------------------------------------
             TAIWAN - LANGUAGES, ETHNIC GROUPS & RELIGIONS
------------------------------------------------------------------------
    Languages              Mandarin Chinese
                           Taiwanese
                           Hakka

    Ethnic Groups          Taiwanese                84 %
                           Mainland Chinese         14 %
                           Aborigine                 2 %

    Religions              Budd., Confuc., Tao.     93 %
                           Christian                 5 %
                           Other                     2 %
------------------------------------------------------------------------
```

VIDEO CASE 9-2   MARESCO INTERNATIONAL CORPORATION[4]

FOCUS ON SMALL BUSINESS

SUBJECT MATTER: International Marketing, Distribution, Importance of Service

Please see the Guide to Video Cases for video length and other information.

AT-A-GLANCE OVERVIEW

Founded in 1983, Maresco International Corporation is an export management company based in Bridgewater, New Jersey. Maresco represented a U.S. manufacturer of low-technology, high-cost forklift trucks in the highly competitive international marketplace. It was facing a situation, in the mid-1980s, wherein the U.S. dollar was at an all-time high relative to foreign currencies. Because of the dollar's value, U.S. machinery manufacturers were having a difficult time competing with products manufactured outside the United States.

Complicating the situation further was a limited U.S. export funding program. This meant that the manufacturer did not have the same economic advantages as companies located abroad who had access to government subsidized financing and loan incentives.

Meanwhile, the manufacturer wanted immediate profitability throughout all areas of the company. Because there was not time to develop a typical long-term international distribution program, Maresco faced a major challenge as to how it was going to represent the company.

To secure immediate profitability for the manufacturer, Maresco developed a trading group to supply spare parts for competitors' machinery. By providing service more efficiently than the competition's distributors, Maresco created instant name recognition and a "service first" reputation for the manufacturer. This, in turn, led to sales and profitability.

DISCUSSION QUESTIONS

1.   *What type of analysis should help Maresco profitability?*

Maresco, as the distributor of the lift trucks, has all the concerns that the manufacturer would if it were marketing its products itself. The primary analysis should deal with estimates of market potential. The long-term exchange rate of the dollar to other currencies is also of concern. However, informal estimates of the nature of the country's political climate, cultural customs, economic situation, and other environmental factors are equally important.

2.   *Assuming the dollar's value will stay high, what pricing strategy could be implemented to be consistent with Maresco overall's "service first" positioning strategy?*

Maresco needs some reason for its high prices, i.e. it needs to justify the prices some way. Offering extraordinary service is one way this can be done. Maresco cannot change the product. It can lend support to high prices with effective promotion, but the product is described as low-tech. There may not be much to talk about in promotions. The problem is the price, but that cannot be lowered. Perhaps customer-friendly payment plans could be put in place to make the price more palatable. None of these solutions is particularly attractive. Some of them are not implementable. Therefore, the "solution" may be to offer more for the money. More what? More service, for example.

Here's what Maresco did. To become competitive, Maresco positioned the manufacturer's lift truck as the "Rolls Royce" of lift trucks. This high-value

---

[4]Excerpts reprinted from *Strengthening America's Competitiveness*, pp. 152-153, copyright 1991 by Connecticut Mutual Life Insurance Company.

approach separated the manufacturer from its competitors, who were focusing on price due to industry price wars. Customers who understood the long-term benefits of buying high-quality machinery purchased the manufacturer's truck.

By developing shared risks among itself and the banks, Maresco implemented a program that used domestic collateral for securing international sales. The manufacturer offered Maresco extended payment terms, and Maresco offered customers pricing discounts if they made payment within a short period of time. By reducing short-term profit levels, Maresco could provide customers with a better purchasing package.

Since starting the program seven years before the video was produced, Maresco has formed distribution channels in over 50 countries and achieved sales on every continent. Sales growth occurred during all facets of the U.S. dollar fluctuation. The manufacturer gained the number one market position in many overseas markets and today is recognized as a major force in the lift truck industry. Maresco itself has grown 258 percent in sales during the last three years to over $8 million. Through the shared risk program, it improved its cash flow position which helped the company structure its credit lines.

In summary, through a name recognition strategy, a shared risk agreement, and creative positioning, Maresco International brought a U.S. manufacturer of low-tech, high-cost forklift trucks into a highly competitive international marketplace and earned the manufacturer immediate and sustained profitability.

10 THE ELEMENTS OF PRODUCTS

CHAPTER SCAN

This chapter is the first of four dealing with the marketing mix variable of "product." The "total product" definition of this mix variable is used, reflecting the fact that all products are more than just a narrowly defined good or service. The intangibles provide much of the satisfaction a buyer receives.

Other topics covered in this chapter include the categorizing of consumer and organizational products, branding, trademarks, labeling and packaging, and customer service, all parts of the total product. Effective marketing requires that all product-related factors be considered. Ethical implications associated with the design and marketing of products are considered.

SUGGESTED LEARNING OBJECTIVES

The student who studies this chapter will be exposed to a wide-ranging introduction to the marketing mix variable of "product" and will be able to:

1. Define "product" and explain why the concept of "total product" is important to effective marketing.

2. Differentiate among convenience products, shopping products, and specialty products.

3. Categorize organizational products.

4. Understand brand-related terminology including brand, brand name, brand mark, trademark, and brand image.

5. Discuss the development of effective brand names.

6. Analyze the importance of packaging in the development of an effective product strategy.

7. Discuss the role of customer service in product strategy.

8.   Understand the ethical implications associated with the design and marketing of goods and services.

CHAPTER OUTLINE

I.   INTRODUCTION

II.   WHAT IS A PRODUCT?

      A.   The Total Product
      B.   Product Differentiation

III. CLASSIFYING PRODUCTS BY THE NATURE OF THE MARKET

IV.   CLASSIFYING CONSUMER PRODUCTS

      A.   Tangibility and Durability
      B.   Consumer Behavior

            1.   Convenience Products
            2.   Shopping Products
            3.   Specialty Products

V.   CLASSIFYING ORGANIZATIONAL PRODUCTS

VI.   THE PRODUCT LINE AND THE PRODUCT MIX

VII. BRANDING - WHAT'S IN A NAME?

      A.   Brands and Trademarks

            1.   Brands
            2.   Trademarks
            3.   Service Mark

      B.   Generic Names
      C.   Brand Image
      D.   A "Good" Brand Name
      E.   Selecting a Brand Name
      F.   Manufacturer Brands versus Distributor Brands
      G.   Generic Brands Provide No Frills
      H.   Family Brands versus Individual Brands
      I.   Combining Family and Individual Brands
      J.   World Brands
      K.   Licensing

VIII. PACKAGING

      A.   Labeling: Telling About the Product
      B.   Legal Guidelines for Packaging

IX.   PRODUCT WARRANTIES

X.   CUSTOMER SERVICE

XI.   ETHICAL CONSIDERATIONS ASSOCIATED WITH PRODUCT STRATEGY

      A.   The Right to Safety
      B.   The Right to Be Informed
      C.   Quality of Life
      D.   Ecology

XII. SUMMARY

XIII. KEY TERMS

XIV. QUESTIONS FOR DISCUSSION (10)

XV.   ETHICS IN PRACTICE

XVI.   CASES

        The following key terms are introduced and used in Chapter 10.   They are
defined in the text's Glossary.

Total product
Primary characteristics
Auxiliary dimensions
Product strategy
Product concept
Product differentiation
Durable good
Nondurable good
Service
Convenience product
Shopping product
Specialty product
Organizational product
Product item
Product line
Depth of product line
Product mix
Width of product line
Brand name
Brand marks
Logo
Trademark
Lanham Act
Service mark
Generic mark
Manufacturer brand (national brand)
Distributor brand (private brand)
Generic product (generic brand)
Family branding
Individual brand
World brand
Brand equity
License
Packaging
Label
Universal Product Code (UPC)
Product warranty
Magnuson-Moss Warranty Act
Right to safety
Right to be informed
Quality of life

THE CHAPTER SUMMARIZED

I.   INTRODUCTION

        The Goodyear Aquatred is an all-season radial tire. The idea is that the
        tire be the best wet weather tire without sacrificing dry road performance.
        The tire has a deep Aqua-Channel that evacuates water from under the tire,
        and visually sets the tire apart from its competitors. The name of the
        tire is easy to say, it is memorable, it is descriptive of the product, the
        tire comes with a 60,000 mile tread warranty, it carries the trustworthy
        Goodyear name ... in short, the Aquatred tire offers buyers a bundle of
        satisfactions.

        This is the first of four chapters dealing with product issues.

II.   **WHAT IS A PRODUCT?**

The product is the "thing" itself, though not necessarily tangible. But many other aspects are part of "the product." It can be a reward for the person willing to buy the product. It can be seen as a bundle of benefits. For example, a room at a hotel at DisneyWorld is much more than just a place to stay. The product, thus, is both the steak and the sizzle. A product is a bundle of satisfactions. And this view shows that a product may be tangible or intangible, good or service.

A.   The Total Product

Effective marketers think of products broadly since each offers a broad spectrum of tangible and intangible benefits that a buyer might gain from a product. This is the **total product**. A product has **primary characteristics**, basic features and aspects of the core product, which provide the essential benefits of the product, e.g. a drill is expected to drill holes. But a product may also have **auxiliary dimensions**, special features or packaging, a warranty, a repair service contract, and so on. Any of these may be particularly important to the buyer.

Such a view allows marketers to segment markets. Different people with different needs may be receiving different sets of satisfaction from the same product.

Exhibit 10-1 demonstrates that Close-Up toothpaste is a core product with associated auxiliary benefits.

Product strategy involves planning the product concept and developing a unified mix of product attributes.

A **product concept** (also called the product positioning concept) defines the essence or core idea underlying the product features and benefits that appeal to the target market.

The marketing strategist selects and blends product core and auxiliary characteristics into a basic idea or unifying concept.

B.   Product Differentiation

Calling the buyer's attention to aspects of a product that set it apart from its competitors is called **product differentiation**.

Product differentiation may be accomplished by making an adjustment in the product to make it stand out from its competitors, or by stressing some intangible benefit the product offers. The difference from competing products need not be scientifically provable. Style changes can be used to show a difference from competing products. If the customers see the variation as important, then the variation differentiates the product from its competitors.

III.   **CLASSIFYING PRODUCTS BY THE NATURE OF THE MARKET**

One of the strongest factors affecting buyer behavior is the nature of the product. Marketers have developed widely accepted product classifications that describe products and, more importantly, buyers' perceptions of them.

IV.   **CLASSIFYING CONSUMER PRODUCTS**

Consumer products are very diverse and may be classified according to a number of criteria. Exhibit 10-2 shows two of these criteria.

A.   Tangibility and Durability

Products may be classified according to tangibility and durability as **durable goods, nondurable goods,** and **services.** Cars exemplify durables, and paper towels nondurables.

Services are products just as are tangible goods. The service industry now accounts for about half of personal consumption expenditures.

There is a goods/services continuum as shown in the text in Exhibit 10-3. A steel girder is "mostly a good," an employment agency's service is "mostly a service," food at a restaurant is somewhere between the two. All are products, however.

```
  Steel              Restaurant's            Dental
  Girder               Offering             Service
|                                                          |
|    GOOD            GOOD/SERVICE           SERVICE         |
|                                                          |
|                                                          |
|---------------------- PRODUCTS -------------------------|
```

Some differences between the marketing of goods and services are:

.   Services are intangible; they cannot be examined or tried before purchase. Marketers have to allow for this, e.g., making projections of what will be delivered. Architects' models of proposed buildings are an example.

.   Services are not separable from their providers. A singer's live performance cannot be truly replaced by another singer's.

.   Services "disappear," cannot be stored, and cannot be resold at another time to another customer. An hour of a dentist's time is "gone forever" if there is no customer. Lowering prices during non-peak times or seasons is a typical marketing response to this.

.   Services cannot be owned or kept. They do not provide possession utility beyond the performance of the service.

.   Most services are delivered by people, thus employee dealings with customers are crucial to success.

.   Services vary widely in quality. The skills of providers vary, one lawyer may be better than another, a tax consultant may not be as sharp at 6 p.m. as he was at 9 a.m. "Quality control" becomes important in achieving customer satisfaction.

B.   Consumer Behavior

Products have been classified in many ways by many authors. The 1924 classification by Melvin T. Copeland is used here (i.e., convenience, shopping and specialty).

Note the following about these classes:

.   They refer to consumer products, not industrial products.

.   They are somewhat descriptive of the products, but are in fact based on the consumer's behavior and need. These product categories are consumer oriented.

.   Like all classifications, exceptions can be found. (To a Rockefeller, "all" products would be convenience products.)

1.   Convenience Products

Convenience products, like disposable pens, have these characteristics:

.   Relatively inexpensive.

- Purchased on a recurring basis.

- Bought without a great deal of thought, and with a minimum of shopping effort.

- Relatively little brand loyalty (e.g., settling for a different brand of cleaner if the one you usually buy is not available or of a higher price).

In short, convenience products are bought at the most convenient location. Distribution is a major element of their marketing mixes, though the other three P's must be appropriate.

2.   Shopping Products

For **shopping products** consumers feel a need to compare products. They seek information and take the time to examine merchandise before they buy. They want to shop for the product and get exactly what they wanted, not settling for what was easily accessible.

- Decisions are not made on the spur of the moment.

- Prices are generally higher than for convenience products.

- Many of these products are seen by other consumers. This involves some risk when deciding on a purchase (e.g., shoes, furniture, etc.).

- There is brand awareness and brand loyalty (e.g., purchasing only Levi's and not substituting them with Wrangler.)

Since people are willing to shop for these products, distribution to the proper location, rather than to many locations, is important. Other mix elements fit the buyer's shopping and purchasing behavior.

3.   Specialty Products

In some cases, consumers do not "shop" for products, they "plot" their purchases. They thus know exactly what they want and will accept no substitutes. The products these buyers want are called **specialty products**.

- Products are often infrequently purchased (e.g., engagement ring, piano, fine china).

- Buyers engage in an extensive search for information and spend considerable time comparing options.

- Brand loyalty can be strong once the buyer's mind is made up (e.g., only Waterford crystal will do).

Since buyers exert great effort to get the products, limited distribution may be appropriate. Other portions of the marketing mix are used to support the product's image.

V.   CLASSIFYING ORGANIZATIONAL PRODUCTS

All **organizational products** (products sold in business markets) have one major thing in common: **derived demand**. The demand for every industrial product depends upon the demand for some other product. Some examples are:

- The auto mechanic's demand for tools rests on the consumer's demand for cars and car repair.

.   The university's demand for chairs and library books rests on the student's demand for education.

The classification of industrial products, shown in Exhibit 10-4, appears more product-oriented than the consumer-products classification. Yet it does reflect the industrial buyer's behaviors and concerns (e.g., buying a building differs from buying a broom).

The text identifies seven classes of organizational products:

1.   Raw materials -- products that have undergone little processing and are close to their "natural states."

2.   Manufactured materials and component parts or fabricating materials -- these have undergone considerable processing and will become part of other products (e.g., wires, spark plugs, sheet metal).

3.   Process materials -- used to make products but do not become part of those products (e.g., acid used to "bathe" machine parts).

4.   Installations -- this is a capital item, a major purchase such as buildings or heating plants.

5.   Accessory equipment -- assists with the operations (e.g., calculators, forklifts, pickup trucks).

6.   Operating supplies -- these are supplies that are used up in operations and are usually inexpensive, such as brooms, pencils and staplers (considered the convenience products of the industrial market).

7.   Services -- work provided by others, ranging from janitorial to legal services.

VI.   THE PRODUCT LINE AND THE PRODUCT MIX

We have been discussing "the product," but few if any marketers offer just one **product item**. They do offer **product lines**, groups of products that are related, such as the Louis Rich food products line, Procter and Gamble's cleaning products line, and Clairol's hair coloring line.

One organization may offer various lines of products.

The term **depth of product line** is used to describe the number of product items within a product group, that is, the selection available. All of the products offered, no matter how unrelated, constitute the **product mix**. The term **width of product mix** is used to describe the number of different product lines within a product mix.

VII.   BRANDING - WHAT'S IN A NAME?

Branding serves both the buyer and the seller. Without branding, customers would have difficulty identifying products desired. Consumers usually are not able to analyze the products they buy so they rely on brands. Brands help sellers build cadres of loyal customers which in turn helps the seller to make the introduction of new products easier and more readily acceptable.

A.   Brands and Trademarks

Despite common misusage, the terms used to discuss branding do have different meanings.

1.   Brands

A **brand** is any name, term, symbol, sign, design, or unifying combination of these, that identifies and distinguishes one product from another competitive product.

A **brand name** is the verbal part of the brand.

Brand marks are the symbolic portions of brands.

A **logo** (logotype) is a brand name or company name written in a distinctive way (e.g., the script used by Coca-Cola.)

2.   Trademarks

A **trademark** is a legally protected brand name or brand mark. Owners of trademarks have exclusive rights to their use.

The Lanham Act declares that brand names cannot be confusingly similar to or used for the same purpose as registered trademarks.

- Miller Lite was declared to have protection for "lite beer" but not for "light beer."

- Coca-Cola has successfully squelched such names as Coola-Cola and Coka-Coola.

- General Motors was not able to block the use of the Cadillac name by a dog food canning company.

3.   Service Mark

Service marks can be registered and protected. They are the "trademarks" of service products. Examples: NBC's chimes, G.M.'s Mr. Goodwrench, and slogans like "Fly the Friendly Skies."

B.   Generic Names

Generic names are part of our language (e.g., water, cat food, flower.) Some generic names were once brand names but "passed into the language."

A holder of a trademarked name may be told by a judge that the name has become generic and that others may use it. This happened with formica, nylon, cellophane, and many others. Holders of the rights to names like Dictaphone, Muzak, and Vaseline usually attempt to make it clear to all that these are registered trademarks, not generic words, in fear that these too, will "pass into the language" and be declared legally generic.

C.   Brand Image

The symbolic value associated with a brand is its **brand image**.

People express themselves in terms of the symbolic value of their possessions. When we say "this is my brand," we are saying that the image we have of a product matches the image we have of ourselves. Thus, much of the advertising is "image advertising" done in hopes that a product will be seen as, for example, "exciting" and be bought by people who want to be "exciting." This topic is treated more fully in Chapter 17.

D.   A "Good" Brand Name

Generally, "good" brand names are:

- Easy to say

- Easy to remember

- Pronounceable in only one way

- Positive in connotation

.   Communicative of product attributes

.   Distinctive

Examples that fit these criteria include: Spic and Span, Fruit'n Fibre, Duracell, Moist and Easy, Jiffy (cake mix,) and Virginia Slims. Other names do not seem to consider these criteria: Qyz, and Vydec.

These four steps typify the process of selecting a brand name:

1.   Identify brand name objective(s).

2.   Generate name alternatives. Screen alternatives for appropriateness.

3.   Research consumer opinion, preferences, and image of brand name.

4.   Conduct trademark search for similar names.

Exhibit 10-5 summarizes some of the characteristics of good brand names.

E.   Selecting a Brand Name

Many characteristics of a good brand name are also characteristics of good brand marks. These include simplicity, few colors, unique, memorable, recognizable whether large or small, and uncomplicated to produce.

Good examples are the Chevrolet "Trapezoid" and the Olympic "Rings."

Brand marks can be effective communicators. Betty Crocker is one such.

F.   Manufacturer Brands versus Distributor Brands

Black and Decker makes and sells tools under its own name. This kind of brand is called a **national brand** or, more descriptively, a **manufacturer brand**.

Black and Decker makes tools which Sears sells under its own Craftsman label. This is a **private brand** or, more descriptively, a **distributor brand**.

Why would Black and Decker sell tools to Sears and create its own competition? It may be easier to sell products to Sears than to individual consumers or businesses. Sears must handle advertising, selling and guaranteeing the products. Black and Decker may be able to smooth out production runs or encounter other savings when it sells tools to Sears. Lastly, if Black and Decker doesn't sell the tools to Sears, somebody else will.

The merchandise is, to Black and Decker, **contract merchandise**.

G.   Generic Brands Provide No Frills

It is possible for a product to carry no manufacturer's brand and no distributor's brand. These are **generic products** or **generic brands**, "no name" products in plain packages, produced and distributed at low cost, some portion of the savings being passed on to the buyers.

The idea is not new. Years ago, customers bought most food products from bins and barrels.

While generic products offer no particular guarantee of quality, a free market allows buyers to decide if the price savings is worth the "guarantee" a national brand provides.

Nonconsumer Generic Products

Many organizational products are, in effect, generic goods. As long as the products meet specifications, the supplier may be unimportant. Many products are traded in bulk internationally without regard for brand names, e.g. wheat and oil.

Suppliers can still use marketing, and consider the total product being offered, however. Good delivery, guarantees, discount policies, etc. are all part of the "total product."

H.   Family Brands Versus Individual Brands

Hunt's, Del Monte and Campbell's uses one name for a whole line of related items. This is **family branding**. It can make the introduction of new products easier, but failures can also be found (e.g., Campbell's try at marketing spaghetti sauce.)

Procter and Gamble (P&G,) for example, puts a different name on almost every product in its mix: Tide, Cheer, Ivory, etc. This is **individual branding**. Reasons for doing this include:

- To protect brands from association with a flop or other disaster (e.g., if something goes wrong with Buicks, GM's other cars might not be badly affected in the marketplace).

- To appeal to different market segments (e.g., Crest toothpaste for the cavity-conscious, Ultra-Brite for the whiteness-conscious).

- To maximize shelf-space in stores. Having Tide, Cheer, Oxydol, etc. gives P&G a greater proportion of the grocer's shelves than just one brand would have.

I.   Combining Family and Individual Brands

Family branding and individual branding can be combined (e.g., Kellogg's Apple Jacks, Kellogg's Mini-Wheats, Kellogg's Corn Flakes, etc.).

J.   World Brands

A product that is widely distributed throughout the world with a single name is known as a **world brand**. Levi's, Marlboro, and Coca-Cola are examples.

K.   Licensing

Brand equity means that market share or profit margins are greater because of the goodwill associated with the brand.

Names like Crayola or Disney add value to a product, and the names hold additional value if the company is sold or if the name is used on other products.

The company with good brand equity may **license** another firm to use the trademark. The name Coca-Cola appears on clothing, Garfield (the cat) appears on clothing, calendars, and notepaper.

VIII. **PACKAGING**

The package is an extension of the product. Sometimes it is more important than the product, as is the hanging dispenser for Shower Mate or the convenient tube on a Glue Stic. **Packaging** involves making decisions about labels, inserts, instructions, and containers.

Packages:

.   Contain the product.

.   Protect the product in transit.

.   Facilitate storage and stacking.

.   Facilitate product use.

.   Serve as promotional tools.

.   Have an ecological function.

The package must, like the product, be "consumer-oriented." Package prototypes should be tested for ease of handling, opening, etc. Channel members should also be considered. Is the package easily broken, subject to leaks, or hard to stack?

A.   Labeling: Telling About the Product

The paper or plastic sticker on a can of peas or jar of mustard is a **label**. As packaging technology improves, the label becomes more important as cans and bottles are less widely used. For frozen foods, for example, the label provides much of the protection for the product. (Technically, such a label is a **wrapper**.)

Either way, the label:

.   Carries the brand name.

.   Carries information about the product and its use.

.   Includes instructions on proper disposal methods.

.   Fulfills legal requirements (e.g., requirements to provide nutritional information.)

Most labels now include the familiar **UPC (Universal Product Code.)**

B.   Legal Guidelines for Packaging

Package design is influenced by certain legal strictures. The F.T.C. dislikes:

.   Packages intentionally designed to mislead.

.   Labels bearing false or misleading information.

.   Packages not providing required warnings.

State laws (such as marking bottles as returnable) cannot be ignored. Packaging's biggest public relations problems are pollution and littering. Biodegradable packages and notices to "dispose of properly" reflect this.

IX.   PRODUCT WARRANTIES

A **product warranty** provides a written guarantee of a product's integrity and the manufacturer's responsibility for repairing or replacing defective parts.

Warranties provide the buyer with a sense that the product is a good one and that its makers stand behind it. They also reduce risk, from the buyer's standpoint. They may lessen the need to find a proper repair shop since locations are usually listed. Unfortunately, warranties can be confusingly written in "legalese." Consumers find them hard to understand. Some marketers have capitalized on this by advertising "plain English" warranties.

The Magnuson-Moss Warranty Act of 1975 addresses some of the difficulties associated with warranties. It:

. Requires that any guarantees be available to buyers before purchase of the product.

. Grants power to the F.T.C. to determine the form in which guarantees are used in promotional materials.

. Stipulates that warranties use simple language and state precisely who the warrantor is.

. Requires that the warranty indicate precisely what products or parts are covered.

. Requires that the warrantor specify what will be done in the event of product defects, how long the warranty lasts, and what obligations the buyer has.

The warranty is part of the "total product."

X.   CUSTOMER SERVICE

Customer service is one element of the product mix. Effective marketing doesn't end with the sale. Indeed, competitive advantages can be built around post-sale service.

XI. ETHICAL CONSIDERATIONS ASSOCIATED WITH PRODUCT STRATEGY

Product strategy, viewed from a macromarketing perspective, reveals certain responsibilities marketers have. Laws require accountability to customers, competitors, and the general public.

A.   The Right to Safety

Consumers have many expectations when they buy a product -- that it works well, lasts as long as expected, etc. Perhaps our basic assumption when we buy a product is the expectation of safety, the avoidance of unnecessary danger. We assume we have a **right to safety.**

A case involved 3-wheel vehicles made by Honda and Kawasaki. The companies agreed to halt sales when consumer safety groups charged that thousands of users were injured monthly.

Yet, some reasonable risks must be taken. Should all possible danger (e.g., poison put in Dr. Scholl's foot powder) be eliminated? If so, at what cost? Still, there is a clear movement away from caveat emptor, let the buyer beware.

A bottom line, of course, is that products that involve unacceptable risks do not profit the marketer in the long run. Failure to reasonably protect consumers is inconsistent with the marketing concept.

B.   The Right To Be Informed

It may be that consumers do not need to be informed (again at increased costs) about every possible aspect of the products they buy. Most would concur that the consumer should not be exposed to gross inaccuracies. The consumer has the right to be given the facts needed to make an informed choice. This is the **right to be informed.**

C.   Quality of Life

As countries develop, they seem to show increasing concern for **quality of life,** characterized by a lessening of economic concern and an increasing concern with a sense of well-being. When this sense is focused on the business community, it translates into a belief that firms should be more than economically efficient. Firms are asked to be efficient and protective of the environment and conservers of natural resources, all at the same time.

Issues of quality of life spring from the idea that citizens have certain rights no organization should be permitted to violate. Citizens and organizations must address this difficult problem.

D.   Ecology

In the past 20 years, society has become aware of issues of ecology and protection of the environment. The clean environment goal could be obtained if that were the only goal. But trade-offs are involved. Examples:

- People want low-priced electric power without the possible dangers of nuclear plants and the problems resulting from burning fossil fuels.

- People want convenient "throwaway" bottles but don't want either litter or "full dumps."

- People want "fast food" but complain that wrappers used by fast food places are a major cause of litter.

- Many packaging products are biodegradable but marketers like fast food restaurants must continue clean-ups near their outlets.

Obviously marketing has a social responsibility to the environment. What is not clear is how that responsibility will be met and who is willing to pay for it. Does society place a higher value on lower-priced cars than on cleaner air brought about by more-expensive-to build cars?

XII.   SUMMARY

The term "product" refers to both goods and services in the consumer and organizational marketplace. Products should be broadly defined to include their intangible, as well as tangible, aspects. Marketers can then understand and attempt to meet buyers' expectations.

Learning Objective 1: **Define "product" and explain why the concept of the "total product" is important to effective marketing.**

Products can be goods, services, ideas, or any other market offering. The total product concept recognizes the many benefits, both tangible and intangible, that each product incorporates. This total product view permits marketers to identify market segments according to benefits received and to adjust products to appeal to those segments.

Learning Objective 2: **Differentiate among convenience products, shopping products, and specialty products.**

Consumer products may be categorized as convenience shopping or specialty goods. Convenience goods are typically inexpensive and purchased at a convenient location with little shopping effort. Shopping goods are purchased after buyers compare of price, quality, and other product attributes. Specialty goods are products for which buyers will accept virtually no substitutes and will go to great lengths to obtain.

Learning Objective 3: **Categorize organizational products.**

The seven classifications of organizational products are raw materials, manufactured materials and component parts, process materials, installations, accessory equipment, operating supplies, and services. They vary in use, purchase, and sale.

Learning Objective 4:   **Understand brand-related terminology including brand, brand name, brand mark, trademark, and brand image.**

A brand is a name, term, sign, or design that distinguishes one product from competing products. A brand name is the verbal part of the brand. A brand mark is a unique symbol used by an organization to identify its product. A trademark is a legally protected brand or brand mark. A brand image is the symbolic value associated with the brand. Manufacturer or national brands are the property of manufacturers; distributor or private brands are the property of wholesalers or retailers. A family brand is a group of products with the same brand name.

Learning Objective 5:   **Discuss the development of effective brand names.**

Most effective brand names are distinctive, easy to pronounce and spell, suggestive of product attributes, and memorable. Possible brand names must be researched for market acceptability and possible trademark infringement.

Learning Objective 6:   **Analyze the importance of packaging in the development of an effective product strategy.**

Packaging offers protection in transit, promotional benefits, and other marketing attributes. Packaging must make handling, storage, usage, and disposal acceptable to the buyer. Packages may convey symbolic meanings to buyers. In some instances, packages may be important as the products they contain.

Learning Objective 7:   **Discuss the role of customer service in product strategy.**

Marketers may create a competitive advantage by emphasizing the amount and quality of customer services. Delivery, gift wrapping, repair, and other customer services all can be important aspects of a product strategy to create a competitive advantage.

Learning Objective 8:   **Consider the ethical implications associated with the design and marketing of goods and services.**

Products, when viewed from a macromarketing perspective, are expected to enhance the quality of life. Products should be safe and not harm the environment. Most agree that marketers have certain responsibilities to customers, competitors, and the general public. However, as with many aspects of marketing, there is not complete agreement about who is responsible for the implementation and achievement of these goals.

XIII. **KEY TERMS**

XIV.   **QUESTIONS FOR DISCUSSION (10)**

XV.   **ETHICS IN PRACTICE**

XVI.   **CASES**

ANSWER GUIDELINES FOR CHAPTER 10 QUESTIONS FOR DISCUSSION

1.   *What is the product concept for the following brands? (a) Prodigy, interactive personal service (b) Domino's Pizza (c) Pillsbury Toaster Strudel (d) Photura camera (e) Pelonis Safe-T-Furnace*

ANSWER:

The product concept (also called the product positioning concept) defines the essence or core idea underlying the product features and benefits that appeal to the target market. Successful strategy requires a blending of primary characteristics and auxiliary dimensions into a basic idea or unifying concept. Students may be encouraged to discuss the core idea, benefits and auxiliary features for each of the products.

(a)   Prodigy, interactive personal service

Interactive personal services, such as Prodigy, are based on the core idea of convenient access and usage of a wide variety of services through computers, telephones, and television sets.

According to an article by Howard Schlossberg in *Marketing News* (October 28, 1991, pp. 1,6), the interactive television industry, using high-tech fiber optics, hopes to eventually provide interactive phone and Cable TV with such services as "Center Screen" and "Main Street." The core idea of "Center Screen" is to provide a choice of when to begin an at-home movie offered through an expanded pay-per-view network of 30 channels. "Main Street" services include shopping, financial, travel, educational, and entertainment accessed through the television rather than a computer.

(b)   Domino's Pizza

"Domino's Pizza Delivers, in thirty minutes," may be considered a core idea of Domino's. While the company also competes on product quality, the primary characteristic is pizza delivered to your door within thirty minutes at a reasonable price. Auxiliary dimensions may include cold Coca-Cola delivered with the pizza and friendly order and delivery personnel. Domino's has also offered free pizzas to anyone not satisfied with the pizza they ordered last time.

(c)   Pillsbury Toaster Strudel

You can almost hear the Pillsbury Doughboy saying, "Nothing says lovin' like my Pillsbury Toaster Strudel." While it may appear difficult at first to define the product concept for a little toaster strudel, ask students to consider characteristics in relation to other breakfast options. For example, the in-home or in-office convenience is superior to a fast food restaurant and perhaps the nutritional equivalent of cereal while providing a heated alternative to cold breakfast foods. Since many breakfast alternatives are high in nutrients, Pillsbury may be described as making a trade-off between nutrition and taste to develop the product concept.

(d)   Photura camera

Photura is positioned as the latest in technology. It is computerized and electronically advanced with a zoom lens. Sophisticated yet easy to use is the basic product concept. There seems to be no end to the ease-of-use concept. At the time of this writing, Canon announced a camera that focuses by sensing the eyes of the camera user and focusing where he or she is looking.

(e)   Pelonis Safe-T-Furnace

The name provides a strong indication of the product concept in this case. Safety seems to be the major characteristic stressed by Pelonis for a product that is, essentially, an advanced form of space heater. The problem with space heaters is, of course, safety. Each winter there are many news stories of families killed, or at least burned out of their homes, by the proverbial "faulty space heater." As long as the safety features can be differentiated by consumers and they continue to perceive risks from other options, the firm can maintain a clear position.

2.   *What characteristics distinguish convenience, shopping and specialty products?*

ANSWER:

Though the system admittedly breaks down under some circumstances (e.g., to a multi-millionaire all products could be convenience products,) the general distinctions among the three are shown below.

Convenience goods, in general:

Are relatively inexpensive.

.   Are purchased regularly on a recurring basis.

.   Are bought almost reflexively without much thought or customer effort.

.   Are bought at the most convenient location.

.   Engender little true brand loyalty.

.   Are associated with marketing mixes that stress intensive distribution.

Shopping goods, in general:

.   Engender customer behaviors such as information seeking and making comparisons, in other words, shopping.

.   Are not associated with spur-of-the-moment decisions.

.   Are associated with decisions made on the basis of fashion or style.

.   Involve "risk," of a social and/or monetary sort.

.   Are associated with brand consciousness and loyalty.

.   Are often closely linked with the store selling them (e.g., a "good store.")

.   Are associated with marketing mixes that stress selective distribution.

Specialty goods, in general:

.   Engender customer behaviors such as careful planning of purchases.

.   Are less-than-frequently purchased.

.   May engender strong brand loyalties (e.g., Waterford crystal) or strong store loyalties (e.g., a well-respected jeweler.)

.   Are associated with exclusive distribution methods.

The major point, however, is that these groupings are consumer-oriented and reflect consumer buying behaviors.

3.   *Evaluate the following brand names: (a) Match Light Charcoal, (b) Arm & Hammer Pure Baking Soda, (c) Almost Home cookies, (d) Scotch Brand video cassette, (e) Kwik-Kopy Printing, (f) Sun-Maid Raisin Bread, (g) Yuban coffee, (h) Diehard batteries, and (i) Handi-Wrap.*

ANSWER:

Some characteristics of a good brand name include these:

.   Easy to say.
.   Easy to remember (mnemonic quality).
.   Pronounceable in one way (at least in English).
.   Has a positive connotation.
.   Suggests what the product is supposed to do.
.   Associates the product with a meaningful image.
.   Sounds distinctive.

(a)   Match Light Charcoal

"Match Light Charcoal" tells almost everyone except the proverbial man from Mars what the product is, how it works, its big advantage over similar products, and associates the product with an image that is meaningful to potential customers.

The name is also easy to say and remember. It is easy to pronounce and is distinctive. While the product leaves something to be desired in that the easy-to-light coals burn out quickly, the name is a very good one.

(b)   Arm & Hammer Pure Baking Soda

"Arm & Hammer Pure Baking Soda" is only "partially" a good name. The "pure baking soda" portion tells the buyer what the product is and that it is "pure." The name Arm & Hammer itself tells us nothing unless some buyers want strong baking soda, whatever that is.

However, the Arm & Hammer name has been around for so long and is so known and respected that it is impossible to evaluate its impact on today's consumer. Good or bad though the name may be, can anybody name another brand of baking soda?

(c)   Almost Home cookies

"Almost Home" is a near-perfect name for packaged cookies. It is easy to read and say. It suggests something good about the product and about what it can do for you -- make you feel like you are "home" again. It lends itself to slogans and jingles. If the name seems a tad long, notice that it has only three syllables, as does "Oreo."

(d)   Scotch Brand Video Cassette

"Scotch" is, like Arm & Hammer, so familiar as to be difficult to evaluate. When you come right down to it, what does the word "Scotch" have to do with video tape? Do buyers want cheap tape, or plaid tape? Obviously, the name is so familiar and so associated with tape in general that people don't think about what "Scotch" might mean other than the fact that the name has been on number one tape products for as long as anyone can remember. In this sense, "Scotch" is an excellent name for a video tape. Consider that the name gave the product "instant familiarity" in the marketplace. What if 3-M had decided to use some other name like "Vid-Ex" or "Minnesota Tape." Would 3-M have had a harder or easier time cracking the video tape market?

(e)   Kwik-Kopy

"Kwik-Kopy" printing is another good name. Its unique spelling, or misspelling, is distinctive and easy-to-say and remember, and defensible in brand-name infringement cases. It connotes exactly what its owners hope to suggest, i.e, on-the-spot copies.

A parallel exists with the new "doc in a box" operations that have sprung up around the country. Students might be asked to check out the names of these. Examples are: "Alert," "Medquick," and "Rapid Response."

(f)   Sun-Maid Raisin Bread

"Sun-Maid" raisin bread trades on the familiarity of the Sun-Maid brand, suggesting that the bread must be good if this grand old name graces it. In addition, the implication is that the best and juiciest raisins go into Sun-Maid's "own" bread, though the name is simply licensed to bakeries.

The Sun-Maid name was originally supposed to suggest that raisins are simply sun-dried grapes (not dried by machine, of course,) and taken care of gently by the lovely bonneted girl on the package. As with Arm & Hammer, this name is so familiar as to be almost devoid of meaning.

Note the similarity to the Scotch video tape example. Which would be easier to introduce to the market, "Sun-Maid Raisin Bread" or some other raisin bread? A recent example of the same thinking is the relatively new Reese's Peanut Butter.

(g)   Yuban coffee

"Yuban" is a name that is relatively easy to say and remember. It is "unique" in that very few words and names begin with "Y" in the English language. The name suggests a South American or Caribbean origin and thus is a good name for coffee, though it does not tell much to the consumer. In this respect, "Taster's Choice" is superior.

Actually, Yuban is an old name dating to the early 1900s. It was revived for use in the 1960s after being out of use for decades. Far from being "Hispanic," it was suggested by the words "Yuletide Blend" used on a "special" coffee sold during the Christmas holidays.

(h)   Diehard batteries

"Diehard" (batteries) is the quintessential brand name. It is made even better by linking the name of the seller to it. "Sears Diehard" tells the customer that a big organization stands behind this great product, that dealers can be found nationwide, and that this battery is Sears' "best."

(i)   Handi-Wrap

"Handi-Wrap" meets virtually every criteria of a good brand name including uniqueness (due to the spelling). It may even connote to some people that Handi-Wrap doesn't get all stuck together, a factor which would diminish its handiness.

4.   *Which of the following brand names for frozen Mexican food would you like to own? Why? (a) Old ElPaso (b) Van deKamp's Mexican Classics (c) Happy Jose's*

ANSWER:

The answer may not be as obvious as it appears. Most students will seize upon "Old El Paso" and with good reason. The name connotes Mexican tradition yet in an "American" setting. The food is thus both foreign and familiar. The name is easy to say, remember, etc. It is a fine brand name.

"Happy Jose's" is also easy to say and remember. It may be appealing to people who go to Mexican-style restaurants with names like "Taco Ed's" and "Benito's." However, "Happy Jose's" conjures up a picture of a chubby, grinning fellow in a sombrero. Hispanic Americans may resent that.

"Van deKamp's Mexican Classics" leaves much to be desired. That the foods are Mexican classics is great but what does a Dutch fellow named Van deKamp know about Mexican foods? Still, Van deKamp is a familiar name, known for other food products, including many frozen foods. The familiarity of the name to many customers suggests that using another name for the Van deKamp line of Mexican foods would have made their introduction far more difficult.

5.   *What marketing strategies and tactics can a company use when it introduces a new product to ensure that its brand name does not become a generic name?*

ANSWER:

As suggested by name experts, a first move might be to name the product with a word or phrase that is defensible from the start -- made-up words with unusual spellings are examples of this strategy. What, after all, is an "Exxon"? What is a "Quisp"? It is a made-up word that can be defended as an "original thought." Several companies with names like "Namelab" have developed computer-based programs to develop such words.

Original (some would say incorrect) spellings are also a mark of originality and, therefore, perhaps more defensible in court. Thus, "Kwik" rather than "Quick" and "Quix" rather than "Quicks" and "Kix" rather than "Kicks." In a case of real significance to the Miller Brewing Company, the firm's "rights" to the word "Light" were struck down but its spelling "Lite" was decreed to belong to Miller alone (at least in the beer product group, and at least for now).

Some strange tactics have been employed by companies seeking to defend their brand names.

.   Recently, companies have begun to use the word "brand" in their advertising. Thus, "Sanka" is now referred to as "Sanka Brand." At one time, Sanka essentially meant decaf coffee so its makers felt it was necessary to protect it.

.   It has been said that Coca-Cola sends investigators to restaurants to ask for a Coke or a rum-and-Coke. These folks, the story goes, test the drink to be sure it's "true" Coke. This may be factual in that, years ago, waitresses and waiters did not say, as they do now, "We have only Pepsi, will that be all right?" when asked for a Coke.

.   Several organizations, especially those whose product names are already generic in use, if not legally generic, run advertisements "reminding" the public that Xerox is not a synonym for photocopying, that there is only one Dictaphone, that Muzak is a registered name and does not refer to all "elevator music." Do these firms feel that the ads will stop people from using the words generically? Probably not. But when a court case comes up, the companies can point to the many ads and dollars spent "educating" the public.

.   Many companies seek to protect names which might become usable by other companies on the grounds that the trademark holder is not actually using it in commerce. They ship a few cases of the product bearing the name to small town retailers. This permits the firm to show that it is, in fact, "using" the protected name.

6.   *Identify which of the following are either generic names or brand names: (a) Aspirin, (b) Fax, (c) Zipper, (d) Sanka, (e) Thermos, (f) Yo-Yo, (g) Pralines N' Cream, and (h) Kitty Litter.*

ANSWER:

Ask students how they might have protected the brand name for each case.

(a)   Aspirin

"Aspirin" is, in the U.S., a generic name. In most other countries, it is a registered brand name of the Bayer Company. In Canada, for example, there is only one aspirin, though many "headache remedies" with other names can be found. In World War I, the U.S. government seized the Bayer Company's holdings in the U.S. (it is a German company) and, in the process, made aspirin a generic name.

(b)   Fax

Fax is a generic name, derived from "facsimile." It would have been a great name to trademark but might, because of its obvious appeal, quickly have become legally generic.

(c)   Zipper

"Zipper" was a trademark of the B.F. Goodrich company. It has passed into the language and become generic. "Zipper" is a good example of a name so perfect for a product that it quickly became generic.

(d)   Sanka

"Sanka" is a registered brand name once greatly in danger of becoming generic. Thus, in recent years its commercials refer to it as "Sanka Brand Coffee." Youngsters who watch T.V. now refer to the product as "Sanka Brand." Sanka's use as a generic word was once far greater that it is today. Sanka was then essentially the only decaffeinated brand. Now there are many, and they are called ... generically ... decaf.

(e)   "Thermos" is, despite its common usage, the name of the Thermos Company (Division of King-Seely) located in Connecticut. The company lost the exclusive rights to the term "thermos," however, because it had come to widely used to mean an insulated or vacuum container. Now, Aladdin, once a competitor, makes and sells the "Aladdin Thermos."

(f)   "Yo-Yo" was a registered trademark of the Duncan Company. Other yo-yo's were sold but could not be marked or identified as "Yo-Yo's." Duncan lost the exclusive rights to the name in the 1970s.

(g)   "Pralines N' Cream" is a trademark. The more common "Pralines And Cream" would be hard to protect.

(h)   "Kitty Litter" is a trademark. Notice that other products of this type
      have names that suggest freshness and odor control. In this they may be
      better names than the original.

      Note: Here are some product names that are still protected: Band-Aid,
      Coke, Jeep, Jell-O, Kleenex, Magic Marker, Q-Tips, Scotch tape, Styrofoam,
      Teflon, Technicolor, Xerox, Windbreaker, Tabasco.

7.   *Give some examples of trademarks that are not brand names.*

ANSWER:

A trademark is a legally protected brand, brand name or brand mark. A brand is
any name, term, symbol, sign, design, or combination of these, that identifies
one product from another competitive product.

The terms "symbol," "sign" and "design" open up a wide range of possible
trademarks that are not names. Some possible ideas:

- The Bell symbol of "the phone company"
- The Red Cross
- Tony the Tiger
- The Chevrolet trapezoidal design
- The Olympic interlocking rings
- The shape of a Coke bottle
- The Schlitz Malt Liquor bull
- The distinctive Coor's (beer) script
- The NBC peacock

8.   *When is it a good idea to use family branding? Individual brands?*

ANSWER:

Family branding is a form of brand extension in which an organization takes
advantage of a familiar brand's reputation and associated goodwill. A whole line
of products is typically given the "family name." Campbell's is an excellent
example of this. Other practitioners include Libby, Del Monte, Heinz, Green
Giant, Ford (cars and many truck models,) and so on.

Family branding does not always pay off, suggesting reasons for using individual
brands.

- It may involve extending a brand beyond limits consumers are willing to
  tolerate. Jolly Green Giant amusement parks failed to catch on, for
  example, as did Campbell's spaghetti sauce.

- If one product proves dangerous or faulty, it might ruin the reputations of
  the other products that bear the family name.

Other situations where individual branding may be suggested include:

- when products produced by a single company differ substantially from one
  another, there may be no benefit from linking them with a family brand.

- when the firm wishes to market several products to appeal to different
  market segments. For example, detergent lines offered by Procter & Gamble,
  Lever Brothers, and Colgate-Palmolive use individual branding and different
  features (bleaching crystals, softeners, low suds, no scent, lemon scent)
  to appeal to different segments.

- when a company believes it is better to lose business to one of its own
  other brands than to the competition.

Some firms use both family brands and individual brands. The name "Kellogg's" is
featured on a whole family of cereals that also have individual names. Finally,
the text also defines a world brand as one common to all countries with Levi's,
Marlboro, and Coca-Cola as examples.

9.   *What are the characteristics of an effective brand name?*

ANSWER:

While there are many successful products whose names don't match up well with the "rules," it is generally thought that good brand names should be:

.   Short.
.   Easy to recall.
.   Pronounceable in only one way.
.   Unique and distinctive.
.   Suggestive of a product benefit.
.   Associating the product with a desired image.
.   Positive in connotation.
.   "Timeless" (e.g., the name of this year's Super Bowl star may be forgotten by next year).

If an organization were interested in protecting its brand name, it might want to consider these four categories of names suggested by Namelab, Inc., an outfit specializing in developing product names.

The most protectable names are the fanciful ones, otherwise meaningless "made-up" words like Exxon, Nerf, and Kotex.

The next most protectable are the arbitrary names, names with no particular relationship to the products they describe (e.g., Arrow shirts, Midas muffler, Comet cleanser).

The third most protectable names are the suggestive names like Accent, Diehard, Lestoil and Sure.

The least protectable names are those which actually describe the product. Examples include Animal Crackers, Tuna Helper and ReaLemon.

10.   *Describe how the basic functions of packaging are performed for the following: (a) Glue Stick, (b) Kode-A Color VR film for color prints, (c) Kiwi shoe polish, (d) Sperry Top Siders, (e) Timex watches.*

ANSWER:

In general, packages perform five functions:

.   Containment
.   Protection-In-Transit
.   Storage
.   Usage Facilitation
.   Promotion

Virtually all packages perform each function, some to a greater or lesser degree. For example, Kiwi shoe paste in a can is different from Kiwi liquid in a bottle with an applicator sponge built into the top.

One way to attack this problem is to ask students to weigh each function performed by each of the packages mentioned and then defend their weighted selections. The matrix below shows our own weights in the form of:

                3 = Significant
                2 = Of Limited Significance
                1 = Of Little or No Significance

FUNCTION:	Contain-ment	Protec-tion	Storage	Facili-tation	Promo-tion
PRODUCT					
Glue Stick	3	3	3	3	2
Kode-A Color Film	3	3	3	1	2
Kiwi Shoe Polish (Liquid With Applicator)	3	3	3	3	1
Top Siders	3	3	2	1	1
Timex Watches	3	3	2	1	1

ETHICS EXERCISE 10

CHAPTER 10 ETHICS IN PRACTICE

Overview

For 21 years, L'Eggs hosiery had been sold in plastic, egg-shaped containers. This product started a revolution in the way national-brand hosiery was sold, going from primarily department and clothing stores to mass merchandise outlets, including discount stores, grocery stores, and drug stores.

The marketing strategy was brilliant, and it revolved around the package. The egg-shaped container was unique, tied in with the brand name, tied in with the slogan "Our L'Eggs fit your legs," connoted brand quality (the egg shell protects a fragile product, and the oval is the most aesthetically pleasing shape), and reduced shoplifting. So why did parent Sara Lee Corporation, in 1991, ditch the packaging sensation of the century in favor of a new, milk-carton style cardboard box made from recycled paperboard?

1.   *Why did the marketers of L'Eggs change L'Eggs' package?*

The packaging shows a silhouette of the signature egg, but it is made entirely from recycled paperboard and has 38% less material. The company claimed in press reports that it was addressing today's consumer preferences: a package that's more compact, easier to read, and that uses less raw material to manufacture. A spokesperson said that the reason for the packaging change wasn't primarily environmental and that the plastic egg, which was recyclable (and 67% of the containers were recycled according to L'Eggs' research,) hadn't hurt sales. The company's market share at the time was at an all-time high of 55%, far ahead of second place No Nonsense at 28%. (Pat Sloan, "L'Eggs Egg Cracks," *Advertising Age*, July 15, 1991, p. 16).

The spokesperson acknowledged that surveys showed that 90% of consumers recognized the environmental benefits of the new package form, and they preferred the new package over the old one two-to-one, citing attributes such as shopping ease, attractiveness, a high-quality look, and environmental friendliness. So, it appears that L'Eggs was just practicing the marketing concept, staying abreast of changing consumer tastes and preferences. (Or, could it be, as J. Taylor Buckley suggested with tongue in cheek in a *USA Today* editorial [7/12/91], that "the L'Eggs chiefs got sick of being embarrassed every time they drove down the street at Easter time and saw yet another dogwood drooping under a heavy festooning of their eggs"?)

2.   *What actions will satisfy the environmental critics?*

The environmental movement is a very broad movement consisting of many components
such as individual consumers, nonprofit organizations, lobbyists, members of
Congress, and hence isn't always unified in its goals and actions (the latter
including lobbying, litigation, coalition building, public relations, research,
and the like). Thus, there will probably always be some elements of this
fragmented, heterogeneous myriad of organizations and individuals who will be
dissatisfied with some environmental aspect of a firm's products and packaging.

It appears in this case that the Environmental Defense Fund will not rest easy
until L'Eggs goes the way of Fizzies, flavor straws, and Bosco. They are quick
to criticize hosiery products, and yet appear to offer no alternative.

L'Eggs' advertising didn't fuss about the environmental benefits of changing from
plastic to recycled paperboard. Spot TV advertising featured the slogan, "A good
egg just got better," talking about attributes such as the slick contemporary
look rather than the "green" aspects.

In an editorial, *Advertising Age* (July 21, 1991, p. 16) opined that the reason
L'Eggs downplayed the environmental side of their packaging makeover was that
they knew from experience that other marketers who made similar changes (e.g.,
McDonald's) got very little, if any, applause when they featured the
environmental aspects of their packaging changeovers. The reason is that any new
package inevitably will displease one or another of the myriad of factions within
the environmental movement. So the thing to do when making a package change,
according to AA, is to downplay the "green" aspect and play up other criteria
such as aesthetics, convenience, etc.

3.   *Do you think the marketing managers or the critics have a "hidden agenda"?*

All environmental critics have as their open agenda greater government regulation
and control. The more radical elements of the environmental movement, the
Greens, (including student radicals, Hollywood activists, peace movement members,
and some scientists) are basically against material progress, technology, and
capitalism, and that they won't be satisfied until these are destroyed and a
socialistic utopia is ushered in. Their hidden agenda is a romantic effort to
reshape society. Other environmentalists are sincere and simply want to leave a
cleaner, more pristine ecology to future generations of men and beasts.

Groups like the Environmental Defense Fund, National Wildlife Federation, Sierra
Club, and Friends of the Earth are what could be termed "establishmentarian
environmentalists", according to *National Review* magazine. Their leadership
consists of affluent professionals whose tone is very moralistic (e.g., pollution
is evil, the result of overreaching ambition and greed) and who view Big Business
and capitalism as the root of all evil. Many of these leaders use the
environmental movement as a springboard from which to launch and extend their
power. This could well be their agenda, although many of the grass roots members
are probably simply doing what they believe in.

CHAPTER 10 TAKE A STAND QUESTIONS

1.   *Is it ethical to market the following products?* (a) Post Coco Pebbles, a
      crisp sweetened rice cereal with cocoa, (b) Channel One broadcasts of
      up-to-date news tailored to students, along with television commercials in
      classrooms, (c) a microwaveable coffee that requires foil-lined cartons to
      preserve product freshness and plastic wrap to ensure the package has not
      been opened, (d) a party cracker that is high in sodium, (e) yellow legal
      pad paper, (f) extended service/labor warranties sold as an extra rather
      than part of the product.

(a)   Post Coco Pebbles, a crisp sweetened rice cereal with cocoa

Some members of the consumer movement and some environmentalists believe that
socially undesirable products are sometimes produced and that these should be
banned. Many of the products in question 1 fall into this realm, Coco Pebbles
being one of them.

This could be viewed as an elitist attitude on the part of the critics.   In effect they feel they know what's best for you and I, while we don't.   Their objective is to reform people by legislation, ridicule, taxation, etc., to make them right and pure.   Their concerns are mostly matters of the body (tobacco, meat, fur, and other "sin" products), not of the soul.   The result is a restriction on consumer choices in the marketplace.   This lessens competition, promotes competitive products, and raises their prices, earning competitors what economists call "economic rents" (noncompetitive profits that accrue from good relations with regulators and influential legislators).

It is true that we have a "right to safety."   The question is: where do you draw the line?   You can probably find a "safety hazard" in almost any food; even nature's fruit contains sugar.   Our obsession with safety leads us to expect government to guarantee the impossible, a perfectly safe world; we've become overly dependent on government to insulate us from all risk.

Would a ban on Coco Pebbles be desirable?   It could be argued that if we banned all sugared cereals, children would eat a healthier breakfast.   Maybe, maybe not. Might they not substitute toaster pastries or donuts instead?   Or load unsweetened cereal with sugar?   Substitutes always exist, and you can't ban all the substitutes.   Parents have the right to feed their children what they feel is best for them.   If the only way to get their kids to eat breakfast is to sugarcoat it, this is probably better than the children not eating at all (Most cereals contain a "healthy" dosage of the minimum daily requirements of vitamins and minerals, although the nutritional value of this has been debated.). Marketers of children's breakfast cereals also argue, and the TV commercials state that the product should be considered part of the child's total diet, and not as an isolated item.

(b)   Channel One broadcasts of up-to-date news tailored to students, along with television commercials in classrooms

Christopher Whittle, chairman of Whittle Communications, launched Channel One in March 1990.   Channel One is a closed-circuit TV network that delivers a 12-minute news-and-information TV program via satellite into middle and high school classes around the country.   Participating schools are loaned $50,000 worth of electronic equipment, including TV monitors, video recorders, and a satellite dish.   Schools are encouraged to use the equipment as a teaching tool, not just as a means for bringing Channel One into the classroom.   In exchange, schools contract that a guaranteed percentage of students will view the news program at the same time every day, without interruption.   Each 12-minute show includes four 30-second commercials from such sponsors as Procter & Gamble, McDonald's, and the U.S. Army.   An advisory panel helped Whittle executives determine which products and sponsors are unacceptable for viewing.

A storm of criticism ensued as this service was launched.   Some of the ethical issues raised were:

.   Is it ethical for advertisers to target a captive audience?

.   Is it ethical for school officials to permit commercial messages to be
      presented in taxpayer-supported public schools?   Educators in several
      states saw to it that it was ruled illegal to use public monies to fund
      schools for the time that students watch news programs with commercials.

Arguments in favor of Channel One advanced by Whittle were:

.   State-of-the-art satellite technology is used to help interest students in
      learning about the world around them.   Those who oppose this are mired in
      past practices and unwilling to exploit new technology.

.   During an era of severe budget cutbacks, few schools can afford the
      expensive equipment Whittle is loaning for free.

.   This is the first television system that really understands who its
      television audience is and can develop its programs specifically for that
      audience.

- Channel One has received overwhelming support from parents and educators. They should have the free choice to take advantage of it.

Arguments against Channel One made by educators, legislators, and watchdog groups include:

- Watching commercials is not an educational activity. The classroom and the curriculum should be a marketplace for ideas, not a marketplace for someone's products.

- Parents entrust their children to the public schools. Channel One is a commercial transaction that violates this trust. We have no right -- legally or morally -- to sell access to our children, even if schools receive some benefit in return.

- Students are required to attend school. Exploiting a captive audience is wrong.

- Classroom time has been paid for by taxpayers. We should not be subsidizing watching TV commercials and the commercial exploitation of children.

- The content of some of these commercials flies in the face of what we're trying to teach our students. For instance, junk food commercials conflict with sound nutritional practices, and ads for expensive brand-name clothes which urge youngsters to succumb to peer pressure contradict our efforts to enhance students' self-esteem.

- Slippery slope -- once the floodgates open, our schools will become prey for endless commercial abuses.

- Teenagers are a very impressionable audience in whom brand loyalties are being formed.

- Under the Whittle contract, teachers can't determine when and how to show the programs. They must run them without stopping at any point for discussion.

- Noncommercial news programming alternatives have recently become available. For instance, Cable News Network and the Discovery Channel are producing commercial-free news and instructional programs especially for students. Teachers can determine when and how to integrate these shows into their classrooms; they don't have this option with Channel One.

(c)   A microwaveable coffee that requires foil-lined cartons to preserve product freshness and plastic wrap to ensure the package has not been opened

Life is full of trade-offs, and this product is a good example. It does use materials such as aluminum foil and plastic which are not "environmentally friendly." Both materials contribute to the ever-increasing solid waste in our ever-crowded landfills. On the other hand, the foil preserves freshness, assuring that the customer gets a higher quality product, and the plastic wrap prevents tampering, a threat to health and life. From a societal perspective, utilitarian calculations could be made in deciding which is the lesser of two evils. But an outright ban on such products probably isn't warranted; it reduces consumer options and chokes off supplies of needed goods. Perhaps the manufacturers could be persuaded (or coerced, if necessary, recognizing that this could raise product prices) to contribute funds to environmental causes in an attempt to get them to internalize the externalities, that is, incur the social costs of the manufacture and consumption of their products.

(d)   A party cracker that is high in sodium.

Again, where do you draw the line in banning products? There are low sodium crackers available, so people aren't being coerced into buying something that might be bad for them. And, for people with low blood pressure, sodium in moderation is desirable. Why restrict their access to a product which will enhance their quality of life and be good for their health?

(e)   Yellow legal pad paper.

The dye in this product is said to be toxic and harmful to the environment.   It leaches out into the groundwater.   Undyed white paper would be better, although in recent years manufacturers have made it less soluble.   Again, a cost-benefit analysis is needed to make a decision.   There is clearly a market for yellow legal pads, which command a higher price than white pads.   Do the benefits received outweigh the harm done to our environment?

(f)   Extended service/labor warranties sold as an extra rather than part of the product.

This is perfectly ethical.   Most products that are sold with extended warranties already come with a basic warranty, which is an affirmation in writing concerning the quality and performance of the product over a specific time frame.   In effect, it is an insurance policy for the customer, guaranteeing a standard of quality/performance.   If products were sold without a warranty, they would command lower prices in the marketplace because sellers would not incur an additional expected cost and buyers would derive less utility from a product lacking this particular type of form utility.

If a standard warranty is offered "free of charge," it isn't really free, rather, the manufacturer has bundled its cost into the total product price.   Extended warranties are a way of segmenting the market.   Through them you can appeal to a group of customers who are willing to pay extra for additional security.   To make the extended warranty mandatory would be to require potential customers to pay a higher price for what in their eyes is little added value (and they might balk and refuse to buy the product.)

2.   A restaurant has a low-fat sausage on its menu.   Its sausage is made from turkey, not pork.   Is it ethical to call it sausage?

This is an issue of the consumer's right to information.   According to most students of business, consumers have the right to adequate information so they can make an informed purchase decision.   It is definitely unethical to deceive the consumer, where deception is defined as causing one to accept as true or valid what in fact is false and invalid.   This is most likely to occur for low involvement purchases, such as sausages, where passive reasoning is used to make decisions.

In the issue at hand, it would seem that a significant number of consumers would be misled by the sausage label (in practice, whether or not this occurs is to be determined by consumer research) since people associate sausage with pork. Still, it could be argued that "what they don't know won't hurt them" and that this is actually a healthier product.   It would be more honest to use a generic descriptor other than "sausage."   This might be wiser from a strategic viewpoint too, since some consumers might be able to tell the difference and will be dissatisfied, while others will read the ingredients (and more and more people are doing this) which might lead some to conclude that the company is trying to pull a fast one.

3.   A "yuppie" pizza is made without tomato sauce.   The dough is covered with olive oil and topped with artichoke hearts and asparagus.   Is it ethical to advertise this as pizza?

This is basically the same issue as in question 3.   To advertise this product as pizza would be to violate consumer expectations as to what a pizza is.   This is misleading and would surely result in many dissatisfied customers.   It would be better to either give the product another generic name or else make it crystal clear that it lacks tomato sauce.

4.   A marketer of high fashion clothing, hoping to conserve the earth's resources, puts a label in its garments suggesting that consumers should not buy products unless they are really needed.   Is this a wise policy?

From a pragmatic perspective this seems self-defeating.   In effect they appear to be saying, "Don't buy our product if you are a good citizen of planet earth." From a socially responsible perspective the message isn't clear.   If consumers don't buy this clothing, will they substitute other clothing that consumes less of the world's resources? Don't all clothes consume resources, be they animal fabrics or artificial fabrics? And, if this company is so socially responsible, why are they marketing this product in the first place?

5.   *According to government studies, bicycles, stairs, doors, cleaning agents, and tables are products that are involved in most accidents. What does this list say about product safety? If a child eats a spoonful of Tide, where does the fault lie? Establish some criteria that a marketer should use to ensure the organization's product is safe.*

This says that no product is 100% safe; life involves risk taking. Zero defect quality is usually achievable only at prohibitive costs. Yet, many people today are suing companies for the risks and hazards which are an inherent part of life. Since we're a compassionate society, we find it hard to say no to people injured for taking reasonable risks, such as climbing up a stepladder. For such products there are conflicting pulls: the need for the product or service at a reasonable price, to be balanced against the basic human desire for safety, to be traded off against the need to keep companies strong and employing people. Yet, the trend seems to be toward a no-fault society in which the manufacturer assumes all responsibilities and passes on all the consequent costs.

For instance, if a child eats a spoonful of Tide, it would seem unreasonable to sue the manufacturer. The typical caring parent should assume the responsibility of seeing to it that the product is put out of harm's way. It would not seem necessary to include a warning label. Again, where do we draw the line? (Diapers - "Warning! Remove baby before disposing of diaper!"; cigarettes - "Caution: do not put lit end in mouth!")

Crawford (*New Products Management*, 3/e) has suggested a list of ways manufacturers get into trouble with product liability/product safety issues:

1.   Some products (such as those listed in this question) have inherent risks associated with their use. These risks are unavoidable in product usage no matter how small (e.g., doors -- "Warning: do not stick hand, tongue, ear, or neck in the jamb of a closing door") or large (e.g., dynamite), the risks might be. Yet, this scribe strongly suspects that if Henry Ford had to bring out his Model T in today's environment, the courts and the regulators would stop him. "Darn thing is dangerous ... why, you could break your arm cranking it!"

2.   Design defects are avoidable. These include designs that can cause a dangerous condition (e.g., a car which suffers "sudden acceleration" problems), designs that lack an essential safety device (e.g., a hair dryer without an overheat cutoff switch), and designs using inadequate materials, which at first perform satisfactorily but eventually wear out and become dangerous (e.g., a radial tire which prematurely wears). The remedy is to examine product design and think of ways it could go wrong.

Products should be designed to be safe in all ways people are likely to use (normal usage).

3.   Defects in manufacture can also be prevented. Inadequate quality control techniques might result in defective individual units even though the product was well designed. The solution is to institute strict quality control standards.

4.   A product might be safe yet have inadequate instructions for use or inadequate warnings against particular uses likely to occur. The "foreseeability" doctrine says that a manufacturer must attempt to foresee how a product might be misused and warn the consumer against the hazards of misuse. This requires both product knowledge and product usage knowledge. Warnings should be conspicuously placed on the product where they are most likely to be seen, should explain the level of danger, and should instruct the user how to avoid the potential danger. Another way to avoid this problem is to not target the product at the wrong users (e.g., industrial strength cleaners sold in retail outlets).

GUIDE TO CASES

VIDEO CASE 10-1   RANDY HUNDLEY'S BASEBALL CAMP

SUBJECT MATTER: Product Concept, Auxiliary Dimensions of Products, Buyer
                            Behavior, Effect of Culture

                            Please see the Guide to Video Cases for video
                            length and other information.

AT-A-GLANCE OVERVIEW

Many major league teams, individual players, retired players, and others
associated with baseball, operate "fantasy camps" wherein older men (40+), and
some women (though this is rare) take part in "spring training" with retired
players they remember from years past. In general, the camps last one week, are
held in Florida or Arizona (like regular spring training), and include a week in
a hotel (meals included), a uniform, instruction, games, souvenirs (such as your
own "baseball card"), and cost about $3,000. This price does not include travel
money to the site. Further, most "campers" spend additional money on "outside"
meals and entertainment. Typical campers are life-long baseball fans who decide
to treat themselves to this program or whose wives (or others) buy the package
for them to mark a "big" birthday (like 50) or anniversary (like 25 or 30).

DISCUSSION QUESTIONS

1.   *Describe Randy Hundley's product concept.*

The core product is a service. More specifically, the core product is the chance
to play baseball at an age when most men no longer have 18 friends who go out and
play ball. The core product also includes the opportunity to play against or
play with major league baseball players who are now retired. The auxiliary
dimensions of the product are equally as important. The baseball uniform,
certificate of attendance, and other tangible elements make the intangible
training tangible. Among the intangibles are pride in being able to perform
athletically, the memories one carries "forever," and "bragging rights" ... the
chance to talk about the training camp and the stars met there.

2.   *How important is the brand name of a baseball camp? Is the "Field of
     Dreams" name better than the "All Star Baseball School of Chicago"?*

The benefits of the baseball training camp extend long past the training itself.
The ability to tell stories that "I played baseball" with the Heroes of Baseball,
or the Chicago Cubs, or another favorite team, is a major part of the consumer
benefit. Therefore, the brand name is extremely important. "Field of Dreams,"
"Heroes of Baseball," and "Chicago Cubs" are all important in making the story
interesting, and are all good names.

For some buyers, however, association with a particular team is important. One
of the authors has an acquaintance who was a life-long Detroit Tigers fan, and
attended the Tiger's fantasy camp. It seemed important to him that it was the
Tiger's camp, not some other team's, or some "generically named" camp.

3.   *Why would a consumer spend $3,000+ to go to spring training and work hard
     when there would be no future chance to play professional baseball?*

To many people, such behavior (with such a price tag) is illogical and
irrational. But to baseball fanatics, has-been jocks and fantasists it makes a
lot of sense. By participating in such an activity, these individuals may hang
on to their youth and live out "Fantasy Island." Additionally, there is some
secret pride at, say, fifty years of age, in being still able to perform even at
a fantasy camp level.

Many individuals have fantasized about playing baseball in the Big Leagues, or at
least against major leaguers. Retired major leaguers are still major leaguers if
they are the ones a fan remembers. To some of us, Mickey Mantle and Willie Mays
are "always" as they were in the '50s and '60s. A wife might buy the product for
her husband's fortieth or fiftieth birthday or twentieth or twenty-fifth

anniversary. This camp appeals to the ordinary Joe and not-so-ordinary Joe (with $3,000+ bucks) who dreams of spring training while sitting at his desk or working construction. "The count is one ball, two strikes, the bases are loaded, the bottom of the ninth, three runs behind, Bob Gibson pitches, you swing ---." A true fan with a decent income might think that once-in-a-lifetime deal is well worth it. George Plimpton has grown rich and famous writing books about these very fantasies. By the way, a coach might be able to take a tax deduction for this as a learning experience.

The Field of Dreams Weekend video shows how strong a motive fantasy can be. In Iowa, at the "field of dreams" game, celebrities played out their fantasy of playing ball with the Upper Deck Heros of Baseball. This portion of the video explains the field of dreams concept. However, as the video shifts to show the real camp, it shows how regular people believe it is a dream come true. They believe baseball makes them feel good. They have a good time. They relive the camaraderie of their youth. The video of the Cubs camp shows the reality of their abilities.

4.   *What social needs have influenced the success of the camps?*

A major social force is reference groups. These groups may be membership, a group of which the individual is actually a part, or aspirational, one whose members are models for an "outsider." Both types of groups influence the success of the camps. By going to a camp, the individual receives the adoration of the membership group (the guys back home who want to know "what was it like?") and fulfills an aspiration. Role playing is also enhanced. If the individual is a "local jock," the camp participation enlarges his athletic role and enhances his image. He becomes even more of an expert on how it really is in "the Bigs." Other factors may include reliving one's youth, enhancing self-concept, etc.

5.   *What part does culture play in the success of these camps?*

All major social institutions have arisen over time as people develop social responses to the particular needs of their society. Sport is a major social institution in the United States and as such is a part of our culture. Baseball is "the national pastime," at least to its fans. Its popularity increases annually. Another aspect of our culture is the concept of winning. Most of us feel that we must be competitive ... and win. Baseball is an accepted way of competing and winning. Pierre Martineau's line "If you want to understand America, you must learn baseball" is probably an overstatement, but the game is a big part of our cultural inheritance and is very important among certain groups in our society.

A major cultural change in this era is the much-discussed emphasis placed on youth. The physical characteristics of youth are the traits desired and sought after by most of the nation's inhabitants. These camps are a part of that movement. Ironically, this product represents a marketing trend of catering to older people.

Lastly, "doing one's own thing" has become quite acceptable. Going to such a camp is doing one's own thing. "Sure, it's a little crazy but, what the heck, I always wanted to do something like this" is explanation enough.

A sub-cultural phenomenon, the historically strong loyalty of Cubs fans might be mentioned. Who would want to go to a Mets or Mariners camp of this sort?

6.   *Using your knowledge of consumer behavior, explain why these camps are*
        successful?

Many of the concepts discussed in Chapters 5 and 6 may be used to help explain the camps' success. In the previous questions, culture, reference groups, and role playing have already been used as explanation variables. Additional concepts such as self-concept and attitudes may potentially explain the consumers' behavior and thereby the success of the camps. Self-concept refers to the individual's perception of himself or herself. The camps help to confirm the self-image one may hold. E.g., "I could have been a great ballplayer if given a chance." An attitude is a learned predisposition to respond in a consistently favorable or unfavorable manner with respect to a given object. The attitude toward baseball is generally positive, i.e., note the popularity of the game.

Given this positive attitude, there are fewer barriers (from the individual and from society as a whole) to participating in such a unique activity.

CASE 10-2   HENRI'S FOOD PRODUCTS INCORPORATED

SUBJECT MATTER: Brand Names, Characteristics of Good Brand Names,
                            Protection of Brand Names

AT-A-GLANCE OVERVIEW

Henri's introduced Yogowhip, a salad dressing with a yogurt base. The product joined Henri's product line of salad dressings and salad toppings. Kraft Foods sent a letter to Henri's management stating that Miracle Whip was a Kraftco trademark that had been used for many years. Kraft objected to Yogowhip being confusingly similar to Miracle Whip and asked for immediate assurance that the Yogowhip name would be dropped. Kraft said it must be "diligent in asserting our rights." Henri's had already spent quite a bit of money and effort on the product, and had seen considerable consumer acceptance of its product. Management felt, "They're not gonna push us around."

Henri's was a small company that had put a lot of money into the brand name. Henri's management was angry with the bluntness of Kraft's demands. Further, the Kraftco trademark was not "whip" but Miracle Whip. Henri's did not believe that the two names were the same or even "confusingly similar." The case notes that Henri's is a very small company by comparison to Kraft. Henri's management resented Kraft's "arrogance."

DISCUSSION QUESTIONS

1.   *Is Yogowhip a good brand name? Why?*

The textbook lists many characteristics of a good brand name. No single brand is likely to satisfy all of these but Yogowhip comes close.

a.   Short, simple, distinctive. (Yes.)
b.   Easy to remember. (Yes.)
c.   Easy to say and pronounceable. (As much as any other.)
d.   Communicates favorable product attributes. (Not unless you have an aversion to the sound of "yogo" or an aversion to "whip.")
e.   Pronounceable in only one way. (Yes.)
f.   Contemporary. (Yes, unless some health or other problem is found to be associated with yogurt.)
g.   Not in use by another firm. (Seemingly debatable given what the case is about.)
h.   Easily translated into other languages. (Seemingly so, at least in European languages, though Latin languages speakers might read "Yogowhip" as "Yogoweep" or "Jogoweep.")
i.   A positive connotation. (Yes.)
j.   Associates the product with an image. (Yes, at least to those who like yogurt.)

In short, the name Yogowhip suggests what the product is, what it contains, that it is good for you (the assumption being that yogurt is good for you), and that it is creamy and, perhaps, light (whipped). Further it is easy to say, read, understand, etc. Still, the problem with Miracle Whip people suggests that it is not perfect.

2.   *What arguments might Henri's give for protecting its utilization of the name Yogowhip? What reasons might Kraftco give for protection of its Miracle Whip name?*

The instructor should be ready for this "answer" -- "The reason Henri's can give for defending its use of the name is that it has money invested in the name, including $50,000 in a television commercial." Of course, a proper answer would also detail possible defenses of the use of the name. Instructors may want to clarify this point before assigning the case.

Here are some defenses that Henri's actually did employ.

. This is simply a threat from a major competitor, attempting to put everything we have worked for in jeopardy. There is no other reason for Kraft's action.

. The attack is based essentially on Kraft's realization that Henri's management knew as much about Kraft operations as did anyone at Kraft and the fear that Henri's small dent in Kraft's business presaged bigger moves.

. Kraft is a huge marketing operation and has sold, in fact, many billions of bottles of Miracle Whip. There is no comparison between this kind of operation and Yogowhip. Henri's has just 75 employees.

. The name is simply descriptive of the product. It has yogurt in it and it is whipped. (Henri's, by the way, makes a companion product called "Yogonaise," a name which has caused no problems.)

. Kraft's original registration of the Miracle Whip name contained a disclaimer of the word "whip." That is, the name Miracle Whip was registered, not the name word "whip." Kraft later registered Miracle Whip Salad Spread under a new trademark law that superseded the original Trademark Act of 1905. This law permitted the registrant to claim right to the word "whip." But, Kraft had not been selling the product so registered for more than five years. This suggested to Henri's attorneys that they might well file a fraud case against Kraft, putting the name Miracle Whip itself in jeopardy.

. Kraft's action seemed to be indicative of an attempt to monopolize the market. Here was a giant going after a gnat. Therefore, Henri's tied an antitrust suit into the total proceedings.

. Lawyers identified many food products that had employed the word "whip" in their names: Quaker Whip, Shur-Whip, etc.

As might be suspected, Kraft used many of the same arguments against its adversary.

. True, there are many products that use the word "whip" in their names but none were spoonable salad dressings. Why did Henri's, faced with a universe of possible names, pick "whip" and fight to defend it if it wasn't expecting to cash in on the (Kraft) protected and famous name of Miracle Whip.

. Kraft is not simply trying to threaten a small company. The facts, from Kraft's side of the fence, are that Miracle Whip is an important trademark to Kraft as witnessed by the billions of units of Miracle Whip sold and the tens of millions of advertising dollars spent.

. Kraft had in fact attempted to remove the original disclaimer of a right to the word "whip," a disclaimer required by the Trademark Act of 1905 and not required under the law of 1946 which superseded the 1905 act.

. Defense of a name in which a company has an obvious interest does not show an attempt to monopolize a market. (In fact, when the case came to trial the judge set this issue aside for future consideration. Henri's did not pursue the matter further.)

3. *Is this issue worth a long drawn-out legal battle for Henri's? What do you think the outcome of the legal case will be?*

In point of fact, this legal matter dragged on for about six years. The trial transcript covered 1700 pages. Legal bills for Henri's were about one and a half million dollars. Henri's owners had made the case a matter of honor for the family owned company, while Kraft had promised to "spend Henri's to death." Kraft was ordered to provide company records to Henri's. Kraft did so by dumping 1.5 million pieces of paper into a 10 by 12 foot room and inviting Henri's lawyers to go through it.

The question "Was it worth it?" ultimately depends on how close you come to winning. Henri's lawyer looked back over his experience with the case and developed six rules that a small company can use in fighting an industry leader. These rules, he now says, could have provided him with a great deal of guidance. They are:

1. The small company must have enough at stake to want to see the fight through.
2. It must make that commitment up front.
3. It must conduct the case throughout as if it expected to go to trial, not just to settle out of court (as most do).
4. It must try to survive the first round intact, without getting buried by the other side's dollars.
5. It must have an issue it can win on, legally and practically.
6. It must really do it ... go to the mat.

How did the case work out? To begin with, Henri's did not settle out of court. Indeed, when Henri's mentioned a figure it would consider in such a settlement ... $14 million ... the lawyer for the other side asked, "What have you been smoking?" Henri's went to the mat. The case went to trial on December 8, 1981. Each side was limited to one week to present its case. It took until August for the judge to hand down a ruling that dismissed Henri's various charges against Kraft such as fraud and unfair practices, but also declared that the name Yogowhip did not infringe on Miracle Whip's trademark. The judgment held that "whip" is descriptive of a manufacturing process. The opinion was upheld a year later by the Circuit Court of Appeals.

11 THE PRODUCT LIFE CYCLE AND BASIC PRODUCT STRATEGIES

CHAPTER SCAN

This chapter focuses on the marketing mix variable "product" and some of the tools, concepts, and strategies that have been developed to help marketers channel their thinking about products. Two tools are treated with emphasis on their use as planning aids. They are the product life cycle and the product portfolio. The fact that these are only tools, not strategies in themselves, is stressed.

The chapter includes discussion of strategies for modifying existing products as well as the use of product line extension and product category extension. The stages involved in the strategic total quality management process are presented in the chapter.

SUGGESTED LEARNING OBJECTIVES

The student who studies this chapter will be familiar with the major product-related planning tools and several product strategies and will be able to:

1.   Describe the product life cycle as a powerful marketing tool.

2.   Specify effective techniques for managing and lengthening the product life cycle.

3.   Characterize the stages of the product life cycle.

4.   Identify strategies for modifying existing products.

5.   Identify the stages involved in the strategic total quality management process.

6.   Understand how marketers use product line extension and product category extension to match products to markets.

7.   Define product portfolio, and show how it can help management
       allocate resources effectively.

CHAPTER OUTLINE

I.   INTRODUCTION

II.   THE PRODUCT LIFE CYCLE

       A.   The General Sales Pattern of the Product Life Cycle
       B.   Profits and the Product Life Cycle
       C.   Do All Products Follow a Product Life Cycle?

III.   THE PRODUCT LIFE CYCLE AS A PLANNING TOOL

IV.   STRATEGY CHANGES THROUGH THE PRODUCT LIFE CYCLE

       A.   The Introductory Stage -- Gaining Acceptance
       B.   The Growth Stage -- Taking Off
       C.   The Maturity Stage -- Reaching a Peak
       D.   The Decline Stage -- Winding Down
       E.   Is There Life After Decline?

V.   STRATEGIES FOR MODIFYING EXISTING PRODUCTS

       A.   Cost Reduction Strategies
       B.   Repositioning Strategies
       C.   Product Quality Strategies
       D.   Product Design
       E.   Implementing a Total Quality Management Strategy

VI.   MATCHING PRODUCTS TO MARKETS: PRODUCT LINE STRATEGY

       A.   Strategies for Expanding the Product Line or Expanding the Product
              Mix
       B.   Eliminating Old Products

VII.   THE ORGANIZATION'S PRODUCT PORTFOLIO

       A.   The Portfolio Model
       B.   Interrelationships
       C.   The Limits of the Product Portfolio Concept

VIII. SUMMARY

IX.   KEY TERMS

X.   QUESTIONS FOR DISCUSSION (13)

XI.   ETHICS IN PRACTICE

XII.   CASES

       The following key terms are introduced and used in Chapter 11.   They are
defined in the text's Glossary.

Product life cycle
Introduction stage
Growth stage
Maturity stage
Decline stage
Product modification
Cost reduction strategy
Product quality strategy
Product enhancement
Product design
Style
Fashion

Fad
Product line strategy
Full-line (broad) strategy
Limited-line strategy
Single-product strategy
Product line extension
Product category extension
Brand extension
Brand equity
Cannibalization
Flanker brand
Enhanced model
Cost reduction strategy
Product elimination
Product portfolio concept

THE CHAPTER SUMMARIZED

I. INTRODUCTION

The black phonograph record looks like an almost extinct species. Because
of cassettes and C.D.s, conventional records now account for just a tiny
portion of U.S. recorded music sales. Vinyl records seem to be at the end
of their product life cycle, compact discs at the beginning of their's.

This chapter explores product-related marketing tools, the product life
cycle and the product portfolio, and some product-based strategies.
Products should be carefully managed from "birth" to "death." Effective
marketing includes withdrawing products as well as developing and
introducing them.

II. THE PRODUCT LIFE CYCLE

The product life cycle is based on the life cycle of all living things.
Products do not "live," but the concept is still a useful one.

The **product life cycle** charts a product's history from "birth,"
introduction to the market, to "death," withdrawal from the market. It is
a sales volume curve and varies widely with product type. Mustard and
baking soda had long lives, FAX machines are just starting theirs. The
product life cycle is associated with product groups such as televisions
sets, rather than with brands or models like an RCA Portable Model D5.
Still, some managers have successfully applied the concept to particular
brands or models.

The "typical" product life cycle is usually drawn with four product life
cycle stages, as shown in Exhibit 11-1. It is important to recall that:

.   The total length of the product life cycle will vary with the product
    type (baking soda vs. Roger Rabbit T-shirts).

.   The stages of any product's life cycle may vary widely in length.

A. The General Sales Pattern of the Product Life Cycle

During the **introduction stage**, the new product is attempting to gain
a foothold, sales are likely to be slow. As acceptance is gained,
rapid growth should occur. At the end of the **growth stage**, sales
should level off, peaking in the **maturity** stage. The product
ultimately loses popularity and acceptance. Market "saturation"
leads to the **decline stage**.

B. Profits and the Product Life Cycle

Many product-related variables can be plotted "against" the product
life cycle. (Inventory, back orders, and prices are among them.) It
is common to show that industry profits can be expected to peak at
the end of the growth stage. (See Exhibit 11-2.) At this point,

firms are making sales and have brought start-up expenses under control. But as the product enters maturity all producers are operating in a static or slow-growth market, so profits of the industry begin to fall, likely because prices are falling as firms try to attract customers.

In the decline stage, the remaining companies try to compete in a shrinking market, driving profit margin lower still. Ironically, the last few companies left may have good profits (though industry profits are low) as they cater to the last surviving, and very loyal, buyers.

Exhibit 11-3 outlines characteristics typical of each stage in the product life cycle.

C.   Do All Products Follow a Product Life Cycle?

The answer is ultimately "yes" -- all products must sooner or later pass through a product life cycle. The product life cycle for peanut butter is very long compared to the product life cycle for talking baseball cards or New Kids on the Block paraphernalia. Exhibit 11-4 illustrates some very different types of life cycles.

In general, marketers would prefer to keep their products in the maturity stage for some time. However, some products are expected to be fads and to have short lives. Cereals and toys named for currently popular characters like The Ghostbusters or the Mutant Turtles are good examples.

Some "short cycle" products can be brought back as the market changes. Disney cartoon films are released every 10 or 15 years when a new generation of kids is there to see them.

III.   THE PRODUCT LIFE CYCLE AS A PLANNING TOOL

The product life cycle has its greatest use as a planning tool. Strategies can be built around it and important information (e.g.-- financial data) graphed against it.

The true value of the life cycle is realized by those who understand the competitive and consumer behavior changes that occur at each stage and why these occur. The cycle highlights the fact that change will occur, and "death" may occur, so the marketing planner had better prepare for the eventualities, preparing product improvements and/or new products. The March of Dimes adoption of birth defects once polio was brought under control is a classic case of an organization adjusting to change to save itself from extinction.

The marketer's general goal is (with the possible exception of some novelty items) to bring the product into the maturity stage and keep it there for as long as possible.

IV.   STRATEGY CHANGES THROUGH THE PRODUCT LIFE CYCLE

Marketers can use the product life cycle as a basis for planning market strategies. Exhibit 11-5 shows how marketing mix variables are likely to be adjusted as the product passes through the life cycle.

A.   The Introductory Stage -- Gaining Acceptance

This is a time of attempting to gain market acceptance. Effort is focused on finding first-time buyers and on making people aware of the product's existence, as well as on developing channels of distribution, appropriate prices, promotional techniques, etc. The product may be altered to get the "bugs" out.

The length of this stage can vary widely. Video games were quick to "catch on;" TV took decades to reach popularity. More recently,

concentrated detergents have had a rapid sales growth (Ultra Tide,
Fab Ultra) even though the first of these products appeared in 1976.

B.   The Growth Stage -- Taking Off

Entering the growth stage suggests a future in the marketplace.
Thus, the number of competitors can be expected to increase,
especially since they can gain market share without having to take it
away from one another, as they would in a mature market.

Cellular phone systems now appear to be in the growth stage. Profits
on these will rise (though not for every company) and peak at the end
of the period. Product quality will be improved and stressed, and
persuasive efforts to create brand preference will become the norm,
as sales rise and costs are brought under control.

C.   The Maturity Stage -- Reaching A Peak

At any one time most products on the market are mature. Competition
is likely to be intense since the market is not growing and most
increases in sales must come from other competitors' shares of the
market. Some producers enlarge their operations by producing private
brand merchandise.

Mature products have the "bugs" ironed out. Changes tend to be in
the area of style. Radios are bigger or smaller or portable or solar
powered. Economies of scale and experience in production and
marketing make many mature products highly profitable.

Marketers should try to learn why products are in the mature stage
(e.g., is it because the market is not growing much or because a new
product is about to make the current product obsolete?)

D.   The Decline Stage -- Winding Down

In the decline stage, sales and industry profits fall. Fewer firms
continue in the market, though some prosper by catering to a
relatively few remaining buyers who are particularly loyal or are
people who truly require the product. There are very few blacksmiths
around, but the buyers of this service really need it and are willing
to pay.

Again, the question "Why?" surfaces. Is the downturn in sales just a
"blip" or is it "for real?" The product life cycle concept helps
marketers to focus on fluctuations and shifts in the markets. It
does not tell them what to do.

E.   Is There Life After Decline?

Some products seem to be in decline or even "near death," but will
then spring back. Many old fashioned food products like Granola,
soup, and honey have found new popularity. A physical fitness craze
can cause the sales of gym shoes to jump, and VCRs have increased
consumer interest in quality color TV sets.

V.   STRATEGIES FOR MODIFYING EXISTING PRODUCTS

Products should be designed to appeal to well-researched target markets,
but products may have to be adjusted to reflect changing market conditions.
Dynamic markets must be monitored so that old strategies can be revised.

Product modification is the altering or adjusting of the product mix. This
typically occurs due to competition, e.g., competitor makes a design change
or a change in the external environment. In 1990 Crayola added eight
bright "neon" colors to its box of sixty-four colors, unchanged for over
thirty years, because kids had taken a liking to bright colors. When some
folks complained about the "lost" colors, Crayola issued a limited edition
"collector's item" box that had the old colors, not the new.

A.   Cost Reduction Strategies

In the maturity or decline stage, firms anxious to "hold on" may
bring about an increased level of competition. Working to redesign
the product to lower production costs would be an appropriate **cost
reduction strategy**. Moving facilities to low wage areas or offering
"stripped down models" may be part of this. Cost reduction does not
mean quality must suffer.

B.   Repositioning Strategies

A **repositioning strategy** changes product design, brand image, or name
in such a way that it alters the product's competitive position.
Reformulating a product without sugar or salt may reposition the
product from a "sweet treat" to a "healthy treat."

A change in the environment or a mistake made earlier can lead to
such a change. Heartwise cereal was forced to change its name (and
position) to Fibrewise when the Food and Drug Administration argued
that the cereal could not be shown to be good for the heart. Other
names and symbols may serve for decades but become inappropriate
modern times ... Sambo, for example. Other companies have added
words like "International" or "Worldwide" to their names to reflect
new interest in international markets.

Repositioning is discussed further in Chapter 12.

C.   Product Quality Strategies

Product quality strategies or **quality assurance strategies** emphasize
market-driven quality as a top priority. In today's competitive
world market most companies must adopt a total quality management
philosophy. Every employee must work for continuous quality
improvement.

What is quality? Once it was defined by engineering standards.
Effective marketers have gone beyond the idea of quality meaning that
the product meets customer expectations, that it is "acceptable."
Rather than having buyers pleased that nothing went wrong, buyers
should experience some "surprises" or find some unexpected benefit in
the product.

Total quality management also stresses continuous product improvement
or **product enhancement**, the introduction of a new and improved
version of an existing brand, to extend a product's life cycle by
keeping it in the growth or maturity stage. Exhibit 11-6 depicts how
Gillette has done this masterfully, introducing new razors that
emphasize improved product performance rather than simple design
changes. Aspects of product quality perceived by consumers are shown
in Exhibit 11-7. Attaining quality requires that top management make
certain that marketing managers communicate consumers' needs to those
with production authority.

D.   Product Design

Product design, a product's configuration, composition, and style,
influences most quality dimensions. Consumer research is required to
assure that the product is pleasing to customers. It is often found
that customer perception of quality is influenced by perceptions of
product attributes that have little or nothing to do with true
quality. Thickness of tomato juice or size of a stereo speaker is
easier to assess than quality of a tomato or a speaker's sound.
Color has been shown to have similar effects on customer perceptions.
That's why Windex is blue rather than clear.

The terms style, fashion, and fad have different meanings. **Style**
refers to a distinctive execution, construction, or design of a
product class. (For example, painting might be of a "modern" style,
some chairs are rocking chairs.)

A **fashion** is a style that is current or in vogue. (For example, rocking chairs may or may not be "in fashion" at any given time.)

A **fad** is a passing fashion or craze that many people are interested in for only a short time, such as a T-shirt from a rock concert.

E.   Implementing a Total Quality Management Strategy

Quality management assumes that the consumer has been brought into the quality improvement process. Marketing research, especially waves of consumer satisfaction surveys, is an integral part of the total quality management strategy. Exhibit 11-8 illustrates the stages involved in the implementation of a total quality strategy.

VI.   MATCHING PRODUCTS TO MARKETS: PRODUCT LINE STRATEGY

The goal of the marketing manager is to develop a total product offering that satisfies the desires of target consumers. A firm cannot satisfy everyone so it must select meaningful market segments that will be profitable. A **product line strategy** involves matching product items to markets. It is, therefore, influenced by the diversity of the market and the resources of the company. An organization that is spread too thin will end up satisfying no market properly. And yet, too limited a product line might have little appeal. Realignment of the product line and the resources involved might solve these problems.

The options and organization faces may be expressed in these terms:

.   The **full-line,** or **broad, strategy** means offering a large number of variations of a product.

.   The **limited-line strategy** entails offering a smaller number of variations.

.   The **single-product strategy** involves offering one product item or one product version with very few model options.

Some general advantages of these strategies are given in Exhibit 11-9.

A.   Strategies for Expanding the Product Line or Expanding the Product Mix

Organizations often develop new products that are similar to existing ones. These may be of two types.

.   A **product line extension** (or **line extension**) is an additional item added to an existing product line to add depth. For example, Procter and Gamble created product line extensions with GumHealth Crest and Antitartar Formula Crest.

.   A **product category extension** strategy involves marketing a new item or line of items in a product category that is new to the company. Ultra Slim-Fast began as a meal replacement milk shake and now markets microwaveable meals and frozen desserts.

A product category extension may be called a **brand extension** if it uses a brand name that is already on one of the company's existing products. The term applies to any situation where the same brand name is used, whether for adding new items to a line or entering a new product category.

Ocean Spray has developed product line and product category extensions. Beginning with cranberry sauce and cranberry sauce in the jelly form, it successfully marketed Cranberry Juice Cocktail, a product category extension. Then it expanded into juice variations, like Cranapple and Crangrape. These additions made good use of Ocean Spray's resources and its well-respected name. Now Ocean Spray sells non-cranberry juices using the well-known brand name.

Expansions using a well-respected brand name suggests the concept of **brand equity**, that market share or margins are higher because of the goodwill associated with the brand. A brand with higher equity will likely be more successful when used for a brand extension in a similar product category, e.g., Ocean Spray Strawberry Juice rather than Ocean Spray motor oil.

But a company's new branded product make take some of its sales from the company's existing products. This is called **cannibalization**.

Product line extensions can fall into the category of **flanker brands**, products likely to be side-by-side on a grocer's shelf. Example: Ocean Spray juices, if placed together, make a nice display for Ocean Spray and serve to deny shelf space to competitors.

An original product item may be offered in an **enhanced model**. This is often a model with "all the bells and whistles." A personal computer with built-in modem, color screen, and great memory capacity would be an example.

An organization might choose a **cost reduction strategy**, especially during the maturity and decline stages of the product life cycle. A "stripped down" version might be developed and offered to the price-conscious consumer. In the area of services, note that Federal Express offers delivery by 10:30 the next day, or afternoon delivery at a lower price.

Other product-related strategies include offering customized products to specific customers or small groups of customers, and producing private brand goods (a form of customization) or a specific model of a branded product for a large buyer. Wal-Mart or Sears may carry a slightly modified Panasonic product so as to be able to say it is an exclusive dealer for that model.

B.   Eliminating Old Products

A sometimes forgotten matter is **product elimination**, removing "old" products from the market. Frequently, getting rid of products that have run their course raises total profits and frees resources to be used to develop and market "new winners," though sometimes elimination of products is a painful process necessitating realignment of resources and personnel. It often develops that markets can be served with twelve products as well as with two or three times that number.

Brands or product items could be dropped because of lack of popularity in the market, low profits, or other reasons.

VII.   THE ORGANIZATION'S PRODUCT PORTFOLIO

Marketing borrows from many other disciplines. One item borrowed and adapted from finance is the **product portfolio concept**. Just as financial experts seek to develop a balanced group of investments, so should the marketer seek to develop a balanced product line. Products grouped into categories within the portfolio will be subject to different marketing strategies and assignments of resources.

The portfolio approach used in the text is the Boston Consulting Group's (BCG). It is illustrated in Exhibit 11-11.

A.   The Portfolio Model

The BCG portfolio model identifies four product types based on high/low growth market and high/low market share of a particular product within that market.

.   High market share product in a high growth market ("star") such as a Sony compact disc player.

- High market share product in a low growth market ("cash cow") such as Spam canned meat.

- Low market share product in a high growth market ("problem child") such as a Sanyo home video recorder.

- Low market share product in a low growth market ("dog") such as Palmolive face soap.

The text makes the point that many, if not most, products on the market at one time are "dogs." Still, they are profitable enough, if unexciting in potential. Example: among many brands of laundry detergent, only Tide is "number one."

"Dogs" can serve a purpose. They may generate some profit, they may be "squeezed" for extra dollars, they may appeal to a group of buyers such as bargain-hunters, and they may be sellable to those customers with little or no resources expended by the organization. Also, a "dog" may occupy a market niche that is easy to defend against competitors.

B.   Interrelationships

All four product types shown in the portfolio can be found within a single organization. Ideally, they will fit together in an interrelated product mix. For example, stars are good to have, but they use up resources to maintain their growth. Cash cows can be used to support this growth.

C.   The Limits of the Product Portfolio Concept

The portfolio model is an attractive and powerful tool for analysis. It must be recalled, however, that "putting products in the right boxes" is not the goal of the portfolio. Once products are assigned to categories, the manager's work has only begun. Now the hard-to-answer questions start.

Examples:

- How much to spend to protect a star?

- When to give up on a problem child?

- Whether or not to hold on to a dog whose competitive picture is at least a stable one?

- How safe is the cash cow from the attacks of competing products?

No tool or theory can replace managerial judgment based on close analysis of the environment of marketing.

A second matter is the reality of the marketplace and of human nature. Maintaining a steady flow of stars, for example, is difficult, to say the least. Some companies, for example Ohio Art, maker of Etch A Sketch, do quite well with a single product and find no success when they seek to develop new products.

VIII.   SUMMARY

Product-oriented strategic tools include the product life cycle (PLC), a range of product-based planning concepts, and the product portfolio.

Learning Objective 1: Describe the product life cycle as a powerful marketing tool.

The product life cycle charts the sales history of individual products from introduction to withdrawal. The stages of introduction, growth, maturity, and decline can be identified and their characteristics described in terms that strongly affect the strategies and tactics of marketing managers.

Learning Objective 2:   Specify effective techniques for managing and lengthening the product life cycle.

Marketing managers must develop strategies for effectively introducing products to the market, encouraging the growth of demand for the product, maintaining the product in its maturity stage, and forestalling its entry into the decline stage.   To bring their products to maturity and avoid entry into decline, marketers can modify a product; develop new uses for it; and manipulate the marketing mix variables of promotion, distribution, and price.

Learning Objective 3:   Characterize the stages of the product life cycle.

The introduction stage of the product life cycle is characterized by large expenditures, an intensive marketing effort, and low profits.   In this stage the marketer must generate product awareness and create channels of distribution.   The growth stage involves large expenditures and increasing competition, as well as rapid sales growth.   The marketer must create brand preferences and promote differential features.

During the maturity stage, sales growth decreases, reflecting intense competition to maintain profitability.   The goal is to maintain or expand the market share.   Decreasing profits and decreasing expenditures mark the decline stage.   Introducing a new and improved product may reverse the declining sales, but termination is typically the final phase.

Learning Objective 4:   Identify strategies for modifying existing products.

Developing strategies for existing products and managing the product mix is an important aspect of product management.   Cost reduction, repositioning, and product quality improvements are often the result of competitive adjustments in the market and passage from one state of the product life cycle to another.

Learning Objective 5:   Identify the stages involved in the strategic total quality management process.

For many years, American corporations did not keep pace with the product quality strategies of a number of overseas competitors.   Many U.S. businesses did not focus on a quality that meets the customers' standards. Today many organizations have implemented total quality assurance programs. They measure quality from the customers' perspective and adjust product strategies accordingly.

Learning Objective 6:   Understand how marketers use product line extension and product category extension to match products to markets.

When no close fit exists between markets and products, the chances of market acceptance are slight.   Individual products and lines of products must be created and managed to achieve acceptance.   However, marketers must carefully consider the costs and other variables that limit their abilities to please buyers.

A product line extension is a new item added to an existing line.   Flanker brands, cost reductions, enhanced models, and customization are strategies for product line extensions.   A product category extension is the addition of a new item or new line in a product category new to the company.

Learning Objective 7:   Define product portfolio, and show how it can help management allocate resources effectively.

The product portfolio identifies four product types: cash cow, dog, star, and problem child.   Each has its own competitive position, its own ability

to generate or use resources, and its own growth potential. The portfolio
focuses the manager's attention on these products. Recognizing the
interrelationships among the products in the product mix should enable
managers to allocate resources more effectively. The portfolio concept
reminds managers of their need to develop and maintain a balanced array of
market offerings.

IX.   **KEY TERMS**

X.   **QUESTIONS FOR DISCUSSION (13)**

XI.   **ETHICS IN PRACTICE**

XII.   **CASES**

ANSWER GUIDELINES FOR CHAPTER 11 QUESTIONS FOR DISCUSSION

1.   *At what stage of the product life cycle would you place the following
      products? (a) cigars (b) coffee (c) pen-based (stylus-activated) personal
      computers (d) theme amusement parks (e) tennis balls (f) slide rules.*

ANSWER:

Students might be advised to review the characteristics of the PLC stages and
Exhibits 11-1, 11-2 and 11-3 before beginning this answer. While there may be
some debate as to exactly where on their PLCs these products are, student
knowledge of the marketplace and of the current marketing efforts of the firms
offering these products should be sufficient to come up with some general
agreement.

It would be possible to actually determine the true PLCs of these products by
locating annual sales figures for each and plotting them over time. Figures
might be found at a good library or obtained from trade associations.

(a)   Cigars

Cigars are in the decline stage despite some help from the Surgeon General. It
is thought that as many as three million cigarette users tried cigars as a result
of the Surgeon General's report on the hazards of cigarettes, joining hard-core
cigar smokers, thought to number about eight million. Cigar sales thus boomed in
1964 peaking at nine billion units, a 25 percent gain over 1963. But sales have
slid ever since because of an "image" problem, rules against cigar smoking,
general changes in attitude toward smoking, and mediocre promotion. Few new
smokers have been attracted.

Cigar sales drop by one-third to one-half billion units per year. The industry
had hoped sales would bottom out but there seems to be no end in sight to the
fall. (Of course, shifts in the environment of marketing could alter this, but
the prospects are bleak.) One problem seems to be that as family members urge
Dad to quit smoking, Dad turns to "sneaking smokes." That's much harder to do
with cigars than with cigarettes.

Advertising efforts involving sexy ladies and macho men have been unable to
reverse the trend. In fact, industry ad money now totals just a few million a
year, though some money has been rechanneled to in-store promotion. The smoke
signals are easy to read. There are few, if any, solutions to the industry's
problems.

Note: The premium-priced cigar market is the only one that has shown any
strength. The "reward" or "symbol of success" approach to positioning cigars may
be the way to go. There is also the "special occasion" market, e.g., the big
banquet. But this is a small market on which to base an industry. And, even at
special occasions, cigars still, by today's standards, "stink up the joint."

(b)   Coffee

Coffee seems to be at the end of its mature stage if not quite into the decline stage.   Coffee marketers continually advertise their product and have tried to place it into new positions, e.g. as a drink that keeps you sharp, as a drink that young adults should drink, and so on.   Coffee sales are not what they once were on a per-capita basis, but the product does not seem to be disappearing.

Still, health-related caffeine scares have affected its sales as has the perception of coffee as an "old folk's drink."   Coffee drinking was once a sign of maturity.   This is no longer true so there is no peer pressure on younger people to drink coffee.

The coffee industry is behaving in a manner consistent with this situation.   Most brands come in instant and caffeine-free versions.   Advertising and other promotions seem clearly aimed at avoiding a slide into decline.   Recent coffee ads (stressing that coffee drinkers move ahead or achieve great things, etc.) are obvious in their attempts to suggest that coffee is not old fashioned and that younger people should drink coffee.   This is said to be intended to counter the ads that made Sanka and other decafs seem "healthy," and by implication, other coffees seem unhealthy.

In short, coffee marketers are doing all the things associated with trying to keep a mature product from falling into decline.   One of the most recent steps, undertaken by several brands, is introduction of "light" coffees that have half the caffeine of regular coffee, but are not decaf.   This was tried in the past, but the current effort is being pursued with greater vigor than before.

(c)   Pen-based (stylus activated) personal computers

We place PCs as a whole at the mid-point of the maturity stage.   The industry behaves as a mature industry ... lots of product changes, improvements, fine tunings, price appeals, heavy advertising, etc.

However, analysts have been fooled before.   The PLC is a unit sales curve.   If unit sales suddenly take a leap upward, the claim that the industry is "mature" appears incorrect.   All this is to say that the market could decide that everyone should have a PC (as appears likely), or even that everyone should have many PCs.   This would drive the PLC into, in effect, a new growth stage.

This happened before.   Television (sets), in 1962 had peaked in sales and appeared to be "mature" or even on the brink of decline.   Then came "perfected" color, tummy TVs, TVs in the kitchen, office, and other locales, cable TV, VCRs, etc.   Television sales spurted upward from what looked, on the PLC curve, to be the beginning of decline.

The question asks specifically about a certain type of PC, the pen-activated models.   These would appear to be in their growth or even late-introductory rather than maturity, stages.   The advertising for them dwells on the revolutionary aspects of these computers, firm prices, and other marks of a product in its beginning stages of the PLC.   However, the text states clearly that the PLC concept is intended to be used with an "entire" product, not variations, brands, or models.   Thus, a question that students should have to answer is whether or not the pen-based computer is a new product, or simply a variation on an old product.

(d)   Theme amusement parks

In recent years amusement parks have appeared to be in a late growth stage or maturity stage.   Six Flags, King's Island, Disneyland, religious theme parks, Opryland, Dollyworld, and many others seem to support this.   Further, in the U.S., citizens generally find themselves with the money and leisure to support such entertainments.

This is not the first growth period for amusement parks.   Old style parks (Coney Island, Palisades Park, etc.) once enjoyed great years.   It is arguable that today's park is so unlike the old ones as to constitute a new product.   This serves to reinforce the perception that theme parks are in the late growth or early maturity stages.

Like the question above, the matter of individual parks vs. established parks should be addressed. Just as it is arguable that a new style of computer is just a variation on an old product, it is arguable that a new theme park may be a new product or a variation on an old product. It is likely, however, that the life cycle concept would be used/misused in this way ... "My theme park, just opened this year, is in its growth stage, but theme parks in general are in their maturity stage."

One matter to be addressed is the state of the national and world economy. If one has a bright outlook one might argue that theme parks are facing a great future as well-off folks seek fun and games. If one thinks things are going to be real bad economically, the opposite projection applies.

(e)   Tennis balls

Tennis enjoyed a boom a few years ago but other sports have, for various reasons, taken away some of the attention once paid to tennis. Still, it continues in popularity and continues to draw new players. The construction of indoor facilities has permitted year-round playing, and the fact that new construction techniques make this possible illustrates the influence of the technological environment on marketing.

The most recent bloom may be off the tennis rose, but it is our belief that due to the continuing interest in keeping "in shape" the PLC stage is maturity. Tennis is unlikely to disappear, as might other "products" in our society. In fact, it will probably boom again. Like billiards, skating, and other activities, tennis is in some ways a fashion item, rising and falling in popularity over time, but always coming back.

The tinkering tennis equipment manufacturers have done with their products such as larger racquets and balls is typical of the maturity stage of the PLC.

(f)   Slide rules

Calculators are easier to use, quicker, and more accurate than slide rules. In other words, there is no reason to have a slide rule unless you live where there are no batteries available. Slide rules provide the perfect example of a product made totally obsolete by technology.

However, there are a very few slide rules still produced for sale in the U.S., and some students may know someone who still uses a slide rule. But purchase, not use, is the key to the PLC. Thus, we place the slide rule at the "extinct" tail of the PLC.

2.   *Try to trace the product life cycle for a brand like Sony compact disc players.*

ANSWER:

The point was made in the text that the PLC is intended primarily to show the "life" of a product as a class, e.g., cassette tape players. However, marketers should be free to make reasonable adaptations to this and other planning tools. In fact, since the sales of all brands of a product combine to build a product's life cycle, it is reasonable to consider the PLC of an individual brand such as Sony. One of the great things about marketing, as opposed to, say, accounting, is that you can do just about anything you want as long as its legal, makes sense, and you get useful results.

Since students are unlikely to have access to the sales figures needed to truly plot the disc player PLC, a descriptive approach may be in order. It should be noted, however, that since the PLC is a unit sales curve it is possible to obtain sales figures and actually plot the curve.

.   Introductory Stage. Focus on early adopters, emphasizing the uniqueness of the concept and the product's ease of use. Special appeals aimed at encouraging trial, such as "visit a dealer," would be used.

- **Growth Stage.** Competition with other brands will increase. Marketers would try to position Sony as the best alternative. Sales should increase as the product gains acceptance.

- **Maturity Stage.** Marketers will call attention to their product's unique advantages (colored models, small version for travel or camping).

- **Decline Stage.** If the decision is to "get out", emphasis would be on price deals to channel members. Gold Circle and K-Mart will buy 1,000 railroad cars full.

3. *What are some typical pricing strategies during each stage of the product life cycle?*

ANSWER:

A "typical" pattern is for prices to be high at the start of a PLC and to decline as competition increases until (finally) prices are low at the very end of the PLC so that inventories may be disposed of. A variation would be for this pattern to continue until the end of the PLC when the remaining company (companies) actually increase prices because the remaining customers are willing to pay "any price" for their favorite product. This occurred in the case of Lydia Pinkham's "tonic" and is frequently seen among parts and repair service providers ... the owner of a classic car is willing to pay quite a bit to keep it running.

Another typical pattern is for prices to be low at the start of a PLC if the product is seen as a substitute for another product whose price is comparatively low. The first U.S.-made compact cars were sold at low prices because Volkswagen and other cars already on the market were being sold at low prices. Prices then could be adjusted as the market dictated.

In the growth stage of the PLC, prices generally fall somewhat as competition heats up. Further, high prices at the start of the PLC may have led to a recouping of R&D costs, permitting the dropping of prices in the growth stage. Note that as competition increases and as buyers become (or think they become) increasingly expert in choosing products, price becomes an increasingly important buying criteria.

In the maturity stage this pattern continues although because of a steadying of the market in general, prices may be expected to stabilize as firms settle into their relative shares of market. Also, product attributes such as style, status, reputation, brand familiarity, etc. become more important than the essentially stable and similar-to-others prices. Note that price changes in this stage are of the "temporary" sort: special sales, cents-off, rebates, coupons, etc.

In the decline stage, as mentioned above, prices may be dropped if management, perceiving the decline, decides to "get out quick," or may rise if the feeling is that remaining customers will buy even at non-bargain prices.

Exhibit 11-5 is of use in answering this question.

4. *What are some typical distribution strategies during each stage of the product life cycle?*

ANSWER:

Again, Exhibit 11-5 is of use. In general, however, the usual pattern is as follows.

In the introductory stage, the firm is likely struggling to set up its channels of distribution. It may be necessary to offer special deals to distributors to get them to take a chance on a new product. Thus, intentionally or not, some type of exclusive dealership system may result. If organizations feel they must do their own distribution just to "get started," direct marketing through mail-order or personal selling may result.

In the growth stage, when it has been shown that the new product has a chance to succeed, dealers should be easier to find. Further, as a mass market begins to grow, more dealers are needed. The result of both forces at work could be a variation of intensive distribution.

In the maturity stage, the product class is firmly established in the market as are various brands. For some products (e.g., chewing gum) intensive distribution could occur. It is also not uncommon for manufacturers to seek to maximize market shares by widening distribution to include all manner of dealer types. TVs, for example, are sold in department stores, discount stores, home centers, in "5 & 10s" like Woolworth's, or even in larger drug stores. For other products, especially products suggesting a fairly heavy investment in inventory (e.g., cars) dealers will seek to "specialize" and manufacturers will seek "good dealers." Thus a form of selective distribution might result.

In the decline stage, if it is recognized as such, distribution is very likely to shrink. Dealers will not want the product and manufacturers will not want to increase distribution.

Manufacturers will probably seek to keep some distribution operative to get rid of products in stock or to maintain a high-profit product being sought by a diminishing number of buyers. Remember that these faithful buyers are willing to seek their favorite product out. Selective distribution is the next result.

5.   *What are some typical promotion strategies during each stage of the product life cycle?*

ANSWER:

Exhibit 11-5 is again of use here. In general, a pattern such as the following one is applicable. Aspects of this problem are touched upon in the text's promotion section.

Promotion in the introductory stage is focused on potential early adopters, influencers, and others appropriate to an effort to set the product on its way. Another part of the strategy is to make the larger market aware of the product. Example: early TVs (often in kit form) were promoted to hobbyists and home tinkers via ads aimed at this sort of person. Publicity describing this amazing invention served to inform the general public about this new wonder.

During the growth stage, the promotional strategy changes. In economics' terminology, promotion is shifted from a development of primary demand to a development of selective demand. This is because of increased competition and because most consumers are now at least familiar with the nature of the product. Thus, brand promotion becomes paramount. It follows that the array of promotional media used would also be broadened.

In the maturity stage, with the market established and comparatively settled, we would expect to encounter promotional strategies aimed at maintaining product awareness, encouraging multiple purchases (2-car family, 3-TV family) and differentiating one product from another ("Laundry detergents are not all alike."). Depending on the product, media is likely to be wide-ranging, a fact consistent with the "reminder" nature of much promotion of mature products.

In the decline stage, promotion is often cut back and then focused on selling off existing stock. Special "deals" may be involved in the process. It is also possible that firms seeking to "milk" a dying market might take some other track, e.g., advertising in special media (especially magazines) with particular appeal to the remaining market. Companies seeking to reverse a decline would be likely to try a promotional program more appropriate to a growth product since a "reversal" of decline is, in effect, a "new growth" stage. Note, however, that decline can be the result of environmental changes the effects of which promotion is unlikely to overcome.

6.   *Does marketing grow in importance as a product matures and moves from the introductory stage through the growth and maturity stages?*

ANSWER:

No, since marketing is always important. Its emphasis on particular goals shifts, of course, as a product moves through the PLC. Exhibit 11-5 illustrates this aspect, as have several of the discussion questions. It might be said that developmental marketing is most important in that it provides the basis for all that is to follow. If it fails in its task, "all is lost." It might be said that marketing in the growth stage is most important in that, at this stage, new competitors are at their most energetic. It might be said that marketing in the maturity stage is most important since that stage of the PLC, and its long-term maintenance, is the goal of marketing management. Also, in the maturity stage, decline may be just a step away. Marketing is most important in the decline stage if it results in saving a product from extinction, and returning it to the maturity stage.

However, the answer must be that marketing is important in all stages of the PLC but important for different reasons and in different ways.

7.   *What guidelines would you suggest for rejuvenation of old brands in the mature stage of the product life cycle?*

ANSWER:

The president and vice-president of New York ad agency, Caldwell Davis Partners, suggest that your "new product" may be your rejuvenated "old product." Old products (like Vicks, Ben Gay, Tide, etc.) are known to be tremendously familiar to consumers. This should be considered before investments in new products are committed. Here are nine criteria suggested by Caldwell Davis.

1.   Does the product have new or extended uses that are underexploited? E.g., A-1 steak sauce on hamburgers, Arm & Hammer baking soda in refrigerators.

2.   Is the category under- or unadvertised? E.g., the "feminine protection" category went from $10 million in advertising to $50 million in one year and "the category exploded, and aggressive advertisers were the beneficiaries."

3.   Is there a better, broader target market? E.g., Marlboro's makers thought so when they switched from the "women's market" to the "macho" market.

4.   Can the product be sold in a more compelling or motivating way? E.g., Pampers didn't sell well until ads switched from emphasizing parents' convenience to stressing babies' comfort.

5.   Can the price be increased to build a franchise with more advertising. E.g., Chivas Regal was a moderately-priced Scotch. The price was raised to the top of the line and extra revenue put into advertising.

6.   Can the price be cut to increase share of market? E.g., Snowy bleach cut its price below Clorox and got a 25% increased share of market.

7.   Is it a generic product that can be branded? E.g., Sunkist oranges, Chiquita and Dole bananas, and Frank Perdue chicken did this with success.

8.   Can the product form or package be changed? E.g., Bold detergent did well as the first of its category to contain a fabric softener. Appeal was largely to price-conscious users of softeners.

9.   Can it be identified with a trend or exploited opportunistically? E.g., Dannon moved yogurt, formally a "health nut" item, to make it fit the health and fitness trend.

Why bother? A new product introduction can cost tens of millions of dollars and a majority of them (some say 65% or more) fail. A few million in advertising can make "old" products like Ivory Soap or Johnson's Baby Shampoo into "new winners."

8.   *How important is product quality to being competitive around the world?*

ANSWER:

Increasingly, U.S. firms must compete on a global scale for markets in the U.S. as well as in other countries. Thus, firms which measure product quality must use global standards as a benchmark. In Chapter 2, the text stressed that U.S.

corporations failed to keep pace with quality offered by international competitors. Today, most U.S. companies adopt a total quality management philosophy for all employees to work for continuous quality improvements. U.S. firms measure quality from the customer's perspective and adjust product strategies accordingly.

Consider the automobile industry and ask students how important product quality is today for firms to remain competitive in the domestic market? Since global competitors have entered the playing field, U.S. firms must catch up with and surpass quality standards to retain a competitive edge.

9.   *What companies have recently implemented cost reduction strategies? Are they always incompatible with product quality strategies?*

ANSWER:

Students may be aware of daily news stories of companies moving to foreign locations to save labor costs or offering products at reduced prices to combat stable sales volume. Stanley Works moved its operations from New England to Puebla, Mexico to manufacture sledgehammers and wrecking bars. Emerson consistently strives to reduce costs in its operations.

A cost reduction strategy does not always mean that quality suffers. Product quality strategies emphasize market-driven quality. Since the level of quality is the degree to which a good or service corresponds to buyers' expectations, cost reductions may actually help a firm provide more satisfactory value to customers in comparison to competitive offerings.

10.   *How important is brand equity to a line extension strategy?*

ANSWER:

A product line extension is an additional item added to an existing product line to provide depth. Brand equity helps explain the reasons for successful brand extensions in the same product line. As the text states, brand equity means that market share or profit margins are greater because of the goodwill associated with the brand. Brand names such as Mrs. Paul's, Harley Davidson, Disney, Ocean Spray or Stouffers depend on the goodwill associated with their established names to aid in the success of new items introduced as part of a line extension strategy. As discussed in the text, Ocean Spray used brand equity from its cranberry sauce to successfully implement a product category extension into juice drinks. Hershey has used its equity to introduce pre-mixed chocolate milk and pudding packs to supermarket dairy cases.

Brand equity can be very important for a line or category extension strategy. However, Procter and Gamble, and others who do not employ family branding, have also exhibited that brand equity is not essential for success with line extension items.

11.   *What are the pitfalls of a brand extension strategy that, for example, extends a name from a hair spray product to a facial cream?*

ANSWER:

Brand extension involves using one established brand name in the introduction of new products. At a limited level, it makes very good sense to take advantage of a "good" name. For example, a new cereal from Kellogg's or a new frozen vegetable from Green Giant probably has a better chance for market success if the familiar brand name is used for the product than if it is not. This, of course, is the idea behind family branding.

Brand extension can obviously be carried too far, but how far is too far is not immediately obvious. The Bell name is respected on telephone and other electronic equipment, but would it be "extendable" to an electric car? Maybe or maybe not. Careful marketing research studies might reduce the level of doubt and increase chances of making the right decision.

In the case at hand, the hair product name, say Clairol, might be so closely allied in the public mind as to be untransferable to a skin cream. If tests show that a great proportion of respondents think of "hair" rather than "personal care" when the name Clairol is mentioned, then the Clairol name should, at the least, be played down: "New Young Skin from Clairol" rather than "New Clairol Cream."

Care should be taken to assure that face cream users are, more or less, much the same market as hair product users. If users of Clairol hair products differ widely in age, race, etc. from the targeted skin cream buyer, the markets may be too disparate to make the brand extension of a meaningful strategy.

12.   *What is the relationship between market segmentation and choice of a single-product versus full-line product strategy?*

ANSWER:

In general, the broader the line carried, the better the chance to please any given customer. But the broader the line, the more expenses are incurred. The more narrow the line, the fewer expenses (other than loss-of-sales) but the less the chance of being able to satisfy the customer. Like all problems in business and in life, risks and tradeoffs are involved here.

Students might be asked to list some of the expenses associated with width of product line, e.g., inventory holding, ordering, size of catalog, sales-force specialization or lack of it, need for overlapping sales territories, salaries, etc.

The text's Exhibit 11-9 sums up many of the advantages and disadvantages of full-line versus limited-line strategies.

13.   *Some homes are now being marketed with cable setups so that computer terminals may be installed. What product strategy does this reflect?*

ANSWER:

In this response guideline, we are taking the view that the cable setups are the idea and product of the home builders themselves. Opinions of the product strategy might vary if one were to assume that the setups are provided by some other marketer, e.g., a computer manufacturer of a TV cable company with grandiose plans.

A home builder including such setups in his or her total product could be seen as attempting to differentiate that product from competing products. Calling attention to this difference would reflect a strategy of product differentiation.

However, the question arises as to whether or not prospective buyers of a house would be impressed with such a feature. It seems to us that a buyer who had or planned to get a computer would like the feature. Buyers not into computers might be impressed with the builder's modern viewpoint and attention to detail. Both buyers might assume that such a feature "shows" that the builder "must have used all the latest advances in building and equipping the house." Further, the setup feature gives the builder and/or realtor an interesting "talking point." A home buyer might imagine that when he or she sells the house this feature will make the sale easier.

Yet it seems that very few people would buy a house solely because of this feature. For most, price, location, schools, shopping, city services, as well as the design and appearance of the house, would be factors of consummate importance. If "everything else is right," the computer setup makes for a nice extra. It seems that this would be true even when most families have computers.

ETHICS EXERCISE 11

CHAPTER 11 ETHICS IN PRACTICE

Overview

Herman Miller is the first furniture maker to pledge not to use rain forest woods in manufacturing. Its management says that to use such woods is unsound environmentally and businesswise. The company implemented this policy even though one of its most popular products, made for forty years with South American rosewood, will be made of other woods until a rosewood source in a sustained-yield setting (i.e. a "tree farm") can be found.

The tropical rain forests are primary forests in regions with heavy rainfall, chiefly but not exclusively found in the tropical regions of Brazil, Bolivia, Columbia, Ecuador, Peru, and Venezuela. Rain forests are significant for their valuable timber resources, and in the tropics they provide sites for cash crops such as rubber, tea, coffee, bananas, and sugarcane. In addition to agriculture, the lush forests are coveted for logging, mining, and hydropower. A quarter of all prescription drugs are derived from tropical plants. (Linda Kanamine, "Rain Forest is Tribe's Heritage," *USA Today*, June 5, 1992. p. 2A.)

Their environmental significance is that they are among the last remaining areas of the earth that are unexploited economically. Furthermore, their destruction threatens the delicate environmental balance of our planet. Though rain forests cover only about 7% of the earth, they are home to half of all plant and animal species (Kanamine, p. 2A). Clear cutting the forests often destroys the habitat, leading to flooding, soil erosion, and devastation of species. Each year 80,000 square miles out of a total of 10 million square miles of rain forest are lost through agriculture, logging, and development (*Endangered Earth*, National Geographic Society, 1992). On the other hand, some would argue that some of these activities which result in deforestation are necessary to further economic development in developing countries. The key is to strike a balance between often competing environmental and economic interests.

Herman Miller pledged not to use rain forest woods, even in one of its most popular and, one assumes, most profitable product items, the Eames chair.

1.   *Why would a company like Herman Miller adopt a policy like this?*

The company could be doing this for self-serving reasons as well as for society-serving reasons. From a self-serving perspective, the firm would realize that more and more consumers are demanding environmentally friendly or "green" goods and are apparently willing to pay more for them (although the extent to which they are willing to do this has been debated). To create environmentally friendly products and to promote them as "green" presents a marketing opportunity. In many industries the opportunity to make plenty of money in the long run lies in the increasing consumer demand for environmental safety. This sometimes involves making some short-run sacrifices (such as temporarily discontinuing the Eames chair) and losing some money along the way. As another example, McDonald's has a policy of not purchasing beef raised on rain forest (or recently deforested rain forest) land, and they make this information available to customers in public relations materials.

It is arguable that a firm might take steps like this because long-run environmental damage might so injure the world and its population that, way down the road, there would be "no people to buy goods." While there is some truth behind this thought, how many of us think that corporate managers really think like that?

From an ethical perspective, the company would recognize that the most moral thing to do is to help the environment and not hurt it with their business actions. Essentially, the earth's safety should never be compromised for the sake of monetary gain. This is for the good of society and is the essence of green marketing. But, the harm done to development and economic growth must also be considered.

CHAPTER 11 TAKE A STAND QUESTIONS

1.   *Are flanker brands and line extensions really needed by consumers?*

This gets back to the issue of needs and wants discussed in Ethics in Practice Exercise 5. The major point there was that in a free marketplace the sovereign consumer decides what is needed and wanted. Flanker brands could not survive in the marketplace unless they met legitimate needs and wants at a reasonable price.

From a consumer perspective, product line extensions provide more consumer choice, variety, and (hence) satisfaction. Specific versions of a product can be developed which better satisfy specific niche markets (enhanced models, cost reductions, customized versions, etc.). This is especially important in mature markets, where consumers might feel like they are being taken for granted if no new products in the category are forthcoming. The familiar brand name assures the consumer that the product will contain the quality they have come to expect from the brand. This provides them with a quick and easily obtained source of information, reducing search and shopping effort.

From society's perspective, the ability to tag product variations with readily accepted brand names serves as an incentive to continue innovating and helps ensure consistent quality in the new products (because "one bad apple spoils the bunch," i.e. the brand's equity).

On the downside, it has been argued that flankers sometimes result in trivial differences; the result is false and misleading differentiation, especially in homogeneous product categories. Nonetheless, minor differences do generally result, which are better able to satisfy at least some customers. A flanker strategy can also lead to higher design and engineering, inventory carrying, order processing, transportation, and manufacturing costs as production must be adjusted to make disparate items, which can result in higher costs passed on to consumers.

On the other hand, promotional economies can be achieved via umbrella advertising, which can offset some of these higher costs. And, especially in the face of excess capacity, manufacturing economies are achievable, especially where standardization of parts in multiple product variations is feasible. So, on balance, the effect of flankers on prices could actually go either way.

2.   *Is it ethical to initiate a cost reduction strategy that requires closing an American factory and opening a factory in a third-world nation?*

As free-trade areas open up, especially with America's neighbors to the south, this kind of a cost reduction strategy is likely to become more common. Under free-trade agreements U.S. manufacturers will import raw materials into other nations with cheaper labor costs, produce products and export them to the U.S., not subject to tariffs (international taxes). From the perspective of the global marketplace, this can be beneficial. First, it is consistent with the concept (discussed in the international marketing chapter) of comparative advantage: a nation has an advantage when it specializes in exporting products it can produce more cheaply than other nations because of its human and natural resources. If all nations implement this theory, standards of living will rise because of the international specialization of labor. Also, it might provide employment to people in the developing countries who might otherwise be either unemployed or underemployed.

On the other hand, it might be argued that workers in the third world countries are being exploited by being paid low wages. However, whether or not this is really exploitation depends on what their alternative employment opportunities are; if they are willing to work for low wages, this would indicate that they lack better employment options.

It might also be argued that U.S. workers lose jobs in the process. While this is true in the short run, over time labor resources in this country will be reallocated to their areas of comparative advantage. Retraining of the displaced workers might be in order, but in the long run they will find alternative employment in industries where their skills, combined with capital, can be exploited. According to Michael Porter's theory of the competitive advantage of nations, industries can then innovate and upgrade to the next level of technology and productivity.

For further thoughts on this issue, see Chapter 16 Ethics in Practice exercise.

GUIDE TO CASES

CASE 11-1 XEROX[1]

SUBJECT MATTER: Supplier Relationships, Competitive Benchmarking, Changes in Market Environment and Corporate Culture, Total Quality Control

Please see the Guide to Video Cases for video length and other information.

AT-A-GLANCE OVERVIEW

Xerox is best known for photocopying, but it is a global company marketing a wide array of products and services, such as financial services, to big and small businesses.

Xerox's predecessor, the Haloid Company, was founded in 1906. In 1949 the company made and marketed the first "dry" copier, and in 1960 the first automatic copier. The company became so successful that it began to think of itself as the ultimate authority in the field. But in the 1970s Japanese competition began to appear, making inroads with less expensive, smaller, and more reliable copiers. (Xerox's machines were more complex and thus more subject to failure.)

In the 1980s, after losing share of market for several years, Xerox saw that it had become a victim of its own success. It had lost its focus on the customer. A "know-it-all" attitude focused on engineering rather than market-driven quality appeared to be the major cause of this lack of focus.

In the late 80s, Xerox turned itself around by implementing a total quality management program. In 1989, the business products and systems division won the Malcomb Baldridge Quality Award.

DISCUSSION QUESTIONS

1.   *From a marketing perspective, why is total quality management important to a company like Xerox?*

For many years, Xerox was the epitome of the well-run corporation. The company was so successful for so long that it began to view itself as the absolute authority in its technology and product fields. It took significant losses in market share and profits for Xerox to recognize that all was not right. Losses in share and profit are sufficient reason to stress total quality management, but there are others.

From a marketing perspective, the company should be on track with the marketing concept. This concept stresses customer satisfaction. Xerox's products are products wherein failures in quality are easily seen. Also, their competitors' better quality is also easily seen. This would not be the case with all products. (For example, quality of nails, insulation, and cement is not immediately obvious to all, but a Xerox machine that is not delivering quality copies is easy to detect.) Furthermore, the failures of a big company are far more widely "advertised" than those of an obscure firm. A "we-know-it-all" attitude is the direct antithesis of the marketing concept. It skates close to the old product orientation that the marketing concept tell us to eschew.

To regain the competitive edge required a complete transformation of the Xerox corporate culture. This transformation had to start with the recognition of the fact that they did not "know it all."

---

[1]This material is adapted from the video from the Association for Manufacturing Excellence.

2.   *What steps would a company like Xerox have to follow to implement a total quality management philosophy.*

A major point in this case is obviously competitive benchmarking. Xerox found that it had become a victim of its own success. Having been so successful for so long the company had lost its focus on the customer. This is an "old story," of course, forgetting about the people who made you great in the first place. In addition, Xerox found internally that a functional focus had replaced a corporate focus. The company seemed to have come to believe that it "knew it all" with regard to its products. As market share and profits fell, the company recognized its errors and changed the way it ran its business. Essential elements of this change include:

.   Competitive benchmarking, by which is meant literally taking apart the competition in order to totally understand how competitors designed and built their products and what it cost them to do so.

.   Implementing new relationships with suppliers on a basis of teamwork. This change meant providing suppliers with technical assistance and training in order to achieve reduced costs and prices. To be able to effectively do so, the supplier base was radically reduced in size.

.   An absolutely essential element to making all of this happen is the active involvement of top management. This involvement includes the recognition by top management of the need for continuous change. The competitive environment will never be static.

Some key concepts should be addressed.

.   Mindset Changes. It is absolutely essential to move from an internal focus to an external, customer focus. This change has to start at the top with senior management. Further, this change requires the recognition that the customers' needs are paramount and will evolve and change through time.

.   Functional Silo Syndrome. The individual functional areas of the firm were achieving their individual goals, but overall the company was losing. People at all levels must work across functional boundaries to focus upon the customers' needs and determine how the corporation as a whole can best meet those needs. Functional goals should then be based on this needs assessment.

.   Competitive Benchmarking. A major element of the change in the corporate culture required the elimination of an NIH (not invented here) attitude. Everyone must recognize that someone else, somewhere else is probably doing something better than "we" are. Therefore, any organization must thoroughly understand its competition. What are "they" doing? In what ways are "they" better than "we" are? How can "we" get better than "they" are?

.   Focus on Total Quality Control (TQC). As the firm seeks to improve its processes and ways of doing business, it must focus on "doing it right the first time." Customers deserve and have a right to expect no less.

.   Supplier Partnerships. In order to achieve all of these objectives, the firm needs to redefine relationships with suppliers.

It must recognize that the relationship must be mutually supportive and beneficial. The firm must provide technical support and training in appropriate areas. In order to do so effectively, it will probably be necessary to reduce the supplier base so that the firm can effectively form and maintain these partnerships.

VIDEO CASE 11-2 WALLACE COMPANY[2]

SUBJECT MATTER: Total Quality, Customer Needs, Relationships with Suppliers

Please see the Guide to Video Cases for video length and other information.

AT-A-GLANCE OVERVIEW

Wallace Co., Inc. is a distributor of pipes, valves and fittings for the engineering and construction industries. Family-owned and founded in 1942, Wallace Co.'s nine regional offices employ a staff of 280 and generated sales of $90 million in 1990.

During the economic downturn, customers, suppliers and competitors were going bankrupt left and right. The company's traditional source of business, engineering and construction firms, was rapidly downsizing. Employee morale was crippled by recessionary fears, and worker's compensation insurance premiums were astronomical. During this time, domestic manufacturers of pipes and valves recognized that their products were not priced competitively with imported products and slashed prices by 20 to 40 percent. Consequently, all existing inventory was instantly devalued -- costing Wallace millions of dollars in capital losses that could not be easily written off.

These problems were later aggravated when two direct competitors filed for bankruptcy under Chapter 11 and then were absorbed by other firms. Such actions essentially enabled those organizations to eliminate millions of dollars worth of inventory debts. As a result, Wallace faced a significant pricing disadvantage in an already depressed market. To compound the problem, the company's credit relationships had ceased due to a bank failure.

Despite extreme financial pressures, the struggling firm decided to invest a principal share of the resources it had remaining on a major quality improvement effort. Key components of this plan included the development of a safety program; "Quality Alert: Safety First, Family First" saved $500,000 in reduced insurance premiums. After engaging a quality training firm, the company invested heavily (8 percent of the annual payroll) in leadership development, company-wide training, employee empowerment, technology and systematic benchmarking and operational procedures such as statistical process control. It also shifted its sales and marketing focus from almost total reliance on engineering and construction to a more diversified, less volatile business base including many maintenance, repair and operations (MRO) contracts.

DISCUSSION QUESTIONS

1.   *Do you agree with Wallace's strategic decision?*

Most students will agree with the decision. The case notes many improvements in the way things were done at Wallace. An integrated, 16-point quality process -- enveloping a customer-driven focus and a heavy reliance on leveraging existing human resource and capital -- was the key to a Gulf Coast distributor overcoming the nation's most severe regional and industry downturn during the mid-eighties. Who can argue with customer focused total quality improvement?

2.   *What are the key principles underlying a total quality assurance strategy?*

Product quality strategies emphasize market-driven quality as a top priority. The text notes in several places that for many years some American corporations did not keep pace with the product quality offered by a number of overseas competitors.

Total quality management is the process of properly implementing and adjusting the product mix strategy (and procedures within the entire business organization)

---

[2]Excerpts reprinted from *Strengthening America's Competitiveness*, pp. 102-103, copyright 1991 by Connecticut Mutual Life Insurance Company.

to assure the customers' satisfaction with product quality. It is a strategy
that expresses the conviction that if an organization wishes to prosper, every
employee must work for continuous quality improvement.

At Wallace, the firm's quality orientation led to several key philosophical
commitments: knowing customer needs intimately and exceeding customer
expectations; competing on the basis of total cost versus price; building
formalized customer and supplier partnerships; and establishing performance
measurements leading to zero defects across all levels of the organization.

As a result of its efforts, Wallace Co. survived hard times and flourished.
Traditionally short-term MRO contracts have been extended for long-term periods
with such firms as Union Carbide, Hoechst Celanese, Monsanto, and Dow Chemical
U.S.A. Long-term arrangements testify to customer satisfaction levels.

From 1987-1990, sales increased 69 percent, profits jumped 740 percent, and
Wallace's market share rose 75 percent due to a dramatic influx of new customers.
The firm achieved the industry's highest worker productivity and a 23 percent
increase in on-time deliveries.

The rewards of the company's excellence were even more than monetary. In 1990,
President Bush awarded the firm the coveted Malcolm Baldrige National Quality
Award in the small business category.

But something happened.

Since the making of the video, Wallace has experienced some difficulty. In 1991,
the company laid off approximately 25% of its work force, and it was deeply in
debt. What went wrong? Large customers had put pressure on Wallace to improve
performance, such as by cutting delivery times. Wallace quality programs
improved from 75% in 1987 to 92% in 1990, but the accomplishment was expensive.
The company's overhead shot up and Wallace increased prices to cover costs.
Customers resisted the high prices. All this, combined with an industry-wide
decline, led to a loss of $691,000 in 1990. The firm's banker became more
conservative with loans to Wallace.

According to *Business Week* (Oct. 21, 1991), the company experienced financial
problems because it spent too much time and effort trying to win the Baldridge
award. Wallace company managers spent a lot of time making presentations about
their quality program, and let some marketing activities slide.

3.   *What is involved in changing an organization's philosophy to total quality
      management?*

Today, with intense levels of global competition, the first step is to recognize
the importance of a total quality management philosophy.

Many organizations have implemented total quality assurance programs. These
programs are not the exclusive domain of marketing managers because production
quality control is an integral aspect of these programs. Other company
operations also enter in. However, in an organization driven by the marketing
concept the definition of quality comes from the consumer.

The philosophy underlying the implementation of a quality management strategy is
epitomized in the following statement by a Burger King executive: "The customer
is the vital key to our success. We are now looking at our business through the
customers' eyes and measuring our performance against their expectations, not
ours."[3] A company that employs a quality strategy must evaluate its quality
through the eyes of the customer. And it must integrate the efforts of
production, billing, marketing, and all areas within the firm.

Another step is to define exactly what is meant by "quality." It used to be that
organizations defined quality by engineering standards. Most marketers don't see
quality that way. Some marketers say that having a quality product or service
means that the good or service conforms to the consumers' requirements ... that

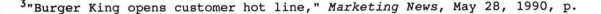

[3]"Burger King opens customer hot line," *Marketing News*, May 28, 1990, p.
7.

the product is acceptable. Effective marketers subscribing to a total quality management philosophy, however, believe that the product's quality must go beyond acceptability for a given price range. Rather than having consumers pleased that nothing went wrong, consumers should experience some "delightful surprises," that is, reap some unexpected benefits. In other words, quality assurance is more than just meeting minimum standards. The level of quality is the degree to which a good or service corresponds to buyers' expectations.

Total quality management stresses continuous improvement of product quality and/or enhancing products with additional features as the product ages. The focus is on improvement, no matter how small. Managers continuously improve product quality to keep their brands competitive. Obviously, a Rolls Royce does not compete with Geo Storm from General Motors. Buyers of these automobiles are in different market segments and their expectations of quality differ widely. Nevertheless marketers at Rolls Royce and General Motors try to establish what quality level their target market expects, and then to market goods and services that continually surpass expectations.

At Wallace, employees were trained to act in the best interest of the customer, and the effort paid off in many ways. In retrospect, the company suffered some bad consequences when, according to some observers, the company became more focused on successful implementation of the program than on its business. Incidentally, some commentators condemn the Baldridge Award because it cannot be won without a great public relations effort which is actually counter-productive to the real work of the organization seeking the award.

12 MARKETING NEW PRODUCTS

CHAPTER SCAN

The focus of this chapter is a discussion of the development and introduction of new consumer and industrial products to the marketplace. For most organizations, new products or variants of old products are necessary to long-range success.

The degrees of "newness" and the characteristics of new product success are discussed. Also covered are the steps involved in developing new products. The related product adoption process is also reviewed.

Finally, the major organizational designs associated with new product developing, testing, and marketing are presented, and ethical problems that may develop in the marketing of new products are discussed.

SUGGESTED LEARNING OBJECTIVES

The student who studies this chapter will be exposed to a wide-ranging discussion of the development and marketing of new products and will be able to:

1. Differentiate among degrees of product newness.

2. Explain why the chances of success and failure for new products are likely to vary considerably.

3. Identify general product characteristics of successful new products.

4. Characterize the stages of new product development.

5. Identify some of the most common reasons for new product failure.

6. Describe the new product diffusion process and list the groups of adopters to which marketing managers must direct their appeals.

7.   Point out the advantages of various organizational forms associated with the successful development and introduction of new products.

8.   Identify some ethical questions about the marketing of new products.

CHAPTER OUTLINE

I.   INTRODUCTION

II.   WHAT IS A NEW PRODUCT?

III.   MANAGEMENT'S PERSPECTIVE OF NEW PRODUCTS

IV.   THE CONSUMER'S PERSPECTIVE OF NEWNESS

    A.   Discontinuous Innovation
    B.   Dynamically Continuous Innovation
    C.   Continuous Innovation

V.   THE SLIM CHANCES OF SUCCESS

VI.   THE CHARACTERISTICS OF SUCCESS

    A.   Relative Advantage
    B.   Compatibility with Existing Consumption Patterns
    C.   Trialability -- The Opportunity for Buyer Testing
    D.   Observability -- The Chance to See the Newness
    E.   Complexity

VII.   NEW PRODUCT DEVELOPMENT

    A.   Idea Generation
    B.   Screening
    C.   Business Analysis
    D.   Development
    E.   Commercialization

VIII. WHY DO FAILURES OCCUR?

IX.   THE ADOPTION AND DIFFUSION PROCESSES

    A.   Innovators -- Being Venturesome
    B.   Early Adopters -- Following the Lead
    C.   Early and Late Majorities -- Riding the Bandwagon
    D.   Laggards -- Bringing Up the Rear
    E.   Nonadopters -- Holding Out
    F.   Use of the Adopter Categories

X.   ORGANIZATION FOR NEW PRODUCT DEVELOPMENT

    A.   The Product Manager
    B.   The Market Manager
    C.   The New Product Manager
    D.   The Venture Team
    E.   The New Products Department
    F.   The New Products Committee
    G.   The Task Force
    H.   Entrepreneurial Enterprises

XI.   ETHICAL CONSIDERATIONS ASSOCIATED WITH THE INTRODUCTION OF NEW PRODUCTS

XII.   SUMMARY

XIII. KEY TERMS

XIV.   QUESTIONS FOR DISCUSSION (9)

XV.   ETHICS IN PRACTICE

XVI. CASES

The following key terms are introduced and used in Chapter 12. They are defined in the text's Glossary.

New product
Discontinuous innovation
Dynamically continuous innovation
Continuous innovation
Relative advantage
Trialability
Trial sampling
Divisibility
Observability
Simplicity of usage
Idea generation stage
Screening stage
Business analysis stage
Development stage
Concept testing
Test marketing
Commercialization
Adoption process
Diffusion process
Innovator
Early adopter
Early majority
Late majority
Laggard
Nonadopter
Product manager (brand manager)
Market manager
Venture team
New products committee
Task force
Intrapreneurial
Product obsolescence
Fashion obsolescence
Right to choose

THE CHAPTER SUMMARIZED

I.   INTRODUCTION

Fuji Optical Systems' DentaCam, the leader in its field, is a dental mirror-sized video system that employs fiber-optic techniques to send a high resolution image to a color screen where it can be viewed by the dentist and patient. It magnifies the image of the tooth and is a great aid in operations such as root canal work in dental education. The dentist can use foot pedals to freeze frames and record images on video disks or print out an instant picture on a video printer. The system also maintains a data base of patient's records and dental images.

II.   WHAT IS A NEW PRODUCT?

The Fuji DentaCam suggests what a "new product" can be. Yet products, from computers to filter cigarettes to lemon-juice fortified dish washing liquid, were once all "new." Is iced cappuccino in a can new? Is the pocket-sized electronic spell checker really new? The marketing concept tells us to view the product as a bundle of benefits. If a product's benefits differ from the bundles of benefits already on the market, then the product is "new." In a sense, an established product that a given consumer or industrial buyer has never before purchased is "new" to that person.

It is clear that the term "new" is a relative one, influenced by individual perceptions.

III.   MANAGEMENT'S PERSPECTIVE OF NEW PRODUCTS

Studies of new products reveal that managers classify newness in terms of two dimensions: newness to the company and newness to the market. Six kinds of new products may be identified from management's perspective. The first three of these (below) are new products with which most companies have little experience.

- New-to-the-world products, those that create entirely new markets.

- Product category extensions, those that allow an organization for the first time to diversify and enter an established market for an existing product category. These products are not entirely new to the market, but the company has had no experience with them. If these products closely imitate competing products, they may be termed "me too" products.

- Product line extensions, additions to existing product lines that supplement the basic items in an established product line. Cost reduction models and variations in flavors and design are examples.

- Product improvements, "new and improved" versions that replace existing ones because they provide improved performance, features, or greater perceived value.

- Cost reductions, those new products that replace existing products but may be produced at a lower cost.

- Repositionings, whereby existing products are positioned to offer a new benefit or a different competitive position, or are targeted to new market segments.

When a product is new to the organization, managers may have to deal with different technology from that of existing products, and/or consumers' perceptions that the product is different from products on the market. Both can mean a need for greater investment in marketing. Exhibit 12-1 illustrates new product situations in terms of technology, consumers' perception of newness, and investment risk.

IV.   THE CONSUMER'S PERSPECTIVE OF NEWNESS

Clearly, there are degrees of newness. One such scheme suggests three degrees of newness.

A.   Discontinuous Innovation

Discontinuous innovations are pioneering products so new that no previous product performed an equivalent function. They necessitate new consumption or usage patterns.

Examples: the original video tape recorder and the Lithium battery pacemaker. These do what no products before them did and necessitate extensive behavior changes. Artificial hearts and kidneys, once perfected, will fall in this category.

B.   Dynamically Continuous Innovation

Dynamically continuous innovations represent changes and improvements that do not strikingly change buying and usage patterns. They constitute the mid-range of the continuum of newness.

Examples: the electric car and electronic word processor. These are genuinely new but do not influence behavior as did the first car and the first typewriter.

C. Continuous Innovation

Continuous innovations are on-going, commonplace changes such as minor product alterations or imitative new products.

Examples: Gel toothpaste and "orangier" Orange Crush. These are certainly at the less innovative end of the newness continuum.

V. THE SLIM CHANCES OF SUCCESS

The "success rate" of new products is difficult to determine because, like newness, it is hard to define. Also:

. Companies do not publicize their failures.

. How much success constitutes success is debatable.

Estimates are available. Examples:

. Some say that 90% of all new product ideas do not become "commercial successes" (a 10% "success rate").

. One study suggests that one successful product is generated per 40 new product ideas (a 2.5% "success rate").

. A product that actually gets to market should have a far better "success rate". One estimate suggests that two out of three new product introductions succeed (a 67% "success rate").

Success rates vary widely from industry to industry. For example, the success rate is high for industrial goods compared with that for consumer goods in part because industrial buyers are better able to tell marketers what products they would like to have.

VI. THE CHARACTERISTICS OF SUCCESS

No one can provide a list of do's and don'ts for product success. At best, such lists have value only as checklists or warnings.

Five characteristics of products that have succeeded are offered for consideration. It is important to note that these must be considered with price, distribution, and promotion matters in mind.

A. Relative Advantage

Products that offer buyers clear-cut advantages over existing, competitive offerings are said to have **relative advantage**.

Examples: A word processor has clear advantages over an ordinary typewriter; a Walkman has clear advantages over other portable radios; Casio's Digital Diary provides a lightweight, pocket-sized information organizer, clearly providing advantages over bulkier notebooks.

B. Compatibility with Existing Consumption Patterns

All else equal, a new product has a better chance for success if it is compatible with existing behaviors.
Examples: CD recordings outperform regular audiocassettes but require purchase of a CD player. A new type of recording tape will be more quickly accepted if it plays on existing tape machines than if it requires that new machines be bought. Frozen foods did not "catch on" until home freezers became common. Kraft's Sun Seasons lettuce remains fresh as it "grows" in its package, but requires no behavior changes of its buyers.

C.   Trialability -- The Opportunity for Buyer Testing

All else equal, a product that is easier to "try out" has a better chance for success than one which is difficult to try. Such a product has **trialability**. A new shampoo is easier to try than a new type of car. Also, the shampoo maker can easily increase trialability by mailing out free samples (**trial sampling**) or reduce purchase risk by providing cents-off coupons.

Trialability is enhanced by **divisibility**, a characteristic that permits a buyer to try a small amount of a new product. A customer can easily try a new soft drink by buying one can of it but cannot buy a "sample" of a pair of $200 running shoes.

D.   Observability -- The Chance to See the Newness

Some products enter the marketplace with attributes that are visible to customers, e.g., the Kodak Photo CD which stores photos on compact discs and plays them on ordinary televisions is a product with **observability**. Sony Walkman and the Black and Decker Workmate (collapsible work bench) are other products whose advantages are easily grasped. This increases the chances of product success.

A new cloth, shop material, or motor oil may have great advantages over existing products but these are difficult to observe. Frequently, testimonial-style advertising is used in an attempt to offset this disadvantage.

E.   Complexity

A complex product starts out with a clear disadvantage. The complexity must be "overcome." Example: The complexity of automobiles, electronic equipment, etc. is offset by the relative ease of operation built into these products. Thus, **simplicity of usage** overcomes complexity and makes a new product more acceptable to consumers.

VII.   NEW PRODUCT DEVELOPMENT

Very few products can be traced to "blind luck," or to "nut inventors" working in basement shops. The "flash of light" is important, but the development of new products is usually a lengthy enough process that five general stages within it can be identified. These are shown in Exhibit 12-3.

A.   Idea Generation

The **idea generation stage** involves a continuing, open-minded search for product ideas that are consistent with organizational objectives and target market needs.

In a large firm or one dealing in complex products, much of this activity takes place in the R and D department. Sony's DataDiskman came from a technology-driven idea. Yet, "outside" suggestions and ideas should not be ignored. New ideas may come from any source, including consumers and industrial buyers.

Idea generation can be encouraged among employees thinking about products that could solve consumer complaints, make a task easier, or provide new uses for existing products. New ideas may flow from an organization's desire to make fuller use of its manufacturing or distribution facilities, or to utilize byproducts of its main business, as meat packers produce people food, but also dog food from what is left over.

B.   Screening

The **screening stage** involves analysis of new ideas to determine which are reasonable and pertinent to the organization's goals and markets.

Thus, some new ideas may not get past this stage. Concern that too quick a decision will be regretted later has led many organizations to allow marginal ideas to slip past this stage in the process. Balancing costs of more investigation against loss of a viable product idea is a delicate task.

At Procter and Gamble the three questions are carefully answered before new product projects are approved.

- Is there a real consumer need for the product?

- Does the organization have the scientific and technological ability to develop the product?

- Is the potential for such a product large enough to offer some promise of making a profit?

Some marketing research tools are appropriate here (e.g., interviews with customers and salespeople and concept testing).

C.   Business Analysis

A product idea that has survived the screening process enters the **business analysis stage** where it is expanded into a concrete business recommendation. This will include specific listings of product features, resource needs and a basic marketing plan.

Quantitative facts and figures are necessary, including market forecasts and break-even analyses. The business analysis stage is a review of the new product from all significant organizational perspectives. It emphasizes performance criteria and chances for success in the marketplace.

D.   Development

A new product idea that survives the preliminary evaluative stages enters the **product development stage.** Product development must be undertaken with the needs of the buyer or user in mind.

G.E. sends engineers who are developing consumer products into the field to talk directly to prospective buyers. This is a form of research known as **concept testing** -- attempting to learn consumers' reactions to a new product idea.

Consumers are presented with a pictorial or written description of a new product and asked their opinion of the product. Dow Jones developed sample copies of a Wall Street Journal Magazine, but found them to be greeted with little enthusiasm by target readers.

In this stage, concepts become in-hand products. They can then be tested as softdrink makers test new formulations on "real people." Results of such tests may lead to reformulation of the product and additional testing.

Test Marketing

Test marketing is an experimental procedure that permits testing new products in realistic situations. It is scientific testing, not just "trying something out." Good test marketing permits management to estimate the success potential of its product and other aspects of its marketing mix. It also allows the identification and correction of problems. Avoidance of costly mistakes is a prime goal of test marketing.

Test marketing is usually expensive. Distribution, media coverage, monitoring sales, etc. take considerable effort. For products that involve sizable investments, test marketing would seem to be a necessity.

Selecting test market locations is not easy. Sites that are representative of the population must be found. Some popular test market cities are Tulsa, Charlotte, Evansville, Little Rock, Nashville, Omaha, and Spokane.

E.   Commercialization

Commercialization refers to the decision to produce and market a product, to "go for it." Thus, the decision involves great risk and commitment of resources. This is the last chance to stop the project and many are stopped at this stage.

It is easy to find products that should have been "killed" before the commercialization stage. Example:

.   One more properly conducted test could have shown that Dow's spray-on, "Liquid Tire Chain," would freeze in its package, rendering it useless in increasing the traction of tires on cars stuck in ice and snow.

VIII. WHY DO FAILURES OCCUR?

The path to commercialization is long. Failures will occur from time to time. Cajun Cola could not compete regionally against Pepsi and Coke; General Mills cereal Benefit failed because of consumer confusion of just what the "benefit" entailed. The text offers these common reasons for product failure.

.   Inadequate product superiority or uniqueness, as when a "me too" product does not offer a relative advantage.

.   Inadequate or inferior planning, such as failing to do proper marketing research to understand consumers' needs, and failure to develop realistic estimates of demand. Example: Fab 1 Shot detergent-softener packets attracted interest but proved too expensive for many families to continue to buy.

.   Poor execution, which may occur when management believes the product is so good it will succeed without resources to support it. Sometimes the firm may simply lack the expertise necessary to make a product a success.

.   Technical problems, as when a product fails because of design or production problems. For example, Hot Scoops, a microwaveable fudge sundae, turned to goop if the oven wasn't set exactly right.

.   Poor timing, as when a company enters a market too early or too late in the product life cycle, or when the environment changes, e.g. a luxury item introduced just as the economy is taking a downturn.

All new products implicitly require forecasting the future and, quoth the sage, "Forecasts are dangerous, particularly those about the future."

IX. THE ADOPTION AND DIFFUSION PROCESSES

The mental process that individual new product adopters experience in the **adoption process** includes: awareness, interest, evaluation, trial, and adoption. Some pass through these quickly, others take more time.

The **diffusion process** is the spread of a new product or idea through society.

Individuals go through the adoption process. The diffusion process takes place as new products are purchased by various groups of adopters (i.e. product spreads through society).

A.   Innovators -- Being Venturesome

Innovators are the first customers to buy a new product. Their
purchase indicates their willingness to change their established ways
of doing things. They constitute a small group that is willing to
take a chance, and tend to be younger, better off, better educated
and to show confidence in "thinking for themselves." Exhibit 12-4
shows this group to be small in number, but their willingness to try
an unproven product is important.

B.   Early Adopters -- Following the Lead

The **early adopter** is a far larger group that follows the lead of
innovators yet has many of the characteristics of the innovators --
income, self-confidence, education. As the first large group of
adopters, they strongly influence the groups to follow. They are a
common target for promotional efforts because of their "opinion
leader" qualities. In a sense, this group filters out the more "far
out" products and ideas that appeal to the adventurous innovators.

C.   Early and Late Majorities -- Riding the Bandwagon

Taken together, the **early majority** and **late majority** groups
constitute about 68% of the total product adopter group. (See
Exhibit 12-4.) They are the "mass market." The early majority
member is the solid, middle-class consumer. The late majority member
is a bit older, more conservative and traditional. By the time this
group adopts the new product there is no longer any risk associated
with the newness, in fact, people in this group may be "forced" by
social pressure to buy a product that "everyone" has.

D.   Laggards -- Bringing Up the Rear

Laggards are the final adopters who have a use for the product but
who have been slow to accept it. Innovations are not welcome to this
group, which tends to be older, more conservative, and traditional.
Example: members of this group often begin wearing recently new
clothing styles when earlier adopters were already wearing other
clothing.

E.   Nonadopters -- Holding Out

Nonadopters essentially never buy particular new products; thus they
contribute very little to their success. They are worth considering,
however, since they suggest that certain marketing activities would
constitute wasted effort (e.g., advertising a new wine or whiskey in
a magazine for Baptists would seem a waste of resources). It is also
possible that modifying the product or marketing mix could make the
product acceptable to this group.

F.   Use of the Adopter Categories

Planners should pay attention to the diffusion process and the
adoption categories. Characteristics of each group's members suggest
aspects of the marketing mix that might be changed to appeal to them.
The characteristics might also serve as bases of market segmentation.

The adopter categories portrayal shown in Exhibit 12-4 is reminiscent
of the product life cycle because gaining adopters moves the product
through its life cycle stages.

X.   ORGANIZATION FOR NEW PRODUCT DEVELOPMENT

New product development is an important key to long-term organizational
success. Organizations should be structured to permit this development to
occur. Unfortunately, managers (of all specialties) tend to get tied up in
day-to-day problems. Studies of new product introductions show that the
most successful companies introducing new products are the ones that have

given the greatest care to organizing for the development of those products.

Here are some "sample organizations" offered with the understanding that variations and combinations are possible and often desirable depending on individual circumstances.

A.   The Product Manager

In this system, a **product manager** or **brand manager** is responsible for planning and implementing the marketing of a single product or brand. The idea is thus to encourage coordination of effort, and serves to identify an individual who is responsible for what goes on. Product managers are usually assigned to existing products, but some organizations give these managers responsibility for developing new products. Other organizations believe that product managers may be too limited by their experience with a few products to be effective in developing new ones.

B.   The Market Manager

A **market manager** is responsible for administering all marketing activities, from forecasting to sales and follow-up, in a particular market. This is typically defined as a customer group, or industry, or a particular application of the product. For example, a tool might be of use in several industries, but differing marketing mixes might be appropriate to each.

C.   The New Product Manager

The **new product manager** form of organization is most likely to be found in a consumer goods company in which marketing issues, rather than technical problems, are paramount. The new product manager is expected to be a creative sort who understands the problems of new product introduction.

D.   The Venture Team

The **venture team** is made up of specialists from the organization's functional areas who are intended to operate as "new business entrepreneurs." The team works independently to develop the "new business venture" and may, if commercialization is achieved, ultimately be assigned to manage it. This prospect, plus financial bonuses, serves as a reward for team members.

Some believe that the independence of these teams, when genuine, results in more truly new products than other forms of organization.

E.   The New Products Department

Unlike the **venture team**, the new products department is a permanent department, headed by a director or V.P. This assigns an organization officer clear-cut responsibility for new product development. The department may be a large one, or a small one that draws needed expert help from throughout the organization. A developed new product is "turned over" to regular departments once the commercialization stage is reached.

F.   The New Products Committee

A **new products committee** is often made up of the heads of the organization's other departments, often under the chairmanship of the CEO. The new products committee approach is widely used, and frequently used even when other approaches, such as new products departments, are in place. These committees create policy, assign priorities, and ultimately make the decision to commercialize the product. Advocates feel this system puts the weight of its high-ranking membership behind new product ideas.

G.   The Task Force

The **task force** is a group whose membership spans numerous departments within the organization. Its "task" is to see that new projects get the support various departments are able to offer. Task force membership is typically assigned in addition to regular duties, and the group disbanded after project completion.

The task force's appeal lies in its ability to transgress organizational boundaries and in the fact that it forces its members to work together to resolve organizational issues that might block effective product development. Its main disadvantage is the need to find the proper membership for such a group.

H.   Entrepreneurial Enterprises

The term "entrepreneur" refers to someone willing to create something new. "Starting small" and succeeding with innovative products still occurs, as the founders of Apple Computers, who began their work in family garages on weekends have shown. These, and other entrepreneurs, had vision, but not the resources to launch their new products in the way a company such as Procter and Gamble launches theirs. Yet their rewards can be great.

Big corporations do not have a monopoly on creativity.

Most successful entrepreneurs "bend the rules" put forth in this chapter (there is more than one path to success, after all), but they are creatively solving the needs of customers. Some large organizations try to instill this entrepreneurial spirit in their product development process by encouraging individuals to take risks by giving them the autonomy to develop new products as they see fit. Such organizations have been said to be **intrepreneurial**.

XI.   ETHICAL CONSIDERATIONS ASSOCIATED WITH THE INTRODUCTION OF NEW PRODUCTS

From a macromarketing perspective one aspect of introduction of new products is the issue of **product obsolescence**, the fact that the consumer may not have the opportunity to buy the old model. Critics of marketing acknowledge the important contribution of some new products but argue that marketers act unethically when they seek to create **fashion obsolescence** rather than **technological obsolescence**. This point may often be valid, but it disregards the fact that consumers have social and emotional needs, not just functional needs.

Planned obsolescence, the intentional designing of products not to last a long time, can sometimes be defended on the grounds that some buyers prefer to buy a cheap lawn mower for a few hundred dollars rather than an expensive lawn mower for several thousand dollars. This is part of the broader issue of the consumers' **right to choose**. Critics may argue that planned obsolescence violates this right by eliminating old products people may still want or by simply "manipulating" consumers. Others argue that if companies act in such a manner and fail to observe the right to choose, competing companies will take advantage of that and offer consumer's what they "really" want. Indeed, the free enterprise system usually operates in just this manner. Various laws such as the Sherman Act help protect free competition and the right to chose.

XII.   SUMMARY

Products differ in degrees of newness and in their chances of success in the marketplace. Marketers must understand the buyers' views of newness, the diffusion process, and the organization needed to develop and introduce new products.

Learning Objective 1:   Differentiate among degrees of product newness.

Managers and consumers view newness differently. Managers classify newness on the basis on newness to the company and newness to the market. Consumers distinguish products on a newness continuum: (1) discontinuous innovations, which do what no other products do and so require new usage patterns; (2) dynamically continuous innovations, which bring significant product improvements to buyers but do not require major changes in usage behavior; and (3) continuous innovations, which offer minor improvements or variations on previously available products.

Learning Objective 2:   Explain why the chances of success and failure for new products are likely to vary considerably.

The chances for commercial success of a new product are generally low. One study shows 90 percent of all product ideas resulting in failure. Another shows one new product emerging from every 40 new product ideas, though nearly two-thirds of actual product introductions are thought to succeed commercially. In general, the consumer product failure rate is higher than that of organizational goods because the consumer market is more dynamic, and organizational buyers are better able to express their needs to marketing researchers.

Learning Objective 3:   Identify general product characteristics of successful new products.

Five characteristics influence a new product's chances for success. Relative advantage is a clear-cut improvement over existing products. Compatibility is the product's ability to fit in with existing consumption and usage patterns. Trialability permits buyers to test the new product with little effort or risk. Observability allows the buyer to see and understand the product's advantages over existing products. Product simplicity (rather than complexity) allows the consumer to understand and operate the product.

Learning Objective 4:   Characterize the stages of new product development.

The new product development process involves five processes: (1) idea generation, the search for a new idea; (2) screening, the evaluation of an idea's suitability to the organization and target markets; (3) business analysis, the detailed study and testing of the new idea; (4) development, the construction and testing of the actual product; and (5) commercialization, the full-scale production and marketing of the new product.

Learning Objective 5:   Identify some of the most common reasons for new product failure.

The marketplace is very dynamic and most new products fail. Some of the most common reasons for failure are inadequate product superiority, inferior planning, poor execution, technical problems, and poor timing.

Learning Objective 6:   Describe the new product diffusion process and list the groups of adopters to which marketers must direct their appeals.

Not all buyers adopt a new product at the same time. The path is blazed by innovators, followed by early adopters, members of the early and late majorities, and, finally, the laggards. Members of the first groups tend to be younger, more adventurous, better educated, and wealthier than members of the latter groups. Each group has characteristics of its own and concerns that the marketer must address.

Learning Objective 7: **Point out the advantages of various organizational forms associated with the successful development and introduction of new products.**

The product manager system assigns the management of a product to one individual who is expected to coordinate all aspects of the marketing process and evaluate the new product's chances for success. The new product manager system, in contrast, emphasizes new products, although the responsibility still rests with one person's hands. Market managers administer all marketing activities related to a market. Under the venture team approach, specialists from several areas in the organization operate as entrepreneurs supporting a new product in the system. Some organizations assign product development to a specialized new products department; others set up new products committees composed of influential persons who can support the effort. The task force approach leads to the creation of a group charged with giving its full attention to the new product from start to finish.

Learning Objective 8: **Identify some ethical questions about the marketing of new products.**

Some people question whether so many new products are needed in our society. The issue of whether product obsolescence, and especially planned obsolescence, is ethical is part of this broader issue dealing with the consumer's right to choose. Physical obsolescence, fashion obsolescence, and technological obsolescence are all factors in this debate.

XIII. KEY TERMS

XIV. QUESTIONS FOR DISCUSSION (9)

XV. ETHICS IN PRACTICE

XVI. CASES

ANSWER GUIDELINES TO CHAPTER 12 QUESTIONS FOR DISCUSSION

1. *What is your definition of a new product?*

ANSWER:

Students may be tempted to answer this question with just about any response, then say that what was asked was, after all, "your definition." This possibility aside, the following approach to this question would seem appropriate.

The chapter shows that there are degrees of newness. Though the inventor of a cure for cancer might receive more favorable notice by historians than the inventor of "Stick-Ups" deodorizer, both inventions can be seen as "new" in one way or another.

From a marketer's point of view, newness is likely to be viewed in terms of newness to the organization and, more importantly, newness to the market. Since a product is defined, in light of the marketing concept philosophy of business, as a bundle of benefits, a new product can be defined as a new bundle of benefits. That is, it is a product that provides a benefit that no previous product provided before.

What then, is a benefit? Is it a lemon scent in a detergent, a strawberry scent in bubble bath, a longer-lived bulldozer blade, or a safer airport radar system? It is all these things if the consumers or buyers of these products see them as providing benefits beyond those already found in existing products.

2. *Classify the type of innovation associated with the following products:*
    (a) A digital safe that uses an LED display and a six-digit computer code,
    (b) A hand checker that consists of a magnetically coded card plus electronic sensors to check hand geometry in order to verify absolute identity for banks and classified areas; card coding and prerecorded hand

data are checked in seconds, (c) A new aerodynamically designed car that has a low-wind-resistance, wedge-shaped body.

ANSWER:

Though other classification schemes could be used, this question can be most easily answered in terms of this scheme:

.   Discontinuous Innovation -- a pioneering product so new that no previous product performs an equivalent function. Some examples would be the first TV, the first automobile, the first "perfected" artificial heart. These do what was not done before and are so new that they alter human behavior patterns. (Students may need explanations about what life was like before TV, but TV is a good example, as are cars, planes, and bicycles.)

.   Dynamically Continuous Innovation -- a product toward the middle of the innovation continuum, between the discontinuous innovation and the "new, improved" version of an old product. These new products represent changes and improvements that do not strikingly change buying and usage patterns. Some examples might include the "perfected" electric car, an appealing product to most but one that will not greatly alter driving behaviors. Similarly, the typewriter radically altered business and then in-home and school behaviors, but the electric typewriter did not effect such changes.

.   Continuous Innovation -- an on-going, commonplace change such as a minor alteration of a product or the introduction of an imitative product. Caffeine-free Coke is "new" in this sense.

Since there is a newness continuum, it is difficult to place all inventions into just three categories, but such an attempt would probably yield the following results.

(a)   The digital safe

If we assume that the digital safe represents some improvement over old-fashioned tumbler locks (for the owner, not for the safe-cracker) the invention could be placed in the middle category, the dynamically continuous innovation category, since there is a change and an improvement, but no radical altering of behaviors.

(b)   The hand checker security device

Wondrous though this is, this product fails (to at least some degree) the "altering of behaviors" test. As such, we would place it in the dynamically continuous innovation category.

However, since the device greatly speeds up an existing process, it would appear to be more highly placed than the digital safe on the continuum of newness.

(c)   Aerodynamically designed, wedge-shaped car

Unless this design is assumed to be something near "perfection," it could be viewed as a low-end dynamically continuous or even a simple continuous innovation. Students should know that wind resistance has been fought by car designers for decades. In the forties and fifties, some cars (e.g., Nash products) were egg-shaped (when viewed from above) to reduce wind resistance. More recently, the Triumph offered the market a wedge-shaped car ("The shape of things to come," but it "went" soon after it appeared.).

Again, if this new design is taken to be the "ultimate" design, it might be placed in the dynamically continuous category. If, for example, it is an otherwise normal car but gets 100 or more miles per gallon, it may well belong in that category. If it is but a small improvement, it moves down the continuum toward the continuous innovation category.

3.   *For the products in Questions 2, identify salient product features that might speed the acceptance of these innovations.*

ANSWER:

(a)   Digital safe

.   Probably the six-digit code can be changed frequently and easily by a non-locksmith.

.   Technological improvements may make it harder for safecrackers to open the safe though, in fact, thieves seem to adapt quickly to such improvements.

.   The safe is compatible with existing usages of safes.

.   Its advantages are easy to observe.

.   It is not, it appears, difficult to work or to understand.

.   The safe fits modern concerns about security.

(b)   The hand checker security device

.   It will demonstrably speed up security checks. This advantage is easy to observe.

.   The machine's workings may be difficult to understand but its results are easily comprehended.

.   The product is compatible with existing behaviors, i.e., security checks are now being made.

.   The product fits modern concerns about security.

.   The identification of persons seems as nearly foolproof as these things can be.

.   The system lends itself to the "cashless society" we hear so much about.

(c)   The wedge-shaped car

.   The product fits current concerns over fuel consumption and the environment (better efficiency - cleaner air).

.   The shape is immediately observable as "different."

.   The fuel efficiency performance, if valid, is easily observed and understood.

.   The car is compatible with normal car usage.

.   The distinctive shape can be a relative advantage if having such a car is a "chic" thing.

4.   *Identify the steps in the new product development process.*

ANSWER:

The steps in the process are:

.   Exploration
.   Screening
.   Business Analysis
.   Development
.   Commercialization

Using the Kodak disc camera as an example, Kodak:

Explored as it tried to design a camera that would take good pictures in a wide variety of circumstances by adding features to roll-type cameras. These proved to be just more things that could go wrong. The Instamatic was one result of the exploration.

Screened as it considered 64 different cameras in a battery of 14 tests, narrowing down alternatives.

Performed Business Analysis when it did a major market research study to see if the new camera's benefits were enough to motivate sufficient sales.

Did Product Development by putting the camera into more than 1,000 U.S. homes, and performed the related studies.

Commercialized the product by the "real test" method ... going to the marketplace where, it was discovered, actual sales far exceeded the most optimistic predictions.

5.   *What takes place in the business analysis stage of product development?*

ANSWER:

The business analysis stage marks a shift in the development of a product away from the technical and qualitative to the financial and quantitative. Break-even analysis, recommendations of specific product features necessary for market success, specific written marketing plans, and inventories of needed resources are undertaken at this time. Formal sales forecasts and buyer research studies are also done.

The product undergoes a transformation from a "concept" to a concrete prototype that can be shown to target customers, discussed with them, and perhaps tried by them.

In short, the business analysis is a review of the new product from all significant perspectives, emphasizing practical applications and chances for success in the marketplace.

6.   *What are the main reasons why new products fail?*

ANSWER:

Transparency 12-8 outlines five basic reasons for new product failure, including: inadequate product superiority or uniqueness; inadequate or inferior planning; poor execution; technical problems and poor timing. In addition, firms may rush to failure through over optimistic projections of potential or through neglecting quality control in developmental stages of a project. To reinforce concepts covered early in the course, new product failures occur due to inadequate research, planning, implementation or control of marketing functions. Managers may fail to understand consumer targets, distribution requirements or competitive reactions. The best of plans may not be implemented properly or early problems may not be corrected due to faulty control procedures.

7.   *What are the benefits and limitations of test marketing?*

ANSWER:

Test marketing permits the marketing organization to investigate its product's performance in a more-or-less real-world setting. It is, in effect, a large-scale experiment. It gives the organization a chance to test its product's market acceptance but also to test the attractiveness of various price levels, the success of various promotions, and the effectiveness of distribution methods. It should be stressed that the test market is not only a product test.

Test marketing has several possible disadvantages. Some organizations eschew test marketing because the products they sell are easily copied by competitors. Some products are so expensive to develop and manufacture that marketers do not test market them. Consider, for example, a new magazine or a new kind of executive jet plane. Such products cost so much to develop that, having sunk millions of dollars into them, the developers would not care to "trust" a go/no-

go decision to a test market. Products not associated with short repurchase
cycles do not lend themselves to test marketing. That is, products not bought
frequently would require very long test marketing periods.

Test marketing is based on the assumption that locales have been found that
reflect the nature of the market as a whole. While careful selection of test
sites can lessen the risk that the test market does not reflect the market as a
whole, the risks associated with such an assumption are clear.

In short, test marketing can provide the best sort of information but test
markets can be risky, difficult to operate and control, expensive, and ... even
when considerable effort is expended ... inconclusive or even "wrong."

8.   *What are the most prominent characteristics of each adopter group in the
      diffusion process?*

ANSWER:

These characteristics are outlined in Transparency 12-10 and consist of the
following descriptions:

Innovators are first to buy new products and typically described as venturesome,
educated, financially stable and willing to take risks.

Early Adopters are local opinion leaders who read magazines and integrate the
social system more than average consumers. This group is a key target for new
product developers.

Early Majority members are typically the solid, middle-class consumers who are
more deliberate and cautious in purchase decisions than early adopters.

Late Majority members are similar to their earlier counterparts but these
consumers are described as older, more conservative, traditional and skeptical of
new products.

Laggards are the last group to adopt a new product. These consumers resist
challenges to tradition, remain oriented toward the past, and may be older as
well as lower in socioeconomic status than other groups.

Nonadopters are consumers who never buy the new product or adopt the new style.

While some people are "laggards" in adopting any new idea or product, most vary
in their adopter classification based on the product category. For example,
college students may be innovators for music, clothing or bungee jumping while
these same students may be in the late majority for lap-top computers.

9.   *Can a new product manager do anything to speed up the diffusion process?*

ANSWER:

To the extent that the product fits the time within a culture, a product manager
can take several steps to assist in the diffusion process.

Transparency 12-4 outlines five characteristics for new product success. Thus,
product managers can formulate promotion strategies or themes to enhance consumer
perceptions of relative advantage over existing options and compatibility with
existing consumption patterns. Product managers can also enhance trialability
and observability through sales promotions, demonstrations or free samples. If
the new product is complex, product managers can enhance the chances of success
through extensive service and education.

From an organizational perspective, product managers must coordinate functions
throughout the company. Thus, these managers must network with key decision
makers in production, engineering, distribution, advertising and sales functions
throughout the company. To the extent the product manager can successfully
integrate ideas from disparate personnel, the manager can possibly speed the
developmental steps for commercialization as well.

ETHICS EXERCISE 12

CHAPTER 12 ETHICS IN PRACTICE

Overview

Gallo Winery, Mogen David, and other marketers of alcoholic beverages have repeatedly come under fire from community and church groups and from legislators for inappropriately targeting vulnerable groups such as alcoholics and underage drinkers. In a similar case in 1989, Gallo was accused of marketing cheap wines such as Thunderbird and Night Train in skid-row districts. In that case, Gallo did discontinue selling those brands in grocery stores, bars, and other outlets in skid-row areas across the United States. But Gallo denied that wines are the source of the trouble, maintaining that the trouble stems from law enforcement agencies that don't enforce existing laws banning sales to habitual alcoholics and obviously drunk party-goers. A Gallo spokesperson said that "history shows that if alcoholics are deprived of one source of alcohol, they will simply find another, regardless of difficulty or cost." And, they continued to market the products in other areas.

In general, the advertising and marketing of alcoholic beverages has been controversial, and there have been many consumer and legislative efforts to restrict or ban the advertising of distilled spirits, wine, and beer. The arguments against alcoholic beverage advertising are somewhat similar to those against cigarette advertising: it seduces susceptible people, glamorizes the activity, and increases consumption as well as abuse of the product.
The alcohol industry responds that the problem of alcohol marketing having an adverse impact on people is nonexistent. It likes to point out that there is a difference between alcohol and drugs like crack, cocaine, and heroin, and that these products should therefore be treated differently. (Note the comparison in the Cisco case to "liquid crack.") The industry points out that it does moderation advertising (the "Don't drink and drive" and "Know when to say when" types of messages). It denies advertising to children (this was an especially tough sell during the Bud Light Spuds MacKenzie campaign) and says that since alcohol is a legal product, there should be a right to promote it; to ban or severely curtail such advertising would be to infringe the advertisers' First Amendment rights to free commercial speech.

These same defenses are used by the tobacco industry. It is debatable whether advertising is a powerful enough force to get kids hooked on drinking -- peer and parental influences, since they are interpersonal, are probably much more influential. Much of the advertising does feature young people and does suggest that drinking will greatly enhance the quality of your life.

Concerning Cisco, there is a legitimate case to be made that teenagers are being deceived, whether or not this is intentional on the part of the marketers. Deception occurs when a false impression is created. Eight out of fifteen victims of acute alcohol poisonings claimed they thought Cisco was a wine cooler, not a highly potent alcoholic beverage.

It could very well be the case that Canadaigua was taking advantage of a psychological principle known as stimulus generalization: people respond similarly to similar things. This explains the popularity of "package knockoffs," i.e., packaging of also-ran brands which strongly resembles leading brands. (For example, compare private label packaging with national brand packaging.) People will reason that what's inside of the look-alike package must be about as good as what's in the well-known package. Hence, Cisco's familiar packaging might entice wine cooler drinkers to give it a try. The sweet taste of the product easily masks the product's potency.

Sand's reaction in this case seems neither moral nor strategically wise, just defensive and arrogant. He could have pointed out that, as in the Gallo case, law enforcement agencies are failing to enforce the laws (in this case against selling to underage drinkers). However, the possibility exists that adults will also be deceived by the package and consume more alcohol than they desire. While Sands might indeed have a case that alcohol marketing doesn't cause teen drinking, in this case if youngsters are actually consuming stronger alcohol than they think they are due to the packaging similarities, Cisco is certainly contributing to the problem. A socially responsible marketer would admit that

Novello has a point, apologize for unintended consequences, and temporarily withdraw the product until it can be repackaged and clearly relabeled as to the product's potency.

CHAPTER 12 TAKE A STAND QUESTIONS

1. *What arguments are given by critics who say product innovations replace perfectly good products currently in the marketplace?*

Nicolo Machiavelli is well known for having said: "There is nothing more difficult to take in hand, or more uncertain of success, than to take the lead in the introduction of a new order of things. For the initiator has the enmity of all who would profit from the preservation of the old institutions and merely the lukewarm defenders in those who would gain by new ones." Within the organization new products meet with resistance; new products people are the change agents of bureaucratic organizations, the inherent function of which is to promote stability and certainty, not change and uncertainty. New products are inherently risky, and most firms promote risk aversion, preferring to be safe, not sorry. All new ideas are threats to the established order of things.

Further, there are critics of new products outside the organization. It is said that the only people who like a change are babies. Consumers too prefer the tried and true (innovators and perhaps early adopters being the exception). Early drivers of cars were admonished to "get a horse" and the Wright brothers were taunted that if "God wanted man to fly He would have given him wings."

Crawford, in *New Products Management*, notes that there are several reasons for resistance to innovation. People desire to perpetuate a general lifestyle or way of doing things. Additionally, change often costs money (e.g., replacing record albums with CDs). And, sometimes there is the desire to hold onto something worthwhile that appears to be threatened by innovation such as social status, a job, or a pleasant way of life.

People in such situations honestly feel that the negatives of innovations outweigh the positives. They might eventually accept new products, but only reluctantly, after many people already have adopted them. Their reaction to new technologies is one of feeling overwhelmed, confused, and full of angst.

Also, there is often a "double-edged" nature to new technology. The same device that increases the number of kilowatts of electricity produced by a ton of coal might also have negative side effects such as creating a pollution hazard or generating dangerous radiation.

On the other hand, it is often argued that innovation enhances our quality of life, and therefore society should be motivated to stimulate innovation. Haven't we benefited from microwave ovens? Personal portable stereos? What about new drugs? The problem is that there will be differences among people in defining "quality of life." There will always be some excess, and one person's excess is another person's dream product.

It might be interesting to ask class members what criteria they use to judge "quality of life." Would they be willing to do without certain recent innovations as CD players, bite-size cookies, AZT, etc.? Has innovation in their lifetime raised or lowered the quality of life?

2. *Pet owners complain that a flea and tick spray is making their dogs sick. Should the marketer take the new product off the market?*

The issue is one of product safety. Whisking the product off the market would probably be premature. It would behoove the firm to first investigate the nature and extent of the complaints. Do the problems occur only for certain breeds of dogs? Only in certain climates or locations? Is the product somehow being misused by some consumers? If the problem is a relatively isolated one, a prominent warning on the package and in the promotions might suffice. If the product is somehow being misused, education is in order. However, if the problem is widespread, a product withdrawal and recall would probably be recommended. Utilitarian calculations could come into play here. Are there good substitutes on the market for those consumers who aren't experiencing problems with the product? Will the firm likely be liable to product liability suits, whether justified or not? Will the Consumer Product Safety Commission step in and force a recall or ban, resulting in negative media coverage?

3.   *A pajama manufacturer develops a new fire-resistant chemical that will not wash out of children's pajamas until they have been washed more than a hundred times. Should this product be marketed as fire resistant?*

Information is needed on how many times most children's pajamas are washed. Given that most children grow rapidly and own several pairs of pajamas, it is probably reasonable to conclude that very few will wear them more than 100 times, and so labeling the PJs as "fire resistant" will be truthful. Research should confirm this, however. It might be wise and more truthful for the company to add some kind of a disclaimer warning that fire resistance is only good for 100 washes, which on average is x months. The latter is easier for consumers to track than the number of washings. If some children do wear their pajamas more than a hundred times, then it would be misleading to label them as fire resistant. It would be socially responsible for the firm to either use the chemical but not tout its fire resistant properties, or use another chemical which doesn't wash out.

4.   *A tampon manufacturer, after it developed and marketed a super absorbent product, learned that the product was related to a serious disease. It withdrew the product from the market when controversy occurred. Should the company be liable for damages?*

This scenario briefly describes the Procter & Gamble Rely tampon case over a decade ago. The Rely tampon was made of new super-absorbent fibers that were supposedly able to absorb seventeen times their own weight in fluid. After test marketing, Rely was introduced in 1979. However, in June of 1980 P&G was made aware of the results of a preliminary study by the Center for Disease Control (CDC) which found that the use of tampons increased the risk of developing a rare disease called toxic-shock syndrome, an acute illness whose signs and symptoms include fever, rash, and hypertension. The CDC alleged that tampons might act as a breeding ground or a carrier of bacteria into the vagina. The bacteria cause high fever, vomiting, diarrhea, and skin disorders, followed by shock. The CDC concluded that there was a statistical correlation between the use of tampons and TSS, but the incidence was too low to warn women to stop using tampons. It also found no link between TSS and any specific brand of tampon.

However, after continued study, the CDC did find cases linking the Rely tampon to TSS during July and August 1980, and CDC announced this in September. In the meantime, P&G conducted its own studies and found no link between Rely and TSS. The September announcement by the CDC brought about various meetings between P&G, CDC officials, and Food and Drug Administration (FDA) officials. When the meetings started, P&G had worked up a warning statement that it was willing to put on the Rely package. However, the FDA wanted complete withdrawal of the product. On September 22, P&G announced that it was withdrawing Rely from the market. The next day the FDA and P&G drafted a consent agreement, in which P&G didn't have to declare the product unsafe or defective, and in fact stated that they had no evidence that it was, though the company agreed to withdraw the product from the market. The motivation for this was in part P&G's fear of being forced by the FDA into an expensive and very visible product recall. The FDA also got P&G to run a big advertising campaign warning women not to use Rely and educating people about toxic shock. The agreement also called upon P&G to buy back any Rely tampons that consumers still had, including those given away as free samples. A public opinion survey conducted after the withdrawal found that the public gave P&G high marks for its quick action, although a number of product liability claims against P&G resulted in the award of damages to claimants.

Did P&G do the morally right thing? It showed concern by conducting its own studies and being willing to issue a warning statement, although we don't know whether the motivation was to protect the company's interests or whether it truly cared about the victims of TSS. In P&G's behalf, it could be argued that the evidence linking Rely and TSS was weak. Nonetheless, the suspicion of a linkage was there. Whether P&G was unwilling to issue a recall because it was truly convinced the product didn't cause TSS or because it wanted to avoid the expense and negative publicity remains unknown.

Should P&G be held liable for damages? Prior to the 1960s product liability legislation in the U.S. was based on the concept of negligence rooted in contract law. Under this concept, liability results if the harm to the consumer was a reasonably foreseeable outcome of the marketer's behavior, i.e., if the manufacturer didn't take proper precautions in production, testing and providing warnings and instructions. Under this standard it is probably reasonable to argue that the TSS problem was not foreseeable, and to note that once P&G learned of the problem they were willing to affix a warning statement to the product.

Today the doctrine of strict (or absolute) liability prevails. This says that a company is liable for damages caused by its product even if the manufacturer couldn't have foreseen the injury. In effect, the manufacturer isn't culpable but must pay damages. Some people say this is wrong since the producer wasn't behaving unethically and since consumers must assume risk when trying new products. In this case P&G might have two possible defenses against strict liability claims: (1) assumption of risk -- if certain buyers learned about TSS and continued to use the product, P&G wouldn't be liable in those cases; (2) product not defective -- P&G could argue that the evidence that Rely causes TSS isn't conclusive.

5.   *According to **New Product News**, marketers introduced 13,244 new products in 1990, including 31 baby foods, 123 breakfast cereals, and 1,143 beverages. Does society need all these new products?*

Many of the points made in question 1 above apply here. Additionally, it should be noted that in food, drug, and health and beauty aids (which most of these new products are), many products are either product line extensions (new sizes, colors, flavors, scents, quality levels, etc. of existing products) and improvements/revisions to existing products. Line extensions were discussed in Take A Stand question 1 in chapter 11.

This leaves us with "new and improved" products. These next-generation products (e.g., "Maximum Strength This," "Advanced Formula That," and "The Other Plus") are sometimes reformulated into superior performance versions, especially if enhanced technology is used. Most are discernibly different in some way, although there is always the problem that some customers preferred the tried and true version. New Coke is a prime example of this.

Also, some differences are said to be superfluous or insignificant. However, the marketplace will soon tell us whether or not this is the case. In highly competitive industries (e.g., food and drugs) where actual performance differences between competing brands are small, companies often tout tiny incremental advantages to keep their brands' images fresh. Thus, Downy offered "More April Freshness" and Pledge offered an "Improved Self-Cleaning Formula." Are automakers' small annual cosmetic changes necessary? Perhaps not, but some buyers seem to look forward to them. In all cases, some sort of psychological value is being added.

GUIDE TO CASES

VIDEO CASE 12-1 CRYSTAL PEPSI

SUBJECT MATTER: Brand Names, Characteristics of Good Brand Names, Protection of Brand Names

Please see the Guide to Video Cases for video length and other information.

AT-A-GLANCE OVERVIEW

As a result of environmental scanning, the Pepsi Cola company recognized a growing preference for light tasting soft drinks and colorless drinks, such as mineral water. Recognition of this trend lead to testing All Sport, an isotonic, lightly carbonated sports drink, and H2Oh!, a sparkling water. In addition to these two products, Pepsi has created a clear cola, a 100 percent natural drink with a unique taste. After two years of research and development in its laboratories in Sommers, New York, and in the field with consumers, Crystal Pepsi was created. Crystal Pepsi is a low sodium, caffeine free soft drink with an intense cola flavor, but it is colorless. Pepsi hopes it will usher in a new era and that Crystal Pepsi will be the first in a new beverage category of the 90s.

Industry observers have noted that regular colas are dark brown only because bottlers has added caramel coloring and that without the caramel coloring, Crystal Pepsi is likely to be perceived by consumers as "healthier" than regular colas. However, it's doubtful that health claims would be made for Crystal Pepsi because this could reflect negatively on Pepsi and Diet Pepsi. In addition, there is an unspoken rule that soda makers not make health claims because such claims simply point out that the products are, in general, not really "good for you." When 7-Up began emphasizing that it is caffeine free, this was considered a serious breech of etiquette by other soda makers. Yet, observers believe that without health claims, the product (Crystal Pepsi) will not be perceived to be substantially different from regular colas.

Furthermore, sales of Crystal Pepsi may cannibalize sales away from other Pepsi brands.[1]

In 1992, Crystal Pepsi was introduced in test markets. Rumors suggest that Coca Cola may be researching the possibility of a colorless version of Tab diet cola.

DISCUSSION QUESTIONS

1.   *Why would Pepsico wish to introduce a product that could take sales away from Pepsi soft drink.*

As a result of environmental scanning, the Pepsi Cola company recognized a growing preference for light tasting soft drinks and colorless drinks. Pepsi recognizes that colas are but one product category in the soft drink product class. Furthermore, soft drinks are just one form of beverage. Pepsi, a company that markets many beverages, recognizes that many of its own brands compete with each other. The company, by introducing Crystal Pepsi to test markets, realizes that if it does not "compete with itself" other competitors may introduce a similar product, beating Pepsi to a potentially important market segment.

In effect, Crystal Pepsi is a product line extension. Students should be reminded that line extensions are additions to existing product lines that supplement the basic items in an established product line. Enhanced models, cost reduction models, and variations in color, flavor, and design are line extensions.

The company knows that all products and brands have life cycles. It sees Crystal Pepsi as a possible "flavor" alternative to other colas.

2.   *Outline the stages in the new product development process for Crystal Pepsi.*

The text indicates the stages are: idea generation, screening, business analysis, development, and commercialization. Neither the case nor the video go into much detail about idea generation except to say that marketing opportunity analysis spotted a trend. The case mentions that other ideas, All Sport, an isotonic, lightly carbonated sports drink, and H2Oh!, a sparkling water, passed through screening. It does not mention ideas that were screened out. The professor might mention Pepsi Strawberry Burst and Pepsi Raging Raspberry as two alternative cola flavors that were considered. Business analysis would indicate that even a 1% share of the soft drink market could be attractive. The video focuses on development, both in the laboratory and in testing the flavor concepts.

The video shows that Pepsico used extensive research in the development of Crystal Pepsi. It shows that the consumer helped guide the process. Pepsi used surveys and focus groups to learn that consumers wanted a lighter and more refreshing drink. The researchers showed the "concept" to consumers, who

[1]Alison Fahey, "Pepsi Faces Cloudy Future for Clear Cola," *Advertising Age*, December 2, 1991, p. 48.

indicated that it should ideally be slightly less sweet, but have the same cola intensity.

Pepsi used 3,000 prototypes (or different product formulations) before they got just the right flavor and crystal clear look. The soda was then put into test market in Colorado and Rhode Island rather than being directly commercialized.

3. *Would it be better for Pepsi to use a name other than Crystal Pepsi?*

As mentioned above, Crystal Pepsi is a product line extension, a variation in color and flavor. This new product is family branded. The Pepsi part of the name connects the new product to an established well-known company. The Crystal part of the name suggests the colorless nature of the product as well as connoting something special as a "crystal" and clean as in "crystal clear." Its research suggested what consumers want, and the name seems to reflect those desires.

4. *Do you think Crystal Pepsi will be a new product success? How would you judge a success or a failure?*

Students will have various opinions. Many will think of the concept as odd. Others will say they like products like Clearly Canadian and think there is a market for the new brand. Some students from Colorado or Rhode Island, where the product was test marketed, may know that initially Crystal Pepsi was a big enough hit to register out-of-stock situations in some markets.

The five characteristics that influence a new product's chances for success in the marketplace are relative advantage, compatibility with existing consumption patterns, trialability, observability, and complexity. The discussion can focus on how Crystal Pepsi meets these criteria. For example, it can be asked whether Crystal Pepsi has adequate product uniqueness. Is it only a "me too" product imitating colas that are already on the market or does it offer the consumer a relative advantage?

However, the professor should stress that the reason for test marketing is to answer the above question. There is so much money at stake that this cannot be an intuitive judgment. As of 1992, Crystal Pepsi was doing well in test markets. However, the enormous amount of publicity and the "bootlegging" of the product by out-of-state visitors who brought some home for their friends had some impact on sales.

CASE 12-2 INTERSOURCE TECHNOLOGIES - E-LAMP[2]

SUBJECT MATTER: New Products, Marketing New Products, Product Adoption Process, New Product Development Process

AT-A-GLANCE OVERVIEW

The E-Lamp, a light-bulb with a life expectancy of 15,000 to 20,000 hours, uses a new technology combining gas and electronics to produce light. In addition to its longer life, it is expected to save enormous amounts of money. Its life span, at four hours a day, will be 10 to 14 years compared to 6 months for an incandescent bulb. A conventional bulb uses 100 watts, but the E-Lamp uses only 25 watts. The bulb doesn't burn out, it dims over time. The cost to operate is .64 cents per four hours whereas the conventional bulb costs 2.6 cents for four hours. Announcement of the bulb by Pierre Villere of Intersource Technologies has led to such a wild response that Villere says "It's pandemonium in here."

The retail price of a conventional incandescent bulb is approximately $2.00 but the E-Lamp will cost between $10 and $20. There are 1.5 billion light sockets in the U.S. and everybody understands how they work. The product looks like it will be a landslide success, but Villere made hundreds of presentations to potential financial backers without receiving any investment. Though development involved a few product glitches these have been all cleared up now, and the dust from the

---

[2]Excerpts reprinted from Kevin Maney, "Technology Helps Build a Better Bulb," *USAToday*, June 8, 1992, B-1 - B2.

publicity stampede is settling. Villere wants to raise another $50 million, in addition to the $6.5 million he raised earlier, to bring the product to market. He is organizing manufacturing activities, and plans to "build a business around E-Lamp." He knows that getting customers to buy a $15 light bulb is his hardest task and is consulting with power companies for help in this area.

DISCUSSION QUESTIONS

1.   *What type of new product is the E-Lamp?*

The E-Lamp is clearly not a totally revolutionary product. It is better than old-style bulbs, but still performs basically the same function and is used in the same way. It fits existing lamps. (Can you imagine the tough task of selling a $15-20 bulb if all the lights had to be rewired to accept the bulb?) At the same time it is not a simple improvement over existing bulbs. It utilizes new technology and its performance far exceeds that of existing products. Thus, since it is a true product improvement but not a revolutionary, lifestyle-changing product, it falls in the middle of the continuum of newness. It is a "dynamically continuous innovation," analogous to the color TV and electric typewriter.

2.   *What theories about consumer behavior would be useful to Intersource Technologies in developing a marketing strategy for the E-Lamp light bulbs?*

The new product adopter categories come immediately to mind. What sorts of people would be likely new adopters of this product? They would be willing to take a risk and spend $20. What sort of person would that be? Possibly younger and better-educated as the text suggests, but in this case we might add that such a person is likely to be technically and/or scientifically-oriented. Readers of popular science magazines who feel they understand the product would be most likely to fall into the innovator and early adopter categories. Also, these people may have friends of the same type who "support" (probably at a low level in the case of a bulb) the purchase of new products. Environmentally conscious people, supported by their reference groups, would favor the bulb.

A fairly recent theory of consumer behavior divides groups of consumers into "dogmatics" and "non-dogmatics." Dogmatics think they know what they want or how things are supposed to be. Non-dogmatics are not hidebound in their beliefs and practices but are willing to consider new information and make their own decisions. Non-dogmatics are what we are after here. Fortunately, as information seekers, they probably read the newspapers and know about the wonders of this bulb.

Theories about how the nature of the product itself might affect adoption are worth considering, especially since they favor this product. Products that are trialable, have observable advantages, fit in with current practices, etc. are thought to have the best chances for success. The E-Lamp, when you come right down to it, is a light bulb. Everyone understands light bulbs and how to use them. This bulb is used identically to the old bulbs yet has easy to understand advantages. Also, some of its payoffs (lower electric bills) are easy to observe. Its long life is not quite so easy to observe since it takes years to realize that the bulb has been in place for a long time, but the payoff is still there.

Price-related theories could be considered too, though these are discussed later in the text. One such theory addresses the problem of the effect of price on a consumer when another, more highly priced substitute item is close by. That is, will you buy a $20 bulb when a $2 is on the next shelf? You have to know something, or be willing to take chances, or be offered a strong guarantee to want the $20 bulb in such a setting.

All this suggests that the E-Lamp would benefit from publicity, testimony from scientists, the recommendation of the power companies, a guarantee from the maker, and other risk-reducing efforts.

Incidentally, one risk is dropping the $20 bulb. How can this be addressed? Return the broken bulb for a new one? Is that reasonable? The reason we mention this is that when the E-Lamp first got publicity, cartoons showing purchasers crying because the bought the bulb and took it home and dropped it appeared here and there. Of course, the price is the "big problem" here, but price is expected to fall as the bulb gains acceptance and production runs become longer and more efficient.

3. *What risks face the adopters of the E-Lamp? How might they be overcome?*

As mentioned in answer 2, the central risk is price related. Twenty dollars for a light bulb is pretty steep, ten or more times the price of current bulbs. There are plenty of risks associated with new products that are not present here, however. The product would not engender the disdain of others. There would be no sneering comments made about a light bulb choice.

The risk related to price should be addressed by offering proof that the product does what it claimed. Since the product must be used before it can be "proved," the proof should be in the form of expert testimonial and manufacturer's warranties.

We might note that many buyers would be willing to try one or two bulbs for those hard-to-reach lights. Almost everyone we talked to mentioned that they would like to have "one of those for the light way up on the wall in the family room." Thus, a coupon strategy comes to mind. A coupon or certificate good for one-half off the bulb (limited time frame) or an offer to send a certificate good for one bulb when proof of purchase is mailed in, might do the job.

4. *Describe the new product development process for E-Lamp up to June 1992? What further steps need to be taken to market this new product?*

This product was developed, as are virtually all new products, in a five-step process: exploration, screening, business analysis, development, commercialization. In this real-world case the process was a bit more disjointed than in a "textbook example" and involved many people and groups other than "the organization." The story is treated fully in this long case.

The case also shows that the stages are sometimes subject to "gut reaction" rather than logical progression from stage to stage. Things were stalled until Pierre Villere "fortunately" had a heart attack, somehow found out about Don Pezzolo, went to California, was "flabbergasted," and pushed a concept that had not been sufficiently pushed before. There is more serendipity in this story than a textbook's five stages of product development can show.

The product, at this writing, is poised for commercialization. It has been introduced to the (news-aware) public as a proven product about to become available. Villere is trying to raise the money necessary to have the product produced and marketed. It is ready to "go commercial."

13 THE MARKETING OF QUALITY SERVICES

CHAPTER SCAN

This chapter describes marketing in the increasingly important service sector of the economy, discussing it in terms of both the profit seeking and not-for-profit organization. "Service" is defined and its basic characteristics discussed. The service marketing strategies of demand management, standardization, and customization are treated.

The chapter also describes classification of services and discusses the need for marketing activities in the not-for-profit area.

SUGGESTED LEARNING OBJECTIVES

The student who studies this chapter will be exposed to a broad treatment of marketing services by profit and not-for-profit organizations and will be able to:

1. Define "service" in its technical, specific sense.

2. Explain the four basic characteristics of services.

3. Understand demand management strategies.

4. Describe the strategies of standardization and customization.

5. Name some of the variables used to classify services.

6. Discuss the need for marketing in the not-for-profit area.

CHAPTER OUTLINE

I. INTRODUCTION

II. WHAT IS A SERVICE?

III.   THE CHARACTERISTICS OF SERVICES

    A.   Intangibility
    B.   Perishability
    C.   Inseparability
    D.   Heterogeneity

        1.   The Strategy of Standardization
        2.   The Strategy of Customization

IV.   THE SERVICE ENCOUNTER

V.   THE MANAGEMENT OF SERVICE QUALITY

    A.   Gap Analysis

VI.   TANGIBLE GOODS WITH A HIGH SERVICE COMPONENT

VII.   CLASSIFYING SERVICES

VIII.   HOW LARGE IS THE SERVICE ECONOMY?

IX.   SERVICE MARKETING BY NOT-FOR-PROFIT ORGANIZATIONS

    A.   Characteristics of Not-for-Profit Marketing

        1.   Slow Acceptance of Marketing
        2.   Production or Sales Orientation
        3.   "Know-All" Philosophy
        4.   Weak Financing

    B.   Target Markets
    C.   Planning Difficulties
    D.   "Majority" Objectives

X.   SUMMARY

XI.   KEY TERMS

XII.   QUESTIONS FOR DISCUSSION (12)

XIII.   ETHICS IN PRACTICE

XIV.   CASES

    The following key terms are introduced and used in Chapter 13.   They are defined in the text's Glossary.

Service
Intangibility
Demand management strategy (capacity management strategy)
Inseparability
Service encounter
Service quality
Expected service--perceived service gap
Gap analysis
Social marketing
Not-for-profit marketing

THE CHAPTER SUMMARIZED

I.   INTRODUCTION

    The chapter opens with a description of Tele-Lawyer, a group of eight attorneys in a high tech office in Huntington, California.   Consumers needing legal advice call 900-INFOLAW, talk to one of the lawyers, and pay a charge of $3 per minute.   Charges are added to the consumers' regular phone bills. The service appeals to people who feel they cannot afford a private lawyer, but also to executives who find the service easier to use than their corporate law offices.

Though 900 service is currently dominated by services offering sports scores and entertainment, the major phone companies believe that 900 service will revolutionize how services are delivered and how products are bought and sold.

II.   WHAT IS A SERVICE?

Chapter 10 defined a product as a bundle of satisfactions. This holds for services. Specifically, however:

A **service** is a task or instrumental activity performed for a consumer and/or a consummatory activity involving consumer participation, such as usage, but not ownership, of an organization's products or facilities.

Instrumental services (typically work performed by others, as by a home lawn mowing service) are purchased to achieve a buyer's goals without direct involvement in the task.

Consummatory services involve the consumer's direct involvement and gratification as the service is used (as when a video tape movie is rented).

Some services combine elements of both these service types, as when a person takes ski or tennis instruction. An instructional task is performed (instrumental) but the consumer is involved and receives gratification as the service is consumed.

III.   THE CHARACTERISTICS OF SERVICES

Four characteristics of services are to be found, whether the service is consummatory or instrumental.

A.   Intangibility

Most services are intangible even if some tangible products are associated with them. (Video tape rental is tied to the temporary possession of the tangible cassette.)

Intangibility means that the buyer of the service cannot see, feel, smell, hear, or taste the service. Intangible things are difficult to comprehend and evaluate. Thus, one job of service marketers is to try to make the intangible tangible.

It has been noted that buyers of (intangible) services are actually purchasing the "promise of satisfaction." They need clues, evidence, and indications that the service's quality in fact exists.

Polished brass railings suggest a quality meal is to be found in the restaurant. Mr. Goodwrench is a tangible symbol that GM service is good service. A familiar brand name, logo, or other symbol (like the Hartford Company's "Stag" and Prudential's "Rock"), or association with a trusted celebrity (Bill Cosby), help consumers believe that what is promised will be delivered. Similarly, the membership card "proves" the customer will get the services offered by the health club, and the "free toothbrush" from the dentist shows that the dentist is concerned about keeping the customer's teeth in good shape.

B.   Perishability

An advertising executive once said, "All our assets go down the elevator every evening." He referred to the fact that the services his writers and artists performed could not be stored; the service "exists" only when the service provider is at work.

Thus, the airline cannot store the empty seats on Flight 117 for later use. The dentist cannot store her services if the patient is a "no show." The empty seats at the theater are "lost forever." Because of this situation, service marketers must plan and implement what are called **demand management strategies** (also, called **capacity management strategies**).

Demand management requires careful forecasting of the need for a service. The patient who waits too long at the doctor's office may seek another doctor, thus scheduling patients is extremely important. Restaurants hire part-time help for peak periods, and may offer discounts to encourage patronage during off-times. Indeed, many service marketers call special attention to their price adjustments precisely because their products cannot be stored for a future time. They must be priced to sell "now." This is clear in the case of Florida hotels, whose rates are higher in the winter and lower in the summer.

Another pricing method is **two-part pricing**. Here the user or buyer of the service pays two prices (e.g., a tennis club member pays a club membership fee and an hourly court fee), i.e., a fixed price and a variable price. Many organizations sell non-refundable tickets or, at least, require reservations, to avoid problems associated with the perishable natures of their service products.

C.   Inseparability

Where goods are marketed, it is not necessary for the producer or manufacturer to be present when the good is sold. This is not the case with services. The service product cannot be separated from the provider of the service.

Inseparability means that the producer and consumer may have to present at the same place and the same time for the service transaction to occur.

The surgeon cannot produce the operation and sell it later, but must promise the service, then be there when the service is "delivered." Of course, the customer must be there, too. Exhibit 13-1 portrays the different order of events between a typical product and service exchange.

Service providers have little flexibility. The amount of product they provide depends mostly on the amount of time they have.

Medical services and other service providers have been slow to consider the marketing mix variable of distribution. Hospitals were located on major streets and the customers expected to "visit the factory." Dentists did much the same thing. Nowadays, however, hospitals have branches, emergency care centers, and ambulatory centers, while dentists are locating branch offices in suburbs and visiting those locations two days a week. Others operate their practices in shopping malls. Banks have many automated teller locations. Universities in rural towns operate branch campuses in commercial centers and even run some programs at specific places of business.

Because service marketers produce a product with skill and pride, they are apt to be, in effect, production oriented. Yet the delivery of service by a person means that the service provider is also a "salesperson." The lawyer, the lawyer's receptionist, the doctor and the nurse, are part and parcel of the product offered to customers. Quality control in service marketing usually means personnel quality ... hiring, training, and management are key elements in achievement of customer satisfaction.

D.   Heterogeneity

Because the service is so closely tied to the provider of the service, great variability among services is likely to result. Reducing this heterogeneity (e.g., regulating the nurses' smiles) is obviously difficult. When buying an airline ticket, the flyer knows only in a general way what to expect from the pilot, attendants, ground crew, and so on. This heterogeneity leads service marketers to one of two general strategies: standardization or customization.

1.   The Strategy of Standardization

The heterogeneity of services encourages some service marketers to try to standardize the service offered. Rooms at the Hyatt Regency in San Francisco are a bit different from those at the Hyatt in San Antonio, but great effort has been exerted to make them very similar (standardized).

The strategy of **standardization** is epitomized by McDonald's restaurants. Personnel are instructed at each location in how to treat the customers. The products offered may not be precisely the same at all locations, but they come close. Many procedures are automated. The need to assure that service levels are maintained at or above standard leads service marketers to carefully select and train personnel, use machines, and monitor consumer satisfaction.

2.   The Strategy of Customization

The strategy of **customization** stresses modifying the service to suit each customer in an attempt to achieve customer satisfaction. Some restaurants pledge to cook the steak "to your order," or you can rent a car, bus, or plane to take you to your chosen destination. Health clubs may develop a fitness program "just for you."

Exhibit 13-2 summarizes major service-related problems and possible strategic responses for each of the four general characteristics of services.

IV.   THE SERVICE ENCOUNTER

A **service encounter** is a period of time during which a consumer interacts with a service provider.

Production of service may take more time than the service encounter (as when an accountant spends hours preparing a tax form, but only a short time presenting it to the client). But the client's evaluation of the service is likely to be based mostly on the physical surroundings (office) and the behavior of the service provider and staff. The tax work may be acceptable, but the surroundings may not be.

Marketers who stress service quality strive to manage the service encounter because evaluation of the service is highly dependent on what takes place during the service encounter.

V.   THE MANAGEMENT OF SERVICE QUALITY

Service quality involves a comparison of expectations with performance. Customers who perceive high quality believe the provider matched their expectations. Marketers who wish to deliver high service quality must see to it that managers and frontline personnel match customers' expectations on a consistent basis.

Managers identify customer service needs and plan the level of service to be delivered. Frontline personnel are then trained and given the responsibility for quality service. Personnel must be motivated to deliver the service planned by managers, and results must be regularly measured against the standards.

A.   Gap Analysis

If customers' expectations do not match the perceived level of
service received, a gap, called the **expected service-perceived
service gap**, is said to exist.

The gap can be "negative" and be a fundamental cause of consumer
dissatisfaction. Or it can be "positive," as when a customer gets
more than expected from a service provider. Marketers use **gap
analysis** to identify the source(s) of the consumers' expected
service-perceived service gap.

Exhibit 13-3 identifies four additional gaps that marketing and
management activities influence.

.   A management perception-consumer expectation gap, wherein
         managers do not understand what aspects of the service
         encounter are important to consumers. Filling the gap is an
         essential part of service quality management.

.   A management perception-service quality gap exists when
         managers know what consumers expect but what they offer is less
         than what consumers expect.

.   A service quality specification-service delivery gap occurs
         when frontline personnel do not perform their tasks according
         to guidelines. Training and supervision of personnel may be
         the answer.

.   A service delivery-external communications gap exists if
         advertising and other external communications promise more than
         the frontline personnel can deliver.

Exhibit 13-4 outlines some determinants of service quality (as seen
from the consumer's point of view.)

VI.   TANGIBLE GOODS WITH A HIGH SERVICE COMPONENT

"Service is everybody's business." Even when the product is coal or gravel
there is still room for intangible elements such as delivery, proper
billing, pleasant telephone manners, and so on. Indeed, most organizations
offer their customers a mix of goods and services. Auto dealers offer a
very tangible product and a major service component. Many people have
bought cars only to be unhappy with the dealers' service departments.
Retailers sell us goods, but we may become annoyed with the service
component ... long lines or nasty clerks, delivery problems, repairs, and
warranties. Admittedly, implementing good service programs can be
difficult.

Marketers of goods, however, should consider the service component of their
offerings and use some of the strategies used by marketers of "pure"
services.

VII.   CLASSIFYING SERVICES

Many criteria provide bases for classifying services. Among them are:

.   Type of market ... ultimate consumer versus organizational/industrial

.   Marketer's mission ... profit seeking and not-for-profit

.   Characteristic of the service ... instrumental versus consummatory;
         the function of the service such as repair, storage, etc., or the
         delivery system employed such as automated versus people-based.

Exhibit 13-5 shows how selected variables related to market segment, type
of organization, or service characteristics, can be chosen to classify
services.

VIII. HOW LARGE IS THE SERVICE ECONOMY?

Service workers are often characterized as "burger flippers" but airline pilots, computer programmers, economists, professors, hairdressers, lawyers, psychiatrists, cashiers, presidents of the U.S., and forest rangers (among many others) are all part of the service economy. Over 80 million workers belong to the service sector, about four times the number in goods-producing jobs, and twenty-seven times the number in agriculture.

The service sector offers a far brighter employment future than manufacturing, but many service jobs are relatively low paying. Over 300,000 cashier jobs will become available during the 1990s but the average weekly wage for such jobs was less than $200 in 1990. However, over 600,000 nurses will be hired in the 1990s at an average projected weekly earning of over $500.

IX. SERVICE MARKETING BY NOT-FOR-PROFIT ORGANIZATIONS

It would be impossible to discuss every type of service marketer but one large group should be addressed ... the not-for-profit organization. Many of these market intangibles, but this is not always the case. The Girl Scouts sell cookies and Goodwill Industries sells all manner of household furnishings. We have already seen, throughout the book, that profit-oriented marketing techniques are adaptable to non-profit organizations.

The term **social marketing** has been used to describe activities intended to enhance the acceptability of social causes, ideas, or desirable behaviors. Some prefer this term to **not-for-profit marketing**. The text uses the two phrases interchangeably, pointing out the differences when necessary.

A. Characteristics of Not-for-Profit Marketing

Social marketing differs from other areas of marketing primarily in the intangible nature of the offerings and the absence of a profit motive. Social marketing may be distinguished in other ways.

1. Slow Acceptance of Marketing

Not-for-profit marketing can be demonstrated to have existed for centuries. (See Exhibit 13-6.) Government, churches, museums, and universities have long been "not-for-profit marketers." However, the terminology used has differed from that of for-profit marketing. Churches make "announcements" but don't like to say they "promote," politicians "give speeches" but don't "sell." The activities are essentially the same though the terminology differs.

The nomenclature is really unimportant but does suggest a reluctance to associate "business" with "the cause." What is lost in this is the opportunity to use marketing knowledge to help "the cause." It has been suggested that marketing itself needs to be marketed to not-for-profit organizations. Many marketing plans for these groups languish in file cabinets because organization leaders were not convinced of the "appropriateness" of marketing to their cause.

2. Production or Sales Orientation

The inseparability of the service from the provider has led providers to be production oriented. This is perhaps more the case in not-for-profit areas where devotion to a cause is prevalent. Nonprofit organizations stand to gain by adopting a consumer orientation rather than a product or sales orientation.

3. "Know All" Philosophy

Managers of not-for-profit organizations often feel they do not need marketing because they know how to handle their problems on their own. Hospitals and universities frequently promote persons with journalism or other backgrounds to what is, in effect, the institution's marketing directorship. This can lead to ineffectual or even negative-results programs. The reverse is possible too, when experienced marketers attempt to aid a non-profit organization without considering the special characteristics of these groups.

4.   Weak Financing

Social marketers rarely have adequate funding at their disposal to accomplish all their objectives. "Businesses," however, are not swimming in money either.

Both types of organizations must contend with the fact that demand for their products affects financing.

Not-for-profit groups frequently are financially weak. Not-for-profit organizations can, like businesses, overcome some of their financial problems if they employ modern marketing tools such as marketing research, and apply them both "upstream" and "downstream." For example, an organization advocating equal employment for the handicapped must generate funds from the government, businesses, and the general public in order to market the concept of equality to the government, to businesses, and to the general public.

B.   Target Markets

Not-for-profit organizations frequently have more than one target market to be served. The zoo wants to attract visitors, donors, government support, and the general public's support.

Exhibit 13-7 shows how marketing efforts in a not-for-profit organization may be geared toward two general publics. These publics are, in fact, markets or customers, though those terms are seldom employed. Words like client, audience, member, or associate, take the place of "customer." In various ways, these publics pay the price necessary to sustain the not-for-profit marketing organization.

C.   Planning Difficulties

Good planning and control require measurable objectives. Businesses can measure success using the "bottom line," but not-for-profit organizations cannot always, and seldom do, use this measure. Operating "in the red" is an undesirable but often acceptable condition.

The intangibility of the objectives sought by many not-for-profit groups, e.g., "equality for handicapped workers," is sometimes used as an excuse for not determining proper marketing objectives. Yet measuring the public's acceptance of such a notion is not much different from measuring the public's acceptance of a product.

Funding agencies are less and less likely to accept vague objectives from not-for-profit marketing organizations.

D.   "Majority" Objectives

Not-for-profit marketers may find themselves facing objectives far larger than those facing businesses. A soap maker may seek just a small percent of the market for its brand of soap, but not-for-profit marketing is likely to seek, in effect, 100% of "the market." For example, the attempt by the U.S. government to convert the country to the metric system will not be complete until the entire country is using the metric system. The American Cancer Society states that its goal is to "end the threat of cancer."

X.   SUMMARY

This chapter discussed the marketing problems faced by marketers of services and marketers who operate in the non-profit sector. Each type of marketing presents unique problems, but these can be overcome by judicious use of traditional marketing strategies.

Learning Objective 1:   Define "service" in its technical, specific sense.

A service is a task or instrumental activity performed for a consumer and/or a consummatory activity involving consumer participation, but not ownership of, an organization's products or facilities.

Learning Objective 2:   Explain the four basic characteristics of services.

The four basic characteristics of services are (1) intangibility -- buyers cannot normally see, feel, smell, hear, or taste a service before agreeing to buy it; (2) perishability -- unused productive capacity disappears in the sense that the provider's time cannot be used again if a customer does not make use of the service; (3) inseparability -- the producer and consumer generally must be present at the same time and place, and the provider of the service cannot be separated from the service provided; and (4) heterogeneity -- providers of services vary widely in their skills, even a single provider cannot perform in the same way on every occasion.

Learning Objective 3:   Understand demand management strategies.

Service providers cannot store their products for future use, so forecasting and managing demand are of key importance. Such strategies as altering prices to attract customers during off-season or off-hour times and two-part pricing (using fixed and variable usage fees) exemplify demand management strategies.

Learning Objective 4:   Describe the strategies of standardization and customization.

Standardization means attempting to control the inherent heterogeneity of services by such means as automation or strict controls on service-providing personnel. Customization involves modifying the service to fit individual buyer's needs.

Learning Objective 5:   Name some of the variables used to classify services.

Services may be classified by grouping them using such characteristics as (1) market segment (for example, consumer versus industrial); (2) sponsoring organization (for example, profit or not-for-profit; or (3) the service itself (for example, equipment based versus people-based.)

Learning Objective 6:   Discuss the need for marketing in the not-for-profit area.

The not-for-profit sector has been slow to adopt marketing, even though it faces many problems that marketing can solve. Marketing itself may have to be marketed to not-for-profit organizations if those groups are to benefit from marketing's philosophy, strategies, and tools.

XI.   KEY TERMS

XII.   QUESTIONS FOR DISCUSSION (12)

XIII.   ETHICS IN PRACTICE

XIV.   CASES

ANSWER GUIDELINES FOR CHAPTER 13 QUESTIONS FOR DISCUSSION

1.   *How might the following services be classified? (a) a city zoo (b) Avis Rent-A-Car (c) a shoe shine (d) a taxi cab ride (e) new false teeth from a dentist.*

ANSWER:

As shown in Exhibit 13-5 in the text, there are numerous ways to classify services. Using this exhibit as a guide, students should be able to classify each service in its appropriate position.

(a)   a city zoo

Characteristics of Market Segment

Buyer	consumer to visit the zoo
	organizations for donations
Organization	entertainment; knowledge
Channel level	consumer

Sponsoring Organization

Mission	not-for-profit, generally
Experience	professional, skilled, & unskilled labor

Characteristics of the Service

Benefit	instrumental in work performed on the animals and facilities; consummatory if the consumer is directly involved and gratified by a visit to the zoo
Delivery	people-based
Function	education

(b)   Avis Rent-A-Car

Characteristics of Market Segment

Buyer	consumer and organizational
Organization	transportation
Channel level	wholesaling for fleets, retailing for consumers and individual organizational buyers

Sponsoring Organization

Mission	profit
Experience	skilled

Characteristics of the Service

Benefit	instrumental in that consumers do not own the rented vehicle, consummatory in that they do drive the vehicle
Delivery	people-based
Function	rentals

(c)   a shoe shine

Characteristics of Market Segment

Buyer	consumer
Organization	personal service
Channel level	consumer

Sponsoring Organization

Mission	profit
Experience	unskilled

Characteristics of the Service

Benefit	instrumental
Delivery	people-based
Function	repair

(d)   a taxi cab ride

Characteristics of Market Segment

Buyer	consumer
Organization	transportation
Channel level	consumer

Sponsoring Organization

Mission	profit
Experience	skilled labor

Characteristics of the Service

Benefit	instrumental
Delivery	equipment-based (cab), people-based (driver)
Function	rental for one ride

(e)   new false teeth from the dentist

Characteristics of Market Segment

Buyer	consumer
Organization	health care
Channel level	retailing

Sponsoring Organization

Mission	profit
Experience	professional

Characteristics of the Service

Benefit	instrumental in that the work to create the teeth is performed by others, consummatory in that customers are immediately gratified and directly involved in fitting and wearing the teeth
Delivery	people-based
Function	personal care

2. *Describe situations where consumption without ownership might be more preferable to consumers than the actual ownership of products.*

ANSWER:

Instrumental services involve work performed by others to achieve a consumer goal without direct involvement in the task or ownership of a product. Examples include lawn care where a company supplies the equipment and customers can avoid purchasing mowers, trimmers, or other products. Medical care is also a clear example of a time when customers would prefer not to purchase X-ray machines, dental drills or stethoscopes. Repair services of all types suggest instrumental service where customers would prefer not to own equipment to fix major problems with automobiles, electronics or appliances. Many customers would probably prefer not to own dry cleaning equipment, industrial sewing machines to upholster old furniture, or dipping vats to strip old paint from wood products.

3.   *Describe a situation in which you paid in advance for a "promise of satisfaction."*

ANSWER:

Any insurance purchase certainly involves a "promise of satisfaction" for future delivery of the service when it is needed. Customers who purchase tickets to sporting events, plays, movies, or concerts also pay in advance for expected satisfaction. Many managed health care plans require people to pay a monthly fee for a promise of medical care delivery. Lawyers and consultants receive retainers before service is delivered. Lawn or swimming pool services may also have customers pay an annual fee in advance of service delivery. College tuition also fits this situation.

4.   *Give three examples of organizations that use slogans or images to impart believability or reliability to the services they offer for sale.*

ANSWER:

Students may need a prompt to start, but generally are able to list several examples of advertisements. A few examples to begin discussion include:

.   "You're in good hands with Allstate"
.   The Prudential "rock" suggests reliability.
.   Delta airlines, "We love to fly and it shows."
.   Cigna property and casualty insurance, "We get paid for results."
.   Tony Randall for anything where persnickety cleanliness is involved.
.   Trafalgar House, a British company, "A World Force in Engineering."

5.   *In what ways do inseparability and intangibility affect marketing planning in the following organizations? (a) a church (b) your local public school board (c) a ski resort*

ANSWER:

(a)   a church

Intangibility means that church members perceive the spiritual aspects of church internally, rather than with the senses. Inseparability is seen in the necessary presence of a priest or pastor as well as the required presence of the customer to receive benefit of interactions with others and spiritual education. Thus, spiritual growth is an intangible idea and the production and consumption of religious teaching are inseparable.

(b)   your local public school board

Intangibility means that the actions of the school board relate more to policy than to physical products. Thus, many aspects of the quality of a school system are not tangible. Knowledge acquisition and level, an environment conducive to learning, and the level of caring provided for students are intangible facets of school board policies. Inseparability is seen in the integrated nature of the school board, its policies and the ultimate quality of the school. School board members must interact with educators, parents and students so it is not possible to separate production of the service from its delivery.

(c)   a ski resort

While the facility, skis, and equipment are tangible aspects of a ski resort's product, the intangible benefit purchased relates more to entertainment, excitement and fun than to possessing a physical product. The expertise of trainers is another intangible component. Inseparability occurs because the producer and consumer must be present at the ski resort for a transaction to occur.

6.   *How does a service's perishability influence pricing?*

ANSWER:

Perishable services cannot be stored or inventoried, thus lost income from empty
seats on airlines, in theaters or medical offices cannot be recovered. Demand
management strategies are used by services to accurately forecast the need for
services and to attempt to balance fluctuating demand periods. As examples, two-
part pricing requires a user or subscriber to pay a fixed fee (for installation
or membership) and a variable usage fee (for tennis court time). Off-peak
pricing may include special sales for normally slow times (e.g., AT&T weekend
rates when demand is lower than during the week; or air conditioner sales in the
winter). Selling the service in advance or requiring reservations are other
means for overcoming perishability.

7.   *How can the following organizations combat intangibility in their product
        and advertising strategies? (a) a health spa (b) a movie theater (c) a
        hairdresser (d) the pub near your university or college*

ANSWER:

While it is important for students to understand the text's points, they should
also reach for creative approaches to adding tangible components to intangible
services.

(a)   a health spa

Health spas can associate the service with a distinct name and/or logo. Spas
should also use other symbolic clues, such as cleanliness of the facility or
design as well as the physical health of personnel to combat intangibility.
Personnel should have business cards which also carry the logo of the spa.
Further, spas may provide supplemental tangible evidence with membership cards,
"keys" to the facility, complementary towels with the logo displayed, or small
gifts such as glasses or pens with the spa's name included. To chart progress,
spas could also consider providing "report cards" which would chart the customer
(measurements, time, weight) over time. Celebrities or local characters may
enhance perceptions as well.

(b)   a movie theater

While patrons do receive a ticket stub, this peripheral evidence does little to
combat the inherent intangibility of experiencing a movie in the theater. Again,
basic considerations include a distinctive name and/or logo as well as clean
facilities. What types of supplemental tangible evidence could a theater
provide? Brochures of upcoming movies which include the movie just seen by
consumers or small free gifts. Theaters could also consider having customers
complete a "critic's" questionnaire and publishing local consumer's reactions to
the latest film or issuing a membership card which accrues to yield a free movie
or refreshments.

(c)   a hairdresser

Again, students should clearly see the need for a distinct image as communicated
by the brand name or logo. The logo should appear on all items sold within the
salon or shop and the store must be clean. Approaches for providing customers
with tangible clues could include: taking a before and after (Polaroid) picture
of each customer; providing a membership card which is punched during each visit
to yield a free hair cut or manicure; free small gifts (brush/comb) with the logo
included; associate the shop with a tangible symbol, such as scissors.

(d)   the pub near your university or college

With a catchy name and/or logo which appeals to local customers, pubs have many
opportunities to provide supplemental tangible evidence. T-shirts, caps,
huggies, mugs, glasses, darts, or other items which bear the logo could be sold
or given away in contests. Cards which entitle the bearer to a free drink after
a certain number of purchases, Polaroid pictures of patrons, napkins, and
pictures on the wall all contribute to the symbolic clues of a pub. Generally,
the internal atmosphere must reinforce the name, logo and "theme" of the pub.

8.   *Do sports figures and celebrities engage in service marketing?   In what ways?*

ANSWER:

Sports figures and celebrities engage in several activities which are similar to service marketing characteristics. For example, the service is intangible if it is entertainment or sports strength and cannot be held as a physical product. The service is also perishable because talent cannot be stored for later use, even though the event can be videotaped. Inseparability is a given since the celebrity must be present at the event and heterogeneity is seen in the varying performances provided. Some sports figures strive for a standardized delivery so that performance is similar during each sporting event. Celebrities may seek customized approaches to tailor the performance to an audience.

Sports figures and celebrities also engage in activities designed to combat the intangibility of their crafts. For example, signing autographs provides a tangible reminder that a fan encountered a celebrity. Peripheral evidence appears in the form of T-shirts, caps or pictures of the stars. Symbolic clues are also seen as celebrities strive to create a unique image. Mr. "T" is associated gold chains; the 1992 Olympic volleyball team all shaved their heads to symbolize unity; and sports teams of all types have clear brand names, mascots and logos to reinforce their image.

9.   *Give examples of the use of the strategies of standardization and customization in the marketing of services.*

ANSWER:

Standardization is desirable for mass marketers where the strategy is to ensure all transactions meet established standards. Thus, airlines hope that each pilot and attendant offer reliable and friendly service to travelers. Chains such as hotels, emergency care clinics, and restaurants attempt to standardize the quality of service offered in each location. Visa, MasterCard, and American Express seek to standardize the acceptance of their credit cards on a global scale.

Customization is appropriate when the service must be modified for each individual customer rather than mass produced. A physician must prescribe a customized treatment for each patient's symptoms. Health clubs may customize a fitness program to suit the patron. Hair stylists might stress a standardized service ("we cut them all the same way,") but more than likely attempt to meet the specific needs of each customer's hair.

10.   *Is it easier to market a service product with a high tangible component than one with a low tangible component?   Why or why not?*

ANSWER:

Difficulty may be in the eye or mind of the student beholder in this case. A service product with low tangibility requires efforts to provide tangible reminders of its existence. It may be difficult to differentiate the service from competitors, to train personnel to consistently deliver a friendly, homogeneous standard, or to supply peripheral evidence of the service.

At first, tangible products with a high service component appear to be the easier of the tasks. The firm has a physical product which consumers can hold and evaluate. However, servicing the product after the sale may not be emphasized. Products can be complex, adequately trained repair technicians may be in short supply, and front-line service personnel typically earn low wages. With a tangible service product for the manager to see, they may omit attention to the critical service component.

11.   *Are there any products that have no service components?   Why or why not?*

ANSWER:

An initial reaction to this question may be that there must be some products containing no service component. However, every product must be exchanged with a provider for something of value from the customer. Service is seen in the customer's ease of obtaining possession utility in the interaction. Service is also included when sellers answer questions from customers about the product, the company's reputation or image, as well as delivery or payment options. Service for consumer products may be associated with a retail store as opposed to the original manufacturer, but a service component exists.

Consider the disposable camera. Customers purchase film which comes with a cardboard camera. While the manufacturer does not come in direct contact with the customer in the store, service is involved in customers' beliefs of the adequacy of the camera, in film development, and in the interaction within the retail store when the product is purchased.

Students should understand the continuum between tangible products and their intangible service components. This continuum is illustrated in the text.

12.   *You are a marketing consultant, and your city or town government has hired you to develop a marketing plan aimed at improving the public image of the local police department. What steps would you take to ensure a smooth introduction of the marketing approach to this organization?*

ANSWER:

This is a topical question of real concern for many governmental agencies. Students should be encouraged to apply the concepts from the chapter to the issue, while actual answers may vary.

A first step may be to research gaps between police department and citizen perceptions of the service provided by the department. As summarized in the text, the following potential gaps could be investigated to provide insight into the current situation faced by the department:

Gap 1 Management Perceptions and Consumer Expectations

Managers fail to understand customer perceptions of important aspects of the service; thus, citizens should be asked what is important to them in police service delivery.

Gap 2 Management Perception and Service Quality Specification

Managers understand expectations but unacceptable standards are planned for service delivery; thus, quality performance reviews must assess service delivery policies.

Gap 3 Service Quality Specification and Service Delivery

Front-line personnel do not perform tasks in accordance with guidelines; thus, police actions would be evaluated in comparison to existing policies.

Gap 4 Service Delivery and External Communications

When communications promise more than front-line personnel can deliver; thus, claims of a crime-free city or the friendliest force in the world must accurately reflect the current departmental personnel.

The next phase of work would involve closing these gaps as well as working to combat intangibility, perishability, inseparability and heterogeneity.

To combat intangibility, police departments have symbolic clues (uniform, badge, car.) Crime watch signs and stickers for windows in houses or honorary badges for children may also indicate ideas for providing peripheral evidence of the service performed. Having celebrities appear with police personnel at community events may also enhance the symbolic clues of the department. Published statistics providing evidence of the department's effectiveness can also offer a tangible reminder of the department's effectiveness.

To combat perishability and insure adequate personnel, demand management strategies could involve forecasting neighborhoods, times of day, special events or seasons when the need for police services is maximized. Small towns may also hire auxiliary, part-time police personnel to fill in during peak demand times.

To combat inseparability, the department may consider multiple locations of offices to offer convenient access rather than the central police precinct where citizens must travel to the service. In many cities, police department offices are appearing in shopping malls. Perhaps a more difficult task would be to train police personnel to view their job as a marketing activity rather than an enforcement function. Thus, hiring and training competent police personnel who also have interpersonal skills is essential.

Police departments use both standardization strategies and customization strategies as aspects of the heterogeneity of the service performed. Tickets are standardized so that any violation receives the same consequence. However, violent situations require police personnel to customize their response.

ETHICS EXERCISE 13

CHAPTER 13 ETHICS IN PRACTICE

Overview

Political candidates spend a lot of money on their campaigns. Laws do not require candidates to substantiate their claims as do marketers of other products. Negative themes are easy to find. Is this proper? Should laws be passed to control political advertising?

Advertising for political candidates is one of the most controversial forms of advertising. Politicians have almost always used promotional techniques, including campaign buttons, slogans ("Tippecanoe and Tyler too," "Keep cool with Coolidge," "I like Ike"), songs, and posters. In the twentieth century new media forms emerged, such as bumper stickers, billboards, radio spots, and the dreaded television commercial. Modern day candidates hire individual members of advertising agencies, campaign managers, political pollsters, and political consultants.

Much of this advertising has always used negative appeals, where the focus is on the opponent's negative characteristics or weak areas. The old axiom is that it is easier to motivate people to vote against somebody than for someone. Since its earliest days, American politics has often been a dirty affair with candidates leveling outlandish attacks on one another, or circulating true but embarrassing stories about extramarital affairs and illegitimate children. In the early days, those attacks were confined to the "smoke-filled rooms." Today, however, the political attacks occur where all can see them.

One of the earliest and most memorable examples of the so-called TV attack ads was run by Lyndon Johnson in 1964 against Barry Goldwater. The implication in the infamous "Daisy" TV spot, which only ran once, was that Goldwater had an itchy trigger finger on the nuclear button. The commercial showed a little girl picking daisy petals off a flower while in the background a technocrat announced a missile countdown. At "zero" a nuclear explosion filled the screen. The spot received much publicity, especially following the Republican's noisy protest against it.

More recently, there was the infamous Willie Horton TV spot in which George Bush's handlers suggested that his opponent Michael Dukakis cared more about criminals than victims of crime. Dukakis refused to immediately return the fire, and when he did counterattack, it was too little too late.

Negative political advertising took off during the 1980s in part because complex issues like crime, drugs, and the federal deficit are far more difficult to understand than simplistic issues like a candidate's extramarital affairs. Also, negative advertising is intrusive enough to cut through the clutter of 15- and 30-second spots that clog the broadcast media. And, conventional wisdom is that attack ads get more news media attention than do positive messages; free pickup on the evening news stretches media dollars further.

There are several reasons why breaches of fairness and honesty are considered so important in political advertising. First, there are long interpurchase intervals. Once we have "bought" a candidate, we are stuck with him or her for two, four, or six years. Second, there is no product warranty or guarantee. Once we have "purchased" a candidate, our only consumer redress is impeachment. Third, and perhaps most significant, there is no claim substantiation. Due to First Amendment protection of free speech, there is no regulation of political advertising; it can be false, misleading, or deceptive, and the media are required to accept all of it at standard advertising rates regardless of content. There are no restraints or regulations to prevent candidates from running even the most vicious attacks. Too, the American Association of Political Consultants has never disciplined a single member for violating its Code of Ethics.

These questions are posed. Is negative political advertising proper? Should any laws be passed or anything done to change the way political advertising is conducted?

There are several criticisms of political advertising in general and of negative attack ads in particular. Concerning political advertising in general:

.   The high costs of media time and space discourage financially poor but qualified candidates from seeking office.

.   Most of the "sound bite" advertising simplifies complex issues. Often incomplete and therefore misleading claims are made.

.   The cost of advertising makes politicians beholden to those who give them the biggest contributions.

Concerning negative attack ads:

.   They focus on the opponent's negatives while failing to discuss the candidate's positives; unfair charges are made about opponents and issues; it has degenerated to mean-spirited bashing.

.   Recent polls suggest that negative advertising harms both candidates and tarnishes the images and credibility of the candidates as well as of politics, causing the public to have less respect for politicians. This is one reason why voters often feel they're choosing between the lesser of two evils, and it might help account for lower voter turnout rates at the polls in recent years.

.   Negative political advertising also drags down the reputation of the commercial advertising community (advertisers, ad agencies, and media).

Nonetheless, negative political advertising has its defenders, especially among those in the business:

.   Some strategists claim that negative ads are a necessary evil, because if you don't use them on your opponent, your opponent will nonetheless use them on you, putting you at a competitive disadvantage.

.   Such advertising does give voters specific information with which to make comparisons among candidates. Roger Ailes, viewed as the master in rough-and-tumble attack ads and the man who guided George Bush's 1988 image transformation from "wimp" to decisive leader, says, "There's nothing wrong with negative advertising so long as it's accurate and fair. It's perfectly right to discuss an opponent."

.   Others argue that the end (election of the "right" candidate) justifies the means: it works, wearing and tearing down opponents and winning elections. This is utilitarian thinking.

Many recommendations have been made for improving the system:

.   Some critics, politicians, and advertising professionals have advocated requiring political spots to be five minutes or more in length in order to adequately deal with complex issues such as foreign policy and economic issues.

- Congress proposed changes in federal law that would require broadcasters to provide free time to candidates for U.S. office who are attacked in political ads. (However, this could be viewed as a violation of property rights by forcing broadcasters to give up valuable air time.)

- Some, such as American Association of Advertising Agencies Chairman Alex Kroll, have suggested using the commercial advertising industry's self-regulatory arm, the National Advertising Review Board, to regulate political advertising. Panelists would review charges of false, misleading, or disparaging advertising leveled by opponents or the public. A review would require a quick turnaround time due to the fast-moving political campaigns where ads might have a life expectancy of a week or less.

- In the 1992 presidential campaign the media started paying closer attention to candidates' ads. Many ran series called ad-watch stories or truth boxes, scrutinizing the candidates' ads. With press scrutiny so intense, several candidates made their ads available to the press before the ads ran in the media.

- Independent civic organizations could be established to monitor and challenge dishonesty in political advertising.

- Any candidate "going negative" would have to personally stand up and say the statements were negative rather than hide behind campaign committees.

- In the 1992 Presidential campaign Ross Perot used 30-minute question-and-answer programs on network and cable TV rather than mud-slinging 30-second commercials.

- *Advertising Age* editorialist Bob Garfield, with tongue at least partially in cheek, proposed that all political advertising should carry the following standard disclaimer: "This has been a paid political announcement. The station is compelled by law to run it, but we have no right and means to verify its accuracy or truthfulness. We encourage you to seek other sources for more complete information. WARNING: POLITICAL ADVERTISING CAN LEGALLY DISTORT THE TRUTH."

CHAPTER 13 TAKE A STAND QUESTIONS

1.   *A doctor's "bedside manner" is part of the service offered to patients. Discuss this product strategy from an ethical perspective.*

This relates to the inseparability characteristic of services. As the chapter notes, service providers (such as M.D.s) traditionally viewed themselves as producers rather than as marketers. Yet, a positive interaction between the service provider and customer/patient might be crucial to retain customers. The quality of contact between doctors and patients might be vital in keeping a competitive edge.

Some who view a doctor's services from a purely technical perspective might argue that this is unethical; a doctor's bedside manner has no impact on whether or not the doctor gives good advice, prescribes the right medicine, or performs other medical duties.

However, quality must be more broadly defined than utilitarian performance to include attitude toward customers, which will certainly affect customer satisfaction. Quality is created during the "moment of truth," the interaction between customers and front-line service providers. Interpersonal skills are vital in high-contact services (where customers are highly involved with the service provider). The relationship between doctor and patient can provide the critical point of difference.

2. *A restaurant customer asks the waiter if the fish on the menu is fresh.*
    Although the fish was frozen, the waiter answers "yes" because he knows it
    tastes great and the customer will love the chef's sauce. Take a stand.

This is a clear ethical lapse. It violates all norms of trustworthiness and
honesty. The waiter's reasoning in effect is a rationalization that the ends
justify the means. This reasoning has historically been used to justify the most
heinous behavior.

The problem with a "little white lie" like this is that, in accordance with
Kant's categorical imperative, when enough people do it, language loses its
meaning. Even though the end result might be acceptable from the customer's
perspective, how would she feel if she knew she was tricked into ordering the
dish? Also, the customer might have some kind of aversion to frozen food. It
would be better for the waiter to be honest with the customer but try to turn the
fish's disadvantage into an advantage by emphasizing the great taste and special
sauce.

3. *Nonprofit organizations which expect to bring about social change, like the*
    National Rifleman's Association, have no business trying to change
    everyone's opinion to their point of view. Take a stand.

Groups like the NRA are involved in what is known as cause (or social or idea)
marketing, which is marketing that seeks to modify public or private behavior;
what is being marketed is a "social product." Some sorts of social marketing are
for noncontroversial causes (e.g., public service campaigns on topics such as
drug abuse, child abuse, crime prevention, and drunk driving).

However, others concern controversial issues such as abortion, environmental
issues, women's rights, pending legislation, and gun control.

Marketing of controversial causes relies heavily on advocacy advertising, which
is advertising promoting an organization's viewpoint on a particular issue of
public concern.

Opponents of cause marketing label it variously as "change management," "behavior
modification," and "social engineering." Arguments against it include:

.   Reports and commentaries on controversial public issues should be presented
    in a journalistic format by the media only. This is more apt to ensure
    accuracy, objectivity, thoroughness, and fairness in reporting.

.   Advocacy advertising encourages biased statements. This can lead to public
    misinformation.

.   Those groups with the most money dominate the debate. This can lead to an
    unbalanced presentation of the issues.

Advocates of cause marketing put forth the following arguments:

.   We can't leave the forum for public debate of controversial issues to the
    media, since it is well known that many media vehicles have a liberal bias
    on most issues and some might have an ax to grind on a particular issue.
    Therefore, balanced presentation on public issues demands permitting cause
    marketing.

.   To disallow issue marketing would be to stifle free speech rights
    guaranteed by the First Amendment to the U.S. Constitution.

.   Advocacy advertising encourages constructive debate of controversial
    issues. This makes for a better informed public.

4. *The 200th anniversary of the United States Constitution was sponsored by a*
    cigarette company. Is a private organization's funding of a public
    governmental event fundamentally wrong? Take a stand.

This is actually an example of the use of advocacy advertising by Phillip Morris
(PM) Company. It was a response to proposed legislation that would limit tobacco
advertising.

In 1988 PM was chosen by the U.S. National Archives and Record Administration to fund the Bill of Rights bicentennial. Philip Morris claimed that it was interested only because it wanted to be a good corporate citizen; in effect, it claimed its efforts were public service promotion rather than advocacy promotion. Also, PM viewed the campaign as an opportunity to carve out a new corporate identity for itself following a decade of acquisitions.

This $60 million image campaign was launched with print and television advertisements concerning the Bill of Rights. One commercial called the Bill of Rights the great American charter of personal liberty and human dignity, and it featured beautifully filmed images of parchments accompanied by the words of John F. Kennedy. Over a two-year period PM also sponsored a national tour of the Bill of Rights and distributed copies of the Bill of Rights to consumers who called a toll-free number.

Critics charged that the Bill of Rights campaign was being used to bolster PM's freedom-to-advertise position and to send a clear message to Congress that PM would actively fight any new legislative efforts to restrict their promotions. By sponsoring this historic occasion, PM indirectly told consumers and legislators that smokers have rights and that PM has the right of free speech and therefore the right to advertise cigarettes. Such ads had been banned from television advertising since the early 1970s. However, the company denied that this was their ulterior motive. Critics also alleged that the sponsorship was a sneaky way to get a banned product advertised on TV.

Given that elements of the tobacco industry had been trying to get a "right to smoke" added to the U.N.'s list of basic human rights, PM's attempt to connect itself to the U.S. Bill of Rights looks even more suspicious.

Although it is tenuous and judgmental to try to determine an actor's motives, the circumstantial evidence suggests that the critics were correct. PM and their ad agency, Ogilvy and Mather, claim that they just wanted the public to realize that PM is a large conglomerate which also markets other products, such as those of General Foods and Miller Brewing. (Beer is another product facing advertising restrictions.) However, PM was pressured by the National Archives to promote its food groups and downplay their cigarettes. It is evident from early correspondence between the firm and the National Archives that PM originally wanted the sponsorship to focus mainly on tobacco products. Is this a case of, to put a spin on a biblical expression, "Let us do good that evil might come"?

GUIDE TO CASES

CASE 13-1   FEDERAL EXPRESS (B)

SUBJECT MATTER: Service Marketing, Tangible and Intangible Aspects of Services, Total Product, Service Gaps

Please see the Guide to Video Cases for video length and other information.

AT-A-GLANCE OVERVIEW

Federal Express company is an innovative company that helped "change the way America does business." Federal Express was the first company to offer an overnight delivery service. However, Federal Express markets more than a delivery service. What Federal Express really sells in on-time reliability. The company markets risk reduction and provides the confidence that people shipping packages will be "Absolutely, positively, certain their packages will be there by 10:30 in the morning."

Indeed, Federal Express sells much more than reliable delivery. Federal Express designs tracking and inventory management systems for many large companies. In other words, Fed Ex customers buy more than just delivery service, they buy a solution to their distribution problems. For example, a warehouse designed and operated by Federal Express is part of the distribution center for a very large computer firm. In other organizations, customers can place an order for inventory as late as midnight and the marketer, because of Federal Express' help, can guarantee delivery by the next morning. Federal Express has positioned itself as a company with a service that solves its customers' problems.

QUESTIONS

1. *What is Federal Express's product? What are the tangible and intangible elements of this service product?*

As the case indicates, Federal Express sells much more than reliable delivery. Federal Express designs tracking and inventory management systems for many large companies. In other words, Fed Ex customers buy more than just delivery service, they buy a solution to their distribution problems. Even customers who ship packages only occasionally get more than delivery. They get the assurance that the package "Absolutely, positively will get there by 10:30" in the morning. They don't have to worry. This is a major benefit. The tangible aspects of Federal Express' service are the pick-up/delivery personnel's uniform, the trucks with the purple stripe, the special Federal Express packaging, the easy-to-fill-out airbill, and many other atmospheric features of the offices and drop-off stations. One of the most important intangibles is friendly service. Also, Federal express drivers "sprint" to and from the pick-up station. This gives the impression that every aspect of Federal Express is geared toward the fastest delivery possible.

2. *What are the elements of service quality for a delivery service such as Federal Express?*

This answer can be structured around the general characteristics given in the textbook.

Access -- Contact with service personnel is easy. For example, using an 800 number to arrange for shipment.

Communication -- The customer is informed and understands the service and how much it will cost. For example, customer understands that the Saturday delivery will arrive before noon, not 10:30 a.m.

Competence -- The service provider has mastered the required skill and is proficient in managing support personnel. The customer believes that people shipping packages will be "Absolutely, positively, certain their packages will be there by 10:30 in the morning."

Courtesy -- Personnel are polite and friendly. All drivers smile and say "have a nice day" after the delivery is completed.

Reliability -- The service is consistently performed to meet standards, and the personnel are dependable.

Credibility -- The service providers have integrity. No one will attempt to steal the package.

Some specific aspects students are likely to mention are on-time delivery, undamaged packages, speed of locating a package that is en route, perceived competence of personnel, and perceived friendliness.

3. *In the service delivery process, where are the possible service delivery gaps?*

If consumers' expectations do not match the perceived level of service received, a gap is said to exist. (The label given to this gap is the Expected Service-Perceived Service Gap.) For example, if a package is not delivered on time, the difference between expected service quality and perceived service quality results in a negative gap. A negative gap is a fundamental determinant of consumer dissatisfaction. When a package is sent "standard overnight" (afternoon delivery) to obtain a lower rate and the package is delivered in the morning, the consumers get better service than they expected.

Marketers use gap analysis to identify the sources of the consumer's expected service/perceived service gap. There are four additional gaps that marketing and management activity influence.

Gap 1 -- A management perception-consumer expectation gap can exist if managers cannot identify or do not understand what aspects of the service encounter are important to consumers. Filling the gap between what customers perceive to be good service and what the company perceives to be good service is essential aspect of service quality management.

Gap 2 -- When an unfavorable management perception-service quality specification gap exists, mangers know what consumers expect but the specifications they plan are less than what the consumer expects. In other words, managers, who should know better, plan unacceptable standards for service delivery. This may occur in production-oriented organizations or in organizations that have not been allocated adequate resources.

Gap 3 -- Service quality specification - service delivery gaps occur when front-line, contact personnel do not perform their task according to guidelines. Service mangers many improve these situations with training and supervision of front-line personnel.

Gap 4 -- A service delivery-external communications gap can exist if advertising or other external communications promise more that the front-line personnel can deliver. A service marketing strategy, like any other marketing strategy, must coordinate all aspects of the marketing mix. To achieve consumer satisfaction, service marketers must deliver what they promise.

In the video Fred Smith indicates that the company is constantly trying to improve service. The video also indicates that Fed Ex is interested in zero failures. Their concern with service quality led Federal Express to win the Baldrige award.

4.   *In what way does technology influence Federal Express' service quality?*

This question is best answered by showing the video which explains the company's cosmos, supertracker, and zodiac systems.

In the video Fred Smith indicates that the use of electronic technology is absolutely essential to improvement of customer satisfaction and to differentiate Federal Express from its competition. Fed Ex says electronic technology is the bedrock of the company. It uses an electronic envelope around telecommunications, and employs computer tracking, scanning, electronic generated labels, and many other technologies. Fed Ex is trying to make all packages "man and machine" readable. Bar code technology is extremely important to Federal Express.

Federal Express' computer tracking system allows a sender to learn if his or her package arrived on time without having to call (and possibly interrupt) the receiver.

Federal Express uses in-process quality control while packages are in transit, trying to avoid problems rather than to react to problems. The video makes the point that the service is "created" right in front of the customers eyes.

CASE 13-2 MILTON SEIFERT & ASSOCIATES[1]

FOCUS ON SMALL BUSINESS

SUBJECT MATTER: Service Marketing, Service Marketing Mix, Consumer Perceptions

Please see the Guide to Video Cases for video length and other information.

AT-A-GLANCE OVERVIEW

When Dr. Milton Seifert started his own practice in 1972, his goal was to satisfy patients with cost-effective, quality care. It was his belief that he would have a good business if he practiced good medicine. When managing his business became more difficult than he had originally perceived, Dr. Seifert formed a business-person's committee of the Patient Advisory Council (PAC).

Seifert's PAC has preserved goodwill in the face of complaints and was the primary reason for a 10 percent discount in Seifert's malpractice insurance. The PAC has also helped promote Milton Seifert & Associates by joining with the practice to put on a community Health Education Forum.

In 1982, many of Seifert's more affluent patients began joining HMOs and leaving his practice. To make a bad situation even worse, overhead rose to 77% and then to 86%. Seifert needed to somehow expand and grow in order to survive.

QUESTIONS

1.   *Identify and evaluate the marketing mix of physicians like Milton Seifert and his associates.*

The product is the medical service. Seifert hired three part-time physicians who shared in his belief that personalized care was not obsolete. Each was willing to provide services at lower-than-market rate. In 1987, Dr. Steven Kind became a partner in the practice and together they increased the practice's availability and productivity while maintaining quality care.

In collaboration with a local mental health and chemical dependency clinic, Milton Seifert and Associates' Health Coordinators were able to meet with a variety of mental health providers, discuss patient concerns, dissolve professional barriers and improve referral patterns.

Today, the Milton Seifert & Associates office employs 15 people and its psychosocial services have been installed in two other medical practices.

Price is the fee paid by the patient. However, acceptance of insurance provider's forms offering payment by the insurance company is part of the price element, along with Visa, MasterCard and other credit plans.

Distribution is direct without any intermediary.

Promotion for most physicians consists of a business card and yellow page advertising. However, pamphlets about health care with the doctor's and clinic's names is another form of promotion. Word-of-mouth advertising, especially for a specialist, is an important source of referrals for many physicians.

2.   *How should Seifert position itself in the health care marketplace?*

Seifert's operation positions itself as offering quality health care with personalized service. Having grown more than 25 percent in the last three years, Milton Seifert & Associates owes its success to an uncompromising commitment to quality and an alliance with its patients. In the medical field a great position is "everything." Permanence, experience, and caring are still very important to

---

[1]Excerpts reprinted from *Strengthening America's Competitiveness*, pp. 78-79, copyright 1991 by Connecticut Mutual Life Insurance Company.

many patients.   People may go to "Rapid Response" for small things, or be less concerned about medical matters when they are young than when they are older, but an aging population needs more health care, and they want it in venues and from persons they feel good about.

3.   *How can service quality be evaluated at Milton Seifert and Associates?*

Service quality involves a comparison of expectations with performance. Consumers who perceive high service quality believe the service providers matched their expectations.

Bedside manner and office personnel have a strong influence on consumers' perception of service quality.   Marketers who wish to deliver high service quality must conform to consumers' service expectations on a consistent basis. Customers who receive quality service come back again.

In organizations that wish to provide high levels of service quality, managers identify customer service needs and plan the proper level of service quality. Managers' analysis and planning leads to specifications for the level of service to be delivered.   Then, nurses and office personnel are trained and given the responsibility for quality service.   Front-line personnel need to be motivated and encouraged to deliver the service according to the specifications planned by managers.   Finally, the results are measured against the standards on a regular basis.

Marketers use gap analysis to identify the sources of the consumer's expected service/perceived service gap.   In addition, several other gaps influence marketing activity.

Gap 1 -- A management perception/consumer expectation gap can exist if managers cannot identify or do not understand what aspect of the service encounter is important to consumers.   For example, patients often want more explanation of their heath problems.   Doctors often overestimate how much time they spend with patients.   That is, they are inclined to think the level of service they provide is greater than it is.   Filling the gap between what customers perceive to be good service and what the doctor perceives to be good service is an essential aspect of service quality management.

Gap 2 -- When an unfavorable management perception/service quality specification gap exists, doctors know what consumers expect, but the specifications they plan are less than what the consumers expect.   In other words, doctors may plan unacceptable standards for time spent in the waiting room.   This may occur in doctor's offices that do not understand the marketing concept.

Gap 3 -- Service quality specification/service delivery gaps occur when front-line, contact personnel do not perform their tasks according to guidelines.

Gap 4 -- A service delivery/external communications gap can exist if advertising or other external communications promise more than the front-line personnel can deliver.   A service marketing strategy, like any other marketing strategy, must coordinate all aspects of the marketing mix.   To achieve consumer satisfaction, service marketers must deliver what they promise.

14 THE NATURE OF DISTRIBUTION

CHAPTER SCAN

This chapter provides a general introduction to the purpose of distribution in the marketing system, with emphasis on how distribution contributes to an effective marketing mix. The fact that all marketers, even not-for-profit and service organizations, engage in distribution activities is stressed.

The functions performed by channel intermediaries are described, along with the major channels of distribution for both consumer and organizational products.

Issues of channel management including vertical marketing systems, channel cooperation and power, and matters of ethics and law are also reviewed.

SUGGESTED LEARNING OBJECTIVES

The student who studies this chapter will be exposed to a broad introduction to the distribution facet of the marketing process and will be able to:

1. Explain the general purpose of distribution in the marketing system.

2. Show how distribution contributes to an effective marketing mix.

3. Understand why all marketers -- even not-for-profit and service marketers -- engage in distribution.

4. Characterize the functions of channel intermediaries.

5. Identify the major channels of distribution used by marketers of consumer and organizational products.

6. Describe the major vertical marketing systems.

7. Differentiate among channel cooperation, channel conflict, and channel power.

8.   Describe some of the ethical and legal concerns associated with the development and management of channels of distribution.

CHAPTER OUTLINE

I.   INTRODUCTION

II.   DISTRIBUTION DELIVERS A STANDARD OF LIVING TO SOCIETY

III.   DISTRIBUTION IN THE MARKETING MIX: A KEY TO SUCCESS

IV.   CHANNEL OF DISTRIBUTION DEFINED

        A.   What a Channel Involves

V.   MARKETING FUNCTIONS PERFORMED BY INTERMEDIARIES

        A.   How Intermediaries Fit in Channels
        B.   Physical Distribution Functions

              1.   Breaking Bulk
              2.   Accumulating Bulk
              3.   Creating Assortments
              4.   Reducing Transactions
              5.   Transportation and Storage

        C.   Communication Functions: Exchanging Information and Title
        D.   Facilitating Functions: The Intermediaries' "Hidden" Tasks

              1.   Extra Services Provided by Intermediaries
              2.   Credit Services
              3.   Risk-Taking

VI.   CHANNELS OF DISTRIBUTION: A SYSTEM OF INTERDEPENDENCY

VII.   ALTERNATE CHANNELS OF DISTRIBUTION

        A.   The Direct Channel
        B.   The Manufacturer-Retailer-Consumer Channel
        C.   The Manufacturer-Wholesaler-Retailer-Consumer Channel
        D.   Channels That Include Agents
        E.   The Direct Channel in Business-to-Business Marketing
        F.   The Manufacturer-Wholesaler-Organizational User Channel
        G.   Business-to-Business Marketers Also Use Agents

VIII.   ARE CHANNELS OF DISTRIBUTION WHAT THE TEXTBOOKS SAY THEY ARE?

IX.   VERTICAL MARKETING SYSTEMS ARE CENTRALLY MANAGED

        A.   Corporate Systems - Total Ownership
        B.   Administered Systems - Strong Leadership
        C.   Contractual Systems - Legal Relationships

X.   MANAGING THE CHANNEL OF DISTRIBUTION

        A.   Determining the Structure of the Channel

              1.   The Marketing Mix Strategy
              2.   Organizational Resources
              3.   External Environmental Criteria

                    a.   Market Characteristics
                    b.   Consumer Preferences and Behavior
                    c.   The Nature and Availability of Intermediaries
                    d.   Other Environmental Factors

B.   The Extent of Distribution: How Many Outlets?

        1.   Intensive Distribution
        2.   Selective Distribution
        3.   Exclusive Distribution

XI.   ISSUES CONCERNING THE INTERDEPENDENCY AMONG CHANNEL MEMBERS

       A.   Channel Cooperation
       B.   Channel Conflict
       C.   Channel Power

XII.   REVERSE DISTRIBUTION

XIII. ETHICAL, POLITICAL, AND LEGAL FORCES IN DISTRIBUTION MANAGEMENT

       A.   Does Distribution Cost Too Much?
       B.   Legal Regulation of Distribution

               1.   Exclusive Dealing
               2.   Exclusive Territories
               3.   Tying Contracts

       C.   Legalities of International Distribution

XIV.   SUMMARY

XV.   KEY TERMS

XVI.   QUESTIONS FOR DISCUSSION (15)

XVII. ETHICS IN PRACTICE

XVIII. CASES

     The following key terms are introduced and used in Chapter 14.   They are
defined in the text's Glossary.

Channel of distribution
Merchant intermediary
Agent intermediary
Conventional channel of distribution
Vertical marketing system
Bulk-breaking function
Bulk-accumulating function
Assembler
Sorting function
Assorting function
Selling function
Credit function
Risk-taking function
Channel interdependency
Jobber
Scrambled merchandising
Multiple channel strategy
Corporate vertical marketing system
Administered vertical marketing system
Contractual vertical marketing system
Cooperative organization
Voluntary chain
Franchise
Intensive distribution
Selective distribution
Exclusive distribution
Channel cooperation
Channel conflict
Channel power
Channel leader, or channel captain

Coercive power
Reward power
Expert power
Referent power
Legitimate power
Backward channel
Exclusive dealings
Exclusive territory
Tying contracts

THE CHAPTER SUMMARIZED

I.   INTRODUCTION

A description of the Carolina Biological Supply Company of Burlington, N.C. introduces this chapter. The company sells everything from human brains to meat-eating plants to one-cell organisms and geological samples. Credit cards are accepted. The company sells mostly to educational institutions, but other customers are welcome.

Much of Carolina's success is traceable to its distribution methods. These play a great part in achieving customer satisfaction, making the organization sizable and successful. The company utilizes a number of channels of distribution and means of transportation to satisfy its customers.

II. DISTRIBUTION DELIVERS A STANDARD OF LIVING TO SOCIETY

The major purpose of marketing is to satisfy human needs by delivering products of various types to buyers when and where they want them and at reasonable cost.

Thus, distribution is of overwhelming importance and accounts for about one-quarter of the price of the consumer goods we buy. It creates time and place utility. Most would agree that it's "worth the price."

Even primitive societies have distribution systems. Though our society is very complex and the distances often quite great, the job is the same: to provide products in the right place at the right time.

III. DISTRIBUTION IN THE MARKETING MIX: A KEY TO SUCCESS

Distribution has become the focus of much attention due to the following:

.   Increasing levels of competition.

.   Cost-consciousness brought on national and world economic developments.

.   Consumer concerns with efficiency in marketing.

Examples of its importance are easy to find.

.   Distribution, rather than production, is now the "biggest part of the business" of major U.S. film studios.

.   Mary Kay and Avon succeeded largely because of their distribution systems.

.   Not-for-profit organizations, such as the Heart Association, distribute both literature and services like blood-pressure checks at libraries, schools, and fire stations.

IV. CHANNEL OF DISTRIBUTION DEFINED

The word channel, derived from the French word for "canal," rightfully suggests a flow of products from producer to buyer. Many intermediary organizations have been developed to aid this flow. The channel of distribution may be called simply a "channel" or a "trade channel" but is always a system of interdependencies, a system that facilitates the exchange process. Intermediaries are specialists in distribution that are external to the producing organization.

A **channel of distribution** consists of producer, consumer, and other intermediary organizations that are aligned to serve as a vehicle to move the product from producer to consumer.

Although the title transfer and physical possession generally follow the same channel of distribution, they need not follow the same path.

A.   What a Channel Involves

All but the shortest (or "direct") channel involves intermediaries. These are organizations that specialize in distribution.

This distinction is to be made between these two intermediary types:

.   **Merchant intermediaries** take title to the products they handle.

.   **Agent intermediaries** do not take title to the products they handle.

Both types perform marketing functions, such as selling, which facilitate the exchange process. Intermediaries may be independent or owned by another organization such as the producer of the products handled.

In service marketing there may appear to be no channel, but there is a direct channel from, say, dentist to patient.

Channel intermediaries form a coalition, each getting a reward for participating cooperatively in the distribution process.

Three terms to be mentioned:

.   **Conventional channel** -- made up of loosely aligned relatively autonomous marketing organizations (wholesalers, etc.).

.   **Vertical marketing system** -- formally organized systems linked by ownership ties or strong contracts or agreements (e.g., a franchise system).

.   **Facilitators** -- functional specialists who offer a service that helps the flow of products but who are not true channel members (e.g., banks and trucking companies).

V.   MARKETING FUNCTIONS PERFORMED BY INTERMEDIARIES

Intermediaries are misunderstood by many. Retailers are often seen as the sole cause of high prices since it is they who collect the consumer's money. Wholesalers perform their necessary and important functions outside of the view of citizens. Thus the "cut out the middlemen" idea gains wide approval.

Though these attitudes go back thousands of years, the fact remains that distribution must somehow be financed. Usually, elimination of middlemen (distribution specialists) will not lower consumer prices since the dollars that go to intermediaries simply pay them for the performance of tasks that must be accomplished regardless of who does them.

A.   How Intermediaries Fit in Channels

Channels vary widely in construction. Not all channels include wholesalers or other institutions. One may use several wholesalers while another uses none. Yet certain functions remain to be performed. If a channel member is "eliminated," the functions performed by that member may be shifted backward (toward the manufacturer's end of the channel) or forward (toward the consumer's end) but the functions remain to be carried out.

The determination of how necessary marketing functions can be carried out efficiently and effectively is the crux of channel design and management.

B.   Physical Distribution Functions

Five major functions of physical distribution are discussed.

1.   Breaking Bulk

Most intermediaries perform a **bulk-breaking function**, buying in comparatively large quantities and selling in smaller quantities. In this way, for example, retailers relieve consumers of the need to buy and store large amounts of goods.

Since producers usually turn out large quantities of products and consumers want to buy much smaller quantities, breaking bulk resolves a discrepancy within the economy.

2.   Accumulating Bulk

Intermediaries may be called upon to perform a **bulk-accumulation function**, to accumulate rather than to break bulk. Intermediaries who do this are often called **assemblers**. Example: Mott's would prefer to buy large quantities of fruits rather than to deal with individual farm owners. An assembler might buy from small farms and accumulate the quantities Mott's would like to buy.

Exhibit 14-1 contrasts the activities of breaking bulk and accumulating bulk.

Some intermediaries perform a **sorting function**, as when eggs are sorted into jumbo, regular, medium, and small categories.

3.   Creating Assortments

Most intermediaries create assortments or perform the **assorting function**.

Examples: a supermarket buys merchandise from many suppliers and presents retail customers with an impressive assortment of goods, a magazine distributor must carry a selection of magazines that is desired by its retailer customers (and by the consumers to whom those retailers sell).

4.   Reducing Transactions

Middlemen, by acting as selling agents for sellers of goods and buying agents for buyers of goods, actually reduce the number of transactions needed to make an economy run.

Example: As a consumer, dealing with one supermarket gets you a vast array of goods. Consider what it would be like to deal with all the producers of those goods. (See Exhibit 14-2.)

5.   Transportation and Storage

Merchandise must be physically moved from the place of production to where it is needed. Further, it usually must be held or stored until desired. Much of this transportation and storage is carried out by intermediaries. This creates time and place utility. Imagine if everyone in the U.S. who wanted Anheuser-Busch products had to travel to St. Louis to get them.

C.   Communication Functions: Exchanging Information and Title

Intermediaries perform important promotional activities to aid the
exchange process.   Their displays and salespeople contribute to the
performance of the **selling function**.   For their own customers,
intermediaries perform the **buying function**.   Throughout all of this,
they will play this role well, imparting product knowledge and other
information.   Located "in the middle," intermediaries are well-placed
to perform the communication function.   It must be admitted that
often they do not properly perform the function.

D.   Facilitating Functions: The Intermediaries' "Hidden" Tasks

Most intermediaries perform various facilitating functions that are
not obvious to the casual observer.

1.   Extra Services Provided by Intermediaries

Depending on the situation, intermediaries are expected to
perform certain "extra" services not part of the basic
buying/selling function.   These include service functions --
repair service, honoring manufacturers' or their own
guarantees; and management services -- as helping customers to
determine appropriate inventory sizes or re-ordering schedules.
These services, if well-performed, can draw business to the
intermediary.

2.   Credit Services

Many intermediaries perform a **credit function**.   Extension of
credit periods such as 30 or 60 days before payment is often
expected.   Accepting credit cards, offering credit plans, and
other credit-related services may be provided.

3.   Risk-Taking

Holding inventory that could spoil or go out of style,
extending credit, and accepting legal risks, are all part of
the **risk-taking function**.   Holding inventories is particularly
important.   Seeking to avoid this risk by hand-to-mouth buying
defeats the purpose of most channels.

Exhibit 14-3 summarizes the basic functions channel
intermediaries perform.

VI.   CHANNELS OF DISTRIBUTION: A SYSTEM OF INTERDEPENDENCY

Channels depend on cooperation among members.   Recognition of
interdependency is necessary if channels are to work smoothly.   The channel
is, in effect, an application of the specialization of labor principle.

The actions of any channel member can greatly affect the performance of
others and of the channel as a whole.   Success is rooted in a "community of
interest," or channel interdependency.

VII.   ALTERNATIVE CHANNELS OF DISTRIBUTION

The variety of channels of distribution is extensive.   Channels are
generally distinguished by the number of intermediaries they include.   The
greater the number of intermediaries the longer the channel is said to be.

Exhibit 14-4 shows the primary channels of distribution of both consumer
and industrial goods.

A.   The Direct Channel

The neighborhood bakery or diner produces its products and then sells
to customers via the direct channel.   Avon does the same, as do many

producers of specialized industrial products. Selling via catalogs
or 800 numbers are uses of direct channels.

B.   The Manufacturer-Retailer-Consumer Channel

The manufacturer to retailer channel is commonly used, especially
when the retailer in question is a large one able to buy in sizable
quantities and deserving of a manufacturer's special attention.
Also, some retailers order their made-to-order products (special
merchandise) direct from manufacturers. Efficiencies that accrue to
manufacturers because of large orders from Wal-Mart or Sears can more
than offset the wholesaling costs the manufacturer may have to
absorb.

C.   The Manufacturer-Wholesaler-Retailer-Consumer Channel

This traditional channel is the most commonly used one for consumer
goods. Such a "long" channel would be necessary for manufacturers
such as Wrigley or P&G who must reach the huge numbers of stores that
carry their goods. To reach each person who chews gum, or even each
retailer who sells gum, would be virtually impossible for Wrigley.

D.   Channels That Include Agents

Commonly employed agent intermediaries are the manufacturer's agent
and selling agent. These do not take title to the goods they sell
but earn commissions by representing manufacturers. Agents may sell
to retailers or wholesalers, depending on circumstances.

E.   The Direct Channel in Business-to-Business Marketing

The very name business-to-business suggests the importance of the
direct channel in this field. The direct channel is one of the most
commonly encountered in the marketing of organizational goods. One
reason is that many of these products require well-informed
salespersons or engineers who can help the buyer properly evaluate
and use the products being sold.

F.   The Manufacturer-Wholesaler-Organizational User Channel

This channel employs a wholesaler who acts something like a retailer,
selling products to users (businesses or other organizations). Names
for this intermediary vary from industry to industry, but **jobber** is a
term commonly used, another is industrial distributor. These jobbers
are merchant intermediaries; they take title to the good.
Distributors of Snap-On Tools, who call on shop owners and sell from
well-stocked vans, fit this description.

G.   Business-to-Business Marketers Also Use Agents

The manufacturer-agent-organizational user channel is often used by
small manufacturers that market one product to many users.
Manufacturers' agents can be used to cover a territory on a
commission basis. Thus they appeal to manufacturers who could not
justify and/or fund their own sales forces. Manufacturers' agents
are also appropriate for use in "thin" market areas, or overseas
markets, where potential sales do not seem to justify use of one's
own sales force.

VIII. ARE CHANNELS OF DISTRIBUTION WHAT THE TEXTBOOKS SAY THEY ARE?

This question was posed by a famous marketing management article by Philip
McVey. Of course, the realities of the world are such that the answer to
the question must be "No."

Textbook illustrations, such as Exhibit 14-4, are too pat and too neat to
be true reflections of reality. More realistic, and confusing, is Exhibit
14-5. Businesses sell to many kinds of customers. Many firms are involved
in several businesses and operate at several levels, e.g., as manufacturer

and wholesaler and retailer, and not always of the same product. Many
manufacturers use a **multiple channels strategy**. Many sellers practice
scrambled merchandising, which is said to occur when one product
traditionally sold in one type of store is sold at many different types of
retail stores. Textbook descriptions, accurate for many situations, cannot
fully describe complexities.

IX.   VERTICAL MARKETING SYSTEMS ARE CENTRALLY MANAGED

In many industries, e.g., fast foods, the vertical marketing system is the
dominant distribution system.

Vertical marketing systems, or vertically integrated marketing systems (VMS
or VIMS), consist of networks of vertically aligned establishments that are
professionally managed as centrally administered distribution systems.
They are centrally administered to achieve technological, managerial, and
promotional economies of scale through the integration, coordination, and
synchronization of transactions and marketing activities necessary to the
distribution function.

There are three types (listed below.)

A.   Corporate Systems -- Total Ownership

The **corporate vertical marketing system** connects two or more channel
members through ownership. Here a channel member actually owns the
system. Examples: Sears and A&P both own manufacturing and
distribution systems. Sherwin-Williams administers a corporate VMS
by owning more than 2,000 retail paint outlets. Thus, for many
products, the marketing system is a corporately owned one.

B.   Administered Systems-Strong Leadership

In the **administered vertical marketing system**, a strong position of
leadership is the source of influence one channel member has over
another. Coordination is achieved by planning and managing a
mutually beneficial program made attractive to all parties by using
discounts or offering aid of some kind. Example: Scott (lawn
products) and Ralph Lauren (men's clothing) can influence those who
deal in their products and thereby administer their distribution
systems. This position of strength can be held by a wholesaler,
retailer, or manufacturer.

C.   Contractual Systems-Legal Relationships

In the **contractual vertical marketing system** leadership is formally
spelled out in contract form. McDonald's headquarters is formally
linked to franchise holders in this way. Three variants on the
contractual VMS are:

    .   The **retailer cooperative organization**, a group of independent
          retailers who combine resources to maintain a centralized
          buying center that acts as their wholesaler. Example:
          Certified Grocers.

    .   The **voluntary chain**, wherein a wholesaler organizes independent
          retailers into a chain-like group that relies on the wholesaler
          for supplies and aids. The member stores may appear to be a
          chain but are, in fact, independent. Example: IGA stores.

    .   The **franchise** maintained by a contractual agreement between a
          franchisor and franchisee. McDonald's is a familiar franchise
          operation, as are Wendy's, Subway, Godfather's Pizza, and so
          on. Non-food franchisors include AAMCO, Holiday Inn, and
          Midas.

X.   MANAGING THE CHANNEL OF DISTRIBUTION

Distribution strategy involves making two major decisions:

.   Determining the structure of the channel.

.   Determining the extent of distribution.

A.   Determining the Structure of the Channel

Many factors can influence this decision.   Three are discussed here.

1.   The Marketing Mix Strategy

The structure of the channel depends in part on the other marketing mix decisions made.   Examples: product characteristics including perishability, need for after-sale service, size, bulk, weight, technical complexity, replacement rate, gross margin and product image.

2.   Organizational Resources

P&G is a wealthy company with resources enough to have its own sales force and to strongly influence its distribution channels.   Church and Dwight (Arm and Hammer baking soda) has far fewer resources and relies heavily on food brokers to sell its product to supermarkets.

Frito Lay's Sunchips was marketed in the same channel as Doritos and other snack foods manufactured by the company. Relationships in the channel were already worked out.   Firms like Frito Lay can spread distribution costs over many products. Smaller firms are unable to do that.

3.   External Environmental Criteria

Many elements of the external environment affect channel selection.

a.   Market Characteristics

The number of customers and average purchase size are important.   If there are many customers, especially buying in small amounts, channels will tend to be long. If there are few buyers, especially buying in large amounts, channels will tend to be short.

b.   Consumer Preferences and Behavior

If customers prefer to buy a product at supermarkets, marketers of that product must adjust their distribution system to meet that preference.   Scrambled merchandising complicates this and may necessitate development of multiple channels of distribution.

c.   The Nature and Availability of Intermediaries

A chosen channel may be unavailable if the needed channel members will not or can not handle the product. Examples: exclusive dealerships may be "the rule" as they are with autos, or certain intermediaries may refuse to carry a product because they feel their current product line or image would be threatened.

d.   Other Environmental Factors

Any environmental variable can affect distribution. Example: In some countries tradition "requires" that distribution of certain products be handled in certain ways.

B.   The Extent of Distribution: How Many Outlets?

Marketers must decide the intensity of distribution their products will have at each channel level. How many wholesalers? How many retailers? There are three general choices.

1.   Intensive Distribution

The **intensive distribution** strategy seeks maximum product exposure. Products that are bought frequently, well-known, and/or "pre-sold" through advertising, are good candidates for intensive distribution at "every possible spot." For example, cigarettes, soft drinks, and chewing gum. Pennzoil motor oil is also intensively distributed to garages, mass merchandisers, and Jiffy-Lube, partly-owned by Pennzoil.

2.   Selective Distribution

The **selective distribution** approach restricts the sale of the product to a limited number of outlets because people are willing to shop for these items and to spend time comparing goods. Examples: Hathaway shirts, Florsheim shoes, Cover Girl Cosmetics, many branded women's clothing items.

3.   Exclusive Distribution

When special selling, repairs, or inventories are required, **exclusive distribution** is often employed. Automobiles, tractors, expensive crystal, Caterpillar tractors would be sold in this way. Exclusive distribution is also found at the wholesale level for a product like Coca Cola, which is intensively distributed but handled by exclusive bottling franchise holders.

XI.   ISSUES CONCERNING THE INTERDEPENDENCY AMONG CHANNEL MEMBERS

The actions of one channel member may greatly influence the other members. Many retailers rely on manufacturers to advertise products while manufacturers rely on retailers to properly display and price those products. Car dealers depend on manufacturers for many activities; manufacturers depend on the dealers for other activities.

A.   Channel Cooperation

The ideal is **channel cooperation**, a situation in which the marketing objectives and strategies of two or more channel members are harmonious.

B.   Channel Conflict

Channel conflict refers to a situation in which channel members have disagreements and their relationship is antagonistic. If the behavior of one channel member is perceived to be inhibiting the attainment of another channel member's goal, there exists channel conflict, a situation in which channel members are antagonistic because of disagreements about the channel's common purpose or about responsibilities for certain activities. Examples:

.   K-Mart in "conflict" with Zayre is horizontal channel conflict since they are at the same channel levels.

.   Manufacturers who sell directly to large retailers may anger wholesalers. This is vertical channel conflict since these two organizations are not at the same channel levels.

It has been argued that a limited amount of channel conflict is good since it may bring about more equitable distribution, and greater balance and stability within the system. But channel conflict is destructive when a lack of recognition of mutual objectives results. Conflict must, therefore, be managed.

C.   Channel Power

One organization in a channel may be able to exert **channel power** over the others and influence their behavior. Such an organization may be termed the **channel captain** or **channel leader**.

The channel captain may be found at any channel level depending on particular circumstances.

There are three types of power which channel captains may exercise.

.   **Coercive power**: the ability to force compliance, usually by economic threat.

.   **Reward power**: the ability to offer a reward, such as a large order.

.   **Expert power**: based on knowledge.

.   **Referent power**: "respect." Anheuser-Busch is trustworthy and has proved itself to have admirable characteristics.

.   **Legitimate power**: as when Godfather's Pizza contractually agrees to perform specific activities.

XII.   REVERSE DISTRIBUTION

It has been pointed out that consumers seeking to recycle waste products become "distributors" or "producers" and users of those products become "customers." This is a reverse channel of distribution or **backward channel**. The ordinary consumer is the first link in the channel rather than the last.

Reverse channels have been very primitive, such as Boy Scouts picking up cans and newspapers.

XIII. ETHICAL, POLITICAL, AND LEGAL FORCES IN DISTRIBUTION MANAGEMENT

Ethical and legal issues, as well as issues of distribution, can be connected with distribution and its macromarketing role.

A.   Does Distribution Cost Too Much?

We have explored specialization of labor in the channel of distribution and have seen that "eliminate the middleman" is an unreasonable demand. If the middleman is removed, the functions of the middleman will remain to be performed and may be performed less effectively and efficiently by a non-specialist. Total costs might very well rise, not fall, if we "eliminate the middleman." Some aspects of distribution may be "nonessential." We could probably live without 7-Eleven-type convenience stores and their high prices. Yet consumers evaluating the various trade-offs involved seem to prefer keeping them in the system.

B.   Legal Regulation of Distribution

In American and international trade, distribution may be subject to legal restrictions, usually to assure that unfair competition does not occur.

In the U.S. three main concerns are to be found.

1.   Exclusive Dealing

Exclusive dealing refers to a restrictive arrangement by which a supplier prohibits intermediaries that handle its product

from selling the products of competing suppliers.
It is easy to imagine situations where makers or distributors
of a very popular product might use their market power to get
other channel members to "play ball" and agree to exclusive
dealings.

Legislation focused on this problem is intended to prevent
channel members from abusing their rights as independent
businesses when the exercise of those rights seriously hurts
other businesses. Exclusive dealing is illegal if it tends to
restrict competition.

Exclusive dealing arrangements are generally legal if it can be
shown that the exclusivity is necessary for legitimate reasons,
e.g., to protect image or because production capabilities are
limited.

2.   Exclusive Territories

A manufacturer that grants a wholesaler or retailer an
exclusive territory may be performing an illegal act. If
granting of exclusive territories is not seen as restricting
competition, such territories are legal. The determination, if
necessary, must be made by our legal system.

Some defenses of exclusive territories include:

.   The investment in a dealership is so great that if no
        "territory" were assigned, no new dealers would want to
        sign on. A Cadillac dealership or McDonald's franchise
        would be examples.

.   The product image is one of exclusivity. A Mercedes
        dealership on every corner would destroy that product's
        image.

.   The product quality is so high that if many dealerships
        were allowed, customers would doubt quality could be
        maintained, e.g., Rolls Royce dealers and repair shops.

3.   Tying Contracts

Tying contracts ("If you buy product A, you must buy product
B") are illegal under the Clayton Act of 1914. But it is
always debatable whether or not a given agreement is a tying
contract. Such agreements are generally not defensible if
competing products of like quality are available. IBM computer
owners need not use "official" IBM ribbons and paper if other
supplies of like quality are available.

Cases involving Dunkin' Donuts (1975) and Baskin-Robbins (1982)
have established that tying agreements may be justified if they
can be proven to be attempts to maintain standards of quality,
enter a new market or industry, or preserve market or franchise
identity.

C.   Legalities of International Distribution

Many restraints and limits on distribution freedom are compounded in
international trade. Usually domestic laws and the laws of the
importing countries must be obeyed as well as those of countries
through which products must travel.

XIV.   SUMMARY

Distribution is a necessary but often misunderstood marketing function.
The common desire to "eliminate the middleman" shows that the general
public has little appreciation for the role played by the channel of
distribution.

Learning Objective 1:   Explain the general purpose of distribution in the marketing system.

A channel of distribution makes it possible for the title or possession of a product to pass from producer to consumer. By common agreement, channel members share the responsibility for performing the basic functions of marketing. Distribution provides time and place utility to buyers by delivering the right products at the right time in the right place. It bridges the gap between manufacturers and final users. In effect, distribution delivers a standard of living.

Learning Objective 2:   Show how distribution contributes to an effective marketing mix.

Effective distribution complements the other marketing mix variables and helps achieve the goal of effective marketing. Perishable products must be distributed quickly, expensive products must be moved to stores or other locations consistent with the value of the products, delicate products must be handled with care, widely promoted and demanded products must be distributed to large and geographically diverse markets. Channel structure in turn influences costs, prices, promotion, and other marketing concerns.

Learning Objective 3:   Understand why all marketers - even not-for-profit and service marketers - engage in distribution.

All marketers, including not-for-profit, service, and for-profit concerns, engage in some form of distribution because there is always some gap between the marketer and the customer that must be bridged.

Learning Objective 4:   Characterize the functions of channel intermediaries.

Channel members perform a variety of functions including breaking bulk, accumulating bulk, sorting, creating assortments, reducing transactions, transportation, storage, communication (selling and buying), financing, management services, and other facilitating services.

Learning Objective 5:   Identify the major channels of distribution used by marketers of consumer and organizational products.

The major distribution channels for consumer goods are (1) producer to consumer; (2) producer to retailer to consumer; (3) producer to wholesaler to retailer to consumer (the most commonly used consumer goods channel); and, (4) producer to wholesaler (agent) to wholesaler to retailer to consumer. The major organizational products channels are (1) producer to user; (2) producer to wholesaler to user; and (3) producer to agent (wholesaler) to user. There are many variations on these basic channel models, many of which involve specialized intermediaries.

Learning Objective 6:   Describe the major vertical marketing systems.

In the corporate vertical marketing system, the members are owned outright by the controlling organization to ensure cooperation and increased effectiveness. An administered vertical marketing system is made up of organizations that follow the lead of the dominant member of the system. In a contractual vertical marketing system, the members are linked to the channel leader by formal contract. In all cases, the purpose of the vertical marketing system is to ensure cooperation among channel members, and the goal is increased effectiveness of the channel.

Learning Objective 7:   Differentiate among channel cooperation, channel conflict, and channel power.

Channel cooperation occurs when channel members share harmonious marketing objectives and strategies. Channel conflict characterizes channels of distribution in which there is some disharmony. Conflict should not go unmanaged. Channel power is the ability of one organization in a channel of distribution to exert influence over other channel members. The most powerful organization is the channel leader.

<u>Learning Objective 8</u>: **Describe some of the ethical and legal concerns associated with the development and management of channels of distribution.**

Several ethical issues arise concerning the macromarketing role of distribution. Many of these have been addressed by laws. Exclusive dealing arrangements can be seen as stopping the distribution of competitors' goods and are thus sometimes illegal. So are territorial arrangements, which may restrict free trade. Tying agreements, which tie the purchase of one product to purchase of another, are in almost all cases illegal.

XV.   KEY TERMS

XVI.   QUESTIONS FOR DISCUSSION (15)

XVII.   ETHICS IN PRACTICE

XVIII. CASES

ANSWER GUIDELINES FOR CHAPTER 12 QUESTIONS FOR DISCUSSION

1.   *What might happen if we eliminated wholesaler intermediaries for the following brands? (a) Izod Lacoste shirts (b) Cutty Sark Scotch whiskey (c) Weyerhauser lumber*

ANSWER:

Technically, intermediaries may include retailers, but in this answer we address only wholesalers.

The key point of this question is that elimination of wholesalers does not eliminate their functions. These must be handled by some other channel member, being shifted backward to the manufacturer or forward to the retailer or consumer. The assumption we are making here is that the channel of distribution for all three products is this one:

MANUFACTURER ---> WHOLESALER ---> RETAILER ---> CONSUMERS

In fact, all three products are distributed via this channel and by other channels as well.

(a)   Izod Lacoste shirts

Elimination of the wholesaler would mean that the manufacturer or the retailer would have to perform these functions: bulk-breaking into lot sizes appropriate for retailers; provide promotional and product information support; storage until the goods are shipped to retailers; delivery of one form or another; and handling of complaints and returns. Because many retailers ranging in size from major department stores to small college bookstores handle Izod shirts, the problem of providing all these services is clearly large and complex. Further, it is difficult to imagine how most of these functions might be shifted forward onto retailers themselves, though Izod's strong market position might permit the company to "encourage" retailers to accept larger orders, thus shifting some bulk-breaking on to them.

(b)   Cutty Sark Scotch whiskey

A situation much like that of Izod's would prevail with Cutty Sark Scotch whiskey. The manufacturer would face greater bulk-breaking, delivery, promotional and other problems. Retailers would have to place larger orders which could be a serious problem for some given the size of many shops, the shortage of extra storage space, the need to pay for larger orders, and the size and weight of cases of whiskey.

Cutty Sark would face serious difficulty were it to lose its wholesalers because the product is produced in one place (Scotland) and sent, in varying quantities, worldwide.   Keeping up worldwide distribution would be "impossible" without wholesalers.

(c)   Weyerhauser lumber

Lumber is sold to many kinds of retailers as well as construction companies, units of government, and other classes of buyers, such as remodeling stores, furniture makers.   Great effort would be needed to supply such an array of customers.   Sales, promotion, storage, delivery and other problems would be complicated by the fact that lumber is a bulky product but cheap in comparison to its bulk.

2.   *Outline the macromarketing functions performed by wholesalers and retailers.*

ANSWER:

There are several macromarketing functions performed by wholesalers and retailers.   For one thing, the roles they play in distribution make them part of the system that "delivers a standard of living to society."   Wholesalers in particular see to it that products from around the country and world end up where they are demanded.

Wholesalers and retailers both typically participate in the major activity known as "resolution of discrepancies."   One of these is "breaking bulk" or "resolution of economic discrepancies."   The typical manufacturer, at one end of the channel, prefers to turn out large quantities of a single item or a limited number of items.   This is "good economics" from that manufacturer's point of view.   However, at the other end of the channel, the consumer wants to buy one or a limited number of items.   Somehow the large amount of product at one end of the channel must be broken down to meet the consumer's demand.   This is what most wholesalers and retailers do.   They buy in comparatively large quantities and sell in comparatively small quantities.   In the special case of "assembling bulk," middlemen buy from many small producers such as small farm operators and sell large quantities to major buyers like food processing companies.   Like bulk-breaking, this is also a resolution of economic discrepancies.

Middlemen of all types also help create assortments.   Retailers, for example, assemble assortments of merchandise suited to their customers.   Though they work behind the scenes, wholesalers perform much the same function.

Middlemen also serve to reduce the number of transactions necessary to affect trade.   Exhibit 14-2 shows that addition of an intermediary to an "economy" that includes five sellers and five buyers cuts the number of transactions necessary for trade to about one fifth of what it would be without the middleman.   Further, intermediaries reduce the geographic distances necessary to complete exchanges in their absence.

Other macromarketing functions that intermediaries provide include communication, exchange, and many facilitating functions.

The contributions of intermediaries to our macromarketing system are less than fully appreciated.   "Eliminate the middleman" is a cry that has been heard for hundreds of years, along with the charge that distribution costs too much.   Reflection may lead us to side with the author whose article posed the question "Does distribution cost too little?" It has been suggested that banking and shopping be performed at home with personal computers.   What implications would this have for channels of distribution?

3.   *At a national bottlers' meeting, the vice-president of marketing for the Dr. Pepper Company said, "No matter how good a job we do, (consumers) can't get Dr. Pepper unless you (bottlers) have made the sale to retailers."   Why would the vice-president say this?*

ANSWER:

Dr. Pepper is sold to consumers by all sorts of retailers ranging from large supermarkets to 7-Eleven-type stores, and from restaurants to coin-operated machines. The "headquarters" at Dr. Pepper could never deal with all of the retailers very efficiently. It is the bottlers who perform such functions as:

.   Manufacturing (of soda at the local level using Dr. Pepper-approved ingredients).

.   Packaging (six packs, cases, etc.).

.   Pricing (to reflect local market conditions).

.   Delivery (via fleets of various trucks).

.   Promotion (to retailers via personal selling and sales promotion as well as some advertising).

.   "Marketing research" at a local level and in the form of feedback to headquarters.

.   Communication (as a link between Dr. Pepper headquarters and retailers and vice versa).

Students will be able to think of other important functions performed by bottlers.

In short, it is hard to imagine a wholesaler doing more than is done by local bottlers. The statement of the vice-president reflects this business reality. If the bottlers don't do their jobs, Dr. Pepper and the vice-president will soon vanish from the business scene.

4.   *A few years ago, Airwick professional products division, which sells a variety of disinfectants, cleaning agents, insecticides, and environmental sanitation products, sold its products through a network of 65 distributors and 10 branch sales offices. The company decided to drop its sales branches. What circumstances might lead to such a change in channel strategy?*

ANSWER:

The answer to such a question usually falls into one of a very few possibilities. The company probably determined that the branches were expendable because the functions they were supposed to be performing:

.   Were not being properly performed.

.   Could be performed by the home office or by the 65 distributors.

.   Conflicted with the activities of the 65 distributors.

.   Were being done more inexpensively by the distributors.

.   Were rendered unnecessary due to environmental change.

5.   *Medical professionals have recently realized that they, like manufacturers, must consider their distribution systems. Hospitals, dentists, and pediatricians might have to make what distribution decision?*

ANSWER:

"Distribution" is broadly defined when one discusses hospitals, dentists, and pediatricians. Here are some "location" decisions facing these three. Some are care-provision decisions; others are business growth decisions.

(a)   Hospitals

.   Location of main hospital and outlying clinics or branches.

.   Hours of operation of various departments, 24-hours for emergency room, 12 hours a day for family health clinic, etc.

- Location and ease of entry of entrances.

- Mobile units for "house-call" purposes, emergency purposes, or sharing expensive equipment and procedures with other hospitals.

- Deliveries of blood, medicines, lab reports, and X-rays to physicians and other hospitals.

- Sending out experts or teams to aid in local health efforts, e.g., speak to groups about exercise or blood pressure.

(b)   Dentists

- Location of office.

- Office hours, weekdays and weekends, evening hours.

- Office hours kept and emergency treatment procedures.

- Scheduling of patients to provide good service.

- "House calls," especially to hospitals and nursing care facilities.

- Mobile units. (Some dentists do operate out of vans.)

- Scheduling of "clinics" for lower-income citizens.

- Going to schools as a guest lecturer.

(c)   Pediatricians

- Location of office.

- Office hours.

- Visits to hospitals and day care centers to provide counseling or treatment.

- Visits to childbirth classes.

- Willingness to make house calls.

- "Branch" offices -- some medical providers do spend certain days in one office and certain days at the other.

6.   *Goldman Sachs is the distributor for the U.S. government's gold coins that compete with Krugerrands. Originally, the gold coins were sold through the U.S. Postal Service, but the distribution situation was not satisfactory. What do you think went wrong?*

ANSWER:

Remember that the U.S. government is that wonderful outfit that brought us the Susan B. Anthony dollar and the I.R.S. We don't mean to sound sarcastic, but it is amazing that the government chose to turn to professional business people rather than to hang on to the distribution of this product until the product was finally "killed." Some things that could have been wrong with the Postal Service distribution process are these:

- The postal employees have no particular knowledge about either selling or gold.

- The Post Office is associated with mail, not with investment.

- The Postal Service has a reputation for "screwing up." (A letter is bad enough to lose, do you want them to handle your gold?)

- Prices of the pieces could not be discovered at the Post Office. The process involved calling the Treasury Department for the price, buying a Postal Money Order for the amount, then waiting six weeks for delivery.

- The Postal Service is, on the whole, an "order taking" business not used to promoting a product. The coins were new and needed promotion from their "retailers."

- The Postal Service sold the coins as an "extra." Employees had little or no interest in whether or not the coin sold. Goldman Sachs would have far more interest.

- Goldman Sachs is probably more flexible in arranging terms of sale than the Postal Service.

7.   *If Sam's Wholesale Club, Price Club, and similar stores sell food, how will Procter & Gamble's distribution system be affected?*

ANSWER:

P&G's distribution will be affected to some degree. A vast percentage of P&G's sales are made in supermarkets, not in small general, neighborhood, or convenience stores. That is, P&G is used to distributing large quantities to large stores. To the degree that Sam's buys more product, the distribution system's capacities may have to be enlarged in certain areas to accommodate the larger quantities demanded.

Currently, P&G uses brokers and distributors, supplementing their efforts with those of P&G's own "missionary salesmen." As supermarkets become larger and more centralized, the point at which P&G will decide to deal directly with them will be reached. Thus, P&G will have to make sure that channel members who now handle its products can handle larger quantities, but Sam's could prove to be so big a buyer that P&G has to deal directly with Sam's (and similar large buyers). P&G's other big sales getters, the institutional and private brand markets, will be unaffected for the most part. If small buyers become even less important to P&G than they are, the company may decide to permit small distributors to deal with them, "cutting them off" in terms of access to and dealings with P&G itself.

Changes, then, should include "more of the same" and enlargement of P&G's ability to deal directly with big buyers. P&G would seem to be the sort of company that will be able to handle changes in its sales environment.

P&G has been in the news recently with its attempts to implement a one-low-price strategy. This has infuriated some supermarkets, but may also be viewed as a reaction to the growing strength of such retailers as Sam's and the consumer's constant search for value in food and other supermarket products. In talking with a personal friend who works in consumer product sales for one of the big manufacturers it was discovered that P&G and others are also focusing on supermarket headquarters and cutting the sales force and service for smaller, less-profitable accounts.

8.   *If you were the manufacturer of the following products what channels of distribution would you select? (a) Facsimile (Fax) machines (b) Automobile mufflers (c) Personal computers (d) Telephones (e) Toy dolls*

ANSWER:

The answers to this question will vary depending on what market one chooses. Are the telephones to be sold to consumers or businesses? Noting this, we make the following suggestions.

(a)   Facsimile (Fax) machines

A manufacturer of fax machines starting out today to distribute his or her product would be faced with a wide array of distribution means. This is because the fax has become so popular so quickly that there are potential buyers ranging from huge companies and governments and commercial buyers to in-home users. The price has fallen rapidly. Individuals are installing them in their cars. They will soon become nearly as commonplace as telephone answering machines.

All this means that the market is fragmented into many segments. The means of distribution selected would depend on the segment to be pursued. Some examples: inexpensive in-home models might be distributed and retailed via mail order methods; office models might be distributed using manufacturers' agents, selling agents, or company-owned sales forces; fax systems for large-scale buyers might best be sold using personal selling methods and direct delivery from the manufacturer.

(b)   Automobile mufflers

Many sorts of dealers buy mufflers intended to be used in the replacement or so-called "automotive aftermarket." The O.E. (original equipment market of G.M., Ford, Toyota, etc.) would be reached via direct dealings with automakers, but the aftermarket includes gas stations, car dealers, do-it-yourselfers who buy at retail, muffler specialists like Midas, and large repair operations like Sears or Wards. All of these needs could be met only by a distribution system that permitted some fine-tuning.

Since the products are varied but not complicated, middlemen might be used almost universally except in the cases of the largest buyers (Midas, Sears) if those buyers insist on buying direct from suppliers. Thus, we have these possibilities:

MANUFACTURERS ---------------------------->   LARGE BUYERS WHO CHOOSE TO BUY
                                              DIRECT

MANUFACTURERS -----> WHOLESALER/JOBBER --->   LOCAL GARAGES, CAR DEALERS,
                                              REPAIR SHOPS, AUTO PART SHOPS,
                                              ETC.

Of course, in both these cases the "customer" remains the car owner. The repair facility simply retails and installs the product. The exception occurs when a buyer purchases the muffler with the intention of installing it at home. Then the dealer performs the retailing function but not the installation function.

(c)   Personal computers

These are somewhat complex products and can be expensive. Many buyers feel the need for advice, instruction, updating on software or add-ons, and a sense that the company stands behind its product and will provide repairs. These needs cannot be met by anything other than a "personal" setting. Most consumers want to go to a "computer store," just as they go to a TV or other appliance dealer, and most industrial buyers want to "talk to somebody." Of course, some buyers are so price-conscious and/or knowledgeable that they will buy mail order. Here, however, the price is the big attraction. In most instances, even if the distributor is owned by the computer manufacturer, a "door to door" approach is not likely to be well received. Small business buyers would probably have to be reached in the same way. Manufacturer's agents or a "non-retail" sales force could be used to approach business customers.

(d)   Telephones

Following the AT&T breakup, most phones are bought rather than leased. "Bought for home use" is virtually a definition of a "retail good." Such a consumer good is most commonly distributed through the "traditional channel."

     MANUFACTURER ----> WHOLESALER ----> RETAILER ----> CONSUMER

Or, when large retailers are involved:

     MANUFACTURER ----> RETAILER ----> CONSUMER

There seems no reason to think that this will not be the case with telephones. These are increasingly becoming "throw-away" models as cheap as $10 or $15. Even the more expensive models rarely exceed $150.

When telephones are sold to businesses, different channels would be needed. Most businesses do not just buy a phone and plug it in. Managers would like to evaluate systems, weighing AT&T's suggestions against those of other suppliers. Thus, a direct channel of distribution is likely to be found, or one that involves a manufacturer-trained agent.

(e)   Toy dolls

With some exceptions, these are mass-market, standardized, relatively inexpensive and uncomplicated items. Thus, the two channels described above for telephones would apply. Rare, expensive, and collector's dolls might require different channels.

9.   *Identify the channel of distribution for: (a) an airline, (b) a bakery, (c) a pizza restaurant.*

ANSWER:

One has to debate some fine points to say anything other than the direct PRODUCER ----> CONSUMER channel applies to all of these. Remember, the channel is the route the product takes from producer to user.

(a)   An airline

For airlines, the channel of distribution is direct because the flyer receives the product directly from the airline. The ticket, which might be sold by a travel agent or even bought and re-sold by the agent, is not the product, so the channel remains direct. To the degree that the agent may "enhance" the ticket, such as by building an excursion around the ticket, does that agent actually deliver the product? No, since the flight itself is still delivered from the airline directly to the flyer.

(b)   A bakery

A bakery, as mentioned in the text, is a "direct distribution system." The manufacturing of bread and cookies is completed and the product sold directly to a buyer.

If we assume that "bakery" means a large Wonder Bread-style bakery, then the distribution is likely to be:

        MANUFACTURER -----> RETAILER -----> CUSTOMER

Some large bakeries freeze their product and distribute through wholesalers.

        MANUFACTURER --> FOOD BROKER --> RETAILER --> CUSTOMER

(c)   A pizza restaurant

A "pizza place" typically sells direct to the sit-down or take-out customer. Though pizza manufacturers may use the same channel variations open to the bakeries, the question asks specifically about a pizza restaurant, i.e., a place where people go to eat.

10.   *What advantages do vertical marketing systems have over conventional marketing systems?*

ANSWER:

There are three kinds of VMS:

.   A corporate VMS involves ownership of other channel members. Sears owns some organizations that produce goods for Sears.

.   An administered VMS is based on a strong position of leadership held by a channel member such as a manufacturer of the very popular Sony products.

.   A contractual VMS is held together by written contracts, e.g., franchise agreements.

A smoothly-operating VMS may achieve technological, managerial, distributional, promotional and other economies of scale. Further, the presence in the system of a "boss" often serves the interests of all by keeping things flowing smoothly (integration, coordination, and synchronization of effort).

Incidentally, it might be worth asking what a "conventional marketing system" is. Surely it cannot be another name for a chaotic mess. Such a system would not survive for long. It is arguable, therefore, that all channels are, to some degree, "administered VMSs." At the least, this suggestion might be worth debating in class.

11.   *Would you use exclusive, selective, or intensive distribution for the following products? Why? (a) Dr. Pepper (b) Lexus automobiles (c) Panasonic videocassette recorders (d) Ethan Allen furniture (e) Fieldcrest Mills towels (f) Michelin tires*

ANSWER:

The point in the text should be noted again, that is, manufacturers could choose an exclusive distribution strategy with wholesalers and an intensive strategy at the retail level. Assuming the interest is at the retail level, the following suggestions are provided.

(a)   Dr. Pepper

This is a convenience good which can be used at any time of the day or night. It competes with Coke, Pepsi, and many others. These products are relatively cheap, uncomplicated, quickly used-up, frequently bought, easy to store, and so forth. Intensive distribution, distribution to and through "every possible means," is the way to go.

(b)   Lexus automobiles

Due to the dealership arrangements with automobile manufacturers and relatively high price, the Lexus may be considered to be exclusively distributed. However, students may suggest selective distribution depending on the size of the city or town. If there is no dealership in a small town which sells the Lexus and the nearest outlet is 90 miles away in the big city, that appears to be an exclusive distribution system. There may be, however, automobiles in lower price lines offered in this small town, which would not appear to be an exclusive distribution system. Students may need to be reminded that even if there are four Chevy dealers in one city there is still an element of exclusivity. One is on the west side, one is in the suburbs to the south, etc. They have "territories," if not very meaningful ones.

(c)   Panasonic videocassette recorders

With the advent of CD players, students may consider the videocassette recorder as an unsought product. However, recorders maintain high usage for many business and customer purposes. Given the price range and Panasonic name, neither intensive nor exclusive distribution seem appropriate. Panasonic is a mid-range brand with a good reputation but it is not the "top-of-the-line"; thus, selective distribution is in order.

(d)   Ethan Allen furniture

Ordinarily, furniture is thought of as a shopping good which suggests selective distribution. Ethan Allen has, however, tried to play on its well-known name to develop a series of dealerships not unlike auto dealerships. That is, around the country exclusive dealerships have been set up in distinctive buildings. These sell only Ethan Allen furniture. It appears that the product's reputation can support such a system. This gives the producer a good deal of control over the dealer. At the same time the dealer, like a car dealer, gets an "exclusive dealership." This is good for the dealer and encourages him or her to basically stock the whole product line.

(e)   Fieldcrest Mills towels

Despite the J.C. Penney ring to the name "Fieldcrest Mills," this is a
manufacturer's brand with a "good image." It is likely to be found in
traditional department stores. Since towels are not products that inspire great
brand loyalty, Fieldcrest Mills cannot employ exclusive distribution, but neither
does it sell branded goods to Penney's, K-Mart, or Sears. Therefore, selective
distribution should be used.

(f)   Michelin tires

Tires are shopping goods. This suggests selective distribution. Further, many
Michelin tire dealers are independent shops with an accent on imported tires and
"performance." This is suggestive of selective distribution, though perhaps at
the "top" of the selective part of the distribution continuum. There are just
too many dealers, at least in populated areas, to defend Michelin's distribution
as "exclusive."

12.   *Identify the possible sources of conflict in a channel of distribution.*

ANSWER:

"Channel conflict" refers to a situation in which channel members are
antagonistic towards one another because of disagreements about the channel's
common purpose or about responsibility for certain activities. The text mentions
that the phrase is most widely used to describe conflict between channel members
at different levels of the channel, or vertical conflict. There is also likely
to be horizontal conflict when two retailers are in a state of conflict.

Ultimately there is one bottom-line reason for the occurrence of channel
conflict. A channel should work smoothly and properly, but behavior of one
channel member may be perceived by other members as inhibiting the attainment of
another channel member's goals or the goals of the channel as a whole. In short,
the conflict is often the result of a channel member's desire to "look out for
number one."

Here are some cases that create channel conflict.

.   Intermediaries are supposed to buy in large quantities but may try to
     practice "hand to mouth buying." This is not what they are "supposed" to
     do. Result ... channel conflict.

.   Manufacturers selling through wholesalers may attempt to keep the largest
     customers for themselves, selling to them directly. Result ... channel
     conflict.

.   Manufacturers may sell stereo equipment to specialty retailers who provide
     high customer service and charge relatively high or full prices. The
     manufacturer also sells to a discounter, most of whose customers seek
     advice at the full-price store but buy the goods at the discounter. Result
     ... channel conflict.

.   A manufacturer of detergent sells name brand goods to wholesalers and
     retailers. But the wholesalers also offer private brand goods to the
     retailers, working hard to sell these goods and not so hard to sell the
     detergent maker's products. Worse, the retailer has its own private brand
     detergent and would prefer to sell that higher-margin product than either
     the wholesaler's or the manufacturer's brand. Result ... channel conflict.

.   A manufacturer (or wholesaler) feels that a retailer should carry all of a
     certain line of goods offered. The retailer wants to carry just the most
     popular types. (This is called "cherry picking.") Result ... channel
     conflict.

13.   *What macromarketing functions do intermediaries perform for society at large?*

ANSWER:

Distribution delivers a standard of living to a society. The developments in the former Soviet Union clearly outline what may happen when distribution systems are inefficient. The inability of customers to obtain products, along with wasted farm products due to inadequate distribution systems, contributed to the fall of the Soviet system.

Intermediaries, as critical channel participants, perform those functions necessary to facilitate the efficient and effective movement of products from producers to consumers. As intermediaries perform physical distribution, communication and facilitating functions for channel members, they contribute to the health of the society at large by insuring products are available when and where they are needed. An intermediary may provide storage, selling or other functions more efficiently than either a manufacturer or a retailer. Further, by reducing the number of transactions required, intermediaries help reduce costs in the distribution function performed for society.

14.   *Under what conditions is exclusive dealing legal?*

ANSWER:

Exclusive dealing refers to a restrictive arrangement by which a supplier prohibits intermediaries that handle its product from selling the products of competing suppliers. Exclusive dealing is illegal if it tends to restrict competition. This is likely to happen when: (1) the arrangement comprises a substantial share of the market; (2) the dollar amount involved is substantial; or (3) the arrangement involves a large supplier and a smaller distributor, where the supplier's disparate economic power can be inherently coercive.

Exclusive dealing arrangements are generally legal if it can be shown that: (1) the exclusivity is necessary for strategic reasons, such as a franchisor's need to protect a product's image; (2) the supplier's own sales are restricted because of limited production capacity.

15.   *Under what conditions are exclusive territories legal?*

ANSWER:

Again, the key point for judging the legality of the situation is the effect on competition. If the granting of exclusive territories does not violate the statutes relating to this point, then limiting the number of outlets within an area may be considered proper. Other defenses include: (1) the investment expected from new dealers is so great that dealers could not be recruited without exclusivity; (2) the image associated with the product demands some exclusivity such as Cadillac; (3) a high quality image is so important that if exclusivity were not employed, consumers would not believe in its quality.

ETHICS EXERCISE 14

CHAPTER 14 ETHICS IN PRACTICE

Overview

A maker of construction equipment has been selling its products in the eastern U.S. using wholesalers who deal with contractors. It plans to expand to the western U.S. using agents to reach wholesalers until the volume of business is large enough to justify creating its own sales force. When agents are hired the company does not inform them of the plan to build up the business through agents, then replace the agents with the manufacturer's own sales force.

The chapter discusses the manufacturer-agent-industrial user channel as common in business-to-business marketing when a small manufacturer markets only one product to many industrial users. The agents (also known as manufacturers' representatives) serve to bring buyers and sellers together, seeking a market for the manufacturer's output. The agents operate on a commission basis and therefore appeal to small organizations with limited financial resources unable to support their own sales force. It should also be noted that manufacturer's representatives typically have close, hands-on knowledge of local market areas, knowledge that can take years of selling to acquire. Additionally, agents don't usually carry competing brands of products.

The case raises this issue: the company does not plan to mention its plans to hire its own sales force after its agents establish a wholesale distribution system for the manufacturer. Is this ethical?

This firm meets the criteria for using agents: it is small and underfunded, and it lacks knowledge of the geographic market so strategically its channel plan makes sense. However, ethically, its intentions are dubious. On the one hand, it could be argued that the agents are earning a commission, and so the construction equipment firm is prospering them. Doing just what the company proposes is "standard procedure" -- it is common in situations like this one. On the other hand, the manufacturing firm is deliberately concealing the fact that in the long run they plan to establish their own sales force. If the agent, at the time it agrees to join forces with the manufacturer, already handles the products of another construction equipment firm, the agent will be competing with their former client. While using the agent, the manufacturer could gain valuable market information from the agent which the agent might be unwilling to divulge if they knew the manufacturer's plans to eventually establish a sales force in the new territory.

Further, it would be reasonable for the agent to assume that the manufacturer has no such plans since they currently don't use a sales force in their other territories. Although the manufacturer could argue that it has no other channel alternative at this time, it would be more ethical to be honest with the agents, hoping they'd nonetheless carry their products and recognizing that they'd be less likely to share valuable information than if the manufacturer kept them in the dark.

CHAPTER 14 TAKE A STAND QUESTIONS

1.   *A liquor wholesaler wishes to purchase five cases of a small California winery's vintage cabernet sauvignon (a red wine,) a wine that has received favorable reviews. The winery says this wine is in short supply and it only ships five case orders if the wholesaler also purchases five cases of its chablis (a white wine.) The chablis is rated as a very ordinary wine, and the wholesaler sells many comparable brands. What should the wholesaler do?*

This situation involves a tying contract, in which a channel intermediary is required for a period of time to buy products which the seller views as supplementary to the merchandise that the buyer actually wishes to purchase. For instance, in the apparel industry, such an agreement might require a dealer to carry a less popular line of clothing in addition to the fast-moving clothing.

As the text explains, there are legal defenses for using tying arrangements when trying to: (1) maintain standards of quality, (2) enter a new market or industry, or (3) preserve market or franchise identity. The first two conditions do not appear operative here, and it is not clear if the third condition is relevant either.

Tying agreements are also ruled illegal when the seller has such economic power in the tying product that the seller can restrain trade in the tied product. Because the winery is small, this condition probably does not apply. Tying contracts are legal when the supplier is the only source of the product (this might be the case here), when the supplier is new and trying to establish distribution (this might apply here), or if the intermediary is permitted to carry competing products (they are here). So, it looks like the wholesaler has no legal recourse. They will probably have to take the tied product (white wine) if they want the main product (the red wine).

Ethically, tying agreements in general are dubious because they restrict the buyer's freedom, lessen competition, might result in higher prices, and are less efficient than "free market" activities. Yet, where a product is in short supply, as in this scenario, these agreements might be a justifiable method for allocating the product; the alternative might be higher prices on the rationed product.

2.   *A supermarket sells many products packaged in aluminum cans and glass bottles. It does not offer any recycling facility or service. Is this responsible?*

When distributors agree to participate in a manufacturer's recycling efforts, they become a participant in a backward channel. The text notes that the major problem with recycling is determining who is responsible for the "reverse distribution" process. For instance, in some cases ecologically concerned civic groups have taken on this responsibility, organizing cleanup days and developing systems and organizations for handling recycling and waste disposal. Also, more and more local governments are creating recycling channels, often in cooperation with waste management companies. Also, some states now mandate bottle deposits and require retailers and local bottlers to participate. Some companies hire intermediaries to pick up their containers from retail outlets and then deliver them to recyclers.

Traditionally, for returnable soft drink bottles, retailers and bottlers form the reverse channel. The allocation of tasks varies, being in part a function of state laws.

Unfortunately, it is not so clear cut as to whether recycling really is the best or only solution to the solid waste problem. The advocates of recycling say that landfills where most trash ends up are filling up, and new land is scarce. Landfills have not proved to be the busy little biodegraders people once thought they were. That makes dumping, which was once cheap, enormously expensive. Recycling not only saves landfill space, it also cuts dumping and burning costs, turns recycled material into cash, and keeps the streets of our cities cleaner.

On the other hand, some observers say there is no shortage of geologically safe, potential landfill sites in the U.S. The not-in-my-backyard (termed "nimby") attitude of most people toward landfill siting has been a barricade. However, if operators offered compensation to people whose property would be in close proximity to landfills, residential and commercial sites that have already been developed would be avoided. State-of-the-art landfill technology makes it possible for all new landfills to be environmentally safe; however, with government-owned landfills there is no incentive to use such technology; private owners are liable for damages they create whereas government operators aren't. (Charles W. Baird, "What Garbage Crisis?," *Human Events*, August 17, 1991, p. 14) Also, the United States incinerates less than 20% of its trash whereas Japan incinerates over 60%. (Baird.) Air pollution from incineration is no longer a problem so this can be a partial alternative.

Nonetheless, recycling aluminum and ferrous metals generally makes economic sense. (This is not true of most paper.) Perhaps the ethical supermarket operator, in addition to encouraging recycling, would also push for privately owned landfills and incineration.

3.   *Wal-Mart notifies manufacturers that it no longer will deal with intermediaries. Its intentions are to deal directly with suppliers. The move squeezes independent wholesalers and brokers out of the picture. Is this right?*

Large buyers like Wal-Mart often prefer to deal directly with manufacturers or suppliers. When they say they will deal with no intermediaries it is possible that a mistake is being made. That is, it is possible (but not likely) for an intermediary to be more efficient and therefore have lower prices than a manufacturer. We can assume that Wal-Mart has determined that manufacturers in general have lower prices than intermediaries. The reason this point is important is that we should be concerned about efficiency in channels and the resulting effect on consumer prices.

Intermediaries are, of course, affected by moves such as these. They may even be driven out of business. This is not necessarily "wrong," though obviously the small wholesaler will feel that the situation is unfair. An element of unfairness is present if intermediaries can never make a sale to Wal-Mart, can't bid on a job, and won't be considered for any business whatsoever. This "freezing out" of competition may be seen as wrong in a macromarketing sense because efficiency might be lost and consumer prices might rise.

However, Wal-Mart is confident that lower prices can be obtained from suppliers than from intermediaries; otherwise, Wal-Mart would not make such a move. In fact, Wal-Mart is probably correct in this belief because of the theory of "economies of scale."

GUIDE TO CASES

VIDEO CASE 14-1 NISSAN MOTOR

SUBJECT MATTER: Customer-Oriented Distribution, Distribution Reflecting Local Needs, Channel Cooperation and Channel Conflict

Please see the Guide to Video Cases for video length and other information.

AT-A-GLANCE OVERVIEW

Nissan Motor was established in 1933 to absorb the businesses of Dat Jidosha Seizo Co., which was the original producer of Datsun brand automobiles.

Nissan ranks second only to Toyota Motor among Japan's largest automobile manufacturers. It is also the world's fourth-largest, being out-paced only by GM, Toyota and Ford in terms of 1990 domestic production.

Nissan's reliance on passenger cars has increased in recent years, with passenger cars accounting for slightly more than 83% of its business in 1989-1991, commercial vehicles about 16%, and bus production staying well below 1%. Nissan is therefore very much a passenger car company, with little dependence on the trends in other market segments. In the passenger car arena, Nissan produces a wide range of vehicles that compete in every major class. It markets many passenger cars ranging from small cars to luxury cars. Nissan sells a range of vans, trucks and minibuses.[1]

Nissan Motors has an American headquarters for its Nissan Division. As with most automobile marketers, Nissan sells its vehicles through a network of independent dealers. There is no wholesaler in this channel of distribution and its retail dealers deal directly with Nissan of America. In the past, local dealers dealt with a district manager who was responsible to the headquarters operation. The Nissan division recently eliminated its district manager system and initiated a localization program to become more responsive to its customers through dealers. In the United States the company established a new plan that established five large geographical regions to manage dealer relationships. In the past, the headquarters operation exerted strong control over its district managers. The new DOM (dealer operations manager) system has been put into place.

The video shows how the new localization plan shifts decision making authority from the national level to the regional level. This plan was designed to help establish a regional allocation of resources and to make allowance for regional differences in making decisions about customers and marketing programs.

---

[1]This material is adapted with permission from Nissan Motor Co., Ltd., Company Report, Donaldson, K.C., Salomon Brothers Inc., 4/13/92.

QUESTIONS

1.   *What are some possible sources of channel conflict between Nissan Division of America and its dealers?*

As the case suggests, the allocation of budgets for promotion and warranty repairs could be a problem if the allocation is not equitable. Conflicts about when things will be done are another source of conflict. For example, dealers are concerned with the speed of warranty claim payments. Another problem could be inventory and the automobile assortment allocated to each dealer. This allocation results from the forecasts at the national level, but there can be regional differences in preferences such as more convertibles in the South, more station wagons in the West.

The dealer's autonomy or empowerment to deal with customer complaints about car problems and warranty repairs can be another major source of conflict that lead to the localization system. The new localization plan shifts decision making authority from the national level to the regional level.

2.   *How might the DOM (dealer operations manager) influence the management of channel conflict?*

The DOM system improves communication between the manufacturer and the retailer. It lets the dealer know the DOM better than under the old system which featured strong control from headquarters. It shifts more decision making authority to the regions. It allows the manufacturer to be more responsive to customers and, in turn, to dealers. This plan was designed to help establish a regional allocation of resources and to make allowance for regional differences in making decisions about customers and marketing programs. Decisions can be made quicker under the DOM system.
Each region is managed by a regional manager. However, the key person in the new plan is the dealer operations manager (DOM) who works closely with dealers in the region. The DOM works with dealers and tries to put dealers' best interests at the forefront. The DOM is empowered to deal with the dealer and to make decisions that are best for the local dealer and the dealer's operations. If there is a need to increase promotion for trucks in a given area, the DOM may make the decision to allocate budgets to this effort without requesting approval from the national headquarters. The DOMs have their own merchandising and marketing budget. Each DOM has a support network of specialists in areas like service operations, who can focus on specific needs. They help analyze the deal with particular aspects of the operation and serve as consultants to the dealers.

As the video shows, the Regional General Manager helps coordinate DOM activities and champion certain product models.

VIDEO CASE 14-2 STOCKPOT SOUPS[2]

FOCUS ON SMALL BUSINESS

SUBJECT MATTER: Channels of Distribution, Gaining Market Entry

Please see the Guide to Video Cases for video length and other information.

AT-A-GLANCE OVERVIEW

StockPot Soups is a manufacturer of fresh, homemade style soup concentrates. The company has 100 employees. The Fortun brothers had 20 years experience in the food business before they founded StockPot Soups in the early 1980s.

---

[2]Adapted with permission from *Strengthening America's Competitiveness* p. 56, copyright 1991 by Connecticut Mutual Life Insurance Company.

The company's product included homemade style soups, such as lobster bisque, chicken flavored vegetable gumbo, cream of broccoli, and clam chowder. Production of the fresh soup product was labor intensive, which drove up the cost of producing the soup.

Grocery wholesalers and retailers often stocked five or six competing brands. Most competitors offered national brands. Like many small start-up companies in their early years, StockPot faced the daunting challenge of convincing distributors to carry its products. Wholesalers simply did not want to carry another soup. This was also true of wholesalers who serviced food services and institutional customers.

QUESTIONS

1.   *Describe StockPot's channels of distribution.*

It is possible that StockPot has channels not described in the case. However, it appears that the company is using, or attempting to use, grocery wholesalers (sometimes called brokers) to reach supermarkets and other retailers. Wholesalers that supply the institutional market (i.e., hospitals, schools, etc.) are also sought by the company. Of course, the key problem StockPot has is getting its products into these channels of distribution.

2.   *What strategy can StockPot use to gain distribution?*

There are things that StockPot can do to gain entry into the wholesalers' lines. Among the things that might be done is to promote the product to consumers, develop demand, and thereby "force" wholesalers to carry the then-popular product. The company might distribute the product directly to institutions and supermarkets; if the markets will accept it, a slotting allowance may have to be paid. The company could offer a major incentive to carry the product to the wholesalers (and retailers, for that matter). Incentives include very large margins (i.e. lower the price charged to intermediaries), or "free product" to resellers which they then sell at full price. That makes the mark-up on these goods "infinite," a very attractive deal.

The question remains, however, whether or not StockPot can afford to do any or all of these things. We are told the company is rather small and new, but lack information about their financial picture.

Like it or not, the marketplace is not always "free," and StockPot may have to choose one or more of the admittedly unattractive possibilities listed above.

3.   *Are there any innovative channels of distribution that StockPot can tap?*

The channels of distribution StockPot is attempting to "crack" are the traditional ones, and these are reluctant and unlikely to change their ways. Innovative channels can be "thought up," but making them work could be difficult, especially over the long run. Still, innovative channels might lead to increased popularity of the product and then to its acceptance by the traditional distributor.

Some possibilities include:

Direct delivery to stores and institutions. This is not impossible, but it is expensive. Nonetheless this is a "fresh, homemade concentrate," not Campbell's soup in a can. Other producers of "fresh" products deliver direct to stores and institutions such as milk, specialty fruits, and vegetables. If this product is unique enough, a similar method might be justified.

StockPot could consider some manner of dealing direct with consumers, though this sounds like an unlikely choice since there is a limit to how much soup a family can use.

StockPot could try selling to restaurants and caterers, perhaps getting them to acknowledge that "We serve delicious homemade StockPot soups." Ultimately, the fame of the product might "force" traditional channel members to accept it.

One good possibility would be to locate distributors of other goods who do not use traditional grocery wholesalers but who deal with supermarkets. Local dairies, specialty distributors (spices, exotic fruits and vegetables) might be induced to deliver soup along with their other products in a "piggy back" deal.

15 RETAILING AND WHOLESALING

CHAPTER SCAN

This chapter continues the investigation of the marketing management problems and opportunities presented by the mix variable "place." It focuses on the two major types of intermediaries, retailers and wholesalers. Retailers are discussed in terms of their ownership, prominent strategies, and retailing mixes. The historical patterns in American retailing, and the theories developed to explain them are addressed.

Merchant wholesalers and agents are described, and their functions in the distribution system explained. The key elements of wholesaler's strategies are discussed.

SUGGESTED LEARNING OBJECTIVES

The student who studies this chapter will be exposed to an overview of the operations of major channel of distribution institutions and will be able to:

1.   Describe the nature of retailing and wholesaling in the distribution system.

2.   Categorize the various types of retailers by ownership and prominent strategy.

3.   Analyze the historical patterns in American retailing and evaluate the theories proposed to explain them.

4.   Understand the nature of retailers' marketing mixes.

5.   Distinguish between merchant wholesalers and agents and describe their function in the distribution system.

6.   Show how both full-service and limited-service merchant wholesalers contribute to the marketing system.

7.   Identify the marketing contributions of agent intermediaries such as brokers, auction companies, and selling agents.

8.   Understand the key elements of wholesalers' strategies.

CHAPTER OUTLINE

I.   **INTRODUCTION**

II.   **RETAILING**

A.   The Importance of Retailing

III.   **RETAILING INSTITUTIONS - TOWARD A SYSTEM OF CLASSIFICATIONS**

A.   Classifying Retailers by Ownership
B.   Classifying Retailers by Prominent Strategy

1.   In-Store Retailing

a.   Specialty Stores
b.   Department Stores
c.   Supermarkets and Convenience Stores
d.   Mass Merchandisers
e.   Other Discount Retailers

C.   Non-Store Retailing

1.   Mail-Order and Direct-Response Retailing
2.   Door-to-Door Selling and In-Home Retailing with Computers
3.   Vending Machines

IV.   **PATTERNS OF RETAIL DEVELOPMENT**

A.   The Wheel of Retailing
B.   The Dialectic View of Retail Development
C.   A General-Specific-General Explanation
D.   Using the Theories

V.   **RETAIL MANAGEMENT STRATEGIES**

A.   Merchandise Assortment
B.   Location, Location and Location
C.   Atmospherics
D.   Customer Services

VI.   **WHOLESALING**

A.   Types of Wholesalers
B.   Merchant Wholesalers

1.   Full-Service Merchant Wholesalers
2.   Limited-Service Wholesalers

a.   Cash-and-Carry Wholesalers
b.   Truck Wholesalers
c.   Mail-Order Wholesalers
d.   Drop Shippers
e.   Rack Jobbers

C.   Agents

1.   Brokers
2.   Commission Merchants
3.   Auction Companies
4.   Manufacturers' Agents and Selling Agents

D.   Manufacturers That Do Their Own Wholesaling

VII.   WHOLESALE MANAGEMENT STRATEGIES

      A.   Selecting Target Markets and Creating Assortments
      B.   Strategic Business Alliances
      C.   Wholesaling in the Future

VIII. SUMMARY

IX.   KEY TERMS

X.   QUESTIONS FOR DISCUSSION (13)

XI.   ETHICS IN PRACTICE

XII. CASES

      The following key terms are introduced and used in Chapter 15. They are
defined in the text's Glossary.

Retailing
Independent retailer
Leased department retailer
Chain store
Corporate chain
Ownership group
Specialty store
Department store
Supermarket
Convenience store
Mass merchandise retailer
Warehouse retailer
Catalog showroom
Warehouse club, or closed-door house
Hypermarket
Off-price retailer
Category discounter
Data-base marketing
Direct-response retailer
Television home shopping
Electronic catalog
Computer-interactive retailing
Wheel of retailing
Dialectic theory
General-specific-general theory
Store image
Atmospherics
Service level
Wholesaler
Merchant wholesaler
Full-service merchant wholesaler
General merchandise wholesaler
General line wholesaler
Specialty wholesaler
Limited-service wholesaler
Cash-and-carry wholesaler
Truck wholesaler, or truck jobber
Mail-order wholesaler
Drop shipper, or desk jobber
Rack jobber
Agent
Broker
Commission merchant
Auction company
Manufacturers' agent, or manufacturers' representative
Selling agent
Sales office
Sales branch
Strategic business alliance

THE CHAPTER SUMMARIZED

I.   INTRODUCTION

After repositioning to compete with more fashionable department stores, J.C. Penney (the country's fourth largest retailer) is trying high-end specialty retailing. One such attempt is its Units subsidiary, a 200-store modular knit clothing chain. Penney's has five other concepts under development: (1) Amanda Fielding, for high quality clothing for over-35 women; (2) Mixit, a Limited-style store now being tested; (3) Tezio, an upper-moderate cosmetics chain aimed at the over-35 woman; (4) Detail, an up-scale bed-and-bath shop; and, (5) Portofino Interiors, for home furnishing, accessories, and home decorating. Success in specialty retailing could help boost Penney's image and have long-term implications for its marketing strategy.

II.   RETAILING

Retailing consists of all activities involved with the sale of products to ultimate consumers.

Though some definitions substitute certain phrases, e.g., "consuming units" (families) for "consumers," retailing is always seen as dealing with people who are acquiring products for their own use. So-called "factory outlets" and "wholesale clubs" are still retailers if they sell to consumers, as are bars, hotels, and ice cream trucks. Retailing is the "final link" in the channel of distribution. As such, bad retailing can ruin an otherwise fine marketing plan.

A.   The Importance of Retailing

Some facts:

- There are about 2.4 million retailing institutions in the U.S.

- They account for well over $1.5 trillion in sales.

- Their sales equal about 97% of personal income.

- About 14% of U.S. workers are in retailing.

- Sears alone had sales of over $57 billion in 1992 if its financial services are included, $32 billion if they are not. Wal-Mart's merchandise sales were about $41 billion.

Exhibit 15-1 lists some of the largest retailing institutions in the U.S.

III.   RETAILING INSTITUTIONS -- TOWARD A SYSTEM OF CLASSIFICATIONS

Retailing is dynamic and its institutions are constantly changing, e.g., Sears was once a mail-order retailer of watches, and "5 & 10s" have all but disappeared. Nonetheless, retailers can be categorized by ownership and product strategy types.

A.   Classifying Retailers By Ownership

Retailers may be classified by degree of integration, that is, by independence, or lack of it, from larger organizations. (Exhibit 15-2 categorizes retailers by ownership.)

- **Independent retailers** operate as single unit entities. Most retailers are of this type. Not all independents are small.

- An independent retailer that owns the merchandise stocked but leases floor space from another retailer is a **leased department retailer**. Though independent, the lessee is likely to operate under the lessor's name, e.g., the camera or fine-jewelry

departments at major department stores are likely to be leased
departments.

. **Chain stores** are members of a group of stores bearing the same
   name and having roughly the same image. Thus, a chain store
   system is two or more stores of a similar type, centrally owned
   and operated. They have been successful in the U.S. because of
   economies of scale in buying and selling which can result in
   lower prices or prices that provide higher margins. The
   financial strength size can give may permit more TV advertising
   and computerized inventory systems.

. The term **corporate chain** is used for a chain with 11 or more
   units. Typically as the number of units increases, management
   becomes more centralized. Larger size provides advantages, but
   smaller chains and independents have flexibility. (W.T. Grant
   and A&P, among others, are large outfits that have had plenty
   of troubles.)

. Retail franchise operations are centrally managed but the
   individual units are independently owned. Franchises, like
   chains, fit the American culture. The U.S. population is
   mobile; if you move across the country, familiar retailer
   franchises like Arby's, and Midas are there "waiting" for you.

. **Ownership groups** are made up of various stores or small chains
   each with a separate name and image. Typically, independent
   stores are bought up by the group but allowed to continue
   semi-autonomous operation. Many famous stores are in fact part
   of such groups. Federated, for example, owns Bloomingdale's,
   Jordan Marsh, Lazarus, and Abraham & Strauss, among others.

B. Classifying Retailers by Prominent Strategy

Retailers may be classified in terms of their most prominent retail
strategies. Two major groups of strategies may be used, in-store and
nonstore. Exhibit 15-3 shows these groupings and their
subcategories.

1. In-Store Retailing

In-store retailers vary in the variety of products they sell,
store size, price level, degree of self-service, location, and
other variables. Each has particular advantages and
disadvantages, and each fits particular marketing situations.

a. Specialty Stores

Specialty stores, also called single-line retailers and
limited-line retailers, can be differentiated from other
retailers by the depth and degree of specialization
reflected in their product lines. Specialty stores focus
on a particular line. Specialty stores do not try to be
all things to all people. Therefore, these retailers
must be sure there are enough potential customers who
seek the few items offered.

Single line and limited-line stores represent the bulk of
retail institutions. Their success lies in the
development of expertise in their product lines, e.g.,
Wallpapers To Go offers wallpapers and all the tools and
instructions to accompany them.

Service establishments, such as banks and restaurants,
may be viewed as specialty retailers.

b.   Department Stores

Department stores are typically large, carry a wide
selection of products, are organized physically and
organizationally into departments, each of which is
headed by a buyer with authority in buying and selling
and who is responsible for the department's profits.

Department stores are characterized by a full range of
services. The services, the typically large building,
and the wide assortment of merchandise necessitate higher
prices and margins than those found in discount stores.
Some consumers seek the services and atmosphere of the
department store but then make their purchases at
discount stores.

Independent department stores do exist, but most are
members of chains or ownership groups.

c.   Supermarkets and Convenience Stores

Supermarkets are much different from the grocery stores
from which they evolved. Old time grocers knew their
customers, personally filled orders, and made deliveries.
A&P discontinued home delivery in 1912, King Kullen (in
Jamaica, Queens, N.Y.C.) placed cans and packages in
aisles and introduced self-service in 1933. Today's
supermarket is a large, departmentalized retail
establishment selling a variety of products, mostly food
items but also health and beauty aids, housewares,
magazines, etc.

The inclusion of non-food items in "grocery stores," and
toys and gifts in "drug stores" was once novel. The
practice was known as scrambled merchandising and the
term remains in use today. Margins on these items tend
to be higher than for "regular stock," though across the
board, supermarket profit margins are low -- 1 to 2% of
sales.

Supermarkets were among the first retailers to use
discount strategies, accenting high turnover and low
prices. Offering few services helps hold prices down,
yet for most retailers personnel costs are the highest
outlay after cost of goods.

Many supermarkets have added take-out prepared foods,
prescription departments, etc. The typical supermarket
now carries over 10,000 product types. Store size of new
operations has grown to at least 50,000 square feet in
the food department alone.

The **convenience store** is a small supermarket. These
stores have grown rapidly in numbers. Their emphasis is
on convenience as most of their names imply (e.g., King
Quik), and they have higher prices and profit margins
than do standard supermarkets. However, their growth and
staying power seems proof that consumers are willing to
pay for their convenience. Convenience stores are
unusual in the retailing world in that they have both
high margins and high inventory turnover rates.

d.   Mass Merchandisers

Mass merchandise retailers, or mass merchandise discount
stores, carry a wide variety of merchandise that cuts
across product lines. They carry a wide variety of
products sold at discount prices.

Supermarkets were the forerunners of mass merchandisers. The term supermarket retailing has been applied to non-food stores that have adopted the supermarket strategy: toys (Toys R Us), lumber (Handy Dan), sporting goods (Oshman's), and many more products. The basic idea is the same: discount strategy positioning, low prices, few services.

As Exhibit 15-4 shows, mass merchandisers usually carry inventories that are either wide or deep, but not both.

Six types of mass merchandisers are described.

- **Warehouse retailers** use their showroom facility as storage space -- a warehouse. They carry far more stock than traditional retailers. Levitz furniture is one of these. The stock on hand permits it to sell "instant gratification" ... the chance to walk out the door with the furniture you want.

  Despite the use of the term "warehouse" they are, of course, retailers.

- **Catalog showrooms** (like Best and Company and Service Merchandise) use catalogs and minimum services accent to the "normal" prices vs. their own "special low price." Sometime the low price is presented in an easy-to-read "code" to accent the "special deal" not available to just any consumer.

- The **warehouse club** or **closed-door house** is a discount operation requiring that customers be "members" in order to enter the store and buy. The method is thought to build store loyalty and should reduce advertising expense since direct mail can be used to reach the members. TV and other media with high waste circulation can be avoided. Warehouse clubs (sometimes called wholesale clubs) may sell to organizational buyers. In such cases they are acting as wholesalers since the goods sold are not for personal use.

- The **hypermarket** (originally, in France, the hypermarche) is a huge operation of 150,000 to 200,000 square feet, selling "everything." A hypermarket is a "super store." Like the smaller supermarket, prices are low and costs are reduced as much as possible. Hypermarkets have been more successful in Europe than in the U.S. but some, like Wal-Mart's Hypermarket USA, can be found.

- **Off-price retailers** are specialty retailers who aggressively promote nationally known brand names at low prices. (Burlington Coat Factory and Dress Barn are examples.) They buy at very low prices in large volumes from manufacturers, who usually don't offer promotion money, extended terms, or return privileges. If the manufacturer operates the off-price store, it is called a factory outlet.

- **Category discounters** (or category killers) are discount stores that specialize in a certain product class or category. Sportsmart, for example, carries virtually all competitive brands of sports equipment at prices even lower than those of mass merchandisers, and offers extensive assortment and great depth in the product they carry.

e.   Other Discount Retailers

Discount operators can be found among many kinds of
specialty store retailers. Crown Books sells every book
on the *New York Times* best seller list at 35% below list
price. Discount jewelry stores and furriers, among many
other kinds of shops, may be found.

C.   Non-Store Retailing

Retailers sell to consumers. This does not require a "store."

1.   Mail-Order and Direct-Response Retailing

Sears and many others do store and non-store retailing. Others
rely on **mail-order** exclusively. Mail-order's big attraction
for customers is convenience, with some outfits even mailing
giftwrapped items directly to the buyer's specified person.
Safety concerns also encourage mail-order shopping.

Many mail-order firms employ computer generated mailing lists
that can focus on selected interest groups, age groups,
homeowners vs. renters, etc. This is called **database
marketing**.

Mail-order retailers are able to reduce some costs mostly
because the customer never sees "behind the scenes."
Warehouses in "bad neighborhoods," and clerks rather than
trained salespeople all keep down costs. However, catalog
expenses can be high and inventories are usually sizable to
permit quick filling of orders before customers decide to go to
a "regular store."

Telephone and television **direct-response retailers** sell all
manner of merchandise, urging consumers to call an 800 number,
filling orders via the mail, and employing advertisements
called saturation campaigns.

Telemarketing is a growing part of direct-response retailing.
It is discussed in Chapter 19 on personal selling.

Home shopping on cable TV involves a "host" describing
products. Consumers call in with questions and/or their
orders. The electronic catalog approach to home shopping is
similar but utilizes videotapes which the customer "asks" to
see via touch-tone telephone.

Another version of home shopping is the interactive videotext
or **electronic catalog**. Unlike live TV, this allows the viewers
to select products they wish to see in any order they choose.

2.   Door-to-Door Selling and In-Home Retailing with Computers

Electrolux, Avon, and others (more recently, Tupperware and
other in-home "party" retailers) have earned great success with
this retailing method. Though sales commissions are usually
high, certain products like vacuum cleaners lend themselves to
effective in-home demonstration. Tie-ins with home computers
and TV cable systems are being tested.

Some communities have moved against unscrupulous door-to-door
salespeople. Local ordinances, generically called Green River
Ordinances after the Wyoming town that passed one of the first
such laws, are in force in many towns. These ordinances
prohibit door-to-door selling, require licenses, or inhibit
such operations in other ways.

Door-to-door selling has decreased in importance in the U.S. but is growing in less-developed countries. Avon is expanding operations in China.

A new development in nonstore retailing is **computer-interactive retailing** through which consumers can shop at home, interacting with retailers via personal computers.

3.   Vending Machines

Vending machines have been availabale for many years. New electronic advances have made them increasingly effective. There is said to be one machine per 40 people in the U.S. Vending machines have traditionally been used to sell small, cheap, easily-preserved, high turnover items. Though some other items have been sold this way, the "competition from other channels" limitation sets limits on their growth. Would you buy a "mystery meat" sandwich from a machine if a Burger King were nearby?

IV.   PATTERNS OF RETAIL DEVELOPMENT

If a "pattern" of retail change could be identified, a means of predicting future developments in retailing would emerge. Three theories are among the most prominent.

A.   The Wheel of Retailing

The **wheel of retailing** hypothesis suggests that new retailing institutions enter the marketplace as low-status, low-price operations, then "trade up" to higher "spokes on the wheel," or "steps on a ladder." Exhibit 15-5 illustrates this. This makes sense because trading up:

.   is the "American Dream." One starts out small and moves up, getting bigger and better.

.   fits the American retailers' tradition of competing using non-price variables like services and decor. These require support from higher prices and higher margins so the institution moves "up the ladder." Then, as one type of store "trades up," the bottom rungs are left open for newcomers to occupy.

It should be recalled that while the "wheel" describes a pattern of institutional change, it does not describe what happens to each and every store. Some experts have suggested that retailers are spending more time and effort on selecting specific target markets and so will be more resistant to the forces that "drive the wheel."

B.   The Dialectic View of Retail Development

German philosopher G.W. Hegel suggested the **dialectic theory,** summarized as follows:

.   A thought or institution exists. This is the thesis.

.   It is challenged by a new idea, the antithesis.

.   The good and bad of both interact and a new combination results, the synthesis.

We see that the department store was once challenged by the spartan discount store, and the discount department store such as K Mart emerged as the synthesis. And, the neighborhood grocery was challenged by the supermarket, one result being the convenience store.

The "wheel" concept pays virtually no attention to competition and response to competition. The dialectic reflects that aspect and may be seen, therefore, as better describing retailing's changing patterns.

C.   A General-Specific-General Explanation

In the U.S., we had many general stores during the country's early years. As the population of cities grew, specialty stores could be supported and appeared (jewelry, book, and meat stores). Now we see huge supermarkets and "all under one roof" shopping malls, the new general stores. This **general-specific-general** pattern may not be as appealing intellectually as those in A. and B., but it does describe what has occurred and is worth consideration. Some have referred to the same idea as the accordion theory, reflective of the expansion and contraction of merchandise offerings over time.

D.   Using These "Theories"

These theories do not purport to explain how all changes in retailing have developed. Their use lies in generating thought. Why do these patterns exist? What market factors contribute to them? The answers to these sorts of questions are important to planners.

V.   RETAIL MANAGEMENT STRATEGIES

Just as there is a marketing mix, there is a retail marketing mix. Exhibit 15-7 shows some of the decision elements retail marketers face in developing a retailing mix. To give a taste of this mix, the totality of which is beyond this text, we will treat four major topics.

A.   Merchandise Assortment

Retailers perform an assorting function -- they combine the goods of many producers to build desired assortments. Consumers and manufacturers are thus spared this task and reward retailers for its performance. From the customer's perspective, assortment is one of the major factors that sets one retailer apart from another. The retailer must match the assortment offered to the customer's desires. Buying mistakes will occur but effective marketing, not guesswork, must be the basis for decisions in this area.

B.   Location, Location, and Location

These are said to be the three most important things in retail success. The saying makes a good point, but is not always absolutely true. Big selections and lower prices can offset the effects of a less-than-perfect location. Still, location in terms of where, but also in terms of retail neighbors, is a key concern. High traffic is important as is the presence of complementary businesses (e.g., a gas station and a diner are more complementary than a gas station and a jewelry shop).

1.   Locating in Shopping Centers

Several types of shopping centers are common.

. The strip of stores set in a parking area.

. The mall built for strolling in a central area.

. The enclosed mall, the technical term for a heated, air conditioned, roofed mall.

Also noted:

. The several sizes of shopping centers: neighborhood, community, and regional (essentially, small, medium, large.)

. The downtown or central business district (CBD,) once a shopping center, has declined greatly in importance since the post-World War II exodus to the suburbs, but some downtown shopping areas, like Chicago's Watertower Plaza, do very well.

C.   Atmospherics

Atmospherics are physical characteristics of the environment, such as the store's interior and exterior appearance, layout, and displays, which contribute to the shopper's mental impression of what the store is. Atmospheres may be planned to appeal to the shopper's five senses. The Hard Rock Cafe is loud and bustling. Exclusive clothing stores are often quiet and plush. Exteriors add to the atmosphere, such as Taco Bell's "Mexican design" building.

Much of what is called "atmosphere" is created by interior design and store layout. Many supermarkets use the grid pattern which permits intensive use of space. The free flow design is common to fashion goods stores. Consideration of newer supermarkets with their emphasis on more open space and the "shoppe" layout (wine shop, gourmet shop, etc.) suggests a move away from the simple grid design.

D.   Customer Services

Customer service offered by a retailer may as important, or more important, than the merchandise offered for sale. Convenient hours, parking, and product information are essential to many retail operations. Giftwrapping, home delivery, repair, credit, and return privileges supplement the retailer's merchandise offerings. A service (e.g. in-home delivery by Domino's Pizza) may be the major reason for selecting a retailer.

Development of the retailing mix involves decisions about the **service level**, the extent of "extra services" that will be offered. The level of service customers expect should be a major determinant of the service level offered. Many retailers regularly survey customers about the amount and quality of services expected.

VI.   WHOLESALING

A **wholesaler** is a middleman that neither produces nor consumes the finished product but, instead, sells to retailers and other institutions that use the product for ultimate resale.

A.   Types of Wholesalers

There are two major types of intermediaries/wholesalers:

. Merchants take title to the goods they sell.

. Agents do not take title to the goods they sell.

Possession has no importance here. The taking of title is the only differentiating feature. Clearly the merchant takes more risks than the agent in that the merchant can "get stuck" with unsold inventory.

Wholesalers act as selling agents for their suppliers and buying agents for the retailers, and others they sell to. They create time and place utility. They must evaluate the needs of their customers and deliver an appropriate total product of goods and services. They must develop methods of performance that suit market conditions.

A recent census of wholesale trade in the U.S. found:

. 467,000 wholesale trade establishments, of which 388,000 were merchant wholesalers.

- 41,000 manufacturer's sales branches and offices.

- 36,000 agents and brokers.

Like retailers, wholesalers act as selling agents for their suppliers and buying agents for their customers. Both create time and place utility, both must deliver an appropriate mix of products and services if they are to succeed.

B.   Merchant Wholesalers

Merchant wholesalers:

- Take title to the goods they sell.

- Account for over 58% of all U.S. wholesale transactions.
- Are independently owned organizations that take title to the goods they distribute.

- Represent about 80% of all U.S. wholesaling organizations.

- Tend to be small; they are 80% of all wholesaling organizations but have less than 60% of the business because the costs associated with wholesaling increase rapidly as the area covered grows larger.

1.   Full-Service Merchant Wholesalers

Full-service wholesalers or **full-function wholesalers**, provide their customers with a complete array of services such as delivery, credit, and market information and advice.

Within this group, three subsets of wholesalers may be noted.

- **General merchandise wholesalers** sell a wide variety of products, e.g., for general stores.

- **General line wholesalers** offer a full array of products within one general line, e.g., grocery items.

- **Specialty wholesalers** reduce the line offered still further, e.g., a coffee and tea, or a spice wholesaler.

Clearly, the wholesaler tailors his or her operations to fit perceived market opportunities. In some industries, tradition or legal constraints may affect the choices of marketing methods available to wholesalers.

2.   Limited-Service Wholesalers

Limited-service wholesalers, or limited-function wholesalers, "cut out" parts of the full array of possible services offered to customers. Their customers may prefer to forego service to achieve a reduction in price.

a.   Cash-and-Carry Wholesalers

Cash-and-carry wholesalers sell on a cash-and-carry basis, eliminating credit and delivery charges. Resultant savings are passed onto customers who forego those services.

b.   Truck Wholesalers

Truck wholesalers, also called **truck jobbers**, usually sell a limited line of items from a truck or van, e.g., snack items to taverns. This provides fresh merchandise and "instant delivery," and frequently involves products in highly competitive markets.

    c.   Mail-Order Wholesalers

Mail-order wholesalers may service small-order customers or deal in items not usually ordered in large quantities.

    d.   Drop Shippers

Drop shippers handle paperwork and credit arrangements but eliminate handling of product by having it shipped to customers directly from the producer. Also called **desk jobbers**. This operation is illustrated in Exhibit 15-8.

    e.   Rack Jobbers

Rack jobbers are merchant wholesalers who set up and maintain racks of merchandise in retail locations. They first came to prominence in the 1930s as an easy method by which supermarket operators could practice scrambled merchandising. L'Eggs, toys, paperback books, and magazines sold in supermarkets or discount houses are examples. A percentage of selling price is paid to the "host retailer."

C.   Agents

Agents may take possession of the goods they deal in but not title. They receive commissions on sales and are expected to have expert knowledge of the market they serve.

1.   Brokers

Brokers are agent intermediaries who receive a commission for putting sellers and buyers in touch with one another and assisting in negotiations.

Brokers are usually "neutral" in the selling process but their commissions are affected by the selling price so it is arguable that they favor seller over buyer. Brokers know their markets and what they "sell" is their expertise. They are found in many fields, such as stocks, livestock, scrap metal, petroleum, and coffee.

Brokers are used on an "as needed" basis. Users need not maintain and pay for a long-term relationship. Because of this, brokers are not a major force in the day-to-day marketing activities of most firms.

2.   Commission Merchants

The **commission merchant** operates similarly to a broker but is given certain powers by sellers such as price bargaining power. They are seen as more in league with sellers than the more neutral brokers. They are found commonly representing sellers of agricultural goods.

3.   Auction Companies

Auction companies are agent intermediaries that often take possession of the goods they deal in, selling them through the auction or bidding process. Art, tobacco, and used mechanical equipment are among the products traditionally sold in this way.

The auction method usually provides the buyer with an opportunity to examine the merchandise, remain anonymous if necessary, and enjoy the "thrill" of the bidding process.

4.   Manufacturer's Agents and Selling Agents

Manufacturer's agents, also called **manufacturer's representatives**, are independent intermediaries that specialize in selling and are available to producers that do not want to perform sales activities themselves.

Manufacturer's agents represent one manufacturer or two or more non-competing producers within a geographically limited area. They work on commission and thus appeal to financially weak companies who need not pay them until a sale is made. Further, because they work in specific geographic areas they may be employed in markets that do not justify use of a manufacturer's own sales force.

Selling agents are much like manufacturers' agents except that they do not limit their activities to specific geographic areas. They sell all the products of the principals they represent. They constitute "external marketing departments" for the firms that use them.

Exhibits 15-9 and 15-10 give an overview of various wholesalers.

D.   Manufacturers That Do Their Own Wholesaling

Much wholesaling is not performed by independent wholesaling organizations. When manufacturers become disenchanted with the work of wholesalers, they may decide to do their own wholesaling. In fact, one-third of all wholesaling transactions in the U.S. is performed by manufacturers themselves.

When manufacturers do their own wholesaling, they usually employ **sales branches** and/or **sales offices**. These vary in only one central aspect: sales branches carry inventory, sales offices do not.

The main reason manufacturers choose to do their own wholesaling can be summed up in the word "control."

VII.   WHOLESALE MANAGEMENT STRATEGIES

Wholesalers, like all marketers, create marketing strategies, analyze market segments, select target markets, and determine a competitive position they wish to occupy.

A.   Selecting Target Markets and Creating Assortments

Wholesalers sell to three basic classes of customers.

.   Retailers who resell the product

.   Other wholesalers who resell the product

.   Organizations in the business market that use the product

Each has different needs, and the wholesaler must determine what product/service mix will be offered to each. Frieda's Finest specializes in wholesaling exotic foods because it cannot compete "across the board" with the giant food distributors; its marketing mix stresses specialization.

B.   Strategic Business Alliances

Wholesalers and clients determine to what extent the wholesaler will be involved in the customer's business. A minimum level would be that the wholesaler will maintain an inventory sufficient to meet the customer's needs. However, customers and wholesalers may create a **strategic business alliance**, a commitment between wholesaler and customer to establish a long-term relationship. A vertical marketing

system is a strong strategic alliance. Some wholesalers provide
customers with computer programs, store design assistance, and
suggested levels of in-store inventory.

C.   Wholesaling in the Future

Wholesalers perform functions that are not easily performed by other
channel members. They must be aware of technological advances that
will help them in their tasks. They must re-evaluate their
activities constantly in light of the changes in the demands of their
customers.

Wholesalers must know their products and their markets. This is what
they have to offer customers. They can make better use of target
marketing and other marketing tools than they have in the past. Like
other marketers, if they adapt to changes, they will experience
success.

VIII. SUMMARY

Retailing and wholesaling are the major distribution institutions that make
our marketing system work.

Learning Objective 1: Describe the nature of retailing and
wholesaling in the distribution system.

Retailers deal with ultimate consumers, people buying products for their
own use. Wholesalers deal with institutions that acquire products for use
in organizations or for resale. Both types of intermediaries buy, sell,
and help to physically distribute products through the economy.

Learning Objective 2: Categorize the various types of retailers by
ownership and prominent strategy.

The retail establishments in the United States may be classified by
ownership, as independents, leased departments, chains, franchises, or
ownership groups. They may also be classified by retail strategy, as in-
store retailers or nonstore retailers. In-store retailers may be further
classified as specialty stores, department stores, convenience stores,
supermarkets, convenience stores, mass merchandisers, warehouse clubs,
hypermarkets, off-price retailers, and category discount merchants. Mail-
order retailers, direct-response retailers, and automatic vending retailers
are the primary nonstore categories based on retailing strategies.

Learning Objective 3: Analyze the historical patterns in American
retailing and evaluate the theories proposed to explain them.

American retailing has evolved to suit an ever-changing environment. Three
theories explain this evolution: (1) the wheel of retailing, which notes
that low-price, low-status stores tend to trade up, leaving space for new
low-status stores; (2) the dialectic view which holds that the challenge of
one type of institution by another leads to the development of a third that
combines characteristics of the original two; and (3) the general-specific-
general theory, which postulates that American retailing began with the
general store, progressed to the specialty store, and returned to the
general store concept with the development of such mass merchandisers as
warehouse clubs.

Learning Objective 4: Understand the nature of retailers' marketing
mixes.

Retail marketers of all types must develop effective marketing mixes aimed
at attracting and satisfying target markets. While the problems retailers
face are somewhat distinct from those of manufacturers and marketers
operating in the organizational sector, the basic principles of effective
marketing can be applied profitably in the retailing milieu. Merchandise
assortment, location, atmospherics, and customer service are of special
importance to retailers.

Learning Objective 5:   **Distinguish between merchant wholesalers and agents and describe their function in the distribution system.**

Wholesalers deal not with final consumers but with organizational buyers, other wholesalers, and, of course, retailers. Independent wholesalers are either merchants or agents. Merchants take title to the goods they sell, while agents do not. In addition, wholesaling activities by manufacturers using sales branches and offices represent an important aspect of wholesaling.

Learning Objective 6:   **Show how both full-service wholesalers and limited-service wholesalers contribute to the marketing system.**

Full-service merchant wholesalers can perform a variety of credit and delivery functions and provide managerial assistance and market information. Limited-service wholesalers perform some, but not all, intermediary functions, eliminating those that particular buyers do not require. These intermediaries can therefore lower their costs of doing business and the prices they must charge their customers.

Learning Objective 7:   **Identify the marketing contributions of agent intermediaries such as brokers, auction companies, and selling agents.**

Agent intermediaries such as brokers, auction companies, and selling agents may offer expert knowledge of the marketplace, provide physical facilities for doing business, give advice to buyers and sellers, and help bring buyers and sellers together. They therefore play important roles in exchanges without actually taking title to the products.

Learning Objective 8:   **Understand the key elements of wholesalers' strategies.**

To a large extent, the wholesaler's strategy is dominated by physical distribution strategies. However, selecting target markets, creating assortments for customers, and developing strategic alliances are important aspects of wholesale strategy.

IX.   KEY TERMS

X.   QUESTIONS FOR DISCUSSION (13)

XI.   ETHICS IN PRACTICE

XII.   CASES

ANSWER GUIDELINES FOR CHAPTER 15 QUESTIONS FOR DISCUSSION

1.   *Give some examples of retailers in your local area that fit the following categories. (a) general merchandise retailer (b) specialty store (c) chain store (d) catalog showroom.*

ANSWER:

This answer obviously must vary from place to place. Some ideas may be offered, however.

(a)   General merchandise retailer

This category includes a retailer offering a merchandise assortment that is wide, that is one that stretches across many generic lines of goods. Thus the category includes everything from the local "general store" found in smaller towns and in some suburbs to larger stores and mass merchandisers like Wal-Mart, Gibson's, K-Mart, IGA "superstores," Otasco, and Zayres.

(b)   Specialty store

These offer a narrowly focused product offering, especially when one product or product line is offered. Examples: Merle Norman Cosmetics, Singer sewing machine stores, a fabric store like Needlewoman, Wallpapers-To-Go, and just about any book store or other shop that limits itself to the product in the store's designation -- meat shop, jewelry shop, fruit stand, peanut vendor, etc.

(c)   Chain store

A chain store system is made up of two or more stores of the same type and having the same name and image. A chain store is a member of such a system. Chains can be large or small, local or international. Examples: Sears, Penney's, Athlete's Foot, Lerner's, Macy's, Wal-Mart, K-Mart. Notice that a chain store can also be a discount store, general merchandise store, etc.

(d)   Catalog showroom

Some include Levitz Furniture, Best and Company, Service Merchandise, "Crazy Eddie," G.E.M. stores, and the Sears and Penney's locations found in small towns that carry "sample" merchandise customers must order from a catalog. Sears calls these "catalog stores."

2.   *Which of the following retailers would tend to utilize free-standing locations? Why? Why would others not use such locations? (a) K Mart (b) McDonald's (c) department store (d) popcorn shops*

ANSWER:

Some exceptions and variations exist especially in the cases of McDonald's and the department store. Exceptions are far less likely in the case of the other two but, as the text notes, location is just part of the retailer's marketing mix. Thus, other variables can make up for "unusual" site selections.

(a)   K Mart

K Marts are almost always free-standing. Some reasons for this include:

.   K Mart needs a certain type of building. These are frequently built to specification.

.   K Mart is "big enough" to attract customers on its own.

.   K Mart prefers to be near malls but mall occupants, especially department store anchors, don't want K Mart. Thus K Mart builds near malls but not in malls.

.   K Mart emphasizes low-prices and convenience. These imply a comparatively low-rent location and a big parking lot.

(b)   McDonald's

McDonald's "traditional" location is a free-standing one near shopping and/or residences. Convenient access is important, as is parking and room for a drive-thru or even a playground.

However, some McDonald's are in malls, in office buildings, or in downtown locations of one kind or another. This is possible because McDonald's can identify market segments to be served by outlets in these places and can vary the hours and services offered to them. Office building McDonald's may be open from 6 a.m. to 6 p.m. only and provide delivery to desk-bound customers within a given distance of the store. Though these units have no drive-thru, they often have a "walk up window" and extra seating to handle lunch and coffee-break crowds.

(c)   Department store

Most students will imagine mall anchor department stores which are not free-standing. Many others are, even in downtown locations where the store building may be physically separate from surrounding buildings. The thing to

recall here is that the department store "wants" to be close to other like
stores.   Some independent stores have been connected by skyways to increase the
flow of traffic between stores.   This is because the merchandise carried is
usually of the shopping goods class.   People want to compare these goods.   It has
often been shown that the "friendly competition" between two shopping goods
stores leads to more sales for each than would have occurred had the other not
been present.

(d)   Popcorn shops

Even the popcorn stands of the pushcart type found in parks or zoos are
free-standing only physically.   They rely on the park, zoo, or fair to support
them.   They are "parasite" outlets.   In malls or large stores, these shops rely
on the drawing power of others.

Few people drive out to the mall to buy a bag of popcorn.   Some free-standing
shops do exist but these are near populous areas or on main travel streets.   Such
shops usually offer something "unique" such as 25 flavors of popcorn.

3.   *What are the advantages of database marketing?*

ANSWER:

Database marketing makes extensive use of computer-generated mailing lists and/or
customer descriptions and purchase information.   There are several examples of
firms using database marketing in the marketing research chapter.   A few
advantages of database marketing may include:

.   allowing a firm to narrowly focus on selected target markets based on
        interest, demographics and/or psychographics

.   relating purchase information with target market descriptions in new
        product development

.   targeting specific geographic areas with promotional campaigns designed to
        reach current non-patrons of the retail store

.   purchasing from a variety of companies which specialize in developing
        targeted mailing lists

.   acquiring their own in-house expertise in designing and maintaining
        continuous research of the market

.   tracking inventory and sales of specific products to better match the needs
        of their target segment

4.   *What are some of the disadvantages of using vending machines as retail
       outlets?*

ANSWER:

This question must be approached from the distributor's point of view.   Note,
however, that the disadvantages to the consumer (e.g., they may keep your money
and give you no merchandise) are, ultimately, the reasons why automatic vending
has not expanded beyond its current bounds.

Some disadvantages and limitations of vending machines, from the seller's point
of view are:

.   Items thus sold are traditionally inexpensive.
.   Traditional limits on machines have required coins though this seems to be
        a thing of the past.   Still, no credit cards or checks are accepted by most
        machines.
.   Items have traditionally been small and comparatively easy to preserve.
.   Items have been high turnover items (so machine owners can make money
        before the public wrecks the machine).
.   Machines are "impersonal" and do not lend themselves to sale of some items.
.   All people have been "robbed" by a malfunctioning machine or received
        disappointing merchandise.

- Machines need servicing and restocking, that means personnel expenses.
- Most importantly, machines face competition from other channels. Most people would prefer to buy most items at a "regular store" where they can see and feel the merchandise, get advice, and have someone to complain to.

5.   *What trends do you predict in non-store retailing?*

ANSWER:

Non-store retailing includes vending machines, telephone sales, door-to-door, mail order, direct marketing via TV and radio, and any other form of retailing that is not done from a "regular" retail outlet. Some particular trends seem reasonable to predict:

- Increase in non-store retailing in general as factors contributing to its growth (2-career families, etc.) increase in importance.

- Improvements in direct marketing seem imminent: cable TV and home computer tie-ins, better quality TV equipment (e.g., 3-D) and better delivery services such as Federal Express. Consumers have already been offered "video catalogs" rather than simple TV shopping shows. Consumers control these "catalogs" using touch-tone phones.

- Non-store retailing "feeds itself." As more people use it successfully, the industry will grow in numbers of customers and frequency of use.

- The "women's movement" or "liberation" contributed to non-store retailing's success in U.S. This should affect life in other countries as well.

- The growth of non-store retailers might cause traditional "big stores" to this market.

- Electronic techniques should permit use of credit cards by card-reading phones, electronic funds transfer, etc.

6.   *Take a look at furniture marketing in the United States and discuss the evolution and development of retailing innovations in this industry.*

ANSWER:

Answers to this question will vary with the amount of research done and the historiographical skills of the student. Some points to be mentioned might include:

- The furniture industry can be dated to earliest colonial days when families made their own furniture.

- Persons more skilled than others soon began producing surplus for sale, the start of a cottage industry.

- Distribution then moved from person-to-person direct dealings to include sale to merchants. Eventually the level of production and growth of markets led to use of wholesale-level intermediaries.

- As the economy grew, better quality furniture was demanded by customers and larger stores.

- Recognition of market segments led to production of furniture for all levels of customer -- wealthy and not-so-wealthy.

- The powerful influence of these segments on the industry (e.g., "the economical buyer") led to discounting, no-frills stores stressing only price, replacement of "free delivery" by some retailers with "free loan of a U-Haul trailer."

- Furniture sold in a variety of ways ranging from traditional department and furniture stores to Ethan Allen exclusive dealerships, from discount stores promising "instant delivery" to catalogs offered by North Carolina manufacturers promising "one-third off list."

.   The electronic catalog would seem to be appropriate to furniture sales with
         shipment direct to consumers from the factory site.

.   Several furniture stores now offer quality furniture kits, finished and
         rather easy to assemble. Vast savings in shipping are at least partially
         passed on to consumers.

7.   *What are the key elements of a retailer's marketing mix? Provide an
         example.*

ANSWER:

Retailers must analyze market segments, select target markets, and determine
their preferred competitive position. A retailer's marketing mix is designed to
establish an image where all aspects of the store (personnel, merchandise,
surrounds, appearance, prices, customer service) reflect the desired impression.

Key elements of a retailer's marketing mix discussed in the text are:

.   merchandise assortment reflects decisions about the product aspect of the
         marketing mix as well as the price levels appropriate for the chosen
         assortment.

.   place as emphasized in the "Location, Location, Location" caveat of real
         estate agents is a key determinant of retailing success

.   atmospherics seem similar to promotion decisions in that the appearance,
         layout, displays and perceptual facets are all designed to promote a
         specific image

.   customer service continues to increase in importance as retailers seek to
         maximize "extra" value within the store and after the sale.

8.   *Do small independent retailing executives have the same growth orientation
         and business philosophies as large corporate executives?*

ANSWER:

This answer assumes that the small independent retailer intends to remain an
independent businessperson, operating one outlet. If more outlets are planned,
we assume that these will be located in the same general market area as the
current facility.

Do both executives have the same business philosophy? They do if they are
successful over the long-term. The business philosophy common to both is the
marketing concept. The fact that their different situations force them to
implement the philosophy differently may cause observers to think the
"philosophies" differ but they are, in fact, the same.

As to growth orientation, assuming the independent retailing executive is at all
growth minded, we do find a major difference between the two. It is likely that
the growth orientation will be locally focused. Concentration on building a
bigger customer base (share of market,) or on opening local branches, is typical.
Growth through better service to the local community is the usual path taken.

Executives in larger organizations are likely to be oriented toward national or
regional growth, or toward a better job for themselves within their large
organizations. They are likely to be more tradition- and policy-bound than the
independent executive and less flexible.

9.   *Find local examples of the following: (a) cash-and-carry wholesaler (b)
         rack jobber (c) manufacturer's sales office and (d) auction company.*

ANSWER:

The "hard part" here is to find these people and organizations locally. Students
should be asked to bring in names, addresses and phone numbers. Some professors
regularly assign students to interview members of these organizations and submit
a written or verbal report.

Where to look?

- Phone book, city directory, Business-to-Business Yellow Pages.
- Retailer-oriented "source books" if these are available.
- Retailers themselves might be asked how they obtain various appropriate merchandise.
- Local manufacturers might be asked how they sell their products.
- Business-oriented periodicals or newspaper sections might carry advertisements that would be of help.

In short, this question is a good exercise in that it can be used to put the student in a situation where his or her inventiveness and resourcefulness can be tested.

10.   *What is the major difference between agents and merchant wholesalers?*

ANSWER:

For some reason this question can always "fool" some students in the class. The distinction, of course, is purely and simply one of title to the goods. Merchants take title to goods, agents do not.

The matter has nothing to do with possession, inventory levels, geography, or anything other than title. Thus, column one in the matrix below shows that agents may or may not take possession, but this does not affect their status as agents or merchants.

	AGENTS NO TITLE	MERCHANTS TAKE TITLE
POSSESSION TAKEN	Auction Companies	"Traditional" Wholesalers
POSSESSION NOT TAKEN	Manufacturer's Agent	Drop Shippers

11.   *What would be the advantages and disadvantages of using manufacturers'*
       agents in the following situations? (a) new company marketing voice
       synthesizer for computers (b) large established company marketing truck
       axles (c) West Virginia coal company selling coal in Pennsylvania

ANSWER:

Certain assumptions will have to be made regarding the situations in which these companies find themselves. However, manufacturer's agents are likely to be used when the company:

- is financially weak and can't afford its own sales force.

- wants representation in a "thin market area" whose potential sales volume does not justify a company-owned sales effort.

- management does not know much about sales and marketing and needs help.

- is moving into "unknown" territory and needs local expertise.

- produces too few products to justify a sales force of its own.

These may be interpreted in terms of the company situations mentioned in the question.

(a)   New company marketing voice synthesizers

Such a company might choose to use agents if it is decided that the firm does not have the resources to pay for its own sales force. Further, the rep may be particularly familiar with the computer industry in his or her territory.

A major disadvantage would obtain if competition for synthesizers is stiff. Then greater control over the sales force would be necessary. There are some manufacturers' agents who represent only one principal. If the company can promise a representative enough sales and/or a big enough commission perhaps the representative would specialize in this company's product, at least for a while, providing it with the "push" it will need.

(b)   Large established company marketing truck axles

Such a company would be likely to use a combination of approaches. To reach repair facilities and other rather small buyers, a channel involving merchant middlemen would be likely, if the product is fairly standardized. Further, these smaller buyers actually need the product if they are to keep their trucks on the road. The personal attention of a manufacturers' agent may not be needed. Also, the established company with regular sales cannot take advantage of some of the agent's major characteristics; it may not be particularly important that no payments need be made until a sale is made.

A company like this may also sell large quantities of axles to manufacturers of small and large trucks, buses, trailers, RV's and specialized trucks like trash-removal trucks. Such manufacturers can be expected to buy in larger amounts than repair facilities and to be more geographically concentrated. Such a situation suggests using a company-operated sales force rather than an agent.

(c)   West Virginia coal company selling in Pennsylvania

If the company is opening up new territories or seeking new customers, the manufacturers' agent approach might be of use. However, since coal is sold in large quantities, shipment would be direct to these large buyers and delivery would be a key matter in attracting and maintaining customers. Thus, once a customer has been "signed up," it would seem that the agent's role would be diminished in importance. The coal producer may begin to regret paying the agent on-going commissions on sales that appear to be "in the bag" and need only an occasional "courtesy call." The manufacturer might then develop a telemarketing system or send out a circuit-riding, missionary salesman-type to replace the agent. In short, after the customer-supplier relationship is established (coal being a standardized bulk commodity sold mostly on the basis of price), personal selling efforts become far less significant.

12.   *What are the most important aspects of wholesalers' marketing strategies?*

ANSWER:

While the point can be made that no one aspect is more important than others because they are interdependent, a few critical areas for wholesalers are discussed in the text.

.   Wholesalers must select target markets and create assortments to satisfy their needs. The three basic options for wholesaler target markets include: (1) retailers that resell the product; (2) other wholesalers; and (3) organizations in the business market that use the product.

.   Strategic Business Alliances, relationship marketing, vertical marketing systems, and channel coordination all seem to be part of the movement in business toward more interdependent organizations. The commitment by wholesalers and other intermediaries to establish long-term relations with suppliers and customers is quickly becoming a necessity in today's business environment.

.   Technological advances have changed the landscape in wholesaling and will continue to affect the distribution of goods and services as organizations strive to increase the efficiency and effectiveness of the system.

13.   *A wholesaler states: "Retailers are our customers. Our allegiance lies with them, not with the manufacturers that supply products to us." Do you agree?*

ANSWER:

To provide the best service for customers, all channel participants must coordinate their efforts. Thus, the publics of a wholesaler include members who are vertically forward and backward from the wholesaler. Strategic alliances, relational exchanges, and long-term commitments describe the current emphasis on developing cooperative relationships with channel participants.

To meet the needs of retailers, wholesalers must perform assortment functions. Wholesalers then must convince various manufacturers that they can provide the desired assortment and level of service required to best meet the manufacturer's needs for a given product. If the wholesaler ignores the supplier in the current environment, the supplier may well find another channel participant who is more willing to coordinate efforts.

A wholesaler's allegiance must lie with all participants from producer to ultimate consumer. After all, part of the wholesaler's function is to assist the retailer in selling products to ultimate consumers. While traditional channels of distribution may have survived with this philosophy, it is no longer viable in the current environment.

ETHICS EXERCISE 15

CHAPTER 15 ETHICS IN PRACTICE

Overview

A Utah ice-cream maker planned to market a frozen novelty item in a 30-store chain in California until the chain's management demanded a $20,000 "slotting allowance." Retailers say that such fees compensate them for finding space in stores and warehouses for new products, entering data into computers, informing individual stores about new products carried, taking a chance on a new product, etc. The allowances also permit them to profit from buying activities in new ways. These allowances are also called by the names "stocking allowance," "introductory allowance," and "street money."

Some of the most expensive real estate in the U.S. is now on retailers' shelves. In the late 1980s a new form of trade promotion emerged -- the slotting allowance. This entails money or free goods being paid by a manufacturer to a retail chain in order to win a slot for the product in the grocer's warehouse and to ultimately slot or place the products on the shelf. This slot money is a flat admission fee demanded by retailers to squeeze products onto their already overcrowded shelves. This contrasts with most other types of trade promotions which are paid to the retailer for some sort of performance or service on his part (e.g., display allowances and advertising allowances) or for special trade payment terms (e.g., sliding scale discounts, free goods). National grocery chains charge a slotting allowance of between $4,000 and $80,000 on top of other traditional trade promotions/trade deals. Slotting allowances are not demanded of well-established products or those backed by extensive marketing research and advertising campaigns. This might have Robinson-Patman implications in the future since the burden of paying slotting fees is put on smaller regional companies that lack the successful track record and promotional firepower of the Procter & Gambles and General Mills of the world.

To add insult to injury, some retailers have also been charging "failure fees" if a new product doesn't capture a predetermined market share within a specific length of time, and some charge "annual renewal" or "pay to stay" fees in order to continue stocking certain items. Some chain buyers have even started charging "presentation fees," which are paid up to $500 for the privilege of an appointment to present a new product. Many of these deals are discussed behind closed doors, and payments are sometimes made in cash.

These tools represent new-found power that food retailers can exercise over manufacturers. Whereas food manufacturers once had power to dictate terms to supermarkets, now retailers have relatively more power -- due to factors such as consolidations and mergers, access to scanner data, and growth of private labels.

Are slotting allowances ethical?

The retailers' arguments in favor of slotting allowances include:

.   They are a response to the proliferation of new products during the past decade. New product introductions are costly for retailers who must incur expenditures such as entering new product information into the computer, finding space in the warehouse, reconfiguring store shelves, notifying individual stores within the chain of new entries, pricing the new products, as well as discontinuation costs such as removing the failed products from the shelves.

.   Most new products fail due to inadequate research during the new product development process. Therefore, it is justifiable to discriminate between large and small stores in administering slotting allowances. If manufacturers wish to avoid stocking fees, they must engage in brand-building activities such as promotion and research.

.   The retail shelves aren't made of rubber; there are too many goods chasing too little shelf space. Where there is a limited supply of space it is fair to charge what, in effect, is rent. Retailers are really in the real estate business, renting shelf space.

Manufacturers cry foul because:

.   A refusal to pay the fee can drastically cut the potential market for a new product.

.   This practice could limit the number of new products which find their way onto retailers' shelves and into shoppers' grocery carts, interfering with consumers' right to choose and stifling innovation. One critic of this practice said: "If we had had slotting allowances a few years ago, we might not have had granola, herbal tea, or yogurt."

.   Slotting fees amount to extortion since nothing of value is received by the manufacturer in return, as is the case with traditional trade promotions. Manufacturers are being held hostage by the trade.

.   The practice discriminates against small producers, who can least afford the payments.

Questions for your students: "If you were a large manufacturer, would you bite the bullet and accept slotting allowances? What if you were a small manufacturer? If you were a supermarket vice-president of marketing, what would be your policy on slotting fees?"

CHAPTER 15 TAKE A STAND QUESTIONS

1.   *A Wal-Mart moves into a small town and many small retail businesses go out of business within a year. Is this right?*

Wal-Mart was dubbed the retailer of the 80s and is likely to continue to be so through the 90s. According to *Fortune* magazine, it is one of America's most admired corporations. Started by Sam Walton as one store in remote northwest Arkansas in 1963, the chain in 1990 had over 1,500 stores and was opening about 130 outlets every year. In 1992 Wal-Mart overtook K Mart and Sears to become the nation's number one retailer.

Wal-Mart has been so successful for several reasons. First, and most important, Sam Walton (who died in 1992 but whose legacy lives on), was a fanatic about customer service. By satellite transmission he talked to all store managers and encouraged them to treat customers with relentless hospitality. Thus, the secret of their success is Wal-Mart's people and how they relate to their customers.

Every employee takes the Wal-Mart pledge: "From this day forward, I solemnly promise and declare that every customer that comes within ten feet of me, I will smile, look them in the eye, and greet them, so help me Sam." Second, Walton used state-of-the-art technology to devise a sophisticated merchandising program. Wal-Mart's advanced computer system handles credit card transactions, inventory analysis, and distribution tracking. The firm also operates 14 distribution centers, where it orders directly from manufacturers and operates its own fleet of trucks. One key to Wal-Mart's third competitive advantage, its low prices, is its efficient network of warehouse distribution centers, which serve its retail stores within a 400-mile radius.

Thousands of small retailers have been outsmarted and undersold by this discount chain. Mom-and-pop stores and regional chains like Woolco, TG&Y, and Gibsons closed many stores as Wal-Mart invaded their territories. Some cry foul and claim that we need to save the little guy from the bogeyman. This is the same war cry sounded by the "mom and pop" grocers against giant A&P, which received price concessions during the 1930s from food manufacturers by claiming it deserved them since it bought in bulk and since it could take its business elsewhere if they didn't give it discounts. As a result, the Robinson-Patman Act was passed, making it unlawful to price discriminate except for cost-justified volume discounts between competing resellers of goods of like grade and quality in interstate commerce, where the effect of such discrimination might be to substantially lessen competition or tend to create a monopoly, or to injure, destroy, or prevent competition.

In both the A&P and the Wal-Mart cases, the small retailers' complaints are really with our free enterprise system. After all, almost every competitive action is designed to enhance a company's position at the expense of competitors' positions. To disallow or somehow restrict Wal-Mart would be to protect inefficient firms against creative competition.

Instead of grousing, the smart small retailers are sharpening skills to fight back, survive, and perhaps even prosper when Wal-Mart comes to town. New competition can be an incentive to break with the old entrenched ways of doing things. A fair number of regional discount chains have fought back against Wal-Mart invasions. Retail consultants now travel the country preaching survival over Wal-Mart by building on a store's individual strengths and exploiting Wal-Mart's weaknesses (e.g., to keep prices low, Wal-Mart sometimes passes up trendy fashion items). They say that retailers must respond by giving unflagging customer service, specialize by filling the high-quality niche left unplugged by giant discounters, and look for value-added ways to build customer traffic (e.g., craft stores can offer classes; hardware stores can do repairs or rent tools or equipment). The kiss of death would be to compete against Wal-Mart on price alone. Although customers are sure to be winners as a result of Wal-Mart coming to town, small retailers can prosper, too, by specializing and treating customers right. However, many small retailers have been unable to do this.

2.   *A major chain store has six supermarkets in a certain city but none on the side of town where many minority consumers live. Should the store open a branch on this side of town?*

Some would suggest that it is unfair to fail to serve poor customers; this smacks of discrimination. However, the marketing concept mandates that we serve customers profitably. The fact is, the poor side of town might not be as profitable due to higher crime rates, lower incomes, smaller buildings in poor condition, higher credit risks, etc.

The free enterprise system is generally considered desirable from a utilitarian perspective because it has permitted the greatest good for the greatest number. However, there is a minority of people who are not always well served. There is some evidence that in the inner cities there are fewer and smaller stores, higher credit costs, lower quality merchandise, and fewer services due to the economics of inner-city marketing. Thus, distributive justice is not achieved.

Whose responsibility is it to rectify this? Does a businessperson have a duty to open a money-losing business in order to serve the inner-city poor? It would seem not; the venture is a business, not a charity. A businessperson has the right to open outlets in locations that would be most lucrative.

Traditionally welfare rights have been a government responsibility, not a business responsibility, although some businesses do meet community needs. To avoid jeopardizing one's retail business, the compassionate marketer should seek charitable alternatives to inner-city retailing such as donations to shelters, food banks, and volunteer educational efforts.

The point of including government within the economic system is to make sure that those who cannot compete successfully are nonetheless guaranteed protection of their rights (as human beings) to provision of their basic needs. Historically, the retail system has not served the poor in inner cities very well; it has been well-documented that, due to an inefficient distribution system, the poor pay more. Government can establish urban enterprise zones in which firms receive lower capital gains tax, tax holiday for a certain time frame, infrastructure support, low-interest loans, and job training. However, some argue that government should only protect civil liberties and does not have a duty to provide people with whatever they need. This, they argue, should be the duty of the citizenry.

3.   A wholesaler refuses to carry a lawn mower manufacturer's product line because the wholesaler already represents a competitor's mower line. Is this legal? Ethical?

This practice is known as exclusive dealing. The manufacturer in effect says to the distributor (usually a retailer, "If you want to carry my brand, you may carry only my brand." This practice as discussed in Ch. 14, is illegal if it tends to restrict competition. If all distributors engaged in this practice, new products in existing categories would never see the light of day. Exclusive dealing arrangements are illegal if: (1) the manufacturer's product has a substantial market share, (2) there is a substantial dollar investment, or (3) the arrangement is between a large manufacturer with market power and small distributors. We don't know if any of these conditions are met in the above situation.

Exclusive dealing arrangements are considered legal under the Clayton Act if the exclusivity can be strategically justified as protection of a manufacturer's image or assurance of intermediary attention to marketing the supplier's item. Justification exists if a new product needs exclusive dealing agreements to strengthen its market position, or if the supplier's own sales are restricted because of limited production capacity. It doesn't appear that any of these conditions are met in this instance.

Therefore, it isn't clear whether the exclusive dealing arrangement is legal in this scenario. If it isn't, the lawn mower manufacturer has the right to take legal recourse. The wholesaler can't refuse to deal with him because he carries a competitive brand. The manufacturer would also have the right to expect the wholesaler to make an equal effort in promoting and selling his brand.

From an ethical perspective, it would seem that some of the legal reasons for allowing exclusive dealing are acceptable. A manufacturer should have the right to ensure that its product is adequately marketed at wholesale or retail if this is vital to sales success. If carrying competitive brands will hinder the intermediary from doing this, exclusive dealing seems to be the solution. If output is limited, exclusive dealing would be a reasonable rationing mechanism. However, if a new product requires little marketing within the channel (e.g., convenience goods), exclusive dealing is unnecessary; the new product should be able to stand on its own legs.

On the other hand, it could be argued that exclusive dealing might restrict buyers' freedom to choose and result in higher prices if competition is hindered. Exclusive dealing could also hinder a seller's freedom to sell in its preferred channels.

4.   A manufacturer of office equipment had used a manufacturer's agent on the West coast to sell to wholesalers for six years. The agent did a good job, and sales volume reached a million dollars in the territory. When this happened a sales representative was hired to replace the agent and the longstanding relationship between manufacturer and agent was terminated. What obligation does the manufacturer have to the agent?

This is a common occurrence. Depending on the industry and other circumstances, it is common practice to terminate the relationship between a manufacturer and his agent when gross commissions reach a level of between $150,000 and up to $1.5 million because it is more economically viable to employ one's own sales force. Because this is a common strategy, the agent should expect that it will happen if sales and commissions grow beyond a certain point. Typically, agents and manufacturers sign an evergreen contract which states that they will continue to do business for the next year unless the manufacturer gives advance notice (typically 30 days to a year) that he will no longer deal with the agent. Terms and arrangements are usually spelled out to ensure a smooth transition in the interim. It is clearly in the manufacturer's self interest not to give too much advance warning to the agent, for then the agent will likely cut back support of the manufacturer's product while seeking alternative sources of supply.

GUIDE TO CASES

VIDEO CASE 15-1 PEP BOYS[1]

SUBJECT MATTER: Retail Strategy, Retail Marketing Mix, Retail Product Line Adjustment, Customer Service, Changing Retail Environment and Technology

> Please see the Guide to Video Cases for video length and other information.

AT-A-GLANCE OVERVIEW

Pep Boys retail stores sell a full range of brand name and private label automotive parts and accessories at discount prices. Most Pep Boys outlets include service centers for automobile maintenance and service, as well as for installation of automotive parts and accessories sold by the company.

Mitchell Liebovitz began working for Pep Boys in 1978. He was named president of the company in 1986. Under Liebovitz, the marketing strategy created a chain of enormous retail warehouses with extensive inventories of discounted items aimed at the do-it-yourself market. After increasing stock in the stores from 9,000 to 18,000 different items, Pep Boys eliminated extraneous items like bicycles. This freed up capital for more car-oriented items.

It has been implementing a new service technician compensation plan. Under the new plan, mechanics receive 32%-38% of the revenue for each service job completed, instead of an hourly wage. In addition, mechanics correct jobs not done right the first time at their own expense.

In 1991, the company introduced a new direct mail advertising/marketing program via its "catabook" to markets. This 48-page booklet features 10,000 of Pep Boys 18,000 items at everyday-low-prices.

Pep Boys implemented a computerized parts catalog. A new automated store replenishment system is being tested. Its point-of-sale computerized inventory control system monitors daily sale of items from each store, so marketers may tailor inventory to a particular local market while setting prices from the home office.

Pep Boys is also testing a new warehouse-style store format which could become the model for future stores.

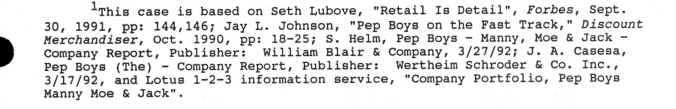

[1]This case is based on Seth Lubove, "Retail Is Detail", *Forbes*, Sept. 30, 1991, pp: 144,146; Jay L. Johnson, "Pep Boys on the Fast Track," *Discount Merchandiser*, Oct. 1990, pp: 18-25; S. Helm, Pep Boys - Manny, Moe & Jack - Company Report, Publisher: William Blair & Company, 3/27/92; J. A. Casesa, Pep Boys (The) - Company Report, Publisher: Wertheim Schroder & Co. Inc., 3/17/92, and Lotus 1-2-3 information service, "Company Portfolio, Pep Boys Manny Moe & Jack".

QUESTIONS

1.   *According to the categorization of retail stores given in the textbook, how
     would you categorize Pep Boys? There are several categories that fit.*

Based on ownership, Pep Boys is a chain store using an in-store retailer strategy
for most of its business. It clearly specializes in automobile parts and
supplies, but it is too big to be a specialty store. Its size, however, puts it
into the category discounter or category killer classification.

2.   *Describe the historical evolution of the automotive parts retailers.   (The
     student should be encouraged to think about the wheel of retailing
     hypothesis.)*

The wheel of retailing hypothesis suggests that new retailing institutions enter
the marketplace as low-status, low-price operations, then trade up to higher
"spokes on the wheel," or "steps on a ladder." The movement from service
stations as major parts suppliers, to specialty automotive stores, to category
discounters like Pep Boys, illustrates this. The American retailers' tradition
is competition using non-price variables like services and decor, not price
competition. Services, decor, and other "extras" require support from higher
prices and higher margins, so the institution moves "up the ladder" to earn those
higher margins. Then, as one type of store "trades up" the bottom rungs are left
open for newcomers to occupy. It should be recalled that while the "wheel"
describes a pattern of institutional change, it does not describe what happens to
each and every store. For example, many small service stations still sell parts
and service.

Pep Boys is also testing a new warehouse-style store format which has shown
excellent initial results and could become the expansion vehicle of the future.
The company is still in the process of fine tuning the mailing of the "catabook"
and tying it to a television advertising program.

German philosopher G.W. Hegel's dialectic theory suggests that a logical pattern
of change is as follows:

.   A thought or institution exists. This is the thesis.

.   It is challenged by a new idea, the antithesis.

.   The good and bad of both interact and a new combination results, the
     synthesis.

This theory doesn't apply to the automobile parts business. The steady
evolutionary process of the wheel seems more applicable to the automotive parts
business.

3.   *Evaluate Pep Boys marketing mix and retail strategy?*

Mitchell Liebovitz, hired as controller of the East Coast division in 1978, was
named president of the company in 1986. He created a chain of enormous retail
warehouses with extensive inventories of discounted items aimed at the
do-it-yourself market. After increasing stock in the stores from 9,000 to 18,000
different items, Leibovitz eliminated extraneous items like bicycles. This freed
up capital for more car-oriented items.

In other words, the company selected a target market and positioned itself as a
low cost supplier with an extensive inventory. The company became more focused
on automotives: "When you need an automotive part, you go to the place you are
most likely to find it ... the place with the larger inventory." Further, Pep
Boys is attempting to increase sales with existing customers through: (1)
one-stop shopping, (2) a reduction in customer complaints, and (3) increased
advertising.

By the end of 1990, the Pep Boys aftermarket automotive chain doubled its size in
5 years, from 159 stores to 318 stores. During the same period, sales rose from
$389 million to over $900 million, and profits increased every year but one. In
an interview, Mitchell G. Leibovitz, president and CEO of Pep Boys, said the
growth was not consciously planned but was a case of analyzing the opportunities

and realizing that, if the 5-year plan worked, the store count would double by coincidence.

Leibovitz gives credit for the growth to a combination of factors, including the leadership of Maurice Strauss, who was not a strong advocate of debt. Low debt and less competitive conditions relegated expansion to secondary importance. Pep Boys, in other words, was conservative in exploiting opportunity in the market.

Pep Boys intends to continue to expand the store base around its existing distribution centers. The stores expect to be in 20 states by the end of 1991, but it will take years to become truly national in scope. The strategy is based on an understanding of the changing retail environment and the need for new institutions to serve new consumer needs.

Catabook is a much more effective vehicle to communicate Pep Boys' larger assortment, its "supermarket" approach to the business. The company has taken advantage of new technology. This is another important trend in retailing.

Currently, in 30 stores, the new system has increased service revenues, decreased payroll expense (as a percent of total revenues), and lowered service time. Also, it has resulted in fewer customer claims and returns. Overall, the new compensation system has positive implications for profitability and customer service. The test program has exceeded expectations and was expanded to all 340 stores. Sears had a similar problem in 1992 which caused much negative publicity and suggested that Sears performed much work that was unnecessary.

Service in Pep Boys' business declined in recent years because people are spending less during the recession and/or engaging in more do-it-yourself work, not because Pep Boys lost its market share to anyone.

The company is poised for expansion, has been able to free up inventory money and keep less inventory on hand due to an improvement in computer systems.

VIDEO CASE 15-2 VONS[2]

SUBJECT MATTER: Inventory Management, Customer Service, Market Segmentation, Positioning, Enhanced Offerings, Atmospherics

Please see the Guide to Video Cases for video length and other information.

AT-A-GLANCE OVERVIEW

The Vons Companies, Inc., based in Arcadia, California, operates 341 grocery stores throughout southern California, and Clark County, Nevada. Vons refers to the region as the "Nation of Southern California" because of its diverse demographic characteristics. Vons is clearly the southern California grocery market-share leader with an estimated share of 26%. The second and third market share positions are probably a toss-up between Luckys and Food-4-Less, while Ralph's share is estimated at 16%.

Vons is a leader in the use of new technology and merchandising techniques. Vons operates both traditional supermarket formats and food and drug combination formats under four different names including Vons, Pavilions, Tianguis, and Williams Bros.

Store design in newer outlets underscores Vons' intention to maximize profitability per square foot of selling space. Selling space is maximized and storage room space is kept to a minimum. Some of the new, larger stores have storage rooms that are the size of those in smaller formats. Vons has achieved this efficiency through its "Densing Up" program and better inventory management.

---

[2]Case materials excerpted with adaption with permission from D. Christopher, *Vons Companies, Inc. - Company Report*, Crowell, Weedon & Co., 5/11/92.

Dense merchandising brings more product to the sales floor and has increased sales per square foot. The strategy is designed to utilize vertical space more efficiently. Extra product is stacked above the aisles, enabling quick re-stocking of high-turnover items. Goods that complement each other are merchandised both in front of, and below, the high-traffic specialty department display cases. For instance, meal combinations are suggested by displaying breads, wines, and tartar and cocktail sauces in front of the fish department. In addition, free-standing displays are used at various points throughout the store to grab attention or to increase the odds of a compulsive purchase.

Vons is the only southern California supermarket offering home delivery from its Pavilions stores. For approximately $12.00 (less for senior citizens). customers may do their shopping over the phone. This service allows Vons to serve senior citizens, handicapped persons, time-constrained consumers, and holiday-, party-, and business-traffic.

Vons operates several food processing operations to serve its stores. It operates a fluid milk processing facility, an ice cream plant, a bakery, a delicatessen kitchen, and distribution facilities for meat, grocery, produce and general merchandise.

QUESTIONS

1.   *What retail classification best fits Vons?*

Vons is an ownership group with several chain store systems in its group. That is, the one company operates several stores under different names, each of them a separate chain store system. Vons could also be described as a supermarket operator.

2.   *Characterize Vons' overall marketing strategy? What role does positioning play in Vons' market strategy?*

Vons is very innovative in the supermarket industry. It clearly segments the market and then positions retail stores to appeal to the different market segments. In fact, a basic idea behind the ownership group concept is that the stores, with various names and images, serve various segments of the market.

Vons operates both traditional supermarket formats and food and drug combination formats under four different names including Vons, Pavilions, Tianguis, and Williams Bros.

Vons operates 341 stores in three distinct retail business units (RBUs): Vons, with 201 stores; Vons Food and Drug, with 83 stores, Pavilions, with 30 stores; and Tianguis, with 9 stores, as well as the recently acquired Williams Bros. chain of 18 stores. Vons stores are primarily in southern California in the markets of Los Angeles, Orange County, Ventura, Riverside, San Bernardino, San Diego, Kern, Santa Barbara, and Fresno. Vons also operates stores in Clark County, Nevada.

The Vons store base is very modern with about 80% being either new or remodeled over the past five years. Traditional Vons supermarkets average 21,000 square feet of selling space and generally include service delis and bakeries. The Vons Food & Drug combination store has nearly 30,000 square feet of selling space, with an in-store pharmacy, expanded general merchandise sections, and an array of service departments.

Pavilions was introduced into the southern California marketplace in 1985 to cater to consumers looking for more of a gourmet selection in their supermarket. The company's 16 Pavilions and 12 Pavilions Place stores target consumers who typically spend more discretionary income on food and food-related products. Pavilions stores have a high-end look and slightly higher prices than the Vons stores. The Pavilions stores feature expanded perishable departments as well as full-service pharmacies and a wide selection of general merchandise, housewares, and health and beauty care items. Many of the stores offer an in-house sausage and smoke shop, bagel shop, and sushi bar. In addition, certain Pavilions and Vons Food and Drug stores sell hot Chinese food from Panda Express, a southern

California restaurant chain. The Pavilions stores average 39,700 square feet of selling space.

The Pavilions format takes an innovative approach to "food fashion." Pavilions stores average 40,000 square feet of selling space. This concept expands the Food & Drug format. Included among the list of departments and services are a cosmetics department, one-hour photo, a flower shop (with the selection of a traditional florist), a top-notch bakery and candy section, European style seafood, sausage shop, smoke shop, catering services, and in-store food service (pizza, Chinese food).

Tianguis (that's Aztec for "marketplace") was introduced in January 1987. It was developed to cater to the Los Angeles Mexican population. Today, four of the Tianguis stores serve a customer base that is 75% Mexican. The other stores include customers from Central and South American countries. Most employees are bilingual and all signage is in both Spanish and English. Tianguis stores capitalize on the growing Hispanic population in southern California. There are over 5 million Hispanics in southern California and Tianguis stores offer a complete selection of foods and merchandise to satisfy their unique tastes. These people tend to buy food from small neighborhood shops -- Tianguis has much better selection and atmosphere. Specialty departments include tortillerias, carnicerias (butcher shop), panaderia (bakery), farmacia (pharmacy), and sachichoneria (sausage shop). The produce department is nearly twice the size of a traditional Vons store with expanded selections of peppers, fruits, and unique bulk goods. There are currently nine Tianguis stores.

Students can be asked to respond to the question "Would it be better if Vons consolidated all its stores under the Vons name?" This brings up the issue of economies of scale for things such as mass advertising versus targeting and satisfying specific needs. For example, Vons could consolidate Williams into Vons since they serve similar markets. The Tianguis stores, on the other hand, serve a totally different market. This makes for a good discussion.

Vons' strategy is to appeal across demographic groups by offering different stores, complete with their own identity, for distinct customer groups. The stores enjoy their own marketing and merchandising programs; however, in order to contain costs and operate efficiently, most functions are centralized. This includes buying, administration, and real estate selection. Management believes that the benefits of operating three RBUs far outweigh the costs as increased sales result in greater efficiencies, thereby lowering total operating costs as a percentage of sales. The three RBUs give Vons an edge because each format appeals to a segment of southern California's diverse population mix. In addition, we believe the various formats uniquely enable Vons to compete against an ever-growing array of competitors.

Vons has begun distributing to the stores from its own distribution network and is also supplying Williams Bros. with Vons' private label merchandise. In addition, the company rounds out its offering with a line of private label products. Vons also sells its own dairy products, under the Jerseymaid and Westwood names, in all stores. Private label products are not focused upon or highlighted in the company's advertising; partially as a result of this, only 13% of sales come from private label products.

The "Join VonsClub and Save" promotional strategy highlights advertised weekly specials and added savings through the acceptance of double-value coupons on a daily basis. The gross margin is not negatively influenced by double couponing as the costs of the program are factored into the company's pricing decisions. In addition, the coupons are scanned at the register for accuracy, reducing the potential cost of giving a customer cents-off for a product that was not purchased. Vons typically passes along savings received through forward and promotional buying and advertises these savings, through in-store promotions and circulars, to reinforce its image of offering good value on quality merchandise. Vons utilizes newspaper, direct mail, television, and radio advertising to get its message across.

In addition to the savings offered through the acceptance of double coupons, Vons has introduced a free membership program that offers customers additional savings. Vons offers two such programs: VonsClub in its Vons stores; and ValuePlus at the Pavilions stores. Vons is one of the only players in its market

to offer this type of program. The free membership program yields Vons many
advantages. It builds customer loyalty by granting rewards for shopping at Vons
through offering special savings that are only available to club members. The
program also provides electronic coupons for further savings. Vons uses the
program in response to competitive openings by advertising promotions that are
available only to club members. In addition, the program provides Vons with
detailed information about its customers, including age, marital status, number
of people per household, and household income.

Vons uses this information to understand its customers' buying habits better, but
information received can also be sold to manufacturers. Vons recently
participated in a test with a manufacturer of a new cereal. Samples of the
cereal and high-value coupons were sent to VonsClub members who used the
competing national brand cereal. Vons received a fee from the manufacturer for
this targeted distribution. We believe there are many possibilities for future
tests of this kind given the array of data Vons has gathered about its customers.

The membership programs have been successful from both an informational viewpoint
as well as profitable on a dollar basis, as evidenced by the fact that of the two
million members, one million are active. These members' average transaction is
typically more than twice the chain average.

3.   *Outline a plan for the athmospherics within each type of Vons store?*

The video is helpful in answering this question. The Pavilions format takes an
innovative approach to "food fashion." Pavilions stores average 40,000 square
feet of selling space. This concept expands the Food & Drug format. Included
among the list of departments and services are a cosmetics department, one-hour
photo, a flower shop (with the selection of a traditional florist,) a top-notch
bakery and candy section, European style seafood, sausage and smoke shops,
in-store food service (pizza, Chinese food), and catering services.

Tianguis stores cater to the rapidly growing Hispanic population in southern
California. There are over 5 million Hispanics in southern California and
Tianguis stores offering a complete selection of foods and merchandise to satisfy
their unique tastes. Promotions are, of course, in Spanish, signs are bilingual,
and stores contain "shops" whose names are in Spanish.

The average gross square footage of a Vons store is 29,200 square feet with
average selling space of 20,500 square feet. In many cases, the store size is
constrained due to location. Stores are physically expanded where possible.
When this is not possible, the company utilizes its "densing-up" program, whereby
more product is added through innovative merchandising techniques.

The densing-up program has been highly successful as it has enabled Vons to add
high-margin merchandise without compromising the stores' atmosphere. The program
was carefully designed so that the store would not look cluttered. In fact,
Vons' innovative shelving designs and adjacencies, together with improved
lighting, have served to make the stores look leaner and neater. We believe
densing-up will enable Vons to improve margins further as additional stores come
on line.

4.   *How important is technology to the retailing of food and drug items?*

Vons is a leader in the use of new technology and merchandising techniques.
Checkout scanners have been used by Vons since 1981. Other operators took years
to automate the checkout process. Vonschek, an automatic check approval system,
has been used since 1987. Vonschek resembles a credit card, yet functions as a
check guarantee card for those writing checks, or enables the customer to "write"
an electronic check. The system has drastically decreased the numbers of bad
checks and check tendering errors, and has improved efficiency at both the store
and administrative levels.

More recently, the Vonschek card is used as a money saving tool by the customer.
Vonschek users are eligible for free membership to VonsClub, while Pavilions
customers qualify for the ValuePlus Club. An extensive monthly handout at stores
lists special marketing and merchandising values. This form of "electronic
coupon" eliminates some of the fuss and aggravation commonly associated with the
coupon usage process. Electronic shelf tag (EST) testing has been going on for

some time. While chain-wide installation would require extensive capital investment, Vons believes ESTs offer significant benefits, including accuracy and pricing integrity, cost savings, and increased efficiency and flexibility, among others. Accuracy and pricing integrity would be enhanced because digital tags and check-out scanners are connected to the same computer system.

Vons is in the process of adding scanning, automated time and attendance, and labor scheduling systems to the stores. These systems should lower costs and improve operating efficiencies at the Williams Bros. stores.

Vons is clearly among the industry leaders when it comes to using technology. The majority of supermarkets today, including the independents through their affiliation with powerful wholesalers, utilize front-end scanning. Vons, however, is one of the few companies using the next generation of scanning -- side bar scanners. These scanners limit the motion required to scan a product, resulting in a decrease in motion-related injuries. In addition, the side bar scanners have a high first-read rate that increases rings per minute by 8%. A faster ring time translates into customer satisfaction as the customer is able to get through the front end faster.

Other examples of the company's daily use of technology include the VonsChek automated check approval system, electronic time and attendance systems, electronic mail to all stores, and computerized labor scheduling.

Technological innovations include electronic receiving for direct store deliveries by vendors. Electronic receiving is expected to be chain-wide by year-end. It should result in an improvement in gross margins and a reduction in shrink. Administrative costs at headquarters are expected to be reduced as some accounts payable positions will be eliminated.

Vons is currently testing electronic shelf tags in six stores. These tags list each product's price and are controlled by a central computer. When the company decides to change a price, it is done automatically by the computer. It is expected that electronic shelf tags will reduce pricing errors and in-store labor expense. The test is still in the initial stages. Due to the high costs of installation ($125,000 per store), a substantial benefit must be shown before the company chooses to roll out the program chain-wide.

Aside from store-level technology, Vons' central buying office monitors warehouse inventory levels and product movement daily so that buyers may analyze and act on information received in a timely manner. In addition, the management control system produces weekly operating data by store and by region. Vons utilizes the detailed data it receives from its systems to determine its customers' purchasing patterns. The company then adjusts its merchandise offering in each store according to consumers' wants and preferences in that particular neighborhood, thereby fulfilling Vons' strategy of catering to individual customers' needs.

To remain an innovative merchant, Vons has been testing VideoCarts in select stores. VideoCarts are shopping carts with a video screen at the front of the cart. The screens are linked to electronic tags in each aisle so that as the customer goes down an aisle the screen on the cart highlights what is on special in that aisle. The screen also displays recipes that can be made with ingredients that may be found in that aisle. The screens can also be used for informational purposes, such as helping a customer locate an item within the store or presenting a map of the store layout. At the checkout stand a menu comes up offering the customers items to keep them amused as they wait in line. Options include movie reviews and various forms of trivia. While we do not believe these carts increase the average purchase amount, they could be useful in providing information about customer traffic patterns and purchasing habits. At this point it is more of a novelty item than a shopping tool, but this will probably change at some point in the future. In any event, Vons remains at the forefront in that it is one of a limited number of retailers testing VideoCarts.

16 PHYSICAL DISTRIBUTION MANAGEMENT

CHAPTER SCAN

This chapter deals with physical distribution which, in its technical meaning, includes the activities involved in moving finished goods from the production point to buyers. Materials management moves raw materials to the point of production. Logistics is the management activity that coordinates the entire process. Such topics as warehousing, order processing, inventory control, and the various transportation modes are discussed in this chapter. The total cost approach is explained.

Distribution takes place "behind the scenes," but marketers can use it to create differential advantages.

SUGGESTED LEARNING OBJECTIVES

The student who studies this chapter will be exposed to a broad treatment of logistics with an emphasis on physical distribution and will be able to:

1. Evaluate the role of physical distribution in the marketing mix.

2. Show how distribution managers can make physical distribution provide maximum satisfaction to buyers while reducing costs.

3. Explain the total cost approach to physical distribution.

4. Compare the modes of transportation available to shippers.

5. Identify the purposes of warehousing, order processing, materials handling, and inventory control.

6. Understand materials management activities and their influence on many marketing decisions.

CHAPTER OUTLINE

I.   INTRODUCTION

II. LOGISTICS AND PHYSICAL DISTRIBUTION DEFINED

III. THE OBJECTIVES OF PHYSICAL DISTRIBUTION

    A.   Establishing Realistic Objectives
    B.   Establishing a Competitive Advantage

IV. A CROSS-SECTION OF THE PHYSICAL DISTRIBUTION SYSTEM

V.   TOTAL COST: A SYSTEMS APPROACH

    A.   Cutting Costs

VI. MANAGING THE COMPONENTS OF PHYSICAL DISTRIBUTION

    A.   Transportation

        1.   Motor Carrier
        2.   Air Freight
        3.   Water Transportation
        4.   Railroad
        5.   Pipelines
        6.   Intermodal Transportation

    B.   Warehousing

        1.   Storage
        2.   Breaking Bulk
        3.   Warehousing Strategy

    C.   Inventory Control
    D.   Materials Handling
    E.   Order Processing
    F.   Protective Packaging

VII. MATERIALS MANAGEMENT

VIII. TRENDS IN LOGISTICS

    A.   International Sourcing
    B.   New Technology
    C.   Unpredictable Energy Costs
    D.   Interorganizational Cooperation

IX. SUMMARY

X.   KEY TERMS

XI. QUESTIONS FOR DISCUSSION (15)

XII. ETHICS IN PRACTICE

XIII. CASES

    The following terms are introduced and used in Chapter 16.   They are defined in the text's Glossary.

Logistics
Materials management
Physical distribution
Systems concept
Total cost concept
Transportation
Motor carrier

Damage in transit
Air freight
Water transportation
Railroads
Diversion in transit
Pipelines
Piggyback service
Fishyback service
Birdyback service
Warehousing
Storage
Inventory control
Economic order quantity (E.O.Q.)
Materials handling
Order processing
Vendor analysis
Just-in-time (JIT) inventory system

THE CHAPTER SUMMARIZED

I.   INTRODUCTION

      Air-Vet entered the very competitive veterinary medicine business
      without the 30 or more regional and district offices typical of
      competitors in that field. Air-Vet had developed a unique storage,
      inventory-control, and delivery system. Research had told Air-Vet's
      managers that veterinarians across the country preferred next-day
      delivery of their orders, but the prospect of maintaining stocks all
      around the country seemed a nightmare.

      Business Logistics Services, a division of Federal Express (like Air-
      Vet, a Memphis company) helped Air-Vet to develop a warehouse and
      overnight distribution system that kept labor and storage costs down.
      Orders of any type can be filled overnight. Telemarketers call vets
      around the country, or the doctors can use an 800 number to place
      orders. It's a just-in-time (JIT) inventory plan for the doctors.

      In every exchange situation some kind of physical distribution can be
      found. Distribution can be the key element in marketing success
      stories.

II.   LOGISTICS AND PHYSICAL DISTRIBUTION DEFINED

      The word **logistics** describes the entire process of moving raw materials
      and component parts into the firm, in-process inventory through the
      firm, and finished goods out of the firm. Though terms are often
      misused, there are some "official" definitions in the area of
      distribution. Logistics management, thus, involves planning,
      implementing, and controlling the efficient flow of both inbound
      materials and outbound finished products.

      Materials management is concerned with bringing raw materials and
      supplies to the point of production and moving in-process inventory
      through the firm.

      Physical distribution is a term used to describe the broad range of
      activities concerned with efficient movement of finished products from
      the end of the production line to the consumer.

      Exhibit 16-1 shows the interrelationship of materials management,
      physical distribution, and logistics.

      Logistics deals with the "big picture," and relies heavily on demand
      estimation (sales forecasting). If a proper forecast shows what sales
      totals are expected and when they are expected, the marketing manager
      can plan for such events and needs as: handling inventories of raw

materials and parts, monitoring inventories, handling and shipping finished goods, disposal of waste and by-products, monitoring and coordinating channel members.

Note that logistics is customer-oriented. It does not start at the factory and work towards the customers; it starts at the customers and works back to the plant.

III.   THE OBJECTIVES OF PHYSICAL DISTRIBUTION

The objectives of PD can be summarized into one general statement of purpose, i.e., to minimize cost while maximizing customer service. This is obviously an ideal as the two goals are generally at cross purposes. As service increases, costs usually increase as well. For example, a vast network of small local warehouses would improve service but be quite expensive to maintain as would a fleet of jet planes based at a central warehouse. The goal of maximum service at minimum cost is unlikely to be met, some compromise or "balancing act" is necessary.

A.   Establishing Realistic Objectives

A good place to start is the marketing concept, which stresses consumer satisfaction. Costs should be evaluated in terms of customer wants. Customers often are found to be willing to pay the cost of better service. Federal Express seems to prove that daily. Others wish to "pay the premium of time," as when consumers buy furniture or appliances and wait for delivery or installation. Others fall in the middle range.

Thus marketing managers need to research and calculate how the customer sees the problem of balancing maximum service and minimum cost.

B.   Establishing a Competitive Advantage

Effective physical distribution can provide an organization with advantages over its rivals, especially in industries where one firm's products and prices are about the same as another's. Salespeople can use rapid delivery as a special appeal, stressing quick service, improved freshness, etc.

Many of the marketing applications of computerization and automation are to be found in the distribution area (inventory handling, billing, etc.).

IV.   A CROSS-SECTION OF THE PHYSICAL DISTRIBUTION SYSTEM

PD consists of several concerns and activities that make up the components of physical distribution. Some examples:

- Inventory Management -- How many suits should a retailer order and when?

- Order Processing -- Sales office personnel arrange for shipping and billing.

- Warehousing and Storage -- Seasonal products, in particular, must be held until they are most in demand.

- Materials Handling -- Literally "physical" movement of goods using forklifts, etc.

- Protective Packaging and Containerization -- Beer is packed in cans, six packs, cases, and onto pallets.

- Transportation -- Shipment of Detroit-produced cars all over the country.

Physical distribution benefits from the **systems concept**. The system must be kept in mind. Storage in a warehouse is not the goal. The goal is to empty the warehouse each time it becomes full. The parts of the PD system affect all the other parts. A "rapid" air delivery across country can bog down at either end if the other parts of the system do not work.

V.   TOTAL COST: A SYSTEMS APPROACH

The systems concept contributed to the development of the **total cost concept** in that the system should operate so that the total cost of the system will be minimized.

When the many factors other than transportation costs are figured into "the system," the cheapest means of transportation may prove to yield the highest total costs. Perhaps expensive air freight usage can reduce the need to hold inventory at storage points. Or, reducing taxes or personnel costs can contribute to reducing total costs.

Customer satisfaction may be more important than reducing dollars and cents. The value of customer satisfaction is difficult to gauge, but the manager must not forget this factor in the effort to hold down total distribution costs.

A.   Cutting Costs

Distribution is a "behind the scenes" activity. Consumers do not see much of it other than its results. This provides many opportunities for cost cutting and improving efficiency.

Some likely sample savings include: automating warehouses, consolidating warehouses, correcting inefficient procedures, utilizing low-cost carriers, moving facilities to low-cost locations, shifting some logistical functions to customers.

VI.   MANAGING THE COMPONENTS OF PHYSICAL DISTRIBUTION

Physical distribution activities must be coordinated with other aspects of the logistical system. Noting that, we treat PD activities, in this section of the chapter, as a "unit." There are six major areas of concern.

A.   Transportation

Transportation decisions involve selecting the specific mode that will be used to physically move products from a manufacturer, grower, wholesaler, or other seller to the receiving facilities of the buyer. The major alternative modes of transportation are shown, in terms of their percentages of ton miles in intercity transport, in Exhibit 16-3. Each has its specific advantages and limitations that must be evaluated by managers making a choice from among them. These are compared in a general way in Exhibit 16-4.

1.   Motor Carrier

In 1980, deregulation of trucking led to more flexible and competitive rates.

Motor carriers (trucks and the far less important "bus freight" companies) are efficient at moving goods over short distances, are flexible in their usage, can be used effectively over long distances, and have a far better record than railroads in the areas of **damages in transit** and on-time delivery. Economic hard times, or other reasons to reduce inventories, actually help the trucking industry as managers are forced to rely on dependable trucking service.

2.   Air Freight

Speed and distance capabilities of **air freight** are great.
In many cases, these advantages compensate for high costs.
Recall that the total cost is the main concern, and air
freight can allow reductions in inventory warehousing
expenses. The trend toward shipping goods "on demand"
obviously impacts air freight.

The growth of international trade has contributed to a
growth in the use of air freight. Further, air freight is
comparatively "gentle" and is heavily used by high-tech
product manufacturers.

3.   Water Transportation

Water transportation is generally the lowest-cost mode of
transportation. However, it is slow, and inland water
routes are subject to freezing in winter. Water seems most
appropriate for bulky, low-value, non-perishable goods. It
is also appropriate for international transport of more
expensive goods if they can be properly protected in
transit.

4.   Railroad

Railroads are best at moving large, heavy, or bulky items.
As shipment size rises, railroads become more attractive to
shippers. However, delivery is limited to places where
tracks are in place. Railroads also have a reputation for
slow delivery and rough treatment of merchandise.

Railroads have tried to overcome their limitations with such
features as **diversion-in-transit** privileges which permit a
customer to specify a final destination after a trip has
been mostly completed.

5.   Pipelines

Pipelines are the most specialized means of transport,
designed to carry specific products. Once built, pipelines
offer an inexpensive means of moving such products as oil
and natural gas. Most of them are, in fact, owned by the
companies that use them.

6.   Intermodal Transportation

Intermodal service combines two or more transportation
modes. **Piggyback service**, whereby loaded truck trailers are
carried by rail to distant spots, then unloaded for local
delivery, is one example. **Fishyback service** carries loaded
containers via water transport, and **birdyback service** does
the same via air transport.

B.   Warehousing

The second major aspect of physical distribution is **warehousing**,
the holding and housing of goods between the time they are
produced and the time they are shipped to the buyer.

The word warehouse has been largely replaced by the term
distribution center to reflect the changed perception of these
facilities. They are not for holding goods; they are places where
throughput is the emphasis.

Many large and small tasks are involved, but they make up two
primary activities -- storage and breaking bulk.

1. Storage

   Storage consists of holding and housing goods in inventory for a certain time period. Storage is usually a necessity because discrepancies almost always occur between cycles of production and cycles of consumption. Storage diminishes the effects of these cycles. Examples:

   - Production of many food products is seasonal but demand is year-round.

   - Demand for wedding gowns, air conditioners and outdoor paint is seasonal, but production is year-round.

   Exhibit 16-5 illustrates the practice of building and depleting inventories over time.

   Storage need not refer to buildings. Magic Chef Corp. had great success with a soft-drink vending machine mostly because it held more product than its competitors.

2. Breaking Bulk

   Typically, large shipments of goods arrive at a warehouse or other location and leave in smaller quantities. This is called "breaking bulk"; an example would be a boatload of Toyotas arriving in California for dispersal across the country.

3. Warehousing Strategy

   Two basic decisions underlie the complicated problem of warehousing:

   - Determining the optimum number, location, and types of warehouses needed.

   - Calculating the proper levels of inventory to be stocked.

   These may be illustrated by two extreme cases between which many possibilities lie.

   - Make large shipments over short distances to high-capacity storage warehouses located near manufacturing points, shipping in small quantities to buyers.

   - Make large shipments over long distances to distribution warehouses located near buyers rather than near manufacturers.

   This is illustrated in Exhibit 16-6.

   Each plan has its own advantages and disadvantages. The "best" plan is the one that:

   - Maximizes customer service.

   - Minimizes cost.

   - Provides a differential advantage.

C. Inventory Control

   Inventory control involves decisions concerning how large or small inventories should be and how overstocking of inventory can be weighed against costly stock-outs.

Sales forecasts and knowledge of past requirements can be used to help determine the inventory level that provides proper service at "minimum" cost. No "perfect" inventory is possible. Three costs, however, can be considered:

.   Acquisition Costs -- the expenses incurred in obtaining inventory.

.   Holding Costs -- the expenses incurred to keep inventory housed.

.   Out-of-Stock Costs -- the losses that occur when customers demand goods the marketer cannot provide.

Computerized inventory control systems have greatly facilitated the task of balancing these costs.

1.   Economic Order Quantity (E.O.Q.)

The familiar E.O.Q. formula considers the buyer's annual demand for units of merchandise, the unit cost of merchandise, the cost of holding inventory, and the cost of placing an order to determe the order size that will minimize total costs to the buyer. The same task can be done in a tabular format, as shown in Exhibit 16-7. Both are shown in the text.

E.O.Q. calculations may not yield a totally reasonable figure, e.g. 408.25 units per order. The manager must then select a reasonable number close to the E.O.Q., but without the formula the manager may not have come close to the minimum cost figures.

D.   Materials Handling

Distribution involves movement. **Materials handling** is the physical handling and moving about of inventory. Of course, such handling increasingly mechanized and automated. In some systems, orders are assembled and packed with almost no human involvement.

E.   Order Processing

Like materials handling, **order processing** is increasingly automated. In many respects avoidance of error in this process is the "main problem." Expedient order processing can lead to economies for the organization.

F.   Protective Packaging

Packaging is important to the product, price and promotion aspects of the marketing mix. Its place in distribution is as important.

Protection of the product in transit is a significant matter but so is ease of handling as shipments are broken down into orders.

Color coding may ease handling difficulties.

VII.   MATERIALS MANAGEMENT

Materials management refers to the activities involved in getting raw materials and parts to the point of production (inbound, whereas physical distribution is outbound.) Evaluation of raw materials and the assurance of a flow of these are the major concerns.

Organizations perform **vendor analysis**, rating alternate suppliers on such attributes as speed of delivery, quality of products, and reliability of service. Exhibit 16-8 lists several logistical criteria for evaluating suppliers.

In recent years, just-in-time (JIT) inventory systems have been
developed. As the name suggests, the idea is to have supplies arrive as
they are needed by an organization, eliminating the need to stockpile
those items.

General Motors and Firestone are among many companies who have adopted
the system, originally developed in Japan. Marketers dealing with firms
employing just-in-time systems must be able to supply smaller, more
frequent shipments to their customers.

VIII. TRENDS IN LOGISTICS

Distribution, like all of marketing, undergoes constant change.
Economic hard times have led many organizations to stress cost control
in this area.

A.   International Sourcing

      Today's buyers of supplies look to the whole world, not just the
      home country; this is also true manufacturing and distribution
      sites.

B.   New Technology

      Computers have made distribution's job easier and more efficient.
      They provide information and the capacity to simulate logistical
      problems.

C.   Unpredictable Energy Costs

      In recent years energy shortages and rapidly changing prices have
      encouraged the drive for efficiency in distribution. Newly
      designed trucks and locomotives have increased fuel efficiency.
      Tandem trailers, longer trailers, and more aerodynamic designs are
      some obviously fuel-related changes.

D.   Interorganizational Cooperation

      Costs have driven some nominal competitors to cooperate in
      providing services to one another. For example, many airlines
      provide ground support services to their competitors so as to
      reduce the need for all companies to offer duplicate services at
      all airports. The Federal Express BLS system, described at the
      start of the chapter, provides a good example of
      interorganizational cooperation, sometimes called third-party
      logistics.

IX.   SUMMARY

The term logistics is broad in scope because it includes both planning
and coordinating the physical distribution of finished goods and
managing the movement and storage of raw materials and supply parts
during the procurement and production processes. Physical distribution,
an activity that can be made more cost effective by the use of
computerized technology and robotics, is a means to obtain a competitive
advantage not easily duplicated by competition.

      Learning Objective 1: Evaluate the role of logistics and physical
      distribution in the marketing mix.

Logistics describes the entire process through which materials, in-
process inventory, and finished goods move into, through, and out of the
firm. Logistics management involves planning, implementing, and
controlling the efficient flow of both inbound materials and outbound
finished products. Materials management is concerned with bringing raw
materials and supplies to the point of production. Physical
distribution provides time and place utility by moving products from
producer to consumer or organizational user in a timely and efficient
manner. Transportation, warehousing, inventory control, materials

handling, order processing, and packaging are the major areas of concern in physical distribution management.

> **Learning Objective 2:   Show how distribution managers can make physical distribution provide maximum satisfaction to buyers while reducing costs.**

The central objective of physical distribution is to keep costs down while keeping the level of service up. Yet the improved service raises costs, and reduced costs lower levels of service. Distribution managers must constantly balance these two elements. The marketing concept suggests that managers determine what level of service will fit the buyers' needs and what prices are acceptable to them.

> **Learning Objective 3:   Explain the total cost approach to physical distribution.**

The total cost concept takes a systems approach to physical distribution. By placing the emphasis on controlling total cost, the manager focuses on how the parts of the distribution system can be used to keep total costs down. Raising expenditures in one part of the system may reduce total costs; lowering expenditures in one part of the system might raise total costs.

> **Learning Objective 4:   Compare the advantages and disadvantages of the modes of transportation available to shippers.**

The five modes of transportation are motor carrier, air freight, water transportation, railroad and pipeline. These vary widely in flexibility, speed, reliability, tendency to damage goods, cost, and other variables. Water transportation is inexpensive but slow, air shipment is fast but often expensive. Trucks are flexible, relatively swift, and have a good reputation in terms of breakage of goods; however, they cannot move the volumes of freight railroads can. Pipelines are efficient movers of certain products but can deliver them only to specific terminals. Intermodal transportation, such as piggyback service, combines the advantages of two or more separate transportation modes.

> **Learning Objective 5:   Identify the purposes of warehousing, order processing, materials handling, and inventory control.**

Warehousing holds merchandise until it is demanded by the market and breaks bulk. Order processing expedites orders quickly and economically. Materials handling moves inventories of products as needed. Inventory control manages inventory so that ideal inventory levels exist most of the time.

> **Learning Objective 6:   Understand materials management activities and their influence on many marketing decisions.**

Materials management is the procurement and movement of raw materials and parts to the point of production. Vendor analysis and just-in-time inventory systems are aspects of materials management that influence marketing mix decisions. International sourcing is a current trend in materials management.

X.   KEY TERMS

XI.   QUESTIONS FOR DISCUSSION (15)

XII. ETHICS IN PRACTICE

XIII. CASES

ANSWER GUIDELINES FOR CHAPTER 16 QUESTIONS FOR DISCUSSION

1.   *Define logistics. What are its components?*

ANSWER:

Distribution, or "place," is one of the four major aspects of the marketing mix. Logistics refers to the entire process of moving raw materials and component parts into the firm, in-process inventory through the firm, and finished goods out of the firm. Logistics Management involves planning, implementing and controlling the efficient flow of both inbound materials and outbound finished products. Two major aspects of logistics relate to the separate phases of the process.

Materials management is concerned with bringing raw materials and supplies to the point of production and moving in-process inventory through the firm.

Physical distribution, as defined by the National Council of Physical Distribution is the broad range of activities concerned with efficient movement of finished products from the end of the production line to the consumer. The purpose of physical distribution is to minimize cost while maximizing customer service.

The definition of physical distribution has two facets that should be emphasized. One is "efficient movement," a term which suggests a focus on actually moving a product. In this sense, PD is set apart from other "place-related" marketing activities like organizing and managing channel of distribution members and their activities. The second facet of the definition worth stressing is the phrase "from the end of the production line to the consumer." This sets PD apart from materials management activities that might involve movement of goods such as raw materials to the place of production or semi-finished materials through the place of production.

The components of logistics might vary in relative importance from organization to organization, but in general they are:

.   Handling and holding incoming inventories of raw materials, parts, and the like.
.   Monitoring stocks, materials, and finished goods inventories.
.   Handling and shipping finished goods to points of storage or intermediaries.
.   Disposing of waste, by-products, and imperfectly manufactured output.
.   Monitoring and coordinating members of channels of distribution.

The mention of the systems concept is appropriate here. These components of logistics should not be viewed singly but as part of a system that works smoothly. Each part affects the operation of the others and the total cost of the system. The system concept helps avoid the pitfalls of sub-optimization.

2.   *Indicate what is meant by the systems concept in physical distribution. In what ways does the use of this concept benefit marketers?*

ANSWER:

The systems concept in physical distribution is little different from the systems concept in other fields. The basic idea is that elements in a system are strongly interrelated and interact in their effects on the achievement of a goal. Within a PD system, the parts may be thought of separately but do not operate separately. They interact constantly, and each part affects the others. That is the very meaning of "system." Remember that the goal of the PD system is "maximized" customer satisfaction at "minimum cost."

In this, the systems concept is closely related to the minimum cost concept discussed in Question/Answer 5. The usual example is that of transportation cost. The "cheapest" mode of transportation may be the most "expensive" when its effect on the system is calculated. The speedy but "expensive" mode might in fact be the "cheapest" given its effect on the system. The "fastest" mode may be very slow indeed if the other parts of the system, that move products to and from airports to customers do not do their jobs.

The use of the systems concept clearly benefits marketers in attaining the goal of maximum customer satisfaction at minimum cost.   Students may find the concept so "obvious" that it is hard to believe it was not always in use.   In fact, it was not.   The old question that transportation people asked themselves was, "What's the cheapest way to move the product from A to B?" Now they know that the answer may well be incorrect in terms of the total transportation system.   Sophisticated thinking, modeling, computer simulation and other methods, have all contributed to great changes in PD management.

3.   *What are the major ways in which an organization can use physical distribution as a means of establishing a competitive advantage?*

ANSWER:

A competitive advantage is some aspect of an organization's marketing mix (4 Ps) that can appeal to prospective customers.   People tend to think of a product or price advantage, but advantages can be found within any of the 4 Ps or within any sub-part of the marketing mix.

PD can be used by most organizations seeking to establish a differential advantage though this may be most common when the product offered is much like its competitors.   For example, raw materials may be similar in quality and price and demand for these relatively uninfluenced by promotion.

Retailers, libraries, dentists, zoos, and museums can use PD to achieve differential advantages by operating "mobile units," extending operating hours, and opening branches.   No good or service, no matter how well designed, priced or promoted, is of use unless it reaches its target market.   Certain companies, museums, doctors, and libraries are so renowned that customers travel the world to see them.   Some stores also have such followings.   Relying on this kind of behavior is risky for most marketers, since customers can usually "switch" if the burdens of providing PD functions for themselves become too great.   Even the Queen of England and the Pope perceive the need to take the "product" to the customers from time to time.

4.   *What is the difference between warehousing and storage?   How do they differ from breaking bulk?*

ANSWER:

Warehousing and storage are two terms that are frequently used interchangeably, though they do differ in meaning.

Warehousing involves the holding and housing of goods between the time they are produced and the time they are shipped to the buyer, and includes all the activities that take place from when the goods arrive at the warehouse until they are released for shipment.

Warehousing involves many activities both large and small, but taken as a whole, comprises two major activities: storage and breaking bulk.

Storage consists of holding and housing goods in inventory, and is necessary because of the virtually inevitable discrepancies that occur in an economy. The Great Lakes freezeover in winter so products shipped via the Lakes must be stored for use (at one end) or later shipment (at the other end) until the Lakes are opened for shipping.

In summary, warehousing may be seen as "including" or "greater than" simple storage.   One warehousing activity is storage.   Both activities, within the constraints of real world considerations, should be minimized by effective marketers.   No one wants to store more products than necessary or for longer periods than are necessary.   Indeed, the term "warehouse," with its image of a dusty, cobwebbed place where nothing ever moves, is being replaced with terms like "distribution center."   Such terms draw attention to the modern view of a warehouse facility as a place where "through-put" or "flow" is more important than simple storage.

(It is worth mentioning that "storage" can be part of production rather than distribution if storage is necessary before the product is bottled and sold, as in the case of Scotch whiskey.)

The question specifically asks about warehousing vs. storage vs. breaking bulk. Specifically, what is the difference between these? In general, the distinctions may be drawn this way.

Warehousing involves and includes storage (holding) and breaking bulk (creating smaller amounts of product appropriate for customer needs).

(1) Products Are Produced	(2) They Move to a Warehouse Facility	(3) They Are Stored Some Period of Time	(4) They Are Reassembled into Order Sizes for Customers	(5) They Are Shipped to the Buyers

(3)   is "Storage."
(4)   is "Breaking Bulk."
(3) + (4) is "Warehousing."

5.   *Discuss the total cost approach to distribution. What are its advantages and disadvantages?*

ANSWER:

The key ideas associated with the systems approach to PD are closely allied to the total cost concept. In brief, the total cost concept looks at the distribution job to be done not in terms of lowest transportation, handling, or other costs, but in terms of all costs and, most importantly, their total or "bottom line."

For example, it is easy to imagine that use of an expensive but quick transportation method might reduce total costs by allowing the diminishing of inventories stored near customers. Shipping an industrial good, even a bulky machine part, by air can reduce total costs if the use of overnight air service eliminates the maintenance of regional warehouses and improves the level of customer satisfaction.

This last phrase, "customer satisfaction," brings to mind the one disadvantage of the total cost approach, its advantages being obvious to even the casual observer of the distribution process. It is possible that a computer-modeling PD manager can become so wrapped up in trying to reduce total PD costs that he or she forgets that one of the costs to be considered is the cost of a lost sale or the cost of a customer who has not been satisfied (i.e., "ill will.") Working the customer's wants and perceptions into a cost model or computer simulation of a distribution system is a difficult business.

The total cost approach can lead to greater customer satisfaction, as when cost savings are explained and "passed along." The PD manager, like all marketing managers, must make sure that the customer's satisfaction, which is more important than a dollars-and-cents reduction, takes precedence.

6.   *An overnight package service and a petroleum pipeline are both common carriers. How do they differ? How are they similar?*

ANSWER:

An overnight package service like Federal Express is likely to be a common carrier in that it is available to all potential users willing to pay for the service and meets any other rules and regulations of usage such as package size, weight, and safety of contents. A pipeline service could also be a common carrier if it accepts a similarly broad array of customers.

Some pipelines are owned by organizations who make use of them exclusively for themselves. Not all pipeline operations are so restricted.

Pipelines have these characteristics:

a)   Specialized, typically can carry only one or two products.

b)   Not easily modified to carry other products (e.g., "slurry" pumping frequently proves difficult).

c)   Expensive to build.

d)   Relatively inexpensive to operate once built.

e)   Limited in general application (natural gas and crude petroleum).

f)   Limited geographic flexibility.   (They can't "go" to places they do not already go.)

g)   Reliability is high unless there is a serious malfunction or accident.

h)   Can be built to serve high-demand areas, can go "almost anywhere" as the Alaska Pipeline shows, though the expense can be great.

i)   Excellent reputation for not damaging their cargo.

Overnight package services use trucks, cars, vans, buses, air, and even "foot power." In general, these characteristics, arranged to follow (a) through (i) above, apply to overnight package services:

a)   Can carry "any" product type as long as basic limitations are observed.

b)   Comparatively easy to modify. Some services have expanded operations to include delivery of packages of 500 pounds, not just small packages.

c)   Not overwhelmingly expensive to "start up." Could use a few vans plus space on scheduled planes or other means of transportation. This is especially true of local and regional services which deliver to only a limited number of cities.

d)   Expense of continued, expanded operation would vary greatly. Federal Express has its own fleet of jets, smaller inter-city services operate with one or two vans.

e)   Wide-ranging application, carry many items.

f)   Geographically very flexible, can "go anywhere" using air, motor, even water transportation.

g)   Reliability is high though not as high as pipelines. Weather, accidents, human error all could affect reliability.

h)   Can "go anywhere"; justified expansion of service area would not be impossible.

i)   Good reputation for not damaging merchandise though, for some services, quality control could be a concern.

7.   *What type of physical distribution system would you use for the following products? (a) Bird of Paradise plants from Hawaii (b) Kiwi fruit and avocados from California (c) Barbie dolls*

ANSWER:

A matter to be established before this question can be answered is where will these products be shipped? The instructor may want to internationalize the question by specifying some distant location like Germany or Nigeria.

For convenience sake, we have assumed a domestic location like Chicago, Boston or New York. This still leaves the question with an international element since Barbie dolls are made in the Philippines.

(a)   Bird of Paradise Plants from Hawaii

Transportation of live and delicate plants would seem to require air
transportation. Quickness of delivery would be necessitated by the fact that
the plants need water and light. Thus, just a few days in transit could
destroy the product. Further, quick handling on both ends of the flight would
be in order. Quickness would seem, in this case, to be primary while cost is
secondary. Customer satisfaction is increased because a dead or dying plant
won't satisfy either the consumer or the organizations selling the plants.

(b)   Kiwi fruit and avocados from California

The fruit can be refrigerated and/or preserved by surrounding it with inert
gases. Such processes will not preserve the fruit forever, but the
opportunity to preserve the fruit means that it can be stored until demanded
and shipped by truck or train. The customers willing to pay for "Fresh Fruit
Flown in From California" can also be accommodated by use of air freight. In
short, the distribution system is quite likely to differ greatly from that
used for Hawaiian plants.

(c)   Barbie Dolls

These dolls are made primarily in the Philippines. Some are also produced in
Hong Kong or Taiwan. The dolls are not subject to spoilage or particularly
breakable unless treated with no care whatsoever. Further, the toy industry
as a whole operates with surprisingly long lead times, though some sell-out
items (like Cabbage Patch Dolls during Christmas of 1983, Nintendo games in
1987, and Batman paraphernalia) do sometimes require extremely rapid delivery.
Barbie dolls have been around for 25 years, and it is unlikely that even a new
variation on the doll would create the stir caused by a brand new "hit" toy.
Lastly, the dolls are very light in weight and quite small.

This combination of elements (lightweight, great distances to travel, etc.)
suggests a distribution system that relies on airfreight to selected locations
in the U.S. and motor transportation to wholesalers and retailers. Though
many toy retailers deal directly with toy makers, other stores work through
toy wholesalers, many of whom enjoy exclusive territory deals with makers of
popular items like Barbie dolls.

8.   *Why do organizations store goods? Provide an example of a storage
      problem faced by a marketing organization.*

ANSWER:

Reasons why various organizations might store goods include:

.   Irregular production facing regular demand, as with agricultural goods.

.   Regular production facing irregular demand, as with air conditioners.

.   The desire to postpone sale of a product until prices are higher.

.   The desire to have products ready to move when a planned promotional
     campaign begins.

.   The need to have inventories handy to meet buyers' "emergency demands."

.   The need to "age" a product like whiskey though this is technically a
     production activity.

.   To gain a competitive advantage by being able to point to stocks of
     merchandise that competitors don't have.

.   To ease problems associated with a "rush season" by having merchandise
     already on premises.

.   To better deal with channel members by handling some aspects of a
     storage problem.

Examples of firms that engage in storage are easy to find and range from
mining companies and auto makers to neighborhood retailers (known, after all,
as "stores.")

9.   *What factors should management consider in determining desired levels of
        inventory? What specific costs should management take into account for
        the following products? (a) cigarettes (b) farm tractors (c) sweaters
        (d) personal computers*

ANSWER:

As with most distribution-related matters, the inventory holding problem is
one of trying to balance the goals of minimizing costs while satisfying
customers. While costs of acquisition costs, holding costs for warehousing,
and spoilage and obsolescence are significant, they also play off against one
another when a firm increases order size or increases frequency of smaller
orders.

The other cost to be taken into account is that of out-of-stock situations. A
sale may be lost if the item demanded is not in inventory. More subtly, ill
will or a bad reputation, may also result. Lost customers may be the result
in either case. The calculation of such losses is difficult.

One way to handle this question is to draw a matrix as shown here and ask
students to identify the costs appropriate to each product and to weigh them
as to relative importance. Then ask them if they are producers, wholesalers
or retailers and whether or not their answer affects their responses in the
matrix.

Cost of:

Product:

	Holding Inventory	Acquiring Inventory	Out of Stock (lost sale)
Cigarettes			
Farm Tractors			
Sweaters			
Personal Computers			

10.   *Define order processing. Indicate how management can use this function
        to gain a competitive advantage.*

ANSWER:

Any aspect of the marketing process can provide a competitive advantage. This
is true of order processing. Though most order processing is "hidden" from
the view of customers, the results of good and bad order processing are not.

Order processing is the procedure followed to fill customer orders after these
have been received at the sales office. The process begins when orders are
received and ends when merchandise has been shipped and bills sent to
customers.

The order processing function has many aspects. Each one is important and
systematically affects the others. Further, each one provides an opportunity
to "mess up." Sending the wrong goods, quantities, or bills, can contribute
to losing customers. These actions contribute to the image of an organization
that "can't do anything right."

On the other hand, doing a good job in this area can give an organization an important plus. Good order processing lends credibility to a firm, gives it a reputation for "not making mistakes," and reflects well on the organization in general. It helps the salespeople next time they call.

An obvious competitive advantage is speed. This permits small firms to compete with large ones. For example, overseas buyers often prefer to buy machine parts through two- or three-person export companies and have them delivered quickly rather than to order directly from GM or Caterpillar and wait for these giant firms to fill the order more slowly.

11.   *What are the advantages and disadvantages of using each of the following? (a) Railroads (b) Trucks (c) Airlines (d) Water carriers (e) Pipelines*

ANSWER:

The advantages and disadvantages of each of these types of transportation can be discussed only in general terms. The relative appropriateness of each depends on the product to be moved, the distance to be traveled, the speed necessary, the desired level of customer service, and so on. Generally, a comparison like that shown in the text's Exhibit 16-4 contrasting these methods may be drawn.

(a)   Railroads

Railroads are "best" for heavy and/or bulky items. They move freight over long distances at low cost, especially when the shipment size is large. Railroads do provide some specialized cars and rates to appeal to certain users.

(b)   Trucks

Trucks are more expensive to use than several competing transportation modes. They provide an effective array of specialized equipment, are quite fast and reliable, and have low damage-in-transit.

The greatest advantage trucks have is their flexibility. They can go "anywhere" with reasonable roads, requiring no particular specialized facility. They can go "door-to-door" with their cargo. Further, shippers can far more easily own their own trucks than railroads, planes, pipelines, or ships.

(c)   Airlines

Air transport is generally the most expensive of all modes but rates near the top in terms of speed, reliability, the ability to span great distances and reach otherwise inaccessible areas, and with gentle treatment of merchandise.

(d)   Water Carriers

Water is generally the cheapest means of transport but is slow and limited to use where ports, waterways, etc. are available. It is very suitable to easily protected, inexpensive, bulky products.

Water transport is also subject to the freezing of canals, ports, and rivers.

Thus, water transportation, compared to other modes, is not particularly reliable. It has a poor damaged-goods reputation.

(e)   Pipelines

Pipelines are largely limited by the goods they carry, the places they go, and the expense involved in building them.

However, once installed, pipelines are comparatively inexpensive to use and very reliable. Given the products they carry, they have the best of reputation for not damaging goods.

12.   *Describe the process for determining (1) the cities and metropolitan
      areas, and (2) specific sites for (a) retail and service units, and (b)
      warehouses.*

ANSWER:

The first step in this process must be an understanding of target customer
locations and needs for service as well as competitive positioning.

Students might be encouraged to use the library, locating books on
wholesaling, retailing, or specific site selection tools. Generally, such
tools may be grouped in terms of the specific tasks for which they are
appropriate.

(1)   Retail and service units

(a)   The B.P.I. and other printed sources of information like the Census of
      Business and County Business Patterns can be used to evaluate cities and
      metropolitan areas in terms of their appropriateness for retail and
      service units. While these have all the limitations of other sources of
      secondary data, they are commonly employed.

(b)   Specific sites within areas can be evaluated in terms of such "micro
      measures" as traffic counts, examination of other businesses, and the
      competitive climate, by mapping customers, and by various survey
      methods.

(2)   Warehouses

Selection of warehouse sites is a problem quite apart from retail or service
site selection. Distributors of products need retail sites near potential
customers. Warehouse facilities need not be near retail customers. The
"hidden" nature of warehousing facilities opens up far more possibilities in
terms of location, distances, facilities, and nature of surroundings. Thus,
for both parts (a) and (b) of this section of the answer, it is to be expected
that a greater stress can be placed on financial and quantitative analysis
than on qualitative judgments.

The two basic options for warehouse locations provided in the text are
summarized in Exhibit 16-6 as well as in Transparency 16-8. In general,
organizations may choose to move large shipments over short distances to high
capacity storage warehouses near manufacturing points. Shipments in smaller
quantities are then sent to buyers. The second option is to move large
shipments over long distances to distribution warehouses located near buyers.
The level of customer service desired, nature of the product, and warehousing
strategy to establish a competitive advantage should be considered.

13.   *What changes in marketing are necessary when a customer adopts a just-
      in-time inventory system?*

ANSWER:

As the text describes, many buyers of organizational goods are adopting the
just-in-time or JIT approach to inventory. This involves a sophisticated
ordering system aimed at minimizing the amount of inventory. Ideally, needed
raw materials and parts arrive at the buyer's place of business "just-in-time"
for use. This implies frequent delivery of smaller lot sizes.

Clearly, if the customer chooses to implement a just-in-time system the seller
wishing to deal with that customer must be prepared to meet the requirements
of the new system. A means must be developed to rapidly obtain information
about buyer needs. It may be necessary to switch from rail delivery systems
to truck or air systems to meet the customer's requirements, including a
strict time frame. It may be necessary to move the seller's storage
facilities, or even production facilities, closer to the customer.

Certain other changes may have to be effected. The salesperson or account
manager will remain in close contact with the customer so that the necessary
product is delivered properly. Further, communication lines generally must

open between various functional areas of the firm. For example, the buyer's quality control department may need access to the seller's engineers. Buyers typically reduce the number of suppliers when engaging in JIT, thus suppliers have an opportunity to increase sales if they can establish the necessary relational elements.

Marketers dealing with customers using a JIT system employ JIT systems of their own. This is because the real essence of the system is to force inventory holding costs "backward in the channel" to the supplying company. The supplying company can force costs backward onto its suppliers.

14. *Is it possible for a retailer to use a just-in-time system?*

ANSWER:

The basic idea of a JIT system is to force inventory holding costs backwards onto suppliers thereby minimizing one's own inventory holding costs. Thus, if a retailer has enough "power" to force inventory holding costs back onto its suppliers it might be in its interests to do so. A large retailer, like Sears or Penney's, would be such an attractive customer to have that suppliers of goods to such a firm would probably cooperate fully with that retailer's just-in-time effort. Other retailers might also institute a JIT system and win supplier cooperation. Of course, as more and more marketers move to JIT systems, they increasingly become the norm. Suppliers will eventually deal with JIT systems and most likely "fall into line."

Retailers of whatever size face a special problem area when it comes to JIT: retailers are largely unable to predict demand. That is, when is "just-in-time" when you are dealing with relatively unpredictable consumers? Manufacturers, operating on fixed production schedules, are far better able to know just when they will require raw materials and supplies. Retailers are able to better predict demand for some goods than others, for example, staple goods and some seasonal goods. But, even in the case of staple goods, their demand predictions cannot be as fine-tuned as those of manufacturers.

As a case in point, winter clothing might be sold in a pre-season sale, during back-to-school days, or at the start of cold weather. The problem of predicting demand is compounded by the dynamic retailing environment. Appliances like fans and air conditioners sell very well if the summer is very hot, not so well if the summer turns out to be rather cool. The same type of pattern can be seen in clothing sales.

Specific mention might be made of the retailer's problems of customer ill will and lost sales. If a customer goes to a store expecting to buy a blue blazer and is told that the money-saving inventory system will have that jacket here in 21.5 hours, the customer is almost certain to go to another store and buy the blazer right now.

In short, just-in-time systems can have an appeal to retailers but making them work in the retailing environment can be tough. Retailers might, therefore, try to implement a "more-or-less-just-in-time" system, or a "close-as-we-can-get-it" JIT system. That is, they can adapt certain aspects of JIT to their businesses. Given their special problems, it is arguable that many retailers have had the closest thing they can get to a JIT system. Most cannot, however, implement a system as tight as that developed by a company like General Motors.

However, major retailers, such as Wal-Mart, are forcing the idea of just-in-time, or Quick Response, on suppliers such as Procter and Gamble. Firms are forging data network linkages with suppliers, that the supplier's computer tracks inventory levels in the buyer's stores. Bar codes, scanner data and networks of information are pushing quick responses to an ever increasing number of retail concerns.

15.   *Summarize the major trends in logistics.*

ANSWER:

The trends can be linked to the "last frontier" mentioned in the chapter's opening. Because so much distribution is done out of the view of customers, many ways to save money and try new ways of doing things are possible without fear of customer concern. This element pervades the major trends found in logistics management.

- International sourcing means buyers are viewing the entire world to determine the most economical sources for supplies.

- New technology includes computerization and automation of both operations and subsidiary activities like information storage and retrieval. Cost reductions through simulation methods also seems to be a fertile area.

- Unpredictable energy costs have fostered new equipment, especially carriers that hold more freight and are more fuel efficient. As a matter of fact, wind-driven "modern clipper ships" have been suggested.

- Interorganizational cooperation, strategic alliances and partnerships between traditional rivals are increasing in number and popularity as firms attempt to manage total costs. Many airlines, for example, fly into airports with no ground crew facilities. The planes are unloaded, fueled and serviced by personnel from other airlines. Cost reductions result from not having to staff every airport visited.

For the class at large: What trends in logistics, other than those reported in the chapter, are evident? What are the major implications of these trends to marketers?

The class may come up with any number of trends they have observed. Many will focus on equipment changes such as automated warehouses where robots do the "picking," or new trailer-truck designs featuring a cab in which the driver is almost supine to permit more cargo to be carried in compartments above the driver. Double, even triple, trailers and streamlined trucks are now commonplace. Use of computer simulations, automatic routing of merchandise and transportation, and the increasingly important JIT inventory systems might be mentioned.

For example, M.S. Carriers is a Memphis-based trucking company. The firm is installing a satellite system so that customer shipments can be accurately tracked. With the system, the company will be able to tell its customers that the shipment should arrive within the next 30 minutes as the truck is at the toll booth on the Interstate Expressway.

The important part of this question is the "implications to marketers" aspect. It is all too easy to marvel at the advances being made and to "predict" that in the future, they will all be carried out to their "logical conclusions." The professor may wish to remind students of wondrous things that have not been accepted by consumers and which have therefore been dropped or shelved. Future marketers should also remember to be consumer-oriented, not production- or "great new innovation"-oriented. Students may not like to be questioned on the trends in distribution that they discover, but they must realize that the customer's wishes and demands are paramount.

ETHICS EXERCISE 16

CHAPTER 16 ETHICS IN PRACTICE

Overview

A garment maker in the U.S. has been under pressure to lower the prices of its product, and has explored the idea of moving much of its production to Asia where labor costs are low. This would cost a loss of 50% of the jobs the company creates in the U.S. The case poses this question: What are the ethical implications of a move of a production operation overseas which will cause a 50% reduction in domestic jobs?

If your students did Chapter 11 Take A Stand question 2, they will recognize that the situation is basically the same, so most of the discussion there is relevant here. The major difference is that in this example the domestic impact is known in advance (a 50% reduction in jobs). As implied there, such an action results in short-term pain but long-term gain for the workers, who will relocate and be retrained to be more productive.

In the U.S., the traditional legal view of the employer-employee relationship has been known as the doctrine of "employment-at-will." According to this doctrine, employees are free to work for whomever they wish, and employers have the freedom to hire whomever they please. Because the agreement is a mutual one, it can be terminated at will, unless there is a contract which precludes this. Thus, if an employer wishes to terminate an employee, he may do so. Unions usually have contracts with employers guaranteeing employment at a certain level for a certain number of years, and permitting a firm to lay off an employee only for "cause." It is generally accepted (and union rules require) that termination be made according to seniority: last hired, first fired.

Fairness requires that an employee not be fired arbitrarily. In this scenario there appears to be a just cause: the firm's ability to survive in the garment industry. If the company keeps its prices at current levels, it will not be able to effectively compete; if, as a result, the firm goes under, all of the employees will go down with the sinking ship.

However, a socially responsible corporation will feel some sense of responsibility for the displaced workers. In fact, some firms have a policy of not firing workers who have been employed a certain period of time; instead, they will shift them laterally. This generous move rewards the firm with increased employee loyalty. Otherwise, it is considered fair (but not required under the doctrine of employment-at-will) for the employer to give the employee as much advance notification of termination as possible. However, advance notification of several months to a year or longer is a contractual agreement in some fields (e.g., in academia). In 1988 a federal plant-closing bill was passed that mandates that any business with over 100 employees must give at least 60 days' notice of any plant closing or major layoff, and several states have passed more stringent bills. When an employer lays off an employee for financial reasons, the firm may, either by contract or unilaterally, give the employee a certain amount of severance pay to provide a financial cushion until the employee finds another job. For instance, in December 1991, General Motors announced plans to cut 74,000 jobs and close 21 North American parts and assembly plants by 1995. Although this announcement received much negative press, many of the layoffs were to come through attrition, early retirements, and buy outs.

CHAPTER 16 TAKE A STAND QUESTIONS

1.   *A company's normal period from order entry to delivery is nine days. A salesperson who desperately wanted to make a sale told a retail customer that delivery could be arranged in five days. Was this right? What should the physical distribution manager do?*

This is not right; it is not fair for a seller to make promises to a buyer that can't be kept, unless the salesperson is sure that delivery time can be made shorter. In this case, the promise seems to be dishonest.

According to the marketing concept, a salesperson's primary responsibility is to serve the customer's best interests. This particular salesperson will certainly not build trust and a long-term relationship with this customer, and negative word of mouth about the salesperson and/or the store could ensue.

Instead, the salesperson should have checked first with the physical distribution manager to see if delivery time could be cut. Perhaps the salesperson could convince the PD manager that this customer has good long-term potential (if this is true), and every effort should be made to speed delivery. But the customer should not be promised five-day delivery unless it is fairly certain that this will be a reality. Alternatively, the salesperson could try to convince the customer that the wait will be worth it. If the customer balks, the salesperson could offer a financial incentive for the inconvenience. For instance, he could agree to either give back a portion of his commission to the customer or ask the sales manager if a discount can be granted.

The physical distribution (PD) manager is being put in a bind by the salesperson. She has no duty other than guaranteeing the normal nine-day delivery; after all, it was the salesperson who made the false promise. In fact, doing nothing to try to speed up delivery might be the best way for the PD manager to teach the salesperson a lesson. Alternatively, the PD manager might consider that the reputation of the firm is at stake, and make every effort to speed delivery. In addition to either of these options, the PD manager could complain to the sales manager. He would have every right to do so since he is feeling the squeeze, and the sales manager has the right to know that an employee does not always treat customers squarely.

2.   *Suppose your petroleum company distributed its crude oil in tankers from Alaska. Knowing what happened to the environment after the Exxon Valdez spilled oil off the Alaska coast, would you continue to ship oil by tanker from Alaska? Would you recommend more pipelines be built across Alaska?*

The oil industry got a bad rap from the irresponsible behavior of Exxon executives in the Valdez oil spill affair. On March 29, 1989 the supertanker Valdez ran aground on Bligh Reef in Alaska's Prince William Sound. The consequence was the largest oil spill ever in North America and an ecological catastrophe, as 11 million gallons of oil spilled into the Sound and spread over a 2,600 square-mile area. The most massive oil cleanup in history was the responsibility of Exxon and the Alyeska Pipeline Service Co., a consortium established by Exxon and seven oil company partners who had built the 800-mile Alaska pipeline in 1970.

Alyeska operated the oil companies' terminal at Valdez and was charged with responding to any oil spill which might occur. However, although on paper Alyeska had a state-approved contingency plan, in practice the company was unable to keep their commitments. The problems were many and too detailed for discussion here; a few examples should suffice. For instance, the firm did not have the promised incinerator to destroy toxic sludge, and pipes on other incinerators they did have were built of a cheap material that leaked routinely. Heaters to separate oil from the water had been dismantled because they were too costly too maintain. There were numerous equipment shortfalls, many due to cost-cutting measures. As one executive commented, "There was an overall attitude of petty cheapness that severely affected our ability to operate safely. I was shocked by the shabbiness of the operation."

Shabby also characterized Exxon's corporate communications in handling the disaster. The most socially responsible action would be to take responsibility for the disaster and actions to make amends. Instead, Exxon spent the first 48 hours floundering around and ducking the press. Exxon chairman Lawrence G. Rawl had nothing to say for a week and even refused to visit Valdez. When he did speak out, Rawl blamed the Coast Guard and Alaskan officials. And, when a grand jury indicted the company for negligence several months later, Rawl argued with the government and others, vowing to fight the case through the courts rather than quietly settling out of court.

In sum, Exxon did not properly prepare for this crisis. A survey indicated that most respondents felt Exxon was slow to react and tried to deflect blame away from the company. Some consumers announced a boycott of Exxon for what they felt was negligence, and Exxon is still facing a variety of lawsuits that could cost billions.

As a result, even oil companies with good environmental records have been tarred with the same black brush as Exxon. In addition, Congress has recoiled from approving new oil drilling sites.

What happened in the Valdez incident need not happen, and so companies should not necessarily stop shipping oil in tankers. It should be noted that double-hulled tankers are less vulnerable to the kind of punctures that caused the Valdez disaster, although they cost significantly more to build. The oil companies would then need to pass on the cost to consumers.

Pipelines are a very good alternative to shipping oil, and they are often used for long-distance hauls of crude oil and its refined products such as gasoline and kerosene, as well as natural gas. Note in Exhibit 16-4 their relative advantages: low cost, although the construction costs are high; reliable delivery; and a good reputation for undamaged goods, although they are slower. Pipelines are certainly less flexible geographically; routes tend to be concentrated regionally, and once built the lines cannot suddenly be moved to deliver goods to different terminals. From an environmental perspective, they are much safer than ships. The only real possibility of damage comes from sabotage and, perhaps, a disaster such as an earthquake. They are supposedly "fail-safe" in that if this happens the whole facility shuts down. Otherwise, environmental problems can be controlled and monitored.

GUIDE TO CASE

VIDEO CASE 16-1 FLEMING FOODS: TECHNOLOGY IN MOTION

SUBJECT MATTER: Physical Distribution, Wholesaling, Materials Handling,
Efficiency and Productivity in Distribution

Please see the Guide to Video Cases for video length and other information.

AT-A-GLANCE OVERVIEW

Fleming Foods is the nation's largest food wholesaler. It distributes to some 5,000 supermarkets and has an estimated 14% percent of the market. Fleming has a tradition of spending to improve efficiency -- the most modern warehouse, computerized systems, laser scanners, etc. Where physical limitations of older facilities make modernization difficult Fleming encourages workers to greater productivity.

The videotape shows the physical distribution activities at Fleming Foods, demonstrating how a major wholesaling operation serves the retail grocery trade. It illustrates an exciting way of automating and computerizing materials. The entire system from order processing to loading of trucks for delivery is illustrated in this videotape. This video doesn't generate much discussion; however, students are flabbergasted by the use of bar-coding technology, automated warehousing, and computerization in the Fleming Foods operation.

QUESTIONS

1.   *Assess the importance of physical distribution to a wholesaler like Fleming Foods.*

The importance of physical distribution to Fleming is made clear by the effort made to ensure that their equipment is the best available. The newest facilities cost $30 million apiece and include IBM computers that sort and assemble orders, laser scanners, and all the rest described in the case. Notice, too, that in older warehouses Fleming has made every effort to increase efficiency to maximum levels.

The real importance of physical distribution in this field of business can be gauged by the traditionally low margins found in the food industry. Even though the industry has sales of more than $42 billion a year, its growth is slow at one percent per year. The well-known supermarket profit margins of one to two percent are lower still at the wholesale level. If profit is to be made, efficiency must be high. Fleming Foods is a perfect example of why PD is the "last frontier of marketing." What better place to cut expenses and increase efficiency than in the PD system employed by a wholesaler in a low margin business!

Other aspects of the importance of PD are, of course, the need to transport many spoilable items, the need to keep stores stocked, and the need to avoid ill-will among customers.

Additional measures of the importance of PD to Fleming are provided by the efficiency-improving techniques in use at their older facilities. The screens telling the worker that he or she is doing a "good job," the extra training for slower workers, the rewards for "best performer," and so on, are not usually associated with traditional warehouses. The fact that the company has actually gotten the approval of the Teamsters for its system attests to the miracle wrought here.

A just-in-time inventory system is important in physical distribution activities these days. The students may be asked "What aspects of Fleming Foods allow it to have a just-in-time inventory system?" The complete computerization of the operation and the use of bar-code technology throughout its system is a plus, almost a necessity, when an organization wants to operate a just-in-time system.

2.   *Evaluate the warehousing and materials handling activities at Fleming.*

The term "distribution center" was intended to draw the distinction between the old image of a warehouse (a dusty place where goods lie stacked about collecting cobwebs) and the modern perception of a storage place that is a vibrant, bustling place where the emphasis is on "throughput." Clearly, the Fleming Foods operation is a distribution center.

Fleming's record to this point speaks for itself. In a slow growth industry it is building $30 million facilities while dealing in measures of efficiency measured in fractions of a cent. Fleming's profit margin is less than one cent on a dollar, yet it finds the means to boost productivity by 11% in the newer warehouses and "automate" its older plants to whatever degree possible.

Fleming shares "industry leadership" with only one other firm and services nearly 5,000 stores. In short, the figures Fleming can throw about are matched by few in any wholesaling field. Fleming is not just doing something right; it is doing everything with excellence.

The methods used by Fleming to encourage workers in its older plants do seem, as the text suggests, "like the worst of all possible time clocks." Some students may wonder how such a system can work since it seems too automated, impersonal, and patronizing. The company is in a tough business, however, and these are tough times. It should be recalled that the Teamsters think it's "the fairest system we've seen." Notice the official doesn't say that he likes it or that it's "fun," just that it is "the fairest." It appears that the warehouse workers at least accept the system and that Fleming management is wise enough to "un-automate" the process from time to time by giving employees "information" and having them meet in "quality circles."

We are calling attention to the fact that these dealings with workers may have short-comings to encourage students to note that the seeming "gee whiz" description of the company may hide some flaws.

Evaluation of Fleming's activities in financial terms is made simple by calling attention to these "bottom line" figures:

.   Despite a less than 1% industrial profit margin and a 1% per year industry growth level, Fleming's profits have in recent years risen by about 15% annually.

.   Although Fleming has spent heavily on new facilities, its earnings per share have grown at an annual average of about 16 percent over the last five years.

.   Fleming's stock trades heavily on Wall Street and its "numbers" are good.

.   Fleming's sales account for about 14% of the total U.S. wholesale food sales.

.   Fleming continues to buy up (at the rate of one per year) smaller
      competitors whose sales average about $500,000 to $750,000 per year.

The instructor might want to accentuate that the case is really about the
total cost concept as implemented by Fleming Foods. The instructor might also
want to note that here is a successfully marketed company unknown to most
students.

17 MARKETING COMMUNICATIONS AND PROMOTION STRATEGY

CHAPTER SCAN

This chapter introduces promotion and its purposes as a communications tool. It discusses the four major facets of promotion and how each plays a role in the promotional mix, each facet supporting the others. The basic model of all communications processes is presented.

The chapter also discusses several general promotional strategies from which marketing planners may select. Budgeting methods are also examined.

Promotional campaigns are described, and the ethical aspect of persuasion is investigated.

SUGGESTED LEARNING OBJECTIVES

The student who studies this chapter will be exposed to a broad introduction of promotion and will be able to:

1. Discuss the three basic purposes of promotion.

2. Define the four major elements of promotion.

3. Describe the basic model for all communication processes, including promotion.

4. Explain the hierarchy of communication effects.

5. Explain how the elements of promotion can be used to support one another in a promotional campaign.

6. Identify the general promotional strategies known as push and pull strategies.

7. Classify the major approaches used by marketing managers to set promotional budgets.

8.   Discuss promotional campaigns and provide examples.

9.   Discuss arguments about the ethics of persuasion in society. Identify several genetal promotional strategies.

CHAPTER OUTLINE

I.   INTRODUCTION

II.   PROMOTION: COMMUNICATION WITH A PURPOSE

       A.   Promotion Informs
       B.   Promotion Persuades
       C.   Promotion Reminds

III.   THE ELEMENTS OF PROMOTION

       A.   Personal Selling
       B.   Advertising
       C.   Publicity and Public Relations
       D.   Sales Promotion
       E.   Packaging: A Product Element That Promotes

IV.   THE PROMOTIONAL MIX

V.   THE COMMUNICATION PROCESS

       A.   Encoding the Message
       B.   Transmitting the Message Through a Channel
       C.   Decoding the Message
       D.   Feedback
       E.   Perfect Communication

VI.   THE HIERARCHY OF COMMUNICATION EFFECTS

       A.   The Promotion "Staircase"
       B.   The Hierarchy of Effects and the Promotional Mix

VII.   PUSH AND PULL STRATEGIES

       A.   Combination Strategies

VIII. DETERMINING THE PROMOTIONAL BUDGET

       A.   The Objective and Task Method
       B.   The Percent of Sales Method
       C.   The Comparative Parity Method
       D.   The Marginal Approach
       E.   The All-You-Can-Afford Method
       F.   The Combination Approach
       G.   Cooperative Promotional Programs

IX.   PROMOTIONAL CAMPAIGNS

       A.   Image Building
       B.   Product Differentiation
       C.   Positioning
       D.   Direct Response Campaign

X.   THE ETHICS OF PERSUASION

XI.   SUMMARY

XII.   KEY TERMS

XIII. QUESTIONS FOR DISCUSSION (8)

XIV.   ETHICS IN PRACTICE

XV.   CASES

The following key terms are introduced and used in Chapter 17. They are
defined in the text's Glossary.

Personal selling
Advertising
Publicity
Public relations
Sales promotion
Promotional mix
Communication
Receiver
Source
Encoding
Decoding
Feedback
Noise
Push strategy
Pull strategy
Objective and task method
Percent of sales method
Comparative parity method
Marginal approach
Vertical cooperative promotion
Horizontal cooperative promotion
Promotional campaign
Image building
Product differentiation
Unique selling proposition

THE CHAPTER SUMMARIZED

I.   INTRODUCTION

The opening of the first McDonald's in Moscow made worldwide news and
generated millions of dollars worth of publicity for the company. Other
types of promotion were also important inside the then-Soviet Union.
Western-style promotion was not familiar in that country. Demand was high
and "pent-up," so coupons and Ronald McDonald were not needed to encourage
patronage. Demand far exceeds supply, yet promotion still served a
purpose. The concept of hand-held foods, not eaten with knife and fork,
had to be explained. Sales counter personnel had to be trained to
communicate with customers in a friendly, helpful way. Promotion is
communication which is always needed, even when demand for a product is
high.

II.   PROMOTION: COMMUNICATION WITH A PURPOSE

Promotion is necessary to reach consumers and other publics with which the
organization interacts. The "better mousetrap" won't bring people to your
door unless people are made aware of the trap and its benefits. Promotion
is communication used to inform, remind, or persuade potential buyers.
Promotion is used to communicate a message by means of personal selling,
advertising, publicity, or sales promotion. Promotion is sometimes
attacked as unnecessary, but how else are consumers to know that
appropriate products, priced right, packaged right, and distributed
conveniently, are available to them?

A.   Promotion Informs

The essence of promotion is communication. Lower prices or better
products are not effective without communication to inform people
about them. The broad purpose of promotion is to inform.

B.   Promotion Persuades

Promotion is communication, but today's world is so full of messages
that plain communication may not effectively promote even the most
perfect products. The competitive situation requires more than just
a simple statement. Though promotion is communication, few
promotions are pure communication. A traditional definition states
more precisely that "promotion is persuasive communication."

C.   Promotion Reminds

Our system leaves competitors free to "tempt" even loyal customers.
Tide, Coke, and Sears, though they have tens of millions of faithful
customers and are number one in their fields, still promote
themselves. Why? To remind people that they are "still around, still
the best, still number one."

III.   THE ELEMENTS OF PROMOTION

Personal selling, advertising, publicity, and public relations are the four
main subsets of promotion. These are of two general types: direct, face-
to-face or telephone, communication, and indirect communication such as
television. It is the marketer's job to determine which communication
method best fits the customer, the situation, and the product being
offered.

A.   Personal Selling

Personal selling is a person-to-person dialogue between buyer and
seller where the purpose of the interaction, whether face-to-face or
over the phone, is to persuade the buyer to accept a point of view or
to convince the buyer to take a specific course of action.

This technique is generally expensive to employ. Salespeople must be
trained and paid. They also spend a good deal of time waiting for
the opportunity to deal with customers. Yet personal selling is the
most flexible technique. It can be focused on the "best prospects"
and adjusted to fit individual circumstances. It provides "instant
feedback."

B.   Advertising

Advertising includes any informative or persuasive message carried by
a nonpersonal medium and paid for by a sponsor whose product is in
some way identified in the message.

Traditional media come to mind: television, radio, and magazines;
but the direct mailing of catalogs, electronic media featuring
computerized ordering, and other direct-response vehicles are
becoming increasingly popular.

One benefit of advertising is its ability to communicate to a large
number of people at once. It can be very cost-effective, advertisers
can control the message being sent, and the message can be sent
uniformly and with great frequency. However, even though the cost
per person reached may be low, the total dollars expended can be very
high. Messages cannot be tailored to each prospect, and direct
feedback is difficult to achieve.

Advertising is discussed in detail in Chapter 18.

C.   Publicity and Public Relations

Publicity is similar to advertising except that it involves an unpaid
and unsigned message, even though it may use the same mass media that
advertising does.

Publicity is news of a sort and is carried "for free" by the media.
The publicized organization does not pay directly for the message.

Publicity always involves a third party, such as a newspaper editor,
and that party has ultimate control over the message. Because of
this, publicity scores high in believability (as compared to
advertising). Of course, organizations can generate and attempt to
control publicity, as when Neiman-Marcus' annual Christmas catalog is
released annually, featuring stunning "his and her" gifts that are
reported in the media.

Publicity can be bad as well as good, even totally false: Procter
and Gamble's problems with stories that it is owned by Rev. Moon or,
alternatively, managed by Satan worshippers; and recalls of autos and
other products. The message is in the hands of the media, not the
marketer. Sometimes, no publicity is best.

Public relations may be described as the organization's attempt to
manage the nature of the publicity it receives.

D.   Sales Promotion

Sales promotion can be defined as those promotional activities other
than personal selling, advertising and publicity that are intended to
stimulate buyer purchases or dealer effectiveness in a specific time
period.

Sales promotion is the "everything else" category of promotion and
includes coupons, sales contests, sales training programs, in-store
demonstrations, give-away hats and T-shirts, and so on. However,
sales promotion is no "poor cousin." Billions are spent on it
annually. Usually, as the definition suggests, sales promotions are
temporary since they tend to "get old" quickly.

Exhibit 17-1 summarizes the characteristics of the four elements of
promotion.

E.   Packaging: A Product Element That Promotes

Packaging is usually discussed as an element of the product facet of
the marketing mix. This book follows that tradition. But the role
of packaging in promotion, especially of consumer goods, must be
acknowledged. In this sense, the package is a communicator and must
reflect the same message communicated by the "traditional" members of
the promotion mix.

IV.   THE PROMOTIONAL MIX

Advertising, publicity, sales promotion and personal selling must all be
integrated and coordinated within the **promotional mix**. Ideally, the mix
would suit the needs of all potential customers, though parts of it may be
aimed at particular customers or groups. Zoos accent publicity and
advertising; business-to-business marketers tend to emphasize personal
selling. Marketers blend the elements of the promotional mix to meet the
information needs of the target customers.

V.   THE COMMUNICATION PROCESS

Communication is the process of exchanging information and conveying
meaning to others. Thus, the goal is a common understanding of the
information being transmitted. The **receiver** is to understand, as closely
as possible, the meaning intended by the **source** (sender) of the message.
The sender must understand the characteristics of the target market, tailor
the message to that market, and choose the appropriate medium to reach it.
Feedback from the market may lead the marketer to vary these elements.

The standard communication model is given in Exhibit 17-2 of the text. It
is stressed that the model applies to all communication, not just
advertising.

A.   Encoding the Message

The message any sender wants to send exists in his or her mind but must be put into some symbolic form before it can be transmitted. This is **encoding**, the process of translating the idea to be communicated into a medium of pictures, words, gestures, etc.   In today's world, there is no way to send a message in its raw or "pure" form.

The Marlboro advertisement in Exhibit 17-3 shows how nonverbal symbolism is incorporated into a promotional message.

B.   Transmitting the Message Through a Channel

Once the sender has encoded a message, it must be sent via some channel of communication, be it mass media or personal.   The sender's job is to pick the medium that will best transmit the message to members of the target market and reach a minimum number of non-targeted receivers.

C.   Decoding the Message

Decoding is the process by which the receiver interprets the meaning of a message.   The message consists of symbols that may mean different things, or nothing at all, depending on the receiver's decoding of the message.   A cigarette ad may be attractive to some smokers, offend anti-smoking people, or be totally "lost" on others.

D.   Feedback

Feedback is the receiver's reaction to the message source.   An advertisement's feedback may be in the form of increased sales or nasty letters from consumers who have seen it.   Personal selling is particularly good in obtaining feedback information.

E.   Perfect Communication

The communication process is "perfect" only if the message that enters the mind of the receiver is exactly the same as the one in the mind of the sender.   This perfection is "impossible" because both parties always have different experiences and frames of reference. However, to the degree that these frames of reference overlap, or are congruent, the message should be transmitted more accurately.   The text refers to this as "commonality in (their) psychological fields of experience."

Noise is the word used to describe any interference or distraction that may disrupt any stage of the communication process.   "Noise" includes everything from audible noise to daydreaming to other distractions.

Exhibit 17-2 shows the steps in the communications process.   Each step is a place where something can go wrong.   The source can be wrong, the encoding and/or transmitting can be wrong, the decoding by the receiver can be wrong.   The marketer's job is to perform each step in the process correctly, while trying to reduce the chance of ineffectiveness.

Effective communication comes from the right WHO saying the right WHAT to the right WHOM through the right CHANNEL.

VI.   THE HIERARCHY OF COMMUNICATION EFFECTS

Promotion seeks to change people or to confirm a desired attitude in them later.   Change is not likely to occur after just a few messages.   This accounts for repetition of ads and for the hundreds of versions of McDonald's commercials and General Motors' Mr. Goodwrench ads.   Promotion is aimed at bringing about responses that can be likened to a "staircase" or series of steps.

A.   The Promotion "Staircase"

As shown in Exhibit 17-4 of the text, the promotion "staircase" is a series of seven steps; from bottom to top, they are as follows:

1)   Potential buyer unaware of the product.

2)   Potential buyer aware of the product.

3)   Potential buyer knows what the product has to offer.

4)   Potential buyer favorable towards the product.

5)   Favorable attitudes develop to the point of preference.

6)   Preference coupled with desire to buy and conviction that the purchase would be wise.

7)   Favorable attitude translates into purchase.

If purchase is reinforced with reward, then repurchase is likely.

Two concepts arise from the "staircase" image.

.   That promotion can be used to "move people along" the series of steps.

.   That different customers are on different steps and require different messages.

The nature of the product affects the marketer's communication plans. A totally new, unfamiliar product faces a different situation than a new flavor of toothpaste. Toothpaste and its benefits do not need explanation, but the very nature of the totally new product does. What "step" of the staircase is the intended receiver on? If they are on a low step they might need extensive factual information, but if they are at the conviction stage they may need just one little piece of information to move them to purchase, such as that prices are about to go up.

B.   The Hierarchy of Effects and the Promotional Mix

No model can show how to organize a promotional mix. We've seen that each mix must match its target market, product, etc. Exhibit 17-6 illustrates, in general terms, however, the relative importance of advertising and personal selling at the different steps in the hierarchy of effects.

.   At the pre-transaction stage of the buying process-generation of awareness, desire and preference is likely to lead to a stress on advertising over personal selling.

.   At the transaction stage, development of conviction and an actual purchase may require great emphasis on personal selling with little reliance on advertising.

.   At the post-transaction stage, we are likely to find that reminders and reassurance rely on advertising and little personal selling. Similarly, in equally general terms, it is possible to note that emphasis on personal selling versus advertising, and vice-versa, can be related to product type.

Each promotional element has relative strengths, but any one of them may be used to accomplish a particular communication objective. Marketers select and combine the promotional mix elements available to them. Large, "wealthy" companies may be able to do things that smaller, less resource-rich companies cannot do.

VII. PUSH AND PULL STRATEGIES

These are promotions aimed at a consumer or at a distributor. There is not likely to be a strict division of this type, but for convenience sake, they are called push and pull strategies.

A **push strategy** emphasizes personal selling, advertising, and other promotional efforts aimed at members of the channel of distribution. The intention is to "push" the product through the channel of distribution. It may be thought of as step-by-step promotion. (See Exhibit 17-7.)

Using a **pull strategy**, a manufacturer attempts to stimulate demand for the product by promotional efforts aimed at the ultimate consumer or organizational buyer located at the other end of the channel. The goal is that demand at the "far end" of the channel will "pull" the product through the channel of distribution.

A. Combination Strategies

An organization would not limit itself to either push or pull strategies if some combination would be deemed effective. Thus, Dr Pepper is advertised to consumers, but Dr. Pepper also sells to its distributors. So a proportion of the promotional campaign for the product is geared toward channel members and has the goal of encouraging promotion by local bottlers.

VIII. DETERMINING THE PROMOTIONAL BUDGET

Several general methods may be used to determine the size of a promotional budget. Their use must be tempered by management's judgment and interpretation of the situation being faced.

A. The Objective and Task Method

The **objective and task method** (also called the task approach) involves two steps:

- Determining the objective or task to be accomplished, such as doubling 1992 sales during 1993.

- Determining the amount of resources needed to achieve the goal.

The approach makes a good deal of logical sense but is clearly "easier said than done."

B. The Percent of Sales Method

The **percent of sales method** involves knowing a sales figure and taking a percentage of that amount. That percentage becomes the promotional budget.

This is probably the most commonly used method but has several weaknesses. Its popularity stems from its ease of use and from the fact that certain "standards" may be available for the budgeter's guidance (e.g., the "average" supermarket spends 1% of sales on promotion). For example, the budgeter takes the sales figure of $100,000 and applies it against the percent of sales figure, such as 7% = a budget of $7,000.

There are two obvious flaws here, though users of the method ignore them:

- Logically, sales should result from promotion (as they do in the task method), not promotion from sales.

- As sales decline, so does the promotional budget; this would work for Christmas trees, but not necessarily for other products.

Two defenses of the system may be made. One is that it suggests that
sales have been made, thus making money available for promotion
purposes. The second is that some industries are so mature and
steady, e.g. electric power, that a mathematical formula fits well,
though it may not in more dynamic environments.

C.   The Comparative Parity Method

The **comparative parity method** boils down to doing what your
competitors do. It is a common method and usually easy to observe in
one's own newspaper or on local TV. Like the percent of sales
method, it is "easy" but does not necessarily reflect market
conditions. Further, it suggests that the competitor is setting your
promotional budget.

D.   The Marginal Approach

Theoretically, the **marginal approach** to almost anything in business
is "best." This method says that the firm should spend promotional
dollars until (at the margin) the additional dollar is no longer
bringing in a sufficient amount of revenues or profit. This makes
very good sense but determining how much benefit was purchased with
the "last promotional dollar" makes the method impractical for most
organizations.

E.   The All-You-Can-Afford Method

The name explains the method. It is particularly appropriate where
risk of business failure is high, as it is with new retail
businesses.

F.   The Combination Approach

In the "real world," many of these budgeting methods may be used at
one time, and not always by choice. The comparative parity or task
method user may be brought to the all-you-can-afford technique by
realities of the market.

G.   Cooperative Promotional Programs

A commonly heard term is "cooperative advertising," but the broader
"cooperative promotional program" is more useful and reminds us that
cooperation applies to all aspects of promotion.

There are two general forms of cooperative programs:

   •   **Vertical cooperative promotion** -- involves channel members of
        different levels (e.g., manufacturer and retailer).

   •   **Horizontal cooperative promotion** -- involves channel members at
        the same level (e.g., several retailers).

The attractiveness of such programs lies mainly in the prospect of
sharing the cost of programs that are beneficial to all concerned.
Problems do arise, however, when there is disagreement over items to
be advertised, comparative emphasis on particular items sold, or who
should decide how promotional budgets will be spent.

Cooperative ads placed by retailers are termed retailer-initiated,
those placed by manufacturers are termed manufacturer-initiated.
Some local media offer lower rates to local businesses placing
retailer-initiated cooperative ads.

IX.   PROMOTIONAL CAMPAIGNS

Good promotion requires a unity of presentation that may be called the
promotional mix. A promotional campaign is part of a firm's promotional
mix, just as a military campaign is part of a total war effort.

A **promotional campaign** is a series of promotional activities with a particular objective or set of objectives.

A campaign must have goals/objectives. Since markets, products, and customers vary greatly, all manner of promotional campaigns are possible, and they might vary with the product's stage in its life cycle. Some examples:

A.   Image Building

People often buy or use a product because the product or brand symbolizes something about themselves or their life-styles. Thus, marketers are properly concerned with "product image," and promotional campaigns aimed at "image building." General Mills, Betty Crocker, Jordache, Calvin Klein, the Girl Scouts, Guess, Obsession and Chanel #5 are all products that are promoted largely through **image building**. However, it must be recalled that the firms using such promotions are doing "all the other things right," contributing to the success of their promotions.

B.   Product Differentiation

A campaign aimed at developing a degree of **product differentiation** focuses on some dimension of a product attempting to show that the feature permits the product to satisfy target customers better than competing products can. A bigger gas tank on a car might be promoted to avoid running out of gas, "miles per tank" versus "miles per gallon."

Along these lines, some advertisers speak of a **USP** or **unique selling proposition** around which a campaign can be built. Examples:

.   Visine "gets the red out" (a unique feature until Murine came out with its own version).

.   Luvs diapers have a "leakguard," and different designs for boys and girls.

Many promotions stress strictly functional features of products as if they were special. Tylenol has many competitors exactly its equal, yet is promoted effectively as somehow better. The key point is you can sell the "sizzle" ... but only if the sizzle means something to the target buyer.

C.   Positioning

Products and brands have "positions" in buyers' minds. Marketers try to get their brands positioned in buyers' minds so that they will see them from a particular perspective. Kentucky Fried Chicken may have a good "chicken position," Wendy's a good "hamburger position," but not vice versa. Avis' position was Number Two and "trying harder." Marlboro is masculine, Virginia Slims is feminine.

Repositioning is also undertaken. Xerox is no longer the "copier company" but, now, the "documents company." Benson and Hedges, producer of cigarettes (once sold with snob appeal), has changed its approach as the cigarette market has become dominated by blue-collar types.

Exhibit 17-8 shows that there are many positioning strategies available to marketers. The central element is using promotion to position a brand relative to the competition.

D.   Direct Response Campaign

The purpose of direct marketing is to obtain a direct response, such as a sale. A **direct response campaign** is conducted specifically to elicit a direct, measurable response, such as an order, donation, inquiry, or visit to a showroom. L.L. Bean engages in a direct response campaign when it sends out its catalog. The availability of highly targeted computerized mailing has increased the prominence of direct response promotions.

X.   THE ETHICS OF PERSUASION

Of all the macromarketing issues related to promotion, persuasion has attracted the most attention, though every element of promotion has been criticized at one time or another.

There is a difference between informative and persuasive promotion. Without informative promotion, we would not know where to get the products we want, whether or not credit cards are accepted, etc. Critics would probably admit this, but argue that it is not right to use marketing, psychology, and expensive ads to persuade consumers to buy something or vote for someone. Cigarette ads, for example, promote an unhealthful product.

Marketers note that an ad for an inferior product usually sells the product only once, and that even the biggest companies have products rejected by the marketplace, despite the alleged power of advertising. Promoting a bad product means people find out about it that much quicker. In general, critics seem to overstate the power of promotion. Did you ever see an ad for a product and not buy it?

XI.   SUMMARY

Learning Objective 1: **Discuss the three basic purposes of promotion.**

Promotion is communication designed to inform, persuade, and remind consumers about the existence and benefits of a product, service, or idea. Without promotion, buyers would have less information on which to base informed buying decisions.

Learning Objective 2: **Define the four major elements of promotion.**

Personal selling occurs when a seller directly communicates a persuasive message to the buyer. Advertising includes any persuasive message carried by a nonpersonal medium and paid for by an identified sponsor. Publicity involves an unpaid message with no identified sponsor delivered through a mass medium. Sales promotion consists of nonroutine, temporary promotional efforts designed to stimulate buyer purchases or dealer effectiveness in a specified time period.

Learning Objective 3: **Describe the basic model for all communication processes, including promotion.**

The communication process occurs when a source encodes a message and sends it through a channel to a receiver, who must decode it and may respond with feedback. Noise may interfere. Each element in the process plays an essential role in the transference of a message from the source to the receiver.

Learning Objective 4: **Explain the hierarchy of communication effects.**

Consumers often move through a six-step hierarchy in relation to a product: awareness, knowledge, liking, preference, conviction, and purchase. Consumers at different steps have different communication needs.

Learning Objective 5: **Explain how the elements of promotion can be used to support one another in a promotional campaign.**

The effective marketer integrates all the elements of promotion -- advertising, personal selling, publicity, and sales promotion -- into a promotional mix. Such a mix is planned to meet the information requirements of all target customers. Each element of the mix performs a task. Some elements may be aimed at the target customer at a lower stage of the hierarchy of communication effects, while others may be aimed at

potential customers near the top of the staircase. Advertising's strength
is in creating awareness and spreading information to a wide audience.
Personal selling is best at moving buyers from liking to making a
conviction to purchasing.

> **Learning Objective 6:** Identify the general promotional strategies
> known as push and pull strategies.

A push strategy is directed towards members of a channel of distribution.
A pull strategy is directed toward consumers in order to stimulate demand
for the product.

> **Learning Objective 7:** Classify the major approaches used by
> marketing managers to set promotional budgets.

In setting promotional budgets, marketing managers can use the objective
and task method, the percent of sales method, the comparative parity
method, the marginal approach, the all-you-can-afford method, cooperative
promotional programs, or combinations of these. Under the objective and
task method, the budget is based on an estimate of the amount needed to
accomplish established objectives. The percent of sales method bases
appropriations on a standard percentage of sales. Under the comparative
parity method, the appropriation is based on what competitors spend. The
marginal approach considers the payoff from the last dollar spent, and the
all-you-can-afford approach uses whatever dollars are available.
Cooperative programs involve a sharing of promotional expenses between
organizations at the same level or at different levels of a distribution
channel.

> **Learning Objective 8:** Discuss promotional campaigns and provide
> examples.

A promotional campaign consists of promotional activities designed to
achieve specific objectives. An image-building approach stresses the
symbolic value associated with the product. A product differentiation
approach emphasizes unique product features. A positioning approach
promotes a brand in relation to competing brands. A direct response
campaign seeks a direct measurable response.

> **Learning Objective 9:** Discuss arguments about the ethics of
> persuasion in society. Identify several general promotional
> strategies.

Every element of promotion has been criticized at one time or another.
Critics argue that it is not right to use promotional efforts to persuade
consumers. However, most people would grant that some advertising is
needed to provide information. Thus, a central issue involves whether
promotions are informative or persuasive.

XII.   KEY TERMS

XIII. QUESTIONS FOR DISCUSSION (8)

XIV.   ETHICS IN PRACTICE

XV.   CASES

ANSWER GUIDELINES FOR CHAPTER 17 QUESTIONS FOR DISCUSSION

1.   *Identify the type of promotion and comment on the effectiveness of each of
     the following: (a) Chicago Cub announcer Harry Cary wears a Budweiser
     jacket on a televised game; (b) a TV ad says "CNN Headline News, if you
     don't have it, call your cable operator to get it"; (c) a Special Olympics
     representative telephones at 7:00 p.m. while you are watching your favorite
     TV show and asks you to make a donation; (d) as a forward receives the
     basketball, the announcer says, "Here comes the Windex man"; (e) at the
     supermarket, a banner announces a scratch-and-win Bingo game; and (f)*

during a corporate takeover attempt, Boone Pickens invites television reporters from major cities to question him during a live satellite news conference. Reporters are allowed to splice in film of themselves for the evening news and make it appear that the local reporter had an exclusive interview rather than a satellite hookup.

ANSWER:

The major types of promotion are advertising, publicity, personal selling, and sales promotion. There are subsets identifiable in these categories, e.g. direct-action advertising, institutional advertising, etc. While it is not too difficult to place the examples of promotions mentioned in the question into one or another category, some students will debate the "right" answer. See the below paragraph (a) for an example of this.

(a)   Harry Cary and the Budweiser jacket

Harry Cary is an old-time announcer who has been on radio and then on television for more than fifty years. Though he announced for the St. Louis Cardinals for years, he joined the Cubs and quickly became a favorite there. He leans out of the broadcast booth during the seventh inning stretch and leads the crowd in "Take Me Out to the Ball Game." He is, in short, a genuine character.

When Harry wears a Budweiser jacket he is engaging in promotion. His jacket, itself, is a sales promotion item for Budweiser. Harry wears the jacket and suggests by means of the jacket, that folks who like the Cubs also like Bud, and that viewers can be like Harry ... a true Cubbies fan ... if they favor Bud like good Old Harry does. Harry is such a beloved old coot that his wearing of the jacket is probably very effective in influencing the market at which it is targeted ... Cubs fans who drink beer. It has been shown time and again that a strong association with a particular image can strongly affect the choice of beer brands. Not every beer drinker who likes the Cubs will drink the beer that supports the Cubs, but a lot of them will.

The fact that Harry is wearing the jacket on TV makes a good case for placing this activity in the category of advertising. Harry is on TV, a mass medium, and wearing a jacket that "talks" about Budweiser, though not actually talking about it himself. Surely Harry is rewarded by the brewer for wearing the jacket and/or the TV station is rewarded. Thus, wearing the jacket could be seen as advertising a paid, non-personal message delivered by a mass medium. Harry could be described as a "walking billboard," an advertisement.

Some students will point out the following other readings of the situation. Some will say that Harry is a salesman and that this example is a matter of personal selling. Well, Harry sure can sell, but this time he's on TV, a mass medium, not selling one-on-one, face-to-face. It will be mentioned that since the jacket is a sales promotion item the whole event is a case of sales promotion. Again, the "message" of the jacket is being delivered via a mass medium in a paid context.

(b)   CNN News

This is an advertisement; it says so right in the question item. Specifically, it is a direct action ad of a sort. CNN wants us to call up a cable operator and get that news program on our TVs.

The ad is most commonly run on CNN's other service, the "all news and talk, in depth" service. It is also carried by local cable systems on such cable-only channels as TNT (another Turner service). Thus, its effectiveness is likely to be limited in that it reaches only people who have cable and who are watching the other news service or another cable channel. Most "regular" TV stations will not carry ads for other TV services, thus it's safe to assume that the CNN ad is seldom seen on TV except on cable service stations. Of course, it will be reaching an attractive target market -- news freaks. CNN also supplies "Headline News" for radio stations and is thus able to advertise itself in that medium.

(c)   Special Olympics telephone campaign

This is a form of personal selling. It is the delivery of what is supposed to be a persuasive message by a real live person addressing the listener directly.

That the person in the question was called during a favorite TV program has nothing to do with the question of what type of promotional message this is. It does have to do with its effectiveness, however. Some people will be annoyed at missing their favorite show, others may be less concerned. But people are willing to help out the Special Olympics and might quickly make a pledge (1) to help the Olympics, or (2) to get back to their program. Imagine what your response would be if you were called by the Special Olympics. Now, imagine your response in the same situation if the caller turned out to be selling storm windows or siding.

Should the Olympics call us at home during our favorite TV shows? Unfortunately, this is the only time that their volunteers can work and the only time we are at home to answer the calls.

(d)   "Here comes the Windex man."

This expression refers to a player who will "wipe the glass (backboard) clean." The use of the name Windex does not refer to a sponsor of the basketball broadcast. Thus, Windex is getting a "free" product plug on the air, a mention that it really cannot control. The situation described here is a matter of publicity. A free plug like this is surely worth something, but its effectiveness in selling Windex is highly questionable. Still, a mention in a favorable context, is surely worth something.

(e)   Supermarket Bingo sign

Though it could be argued that the banner is "advertising" the Bingo game, it is more accurate to describe it as part and parcel of the Bingo game itself, a sales promotion.

Its effectiveness in generating awareness of the game cannot be easily judged. Yet the use of such signs does suggest that they are effective parts of the total sales promotion game.

(f)   Boone Pickens

This situation is one that fits publicity perfectly. Boone Pickens is certainly spending some money on this, but the distribution of his message is essentially free and thus matches the definition of public relations/publicity. That the reporters are able to pretend they were there in an exclusive interview with Mr. Pickens merely serves to make the publicity package a better one. Movie stars do a similar "trick" when promoting new movies and shows.

The effectiveness of the interview depends on how well Mr. Pickens is able to field questions. Effectiveness in getting the Pickens' face and story on the air was very great. Most reporters seldom get a chance to interview a person in the national news "personally." This same technique has been in use on radio for years. A performer about to open in town sends a tape to disc jockeys and a list of interview questions. The disc jockey then introduces the performer as if he or she were actually there, then begins to ask questions that are answered on the tape. Some radio funnymen have been known to "ask" the questions out of order or to alter the questions to make the performer appear to be an idiot. This shows how publicity, which is not fully controlled by the source, can have an unintended result.

2.   *What is sales promotion? Give some creative examples of sales promotion.*

ANSWER:

Sales promotion is a catch-all or "other" category. It can be defined as:

> Those promotional activities other than personal selling, advertising and publicity that are intended to stimulate buyer purchases or dealer effectiveness in a specific time period.

The "specific time period" is mentioned to accent the temporary nature of these promotions. They are temporary because they will "get old." For example, one common sales promotion is the dealer listing, the offer by a producer to list in ads the dealers willing to stock certain goods. Thus, TV ads tell us that the

K-Tel pocket fisherman is available at "K-Mart, Gibson's, Wal-Mart, and other fine stores."

Imagine approaching K-Mart with yet another "great deal" like "Hey, we will mention you on our TV ads." Such a promotion is now expected by K-Mart and is no big deal. Some retailers may, in fact, expect an outright payment for carrying a product. Thus, the most effective sales promotions are usually those used on an on-and-off basis. This is true of sales promotions aimed at consumers. A 25-cents-off coupon for Maxwell House coffee is a ho-hum item. Of course, Maxwell House continues to issue the coupons, violating the "temporary" rule of sales promotions, because all other coffee marketers issue coupons constantly.

Creating new sales promotions is difficult because so many promotions have been run into the ground. Variations on common promotions might be considered creative. Examples:

. Coupons that offer a "secret amount" off the price. The consumer has to rub off the seal to determine the amount.

. Store issued coupons that are good only for certain times of day, e.g., from 6 to 8 p.m. when family suppertimes are keeping store traffic low.

. "Mystery" sales incentives for industrial salespeople such as an all-expense trip to "?" guaranteed to be worth $4,000.

. Student-oriented "fun and games" at Fort Lauderdale for spring break. Tugs of war, trivia contests, and free product giveaways all have been used with success.

3.   *Using the communications model in Exhibit 17-2, give examples of the encoding and decoding that might take place during the personal selling process.*

ANSWER:

If we assume a one-on-one, face-to-face meeting between a salesperson and a potential buyer of industrial goods, we might have, on the salesperson's side, the desire to:

. Transmit information about a product and its benefits.
. Suggest that the salesperson really knows what he or she is talking about.
. Demonstrate a "professional attitude."
. Demonstrate "honesty" and "sincerity."
. Repeat key points about the product, price, delivery system, etc. since repetition is necessary.

This would suggest the following sorts of encoding.

. Portrayal of information about the product and its benefits via spoken and written words, pictures, diagrams, catalogs and pamphlets, scale models, and "love letters" (endorsements by satisfied customers.)

. Suggestion of product knowledge by statements relating to: education ("When I was in engineering school ...."), years of experience, acquaintance with the marketplace, and specific problems the customer is likely to be facing.

. "Professionalism" suggested by manner of dress, competent discussion of situations, sticking to "problem solving."

. "Honesty" and "sincerity" suggested by speaking style, earnest attitude, facial expressions, manner of speech and "body language."

. Repetition of key information by introducing "another look" or "a review of benefits."

On the customer's side of the desk, a good deal of "decoding" is taking place. If the salesperson is doing a good job of transmitting information, in a manner that suggests good knowledge of the product, "professionalism" and "honesty," and representing information as needed, the receiver is likely to "decode" something close to what was "encoded." The match between the two depends on the frames of reference of each participant, time pressures surrounding the situation, simple "human chemistry," and much more. Clearly, since the encoder is trying to sell something, it is more the encoder's task than the decoder's to try to assure good transmission of information.

The complicated nature of this diadic relationship should be acknowledged by stating that the receiver (customer) is very likely encoding reactions to the salesperson's performance in the form of glances, nods, questions, clock-watching, etc. The salesperson must decode these and more formal statements or questions at the end of the presentation.

The flow of encoded and decoded messages is likely to be rapid and extensive. Perhaps a classroom exercise could be used. Have two students act out a salesperson's call on a customer, even for one or two minutes. See if the rest of the class can note or count the (probably tens or hundreds) of encoding-decoding events occurring.

4.   *What is "noise" in the communication process?*

ANSWER:

"Noise" is a very broad term used by communication theorists to encompass all sorts of interferences that contribute to a sender's message not being received clearly by a receiver. In short, anything that "messes up" the communication process is noise. Consider a person driving to work listening to the radio. An advertisement comes on. What kinds of "noise" might make the ad a less-than-perfect communication? Answer: so many things that it is nearly impossible to list them. Some examples:

.   Horn from nearby car.
.   Driver thinking about the time.
.   Driver watching traffic or reading billboards.
.   Passenger talking.
.   Driver thinking about last song on radio or last night's ball game on TV.
.   Driver rehearsing a "give me a raise" speech.
.   Ad makes listener think of another brand of the product in question.
.   Radio is insufficient to transmit the message sender sought to transmit.

5.   *How does selective perception enter into the communication process?*

ANSWER:

This question relates this chapter to the consumer behavior material in earlier chapters. Selective perception is the process whereby individuals view exactly the same object, or message in different ways because of their backgrounds, experiences, and interests. Different people may not see the same things because of this phenomenon. People who favor Bill Clinton for president interpret his speeches, positions, and background differently than do people who think George Bush should be president. A person whose beliefs and experiences are such that they don't like any politician at all may ignore the two men entirely except to announce that "they are all crooks."

Many examples can be found in our reactions to all forms of communications. A class poll on which TV ads they like best will show this to be the case.

.   Most people like Bill Cosby; a few can't stand him.
.   Some may like Michael Jackson; others will say he's a creep.

Classroom discussions along these lines leads class members to see why there are so many different products, messages, and prices to be found in our marketing system.

6.   *How does a push strategy differ from a pull strategy?   Give some examples from your experience.*

ANSWER:

A push strategy is aimed at channel of distribution members to get them to participate strongly in promoting the product in question.   The flows of merchandise (M) and of promotional efforts (PE) are as follows:

```
                    M              M              M
Manufacturer -----> Wholesaler ----> Retailer ----> Consumer
                   PE             PE             PE
```

The pull strategy involves "skipping over" channel intermediaries to reach a customer, usually the consumer, who is further on down the channel.   The flows of merchandise and promotional efforts then become:

```
                    M              M              M
Manufacturer -----> Wholesaler ----> Retailer ----> Consumer
               >................. PE ..................>
```

The idea, of course, is to develop demand so that products will be "pulled" through the channel of distribution.

Examples from the classes' own experiences might include things like these:

.   An ad encourages the consumer to go to the store and ask for a new product (or, to "insist" on Bayer aspirin).   This represents a pull strategy.

.   The radio announcer says, "Tell Bill down at Bill's Used Car Lot that Jim Fields from WCUE sent you."   This is a form of pull strategy since it may increase demand for WCUE's product, advertising time.

.   Workers at McDonald's are visited by a regional manager and taught to ask all customers if they would like to try a new McDessert today.   Push strategy.

.   The retail sales clerk works extra hard to sell Bulova watches during periods when Bulova is offering an extra bonus for each watch sold.   Push strategy.

7.   *Comment on this statement: "Promotion mirrors the values and lifestyles of the target consumers."*

ANSWER:

The marketing concept tells us that we cannot "create" needs and wants and that marketing will best succeed if it reflects and is associated with the lifestyles and values of the buyers to whom the appeal is being made.   Thus, the statement would be better put, "Promotion should mirror ...."   Generally, advertisers follow this precept.   Thus, teenagers may see themselves as similar to the bike-riding, fun-loving youngsters in the Coke and Pepsi ads, children may see themselves as having fun with Legos, and parents can identify with the couples on TV trying to get the teenagers and children to stop riding bikes and playing with Legos long enough to eat a good breakfast or lunch.

8.   *For each of the following brands indicate whether the primary promotional strategy is image building, positioning, or unique selling proposition. (a) Mountain Dew soft drink, (b) Cooper Tools (e.g., crescent wrenches, Lumpkin measuring tapes, Nichols saws), (c) SunLight dishwashing liquid, and (d) BMW convertibles.*

ANSWER:

Most promotional strategies involve elements of several approaches to execute those strategies.   For example, the soft drink Slice, which contained "10% real fruit juice" suggests a unique selling proposition in that, at the time it was introduced, it was the only bottled drink of that type.   On the other hand, the promotions for Slice also positioned it vis a vis other soft drinks ... healthier than Coke, Pepsi and other drinks of the sort but also not a straight juice, more of a fun drink or a treat. On the third hand, the image of the product as a somehow healthy substitute for regular sodas was also enhanced by the ads and other promotions.

(a)   Mountain Dew soft drink

Most advertisements for this product show fun-loving young people gamboling about in an outdoor setting while the mild, happy country music plays in the background. The packaging uses two colors, green to suggest the nature of the product, a lemony drink like 7-Up, and yellow, a bright, happy color. Further, the very name Mountain Dew suggests both "pure/refreshing" and something a bit bold and daring since Mountain Dew is another name for bootleg "white lightning." Thus, it seems reasonable to say that the major thrust of the promotional strategy is image-building.

(b)   Cooper Tools (Crescent wrenches, Lumpkin measuring tapes, Nichols saws, etc.)

It is difficult to sell tools via advertisements. Most tools are sold via hands-on examination with some assistance from a salesperson or friend/co-worker who gives advice. The advice usually consists of comments like "Crescent is the best" or "Lumpkin has been around for a long time" or "Nichols cost more but you get what you pay for." Thus, promotion focuses on showing these tools to be quality, top-of-the-line, "lifetime investment" types of tools. The salesperson's comments and the advertising done for these tools stress this quality appeal. While this might be a matter of image building, it seems more appropriate to say that these promotions position the products as "the best." The best compared to what? Compared to all the rest. This establishment of a spot in the market is positioning.

(c)   Sunlight dishwashing liquid

Sunlight is a liquid dishwashing product also made in a powdered version for use in dishwashing machines. The claim to fame of the liquid is that it contains lemon juice, not just a scent but real lemon juice which supposedly cuts grease and smells good in the bargain. Ads for the product stress this marvelous quality. Real lemon juice is not found in other dishwashing liquids. The major emphasis of promotion for this product is the unique selling proposition.

(d)   BMW convertible

BMW ads generally stress product quality, performance, and panache. In one TV ad, a handsome man, accompanied by his lovely "classy" wife, are driving down a beautiful highway along the cliffs near the ocean. The couple is dressed in the best clothes ... going-to-the-governor's-home-for-dinner sort of wear. These folks are rich, but classy rich. No Cadillac or Lincoln for these people. They are "quality" all the way. The man must have gone to Harvard or Princeton, the woman to Smith or Radcliffe. Clearly he owns an important business, is a respected lawyer or surgeon, or is a senator whose family has always had money.

Suddenly a curve in the road, a traffic mess-up ahead. A couple of clowns sliding their cars around. The BMW couple sees this, the driver (the man) and the machine (the BMW) spring into action. The responsive steering, amazing brakes, etc. permit our hero to execute some professional driver-type maneuvers. The man and his car whip around the various accident-prone peons and their lesser automobiles and the classy people come to a safe stop well past the accident. Do they laugh at these fools who nearly screwed up their big night out? Curse them for getting in the way? Noooo! The last thing we hear is the rich folks deciding to go back to see if anyone was hurt.

In short, while BMW ads do tell readers and viewers about the car's special mechanical properties, and while there is some element of positioning involved here, the ad described, and other BMW promotions are primarily image-building ads. The ad discussed above clearly aims to show us the kind of people who drive BMWs ... handsome, classy, well-positioned in society, well-connected with the upper-crust, great drivers, well-educated, and caring people.

ETHICS EXERCISE 17

CHAPTER 17 ETHICS IN PRACTICE

Overview

Every Sunday afternoon at Rider College, a small non-state supported school in
New Jersey, eight students, paid $5 per hour, call college prospects (who are not
expecting the calls) and promote Rider from the student's point of view. These
student telemarketers are trained and supervised like any other sales force.
Applicants to the college are called again by a faculty member in his or her
major field to talk about course schedules. Should colleges engage in such
activities?

More and more colleges and universities are becoming sophisticated marketers.
This has been especially true in the past decade or so, as a declining market of
college-age students and diminishing enrollments have led to higher levels of
competition among schools of higher education. While university marketing
activities were once largely limited to college catalogues and campus visits
coordinated by the admissions counselors, today the latter have become
sophisticated marketers, often employing advertising agencies and using a wide
range of media such as newspaper and magazines, radio and television spots, open
houses, and telemarketing.

The ethical issue in this case is not the use of marketing activities by
colleges; very few people have a problem with that. In a highly competitive
environment, most nonprofits use marketing techniques as they vie for the time
and dollars of their target markets. The marketing communications they use are
an acceptable practice for getting persuasive information into the marketplace.
However, telephone marketing in general, and especially when used by
not-for-profit organizations, is a controversial practice.

There are two forms of telemarketing. Inbound telemarketing is where customers
respond to an ad and place an order via mail or a toll-free telephone number.
What we have in this scenario is outbound telemarketing, where sellers call on
prospects and make a sales presentation. Although for years telemarketing had an
unsavory reputation and was associated with boiler room scams, today it is one of
the fastest growing marketing methods, especially in business-to-business
marketing. Nevertheless, it is still the most controversial form of direct
response marketing.

Should colleges engage in marketing activities like telemarketing?

More and more colleges are, in fact, using telephone marketing, employing current
students and, to a lesser extent, faculty. There are several reasons why a
college might decide to use telemarketing:

.   Personal contact: Next to in-person selling, telemarketing is the most
     personal medium. This is an advantage for the seller since she can tailor
     the message, and it is an advantage for the prospective student since he
     gets personal treatment, questions answered, etc.

.   Flexibility: It is not a case of "One message fits all." The seller can
     adjust the message in light of feedback from the prospect. This is also an
     advantage to the prospects since they can give feedback and suggestions.

.   Measurable: Based on prospect response (e.g., inquiries for more
     information, orders), the seller knows how well the sales pitch is working.

.   Speed: Telemarketing works much more quickly in reaching prospects than
     does personal selling. Thus, more prospective students will have the
     opportunity to receive personal communication about the school.

.   Low cost: Especially compared to personal selling, this is a low-cost
     medium. And, students and faculty are working for low wages.

.   Targeted: The prospect list is usually highly targeted.

However, there are several reasons why a college might have second thoughts about using telemarketing.

.   Telemarketing is generally considered the most intrusive of all selling methods.   It interrupts family and business activities, causes people to walk up and down the steps, summons us from the shower, etc.

.   Negative image: It might be a turnoff to some prospects, thereby backfiring. Consumers particularly dislike this form of advertising, viewing it as an invasion of privacy. When the phone rings, we expect it to be a friend or relative, and instead it turns out to be another salesperson.

.   Not using highly trained personnel: It is generally recommended that the caller be trained in communications skills, have a thorough knowledge of the product, and be well versed in commonly asked questions. How many students will fit the bill after the (presumably brief) training period? What about faculty who aren't trained? On the other hand, who better to call college prospects than students and faculty? Would a highly-trained telemarketing professional be more acceptable to prospective students?

The ethics of telemarketing in this situation turns largely on how it is used. Probably many prospective students who are seriously considering Rider College would be glad to get a call from a friendly student voice on the other end willing to offer helpful advice and information. However, if the telemarketers are cold calling (rather than following up on leads), the phonecall is likely to be viewed as intrusive and pushy by a significant number of prospects. One would suspect that an accepted student who has not yet made her college choice decision would find it premature and pushy to have a faculty member call to discuss her schedule, although some prospects might value the information and opportunity to interact personally with a "real live" professor.

Probably the best way to handle this scenario is to ask your students by a show-of-hands vote how they would react, first to students, and then to professors calling. Then, ask individual students under what conditions each call would be acceptable.

CHAPTER 17 TAKE A STAND QUESTIONS

1.   *Walt Disney Company will not allow its films to be shown in movie theaters showing commercials before the film. Should movie theater personnel be upset?*

Advertising in movie theaters (variously called film advertising, theater advertising, and cinema advertising) has been around since long before TV, is very common in Europe and in Asian countries, and in the U.S. is a rapidly growing but controversial practice. Commercials shown prior to the movie and previews, called "trailers," have apparently largely replaced cartoons. They are similar to television commercials but are generally longer (45 to 120 seconds) and better produced.

Organizations such as Screenvision handle distribution of these commercials. Companies have placed commercials at the beginning and of films on videotape and have ads on the boxes containing the rental tapes.

From an advertiser's perspective, there are several reasons to use theater advertising:

.   Creative advantages: High quality reproduction (e.g., Dolby stereo, large screen) and entertainment value (people in theaters have a low tolerance for hard-sell messages; therefore most theater ads use drama and MTV techniques).

.   Impact: Attention and concentration are generated by the theater environment. The large screen has for a compelling image that commands total attention.

.   Low clutter: Usually only one, two, or three commercials are shown, and they are shown before the feature begins so there is no interruption.

. High recall: Research shows that theater advertising has much higher recall levels than TV advertising.

. Geographic and demographic targeting: The style and mix of commercials can be tailored to the audience, e.g., movies thought to appeal to teenagers open with MTV-like ads.

. Captive audience: No remote control and few "bathroom breaks."

However, there are some disadvantages to using this advertising medium:

. It is fleeting: Here now and gone the next minute, like radio and TV commercials.

. Low attention: Ads run while people are talking and trying to find their seats.

. The commercials are often resented by movie patrons: This is the only form of advertising not requiring even a grudging consent on the part of the potential viewer. Most other ads we can control by changing the channel or turning the page. Irritation is probably the major problem; people feel that because they have paid to see a movie, advertising is an intrusion. Moviegoers have been known to picket outside movie theaters to express their dissatisfaction that movies are shown. People have also been known to boo and hiss when the commercials come on. This dissatisfaction could rub off on the advertised product.

The decision to run commercials is usually not up to the individual theaters but is made by the motion picture companies and the distributors (i.e., the movie theater chains) who handle the films. Some don't run them for fear of offending their audiences, while others, such as Cineplex Odeon, welcome commercials.

A few years ago Disney executives discovered research indicating widespread discontent with commercials in theaters. As a "public service," they decided to keep their films out of venues that run the ads. The decision by Disney was hailed by some creative people in the industry.

In addition to the intrusion factor, critics of this practice feel that the creative content of movies is compromised by commercials. Writers become subservient to the advertisers. A little bit of advertising money works like a habit-forming drug; more and more of it is desired until the entire industry is hooked, sending quality down the toilet.

On the other hand, the research Disney used to make its decision has questionable validity. A savvy (and unethical) researcher can usually phrase a question to get almost any answer she wishes. For instance, a survey that asks, "Would you be willing to pay higher ticket prices to offset lower theater revenues caused by Disney's ad ban?" would likely elicit findings at odds with Disney's.

It could be argued that consumers, not studios, are best suited to decide whether ads will be shown in theaters. Advertisers are very sensitive to public opinion; witness the sponsor defections from controversial TV shows. The marketplace is best served when operations can run unrestricted.

For instance, patrons in upscale areas might be willing to forego commercials and pay higher ticket prices, whereas moviegoers in lower-income neighborhoods might be willing to endure a few commercials to receive lower ticket prices.

Disney's attitude is bullying and coercive. It is interesting that they conveniently forgot to survey consumers on product placements (question 2 below) from which they derive revenue and with which their movies are filled. Yet their stance on trailers might encourage those who wish to ban these even less intrusive ads from which they derive revenues.

2. *Because a brand shown in a movie has some promotional benefits, some movie studios charge product placement fees. For example, $20,000 for a visual, $40,000 for a visual and an actor mentioning the brand name, or $60,000 for an actor actually using the product. Is this ethical?*

This practice, known as product placement, is a minor but growing part of the promotion industry. A number of companies have paid to have their products shown or used in movies, TV shows, and video games. These cameo appearances were believed to take off in the early 1980s after Reese's Pieces was used as bait to lure the extraterrestrial in the film "E.T."; sales of the product subsequently soared 70%, and the candy was added to concession stands in 800 theaters.

Major movie studios have in-house product placement; they send scripts to ad agencies and advertisers with the suggested placement. Sometimes the agencies and advertisers will edit the scripts to suit their wishes. Other movie studios use product placement agencies which basically do the same work as an in-house operation.

From a marketer's perspective, there are several advantages to using product placements:

. Exposure: Moviegoers are very attentive audiences. Also, the increased home video rental and network and cable TV venues in which movies are viewed can greatly expand exposure for a single movie. Also, exposure is not subject to channel switching -- at least not in the theater.

. Frequency: The placement can be repeated within a movie as well as among different movies and TV shows. Also, some people watch their favorite movies several times in videocassette.

. Favorable imagery: There can be a halo or rub-off effect when a beloved character uses or is associated with a product.

. Recall: This is significantly higher for products placed in movies than recall of TV commercials.

. Intrusiveness: These ads are relatively innocuous.

On the other hand, there are some potential drawbacks to product placements:

. Selective attention: Because they are relatively inconspicuous, product placements might go unnoticed.

. Limited message: The product benefits cannot be discussed, and detailed information cannot be provided. Rather, appeals are limited to association with the movie and its characters, product use, and enjoyment.

. Adverse public reaction: This is the real ethical issue. Some movie fans believe that the wall of separation between program content and commercials should remain standing. Many moviegoers and television viewers are outraged that product promotions are being inserted into movies without their awareness.

Some people might put product placements on the same level with subliminal advertising (although, of course, it isn't the same thing) and use many of the arguments against subliminal advertising against it. (See Chapter 5 Take A Stand question 5.) As with embeds and subliminal stimuli, this would violate the consumer's right to know.

However, because the products are in plain view, there is no intent to deceive. There is no intrusive hard sell; the "ads" are presented in a soft-sell, sugarcoated form. Finally, as with theater commercials, product placements might result in lower ticket prices. In this case, it would be because movie studios derive revenues from placements and can hence afford to charge a lower price to movie theaters and can afford to produce more movies.

3.   *A tobacco company hands out free samples of a smokeless tobacco (snuff) at a college football game. Is this ethical?*

The merits and demerits of tobacco promotion have been discussed in Chapter 2 Take A Stand Question 2. Points arguing for a ban on sampling snuff at college football games are:

. Many spectators will be young and impressionable. Although the

effectiveness of advertising in changing behavior of adolescents and young
adults is open to question, putting free samples in their hands could be
quite tempting. Like cigarettes, snuff is addictive, not to mention
hazardous to one's health (it causes mouth and tongue cancer).

. Sampling the product at a respected institution such as a university might
put a stamp of approval on the product, signaling that the university
endorses it.

. The product is filthy; people will be spitting it out all over the place
and spittoons are pretty rare these days.

On the other hand, the snuff promoters could argue that:

. It is a legal product and most attendees are 18 or older. Hence, the
promoters should have the right to sample.

. Slippery slope -- what will be banned next from sampling? For instance,
candy isn't exactly healthy.

. They are promoting only to those who have already decided to use the
product and to those of age. (Do they intend to "card?") They will not
attempt to persuade nonusers to try snuff.

. People over 18 have the right to have access to free products if producers
are willing to give them away. To disallow the sampling is paternalistic
and suggests people aren't capable of making their own free choices.

4. *Public television stations don't allow commercials, but they mention the
name of sponsors of programs at the end of the programs. Should this
practice be stopped?*

Although the common perception is that public television is "commercial free," in
reality the Public Broadcasting System (PBS) has permitted advertising since the
mid-70s. Traditionally, commercial sponsors supported or underwrote PBS programs
through grants, and their donations were acknowledged in credits at the beginning
and end of the shows. Although this still occurs, public TV also turned to more
traditional advertising to compensate for the cutback in federal funding that
occurred during the Nixon administration and to more effectively compete with
commercial television.

Advertisers like PBS because it attracts a large upscale audience and because it
adopted a fairly consistent programming schedule in the early 80s.

Current FCC guidelines permit commercials on public television only during the
local 2.5-minute station breaks. Each station maintains its own acceptability
guidelines. Some stations run the same ads that appear on commercial TV (e.g.,
AT&T) while others only accept noncommercial ads that are "value neutral."
Although there is no effort to sell anything in these ads, the messages may
include non-promotional corporate and product logos and slogans; business
locations and telephone numbers that aren't used for telemarketing; and brand
names, service marks, and logos.

Whether any, some, or all of this commercial activity is appropriate or not is
not really determined by moral values so much as by personal tastes and
preferences plus one's own philosophy of the proper role of public television.
The original idea underlying public television was that the marketplace was not
providing "quality" programming, so the federal government would fill the void by
providing a commercial-free environment paid for out of public funding (read:
your tax dollars and mine) and private contributions. Since public television is
partially paid for out of federal taxes, the question is whether or not viewers
are willing to endure more commercial messages in return for lower taxes. Two
other facts might be useful in helping your students to decide on an answer: (1)
the audience for public television is mostly upscale and (2) the television
marketplace has changed tremendously since PBS was founded in the 1960s (cable,
pay per view, more independent stations, etc.)

5.   *H.G. Wells claimed that "advertising is legalized lying." Do you agree?*

This question relates to the last section in the chapter on the ethics of persuasion. H.G. Wells' statement illustrates a total lack of understanding of the role of advertising as an instrument within a company and as an institution within society. Yet, many people would agree with Wells. (Ask for a show of hands as to how many of your students agree with Wells. Then, ask for specific examples of ads which lie.) Advertising is the most criticized business function; its visibility makes it an easy target. Some quotables similar to Wells:

.   "Advertising will be seen in the history books as one of the real evil things of our time." -- Malcolm Muggeridge.

.   Advertising is "the single most value-destroying activity of business civilization." -- Robert Heilbroner, Economist.

.   "Don't tell my mother I work in advertising. She thinks I play piano at the whorehouse." -- Jock Elliot, former chairman at Ogilvy & Mather advertising agency.

The credibility of advertising among the public leaves something to be desired. We still have visions of hucksters selling snake oil. The public thinks that advertising professionals are no more honest than used car salespeople, no more ethical than local political hacks, insurance peddlers, labor union racketeers, and pawn shop proprietors.

But by its nature advertising need not be (and usually is not) this way. The basic role of advertising is communication. Its two most fundamental functions are to inform and to persuade. It is the persuasive role of advertising with which people have a problem. To consumers, informative ads make the process of search for information more efficient, increasing knowledge, and thereby allowing for a more perfect marketplace. However, persuasive ads are viewed as an economic waste of resources (competition is seen as strictly a zero-sum game, and so advertising is described as "combative," competitive, "superfluous," and the like) and as manipulation (puffing, misleading, exploitive, etc.).

However, virtually all communication contains some persuasive elements. Both informative and persuasive communication are vital and indeed necessary ingredients of the decision-making processes in other walks of life such as politics (politicians orate), religion (ministers preach), education (parents and teachers criticize), the media (newspapers editorialize), and the marketplace. If you believe that consumers are sovereign and able to make up their own mind, then persuasion is not coercion. People build up immunity against advertising's persuasions via selective perception. And, it is not propaganda if people are aware of its persuasive intent; contrast this, however, with much publicity and other public relations work.

In short, persuasion is a legitimate activity when dealing with responsible, thinking consumers able to make up their own minds, as long as it is honest and promoting a legal product. However, Wells suggests that most or even all advertising is dishonest. Is he right? Persuasion does allow for some exaggeration and embellishment (so-called puffery, based on subjective opinion, not fact. But in a society of the superlative, it is not unusual for advertisers to praise their product. Reasonable people know that puffery is just a way of showing enthusiasm.

On the other hand, sometimes there is a fine line between puffery and deception. The misled or manipulated person acts differently than they would have freely chosen had they known the truth. For instance, sometimes advertisers are able to get away with so-called "weasels" or small deceptions, e.g., "temporary relief in many cases"; parity claims such as "no brand works faster" (maybe no brand works slower either).

Fortunately, there are various regulatory mechanisms to police advertising; as a result, the vast majority of ads are above board. These mechanisms include the Federal Trade Commission (rules against deceptive advertising in interstate commerce) and other government agencies, media clearance departments, advertising industry self-regulatory agencies such as the Better Business Bureau's NAD-NARB and consumer watchdog groups and individual consumer complaints. Misleading advertising is not only unethical, it is stupid: it contradicts consumer experience, which will result in no repurchases and negative word of mouth. In the long run advertising only works when it reinforces the experiences and impressions of satisfied customers.

Advertising causes a bad product to die more quickly than it otherwise would since it hastens trial. The take-the-money-and-run school of advertising only works for fly-by-night operations, not legitimate companies in business for the long haul.

GUIDE TO CASES

VIDEO CASE 17-1 NEW PIG CORPORATION[1]

FOCUS ON SMALL BUSINESS

SUBJECT MATTER: Marketing of New Products, Direct Marketing, Product Names.

Please see the Guide to Video Cases for video length and other information.

AT-A-GLANCE OVERVIEW

New Pig Corporation was founded in 1985. It is a manufacturer of industrial absorbents, and employs 175 people in Tipton, Pennsylvania and Reno, Nevada. Annual sales exceed $18 million.

The company designed an innovative method for absorbing fluid leaks in industrial machinery. It invented spongy socks and pillows that are used to absorb oils and other liquids that get spilled around machines in factories. Although this low technology solution to a problem was simple, it was revolutionary.

The firm obtained 40 wholesale distributors, but sales volume was very low. Distributors indicated their lack of marketing success was because the New Pig Corporation's pig product was an unknown product with a strange name. The company had a superior product that was proving hard to sell.

To overcome these hurdles, it was suggested that the product be marketed in an unconventional way. It was suggested that direct marketing used to promote and distribute the product.

QUESTIONS

1.   *Is the use of direct marketing, direct distribution, and direct mail-advertising, a sound idea for New Pig? What are the strengths and weaknesses of this strategy? Would another promotional mix be better?*

The idea of direct marketing is a sound idea. The process works well for many companies. Will these methods work with a product like industrial absorbents? There are reasons to say that it would. First, the product is unique and superior to others. Thus, it should be "in demand" if only the company can get the word out. Using distributors could be inappropriate since distributors are famous for selling things that are easy to sell and not new, unfamiliar products. Arguably, the best way to introduce a new product is to "take matters into your own hands." Secondly, the product is low tech, i.e. it doesn't necessarily require detailed explanations and personal contact by a salesperson. Selling low tech products like janitorial supplies is usually done in person, but those products are homogeneous and have many competitors. This product does not.

[1]Excerpt adapted permission from *Strengthening America's Competitiveness* p. 93, copyright 1991 by Connecticut Mutual Life Insurance Company.

The weaknesses of such a strategy may boil down to the fact that even a low tech product can require some personal selling, at least to get the first sale. Office supplies, like copier paper, can be sold (orders taken) over the phone, but the first sale to a given client may require personal contact. Would some other promotional strategy be better than direct-mail? Probably a combination of direct mail and personal selling would be best, with personal selling being used to make the first contact, and mail or phone used to replenish customer supplies. However, the company may feel that a relatively cheap product could not "carry" the expense of a personal sales force. So, it would not be reasonable to follow the direct marketing route.

Here's what actually happened. To overcome the low sales volume and lack of name recognition, the company devised an entirely new strategy. Defying conventional wisdom, the company marketed its product by mail-order. After developing creative promotional materials that exploit the firm's unconventional name and its product's superiority, the company sent out a comprehensive mailing, encouraging prospective customers with lifetime product guarantees and 45-day free trial periods. As orders flowed in, the firm increased production capacity by designing custom machinery from existing tooling. After some experimentation, the firm efficiently met production quotas.

As a result, through highly-resourceful marketing tactics, New Pig Corporation overcame a lack of production and distribution capabilities to become one of the fastest growing companies in the nation.

2.   *Is this a push or pull strategy?*

Direct marketing need not be a push strategy, though the word seems to describe much of direct marketing. By advertising to potential buyers, whether by mail or TV, and hoping orders will follow, a company is following a pull strategy. Since we know that New Pig also offered several push-like incentives, e.g., 45-day free trials, it could be said that the company utilized a combination strategy that combines elements of push strategy even though pull strategy is very much in evidence.

3.   *What promotional message should New Pig try to communicate through direct mail?*

The message should be one of product differentiation. The product offers a unique selling proposition that can provide substantial competitive advantage. As discussed in the chapter, other communication strategies such as positioning overlap the USP strategy and the product benefit can be positioned in the buyers' minds relative to competition (or not using the product). Further, encouraging prospective customers with lifetime product guarantees and 45-day free trial periods is a strong message in a direct mail campaign.

4.   *Should New Pig change its name?*

The name has an attention-getting quality and is memorable because it is so unusual. It does not communicate the product benefit until the buyer understands the product, i.e. that the product "eats up spills." However, after the benefit is understood it has a great recall quality because it actually does explain that the company no longer has to be a "pig" in its manufacturing operations.

CASE 17-2   ACTION FEDERAL SAVINGS AND LOAN

SUBJECT MATTER: Public Relations, Promotional Strategy

AT-A-GLANCE OVERVIEW

Action Federal has thirteen branches in a southeastern state, a state that had been suffering through a recession in its economy. The branches varied from sizable downtown locations to small suburban settings. Stories of bank failures had been common during this period. One day in January 1992, a K Mart assistant manager in the capital city refused to cash checks from Action Federal. A rumor quickly spread that Action was bankrupt. This began a "run" on the bank, and stories about the run further fueled rumors. The rumor was totally false, but accounts were being closed and millions of dollars withdrawn. Action needed an appropriate promotion strategy to quell the rumors and restore public confidence.

Instructors may or may not wish to call attention to two points. One is that the name of the organization is Action Federal S&L. Banks and S&L's may not use the word "federal" in their names unless they are chartered federally. To be federally chartered, a bank or S&L must be a member of the FDIC or FSLIC. Therefore, Action's depositors are insured by the federal government. This was not the case in the Ohio S&L closings that occurred during the mid-1980s nor in the later Rhode Island S&L situation. Those S&L's were insured by the states via inadequate funds and was misrepresented to depositors as essentially a federal insurance program. The problem faced here is more a marketing one than a financial one since Action Federal deposits are insured by the FSLIC.

The second point is that the promotional strategies Action needs should be both short run and long run in their focus. First stem the tide of mistrust, then repair the damage. Students will focus on the short term and largely ignore the long term unless reminded. One approach might be to allow this to occur, then turn the discussion specifically to the long-term strategy required.

Instructors may not wish to mention either of these points, permitting the students to discover them for themselves.

QUESTIONS

1.   *Design a promotional strategy for Action Federal Savings and Loan.*

This case provides a good example of how publicity can be negative and how the truth or lack of truth associated with it is virtually irrelevant over the short run.

In this case, the publicity received is the villain of the piece, and it will take a strategy focused on publicity to address the problem. Action Federal is not bankrupt. The strategy portrayed here might have been quite different had the corporation been in real economic difficulties.

Action has to "get the truth out" by whatever means it can. This includes "personal selling" by bank employees as they deal with fearful customers, "publicity" in the forms of interviews with reporters and other people in positions to influence publicity, "sales promotion" activities to the extent that these can be implemented in a short period of time, and advertising that supports the corporation's effort to spread the true story. Overall, it could be said that a combination promotional strategy, with greatest emphasis on the "pull" portion, would seem to be appropriate.

Some specific suggestions may be made in the context of the overall strategy: The governor or top banking officials could participate in Action's press conferences. These officials should be happy to help the bank in this situation. Local media people who have particular credibility could also be of assistance. For example, the local paper's financial columnists could be brought into the situation. Other credible people, like the dean of the state university's business school, could be asked for aid.

Other tactics might include developing a simplified financial statement that proves the corporation's financial health. Officials of other banks and S&L's might be willing to witness to the good standing of the Action Corporation in the hope that, should they be in a similar state, Action would help them.

In short, since Action is not broke the strategy must be to get the truth out in the most credible ways. The essence of promotion is communication. Promotion is the key element of the marketing mix at this time.

2.   *How important is timing in this situation? How will it influence the promotion strategy?*

Public relations has developed in three stages, much as has the marketing concept. The "final stage" has been to realize that stonewalling, lying, and using misleading information is almost always a terrible mistake. In short, the truth ... and the truth right now ... is the generally accepted and recommended

pattern of behavior.   Timing for Action Federal is a major problem. That is, with
literally each minute the problem gets worse for the firm, financially and
publicity-wise.   Action is faced with the classic "snowball effect":   each person
who withdraws funds contributes to the problem in dollar terms and in terms of
making the problem more visible to the public.   Action Federal must act today.

The promotion strategy is certainly affected by this urgency, as are the tactics.
Promotional efforts that require long lead times such image building TV
commercials would be difficult to employ.

Stemming the flow of withdrawals, Action's management will also have to think
about a long-term promotional strategy.   Once things are back to near-normal,
Action Federal will have to investigate the effects of the run on its image.   It
will then have to develop a promotion strategy to strengthen its perception by
the public.

Instructors may want to make this point before assigning the case so that
students will answer question 1 in long- and short-terms.   Otherwise, most
students will focus on the short-term problem and ignore the longer term.
Another approach would be to permit the students to dwell on the short term, then
restate the questions posed in the text so that classroom discussion can be
turned to the long term.

Here's what really happened:

Because the S&L involved in this case was federally insured it was not in danger
of being unable to "cover" its depositors.   However, its reputation could be
permanently sullied.   The "real" S&L is in Oklahoma, a state where the oil
business was in a period of decline and people were in such a mental state that
"the slightest little thing sets them off," according to a company
vice-president.   The vice-president relates that "as soon as we saw lines forming
we knew we had to do something."   Here are some of the things they did:

.   The firm happened to have just finished producing three 10-second
     television spots emphasizing the S&L's financial strength.   The marketing
     V.P. directed the advertising agent used by the S&L to saturate the market
     with the ad without worrying about getting good time slots.   The S&L, in
     short, blitzed the market.

.   The S&L took the approach that it had nothing at all to hide, and directed
     all employees to be totally honest with all questioners.

.   After the "run hysteria" died, down the S&L's CEO appeared in newspaper and
     TV ads thanking the public for its support "during the difficulty and
     confusion of the past several days," and reporting "first quarter earnings
     of $1.35 million" and the expectation that second quarter earnings would be
     twice that figure.   The ad was introduced on TV (and in large print in
     newspaper ads) as "A WORD FROM THE PRESIDENT OF OKLAHOMA'S LARGEST AND
     STRONGEST SAVINGS AND LOAN."

.   As a little icing on the cake, the S&L actually refunded $91,000 to
     depositors who had withdrawn certificates of deposits and paid the penalty
     fees required by the government for early withdrawal.

18 Advertising and public Relations

CHAPTER SCAN

Marketing is an art and a science. Advertising is the area of marketing where art is most obvious. This chapter differentiates among different types of advertising and traces the development of advertisements from the setting of a communication goal through media decisions. It also shows how advertisements are likely to change over the course of the product life cycle.

The chapter also discusses advertising appeals and several commonly used execution formats, the relative advantages of various media, and the measurement of the effectiveness of advertisements.

Finally, public relations and the management of publicity are described, and several ethical issues involving advertising and publicity are discussed.

SUGGESTED LEARNING OBJECTIVES

The student who studiesd this chapter will be exposed to a discussion of the advertising portion of the promotional mix and will be able to:

1. Understand the purpose of product advertising, direct-action advertising, and institutional advertising.

2. Know the difference between primary and selective demand advertising.

3. Discuss the stages in the development of an advertisement.

4. Analyze the role of communication objectives in the advertising process.

5. Show how advertisements for a product are likely to change over the course of the product's life cycle.

6. Define advertising appeal and describe several commonly used execution formats.

7.   Compare the advantages and disadvantages of various advertising media.

8.   Explain how advertising effectiveness is measured.

9.   Identify the nature of public relations and explain how publicity should be managed.

10. Discuss several ethical issues involving advertising and publicity.

CHAPTER OUTLINE

I.   INTRODUCTION

II.   THE NATURE OF ADVERTISING

A.   Product Advertising
B.   Institutional Advertising

III. PLANNING AND DEVELOPING ADVERTISING CAMPAIGNS

A.   Communication Goals for Advertising
B.   Specific Advertising Objectives
C.   Advertising Objectives and the Product Life Cycle
D.   Advertising the Mature Product

IV.   CREATIVE STRATEGY

A.   What to Say - The Appeal
B.   How to Say It - The Execution of the Appeal

1.   Storyline
2.   Product Uses and Problem Solutions
3.   Slice-of-Life
4.   Demonstration
5.   Testimonials
6.   Lifestyle
7.   Still Life
8.   Association
9.   Montage
10. Jingle
11. Other Formats

V.   PRODUCING AN EFFECTIVE ADVERTISEMENT

A.   Copy - The Verbal Appeal
B.   Art - The Visual Appeal
C.   Copy and Art Working Together: The AIDA Formula

1.   Attention
2.   Interest
3.   Desire
4.   Action
5.   How the AIDA Formula Works

VI.   MEDIA SELECTION

A.   Mass Media and Direct-Marketing Media
B.   Which Media?
C.   What Scheduling?

VII. MEASURING THE EFFECTIVENESS OF ADVERTISING

A.   Developing Messages and Pre-testing Advertisements
B.   Post-testing Commercials and Advertisements

1.   Measuring Brand Recognition and Recall
2.   Measuring Change in Attitudes About a Product

     C.   Generating Inquiries About a Product
     D.   Sales as a Measure of Advertising Effectiveness

VIII. PUBLIC RELATIONS

     A.   Publicity

           1.   News Releases
           2.   Press Conferences

     B.   Other Public Relations Tasks

IX.   ETHICAL ISSUES IN ADVERTISING AND PUBLIC RELATIONS

     A.   Deceptive and Misleading Practices

           1.   Misleading Advertising
           2.   Bait and Switch
           3.   Puffery

     B.   Public Standards
     C.   The Quality of Children's Lives

X.   SUMMARY

XI.   KEY TERMS

XII. QUESTIONS FOR DISCUSSION (15)

XIII. ETHICS IN PRACTICE

XIV. CASES

      The following key terms are introduced and used in Chapter 18. They are defined in the text's Glossary.

Product advertisement
Direct-action advertisement
Indirect-action advertisement
Institutional advertisement
Communication goals
Generic, or primary, demand
Primary demand advertising
Selective demand advertising
Creative process
Advertising appeal
Advertising theme
Execution format
Storyline format
Slice-of-life format
Demonstration format
Comparative advertising
Testimonial
Spokesperson
Lifestyle advertisement
Still-life advertisement
Association advertising format
Fantasy
Montage format
Commercial jingle
Copy
Art
AIDA
Media selection strategy
Media schedule, or media plan
Reach
Frequency
Gross rating points (GRPs)

Pre-testing
Post-testing
Recall tests
Unaided recall
Aided recall
Related recall
News release
Press conference
Misleading or deceptive advertising
Bait-and-switch advertising
Puffery

THE CHAPTER SUMMARIZED

I.   INTRODUCTION

Fog City Diner, an art deco restaurant in San Francisco, was featured in a
Visa advertisement. Media spending was five to six million dollars. The
restaurant, whose popularity had flagged until the commercial began
running, has had a tremendous surge in business. Advertising is powerful
indeed, and its effects can go far beyond the advertiser's original intent,
as this story shows.

II.   THE NATURE OF ADVERTISING

Communication experts identify these two types of messages:

Advertising is a persuasive message carried by nonpersonal media and
paid for by an identified sponsor. There are, then, two
considerations -- the message and the medium. Advertisements get no
immediate feedback, as can salespeople, but their advantages, such as
control over timing, outweigh this disadvantage when they are used in
the right way. Often the advertising message must be presented to
people who really don't want to hear or see it, or in the face of
many competing messages. Advertising must be, therefore, creative
and innovative to overcome these obstacles. Advertising can be a
topic of conversation, and thus an influencer of word-of-mouth
communication. Advertising can help publicize a public relations
event, help a salesperson get "a foot in the door," and perform other
functions.

One way of categorizing advertising is as product advertising or
institutional advertising.

A.   Product Advertising

A **product advertisement** advertises a specific product, e.g., Ford
trucks, and suggests that viewers act now and get a Ford truck
"today." This is also a **direct-action advertisement**, or **direct
response** advertisement. It features a specific product and attempts
to elicit an immediate response. Some ads of this type permit a
means to respond immediately -- return the card, call the 800 number,
and use your credit card.

An ad intended to bring about sales or some other action in the
longer run (e.g., "Vacation in Jamaica this year!") might be called
an **indirect-action advertisement**.

B.   Institutional Advertising

Institutional advertisements do not stress a particular product but a
larger institution as a whole ("Better Living Through Chemistry,"
"Sears Has Everything," or "Baseball Fever ... Catch It"). The goal
is promotion of goodwill rather than sale of a specific product or
baseball team.

III. PLANNING AND DEVELOPING ADVERTISING CAMPAIGNS

Exhibit 18-1 shows the flow of interconnected decisions that contribute to an effective advertising campaign. These are discussed below. Effective advertising campaigns must be developed as part of an overall marketing strategy and be tightly coordinated with other facets of the promotional mix.

A.   Communication Goals for Advertising

Goals must be decided before any work is begun. Advertising is a form of communication and has four broad **communication goals**:

. To generate attention
. To be understood
. To be believed
. To be remembered

If these are not met, no other goal can be met (as in creating a "romantic image" for a product.)

B.   Specific Advertising Objectives

Many "popular" ads that "everybody loved" have disappeared because they did not contribute to achieving specific objectives like increasing sales or building repeat business. "Great ads" that fail such tests are great only in a creative sense, not a business sense.

C.   Advertising Objectives and the Product Life Cycle

The objectives to be met by advertising vary over the course of the PLC (see Exhibit 18-2). At the start, the need is to develop **generic demand**, or **primary demand**, for the product class as a whole. That is: "This is what a VCR is. This is why you might want a VCR." This kind of advertising is called **primary demand advertising**, or pioneering advertising.

D.   Advertising the Mature Product

As products move beyond the introductory stage, ad objectives and campaigns invariably change. Ads no longer need to explain what the product is, they try instead to tell why a particular brand and/or model is the best of this product type. This is **selective demand advertising**. Messages tend to become more symbolic as the product moves to and through the maturity stage of the PLC since:

. Customers know now what it is and there is little need to explain it.

. Market segments and product positionings more greatly influence the nature of the appeal. Symbols are likely more important than facts at this stage.

For mature products the most common advertising objectives are to:

. Increase the number of buyers by converting buyers of competing brands, and appealing to new market segments;

. Increase the rate of usage among current buyers by reminding them to use the brand, informing them of new uses for the product, enhancing brand loyalty and reducing brand switching among current customers.

IV.   CREATIVE STRATEGY

Though the **creative process** is necessary in all aspects of marketing, the term has come to be particularly associated with advertising. Exhibit 18-4 attempts to show that while the answers to the questions "What to say" and "How to say it" are based on research and serious thought, there remains that hard-to-describe creative spark that contributes so much to developing advertisements and ad campaigns.

A.   What to Say -- The Appeal

The **advertising appeal** is the central idea of an advertising message.

The purpose of the appeal and of the advertisement is to tell potential buyers what the product offers and why it is, or should be, appealing to them.   Whether it has "sex appeal" or it "cures morning mouth."   The appeal may be straightforward -- "Removes hair from legs," or may stress an image -- "For today's young-at-heart woman."

When an advertising appeal is used in several different ads to provide continuity to an advertising campaign, it is called an **advertising theme.**   Whether straightforward or "catchy," the theme shows us that creativity is the lifeblood of advertising.

1.   An Example from the Brewing Industry

Beer marketers show great creativity in their advertising such as:

- Dixie is a "Part of Southern Living."
- Lone Star is the Texas beer, complete with armadillo.
- Lowenbrau is for special occasions ... "tonight."
- Bud Light shows singles having fun.
- Coors stresses high quality.

Competition is the reason.   They can't all just say that "It tastes great."   They must try to show consumers that they have distinctive competitive positions.   Creativity is an advertising tool AND a competitive tool.

B.   How to Say It -- The Execution of the Appeal

Swanson tried to sell TV dinners by showing exhausted women with no time to cook anything else.   It did not help sales because it seemed that women would rather not be reminded of how tired they are. Detergent and other "work related" ads follow this lesson.   They show peppy, happy users, not people cursing and sweating.   How you say it is as important as what you say.   How you say it, the style of the commercial message, is the **execution format** (see the examples listed below).

1.   Storyline

The **storyline advertisement** gives a history or tells a story about the product.

Examples: Saturn auto ads show how a town, a company, and its workers changed to build a new kind of automobile; vacation spots are shown in all their historical glory as the "home of kings" or some such.   Often use of an unseen announcer doing a voiceover makes the product the "hero" of the story being told.

2.   Product Uses and Problem Solutions

Some ads tell, in a straightforward manner, why the product is a solution to a problem and/or how the product is used to obtain that solution.

Examples: Crest fights tooth decay if used daily; Texaco gasoline will stop your car from pinging.

3.   Slice-of-Life

The **slice-of-life** ad dramatizes a "typical" setting where "real people" use the product with success.

Examples: Most laundry detergents, also breath fresheners, use this dramatized approach to the problem-solution format.

4. Demonstration

Some products particularly lend themselves to the **demonstration format.**

Examples: Locks that don't break open even after being shot with a Howitzer; ballpoint pens being shot through planks to show that they are tough even if they are disposable. Timex and Bic pens used these sorts of demonstrations for years.

A variation on this is **comparative advertising,** where one brand of a product is contrasted with another and demonstrated to be better.

Examples: Detergent whiteness tests, soft drink and beer taste tests, and Coke versus Pepsi. The FTC has lent support to this type of ad in the belief that the approach is good for competition.

5. Testimonials

Testimonials and endorsements have an individual, usually a celebrity of some type, state that he or she owns, likes, uses, or approves of the product in question. It is hoped that the **spokesperson** will be seen as an expert and/or an honest person who wouldn't lie about such things.

Examples: Leonard Nimoy (Mr. Spock) is an "expert" on matters of science. Bill Cosby and James Garner are so nice they can be believed no matter what the topic. Merlin Olsen sells FTD flowers. Some spokespersons, such as the Pillsbury Doughboy and the Keebler elves, are not even real but are, it seems, believable.

6. Lifestyle

The **lifestyle advertisement** shows scenes or sequences of situations intended to reflect the target market's lifestyle.

Example: Young people like hamburgers so Burger King and McDonald's both show people of this age group dropping in for a hamburger after a basketball game, movie, or day at the beach.

7. Still Life

Still life advertisements portray the product in a visually attractive setting. The format is used frequently in reminder advertising because the major goal is to reenforce the brand name.

8. Association

The **association advertising format** attempts to draw a relationship between a situation and the product. Sailing, Western scenes, and romantic scenes are all frequently used to sell coffee, beer, liquor, and cigarettes. Fantasy is a special case of the association format. It serves to associate the product with glamour and with dreams and hopes.

9. Montage

The **montage format** blends a number of situations together in a series of pictures or swirl of colors to suggest excitement and so many "payoffs" that it is almost impossible to show them all.

Example: Ads for vacation spots, such as Jamaica, use this format.

10.   Jingle

Commercial jingles have great memory value. Most of us, especially with a bit of help, can remember them nearly word-for-word even after they have been out of use for some time.

11.   Other Formats

Many other formats are possible: animation, special effects, computer graphics, etc. The discussion, to this point, should help the student to think of other formats and the way they work in effective marketing programs.

V.   PRODUCING AN EFFECTIVE ADVERTISEMENT

Advertisements consist of visual, verbal, and/or audio elements. How these are used depends on the people designing the ad and the medium they plan to use. The ultimate consideration is that ads reflect advertising objectives.

A.   Copy: The Verbal Appeal

The term **copy** refers to the words in an advertisement.

Even in TV or magazine ads, copy is likely to retain supremacy over other elements of the advertisement. Almost always, it is copy that gets the message across. Though we may see that one pile of laundry appears to be brighter than the other, the copy assures us that this is the case.

While some suggest that "too much" copy scares off viewers of print media ads, it is true that if the target reader is interested, he or she will read the copy. Thus, the bald man will read the lengthy ad about a cure for baldness.

B.   Art: The Visual Appeal

The term **art** is broadly used to mean all aspects of an advertisement other than its verbal portions.

Graphs, charts, pictures, and layout (including the use of white space) are all "art." Art is used to attract attention or to focus attention on key features of the product or the message. White space generally suggests quality, clutter and crowding suggests a discount or "cheap" image. Note the use of white space (or a simple color background highlighting an object) in newspaper and magazine ads.

C.   Copy and Art Working Together: The AIDA Formula

Most ads (except radio, of course) feature copy and art. These must work together to achieve a goal. A commonly used "formula" that encompasses this idea is AIDA (Attention, Interest, Desire, Action).

1.   Attention

An effective ad must draw attention. Copy can be used to do this as can eye-catching art or a picture that makes the viewer pause to wonder "What's going on here?" Radio relies on words to attract attention, perhaps using a mysterious or humorous beginning to attract the listener's interest.

2.   Interest

If the attention-getter is strong enough, interest should follow, but it may be necessary to help it along such as by describing how the product can be of use to the viewer or listener.

3.   Desire

Most ads try to arouse desire by showing a result of product
use that is thought to be desirable by the target viewer.
Example: The "pay-off" for the man who hires ChemLawn to
green-up his lawn is shown to be relaxing in a hammock while
his poor, suffering neighbor struggles in the hot sun with
chemicals and equipment.

4.   Action

Notice that most ads include a call for action. Examples: (1)
Phone ChemLawn today; (2) find HFC in the white pages of your
phone book; (3) call this toll-free number for the name of the
Toro dealer nearest you. Provision of a toll-free number or a
note that credit is available help make action easy to take.

5.   How the AIDA Formula Works

The four-step AIDA formula is based on an understanding of
consumer behaviors and mental processes. It is a good, common
sense tool, and serves as a guideline for ad writers. Of
course, one exposure to even a good ad might not bring about
the desired result. Repetition of the message may be needed
for it to "sink in." Further, the target consumer's situation
might change from day to day (a payday or a tax return may
arrive) and he or she might then see the message in a different
light.

VI.   MEDIA SELECTION

Media selection strategy rests on the message to be transmitted, the
audience to be reached, the effect intended, and the budget available. Two
overall questions may be posed:

.   Which media will efficiently get the message to the desired audience?

.   What scheduling will neither bore the audience with repetition nor
     make it too easy to forget the message?

A.   Mass Media and Direct-Marketing Media

Exhibit 18-5 shows the individual media, both mass media and direct-
marketing media. Technological advances have greatly improved the
selectivity of direct-marketing media such as direct mail. Access to
data bases, the ability to customize and personalize messages
(referencing family members, for example), and identifying loyal
customers or customers loyal to other products, are all part of this
improved technology.

B.   Which Media?

Certain media lend themselves to certain tasks. Print media
generally permit lengthy messages, radio and billboards are best for
quick reminders, etc. These sorts of advantages and disadvantages
are summarized in Exhibit 18-6. Once it has been decided what to
say, the planner's attention can be turned to where to say it: what
medium or combination of media would be best? At this point the
media expert becomes a market expert, determining which medium or
combination of media will best reach the target market. A good
example is Crayola, which addresses some of its ads to mothers and
some to children.

1.   Media Strengths and Weaknesses

See Exhibit 18-6.

C.   What Scheduling?

The **media schedule** or **media plan** is a time schedule identifying the exact media to be used and the dates on which advertisements are to appear.

Selecting media vehicles involves considering **reach**, the number of people exposed to an ad in a given medium. Of course, cost considerations must also be taken into account. Another matter is repetition or the **frequency** of the advertising message in a given medium within a given time period. These two variables can be combined to calculate **gross rating points** (**GRPs**) which is reach (in percentage points) times frequency. For example, four placements on a news show that reaches 25 percent of the market equals 100 gross ratings points. Again, realities such as the budget, the target market, etc., must be considered by the marketer.

VII. MEASURING THE EFFECTIVENESS OF ADVERTISING

It is very difficult to measure the effectiveness of advertising. Tools to do this exist but they are not at all exact measures. However, the costs of advertising are so great that it is not a good idea to ignore even inexact measuring tools.

A.   Developing Messages and Pre-testing Advertisements

Ads can and should be subject to **pre-testing**. "Roughs" of ads may be shown to groups of people much like those for whom the "finished" ad is intended. Different spokespeople may be taped and shown to consumers, thus checking the effectiveness and believability of the spokespersons. Example: Raquel Welch did not "test well" for a home-use hair coloring kit because the sample viewers did not believe she would actually use an in-home-use product. Versions of ads may be tested in actual home settings (in-home projector tests) or in specially set-up buses or trailers (trailer tests).

B.   Post-testing Commercials and Advertisements

Ads can be subjected to **post-testing** to see if they have met their objectives, though absolutely accurate measurement is impossible. Notice that established objectives are needed if success is to be gauged.

1.   Measuring Brand Recognition and Recall

Ads must be noticed and brands made familiar or they cannot be called successful. Thus tests of brand recognition and ad **recall tests** are common measures of ad effectiveness. The two general types of tests are **unaided recall** and **aided recall**. Another type is **related recall**, a test wherein respondents are asked to describe, or "play back," ads. The ones best described would appear to be the most remembered. The Starch Advertisement Readership Service uses respondent recognition of print media ads to make similar judgments.

2.   Measuring Change in Attitudes About a Product

Effective advertisements can contribute to changing attitudes about a product. This suggests a two-part study of measuring attitudes before and after exposure to a message. The general format is to ask questions about a product, then show the ad messages to the subject, then ask a similar batch of questions. This serves to give some indication of the clarity and effectiveness of the ad.

C.   Generating Inquiries About a Product

For some ads (such as direct mail ads), the number of inquiries generated is a good measure of effectiveness, and the inquiries

probably come from people actually interested in buying the product.
Coupons returned might also be counted.

D.   Sales as a Measure of Advertising Effectiveness

Why not measure ad success with sales totals alone? Ultimately, of
course, sales is a measure, but sales of many goods and services rely
on the state of the economy, derived demand, or some other variable
rather than ads. Some ads, too, are intended to generate long-term
results making sales a difficult-to-employ measure of their effects.
Perhaps advertisements featuring a coupon or 800 number do permit a
fairly direct measure of sales effectiveness.

VIII. PUBLIC RELATIONS

Publicity is "free" but controlled by an outside party such as a newspaper
editor. However, it can be as effective as advertising and so should be
planned. This is often the duty of the organization's public relations
department. The purpose of public relations is to actively manage
publicity to maintain a positive image. After all, publicity can be good
or bad.

A.   Publicity

Publicity can serve many purposes, e.g., to provide consumers or
other public interest groups with useful information, to change
attitudes, or to combat negative publicity.

In any event, to get in the news the information must be newsworthy,
as when Magic Johnson was asked to work on the government's AIDS Task
Force.

1.   News Releases

A **news release** is typically a brief summary describing a
newsworthy aspect of a new product (e.g., a candy bar that
won't melt when the temperature reaches 100 degrees and that
"proved itself" in the desert during Operation Desert Storm).
News releases are usually designed to be used with ease by
editors and others.

2.   Press Conferences

The **press conference** is used when the organization wishes to
make a specific announcement before representatives of the mass
media, as when a pro football team introduces its newly signed
college All Star.

B.   Other Public Relations Tasks

All messages about the organization affect the public's perceptions.
Thus, managers must not overlook the coordination of public relations
with other forms of promotion. Sometimes public relations (such as
by the government) is really sales called by a different name.
Exhibit 18-8 illustrates the fact that public relations includes more
than just publicity.

IX.   ETHICAL ISSUES IN ADVERTISING AND PUBLIC RELATIONS

Advertising and public relations are frequently the focus of ethical
debate.

A.   Deceptive and Misleading Practices

Society grants consumers the right to be informed and prohibits
deceptive practices that intentionally mislead consumers, e.g., what
are the odds of winning a sweepstakes?

1.   Misleading Advertising

An area of particular concern is **misleading** or **deceptive** advertising. The F.T.C. Act of 1914 makes it illegal to run dishonest advertisements. Other laws and court cases aimed at the worst cases are many. Consumerism draws additional attention to the matter.

It is difficult to say what is "misleading." Is sugar or NutraSweet lower in calories and better for your teeth? The Sugar Association claims that sugar is best and that NutraSweet ads are misleading. NutraSweet's maker does not agree.

2.   Bait and Switch

Bait and switch involves advertising a product at a very low price then trying to switch a buyer to higher-priced products. But who would expect a salesperson not to try to sell higher priced or unadvertised products? Probably a clearly unethical practice would be using an unavailable product as the "bait."

3.   Puffery

Puffery is the practice of stating opinions or exaggerations in an advertisement or other promotion. "Most exciting movie ever!!!" is an example. Where does acceptable puffing stop and lying commence? The F.T.C. or a judge may have to decide.

B.   Public Standards

Matters of law and ethics are often based on beliefs as to what is right and proper, or on what somebody thinks public standards are. Should ads be "sexy?" Should liquor and tobacco be advertised? Should some products be denied to minors? Some condemn certain TV shows; others say "Turn it off if you don't like it." Some part of this difficulty may be addressed by noting that many market segments exist. If you think Preparation H ads are disgusting, is it possible that people who need the product do not?

C.   The Quality of Children's Lives

Marketing to children is almost always controversial. Advertisements are seen by some as causing problems in children's lives, or as misleading susceptible youngsters. Others see the process as one of socializing children, preparing them to live in this world. Food products, like sugar-laden cereals, are a favorite target, but cereal producers argue that the bowl of Frosted Flakes should be considered as just a part of the child's total daily intake.

X.   SUMMARY

Advertising is the promotional activity in which the art of marketing is most visible. Public relations involves the management of publicity, along with many other aspects of an organization's relationships with its environment.

Learning Objective 1:   Understand the purpose of product advertising, direct-action advertising, and institutional advertising.

Product advertising promotes the attributes, benefits, uses, and images of specific products. Direct-action advertising encourages immediate action. Institutional advertising promotes an organization or industry as a whole, stressing goodwill, image, and contributions to society, or stimulates generic demand for a product category.

Learning Objective 2: **Differentiate between primary demand and selective demand advertising.**

Primary demand (or generic demand) advertising promotes a product category without stressing particular brands. Selective demand advertising accents a particular brand.

Learning Objective 3: **Discuss the stages in the development of an advertisement.**

Advertisements are developed in six basic steps: (1) setting objectives consistent with the marketing strategy, (2) determining a creative strategy, (3) developing the advertising message, (4) formulating a media selection strategy, (5) measuring effectiveness and (6) setting the advertising budget. Creativity is at work throughout the process.

Learning Objective 4: **Analyze the role of communication objectives in the advertising process.**

Because advertising must communicate with target markets, its communication goals must be clearly defined. All advertisements must gain attention, be understood, be believed, and be remembered.

Learning Objective 5: **Show how advertisements for a product are likely to change over the course of the product's life cycle.**

In the introductory stage, advertisements must help to develop primary demand for the product category by explaining what the product is and how it works, with little stress on brand name. In the growth stage, they seek to develop selective demand for particular brands and models. In the maturity stage, they stress product images or features that set the product apart from its competitors in order to maintain market share and enhance brand loyalty. During the decline stage, advertising efforts help phase out the product.

Learning Objective 6: **Define advertising appeal and describe several commonly used execution formats.**

The advertising appeal conveys information about product benefits to the target audience. After answering the question "What to say?," the marketer must answer the question "How to say it?" The execution formats include: storyline (a story about the product or its history); product uses and problem solution (how a product can be employed to solve a problem); slice-of-life (a dramatization of how the product solved a particular problem); demonstrations (how the product is used); testimonials (spokespersons attest to the product's worth); lifestyle (links a product to the target customer's own or aspired-to lifestyle); still life (focuses on visual aspects of the products); association (draws an analogy to convey a message); montage (blends a number of visual effects); and jingles (especially effective as memory aids).

Learning Objective 7: **Compare the advantages and disadvantages of various advertising media.**

Each medium has advantages and disadvantages. Magazines and newspapers, which permit the customer to reread a message, are suitable for longer, more complicated messages. Magazines can carry clear pictures better than newspapers. Radio seems best suited for reminders or other short messages for specific target groups. Television permits the use of music, motion, and color. Outdoor advertising is appropriate for short messages but may be limited in its reach. The appropriate mix of advertising media depends on the advertising budget and objectives.

Learning Objective 8: **Explain how advertising effectiveness is measured.**

Pre-testing evaluates effectiveness before an advertisement is placed in the mass media; post-testing determines if the actual media-run advertisement achieved its objectives. Sales are the ultimate measure of effectiveness, but the relationship of advertising to sales is difficult to measure.

>   **Learning Objective 9**: **Identify the nature of public relations and explain how publicity should be measured.**

Public relations is the managerial activity that identifies, establishes, and maintains beneficial relationships between an organization and its publics. Its specific purposes are to enhance the organizational image and to convey product information. Favorable publicity can have the same impact as advertising. Hence, effective marketers plan publicity with as much care and consideration as they give to the rest of the promotional mix.

>   **Learning Objective 10**: **Discuss several ethical issues involving advertising and sales promotion.**

Our society grants consumers the right to be informed and prohibits deceptive practices and promotions that intentionally mislead consumers. Hence, deceptive advertising is illegal; but it may be difficult to identify. Questions about what public standards should be used in advertising may also present ethical dilemmas for marketers. Another issue involves advertising to children. Children are a special public, and there is disagreement about whether advertising aimed at this public is ethical.

XI.   KEY TERMS

XII.   QUESTIONS FOR DISCUSSION (15)

XIII. ETHICS IN PRACTICE

XIV.   CASES

ANSWER GUIDELINES FOR CHAPTER 18 QUESTIONS FOR DISCUSSION

1.   *Indicate whether the advertising in the following instances is aimed at indirect or direct action: (a) Macy's holds its Fourth of July sale; (b) Nintendo advertises that its home unit would be a nice Christmas gift; (c) "Hertz is Number One for Everyone" car rental ad is launched; (d) the California raisin growers promote raisins as a snack food.*

ANSWER:

It can be argued that even a direct-action advertisement has some indirect action effect. Thus, a direct action ad like "Buy a Sears refrigerator this week during Sears' Special Sale Days" has some indirect or long-term effect in that a person who does not need a refrigerator now might, years later, recall that Sears has refrigerators and has sales occasionally, then proceed to buy a Sears refrigerator. There is a saying to this effect, "All ads are institutional ads," which is intended to remind us of this likely long-term effect.

(a) Macy's Fourth of July sale

Macy's Fourth of July sale is primarily a direct action ad intended to build traffic on this "special sale day." Most stores in Washington, D.C. have "super" sales on Washington's Birthday with the same intent. However, there is a bit of indirect sale effect in both of these in that each annual sale carries on and adds to a tradition. Someone seeing Macy's ads may not go to the sale this year but may decide to go next year for sure.

(b)   Nintendo's home unit

Nintendo's ad suggesting its home unit as a Christmas gift is almost entirely a direct-action ad. An 800 number would make it almost 100% direct action. However, the expected response (lots of sales) and the rest of the marketing mix (e.g., easy availability at nearby stores) may negate the need for an 800 number.

Some viewers of the ad may resolve to buy a Nintendo right after the Christmas rush when "prices go down." Even in this case, however, we still see this as an almost entirely direct-action ad.

(c)   "Hertz is Number One for Everyone"

"Hertz is Number One for Everyone" is an indirect action ad in that it is essentially an institutional, image-building ad. The slogan does not instruct listeners to rent a car today, or even soon, nor does it accent current rates or other deals.

The slogan itself is of some debatable value in that the phrase "For Everyone" seems to go against the basic tenets of market segmentation. Campaigns that are aimed at everyone are often symptomatic of "what went wrong" in textbook case studies.

(d)   California raisin growers

The California raisin growers have attempted to promote raisins as a snack food for years, long before the advent of the dancing, singing Claymation "California Raisins." Similar efforts have been undertaken by producers of other fruits including prune growers. That group ran a series of quite humorous ads about prunes.

The raisin promotion is essentially a direct action effort aimed at increasing the consumption of raisins; however, it has some indirect applications as well. If people try raisins now, or try them again if it's been awhile since they had some, it is hoped they will continue to use raisins as a snack food far into the future. Their use of raisins will be passed on to their children, etc. So, there is an indirect action aspect to the promotional effort.

The famous dancing raisins won a lot of recognition. The ads were clever, the characters appeared on t-shirts and other items, and the ads were a big success. At this writing, the jury is still out on how successful over the long run the attempt to win raisins a spot in the snack food line-up will be. The times are right: health conscious society, "natural foods" preferences, avoidance of sugar, etc., are all in place. But many famous ads have gone by the wayside when it was discovered that people loved the ads and the characters in them, but weren't buying the product they sold.

2.   *When does advertising stimulate primary demand? When should it?*

ANSWER:

There are many situations in which advertising can be or should be used to stimulate primary demand. Some examples include:

.   When a product is so new to the market that it must be explained and introduced to potential buyers.

.   When all suppliers can profit from stimulation or diminution of demand, e.g., "Shop Rolling Acres Mall" or "Conserve Natural Gas."

.   When one supplier has such a big portion of the market that advertising the product class makes as much sense as advertising the brand, e.g., "Cranberry Juice for Breakfast."

.   When the public interest at large can be served -- "Support the college of your choice."

.   When demand for a product (e.g., ink) is being affected by a decline in demand for a product from which its demand is derived (e.g., fountain pens). The ink-supported ad might encourage the use of fountain pens: "Nothing looks like, nothing writes like, a real pen."

.   When demand is cyclical or highly restricted by time in some way. "Orange juice isn't just for breakfast any more" is a good example of the latter. The cranberry industry's success in selling berry-products throughout the year (thirty years ago few sales were made other than at Thanksgiving and Christmas) is an example of the former.

Note that most ads, even if they mention brands specifically, do serve to stimulate primary demand by reminding those who see or hear them of the product class and, perhaps, inspiring a search for the product which ends in the purchase of another brand.

3.   *Inspect several TV commercials and determine what the advertising objective is for each one.*

ANSWER:

This is clearly an "individual project," but it can also be accomplished in class by: discussing familiar ads, using magazine ads, using the ads in the text, or choosing advertising transparencies to discuss in class.

4.   *Identify three institutional advertisements and explain their purpose.*

ANSWER:

This is, like 3, an individual project. However, the book does show some ads that are primarily institutional. Others could be brought into class and are also included in the advertising transparencies for the text.

5.   *Identify some beer advertisements other than those mentioned in the textbook and compare them to the ones shown in the textbook.*

ANSWER:

Again we have an individual project but one that can have a special local flavor. Though regional breweries have been disappearing in recent decades, many rely on a local flavor in their ads. Further, even large brewers inject local colorings into their ads, e.g., campus motif or local geographic or man-made "sights" such as the St. Louis arch or the Alamo. Other ads might be found to emphasize beer attributes not mentioned in the text. Meisterbrau has accented price "As good as Bud, but much cheaper." Other beers do this less directly. The Blatz and Schlitz tastes test "showed" that Blatz to be as good as beers with far more exalted reputations. Others do much the same. The success of this approach has inspired local imitators like Goebels (a "reasonably price" Mid-Western beer).

6.   *Does the AIDA formula have more relevance for the writing of advertising copy or the visual art aspect of advertising?*

ANSWER:

The AIDA formula -- Attention, Interest, Desire, Action -- reflects human nature rather than advertising or the thinking of advertising experts. We all use "the formula" in regular conversation. Street peddlers in Babylon used it when "calling their wares" making noise to attract attention, and using words describing the wares and their prices to arouse interest and desire. George Washington was the focus of "the formula" when he encountered a tavern sign at the "Bucket-O-Ale" in Williamsburg. Thus, the formula has, and has had, a great deal of appeal for writers of copy and for those using pictures to get their messages across.

As the text suggests, the elements of a promotional message should work together. Most messages, other than those on radio, have verbal and visual aspects that can combine to "do the job." AIDA works for both.

7.   *Describe the steps in developing a creative strategy.*

ANSWER:

Describing the development of a creative strategy is probably easier than actually developing one. This admitted, we move on to a description of the creative strategy remembering that the discussion must perforce be flawed by the near impossibility of describing the "creative spark," the ineffable talent that contributes so strongly to the process.

The text describes the development of the creative strategy in terms of:

- What To Say -- The Appeal
- How To Say It -- The Execution

This last section includes a discussion of the various formats that might be employed.   This is covered in the text.

Another way of looking at the process is presented below.

- Assess marketing communications opportunities.
- Analyze marketing communications resources.
- Set marketing communications objectives.
- Develop and evaluate alternative marketing communications strategies.
- Assign specific marketing communications tasks.

While for our purposes we might substitute the word "advertising" for "communication," students who have gone this far through the text should be able to see that advertising is but a part of the total communication mix.   It should, therefore, be evaluated in terms of and be consistent with that mix.   Perhaps the above steps should be discussed in class so that this point may be brought home.

8.   *What type of spokesperson would you utilize in a testimonial advertisement for each of the following products: (a) Campaign against alcohol abuse; (b) Campaign to encourage cigar smoking; and (c) Campaign for high quality luggage.*

ANSWER:

"Spokespersons" can be famous people (celebrities of one kind or another), "real" people (little-known actors or non-celebrities or folks like you and me), or animated spokespeople like Tony the Tiger.

(a)   Alcohol abuse

Veteran actor Jason Robards, a reformed alcoholic, speaks honestly in his ads against alcohol as have Dana Andrews, Betty Ford, Elizabeth Taylor, and some rock performers and athletes.   Might as well have someone who knows what they are talking about.   Many other celebrity possibilities come to mind.

"Real" people have also been effective, non-celebrities who talk about how alcohol has ruined their lives either because they, or members of their families, drank to excess.   Not all persons doing such ads are alcoholics, some are paid actors, but they "look right" for the part.

"Imaginary" spokespeople might be used to appeal to children to watch out for demon rum.   Popeye and the Star Wars robots have been "employed" to do health-oriented ads of this type, though the target is usually smoking.   These days, however, young children have to be warned about drugs, drinking, pregnancy, AIDS, etc.

(b)   Cigar smoking

Cigar smoking has been in rapid decline.   George Burns has been used to promote cigars, as have younger, typically non-celebrity people.   Cartoon or other imaginary characters are not beyond possibility, though these would probably have to be invented for the occasion.   No one would jeopardize the future use of Mickey Mouse or Popeye by putting them in cigar ads.   Even Mark Twain quit smoking pipes in 1983.

(c)   Campaign for high quality luggage

We are taking the position that "high quality" refers to workmanship and expense, that the product is top-of-the-line stuff.   (If "high quality" is taken to mean "unbreakable," other answers might follow.   After all, Samsonite used a gorilla playing with its tough suitcases as a "spokesperson" of a sort).

Expensive luggage would most likely be associated with travel to glamour spots like San Francisco, Paris, Rome, or Rio.   This suggests that the spokesperson be someone perceived as the type who makes exciting trips to such places or someone who looks like they do. Movie and television personalities associated with glamour, like the women in "evening soap operas" or perhaps Elizabeth Taylor or a younger equivalent, come to mind. Lesser known actresses and models (or even unknowns) who look the part could also be used. (Do you remember Rhula Lenska, a British actress, unknown in the U. S., who was on TV ads for several years?) While the ad is for Quality Hotels rather than luggage, the Penguin character from the Batman movie is a spokesperson.

It is often wise to use Chuck E. Cheese, Mr. Munch, Captain Crunch, various cartoon characters, characters invented to fit a particular product, and other "controllable" sorts of characters. They can be fun-loving, wisecracking symbols of joy, and hold a cartoon character fascination for kids and adults. Yet they have no lives of their own to be embarrassing to shop owners nor do they refuse to make certain ads or to appear at grand openings, and they never hold out for more money.

9.   *Suppose you are the creative director for an advertising agency that has just landed the Cleopatra Soap account, a new introduction to the market. Suggest a creative advertising strategy.*

ANSWER:

Cleopatra is a name that has been associated with beauty for over 2,000 years. It is safe to assume that the soap is a "beauty bar" aimed at women. This suggests that the basic advertising strategy be one of developing awareness (this is a new market entry) but awareness of the product as a special sort of soap ... say, luxurious, special, for "beautiful women." It is likely that the soap is a bit expensive, thus the basic theme is likely to be something like, "Cleopatra soap. For special women who care about their beauty ... and think it's worth the price to care."

The major difficulty here is that there are many soaps of all types on the market. Thus, part of the strategy must be to set Cleopatra apart from the others. If we assume that it has no unique-to-the-market ingredient, the difference will have to be less concrete. The product could be shown to be the soap that beautiful jet-set women use, in a montage advertisement showing the glamorous capitals of the world.

Like many of the questions included in this chapter the answer depends very much on the individual writing it. Thus, whatever the student proposes should be defended against such questions as: What is the target market? How will the ads change as the product gains familiarity? (And so on.)

10.   *What advertising media would you select for the following products? Why? (a) A local zoo (b) Local amusement park (c) Local clothing store (d) National soft drink.*

ANSWER:

In this answer we have focused entirely on advertising though, obviously, some other promotional means would likely be used and must be kept in mind.

(a)   Local zoo

Local zoos tend not to have huge advertising budgets thus any low-cost advertising means that might be available should be considered. Example: "Piggybacking" with other local "community assets" such as the Y, the Art Museum, or other groups that have or use ad media (like newspapers or newsletters.) Direct mail pieces, if a good list is available to people who go to local attractions. Of course, any free publicity should be obtained, but this is not advertising.

Most people in the area are likely to know of the zoo's existence. What is needed is ad media that can be used to remind people to go to the zoo. Billboards and brief radio spots would seem to be in order. Some TV stations do sell brief spots for local advertisers. Though TV is thought to be expensive, such local spots may be bargains.

(b)   Local amusement park

Amusement parks in general need to show the "great fun" they offer, especially since such parks usually cost a fair amount of money to go to once all the snacks and other extras are added in. Thus media that show that the fun is worth it are required. TV is such a medium. Cleverly designed billboards, e.g., showing a roller coaster in action, also serve the purpose. Radio "reminder" ads would supplement the other two media as might newspaper ads containing admission discount coupons.

(c)   Local clothing store

Local clothing stores, and other retailers, use newspapers most heavily of all media. This is because likely customers look to newspapers as a traditional source of information about sales. Too, newspapers can show pictures of clothing for sale ... not great pictures but magazines, except for local magazines (if any,) don't make economic sense for most local stores. Further, the lead time for placing newspaper ads is very short.

(d)   A national soft drink advertiser

Such an advertiser, with a national market made up of many customers, could use any media. TV, radio, magazines, newspapers, billboards, and many lesser media are all used, though some are left to local bottlers, e.g., newspapers so that locally sponsored coupons may be provided, and billboards with their emphasis on local markets.

Of course, to say that all media might be used is overdoing it a bit. Vehicles within media (e.g., particular radio stations, magazines, or TV shows) might be known to have special appeal to certain target groups. Much time and effort is spent on identifying these.

11.   *What are some reasons for pre-testing and post-testing specific advertisements? What are the best ways to do the testing?*

ANSWER:

Ads should be pre-tested for effectiveness, clarity, and general acceptability by the target markets. On a local level, we often find newspaper ads, campus announcements of meetings, etc. that are:

.   Ineffective, e.g., written in an ink that is almost impossible to read or incapable of doing the job.

.   Unclear, e.g., is the admission for the dance $8 per person or couple? When is the dance and where? The people who made up the sign forgot to put that information on it.

.   Unacceptable in that they have an aura of snobbishness, or some other unattractive aspect.

In general, then, pre-testing is used to discover which of several messages and/or media choices is best to get the message across and to determine if the message is proper and complete, given the communication goals. Pre-testing usually takes place in face-to-face situations, e.g., malls, or in media-like tests such as research done using theaters to show commercials to panels.

Post-testing is associated with determining whether or not the objectives of the advertisements were met. Surveys taken in late 1988 and early 1989 may indicate that sales have gone up by 1/3 in four months, that brand name recognition has doubled, etc. If these were the goals of the ads being run, it would appear that they are good ones.

Consider the following item.

ARE YOU GETTING RESULTS?

Achievement of advertising objectives is the standard by which to measure success.   Consider these different advertising objectives and the associated results.

OBJECTIVE: To introduce a new premium beer -- Christian Schmidt Classic.

RESULTS: The introductory TV commercial scored 64% on Favorable Buying Attitude vs. a beer norm of 25%.

OBJECTIVE: To shift emphasis from consumer usage of Yellow Pages to a program encouraging advertisers to run larger ads.

RESULTS: A 75% awareness of the advertising message among business customers, and a 15% or greater annual sales increase since the inception of the program.

OBJECTIVE: To introduce a new SKF spherical bearing design.

RESULTS: Over 1,000 qualified leads, the highest readership scores in the product category, and a significant increase in the perception of SKF as the leading innovator in bearings.

OBJECTIVE: To maximize sales by introducing a variety of lottery games designed to appeal to the broadest possible audience.

RESULTS: Pennsylvania Lottery sales have grown by millions each year.

OBJECTIVE: To increase awareness of the Exide Edge car battery (a low interest category), by 50%.

RESULTS: In 12 weeks, awareness increased 125% (from 24% to 54%). Distribution grew from 30 dealers to 200 dealers.

Based on information in an advertisement for Lewis Gilman, 1700 Market Street, Philadelphia, PA 19103.

12.   *An urban university is planning on advertising its educational programs in local newspapers. What type of creative strategy would you utilize? Be specific.*

ANSWER:

A newspaper ad would need to attract attention. It would seem to "hang its hat" on something that could remain with the reader and get him or her thinking about:

.   Going (or going back) to school and,
.   Going to XYZ College because it is good and/or cheap and/or convenient.

Here are some ways schools have sought to respond to the creative strategy question of "what to say?"

"Is there life after work?" University of Akron

"Be a road scholar." University of Akron

"A degree of excellence." LaSalle University

"For now . . . For life." Kent State University

"Opportunity. It's happening for you at Roosevelt." Roosevelt University

"Weekend college is the only way I could complete my college degree." North Central College

"For the big change in your life ... Now is the time ... Governors State University is the place ... Wishful thinking won't get you the things you want out of life." Governors State University

"Any school can satisfy the masses! Lakeland College serves you, the individual." Lakeland College

"Build your Career at the City Colleges of Chicago." Chicago City Colleges

"Loyola University is the MetroVersity," Loyola University of Chicago

"Build your future by degrees. Moonlight at Northwestern" (and) "If you can afford night school, you can afford Northwestern." Northwestern University

13.   *What type of marketers emphasize public relations in their promotional mixes? Why?*

ANSWER:

One answer to this question is that marketers who are not financially well-off are likely to emphasize public relations because public relations is "free."

Another, more common situation, is that marketers who do advertise extensively often use public relations to supplement that advertising. For example, I.B.M., Disneyland, General Motors. All these, and many more, advertise their products but never pass up a chance to gain favorable publicity ... a new voice-activated P.C., the fact that the umpteenth millionth visitor has passed through Disney's gates, or the development of an electric car ... all these will "make the news."

The IBM situation shows how public relations can help a personal sales force. The sales person from IBM has an advantage over sales people from other companies just because everybody knows, via publicity, that IBM is a leader in its field and produces quality products.

The phrase "award winning" is tossed around by manufacturers, authors, radio and TV stations, newspapers, magazines, and so on ... the awards they have won are publicity.

Another type of marketer is likely to make heavy use of public relations ... the marketer of a personality like Madonna, Prince, Michael Jackson, and so on. Many of these people do outrageous things, pretend to be "involved" with other famous persons, and so on, simply because they are what used to be called publicity hogs. In fact, of course, they are using public relations as a big part of their promotional mixes.

In short, any marketer whose product can be considered somewhat newsworthy, new mall developer to movie starlet, could emphasize public relations in its marketing mix.

14.   *Discuss how a political candidate for national office might develop strategies for both advertising and public relations.*

ANSWER:

Political candidates, these days, must spend a great deal of money on advertising. Even local elections can consume considerable advertising budgets since so much of the advertising is likely to be the most expensive sort - television.

It is therefore important that advertising dollars be spent where they will do the most good. Target markets must be selected and reached. Advertisements must cater to the desires of particular market segments (groups of voters). Thus, advertisements in *Senior Citizen News*, or on stations in Florida, tend to emphasize the candidate's concern with issues facing the elderly, like health care and Social Security.

However, the strategy must be internally consistent to avoid problems and to preclude the opposition from seizing on inconsistencies in messages and capitalizing on these.   How often do we hear things like this ... "He said he's going to balance the budget when he was talking to group A, but then he promised to spend billions on defense when he was talking to group B."

This need to avoid giving the impression of being inconsistent (or worse, dumb or a liar), and to avoid giving the "other guy" a stick to beat you with, requires development of a good, overall promotional strategy.   And that includes public relations.   Giving a speech in Toledo is public relations since, one hopes, that speech will be covered "free" by the local media.   But the media is famous for carrying only short excerpts of what is said, and for emphasizing slips of the tongue (just ask Dan Quayle).

In fact, in the 1992 election, President Bush was attacked (negative public relations) for not visiting certain cities to speak (one was Toledo, Ohio).   The reason for not visiting was that these cities were doing poorly economically and almost certain to vote for Clinton.   Why then should Bush waste time speaking in them?   One reason is he was castigated for not giving speeches in places that were admittedly hostile to him.

Development of a political promotional strategy is much the same as developing any promotional strategy.   One needs an objective, information about the market and the segments it contains and how to reach them, information on the availability of resources, a means to monitor changes in the market and the market's reaction to the candidate's promotion, and that ineffable thing "the creative spark."   It was the "spark" that led to successful slogans like "New Frontier," "New Deal,"   "The Only Thing We Have To Fear is Fear Itself,"   "There You Go Again, Mr. President," and "I Knew Jack Kennedy And You Are No Jack Kennedy."

15.   *Provide some examples of unethical advertising and sales promotion efforts? Why are they unethical?*

ANSWER:

Students will, of course, vary in their answers to this.   The whole point of ethical problems is that they are viewed differently by different people.   Among the possible ads that may be considered unethical are any for "sin products" like alcohol or cigarettes.   (The authors of the text have received letters from professors here and there complaining about our use of tobacco and alcohol products as examples in the text.)   Ads for sports cars feature dangerous products.   Ads for just about anything at all encourage use of natural resources and the creation of garbage in one form or another.   Ads for something "new" encourage people to throw out older but serviceable products and buy the new product.   Ads that show well-off people inspire the poorer person to turn to crime to get what the rich people have, or, at minimum, show that person how rotten his own life is.   In fact, almost any ad you can find suggests some ethical difficulty.   Ads suggesting you go to church this week are seen, by the atheist, as the most unethical rip offs.

More likely to raise ethical questions are ads glamorizing products that are dangerous or "bad for you," especially if these are aimed at particular market segments, especially children.   Cigarette ads aimed at women are "bad" in that cancer rates high among women.   Ads that might be seen by poor people are "bad" because they encourage them to spend what little money they have.   Several clergy members have made headlines by forcing state lottery commissions to remove advertising billboards from poor neighborhoods, though it is arguable that the poor can improve their lives greatly by winning the Lotto.

Sales promotions can also be seen as unethical.   Most would agree that a sweepstakes or contest that is "rigged" is unethical.   But how about the sweepstakes where the chances of winning are one in several million (or more)? What about the "free gift" in a box of candy?   The gift is worth next to nothing and the candy is bad for you in the first place.   What about a free T-shirt with a product name on it?   The wearer is a "fool" for providing "free advertising" for the product.   And, the product is often a cigarette or beer -- products that are bad for all of us.   How about Coca-Cola trademark shirts?   We pay to wear that "free advertising."   Further, Coke is not good for us, containing only sugar or potentially harmful sugar substitutes.

ETHICS EXERCISE 18

CHAPTER 18 ETHICS IN PRACTICE

Overview

This case involves a Swedish copywriter who attained notoriety on Swedish TV when his anti-pollution commercial caused what the Swedes call a "folkstorm." To demonstrate what detergents do to our water supply a tank containing a carp was "dumped" with detergent, leading to a gasping death for the fish, dramatized with sound effects. Then the fish is plucked from the water and thrown into a sizzling frying pan to illustrate how poisons can get into people via the food chain. The fish (four in all were involved in the shoot) had been drugged to ease their pain, but the "Goldfish Spot" caused an uproar, including threatening and sometimes tearful phone calls.

So Swedes said they learned a valuable lesson and now use only small amounts of detergent when doing laundry; others were, as stated above, up in arms. The copywriter claimed this was the kind of reaction he hoped to create, and said that many people now think of the poor fish (and the fish they eat) whenever they use laundry detergents, therefore using them sparingly.

The case poses three questions.

1.   *"Do you find this commercial objectionable? Why?"*

You might want to begin by asking for a show-of-hands-vote on how many of your students find this ad to be disgusting. Then, based on the vote, ask how many think its okay to run it. Would those who find it objectionable nonetheless run it if most people thought it was okay? If most people thought it "worked" in terms of achieving the advertiser's objectives?

This ad involves a matter of personal taste. What repulses one person might, indeed, convince another. Unfortunately for the advertiser, there is a wide variation in what people consider to be in good taste, since this is a matter of subjective interpretation and opinion, a matter of personal preference or inclination. This is true in matters of dress, music, and other things as well as advertising.

Consequently, creating general guidelines for good taste in advertising is difficult. Taste is a function of the audience, the culture (e.g., the U.S. vs. Sweden), the subject being advertised, the medium (e.g., Playboy vs. Reader's Digest), and other situational variables such as time of day (laxative ads at dinnertime) and whether the viewer is alone or with others when viewing the ad. For example, ads for menstrual protection products can be embarrassing when viewed in mixed company. Also, taste varies over time. What is considered offensive today might not be found offensive tomorrow.

The best advice for an advertiser is to consider these factors: be aware of public standards of decency and pretest the advertising with the target market. Also, consider your own personal standards. As David Ogilvy once said, "Never run an advertisement you would not want your family to see," and as the Bible says, "Never follow a crowd in doing wrong." Or, as another bit of sage advice goes: "When in doubt, don't."

2.   *If a similar ad were produced in the United States should it be allowed to be shown during prime time viewing hours?*

Again, the factors above in question 1 need to be considered by the advertiser. It would probably be more desirable to leave the decision up to the advertisers and their agencies and to the media. Many in the media reject certain ads for being what in their own estimation are in bad taste. Taste is generally best left to the marketplace, which represents public standards for acceptable taste and in which consumers vote with their dollars, rather than to an elitist group of government regulators whose standards might be at odds with the majority and who are subject to special-interest influences. Furthermore, though once TV and other censors were very powerful, they are not as powerful today. There is probably a reason for this, and that reason has a lot to do with the free market.

Though we do hear of groups organizing to have certain commercials and programs stricken from the air the effectiveness of these groups is spotty at best.

Taste is difficult to legislate or regulate. You usually must tolerate some bad taste if you want free speech, although consumers should be encouraged to complain to the advertisers or media vehicles that run the ads if they find certain ads to be in bad taste.

3.   *When the purpose of an advertisement is to create a better society for*
       everyone, does the end justify the means?

This is, in effect, utilitarian thinking: act so as to produce the greatest good for the greatest number. The focus is on the consequences or end results of an action (especially in terms of societal welfare) and not on the means in determining its moral worth. In business, many unethical decisions are made by sincere and honest people who are strictly results-oriented. However, one must be sure that there are no unanticipated negative consequences, which tend to occur over time and hence are difficult to foresee in advance. In this case, for instance, might children and sensitive people suffer psychological damage if exposed to the commercial? Might people become desensitized to killing animals? A minority of people (and animals) could suffer so that the majority is better off in terms of less environmental pollution. Ends-justify the-means thinking is akin to saying "Let us do evil, that good may come." (Romans 3:8)

CHAPTER 18 TAKE A STAND QUESTIONS

1.   *Singer Madonna wrapped herself in an American flag, but was otherwise*
       scantily clad, during a public service announcement urging young Americans
       to vote. Is this right?

This, like the fish kill ad, seems to be an ad based on an ends-justify-the-means mentality. The ends -- getting more young people to vote -- are desirable to all who believe in our democratic political system (and few would argue with that). The means are more questionable and are largely a matter of public standards of good taste. (See question 1 above.) To the best of the authorss recollection, this incident did cause some discontent among middle-age and older Americans. They felt that the ad was disparaging to the U.S. flag. Similarly, Madonna's "Like a Prayer" Pepsi commercial was found by some to be offensive since a video of the same name was considered by some to be blasphemous to the Christian religion because it mocked the crucifixion of Christ. However, the young folks by and large weren't offended.

A generally accepted legal and moral standard in branding, packaging, logos, and other brand communication elements is to not disparage people, beliefs, institutions, or flags or insignia of the U.S. For instance, recently the U.S. trademark office refused to grant a trademark for the company name and logo of Old Glory Condom Corp. The logo, which featured a flag shaped like an unfurled condom, was said by the federal agency to have the potential to "scandalize or shock the conscience" of the public. Some argue that this ruling violates constitutional rights to free speech, although, as anyone who has ever falsely yelled "fire!" in a public forum knows, free speech rights are not absolute. Further, many wonder how far free "speech" can extend ... to actions, ads, "art," protests, pornography?

Others would argue that there is a market for Madonna's antics. True, but regardless of the target market, the Madonna commercials were viewed by a significant sector of the general public whose standards should be considered.

Still others would hold that standards are relative and changing. In another day and age, a pop star like Madonna would be run out of town. Today she is the subject of adulation, lionized and venerated. Does this make the advertising acceptable?

2.   *A consumer advocate wishes to create a center for the study of*
        commercialism because the public needs to be aware of the insidious nature
        of advertising. "The whole emphasis of our society has become "buy, buy,
        buy'" she claims. Do you agree?

There are two criticisms of advertising embedded in this statement. First is the
notion that advertising is "insidious," i.e., works harmfully in a covert, sly or
subtle manner. It seems to be suggesting that advertising is seductive and
manipulative in how it works. The discussion of Chapter 17 Take A Stand question
5 can be applied here.

Also, the argument is often raised that advertising is exploitive, i.e., it
stimulates people to act in ways that are contrary to their self-interest. The
suggestion that marketing (and advertising) can manipulate the masses and can get
us to buy unwanted products has been dealt with in the Ethics in Practice issue
for Chapter 5. Again, the issue boils down to free choice and consumer
sovereignty. There is a difference between making someone buy and presenting a
product attractively to increase desire for it.

In life, manipulation is often hidden or secretive. What's the purpose of a wink
other than to manipulate? Why do we bother to spritz ourselves with perfumes and
colognes other than to make our presence somehow larger or stronger than it
otherwise would be? Why do we dress ourselves in dandy clothes? If a person
admires your new outfit, do you admit that you're wearing it to make an
impression? No, you probably modestly say, "Aw shucks, it's just something I
pulled out of the closet."

However, in advertising such secretive manipulation is impossible. We all know
the sponsor (unlike publicity/public relations, which does in a sense tend to be
insidious), and we all know that sponsors have a bias, which we are willing to
weigh when evaluating the message. Unless you believe in subliminal advertising
(see an earlier Take A Stand question), you cannot reasonably say that
advertising is insidious.

A second criticism in the "consumer advocate's" statement is that advertising
makes us materialistic by stressing material gratification at the expense of
intellectual and spiritual values. However, emphasizing these is the job of
educators, intellectuals, preachers, and evangelists, not commercial advertisers.
Advertising is also said to ignore nonmaterial interests such as love, freedom,
and other "higher values." However some (notably public service) advertising
does deal with this. Otherwise, this is out of advertising's domain. And, it is
said to create a "consumer culture" in which commodities are more important than
people, or at least in which good become overvalued means for acquiring social
ends such as love and friendship (e.g., an ad targeted to children: "Make
friends with Kool-Aid").

While it is true that advertising often stresses materialism (How can it not,
since most of it is ultimately designed to sell things?), it is wrong to say that
it causes us to be materialistic. Again, the principle of consumer sovereignty
suggests that wants originate deep within the consumer psyche, not the producer
or the product. As we've seen, marketers create want satisfiers, not wants. The
advertising industry responds that "advertising is another word for freedom of
choice." As Michael Schudson has pointed out in *Advertising, The Uneasy*
Persuasion, "Demand is almost never created -- it can only be discovered and
exploited."

Materialism is a result of (1) affluence and (2) unlimited wants and needs.
Advertising certainly reinforces this materialistic bent. It does perpetuate the
consumer ethics and capitalism. However, where do you draw the line on excessive
materialism? Who is to say what really are, as John Kenneth Galbraith calls
them, "wicked wants"? It is interesting to note that Galbraith and other critics
use advertising to hawk their books.

Much of this kind of criticism of advertising is really a criticism of the state
of our society, which it reflects, as well as of capitalism, whose most visible
member is advertising. Perhaps we are too materialistic and hedonistic, putting
too much emphasis on self, living for today, etc. These are important issues
which should be open to discussion. And, we can legitimately oppose certain
forms of advertising which unnecessarily overemphasize self-indulgence, vanity,

and a "you can have it all" mentality. But let's not pass the buck solely to advertising. Let's not kill the messenger instead of dealing with the bad news.

3.   *While visiting in Kentucky, an outdoor advertising executive saw a billboard for a car dealer that claimed "We'll beat the pants off any deal in town." The billboard featured a mannequin with undershorts down around its ankles. The executive decided to use a mannequin with its pants down and the same lowest prices in town theme for an automobile dealer located in another state.*

There are two issues here. First is the matter of poor taste. Points raised in the scenario at the beginning of this exercise can be reiterated here. The ad will certainly get attention, and some might call it cute. What is noteworthy is that the ad is appearing in a mass medium where it will be seen by virtually everyone, including children. Do parents want their children exposed to this? Better either copy test or else find out the reaction in this market -- did the original advertiser get a bagful of negative mail?

The second issue is copycat advertising. A general complaint is that too much advertising is of the look-alike, sound-alike, act-alike variety. Copy writing seems sometimes to mean copying others' writing. Witness your typical car commercial: screeching tires, vehicles roaring down country roads or bumping violently across rough terrains and sloshing through obligatory mud puddles on rain-slicked mountain roads, dramatic sunsets, and hot women running their nails across gleaming red fenders. Ad nausea. Ad oblivion.

Legally, ideas are hard to copyright. The Library of Congress provides controls for copyrighting coined words, slogans, illustrations, characters, photographs, and other distinctive elements of ads. Although a copyright prevents an entire ad from being ripped off, it doesn't prevent others from using the general concept or idea of the ad or from paraphrasing the copy and expressing it in another way. So, this advertiser is probably safe on legal grounds.

Strategically, such formula advertising is questionable; it's too easy to get lost in the clutter. Perhaps the research suggests that everyone in the category should do the same thing, but it's probably best to avoid the swamp of sameness.

Ethically, in the same market doing cookie-cutter advertising is dubious since in a sense it is theft--stealing another's ideas. However, in this case the ads will be seen almost exclusively by another group of consumers, so perhaps it could be justified. But, isn't an advertiser paying the ad agency for original ideas to solve her advertising problem?

4.   *Beer is advertised on a televised college football game.*

The marketing of alcoholic beverages is discussed in the Chapter 12 Ethics in Practice exercise. Key arguments raised against alcohol advertising pointed out in that discussion include:

•   It seduces vulnerable people.
•   It glamorizes drinking.
•   It increases consumption, and in some cases, abuse of the product.

The alcoholic beverage industries counters that:

•   They also do moderation advertising (e.g., "Don't drink and drive").
•   They don't aim advertising at children.
•   A legal product has the First Amendment right to free commercial speech, including advertising.

A televised college football game potentially has some people under 21 (legal drinking age) in the audience. Also, an activity which is possibly detrimental to one's health and which will certainly hinder one's athletic performance is being tied to an athletic event. Some argue that the constant linkage between beer commercials and athletic events sends the wrong message to the wrong audience -- that drinking is somehow the "cool" thing for athletes to do (only ex-jocks may appear in TV commercials according to industry self-regulatory rules). Incidentally, this "wrong message to the wrong audience" argument is also leveled against college promotions, celebrity endorsers, musical- and sporting-event sponsorships, and alcohol ads built around race-car driving and other activities that can be lethal when combined with alcohol consumption.

One recommendation to deal with this problem has been to put health warnings in alcohol ads. Another possibility is to match alcoholic beverage ads with an equal number of pro-health and pro-safety messages. When he was Surgeon General, Everett Koop called on alcohol marketers and colleges to voluntarily curtail such practices rather recommending passage of restrictive legislation.

The beer marketers respond that they advertise on such events because the audience's demographic characteristics skew heavily toward their target market (adult males). Virtually all ads can, and probably are, seen by children. However, children start drinking for other reasons, especially interpersonal influences. And, advertisers say, there is no implicit message that to be a good athlete, you should drink.

5.   *A retailer of roller skates uses the following attention-getting headline: "Kick some Asphalt" and pictures an action shot of a helmeted skater.*

This is again a matter of taste. This is the kind of ad that is regularly taken to task in Advertising Age by readers who submit examples of "ads we can do without." Some examples of candidates for the Advertising Hall of Shame you can ask your students about:

. BRC The Sporting Place -- a picture of a woman in a bathing suit, with the focal point being her buttocks, headlined "Get A beach Bum for $99." (A bummer?)

. Jovan Musk Oil For Men -- "If you want it, wear it." (A double entendre.)

. Vivitar's TEC 35 -- "A camera for people who don't know their ASA from their elbow." (From an advertiser who doesn't know good taste from bad taste?)

. Majestic Counterpot Jewels -- a picture of a woman clutching her bare breasts, headlined "What do you mean they're not real? Even your jeweler won't know." (Who is the "boob" who wrote that one?)

. Electrolux vacuum cleaners -- "Nothing sucks like an Electrolux." (Sweep it away?)

. Price Pro sporting goods -- a picture of footballs, baseballs, tennis balls, etc., headlined "We've not only got the lowest prices, we've got the balls to prove it." (A fun pun?)

Does such bad vertising sell products? It probably gets attention (not to mention occasional publicity in *Ad Age*), but whether it motivates customers to buy is questionable. Plus, it could be offensive enough to some potential customers to turn them away.

Another related issue is the violent overtones in this ad. Whether this will cause some viewers to become violent is debatable, but there is an unequivocal linkage between violence on TV shows and violence in society. A socially responsible marketer would refrain from being associated unnecessarily with violent activities.

GUIDE TO CASES

VIDEO CASE 18-1   FALLON McELLIGOTT (B)[1]

SUBJECT MATTER: Advertising, Agent-Client Relationship, Developing
                  Advertisements, Creativity

          Please see the Guide to Video Cases for video length and
          other information.

AT-A-GLANCE OVERVIEW

Fallon McElligott is an advertising agency know for its creativity. It is also
known as somewhat of an outsider because its headquarters are in Minneapolis-St.
Paul rather than New York. Although it is not located on Madison Avenue in New
York City, its clients include some of the world's major advertisers. Lee
Apparel Company, Porsche, Timex, and Continental Bank are among its accounts.

Its perception/reality advertising campaign for *Rolling Stone* magazine is
considered an advertising classic. *Rolling Stone*'s customers, advertising agency
media buyers, thought its audience was composed of a bunch of old hippies from
the '60s without much money or interest in purchasing much of anything, let alone
upscale items. The advertising campaign (See Case Exhibit 19-1) juxtaposed old
hippie images with actual characteristic and buying patterns of *Rolling Stone*'s
readership. This advertising was not only creative, it served a marketing
objective extremely well.[2]

The agency's mission statement comes up every day on its Macintosh computer
system. The computer screen indicates Fallon McElligott's mission is:

> "To be the premier, award-winning agency in America that produces
> extraordinary effective work for a short list of blue chip
> clients."[3]

The focus is on doing good creative work and the agency's entrepreneurial nature.

Fallon McElligott has 144 full-time employees. The agency does not have an
organizational structure with multiple levels of management. There are no vice
presidents in an industry where the title of vice president is commonplace.
Titles, such as management supervisor, account supervisor, and account executive,
reflect functional activity. The agency focuses on creating great advertising
rather than chain of command decisions and power struggles for senior positions.
At Fallon Mcelligott, cultivating a star system and giving recognition for
authorship are important.[4]

Like account personnel at most advertising agencies account personnel at Fallon
McElligott deal with the clients. At Fallon McElligott, however, the focus is on
creating a partnership with the client. The job is to be involved in the
client's business and to be problem solvers. They work with research personnel
to analyze available information to help understand the client's marketing
communication task. They communicate the client's needs to creative personnel
and media personnel.

Fallon McElligott's media strategists and planners develop media strategies to
match the client's objectives. Media personnel buy media time or space from

---

[1] We greatly appreciate the help of the professionals at Fallon
McElligott, especially Mary Ann O'Brien, in the preparation of this case and
the accompanying video.

[2] David M. Steward, "Twin Piques," *Advertising Age*, June 3, 1991, pp.
20c-25c.

[3] Joyce Rutter Kaye, "Group Therapy," *Advertising Age*, July 2, 1990, pp.
s16-s17.

[4] Ibid.

media representatives. The job entails sharing target market information with media representatives, finding the best match, and negotiating the best deals.

Fallon McElligott's creative success has also work in the marketplace. For example, advertising for Lee Jeans helped increase market share from 14.6% to 22.1% during the back-to-school selling season.

QUESTIONS

1.   *Is a Minneapolis location a disadvantage in the advertising agency business?*

Many advertising agencies are located in New York, Chicago, and L.A. However, Minneapolis does offer some advantages for midwestern clients and clients that do not want a "New York" look. Further, there may be some perception that an agency removed from glitz and glitter has a better "feel" for the "real people" or for the "heartland." Too, there may be some sense that the agency is cheaper than one paying New York rents, though this may not be the case.

In the video, the following question was asked. The answer tells what the agency thinks are good characteristics for a client to have. None of them have to do with location of the client or the agency. They don't suggest companies that "look down" on smaller, less glamorous cities.

Q.   What do you expect from a client?

      Companies who have a good product.
      Companies who are smart and aggressive.
      Companies who have a strong self-image.
      Companies who need and are committed to advertising.
      Companies who are seeking a long-term marketing partner.
      Companies who understand, want and appreciate quality.
      Companies who are financially sound, and encourage their agency to earn a
      fair and equitable profit.

2.   *Evaluate Fallon McElligott's mission statement.*

Here is the mission statement.

      "To be the premier, award-winning agency in America that produces
      extraordinary effective work for a short list of blue chip clients."

This is a good statement in that it describes a goal (premier, award-winning), a means (extraordinary effective work), and a limit that suggests how this agency can do this (working for a short list of blue chip clients). Working for a short list of clients is not unique to this agency. Many others do the same thing. A risk involved is that the loss of a client or two from a short list can be serious. This agency obviously feels that "extraordinary effective work" will help prevent client loss and/or draw new clients if old ones are lost. The trick is maintaining the performance of extraordinary effective work over time.

In the video the following questions were asked about the agency philosophy.
Here are the answers provided.

Q.   As a business enterprise, what are the objectives of your agency?

To be successful as a business, we felt we had to offer a difference. We had to be unique. We had to have a goal, a product, and an identity that together would set us apart. We opened our doors with the following mission statement, which now comes up on each employee's personal computer each morning.

This mission works for us in two ways. The awards won on behalf of our clients work as a marketing device for the agency. Second, the commitment to effective work keeps us focused on developing advertising that breaks through the clutter. It is critical to our goal that our advertising wins in the marketplace for our clients. Without their success, we could not realize our other business objective, which is to make a fair profit.

Q.   What business strategy has your agency adopted for achieving these results?

To provide an environment to achieve our goals, we have chosen to limit our growth. We plan never to have more than 25 clients, so we choose them carefully (as we assume they choose us). Because our desire is to be full marketing partners with our clients, living their business with them, we like our growth to come 60% from existing clients, 40% from new business. We try to choose clients with whom we will share a common focus and common values to guarantee an effective and rewarding partnership.

We have also chosen to use our creative resources in what we believe is the best way for our clients and for our people. We focus on advertising, which is our strength. We recognize our clients' needs for promotional, direct marketing, and other communication needs, but we do not think we are the best resource for many of those needs. We prefer to work with our clients -- and their other suppliers -- to ensure that all those needs are being met by people whose commitment to those parts of the marketing mix parallel our own commitment to advertising.

Q.   What do you consider to be the principal product your agency sells? What is the main competitive advantage it has over other agencies?

Creative leverage is Fallon McElligott's principal product and our competitive edge. That is what we best provide and that is what our clients need and want. Through imagination we create advertising which extends our clients' advertising dollars and lets them work harder. In an age of tightening budgets and perceived parity among products, it is the one way to increase the power of your advertising budget without increasing the size of it. We have the passion, the driving commitment, to provide this leverage for our clients. It's the reason we all come to work every day.

Q.   What is your agency's philosophy regarding what makes advertising effective?

Our philosophy is simple. There is no formula for effective advertising. We try to provide the best work possible for a sound marketing strategy. We believe in the power of brand names and brand identities. Advertising should do all it can to shape and strengthen a brand franchise.

We also think that great advertising has humanity. It is honest. It illustrates that our clients are people as well as products, people who understand the needs of consumers and want to satisfy them. Great advertising is bold -- and likeable. It makes people nod, and smile, and talk. It tells them the truth, with simplicity and with charm. It respects them.

3.   *What is the nature of the relationship between an agency and the client?*

In the video the following question was asked:

Q.   Discuss the role of the account executive as it relates to your clients' day-to-day business issues and internally within your agency's structure.

The Fallon McElligott account team will be the core of our marketing partnership with you. Their involvement in client business goes well beyond advertising issues. Our account teams are problem solvers, generalists who learn and monitor the consumer perspective on their clients' products and services. They become as deeply involved in a client's business as the client allows. It's their commitment and it's our promise.

They are facilitators. Within the agency, they are the stewards of your business, your internal representatives. They orchestrate the full resources of the agency in order to provide the services each client requires. This means filling whatever role he or she has to fill, becoming involved in any and all parts of the marketing mix in order to make the client/agency relationship work. We don't talk about "your" business, we talk about "our" business, because that's how we feel about our clients' business.

We think this relationship works two ways, too. The best sales people for our product are our clients.

Q.   Describe your account service structure.

One of the founding tenets of the agency was that top management stay in the business of serving clients and managing advertising on a day-to-day basis. Thus, our structure is less hierarchical than most, and we will never have more than 25 accounts. Pat Fallon (Chairman), Steve Sjoblad (President), and Fred Senn (principal/management supervisor) are actively involved in managing accounts.

We have no vice presidents in an industry where vice presidents often constitute a majority. Our titles are functional: management supervisor, account supervisor, account executive. We have no formula for staffing an account other than "whatever it takes." Thus, you'll find two very senior management supervisors co-managing an account where strategic counsel is critical. And, on the other hand, we have a multi-brand client with a total of 14 account people assigned. Compared to most agencies, we staff lean, but with more senior people. Excluding the assistants, and those in our training program, the average account services professional has 9.7 years of experience, nearly double the industry average.

4.   *What steps are necessary for an advertisement to be created by an advertising agency of a client? What role does the agency play in making creative decisions and selecting media?*

The advertising agency/client relationship is a difficult one to describe. Ideally, it is one of trust, especially of the agency by the client. The agency is supposed to know what it is doing; the client is supposed to have carefully selected the agency; and the client is, therefore, "in the hands" of the agency. Unfortunately, it doesn't always work out this way. The client is likely to second guess the agency, question it, argue with it, and so on. The agency, for its part, is likely to either take the stand that "we are the creative people here, so leave us alone" or to cater to the client, sometimes going against its own beliefs about what is good for the client so as not to anger the client.

Ideally, the agency would know the client and its product and follow the steps needed to create an advertisement that is consistent with such considerations as the product's stage in the PLC, the available funds, the advertiser's objectives, and so on.

The creative process itself involves answering several questions (admittedly easier to ask than answer).

What to say? What will the appeal be? What will the theme be?

How to say it? What will the format be?

What will the copy say? That is, what will be the verbal appeal? And, what will the visual appeal be ... the art?

What steps are needed to pretest the ad? To posttest it? How can effectiveness of the ad be measured?

Obviously it is improper to create an ad without having some idea of where it will run. In what markets? Via what media? Hence, the question of media selection cannot be handled separately from "creative" questions. A great ad developed with the idea that it will run on TV may not be so great if there is not enough money to put it on TV. The decision to run the audio portion on radio, though this is sometimes done effectively, doesn't make a good TV ad into a good radio ad. Thus, media selection is part of the agency's job, as is media scheduling. Most agencies of any size, therefore, employ media specialists.

5.   *Are there any special considerations that should be considered when an agency manages creative personnel.*

The temperamental artist stereotype, like all stereotypes, has some basis in fact, though a look at the attire of an artist at an agency and of an artist in the advertising department of a tire company draws some interesting contrasts. The same is true of copywriters.

Creative people do need "space." They need time to be creative. While an accountant can sit down and do the books from 9 to 5 each day, it is far more difficult, from most perspectives, to walk in, sit down, and do some great creative work "on demand." Thus, to a point, creative types need time and patience from their managers if they are to do their best work. Of course, it has been demonstrated time and again that free rein ("Come in whenever you want to. Spend the day thinking on the golf course.") doesn't work either.

A delicate balance must be struck by managers of creative people between "free rein" and (a little bit, at least, of) the whip.

VIDEO CASE 18-2   LEE JEANS

SUBJECT MATTER: Marketing Mix Objectives, Creative Strategy, Media Strategy

> Please see the Guide to Video Cases for video length and other information.

AT-A-GLANCE OVERVIEW

In the 1980s, many jeans makers focused on high fashion jeans. As the baby boomers aged to 30 and 40-something, the market for jeans declined. Younger people, especially teens, are the heavy users of jeans. Lee sold to many segments of the market so as the market as a whole declined so did Lee's sales. One segment wherein Lee was strong was women aged 25-54, seen as a poor segment for a denim company in a fashion-driven market. So Lee began to target younger consumers with its fashion jeans. This resulted in production and delivery problems and alienated retailers. They began to carry just one or two styles of Lee jeans, often as loss leaders. Many stopped carrying Lee altogether. Three questions faced Lee.

> How to stop sales volume and market share from declining?
> How to restore the power of the Lee brand?
> How to impact retail distribution?

Research was conducted with women aged 25-54 and uncovered strong loyalty to the Lee brand based on belief that Lee offered superior fit and quality. It also showed Lee had failed to develop an emotional relationship with the customer. But then, neither had other brands (in this segment). It also appeared that women in this group viewed jeans as work jeans (e.g., for yard work), casual jeans (e.g., for shopping), and dress-up jeans for social occasions. Lee determined that it was the only brand that could be associated with all three situations. Lee also knew comfort was extremely important. Women believed that coming home to their jeans at the end of the day in office or other attire was a pleasurable experience.

QUESTIONS

1.   *What overall marketing mix objectives would you set for Lee jeans?*

The marketing mix for Lee jeans must, as the text stresses throughout, be consistent. Its components must work together. Students should decide first what target market is going to be pursued, what information is known about the target market, and what strengths Lee has.

Admittedly it is different to discuss the aspects of a marketing mix under separate headings, but here are some ideas.

A reasonable assumption here is that Lee wants to build on the strengths it has, and not reposition itself in the market. If this is the case, what are the strengths Lee has? What does it know about the jeans market?

a.   The market has declined somewhat as the number of teenagers, the heavy user segment, has dropped.

b. Lee has appeal across the market, though the segment "women, 25-54" has the strongest brand loyalty to Lee. But, this segment is not seen as particularly desirable by fashion jeans makers.

c. Lee's attempt at a "fashion focus" did not meet with much success, although this could be due to bad execution.

d. Lee is seen by the "women, 25-54" segment as making superior fitting, well-made, quality products, but had not established an "emotional bond" with its customers. However, neither had any other company.

e. Lee is the only brand seen as appropriate for all three jeans-wearing occasions. Of course, Lee is also a name that has been around for a long time. Lee jeans are associated with fit and comfort, and comfort is a major point in consumer evaluation of jeans.

It would make sense to try to capitalize on Lee's strength ... its position as a long-time maker of quality, well-made, comfortable jeans for a brand-loyal market segment.

PRODUCT   Product-related objectives would include continuing to offer comfort and quality, with quality understood to be related to price. Since Lee is facing an older and aging segment, the product may have to be altered somewhat to maintain the image of comfort and quality. Softer materials may be preferred, and one is reminded of the jeans ads that say "ours are just a skosh bigger." These ads claim that the buyer can buy the "same size you always bought" but still be comfortable in the "skosh bigger" jeans. Overall, the objectives in the product portion of the mix should show a stress on quality, comfort, and the other product-related characteristics Lee's target market prefers.

PRICE   Lee's effort to sell fashion products was not a success. This lack of success could have flowed from a number of factors, but one matter of importance could have been price. Lee's image seems to be one of comfort and quality. "Quality" doesn't have to mean the greatest and most high-priced quality. Quality can mean "real good for the money." Also, the case's description of the women who prefer Lee suggests that not everyone in this age group is a professional, working woman with a good income. To appeal to the non-affluent woman, prices should be kept at reasonable levels. Lee might want to conduct additional research to see if it can link "quality" to "price" more exactly. That is, its customers want comfort and quality, but how high can Lee, an non-fashion company, go with its prices? That is, what is the appropriate price as defined by the market?

PLACE   Lee's lack of a fashion image, and the description of its target market and the several ways in which they use jeans, suggests that the "proper" outlets for Lee are outlets where quality seekers (and reasonable price seekers) are likely to shop. "Fancy shops" do not seem appropriate. Stores along the lines of Sears, Penney's, and the up-scaling K-Mart or other like outlets, would appear to be appropriate, though it would be nice to have more information about customer preferences. Lee "shops" within Sears stores are a possibility. As mentioned above, Lee is an old, reliable name in this product line. "Fashion" is difficult to conjure up when the name Lee is mentioned.

PROMOTION   Though there are many subsegments within the market segment "women, 25-54" certain media do focus on this group. Women's magazines abound, and each can provide information on its readership. Many TV shows are known to appeal to this group. Lee will, of course, use some amount of personal selling to get its products into the appropriate stores, and students will be able to think of some sales promotion activities that might be useful.

2.   *What creative strategy for advertising would you recommend?*

The strategy must match the target market. If we assume, as we did above, that
Lee will pursue the "women, 25-54" segment and its parts, the advertising
strategy must yield advertising appropriate to (1) this segment, (2) the product,
and (3) the company.

What to say? The ads should stress facts and perceptions about the product that
are important to the target market. We know that members of this market want
value and quality, but that comfort is especially important. A message along the
lines of the aforementioned "just a skosh bigger" idea may be most appropriate,
especially in ads aimed at the older end of this segment.

How to say it? "Comfort" is hard to prove in an ad, but the various execution
possibilities do bring to mind ways in which this might be done. The storyline
format could be used to trace the long history of jeans and Lee jeans in
particular. A powerful statement can be made by demonstrating that the company
has survived for a long time. Problem solutions can be offered ... "Jeans
uncomfortable ... Lee's new jeans for women are designed a whole new way to fit
a woman and a woman's lifestyle." Slice of life possibilities come to mind,
showing "settings" where Lee jeans for women are in use. Demonstration can show
that Lee jeans are cut differently than others ... "Why wear men's jeans?"
Testimonials are possible too, if Lee can afford them. Maidenform sold bras to
older, "full-figured" women using the testimony of Jane Russell, a movie star
from the 40s and 50s that older folks remembered mostly for her large, umm,
figure. Most of the other formats could at least be considered, though the
montage format, so often used to suggest glamour, may not be easily employed.

3.   *What media strategy would you recommend?*

As mentioned above, if Lee decides to pursue "women, 25-54," there is no shortage
of media with appeal to this group and subgroups within it. Magazines come to
mind. Students may not know that the circulations of these magazines are very
large. A list of the top 100 magazines starts with *Modern Maturity*, and *TV
Guide*, but once past the first 4 or 5 titles, one encounters title upon title of
"women's magazines," like *Good Housekeeping*, *Family Circle*, etc. For
subsegments, there are *Working Woman* and many other books aimed at these groups.
Also, some sports-oriented magazines have many women readers. Magazines supply
potential advertisers with information on "who our readers are."

Television has many popular shows ("Roseanne," "Murphy Brown") that appeal to
certain women in this age group. However, the expense involved may be seen as
prohibitive. Newspapers are a possibility, but lack the color and photo quality
of magazines. Also, people reading the paper are more likely to be looking for
jean sales than for Lee jeans. Radio lacks the visual impact needed for this
product, but may play a supplementary role. A number of firms play the audio
portion of their TV ads on the radio as reminder advertising, but usually only
after the ads are well-known thanks to TV. Billboards are worth a thought, but
they are not as focused as magazines.

In short, a media strategy should focus on the segment the company hopes to
reach. Selectivity of media is most important in this question.

•19 PERSONAL SELLING, SALES MANAGEMENT, AND SALES PROMOTION

CHAPTER SCAN

This chapter deals with personal selling and relationship management. It discusses the purposes and applications of personal selling and the several types of sales positions. The marketing concept has made for a "new" role for sales, one of identifying and solving customer problems, thereby contributing greatly to the operations of the modern firm. The steps in making a sale are outlined with emphasis on the fact that the marketing process doesn't stop when the sale is made.

The chapter also deals with sales management -- the tasks and duties of those who select salespeople and manage their activities. The ethical issues that face sales personnel are addressed.

Sales promotion and the major sales promotion tools are also explained.

SUGGESTED LEARNING OBJECTIVES

The student who studies this chapter will be exposed to a broad view of the personal selling task, sales management, and sales as a career and will be able to:

1. Describe the role of personal selling and relationship management.

2. Identify marketing situations in which personal selling would be the most effective means of reaching and influencing target buyers.

3. Show how the professional salesperson contributes to a modern marketing firm.

4. Outline the steps involved in making a sale.

5. Explain why the marketing process does not stop when the sale is made.

6. Characterize the major aspects of the sales manager's job.

7. Classify the various forms of sales compensation.

8. Identify some of the ethical issues facing sales personnel.

9. Identify the purposes of sales promotion and explain how the major sales promotion tools work.

CHAPTER OUTLINE

I.   INTRODUCTION

II.   PERSONAL SELLING DEFINED

III. IMPORTANCE OF PERSONAL SELLING

IV.   THE CHARACTERISTICS OF PERSONAL SELLING

A. Personal Selling is Flexible
B. Personal Selling Builds Relationships
C. Some Limitations of Personal Selling

V.   THE TYPES OF PERSONAL SELLING TASKS

A. Order-Taking
B. Order-Getting
C. Sales Support

VI.   THE CREATIVE SELLING PROCESS

A. Step One: Locating and Qualifying Prospects

1. Locating Prospects
2. Qualifying Prospects

B. Step Two: The Approach
C. Step Three: The Sales Presentation
D. Step Four: Handling Objections
E. Step Five: Closing the Sale
F. Step Six: The Follow-Up

VII. SALES PEOPLE AS FUTURE MANAGERS

VIII. EXECUTIVE SELLING

IX.   SALES MANAGEMENT

A. Setting Sales Objectives
B. Organizing the Sales Force

1. Geographically Based Sales Territories
2. Organization by Customer Type
3. Organization by Product Line
4. Organization by Selling Tasks

C. Recruiting and Selecting the Sales Force
D. Training the Sales Force
E. Compensating the Sales Force

1. The Compensation Continuum
2. Straight Salary or Wage
3. Straight Commission
4. Commission with Draw
5. Quota-Bonus Plan
6. Salary Plus Commission

F. Motivating the Sales Force

The following key terms are introduced and used in Chapter 19. They are defined in the text's Glossary.

Retail selling
Field selling
Telemarketing
Inside selling
Relationship management
Order taker
Suggestive selling
Order getting, or Creative selling
Pioneering
Account management
Missionary sales personnel
Sales team
Account service representative
Creative selling process
Prospecting
Qualifying
Approach
Sales presentation
Handling objections
Closing
Closing signals
Trial close
Follow-up
Sales management
Sales objectives
Sales territory
Field sales manager
Straight salary
Straight commission
Commission with draw
Quota-bonus plan

Salary plus commission
Call report
Trade show
Contest
Point-of-purchase materials
Cooperative advertising
Allowance
Product sampling
Rebate
Premium

THE CHAPTER SUMMARIZED

I.   INTRODUCTION

By way of introduction, this chapter begins with an accounting of Joe
Privitera, a 28-year-old computer salesperson with Unisys. He details his
workday, a long one involving a good deal of follow-up and relationship
building. His discussion of what sales has taught him involves such points
as the challenge of calling on new accounts, learning to adapt to
situations and take rejection, "aggressive listening," the importance of
product knowledge, the importance of helping customers, the need to deal
with several peoples' needs simultaneously, and the importance of
developing long-term relationships.

II.   PERSONAL SELLING DEFINED

Personal selling is person-to-person dialogue between buyer and seller.
Like advertising, the salesperson's job is to remind, inform, and/or
persuade. To reach potential and existing clients is the goal of selling.
Salespeople are "the front-line troops in the battle for customers'
orders." They communicate the company's offer and show perspective buyers
how their problems can be solved by the product.

Many kinds of business and other organizations use personal selling. All
are familiar with **retail selling** -- selling to ultimate consumers. In
contrast to most retail selling, **field selling** is performed by an outside
salesperson who typically travels to the potential buyer's place of
business. **Telemarketing** involves using the phone as the primary means of
communication. **Inside selling** is similar to most retail selling and
involves selling in the employer's place of business.

III. IMPORTANCE OF PERSONAL SELLING

Personal selling is the most widely used means of communicating with
customers. An organization, even a two-man machine shop, must have some
personal contact with customers, even if it is just talking with them in
the shop. CPA firms use their partners mostly to gather new business.
Doctors and dentists deal with customers (called "patients").

In terms of dollars, personal selling is the foremost promotional tool, far
exceeding advertising in spending. This is because of the great numbers of
salespeople and the expenses associated with recruiting and maintaining
them.

Selling is most important in terms of employment. At least 10% of the U.S.
work force is in sales. The salesperson is the catalyst that makes our
economy function.

IV.   THE CHARACTERISTICS OF PERSONAL SELLING

Personal selling has two important characteristics: it is flexible and it
builds relationships.

A.   Personal Selling is Flexible

The word that describes the advantages of personal selling over other
means of promotion is flexibility.

- The presentation can be adapted to situations or clients.

- The salesperson can answer and overcome objections.

- The salesperson can focus on points of customer interest and ignore points not of interest.

- Direct and immediate feedback is elicited.

- Information about needs, product modification possibilities, activities of competitors, etc., can be obtained.

Personal selling flexibility allows concentration of effort on the best, biggest, or "most-ready-to-buy" customers -- a big advantage over mass media. Personal selling is a selective medium.

B.   Personal Selling Builds Relationships

The text has stressed that the relationship between buyer and seller does not end when the sale is made. Long term success depends on building a good relationship with the buyer. The term **relationship management** refers to the sales function of managing the account relationship and ensuring that buyers receive the appropriate services. The salesperson is the key in relationship management, making sure the product solves customer problems and contributes to the success of the customer's organization.

C.   Some Limitations of Personal Selling

Personal selling is not without limitations.

- It cannot economically reach mass audiences. Advertising is more appropriate for mass market products.

- Costs are generally high, especially cost per call, since recruiting, training, paying, and supporting salespeople is expensive. Estimates run to $300 and more "average cost per call."

- Recruiting, training and monitoring salespeople is difficult work.

Despite these problems, the many advantages of personal selling can offset the high cost per sale; for many products, personal selling is the only way a sale can be made.

V.   THE TYPES OF PERSONAL SELLING TASKS

Marketing managers must decide which skills go with which selling jobs so it is useful to distinguish between the selling assignments. There are three basic categories: order taking, order getting, and sales support.

A.   Order-Taking

Many people are engaged in routine selling tasks; they "sell" what their customers ask for, writing up orders and assuring good order processing. They are **order takers**. Essentially, their goal is to be pleasant and helpful, though they may engage in **suggestive selling** ("Do you want fries with that?"). Primarily, however, they keep sales ... they don't make sales.

Order-taking sales jobs are of two major types: "inside" and "outside" (or "field"). An "inside" job might be exemplified by an auto parts store clerk who gets the customer what he or she needs, provide some advice, and may even "sell" a tool or lubricant suited to the repair job. Telemarketing is an activity of many inside order-takers who use the telephone as their primary means of communicating with customers.

The "outside" job of the order-taker might be exemplified by the salesperson working for Campbell's Soup. The question he asks customers is essentially, "How much do you want?" There is room for such salespeople to improve sales figures, etc. Compared to selling corporate jets to company CEO's, however, this is still an order-taking job. Order taking requires less persuasive skill than order getting and compensation generally reflects this.

B.   Order-Getting

Order-getting, also called **creative selling**, requires that salespeople find and analyze customers to discover how products offered might solve the customer's problems.

Creative selling calls for the ability to interpret product and service features in terms of benefits and advantages to the buyer and persuade and motivate the buyer to purchase the right quality and volume of products or service.

The order-getter's job is to make the sale. As would be expected, such salespeople generally earn more than do order-takers, and their sales can take far longer to make and far greater effort. An IBM salesperson selling a new computer system to the State of Pennsylvania or any other big customer could spend years in the effort.

Order getters may specialize in certain selling situations. Those who focus on new business generation are sometimes called **pioneers**. In contrast, **account managers** concentrate on maintaining an ongoing relationship with existing customers. In many organizations, creative selling types are expected to do both kinds of work.

Exhibit 19-1 classifies the job activities of order-getters.

C.   Sales Support

Sales support people are involved in specialized selling situations. Examples:

.   Missionaries or **missionary sales personnel** build goodwill by "checking-in" with customers to be sure all is well. They are employed by manufacturers, most of whom distribute using intermediaries, to perform a kind of public relations function.

.   "Detailers" are used by pharmaceutical companies to call on doctors to provide them with product information.

.   "Sales engineers" or "technical specialists" may be needed to support salespeople selling technical products in specific situations.

.   Some firms have sales experts or "master salespeople" available to help a sales force member who is not quite able to close a sale (these are commonly found in auto and real estate sales). Note: These salespeople, no matter what their official title, are known in sales parlance as "closers."

In many organizations there is a recognized **sales team**. The person who "made" the sale may have had the road smoothed by a missionary and helped by a master salesperson and a engineer.

The **account service representative**, someone at company headquarters who answers customer questions, etc., can also be an important part of the sales team.

VI.   THE CREATIVE SELLING PROCESS

Except for the totally "canned" sales presentation, defended by its users on the grounds that it is the "best possible" presentation and has been tested as such, sales presentations generally involve some measure of creativity.

A "picture" of the **creative selling process** is shown in the text, Exhibit 19-2, and is discussed below.

A.   Step One: Locating and Qualifying Prospects

Even established salespeople are expected to generate new business. New accounts must be sought. But trying to sell to persons with no funds or interest in the product is fruitless. Potential customers, not just people nice enough to listen, are what is desired.

1.   Locating Prospects

Locating likely new customers is called **prospecting**. Sources such as association membership lists, lists of conference attendees, etc., can all be used in the effort. The number of prospecting tools and methods is "unlimited."

2.   Qualifying Prospects

Prospects must be found to be in need of the product and able to pay for it. The person contacted must be found to have some buying authority or influence. Determining that conditions such as these are met is termed **qualifying** the prospect. Included here is the determination of such factors as likely customer size, potential order size, "softness" of current buying commitments, etc.

B.   Step Two: The Approach

The **approach** involves making an initial contact and establishing rapport with the prospect. With old accounts this may involve a simple phone call; for possible new customers, more is involved. Usually success in the approach is the basis for effective communication by letter, phone or personal visits. A common approach is something like, "I hear you are spending $X per year for raw material Y. We can cut that by 10%. Let me show you how." The goal is to attract the buyer's attention.

Personal matters can be researched, too. Carrying a cigar into a nonsmoker's office can ruin an otherwise well-planned approach.

C.   Step Three: The Sales Presentation

The **sales presentation** is the salesperson's attempt to persuasively communicate the product's benefits and explain appropriate courses of action to the potential buyer.

Typically, the presentation begins with an attempt to gain the prospect's attention. Statements, models, or the product itself are commonly used, followed up with the development of interest via descriptions of the product or demonstrations of its effective use. These steps are aimed at generating desire to purchase the product. Note that these steps are not always verbal -- "body language" is involved.

D.   Step Four: Handling Objections

The customer will have problems, questions, and objections which must be met, yet they are opportunities for the salesperson to listen and learn from them. In fact, a sales talk that is a dialogue with a customer does not give the customer an opportunity to sit quietly, then say "No."

Objections tell the salesperson what points need to be more strongly stressed -- what points are important to the customer. These may be things not previously encountered by the salesperson. Also, they can be "turned around" to become selling points. They may be accepted by the salesperson, but with a reservation. ("Expensive? Yes. But it lasts 10 times longer than the one you are now using.")

Questions and objections may also show how close the prospect is to making a decision.

E.   Step Five: Closing the Sale

Closing means bringing the sale to a finish. Many salespeople seem to "forget" to close the sale; for whatever reason, they find it hard to stop selling and ask for the order. The **trial close** is a tactic intended to draw information as to whether or not the client is ready to make the deal, e.g., "Do you prefer the standard over the deluxe?"

The main thing is that sooner or later, this step must be taken.

Examples of closing signals/statements are listed in the text. Five closes are described:

- "Narrow the alternatives" -- ask something like "Do you want A or B?"

- "Direct" or "straightforward" -- simply request the order.

- "Assumptive" -- act as if an agreement has been reached.

- "Standing room only" -- imply that time is running out, that the product or the low price will not be available much longer.

- "Summative approach" -- list, perhaps on paper, advantages and disadvantages, leading up to asking for the sale.

F.   Step Six: The Follow-Up

The professional salesperson knows that the job isn't done when the customer says "Yes." Appropriate **follow-up** (delivery, installation, parts, repair, supplies) is needed if anything other than a one-shot sale is desired.

VII.   SALES PEOPLE AS FUTURE MANAGERS

Sales experience is often required for upper-level management positions. Such experience suggests an opportunity to become customer oriented. A discussion by the manager of systems development for Amoco Corp. shows the value of sales experience early in one's career.

VIII. EXECUTIVE SELLING

In some industries, executives may be the most important salespeople. With the trends toward long-term relationships between buyer and seller, this is more than ever likely to be the case. If decision makers at the buying organizations are top-level executives, they are likely to want to deal with their counterparts at selling organizations.

XI.   SALES MANAGEMENT

Sales management is the marketing management activity of planning, organizing, directing, and controlling the personal selling effort. The major activities involved are shown in Exhibit 19-3.

Sales management is particularly important since so many salespeople, especially those not in retailing, work "on their own." The emphasis is generally on planning rather than on control of day-to-day activities.

Sales managers, like other managers, are assigned to particular corporate responsibilities. For example, sales managers may be assigned to more direct selling jobs (as when a particularly important sale needs to be consummated).

A.   Setting Sales Objectives

All managers start their assignments by determining what **sales objectives** are to be met. How can a manager know, for example, how many salespeople to hire unless the objectives they are to obtain have been set? Objectives should be as follows:

.   Precise ... so the goal is clear.

.   Quantifiable ... so when a goal is reached, all know it.

.   Inclusive of a time frame ... otherwise "forever" is the time allotted to achievement of the goal.

.   Reasonable ... in that they reflect reality.

Objectives can be expressed in many ways, such as dollar sales, share of market, calls per sale, calls per day, etc.

B.   Organizing the Sales Force

Some form of organization of sales efforts is necessary:

.   to properly use sales resources.

.   to avoid duplicate calls on clients. These waste time and effort and can annoy customers.

A sales territory system is one way to organize efforts. Territories need not be strictly geographical; they can also be set up in terms of customer type or size, even alphabetically using client names.

1.   Geographically Based Sales Territories

An example of a geographic sales territory set-up is shown in Exhibit 19-4 of the text.

District and regional sales managers accountable for the activity of sales personnel in specific areas are called **field sales managers** because they work with people "out in the field."

No matter what method is used to create the territories, the sales manager who develops them is likely to be concerned with obtaining a degree of equality among them in terms of such variables as physical size, number of customers, potential for new business, size of existing accounts, etc. Why? Because personnel problems develop quickly when some salespeople get "good territories" and others get "bad territories."

2.   Organization by Customer Type

If an organization specializes by customer type (e.g., petrochemical users vs. other chemical users). several salespeople may cover the same territory. Such a plan is justified if the customers will be better served by dealing with a specialist.

Note that an element of geography is found within this plan, i.e., specialization within some area of the country or world. This means that a combination approach to creating sales territories is, in fact, commonly employed.

3.   Organization by Product Line

A company with a wide product line may organize its sales force in terms of that line. This may have payoffs in terms of permitting specialization in particular products. A result, however, is that several salespeople may call on the same firm though. If there is specialization of buyers as well as of sellers, this need not cause annoyance to clients. Companies using this approach obviously have decided that the advantages are worth the "waste" of duplicate calls on clients.

4.   Organization by Selling Tasks

Some people seem best suited to sales maintenance (e.g., the "order-taker"), others to sales development ("order-getting" or "new accounts"). Organizations can be set up to take advantage of these differences by assigning the right people to these tasks.

C.   Recruiting and Selecting the Sales Force

Finding the right salesperson begins with an analysis of the job to be done. There is no "born salesman" who is acceptable in all situations. Even though certain sales jobs are associated with high rates of personnel turnover, some individuals pursue long careers in these slots. Getting the right people seems the key.

With regard to sales aptitude or personality tests, this can be said: No test proves an applicant will or will not be a good salesperson. Tests may "flag" areas of concern and may, in the aggregate, increase the odds of making a proper choice.

D.   Training the Sales Force

Training varies from the "sink or swim" approach to sending neophytes out with "an experienced man," to extensive in-class training systems.

Few would recommend the "sink or swim" method. At the minimum, some training in company policies and practices, industry and competitor background, and product knowledge and selling techniques seems to be in order. Work as an account service representative (sales correspondent) is often used to familiarize newcomers with how things are done.

On-going training and refresher courses are used with great success to introduce new products or provide a break in regular schedules.

E.   Compensating the Sales Force

The ideal pay plan would include these features:

.   Simplicity (so as to avoid misunderstandings and disagreements).

.   Regularity (so employees would be able to count on receiving their pay).

.   Security (so as to avoid undue concerns about income).

.   Incentive (to encourage performance).

.   Control (to permit managers to direct sales activities).

.   Optimization of order size (Too much incentive can result in over-selling and disgruntled customers.).

There is no one compensation plan that reflects all these ideals; however, there are many that do reflect some of them.

1.   The Compensation Continuum

Compensation plans range from the "pure incentive" of the straight commission plan to the "security and regularity" of the straight salary or wage. The text's Exhibit 19-5 shows the nature of this continuum.

2. Straight Salary or Wage

The **straight salary** payment plan does not directly tie wages to sales performance, but rates high on the other attributes of the "ideal plan." It seems to be virtually required when sales opportunities are not equal (e.g., among employees at a Kmart or Woolworth's) and/or where sales help is expected to do nonsales work like stocking shelves.

3. Straight Commission

The **straight commission** plan rewards only sales performance; it fits jobs where the only requirement is to sell. It can have the advantage of simplicity, but management is frequently tempted to "play around" with the commissions. Raising them for items that are hard-to-sell while lowering them on easy-to-sell goods is a common example. The system gives the salesperson little security and the incentive value quickly turns sour if a "dry spell" is encountered. Finally, managers using the straight commission method cannot know what this aspect of selling expenses will cost in total dollars but only as a percent of sales.

4. Commission with Draw

The **commission with draw** compensation method is a compromise plan between the two extremes, a variation on straight commission except that there is a drawing account against which salespeople may draw in slow periods. However, the draw must be paid back once commissions return to higher levels.

5. Quota-Bonus Plan

Under the **quota-bonus plan**, evaluation of salespeople and managers is based on contribution to attainment of prescribed goals and objectives. These must be specific and measurable.

Another compromise plan, this gives the salesperson a quota to meet. For sales beyond this quota amount, an incentive (or bonus) is paid. This plan has considerable appeal, but friction can arise if salespeople feel that bonuses are set too low or quotas raised too high. Cuts in the size of the territory affect the chance to make the quota, also affecting attitudes.

6. Salary Plus Commission

The **salary plus commission** compromise plan is a common sales pay plan in the U.S. in part because it is so heavily used in retailing. The salary, or hourly wage, is seen as providing regularity, security, control, etc., while the commission provides incentive.

F. Motivating the Sales Force

Successful salespeople tend to be self-motivated. They enjoy the challenge of selling; however, most need occasional support from management. Morale swings can be wide in sales work.

The element of sales promotion comes in here. Conventions, sales meetings, sales contests, etc. all have their place in the motivation effort.

G.   Evaluation and Control of the Sales Force

Corporate and regional sales plans rest, ultimately, on local
efforts. Managers must develop instruments of control that provide
feedback from people in the field.

Data on the performance of salespeople can be in the form of sales
totals but also in the forms of:

- calls per week or day. (Most companies require salespeople to
  keep a log of their activities known as a **call report.**)

- increased or decreased sizes of orders.

- orders per sales call ("batting average").

Many other measures can be and are used. Such measures are important
so that goals and performances can be discussed in meaningful terms.
"Not too good" is not a very useful evaluation. Thus, sales quotas,
call reports, logs, etc. all have their place in evaluating the sales
force. They can also be of use in evaluating the methods of sales
management such as the territories or compensation plans.

Quotas can be motivational tools. IBM sets its quotas such that 70%
to 80% of salespeople reach their goals, giving them confidence
rather than a sense of being a "loser."

H.   Management of Sales Agents

Many firms use agents rather than their own sales forces; still,
these agents need some "sales management." They need training,
motivation, evaluation, etc. Admittedly, managing persons not under
one's direct control requires modification of traditional sales
management tools. Still, a smooth working relationship is worth the
effort.

X.   ETHICAL ISSUES IN SALES AND SALES MANAGEMENT

Salespeople may be frequently faced with ethical and legal issues, ranging
from serious (legally punishable) matters dealing with price discrimination
or price fixing to "little white lies." A starting point must be for the
sales force to know the law, but this is not enough. Companies that have
adopted the marketing concept usually let their salespeople know what is
expected of them. Companies may have a code of conduct involving honesty
and forthrightness in dealing with customers, the keeping of promises, and
avoidance of deception.

XI. SALES PROMOTION

The typical purpose of sales promotion is to bolster other elements of the
marketing mix, as when a sales contest is used to motivate a sales force.
Other examples include:

- promotions used to encourage a wholesaler's sales force to sell more
  aggressively to retailers.

- a promotion aimed at getting retailer cooperation with a consumer-
  targeted promotion. A promotional allowance could be given to
  retailers who permit a display to be set up in their stores.

- a promotion aimed at consumers, like offering toys with the purchase
  of a meal at McDonald's.

The marketer planning a sales promotion should carefully determine the
organization's objectives and create a budget that can realistically be
expected to achieve them. Some sales promotions are not "big ticket"
items, thus sales promotion may prove especially useful for smaller
organizations.

A.   Sales Promotions Aimed at Wholesalers and Retailers

Promotions of this sort are intended to motivate channel members to make special efforts on behalf of a product by devoting more space, salespeople, or other resources to the product. Trade shows, contests, displays, and cooperative promotional programs are among the most common promotions.

1.   Trade Shows

Trade shows are scheduled throughout the year across the country at hotels and convention centers. Typically, booths are set up at which marketers can display wares and meet customers. These are temporary bases of sales operations. Most shows are set up much like the boat and car shows consumers attend, though attendance is limited to members of the "trade."

2.   Contests

Contests may be used at any level of the channel to encourage members to increase sales or to stimulate individual competition among salespeople. The contests lend excitement to the sales job and provide a chance to earn recognition and prizes or extra compensation.

3.   Display Equipment and Point-of-Purchase Materials

Display equipment and other **point-of-purchase materials**, such as the L'Eggs rack and packing crates that can be used as display cases, help sellers conveniently display the product. Clocks, statues, paper cutouts, and many other point-of-purchase materials are commonly encountered.

4.   Cooperative Advertising and Promotions

Though **cooperative advertising** programs vary from case to case, the common denominator is that suppliers share promotion expenses with their customers. If a wholesaler or manufacturer shares costs with a retailer, both receive a benefit. The supplier's product is featured and the retailer's store is accented in an ad paid for by each (as in a 50/50 program.)

5.   Allowances

Allowances are reductions in price, rebates, merchandise, or other things given to intermediaries for performance of a specific activity or for placing a large order. E.g., an amount of free merchandise is given to retailers who agree to feature the product in point-of-purchase displays.

B.   Sales Promotions Aimed at Ultimate Consumers

A promotion aimed at the consumer can take many forms. Examples include providing products to be auctioned off at charity functions and contests. (See Exhibit 19-6.) The purpose is always similar -- to attract attention and perhaps encourage a product trial.

1.   Product Sampling

Product sampling involves providing a free sample of the product to consumers to stimulate product awareness and provide first-hand experience with the product, e.g., miniature packages of detergent mailed to consumers' homes.

2.   Coupons

Coupons generally offer price reductions of some sort and are intended to stimulate short term sales by attracting new

buyers, encouraging brand-switching, and encouraging current
buyers to purchase.

3.   Rebates

A **rebate** is a price reduction designed to induce immediate
purchase, except that the consumer gets money back from the
manufacturer rather than a price break at the retail level.

4.   Contests and Sweepstakes

Contest participants have to complete some task. The Pillsbury
Bake-Off is a contest. A sweepstakes is a game of chance.
Both are intended to encourage purchases of the products
involved.

5.   Premiums and Self-Liquidating Premiums

A **premium** is a product offered free or at a reduced charge if
another product (the key brand) is purchased. A concert that
is free after a baseball game is an example of a premium.
Self-liquidating premiums are obtained by using proof of
purchase and/or cash. For example, a cap can be obtained for a
dollar when proof of purchase is mailed in with the money. (In
other words, from the company's perspective, the premium "pays
for itself.")

6.   Point-of-Purchase Materials

Banners, cut-outs, pamphlets, and other things that provide
product information at the point of purchase fall into this
category. New technology has made some of these quite "high-
tech."

XII.   SUMMARY

Professional selling is the basis on which most organizational successes
are built. Selling is most effective when it involves identifying and
fulfilling customer needs on an individual basis, thus reflecting the
marketing concept. Sales promotion supports other elements of the
promotional mix by stimulating sales over short periods of time.

**Learning Objective 1: Describe the role of personal selling and
relationship management.**

Personal selling occurs when a seller "personally" tries to persuade a
prospective buyer to purchase a product. A salesperson is a professional
who can effectively communicate the benefits of a product or service. The
salesperson should provide current information about the company's products
and services to present customers and also convey a sales message to
potential customers. The sales message must be made flexible -- adapted to
the individual needs of each prospective buyer. Relationship management
refers to the sales function of managing the account relationship and
ensuring that the buyer receives the appropriate services.

**Learning Objective 2: Identify marketing situations in which
personal selling would be the most effective means of reaching and
influencing target buyers.**

Personal selling is effective because the salesperson can adjust the sales
message on the basis of direct verbal and nonverbal feedback and close the
sale. Personal selling concentrates on the best prospects and is therefore
more effective than advertising in completing a sales transaction.
Personal selling works better than other forms of promotion for technical,
expensive, innovative, or complex products. It is effective in selling to
channel intermediaries and organizational buyers. However, it is
inefficient in reaching mass market consumers of frequently purchased
products.

Learning Objective 3: Show how the professional salesperson contributes to a modern marketing firm.

There are three kinds of selling tasks: order taking, order getting, and sales support. Order takers do little creative selling. The professional order-getting salesperson must apply the marketing concept by identifying customers' problems and solving them individually with the organization's products, terms of sale, and other benefits. Sales support personnel engage in special activities such as providing service and expertise.

Learning Objective 4: Outline the steps involved in making a sale.

The steps involved in making a sale are: (1) locating and qualifying prospects, (2) making the approach, (3) making the sales presentation, (4) handling objectives, (5) closing the sale, and (6) the follow up. Salespersons are often supported in their jobs by technical specialists and account service representatives.

Learning Objective 5: Explain why the marketing process does not stop when the sale is made.

Obtaining an order is the beginning of an organization's relationship with a customer. Satisfied customers provide repeat sales and positive word-of-mouth recommendations. To ensure an enduring buyer-seller relationship, sales personnel should follow up on orders to guarantee that they are delivered in proper condition on schedule and that post-sale services are performed.

Learning Objective 6: Characterize the major aspects of the sales manager's job.

Members of the sales force must be managed so that their efforts are directed toward organizational goals. A sales manager is responsible for (1) setting sales objectives, (2) organizing the sales force, (3) recruiting and selecting sales personnel, (4) training the sales force, (5) developing an effective compensation plan, (6) motivating the sales force, and (7) evaluating and controlling the sales force.

Learning Objective 7: Classify the various forms of sales compensation.

Sales personnel may be compensated by use of a straight salary method, a commission based on sales, or a combination of these plans, such as a commission with draw, a quota-bonus plan, or a salary-plus-commission.

Learning Objective 8: Identify some of the ethical issues facing sales personnel.

The ethical issues facing sales personnel are as numerous as those involved in any human interaction. In general, companies expect their salespeople to comply with the law and be honest and straightforward in all their dealings.

Learning Objective 9: Identify the purposes of sales promotion and explain how the major sales promotion tools work.

Sales promotion programs support other promotional elements, which in turn support the sales promotion. At the wholesale and retail level they include trade shows, contests, point-of-purchase displays, cooperative advertising, and allowances. Popular sales promotions at the consumer level are product sampling, cents-off coupons, rebates, contests and sweepstakes, premiums and self-liquidating premiums, multiple-purchase offers, and point-of-purchase materials.

XIII. KEY TERMS

XIV. QUESTIONS FOR DISCUSSION (14)

XV. ETHICS IN PRACTICE

XVI.   CASES

ANSWER GUIDELINES FOR CHAPTER 19 QUESTIONS FOR DISCUSSION

1.   *For each of the following, tell whether you would expect the salesperson to be an order-taker or an order getter: (a) selling cable TV subscriptions to homeowners; (b) selling industrial power tools to purchasing agents in the aircraft industry; (c) selling blocks of Oakland A's season tickets to businesses that entertain customers at the games; and (d) selling paper product supplies to office supply stores.*

ANSWER:

There is no "easy" answer to this question. In fact, jobs might be arrayed on a continuum from "most order taking" to "most order getting." The class might try to develop such a scale before going further. Example:

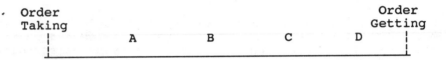

where "A" is, perhaps a retail sales job in an auto parts store, "B" a shoe salesperson in a woman's shoe shop, "C" a person selling an industrial cleaning service to a factory-owner currently employing people to do that work, and "D" a salesperson for IBM attempting to sell a computer system that will control and keep track of traffic patterns for the city of Chicago. Incidentally, when the class has established its continuum, they might be asked if the rankings of sales jobs might change if the sale were not to a new customer but to an established, regular customer. Of course, depending on the sales positions selected, the rankings would change.

On a continuum like the one shown above, the sales jobs mentioned in the question might be placed as follows.

a)   Cable TV

The sale of this product is not an extremely difficult task, though not as uncomplicated as "selling" milk and bread to a grocery buyer. The fact is that cable TV is familiar to virtually everyone and, in any given area, a monopoly may have been granted to a cable company thus eliminating competition. Such services are quite heavily promoted and are supported by price specials like "free installation" or "two months free service."

Though a seller of a cable system may have to exert some effort to "talk people into it," the job falls near the order-taker end of the spectrum. This accounts for the fact that "sale" of these services is often entrusted to college students who essentially canvass neighborhoods.

b)   Industrial power tools

This task falls near the order-getting end of the spectrum. The special needs of buyers must be understood and addressed. Buyers probably have supplier preferences which must be overcome. Specialized tools may have to be designed to fit specific needs. While there may be products that are more difficult to sell, this is definitely an order-getter job.

c)   Oakland A's season tickets

This selling activity falls toward the middle of the range, yet is clearly on the order-getting side of the mid-point. Even when a team is at or near the top of its league or division, as the A's have been lately, the investment in dollars and time associated with season tickets is great.

While it is true that many buyers routinely buy blocks of tickets, and businesses that want to buy tickets for summer events don't have a lot to choose from besides baseball, it is also true that:

.   In this case, buyers could buy S.F. Giants tickets. Other sports tickets are also a possibility where teams operate.

.   Possible buyers, other than past buyers, are probably numerous but will have to be located.

.   The appropriate person to talk to has to be found.

.   Ways to use the tickets have to be developed, e.g., company outings, give to clients, entertain visitors, donate to kids' organizations, etc.

.   Businesses may have to be convinced that clients want to go to the games.

Incidentally, the Oakland A's, and many other teams in all sports, produce videotapes to be shown to perspective business buyers. These may be available for use in class.

d)   Paper products to office supply stores

Normally, this would be an order-taking sales job, replenishing supplies as they are worked off. It could be handled over the phone; however, the job may be more complicated in that it would involve checking to see if new suppliers are "moving in" on the client. Personal sales calls and knowing the market are thus necessary.

In some cases, selling these products could be "creative." For example, getting the first order and/or getting the business away from a competitor is not simple order-taking. This product line and the situations which might surround its sale lead many sellers to have two sales forces. The "boss" or some experienced salespeople might constitute the outside/order-getting sales force while telephone order-takers or less "high powered" salespeople handle the routine orders.

2.   *How would you prospect and qualify accounts if you were selling each of the following: (a) Chain saws to hardware wholesalers, (b) Installations of cables for office computer networks, (c) Life insurance, and (d) Executive jet aircraft?*

ANSWER:

Prospecting and qualifying tools and techniques are limited "only" by the imagination of the salesperson. Telephone books and directories, government publications, leads from current customers, and just about "anything that works" can be used for prospecting and qualifying purposes. Because prospecting is the more general of the two activities, qualifying is often more organized or "quantitative." A firm might determine, for example, that buyers of product X are of particular interest at this time only if they buy in quantities beyond a certain amount, produce a certain number of products, or buy from more than one supplier. The seller may set such criteria at will, of course, as long as use of these is a help in deciding the prospects worth pursuing.

a)   Chain saws to hardware wholesalers

Prospecting for (i.e., locating, these wholesalers is a relatively easy task. Mailing list brokers might be used, as well as lists of trade association members. Industry "source books" (These answer the retailers' questions of where to obtain merchandise.), registration lists from "hardwaremen's" conventions, and numerous government business-oriented publications could all be used.

Qualifying would, as mentioned above, depend in large measure on the goals of the seller. Factors which could be easily discovered and used in qualifying these wholesalers might include size of territory covered, Dun and Bradstreet ratings, credit records, sales volume, reputation with retailers and manufacturers (Though this could be "gossip," it is still used.), whether or not the organization is part of a larger firm, and numbers of retail customers.

b)   Cables for office computer networks

The seller of an installation service like that mentioned in the question will (more than likely) be selling to computer manufacturers and/or their sales organizations than to the users, or office operators, themselves. Locating computer manufacturers and their offices in any area is a relatively simple task since such manufacturers and dealers are relatively few in number when compared to offices and stores that use computers, for example. These computer suppliers can probably be found quickly using a phone book, city directory, or (the newer) "business to business" yellow pages.

Since the number of potential customers is fairly small, qualifying them would likely involve direct calls, in person or even by phone, though the personal approach would seem to have more appeal. Questions to be asked would focus on how this installation is now handled (own work force or sub-contracted,) prices paid, level of contentment with current method, service, guarantees, etc.

(c)   Life insurance

A life insurance salesperson may target customer markets for individual policies as well as organizations for group policies. In either case, continuous prospecting is critical to long-term success. Endless-chain-referral is used when these representatives ask a customer to refer them to a friend or co-worker. "Bird dogs" are people whose position provides a center of influence for information about people moving into the town, businesses which may need coverage, or to change providers. Life insurance salespeople establish relationships with people who can provide a continuous source of prospective names. Other sources include newspaper announcements of life events (weddings, graduations, promotions, births) for consumers and business directories to form mailing lists of prospective organizations.

Qualifying may occur for business clients before an initial face-to-face interaction based on the size of the firm, financial statements, or personal referrals. For customers, life insurance salespeople generally complete a standard list of questions (in person or over the phone) to insure initial qualifications or risks associated with issuing a policy.

(d)   Executive jet aircraft

This industry seems small enough to compel efficient database marketing. Beginning with no prior history, lists such as the Fortune 500 in industry and services may provide a starting point. Information services such as Dun & Bradstreet or others would sell mailing lists based on specified criteria. Multinational corporation executives may be prime prospects. Magazine articles and purchased lists of names may also be helpful.

Qualifying may begin with knowledge of current purchasers of executive jet aircraft, i.e., minimum dollar assets, number of trips per month, or benefit derived from ownership. Interviews by salespeople would probably be required to assess awareness, interest, or ability to purchase the organization's jet.

3.   *"Salesmen are born, not made."* *Comment.*

ANSWER:

This statement has a lot of appeal because of its simplicity. While some people are more "outgoing" than others, or less intimidated by the salesman's "less than 100% success rate," or more intrigued by the challenge involved in sales work, the statement is false because of the following considerations:

.   There are many kinds of sales jobs mentioned in the text. Some call for "aggressive" behavior, others for friendly chats, others for little more than checking out orders. There is no "born salesman" who fits all of these roles, and there are roles enough for just about any type of person (at least, given that sales training is available).

.   All salesmen would admit, if pressed, that they do not just go out and "snow" the customers. They in fact train, prepare, study the customers and their needs, study the products for sale, and rehearse their presentation.

. Companies spend a lot of money on sales training programs, many of which deal specifically with narrow selling situations - "What do I say if the customer asks this question?" These firms, and their salesmen, would not invest the money and effort if these programs could be avoided by simply hiring "born salesmen."

. Tests that supposedly identify "sales types" may, in the aggregate, stack the odds in favor of the user of such tests but virtually no one, not even the people who sell the testing procedures, claims the tests will find "salesmen" and eliminate "non-salesmen."

. To say that there is such a thing as a "born salesman" is stereotyping and most educated people eschew that.

. To say that there are "born salesmen" will get you in trouble. These days, we say "salesperson."

4. *What are the steps in the personal selling process? Which is the most important step?*

ANSWER:

There are six steps in the selling process, according to the text. We might add one at the start of the process: "preparation." We would then have:

Preparation
|
Locating and Qualifying Prospects
|
Approach
|
Sales Presentation
|
Handling Objections
|
The Close
|
Follow-Up

These are described in the text.

Which is the most important? One approach would be to ask "Which can be left out?" The answer, of course, would be "none." No subsequent steps can succeed without preparation, no objections can be handled unless the customer is found, etc. Since we are dealing with a logical, step-by-step process, ALL are important.

However, this is a business text so we must admit that a bottom-line answer would be "The Close." There may not be a sale made to every potential customer on every call, but the purpose of a sales call is to make sales. Thus, the close is arguably "the answer" in that it is the sale that drives the whole process and on which the organization rests.

As marketers, we could also make a case for the "follow-up," since it is here that we learn about customer satisfaction with the product. Of course, "locating and qualifying" means we are trying to find customers whose needs we can satisfy. Thus, this stage could be "most important." Best to go back to the original answer ... all are important.

5. *Handle the following objections: (a) "The price is too high." (b) "I don't have enough money. I'll have to wait a month or two." (c) "I'm just not certain if I need one or not."*

ANSWER:

This is a good question for classroom role-playing. The question does not state the nature of the sales situation, whether consumer or industrial. This should be established before the role-playing begins.

Among the possible responses to the cited objections are those mentioned below. Since some of the class will find themselves in the buyer role, they should be encouraged to respond to the responses.

(a)   "The price is too high."

. "The price is high, but not too high given what you get."
. "The best quality costs a bit more, of course."
. "Not when you look at these cost-savings figures I've brought you."
. "Your competitor, XYZ Company, uses this and look how they have kept prices down."

The attempt should be not to argue. Thus shouting, "It is not too high!!" is definitely the wrong response. The possibilities mentioned here are intended to show some agreement that the price may be a bit high (after all, the customer knows that) but not too high given the product benefits. In the TV ads for Curtis Mathes products, students may have seen this approach. CM, and many other advertisers, say, "Yes, this is an expensive appliance but look what our price includes." A list of extras -- that competitors charge for -- is shown and, lo and behold, CM is the much better deal. In automotives, Volvo, and many other brands, stress long life.

The "boomerang" approach to overcoming this objection, where the objection turns into the reason for purchase, might result in the following:

. "That is the very reason you should buy this product. In ten years when your neighbor has purchased four replacement units, you'll still be using our product."

(b)   "I'll have to wait a month or two."

Here the salesperson might adjust the marketing mix, particularly the price variable. If the buyer's statement is not just an excuse to get rid of the sales rep, the sale has been made, it's just the terms we have to work out.

. "We have a regular arrangement with First National to finance this."

. "Our postponed payment plan can let you get the advantages of this product but work out your own payments. Plan A involves a down payment with later installments, B no down payment, and installments don't start for two months, etc."

. "I know you can use this and I appreciate the cash crunch. A little down payment now will lock in this sales price. It won't go up. Then we'll work out the payments."

(c)   "Not certain if I need one or not."

The question to be answered is why the customer is not certain. If this can be determined, the salesperson can focus on those areas.

. "Let me run these cost savings figures up again. They make a good point."

. "You don't have to worry about new requirements you might encounter later. This machine can be expanded with add-on modules."

. "This computer can be used by every department in your organization."

The traditional "T-Account" or "Ben Franklin" close may also be useful in this situation:

. The salesperson says: "Let me give you this piece of paper and pen. Draw a big T the size of the sheet. On the left side write 'benefits' and 'disadvantages' on the right. I'll start by summarizing what I understood from you." The list should be longer on benefits than disadvantages for the uncertain customer to clearly see the positive aspects.

The salesperson may also benefit from the SPIN (situation, problem, implication, need-payoff) approach to presenting the benefits of the product in relation to needs, as follows:

Situation: "You've had 100 complaints from your customers about billing errors, is that correct? Your employees are working 10 hours overtime per week to keep up with the paperwork?"

Problem: "You're losing customers and your compensation expense is costing you money, right?"

Implication: "These problems will only get worse as your business continues to grow."

Need-payoff: "This computer will save you money in the long run by eliminating those customer complaints and the overtime you pay now. Our training program will insure your employees can use the machine. In time, you can add components as your business grows.

6.   *The sales volume of a man with 25 years of experience begins to slip. How would you motivate him to work hard?*

ANSWER:

First, some obvious matters would have to be cleared up, especially since more and more organizations are moving away from the "traditional" response to a situation like this, e.g., "Fire the bum!" to the more modern response of finding out what's wrong.

Some possibilities include:

.   a slump in the economy affecting his sales.

.   sales were very high before the "slip" thus it is possible that the "slip" merely reflects overstocked clients.

.   salesman has been introducing new products or cultivating new customers, both "good" things.

.   salesman is having "personal problems" at home or with self: sickness, drinking, etc.

Given that these first situations do not apply and that the salesman simply appears to be losing steam, various approaches to motivate him might be used. Some things that many successful organizations do include:

.   Hold formal sales meetings in a "special spot," not at the home office.

.   Bring the "on the road" salesman in to the home office for a week.

.   Send a sales management-type to the salesman to work with him.

.   Employ some non-overused sales incentive plan, e.g., trip to Paris.

The main purposes of such methods are to provide the salesman with a change of pace, a time of refreshment and, maybe most important, show him that the company cares about his contribution.

Of course, some strictly "mechanical" things might be in order. E.g., the compensation plan, product line, territory set-ups, and other variables should be checked out.

In general, "burn-out" is not uncommon. Salesmen do become less "hungry." However, it often happens that the same motives that made the person a "good seller" can be used to reactivate him. These include pride in accomplishment. Thus many programs focus on a chance to "prove you are still the best," or the offering of a challenge such as sales development or another specialized activity.

7.   *How can a sales manager determine the number of salespeople to hire? Be creative.*

ANSWER:

Students can be asked to develop some "formulas" to do this job. In fact, the usual methods used to determine the number of salespeople to hire are relatively simple. Examples:

.   Study the job to be done, the territory to be covered, etc. Hire some salespeople to handle the job and add or subtract as experience warrants. (Sounds pretty unprofessional, but this is common.)

.   Use a "marginal approach" hiring salespeople until it appears that the added salesperson (at the margin) is not generating enough revenue to "justify" him or her. While the marginal approach has a strong intellectual appeal, it is easier said than done since the variables involved in making for a good sales week, month, or other period are so hard to judge. Who is to say whether or not the last person hired was a dud or not? In other words, a different person in that same slot might have done far better.

.   For the formula-oriented person there is the "equalized workload method." Here the sales task is "added up" as follows:

1)   Need to make 12 calls per year on 1,000 Class A customers (12,000 calls).

2)   Need to make 6 calls per year on 1,000 Class B customers (6,000 calls).

3)   Need to make 2 calls per year on 1,000 Class C customers (2,000 calls).

4)   "Average salesperson" can make 600 calls per year.

$$\frac{\text{TOTAL CALLS TO BE MADE}}{\text{AVERAGE CALLS PER YEAR}} = \frac{12K + 6K + 2K}{600} = \frac{20,000}{600} = 33\ 1/3 \text{ salespeople needed}$$

A problem here, besides the need to find 1/3 of a salesperson, is that the formula, as stands, does not permit any "slack." Some space for developing new business, introducing new products, collecting information, etc., would have to be built in.

Another alternative is to divide the sales forecast for a territory by an estimate of the productivity of each salesperson. For example, a company forecasts sales for the first year of operations as $2,500,000. It consults *Sales and Marketing Management* magazine to discover that the average salesperson in this industry sells $72,000 per year. Thus:

$$\frac{\text{FORECASTED SALES}}{\text{AVERAGE SALES PER YEAR PER REP}} \quad \frac{\$2,500,000}{\$72,000} = 34.7 \text{ salespeople}$$

The firm may then hire 15 or 20 salespeople to begin as judgment always plays a part.

8.   *Over a five-year period, a company keeps the same sales personnel in the same geographical territories. What problems might this create?*

ANSWER:

Territories are assigned after a number of variables have been weighed. Among them are these: physical size of the territory, transportation within the territory, the number of current and potential customers within it, the general economic state of the territory, and the territories' sales totals and potential. Though many companies have labored long and hard, and used computers to try to equalize territories, inequities almost always result.

The problems which keeping the same people in the same territories for five years or more might create are not so much associated with the "five years" as they are with possible innate differences in the territories themselves or with personality clashes, jealousies, or things just "going wrong." Many salespeople service the same territories for decades. The old adage, "Know the territory," seems to suggest such a practice and many companies keep people in their home territories "forever." Clearly, this pays off for those firms or they wouldn't do it.

We are concerned, however, with the problems such a policy might create. Some possibilities include:

. When territories are somehow unequal, or perceived to be, jealousies over who has the biggest or best territory may occur.

. A salesperson might not fit into the territory for any number of reasons, not feel "at home" and allow this to affect his or her work.

. The salesperson might not get along with some key customers in the territory.

. The salesperson might get along so well with customers that he or she loses a sense of "challenge" or fails to develop new customers.

. The salesperson might feel "forgotten" in some remote territory and suffer failing morale.

In short, the reasons why a salesperson might profit from long tenure in a given territory can be turned on their heads to become disadvantages. This is one reason why so many companies carefully select and monitor salespeople in an all-out attempt to get the "right person in that territory."

9.   *Why do most college students avoid careers in personal selling?*

ANSWER:

Actually "most" may try to avoid sales careers. Many do not succeed. A large proportion of college students end up in sales whether they want to or not. This is especially true of students as a group if we drop out engineers and accountants, since these have fixed career paths for which their training has (rather narrowly) prepared them. Still, sales is, at least initially, often a "job of last choice" and, in terms of this question, many students enter sales not as a career but as a step to something they think of as "management."

Some reasons for this attitude might include the following:

. Perception of sales as low-prestige.
. Stereotype "Willie Loman" image of door-to-door peddler.
. Experience with low-level retail sales positions or with door-to-door sales of some type.
. Lack of understanding of the nature of a sales career at higher levels.
. Fear of failure because performance is subject to direct measurement (sales volume).
. Lack of understanding of sales as a career starter.
. Don't want to work "on commission."
. Don't understand vast array of sales jobs that exist.

.   Don't appreciate that salespeople are among the most highly paid
       individuals in business.
.   Belief that sales is the last resort for those who "can't get another job."

This is a good question for class discussion. Who knows the answer better than
our students? Further, many articles can be found that deal with this matter.
It is a good topic for library assignments.

10.   *What average cost per contact do you think is involved in having sales
       representatives personally visit customers?*

ANSWER:

The figure of $300 per call for industrial products is commonly bandied about.
Other estimates are available, and rise annually, from such sources as *Sales and
Marketing Management* magazine. The estimates go as high as $250-$350 on the
average and the range goes as high as $500 or $750 (occasionally more) depending
on the nature of the product, the length of the average visit, and the
salesperson's background (e.g., Ph.D. in nuclear physics) and salary.

These figures are, of course, estimates. They should not be seen as proof that
every time a knuckle hits an office door, $200-$750 suddenly "goes" somewhere.
Yet, the cost is high. Students should be asked what contributes to this. Some
possibilities:

.   Salary.
.   Training costs and time.
.   Car, lodging, entertainment expense, etc.
.   Waiting time spent in office lobby.
.   Travel between appointments.

11.   *How important are personal appearance and proper dress in personal selling?*

ANSWER:

This question is something of a "red herring" in that students are tempted to
discuss the obvious matters of dressing well, shining shoes, looking healthy, no
bad breath, no smoking in the customer's office unless the customer suggests it,
etc.

Yet, while we'd all like to look good, what is "proper" dress in one selling
situation may not be proper in another. A person selling IBM executives
financial advice, insurance, or just about any personal or corporate-related
product should probably be wearing a blue suit, white shirt, and conservative
tie. But a person selling that same executive a lawn mower, a mowing service, or
tree-removal service should wear work clothes or perhaps a uniform of a sort.
Thus, the proper dress is situation-specific.

Would you buy the tree-removal service from a fellow in a Davey Tree Co. uniform
or from a man wearing a $600 dark suit, a $120 shirt and a $75 tie? Would you
buy life insurance from a guy in a set of mechanic's overalls and a baseball cap?
Note that in most cases the "sales uniform" may change but we still expect some
points of commonality: clean clothes, reasonably neat appearance, minimum body
odor and bad breath, etc.

We should also make the point that there are suits and there are suits. Most
students will recall Herb Tarlak, the salesman on the TV show re-runs of "WKRP"
and on the syndicated "New WKRP." He wore suits and ties, but they were so bad
as to be part of the joke "salesman" persona the actor projected. There ARE
suits like that -- some of the students may have them. Female students we have
encountered wear the clothes and make-up of a motorcycle gang groupie. We assume
they are as dumb as they look, yet they surprise us on examinations by being
first in the class. Obviously, their choice of clothes will hold them back in
the world. Many students need some guidance in this area.

12. *Many salespeople take clients to restaurants for lunch. What should a young salesperson be told about entertaining at lunch?*

ANSWER:

Basic information begins with reimbursement expectations from the salesperson's organization. Limited reimbursement plans may limit the amount which can be spent while most companies will expect receipts.

Young salespeople may not be aware of the importance of atmospherics in selecting a location for the lunch. Asking for the customer's preference may be a safe beginning, but the salesperson should have options pre-selected which offer a quiet ambiance, relatively quick service, and quality food.

Alcohol consumption at lunch has become a sensitive issue. If the customer orders an alcoholic beverage, the salesperson may also do so to be social. Current sensibilities seem to suggest that it is O.K. not to drink even if others are doing so. An interviewing tactic to assess a college applicant's ability to handle alcohol occurs over a luncheon interview. The unsuspecting applicant appears to hear from a salesperson that the sales manager will be delayed. The two of them will have lunch and a glass of wine and await the manager's arrival. An hour later, another salesperson arrives to relieve the first and another round of drinks is ordered. The applicant who received the job was the only one of ten who had one glass of wine with lunch, drank soft drinks the remainder of the afternoon, and entertained four salespeople who had a great time. By the time the manager arrived, all the other potential salespeople were too drunk to talk.

Many salespeople must entertain at lunch and dinner. However, the key is to recall the purpose of the visit: the customer's happiness and subsequent goodwill or order.

13. *Some sales promotions are geared toward stimulating activity among wholesalers and retailers; others are geared toward influencing ultimate consumers. How do the objectives of these types of promotion differ?*

ANSWER:

The objectives of the two forms of sales promotion are more different than the methods themselves. It is clear that both types of promotion can employ contests, give-aways, displays (at trade shows for retailers, in stores for consumers, etc.).

The objective of sales promotions aimed at wholesalers and retailers is to win their cooperation in the marketing effort. A sales contest approach might be used to encourage retail salespeople to sell the product more aggressively. Rewards are often in the form of a bigger commission or "push money" of some kind (extra bonus on each sale). These monetary rewards may be replaced in some cases with attractive rewards of some other type, e.g., trips, merchandise, or other prizes.

Sales promotions aimed at consumers are intended to stimulate sales, especially over the short run. Of course the marketer hopes that these purchases will result in the winning of a number of long-term customers, but the immediate goal is more sales right now.

14. *For each of the following sales promotion tactics, give your opinion on the promotion's likely effectiveness: (a) A rebate offer on an automotive battery; (b) Four pairs of pantyhose in a package for the price usually charged for a three-unit package; (c) A sweepstakes contest for a regional airline; and (d) A free screwdriver with a can of WD-40.*

ANSWER:

(a) A rebate offer on an automotive battery

The rebate offer has these advantages: (1) temporary lowering of price until the offer is withdrawn; (2) some batteries will be sold to customers who do not submit the paperwork to receive the rebate; (3) the rebate is a "hook" to be used in advertising and point-of-purchase materials; and (4) the retailers and

wholesalers like the program because the maker pays the rebate so the retail
price remains steady as does the margin. The retailer, in effect, sells a
lower-priced product but does not have to absorb the lower price. The
effectiveness of the program would probably be significant among one group of
consumers: those who need a battery and/or those who think their battery is
getting old. If you don't need a battery, a rebate isn't going to entice you to
buy one.

(b)   Four pairs of pantyhose in a package for the price usually charged for a
      three-unit package

The four-for-the-price-of-three pantyhose package can be less effective than the
rebate. In the case of the rebate, the customers see they are getting a reduced
price because a check for $X arrives in the mail one day. A four-for-the-price-
of-three deal is less obvious, unless one is sure of what the real price for
pantyhose is supposed to be. Further, in the battery case, the company handed
out real money. The pantyhose people may be seen as handing out their own
product, a product that it has warehouses full of, and anyhow this may be a way
to get rid of some old or imperfect stock. In short, everybody wants something
for nothing but the reward in the case of the pantyhose is less obvious than the
rebate money. On the other hand, buyers of pantyhose may decide to stock up;
that is, you don't have to need pantyhose today to buy pantyhose. Purchase of
this product can be an impulse purchase. Probably a four-for-the-price-of-three
deal would prove attractive. There is not much risk involved, and a rebate on a
relatively inexpensive product may seem to be more trouble than it is worth.

(c)   A sweepstakes contest for a regional airline

The sweepstakes is attractive to all of us. One imagines that the prize is a
first-class cruise through the South Seas or some such thing. The sweepstakes is
usually used to attract attention, especially is this case. In a contest like
this, consumers are typically asked to sign up or fill in a card ... not buy a
plane ticket to Europe or make a purchase as could be the case with a low cost
consumer goods item.

One other problem is that most of us have the sneaking suspicion that the contest
is "fixed," or that "nobody ever wins," or that we sure as heck will never win.
Of course, in most instances there is a winner, but the chances of winning appear
to the average person to be about the same as the chances of buying a $23 million
winning lottery ticket. Still, many, if not most, are willing to take a chance
if there is essentially no investment. Therefore, if the purpose is to make
people aware of the airline or to get them somehow "involved" with the airline, a
sweepstakes could be reasonably effective.

(d)   A free screwdriver with a can of WD-40

The free screwdriver is a low-cost item. Most people know that even a consumer
can buy a screwdriver ... a cheap one ... for at least fifty cents. We all know,
too, that the WD-40 people bought "n" million of these screwdrivers for this
promotion, which means they paid pennies apiece. Also, buyers of WD-40 are often
home handymen ... folks who have many screwdrivers already. Yet, a handyman
could always use another screwdriver. They have a way of disappearing. As
mentioned above, the appeal of something-for-nothing is strong, and no one will
rip the screwdriver off and leave it at the store, but this is still a "so what"
deal. Of course, since the WD-40 itself is a low-cost item, it is a real
challenge to think of something better to tie to the product.

ETHICS EXERCISE 19

CHAPTER 19 ETHICS IN PRACTICE

Overview

A sales manager tells his sales force that he is under a lot of pressure to
increase sales for the quarter, which ends in one week. A sales person has a
prospect who has mentioned that she is almost ready to buy. The salesperson
calls her, invites her to dinner, orders the best of everything, and sprinkles
the conversation with disparaging remarks about the competitor's way of doing

business. Not all the statements are completely accurate. The salesperson usually doesn't do things this way, but wants to make a quick sale to help the sales manager increase sales.

There are several ethical issues common to many of these situations:

.	Balancing one's loyalty to one's superior and to the firm with the right of customers to receive accurate information.

.	The right of a supervisor to pressure an employee to such an extent that the employee will feel the need to cut ethical corners.

.	The right of a competitor to be free from untrue disparaging remarks and unfair competition.

.	Does a salesperson have a responsibility to his/her superior to make a sale even if it means compromising his/her own ethics?

.	What sales practices are necessary for building trust and long-term relationships?

.	To whom is the salesperson's primary responsibility: the customer, himself/herself, the manager, or the company?

The question posed is is: it ethical for a salesperson, who is under pressure from her sales manager to make quick sales, to take a prospect out for dinner, and to make misleading statements about the competitor's products?

It is easy to apply situation ethics in a case like this, rationalize, and say, "Well, after all, I'm under pressure from my boss, and he'll be pleased with my performance, so under the circumstances it's okay to stretch the truth somewhat to make a quick sale to help the sales manager out."

This is stepping over the ethical line for several reasons:

.	From the standpoint of common morality or absolute values, you are lying/deceiving. It doesn't matter how little or how much you stretch the truth -- a lie is a lie. Lying increases (what in economics-speak is known as "transactions costs"), making exchange less efficient.

.	The salesperson is violating his or her own normal standards (note that the salesperson would not normally do this). Expediency is no excuse to violate one's standards of conduct.

.	Ordinarily, it is considered acceptable to pay for and receive such customary business amenities as meals, provided the expenses are reasonable (which they might not be in this case). However, there is a point of unacceptability.

If the purpose of gifts and entertainment is more than just goodwill and may unduly influence the recipient or make that person feel obligated to return the favor by giving the company the business, then they are unacceptable. (Gene R. Laczniak and Patrick E. Murphy, *Marketing Ethics: Guidelines For Managers*, Lexington, Mass.: Lexington Books, 1985, p. 122.)

The purpose of the expensive meal in this case seems to be to create a feeling of obligation, i.e., it seems to be a bribe. A bribe creates a conflict of interest, i.e., a situation where a person must choose whether to advance his or her own personal interests, those of the company, or those of some other groups. The prospect was pretty much convinced that going with the competitive supplier is best for his/her company, but now a personal interest (owing this salesperson "one" since he or she treated her to a nice dinner) conflicts with doing what could be in his/her firm's best interest -- buying from the competitor. In the U.S. it is generally accepted that one shouldn't accept bribes, personal payments, gifts, or special favors from people who hope to influence the outcome of a decision. (O.C. Ferrell and John Fraedrich, *Business Ethics: Ethical Decision Making and Cases*, Boston: Houghton Mifflin Company, 1991, p. 22.)

. This is unfair competition: it involves lying to a competitor's potential customer. The Sales and Marketing Creed of the Sales and Marketing Executives, International states that "I shall not knowingly participate in actions, agreements, or marketing policies or practices which may be detrimental to customers, competitors, or established community social or economic policies or standards." The salesperson's behavior seems to violate this professional ethical standard.

CHAPTER 19 TAKE A STAND QUESTIONS

1. *Are the following sales activities ethical?*

a. *A salesperson skips lunch but adds the typical $10 charge to his/her expense account.*

This is certainly easy to rationalize ... "Well, they budget for it, and they expect me to take it. They would have paid for it anyway. It's a normal cost of business. They won't miss it. They owe it to me." Fact is, this is an example of padding an expense account. By claiming to have incurred an expense never taken, the salesperson is lying to the company. No supervisor will be pleased with this.

b. *In a hotel bar, a salesperson recognizes a sales representative from a competitor and they discuss each company's prices, discounts, and terms of sale.*

Unless what they are discussing is nonproprietary information this is unethical, since it violates several standards of common morality:

. Confidentiality: a salesperson is entrusted with certain information to be divulged only to selected parties. To give this out to unauthorized persons is to breach the trust of the employer.

. Loyalty: a salesperson is an agent for the company and should do what is best for the firm (as well as what is best for the customer, society, etc.).
It is not clear whether this salesperson's actions are in the firm's best interests.

. Fairness: The sales and Marketing Creed of the Sales & Marketing Executives International says, "I shall not knowingly participate in actions, agreements, or marketing policies or practices which may be detrimental to customers, competitors, or established community social or economic policies or standards." This kind of collusive behavior (acting jointly to achieve monopolistic goals) can harm consumers who might end up paying higher prices, get less desirable terms, etc. It would also be unfair to competitive firms which lack access to the information these two companies have shared. It is an anticompetitive practice, giving these firms an unfair competitive advantage.

. Price collusion, i.e., agreeing on prices to charge, which might at least implicitly be what these salespeople are up to, is generally illegal and is immoral, even if subtly done and cannot be proven, as might be the case here.

c. *A Christmas gift worth $50 is given to a purchasing agent who is responsible for buying at a major account.*

Again, this could be construed as a bribe. It is often difficult to determine when the point of unacceptability described in the Ethics in Practice case above has been crossed, unless laws make that clear. Is the motive behind the $50 gift goodwill, or is it to unduly influence the recipient? That is the key.

Some companies, such as IBM, have very rigid policies against accepting any gifts which might be reasonably supposed to have a connection with business relationships. Only customary gifts of nominal value are acceptable to such firms. Is a Christmas gift customary? Is $50 of nominal value? These are judgment calls if the company's guidelines aren't specific (which they probably should be). When in doubt, it is best to consult with one's manager before giving or receiving such gifts. (It might not always be better to give than to receive!)

d.   A salesperson offers a customer (who is "difficult to deal with") a higher discount than the typical prospect.

This could be considered a discriminatory action. It violates standards of fairness in that it disadvantages the customer's competitors. Specifically, it is a form of price discrimination and could run afoul of the Robinson-Patman Act (discussed in an earlier ethics scenario), which disallows the practice of unfairly offering attractive discounts to some customers but not to others for tangible goods of like grade and quality and where the result is an adverse impact on competition. The fact that the customer is tough to deal with would probably not be a legitimate excuse (as would be the cost-justification defense) to price discriminate. In fact, the discount appears in a sense to be a bribe to get the business.

GUIDE TO CASES

VIDEO CASE 19-1 MEAD JOHNSON-PHARMACEUTICAL SALES

SUBJECT MATTER: Sales Strategy, AIDA Formula, Missionary Sales, Sales Presentation

Please see the Guide to Video Cases for video length and other information.

AT-A-GLANCE OVERVIEW

The objective of this video case is to show how a personal selling strategy is developed and implemented. It shows a sales presentation and demonstrates the AIDA formula. The original purpose of this tape was as a sales training film.

Mead Johnson manufactures and markets pharmaceutical drugs. Company sales personnel typically sell to physicians because, even though the physician is not the ultimate consumer, the physician make the prescription decision. The task requires that the salesperson build goodwill with physicians by distributing information and by checking to ensure that the physician is being satisfactorily serviced by the company or pharmacy distributing his products.

This case is best utilized by showing the video materials before the discussion.

One of Mead Johnson's then-new products, Naturacil, is a bulking agent which competes with older (more established) brands, such as Metamusil. Its primary advantage is that it is a chewable bulk laxative, which does not require any mixing of ingredients.

When Naturacil was being introduced to the market, Mead Johnson's sales management established objectives for each of their target markets. The objective was to introduce Naturacil to all targeted physicians and to make Naturacil the first choice bulking agent. Thus, the company wanted to create brand awareness and replace Metamusil as the physicians' first preference. The salesperson's primary task was to provide information and to encourage product trial by providing free samples.

The objectives for retail pharmacy were:

1.   to increase pharmacy generated unit movement.
2.   to get the retailers' cooperation to put up point of purchase displays.

QUESTIONS

1.   *Using the descriptions in this chapter, how would you classify the
      Mead Johnson sales personnel?*

Missionary sales personnel typically sell to physicians because the physician is
not the ultimate consumer. The task requires that the salesperson build goodwill
with physicians by distributing information and by checking to ensure that the
physician is being satisfactorily serviced by the company or pharmacy
distributing his products.

The objectives for retail pharmacy were specific. Students should be asked if
they remembered how the sales objectives were stated. It was very specific:
Contact 20 retail pharmacists. This also could be seen as missionary sales,
since pharmacies could be buying their stock through wholesalers. In this case,
Mead Johnson salespeople would be missionaries. If certain pharmacies are buying
via direct dealings with Mead, the salespeople are not missionaries in the usual
sense of the term; however, the Mead salesperson would still be doing missionary-
like work.

2.   *How important will it be for the salesperson to create a good first
      impression with the physician? What type of approach would you
      expect the salesperson to use?*

In the videotape, the importance of the salesperson creating a good first
impression is discussed. In terms of the steps of the personal selling process
mentioned in the textbook, what is being suggested?

The suggestion is that it is important to approach the physician properly.
Dealing with physicians in this manner is sensitive business for the missionary
(called a "detailer" by many drug companies). Doctors are usually very busy and
are reluctant to deal with salespeople unless there happens to be no patients in
the waiting room.

Since doctors see themselves as taking time from important work and giving it to
the salesperson, the salesperson had better appear to be worthy of that
attention. Certainly a professional appearance and demeanor is important, as is
an appropriately "respectful" attitude for the healer. The approach cannot be
loud or hard-sell-like. Usually, the salesperson approaches the doctor with
respect and gratitude for his/her time, quickly describes the new product,
provides some brief technical pamphlets, and offers a bunch of free samples. The
doctor, of course, can then give these to patients and appear to be a "good guy."
Observe these detailers at the doctor's office. The whole business is over very
quickly. The salesperson may have waited quite a while, but the "sale" often
takes just a minute or two.

3.   *Do you think the AIDA approach could be used during the sales presentation?*

Yes. But in a modified and shortened form. After seeing the video, the student
may be asked the following question: "What type of approach does Jack use with
Dr. Garrett?"

It's obvious that he has called on her many times before; therefore, the most
basic way of making a good impression is to say, "Hello. How are you doing
today?"

How does Jack (the salesperson) get the doctor's attention?

The demonstration kit allows Jack to show the problems with the existing market
leader and other competitive brands.

How does Jack generate interest?

He not only talks about the products' advantages but shows illustrations and text
from a booklet that will ultimately be left with the physician. Jack provides
statistical facts to demonstrate his point even further.

How does Jack generate desire and action?

This is less obvious than attention and interest mentioned above. The doctor need not desire the product personally, but the presentation can make the doctor see that the product is a good one and can help the doctor do her job. This is so because the action to be taken, prescribing or recommending, or giving out the free samples, must be done in the future. However, there is good reason to assume that free samples taken will be given out, thus appearing to be a recommendation from the doctor.

Again, this sales contact is very "delicate" in the sense that the doctor holds a respected position in the community (even today) and probably feels "worthy of respect."

4. *Do you think the physician will raise any objections? What are some techniques that a sales person uses to overcome objections?*

Did Jack overcome any objections or use any closing techniques?

Remember how Jack asked the doctor her reaction to Naturacil. This was an opportunity for him to overcome any objections or to "close the sale."

Remember how Jack asked for the order by asking, "Will you recommend Naturacil to your patients?"

Remember also how the developing of action was accomplished in the sales presentation. Jack left the "Naturacil prescription" display so the patients could try the product at a reduced price. Thus, the sales promotion device stimulates action. It also serves as a reminder to the physician that Naturacil is her preferred brand.

How important is the use of the demonstration kit?

This is an aspect of the sales presentation that most students will see as positive. A discussion about the kit provides the instructor an opportunity to use students' answers as springboards to discussing the fact that a sales presentation is not merely a one-way lecture, but a interaction between the salesperson and the client.

VIDEO CASE 19-2   OIL TECHNOLOGY INCORPORATED[1]

FOCUS ON SMALL BUSINESS

SUBJECT MATTER: Organizational Marketing, Derived Demand, Applicability of Personal Selling

Please see the Guide to Video Cases for video length and other information.

AT-A-GLANCE OVERVIEW

Oil Technology Incorporated is located in Hobart, Indiana. It was founded in 1982 to market on-site oil recycling for the steel industry.

From the start, the company faced market resistance. Many potential customers saw no need for the service of "on-site recycling." While Oil Technology understood the need for oil recycling, little research had been done to develop techniques to accomplish it. The industry was so new, and information was changing so quickly, that it was difficult for the company to plan exactly how to accomplish their goals. Pricing, employee job descriptions, and client contracts could all be moving targets. While the company was grappling with these issues, its major account ground to a halt under a six-month work stoppage.

---

[1]Excerpts reprinted from *Strengthening America's Competitiveness*, pp. 45-46, copyright 1991 by Connecticut Mutual Life Insurance Company.

This made survival an issue, but management persisted. Management made a tremendous commitment to research, which helped to greatly improve the quality of their service.

QUESTIONS

1.   *To what extent does derived demand influence Oil Technology's sales?*

This is a major factor. If the companies Oil Technology has as customers are not working at full capacity, the amount of oil recycling they need is reduced. If the customers cease operations all together, as happened when the six-month work stoppage occurred, demand for Oil Technology's service is completely eliminated. On the other hand, when customers are in full operation, demand for Oil Technology's services should be very high. The potential for "boom and bust" is very clear, and suggests that companies like Oil Technology should try to do something to predict demand or even level out demand, such as by finding new applications for its services. This may not be as difficult a task as it seems given today's accent on the environment.

2.   *How important is personal selling in Oil Technology's promotional mix?*

As with most business-to-business marketers, personal selling is the major promotional element, especially when some customers (as mentioned above) see no need for the service Oil Technologies can provide.

The company "customizes" its product for prospects, thus personal selling and the ability to close a sale is important. Although the case does not mention it, it may be that negotiation of the price is an important activity that takes place during personal selling. It is also likely that potential buyers have questions about technical matters, about the availability of service when they want it, about the satisfaction levels of other customers, and so on. These are best addressed by personal selling.

Also, how many companies need Oil Technology's services? What companies are they? Do big companies need it more than small firms? Who will be the best prospects, biggest users, steadiest clients? Answering these questions and reaching those customers suggests personal selling over any other promotional tool.

3.   *Should relationship management be a major consideration for Oil Technology?*

Yes. This business is a service that is on-going. In many respects the best customer is the one the company can work with over long periods of time; hence, a good relationship is essential. This also illustrates the need for personal selling rather than other forms of promotion.

Company sales have grown 400% in the last three years, making Oil Technology the leader in on-site oil recycling for the steel industry.

20 INTRODUCTION TO PRICING CONCEPTS

CHAPTER SCAN

This chapter introduces the concept of price as a factor in our economy and as a marketing tool. Price elasticities are also discussed.

The chapter defines price, tells the names used to describe prices, and explains the relationship of price to the other pieces of the marketing mix and to the organization's objectives.

SUGGESTED LEARNING OBJECTIVES

The student who studies this chapter will be exposed to a broad introduction to the matter of price and will be able to:

1. Define price and be able to discuss it.

2. Tell how price interacts with the rest of the marketing mix.

3. Analyze price's place in our economy.

4. Outline the fundamentals of pricing strategy.

5. Characterize the relationship between price and organizational objectives.

6. Relate the demand in a target market to the prices charged.

7. Understand that demand and cost considerations influence pricing.

8. Differentiate among price elasticity, inelasticity, and cross-elasticity.

CHAPTER OUTLINE

I.   INTRODUCTION

II.   WHAT IS PRICE?

III.   PRICE AS A MARKETING MIX VARIABLE

     A.   Dealing with Competition
     B.   Price and Marketing Effectiveness

IV.   PRICE IN THE ECONOMY

     A.   Demand Curve
     B.   Supply Curve

V.   THE FUNDAMENTALS OF PRICING STRATEGY

VI.   PRICING OBJECTIVES

     A.   Income-Oriented Objectives

          1.   Target Return on Investment
          2.   Maximize Profits
          3.   Sales Objectives

     B.   Competition-Oriented Objectives

          1.   Avoid Competition
          2.   Meet Competition
          3.   Stabilize Prices

     C.   Objectives Related to Social Concerns

VII.   TARGET MARKET CONSIDERATIONS

VIII. KNOW YOUR DEMAND

     A.   Price Elasticity of Demand
     B.   Cross-Elasticity of Demand

IX.   KNOW YOUR COSTS

X.   SUMMARY

XI.   KEY TERMS

XII.   QUESTIONS FOR DISCUSSION (11)

XIII. CASES

     The following key terms are introduced and used in Chapter 20.   They are defined in the text's Glossary.

Value
Barter
List price
Price competition
Nonprice competition
Demand curve
Supply curve
Pricing objective
Return on investment (ROI)
Turnover
Market share
Price stabilization
Price elasticity
Cross-elasticity
Marginal analysis

Marginal cost
Marginal revenue
Average cost

THE CHAPTER SUMMARIZED

I.   INTRODUCTION

Roses generate $1.6 billion in U.S. sales annually. A small but growing share of this is generated by roses-only shops, selling roses for $6 to $16 per dozen (vs. perhaps $50 or $60 in traditional florist shops). Bigger cities now have shops called "Rosa Rosa," backed by Central and South American rose farmers who want to sell their total crop, grown year-round, in the U.S.

The impact on U.S. growers has been strong, but importers are doing very well, now accounting for 40 percent of rose sales in the U.S., up from 2% twenty years ago. The American Floral Council, fearing that lower prices might mean Americans could come to think less favorably of roses, now advertises that "A rose is a rose even when it's a bargain." U.S. growers complain of "dumping" by the Latin Americans.

The story illustrates much about pricing, including its use in entering a market. Proper price can mean the difference between success and failure.

II. WHAT IS PRICE?

Marketing involves the exchange of something of value. **Value** is quantitative measure of the power one good or service has to attract another good or service in exchange. When goods or services are exchanged without money changing hands, the trade is called **barter**.

Price is a statement of value, most commonly expressed in dollars and cents, though it would be possible, if unwieldly, to express the value of everything in terms of everything else.

Price has many names: rent, fee, donation, tuition, honorarium, vote, etc. Marketing involves exchanges of things of value and the name most commonly used to express value is price.

III. PRICE AS A MARKETING MIX VARIABLE

Ultimately, price "pays" for all of a firm's activities. Price is a prime determinant of sales revenues, but its relationship to the other facets of a marketing plan cannot be forgotten. It is an especially flexible element of the marketing mix because, generally, it can be changed rapidly in response to changes in the environment.

We noted that price is an economic tool. It is also a marketing tool. Many marketers provide lists of their products' prices to establish a basic price for each, hence the term list price. Adjustments can be made seasonally or for other reasons.

.   A high price can add status to a good.

.   A low price can suggest a bargain.

.   A coupon or rebate may encourage purchases.

Pricing policies really cannot be discussed apart from other marketing mix variables. Pricing must support the firm's other marketing strategies and must be supported by them. Example:

.   Maytag produces (1) quality products, at (2) quality prices, (3) promoting the years of trouble-free service buyers can expect, and (4) distribution through a system of dealerships consistent with all the other elements of the marketing mix.

A.   Dealing with Competition

Price competition is especially strong in industries where products are not distinctive, e.g., raw materials. Price is less important where other distinctions can be drawn. Further, reliance on low price alone presents the difficulty of competitors simply lowering their prices. Example:

.   Datril "went after" Tylenol with a low price and an ad campaign that said the two products were the same (they are) but that Datril was half the price. Once Datril was perceived by Tylenol as "a threat," Johnson & Johnson lowered its price to Bristol-Meyers' Datril's price. This wiped out Datril's "advantage" and forced a redoing of all Datril ads. One lesson is that price is flexible and can be quickly adjusted to changing situations.

B.   Price and Marketing Effectiveness

Obtaining and sustaining a relatively high price indicates that the marketing plan behind the price is sound. Lego building blocks are offered at "high" prices but, because of other factors, far outsell competitors. **Nonprice competition** allows marketers to emphasize other marketing mix elements rather than relying solely on price to gain customers. Federal Express is fairly expensive, but the total product it offers is "worth it" to many users. UPS uses price to position itself as a slightly cheaper competitive service.

Proper pricing supports promotion, distribution, and the product offered. On the other hand, these variables support the price being charged.

IV.   PRICE IN THE ECONOMY

The major purpose of price in a free economy is to help allocate goods and services to members of society. Most items are distributed to those who:

.   demand the products,

.   and have the ability to pay for them.

Thus, wealthier citizens are better able to have certain products. The price system "allocates" most products in this way. In addition, price helps to determine the quantity of goods and services that will be produced and marketed.

A.   Demand Curve

The relationship of price and quantity demanded may be shown in tabular form. The **demand curve**, or schedule of demand, represents the relationship between the prices suppliers might charge and the amount of product desired at those prices shown in Exhibits 20-1, and 20-2). In general, as price rises, quantity demanded declines.

While marketers would be greatly aided by knowing exactly the demand schedule they face, this usually is not the case. But some assumptions must be made nonetheless.

B.   Supply Curve

The **supply curve** shows the amount of goods and services marketers are willing to supply at various prices. In general, as prices rise suppliers are willing to supply more products (Exhibit 20-2).

The intersection of these curves shows the market price and quantity produced for a product (Exhibit 20-2).

Note that this discussion (as in an economics text) is of an industry, not an individual organization.

V.   THE FUNDAMENTALS OF PRICING STRATEGY

Many mathematical tools have been developed to assist marketing managers in the task of pricing. Though costs and other quantitative matters are important, few managers would set their prices using these tools exclusively. Judgments about the likely reaction of buyers and competitors come into play.

Pricing alternatives must be evaluated in terms of competitors' actions and anticipated buyer reactions to prices. In short:

.   Determine your pricing objectives.

.   Know the importance of price to your target market.

.   Know your demand.

.   Understand your costs.

.   Determine your pricing strategy.

Other matters would have to be considered including other marketing mix decisions, environmental forces, competition, legal matters, etc.

VI.   PRICING OBJECTIVES

Pricing objectives must be coordinated with the organization's other marketing objectives. Managers must know what prices are intended to accomplish, why certain prices should be charged, and how they might be changed from situation to situation. Every price and pricing strategy should have a reason behind it. Prices are supposed to help bring about a result; this result is the pricing objective. Twelve such objectives and the related pricing strategies are shown in Exhibit 20-3.

Exhibit 20-3 is intended to show that pricing (and other marketing mix) objectives flow from overall corporate objectives. Our focus in this chapter is pricing, but price cannot be treated apart from other aspects of the firm's operations. Some objectives and related pricing steps are shown in Exhibit 20-4.

A.   Income-Oriented Objectives

These objectives may be long- or short-term, but must be consistent with the long-term profitability dimension of the marketing concept. Also, short-term changes in the environment may hinder achievement of an income target. Ultimate achievement of the desired profit level should remain the objective.

1.   Target Return on Investment

Return on Investment (ROI) is the ratio of profits to assets (or net worth) for an organizational segment, product line, or brand. (Appendix A -- Arithmetic for Business Analysis -- shows how to calculate this, as well as other financial measures.)

The ROI can also be termed the profit target in that if management decides that a certain ROI is needed, prices must be set with that return objective in mind. Choices between and among marketing opportunities can be made easier using ROI.

Turnover is sales divided by average inventory.

Turnover is important to many marketers, and influences ROI. Example: a grocery store may have a low profit margin but a high ROI because of rapid turnover.

Note: Judgment is a big part of all of this. What is or is not an acceptable ROI is something of a "judgment call."

Further, if an ROI calculation yields a proposed price, judgment still comes into play:

- Will the market accept that price?

- Is the ROI price too low?

- Should the ROI price be raised so that later markdowns can be taken?

- Should different prices be charged to different customers?

- How will competitors react to this price?

ROI makes comparing possible prices somewhat easier, but ROI methods only suggest a price ... they do not determine it.

2.   Maximize Profits

It is not hard to find sellers who charge "all the traffic will bear." But businesses who seek long-term survival cannot do this. Customers will eventually stop buying and seek substitute goods. Further, competitors will be drawn to the market if high profit items can be sold. Pricing to obtain long-term profit is consistent with the marketing concept.

3.   Sales Objectives

Many sales objectives are possible (Exhibit 20-4). Prices may be set to encourage sales growth, to maintain or increase market share, or to help a product survive difficult economic times.

Market share is the percentage of total industry sales accounted for by a particular firm or product.

Caterpillar and Coca-Cola have huge shares of their markets. For financial reasons, and even reasons of "pride," these firms set their prices with the goal of maintaining market share firmly in mind.

Prices may also be set, e.g., cut, to increase market share. Some risks include:

- Competitors move to match prices.

- A price war is set off.

- Customers think price cut = quality cut.

Thus, price cuts (sales, coupons) are generally temporary.

B.   Competition-Oriented Objectives

Competition plays a significant role in pricing situations. Some specific examples follow.

1.   Avoid Competition

Some sellers keep prices down so as not to attract new competitors to their markets. Better to be the only shop in town and make reasonable profits than to make large profits and attract competition.

2.   Meet Competition

It may be necessary to price at the levels charged by competitors. Rare is the situation where competitors' prices need not be considered. For example, a new brand of coffee, unless it is very unusual in some respect, almost has to be priced at about the same price as other coffees. Where a product is more expensive than competing products, the price must be supported by other marketing activities. For example, Rolls Royce cars are very expensive but also well-made, well-advertised, distributed, and repaired with care, etc.

3.   Stabilize Prices

Price stabilization could be the goal of matching competitors' prices. This avoids price wars (e.g., in most towns, gasoline prices are roughly the same at most gas stations).

C.   Objectives Related to Social Concerns

Many organizations set prices on the basis of social, not economic, concerns. Schools, zoos, and museums are good examples. Some profit-seeking firms may seek to "save the hometown" by pricing in a way that permits them to meet the payroll and preserve jobs.

VII.   TARGET MARKET CONSIDERATIONS

The most significant of factors affecting pricing decisions is the target market. The question becomes, "Who are our customers and what do they want the price to be?"

The customer does not necessarily want the price to be low. Rolls Royce cars are expensive in part because Rolls owners expect (even want them to be) expensive. High prices lend a sense of pride in "having the best." Even mundane products like jeans, irons, baby food, etc., reflect this phenomenon. When J.C. Penney's "plain" jeans or "Fox" shirts sell to people unwilling to pay for designer jeans or Ralph Lauren's "polo player" shirts or for "alligator" shirts, it is because these are aimed at different target markets.

VIII.   KNOW YOUR DEMAND

Market sensitivity to price is defined by its price elasticity of demand.

A.   Price Elasticity of Demand

Price elasticity measures the effect of a change in price on the quantity of a product demanded, or the percentage change of quantity demanded induced by a percentage change in price.

Illustrations in the text show that as prices go up or down, changes in demand may vary widely. Changes in demand that are slight occur when demand is price inelastic; greater changes reflect demands which are elastic. Perfect inelasticity is portrayed when the demand curve is perpendicular to the base (quantity) of the graph, showing that the product (e.g., a dose of a life-saving medicine) will be demanded at "any price." Perfect elasticity is portrayed by a curve that is horizontal to the base of the graph.

Exhibits 20-5 through 20-8 illustrate these various price elasticities of demand.

It is difficult to determine exact demand curves/schedules, but information published by trade associations, and other marketing research information, should assist in this chore. Experimentation with prices, an on-going phenomenon for some marketers, may yield information about price elasticity of demand.

B.   Cross-Elasticity of Demand

Demand for some products is linked strongly to demand for others ... turkey and cranberry sauce, for example. Other cross-relationships can be found. For example, if the price of beef rises and demand falls, buyers might increase their demand for fish. This is referred to as **cross-elasticity**.

IX.   KNOW YOUR COSTS

Though marketers should be consumer-oriented, not cost-oriented, costs do provide a "floor" on which to build a marketing strategy.

Marginal analysis attempts to determine the cost and revenue associated with the production and sale of each additional unit of a product. If costs are less than revenue, it makes sense to produce and sell "one more unit"; if costs are greater than revenue, it does not. Therefore, a firm would try to operate where marginal cost = marginal revenue (MC=MR). This is illustrated in Exhibit 20-9.

X.   SUMMARY

Marketing involves the exchange of something of value. Value is generally represented by price. Price has an important role in the marketing mix and in the attainment of marketing objectives.

Learning Objective 1: **Define price and discuss it.**

Price represents value, which is the power of one product to attract another in an exchange. Price enables buyers and sellers to express the value of the products they have to offer.

Learning Objective 2: **Tell how price interacts with the rest of the marketing mix.**

In an effective marketing mix, product, distribution, promotion, and price decisions must be consistent with and supported by one another. For example, a high price is consistent with high product quality, strong image-oriented promotion, and exclusive distribution in prestige stores.

Learning Objective 3: **Analyze price's place in our economy.**

Price plays a major role in the allocation of goods and services in market economies. In addition, price encourages or discourages demand; it often imparts a symbolic value to products that can easily be perceived by buyers; it helps achieve financial or market-share objectives; and can be used as a rapid-response adjustment to environmental changes.

Learning Objective 4: **Outline the fundamentals of pricing strategy.**

In setting prices, it is important to (1) determine your pricing objectives, (2) know the importance of price to the target market, (3) know your demand, (4) understand your costs, and (5) determine your pricing strategy.

Learning Objective 5: **Characterize the relationship between price and organizational objectives.**

Organizational objectives are the basis for pricing policies and are achieved partially as a result of those policies. Price affects income generation, sales, competitive moves, and attainment of social objectives.

Learning Objective 6: **Relate the demand in a target market to the prices charged.**

The price of a product must suit the target market. For example, the decision to target potential buyers of extremely expensive jewelry means that prices charged can be high if they are supported by the appropriate product quality, promotion, and distribution policies.

Learning Objective 7: **Understand that demand and cost considerations influence pricing.**

Marketers need to know how many people will buy their product and how much it will cost to meet this demand. Cost provides the "floor" on which to build a pricing strategy. Marginal analysis is a technique that helps marketers determine the cost and revenue associated with production and sale of each additional unit of a product.

Learning Objective 8: **Differentiate among price elasticity, inelasticity, and cross-elasticity.**

Price elasticity exists when the relative change in quantity demanded exceeds the corresponding change in price that brought it about. Price inelasticity exists when the change in quantity demanded is smaller than the change in price. Cross-elasticity exists when price changes for one product affect demand for another, as when a rise in the price of meat contributes to an increase in the demand for fish.

XI.   KEY TERMS

XII.   QUESTIONS FOR DISCUSSION (11)

XIII. CASES

ANSWER GUIDELINES FOR CHAPTER 20 QUESTIONS FOR DISCUSSION

1.   *What are some other names given to "price?" Why are these names used instead of price?*

ANSWER:

"Price" is an expression of value. It is, in effect, "what is exchanged" when an exchange occurs. We pay a "price" when we invest our time or votes in a candidate's campaign, for example. However, price is usually expressed in monetary terms; even limited to money, the word "price" has many synonyms. Among them are: rent, fee, tuition, commission, honorarium, charge, premium, etc.

Why do some sellers avoid the word "price?" There are two general causes for this. One is tradition. "Rent" is a word that has been around for centuries and remains in use. "Fee" is another such word. "Honorarium" is a Latin word, so it obviously has a long history. However, even in Medieval times (to which current usage of the term "Honorarium" can be traced), there probably was (as there is today) a desire on the parts of certain "professionals" to avoid the appearance of charging a "price" for their work. Doctors and lawyers thus have fees, professors doing off-campus lectures charge (make that "accept") honorariums, and so on. Perhaps the cleverest of all names for "price" is "donation."

2.   *What is the main macro-marketing function of price in the economy as a whole? Differentiate between that function and the role of price as a macro-marketing tool.*

ANSWER:

Price, by whatever name, serves this major function within an economy: it serves to allocate goods and services to members of society. This fact may generate some debate in class but, like it or not, the rich can drive Rolls Royces and the poor generally cannot. It may prickle the conscience, but the better-off person can drink bottled water if the local water is contaminated while the less well-off may continue to drink contaminated water. The better quality food and housing is also claimed by the wealthy. Thus, with certain exceptions, price allocates goods and services to those who want them and can pay for them. While the marketer recognizes this role of price in an economy, such a portrayal is generally not seen as broad enough. Price is an "economic tool," but it is also a "marketing tool." Some examples:

- Price may be used to help establish a product image, be it "status" or "economy."

- Price cuts may be used to attract new customers.

- Prices may be varied, as they are in quantity discounts, as a "reward" for large purchases.

- Prices may be varied to level out demand fluctuations.

- Prices may be used as competitive "weapons."

- Price may be used in support of other elements of the marketing mix.

3. *"A high price policy needs supporting policies." Explain.*

ANSWER:

It would be the rare buyer who would purchase a product just because it is expensive. Even the "show off" needs something other than high prices to attract him or her. Status value, a quality product, a product image augmented by great ads, excellent sales and service personnel, and a good reputation, are among some of the factors that could support or help support a high price.

In short, the policy of charging a high price cannot stand alone. The price can be high only when the selling organization "delivers the goods" in one way or another. The Rolls or Ferrari can be expensive, but it must also be properly promoted, distributed, and well-built. In some way, it must be "worth the money." Thus, the high price must be supported by the selling organization's other (nonprice) activities.

4. *Give some examples of situations in which price might not suit other aspects of a firm's marketing plan.*

ANSWER:

In gross terms, in light of the fact that a firm's marketing plan is the "given" in this question, a price can be (a) too high, (b) too low, or (c) just right. Since situation (c) is not germane to the problem, the other two must be considered.

(a) Too High

Prices may be "too high" because of the decision of a marketing manager or because of cost or other manufacturing/marketing considerations. In the latter case, the cost of making and marketing the product is such that the selling price necessary to cover these costs and a reasonable profit ends up being beyond the range prospective customers are willing to pay. We encounter this frequently in international marketing when an otherwise "good" marketing mix runs afoul of shipping, manufacturing, or other costs and/or taxes and duties that drive the price of the product involved to unacceptable levels. The price ends up "out of synch" with the rest of the marketing plan.

Prices may also be "too high" because of a miscalculation by a marketing manager who, using research data or "gut feelings," sets a price that proves unacceptable to the market. However, since price is the most flexible aspect of the marketing mix, it can usually be dropped to obtain a better "market fit." The very common "sale price" or "mark down" exemplifies this situation.

(b) Too Low

Prices can be too low in the sense that they do not cover costs and a reasonable profit. This can often be blamed on a miscalculation by a marketing manager or on faulty data. It happens that most markets are changeable enough that projected sales totals can be way off the mark. Since (as seen in the next chapter) many prices are based on a calculation of the quantity of products to be sold, if those target quantities are not sold, loss will result. If the product, promotion, distribution, or research is "wrong," the price will be "out of synch."

Prices can be too low in the sense that they cover cost and some profit but could have been higher and generated a greater level of profit. Interestingly, when prices are "out of synch" in this manner, the market (at large) adjusts the price upward even if the marketing firm itself does not. Ticket scalpers provide an example of this phenomenon.

5.   *Why does the consumer often view price as the most important part of a transaction?*

ANSWER:

Among the reasons why price receives the brunt of consumer attention are:

. Price is generally obvious and out in the open.

. Price is usually understood by consumers while other aspects of a product or transaction are not.

. People generally do not fully understand the "quality" of the products they buy and so use price to gauge that quality.

. The seller gets "paid" by the price the consumer pays and the consumer often attempts to figure out the seller's "cut."

. Price includes credit and payment terms that are of major interest to buyers.

. Price is a feature of the transaction that is often heavily advertised or stressed in sales messages.

. Most people must give up other options once they have agreed to pay a given price.

. Many people devote time to comparison of price.

6.   *Consumers can rent everything from houses, yachts, and luxury cars to televisions and other home appliances. What price-related advantages might renting bring to consumers? What aspects of buyer behavior are brought into play when a consumer compares renting a TV or refrigerator to buying such items?*

ANSWER:

The most obvious price-related advantage of renting is the fact that one need not come up with an amount of money equal to the purchase price or required down payment. Business students may think of this advantage in terms of its financial implications for those who have alternate ways to use their money, i.e., why tie up a lot of money when you can invest it somewhere else and receive a higher rate of return? In fact, of course, many renters look at renting as a means to "pay as you go." That is, they can't afford to buy a house or to put a down payment into a house, but they can live in a house for X dollars a month.

Depending on the rental situation and the product involved, certain other price related advantages are associated with renting rather than purchasing. Among them are:

. Avoid having to pay for "extras" such as heat, water, etc., since the rent pays for these in one lump sum each month. This reduces risk and also reduces "bother" for the renter.

. Avoid having to repair the item in question since, in many rental situations, this is covered by the party who owns the item. As above, this reduces the risk to the renter, both financial and in terms of "bother."

. Avoid having to pay for new items if the rented one is superseded by a new model. For many renters, one attraction of renting ... whether house or appliance ... is the opportunity to move on to a new house or have a new model appliance without having to get rid of the "old" item.

.   Avoidance of the feeling of being "tied" to a house or other item. Many
         renters rent to avoid the sense of having so much "in" a house or other
         product that they can't afford to get rid of it when it gets older. This
         seems to be a major appeal of car leasing deals.

As can be seen from the advantages of renting, the aspects of consumer behavior
most influencing the rent-or-buy decision are risk-avoidance in several
manifestations and a desire to have "the best I can at the price I'm willing to
pay." Unfortunately this way of fulfilling needs and wants leads to large
monthly payments to be met. Indeed, running up purchases on credit or using a
credit card is really a form of renting, since the debtor has "bought" the
appliance (or whatever) but arguably rents the products bought from the
organization providing the credit arrangements.

7.   *Days Inn of America, a chain of 325 motels, adopted a slogan for use in its
         advertisements: "Inexpensive, but not cheap." What does this slogan say
         about Days Inn motels, their prices, and the target market Days Inn is
         trying to attract?*

ANSWER:

The slogan is intended to suggest value at a reasonable price. The term "not
cheap" tells the reader or listener that the motel is not physically cheap (that
is "schlocky"), but that it is clean, adequately comfortable with several
amenities included. It's not the Ritz, but it's no dump either. Further, the
slogan tells customers about the price. The price is "inexpensive." This
indicates that the price is not super low. This is not a flop house, after all.
Yet the price is suggested to be much less than the other major motels that
compete with Days Inn. Those places may try to charge the traveler $60, $80,
$100 or more per night; but not good old Days Inn. Management there knows that
its customers want a good value but that they also want a "nice" place to stay.

Who is the "they" to which Days Inn is directing the appeal? What target markets
could be expected to respond to this slogan? In general, any individual who
wants to stay at a "decent" place without spending a great deal of money would
like what Days Inn is seemingly able to offer. Such people would be found in
these target market groups:

.   Less-than-top-level business travelers who cannot justify staying at
         expensive hotels. This large group includes several subgroups who might be
         reached by specific media (such as *Inc*, the magazine for business owners).
         Subgroups would be: salespeople with limited expense accounts or per diem
         limits; owners of businesses who are not willing to pamper themselves;
         occasional business travelers who are "afraid" to call other possible
         hotels only to find themselves "stuck" with an expensive room; business
         travelers of all sorts who have had bad experiences with "cheap" motels.

.   Families traveling on a limited vacation budget. Such people do not want
         to put their spouses and/or children into a "cheap hotel," nor do they wish
         to spend a lot of money.

.   Retirees, a group which travels a good deal, might also be wary of "cheap
         hotels," especially since there might be some question about the security
         of such places. These travelers, like families, may want to hold down
         expenses, and ... because they can recall the good old days ... might be
         shocked at today's prices at Marriots, Howard Johnsons, Hiltons, and other
         hotel-motel chains. This group could be reached by "senior citizen" media
         like *Modern Maturity*, now the number one U.S. magazine as measured by
         circulation.

8.   *The price a firm charges for its goods or services often depends primarily
         on how the customer is expected to react to the price charged. In what
         situations have you, as a customer or seller, encountered this approach to
         pricing?*

ANSWER:

Since most students have greater experience as customers than as sellers, the following examples are largely from the buyer's perspective. They can easily be reversed to reflect the seller's perspective. We have all heard:

. "Buy a 1993 Ford now. The 1994 models will cost more."

. You ought to get one of these now. The price is going up next month."

. "This is our pre-Christmas price."

. "The prices of these condos will be higher as soon as the building is done."

. "Ten percent off the lawn care service if you sign up before April 15."

. "The price on these winter coats will go down in the Spring, but there's no way of telling if the coats will be in style next year."

. "Coupon expires on May 1. Use it now!"

. "Sure it costs more, but you want the best." "It's the only one of its kind available in this state."

. "The price is low because we buy in huge lots."

. "Low overhead means lower cost to you."

. "Buy direct from the factory."

. "Too expensive? Let me talk to the manager. I'll see what I can do."

. "We give you six months to pay."

9.   *Differentiate among organizational objectives, marketing objectives, and pricing objectives.*

ANSWER:

Exhibits 20-3 and 20-4 show the difference between company objectives, marketing objectives, and pricing objectives. All are determined by managers and all should have the usual characteristics of good objectives. That is, they should:

. be realistic.
. be specific and quantified.
. include a time frame.

Yet they vary in their "broadness."

Organizational objectives are intended to encompass the whole organization. They describe the "mission" of the company as a whole.

While most marketers give to marketing a position of primacy among the firm's operational objectives, others would include financial and manufacturing objectives. It is at this level that we find marketing objectives. Fulfillment of these contributes in a major way to achievement of the company objectives.

Marketing is conveniently broken down into the 4 Ps. For product, place, promotion and price, there will be objectives, though we acknowledge that these cannot be set without consideration for each other. At this level, we find the pricing objectives mentioned in the questions. These objectives lead to the determining of pricing policies and strategies, then to the determination of actual dollar and cents figures.

The area encompassed by the levels of objectives declines in size as we move from company objectives to pricing objectives and down to the actual prices themselves. So, ordinarily, do the time frames covered diminish, as might the rank of the managers making the decisions.

10.   *Why must managerial judgment play a role in determining prices even though many mathematical techniques for that purpose have been developed?*

ANSWER:

Price is, with promotion, an extremely visible portion of the marketing mix. It is arguable that it is the factor to which consumers pay the most attention. It is certainly one they evaluate closely and often the one by which they evaluate the product offered for sale. Price may be the key factor in appealing to a particular target segment of the market. For these reasons alone, a marketing manager would be unwilling to trust price determination to a mathematical tool. The prices such tools appear to suggest may be too high or too low given the realities of the market as an experienced manager understands them to be.

A second matter, relating to the mathematical tools themselves, should be mentioned here though the subject comes up again in a subsequent chapter. It is that the formulas and tools available to "determine prices" are only as good as the information used in them. Many rely on an estimation of demand to be used in setting the price. This raises three issues:

.   Prices should be strongly influenced by demand; yet in formulas relying on demand estimates, price is fully determined by demand.

.   Most price-determining formulas rely strongly on cost figures. Cost-orientation is not marketing; demand-orientation or market-orientation characterizes the field.

.   If the estimate of demand is off by any sizable amount, the calculated price will be far from the amount appropriate. Imagine what happens when a formula uses an expected sales total of 1,000 units and actual sales turn out to be 500 or even 250 units.

For these reasons, marketers use these formulas best when they use them to get "ballpark figures" or "starting points" and then apply their own managerial judgments.

11.   *How can target market considerations affect a firm's pricing policies?*

ANSWER:

Though costs and other variables will, of course, affect pricing policies "in the real world," consideration of the organization's target market should be the major factor in pricing policies. This is called for by the marketing concept's insistence on customer-orientation.

Some examples of how target market considerations can affect a firm's pricing policies would include:

.   The comparative wealth of the market would indicate whether high or low prices are appropriate.

.   The status-sensitive nature of the market would also have an obvious influence on pricing as would level of fashion-consciousness.

.   The degree of price elasticity or inelasticity displayed by target market members would affect pricing.

.   The sheer size of the target market would affect pricing policies in that mass marketed items generally are priced "reasonably" both to appeal to the mass market and because of economies of scale.

.   The market's preference for product variations would affect pricing. A desire for "specially made-to-order goods" must be paid for.

In large measure, many pricing policies and practices are influenced by these two target market-related questions:

.   "What does the market expect to pay?"

.   "What does the market think this is worth?"

ETHICS EXERCISE 20

CHAPTER 20 ETHICS IN PRACTICE

Overview

The chapter opened with a discussion of how roses-only stores sell imported roses
in the U.S. at very low prices. Some U.S. producers of roses feel that roses
will become so widely available that they will saturate the market and roses will
lose their appeal and image as a special flower. Some of these producers want
the government to restrict importation of roses into the U.S. The case poses the
questions of how the reader would feel about this if the reader were an American
rose grower, a retailer selling roses imported from South America, or a consumer
who wants to buy roses for mother's birthday.

The Ethics in Practice Case illustrates that whenever government intervenes in
the marketplace, whether it be by price controls, import restrictions, or
whatever, the natural workings of the free marketplace are circumvented, and some
groups prosper while others suffer. Generally the groups who prosper (e.g.,
domestic rose producers) are highly involved, well-organized and unified;
therefore, they push for the interventionist legislation, which earns them what
economists call economic rents. That is, noncompetitive profits that accrue from
good relations with regulators and influential legislators. The majority who are
disadvantaged by the legislation (e.g., consumers) are diffused, scattered, less
involved, and unlikely to take action in their own favor.

Also explored in this case are the ethics of dumping and of charging a relatively
high price to create connotations of high quality.

How would you feel about the government passing laws to restrict the importation
of roses into the United States if you were an American rose grower? A retailer
who imports roses into the United States from South America? A consumer who
wants to buy roses for your mother's birthday?

Before the invasion of Latin American rose growers, domestic rose growers were
apparently earning handsome profits. With supply mostly restricted to domestic
producers and a strong demand, rose producers were able to charge a pretty penny
for their wares. However, when the foreign rose growers entered the retail
market in the U.S., several things happened. First, supply increased, since
previously the foreign producers were not able to sell their entire crop.
Second, the cost of rose production apparently declined, since labor costs are
lower in Latin American countries. Hence, there was increased supply as well as
lower costs, both which shifted the supply curve to the right, increasing supply,
resulting in a lower market-clearing price for roses.

American rose growers would be as pleased as punch with restrictive legislation.
Supply would decrease and they would no longer face producers with a lower cost
structure. Prices would rise (and correspondingly, revenues would grow) and
their market share would increase. Because domestic rose growers are
well-organized through the American Floral Marketing Council (and probably other
trade groups), they could lobby for restrictive legislation to keep the
"cutthroat" competition out. But on what basis?

They could charge the Latin American growers with using price "dumping." Dumping
occurs when a firm sells a product in a foreign country either at a price below
its domestic price or below the full cost of production (including profit).
Dumping is a combination of price discrimination on an international basis. That
is, lower prices are charged in foreign markets than in domestic markets.
Dumping is also predatory pricing -- pricing low so as to unfairly hurt
competition. This is illegal if the intent is to drive competitors out of
business, but legal if the purpose is simply to cause temporary pain for a
competitor. Dumping is illegal under GATT (General Agreement on Tariffs and
Trade) regulations and the laws of many nations.

In response to dumping, the United States historically has added import tariffs to dumped products to bring their prices in line with those of domestic products. The U.S. can also institute quotas and other trade barriers. From the information in the case, it is not clear whether the rose growers are actually dumping; and in practice, this is often difficult to determine.

The other reason why domestic rose growers wish to bid the foreign growers good riddance is that the low prices are hurting the quality image of the roses. In many product and service categories there are price-quality relations -- high prices are believed by consumers to be correlated with higher-quality products. That's why sales of some products increase after a price increase (contrary to the law of demand). This is especially true where consumers are not knowledgeable. It is difficult to objectively evaluate product performance and/or consumers' lack of confidence to make such evaluations; perceived risk is high, and there are perceived quality variations among alternatives. Roses seem to meet many of these conditions.

Are higher prices associated with higher quality? Unfortunately, the jury is still out -- some research says yes and some says no, though the perception seems to hold true in some product categories but not in others. Economic theory suggests that higher prices are associated with higher quality since higher prices would reflect higher production costs and higher demand. However, is demand higher because the product is better or due to perceptions shaped by pricing, promotion, and distribution? If so, is it ethical to create quality perceptions through the marketing mix and therefore make it possible to charge a higher price? Critics say no, since no tangible value is being added. However, supporters say that intangible psychological value is being added -- brand image, snob appeal, whatever. So, in a sense, people are "getting what they pay for."

The response of a retailer who imports roses from South America to any restrictive legislation would be positive, especially if that retailer was vertically integrated and also grew his own roses. Domestic retailers also face competition from the Latin American growers -- retailers who undercut their prices by selling at wholesale, and securing restriction of competition would be in their self interest. They would possibly join the growers in lobbying for restrictive legislation.

Consumers will be harmed by the proposed law because they will lose access to a source of quality, lower-priced roses. Restricted competition and less supply will mean higher prices. For this reason, most economists aren't opposed to continuous dumping, for it is an opportunity for a country to take advantage of a low-cost source of a particular good and to specialize in others. (Warren J. Keegan, *Global Marketing Strategy*, fourth edition, Englewood Cliffs, N.J.: Prentice-Hall, 1989, p. 409.) However, the common type of dumping is a sporadic type which is unpredictable and harms the orderly development of enterprise within an economy, injuring domestic business. This case seems to involve continuous dumping, which is in accordance with the notion of international comparative advantage. Perhaps some domestic growers will be harmed, but domestic resources can be allocated more efficiently to other sectors.

In the matter of the effect of cheap roses on consumers, one partially "off-the-wall" argument could be made. That is, that imported roses drive down the price of roses, thus consumers lose out because they are denied a product that was once attractive and "high class" (i.e., what they once sought as special has become commonplace). Thus, it could be argued, restrict importation of roses and keep the prices higher "where the consumers want them to be." While this argument for import restriction is certainly weak, it has been used by business in the past to defend high prices, e.g. in support of the now defunct Fair Trade Laws.

CHAPTER 20 TAKE A STAND QUESTIONS

1.   *Supply and demand theory suggests that prices should be at a level that "all the traffic will bear." Is such pricing ethical? Is it good for society?*

There is a discussion of this issue under the section of the chapter entitled "Income-Oriented Objectives," one of which is "Maximize Profits." The word "profits" conjures up images of selfish greed. A defense of the profit motive

was given in the Chapter 2 Ethics in Practice case question 1. Key points from
that discussion are:

. Profits provide an incentive for producers to be efficient and responsive
to consumer needs, and to work hard.

. Profit is a reward for risk taking, such as launching new products or
trying innovative marketing strategies.

. The profit motive has created greater wealth than any other economic
system.

From a macroeconomic perspective, when firms charge "all that the traffic will
bear," what they are doing is charging the market-clearing price, i.e., they are
matching supply and demand. If they were to charge a lower price, shortages
would be created. Thus, price performs the important societal function of
allocating society's resources. If firms in an industry are earning fat profits
("extranormal profits" in the economist's lingo) this attracts other enterprises
to the industry, with the result that price will be lowered (due to increased
supply) and perhaps quality will improve, innovations will spring up, etc. as the
new firms try to compete more effectively and efficiently. Consumers play an
important part in the resource allocation process by voting with their dollars.
If they believe that a seller has established a fair price for the object of
exchange, they vote for (purchase) the product. Firms that don't effectively
satisfy needs and wants at a desired price cannot compete effectively for
resources and will go out of business or switch to producing another product.

The special situation is that of the profit-maximizing monopolist, where a single
firm dominates an industry (e.g., regional utilities, new products). Although
unregulated monopolists set prices in accordance with market demand and their own
cost structure, they do charge higher prices and restrict output in comparison to
other market structures. It should be noted that even a monopolist must set
prices to be consistent with value perceptions. For instance, if the U.S. Postal
Service tried to set prices beyond what consumers are willing to pay, the volume
of mail would decline and alternative forms of message delivery (e.g., fax
machines) would become more popular.

As the text suggests, a monopolist (or any marketer) who creates perceptions of
price gouging could be faced with boycotts, bad public relations, or government
regulation. In fact, most monopolies are regulated (e.g., cable T.V. companies,
power companies). Prices are set by government fiat so as to yield a "fair"
target rate of return and to charge "fair" prices (where government bureaucrats
define what is "fair").

The smart marketer will realize that there is a difference between maximizing
short-run profits (charging what the market will bear) and long-run profit
maximization (which considers possible adverse reactions to high prices and
profits, such as competitive entry, government regulation, and the like).

A case where there are perceptions of companies trying to squeeze as much money
from people as possible is pricing of new drugs. Setting initial steep prices on
drugs is common (skimming) because drug companies wish to recoup their initial
high development costs. However, this can lead to problems. For instance,
Burroughs-Welcome developed a life-prolonging drug for AIDS patients, AZT. AIDS
activists demonstrated against the company in several cities, claiming they were
"corporate extortionists" because the initial cost of AZT was $10,000 for a
year's supply. The company responded by lowering the price to $8,000, but the
protests continued because many AIDS patients couldn't afford the treatment. The
average price later dropped to about $3,000. Recall that price does drop over
time even with a skimming strategy. The company now provides the drug free to
many needy patients and provides discounts to government agencies that purchase
the drug.

Where should drug companies draw the line on profit goals for new drugs?
Enlightened firms use ethical pricing, defined as pricing so as to avoid taking
undue advantage of inelastic demand, but where to draw the line isn't clear.

Is an accelerated approach to recouping profits justifiable? For instance,
Medtronics held the line on price when it introduced the world's first pacemaker,

and Gerber supplies a specially formulated product free of charge to children who cannot tolerate foods based on cows' milk. What responsibilities do pharmaceutical companies have to victims of diseases? Do they have the right to decrease profits (and hence shareholder wealth) for the good of others? Will the increase in goodwill be worth it to the firm? Will government intervention decrease the incentive to develop expensive (but important) new drugs or will it serve society?

2.   *"Consumers want lower prices. If the marketing concept means being oriented toward the consumer, prices should be lowered."* Comment.

This statement reveals a lack of understanding of the marketing concept, which suggests that a producer serve and satisfy customers profitably. The AMA definition of marketing notes the need to satisfy both buyer and organizational objectives. If a firm followed the logic of this statement to its ultimate conclusion, it would give the product away! This would maximize customer satisfaction. However, the purpose of the marketing concept is not usually philanthropy. Customer satisfaction is a means to achieving the organizational goal of profitability, not an end in itself. As Ted Levitt has said, "A business is about only two things -- money and customers." You can't forget the money.

GUIDE TO CASES

CASE 20-1   LLOYD MANDEL FUNERAL DIRECTION[1]

SUBJECT MATTER: Service Marketing, Price Elasticity, Consumer Perception of Price, Relationship of Cost to Price

AT-A-GLANCE OVERVIEW

Lloyd Mandel Funeral Direction is located in Skokie, Illinois. It's not like most traditional funeral parlors. It is located in a strip mall, next to a hearing aid store. From this modest storefront, Mandel averages a funeral a day ... 365 a year. Why is he successful? He's inexpensive. He rents space in traditional funeral parlors and charges $1,350 for a gravesite and service. He undercuts the nearby traditional shop by $1,000. (His father is a partner in the older business.) Mandel advertises that he can complete a funeral without using a chapel and save the buyer $2,000.

The funeral business is clearly changing. Once most bodies were embalmed for viewing. Now that is thought to be about 30 percent. Cremation has doubled in popularity during the past 14 years, knocking a big hole in the profitable casket business. Many clients arrange no services other than immediate cremation or burial. Funeral directors are looking for new ways to make money since "the economic underpinnings of our business are deteriorating."

Students usually discuss this case very well. Most have pro or con opinions on the funeral "industry," stories to tell, preferences to voice, and so on.

1.   *How price elastic is a funeral service?*

This is a perfect example of price and its relationship to market segments. For some people the price of a funeral "doesn't matter." These buyers have such reasons as "Mom deserves the best," "Do just what you did for Dad," "This is our tradition," or "What would the neighbors say?" For these people, to scrimp on a funeral service is either an insult to the deceased, an indicator of their own "cheapness," or both. Even here, however, there is some top price at which consumers begin to balk. They might go for the $5,000 casket but not the $10,000 model. We might mention that there is an element of "hysteria" here, too. The "hysterical" segment, as unscrupulous funeral directors know, will "go for anything."

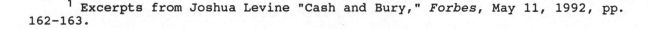

---

[1] Excerpts from Joshua Levine "Cash and Bury," *Forbes*, May 11, 1992, pp. 162-163.

Other people may not have enough money to be so "generous." These people would be price sensitive. It is sad to read about families that cannot afford a "proper" funeral, and most of us would prefer not to be dumped in a hole with a bunch of other stiffs (like Mozart in the movie "Amadeus") even though we "know" it won't make a heck of a lot of difference.

Other people can afford a "nice" funeral but feel that flowers that last one day, a limo ride that lasts a half hour, etc., just isn't worth it. Still others, because of their views on life and death and the ceremonies that can surround death, opt for "instant cremation -- and that's the end of it."

The fact that older funeral homes still survive down the street from Mandel's operation supports the notion that segments are important in the funeral business. And, where there are segments there are different levels of price elasticity.

Of course, Mandel's success also suggests that the times "are a'changin."

2.   *How well does Lloyd Mandel know his market?*

Very well. He's doing a funeral a day, grossing over half-a-million dollars per year, has no investment in building or equipment, and operates out of a store front. Though this kind of funeral operation doesn't appeal to the traditionalist, Mandel sees that it has great appeal to a particular segment of the nation's biggest market ... the people who are going to die, and great appeal to another huge segment ... the people who know people who are going to die.

3.   *How important is cost a typical funeral home's pricing strategy? How important is cost in Lloyd Mandel's pricing strategy?*

A traditional home has high prices but also several high-cost investments. While the mark-up on caskets is great, the caskets themselves still cost about half of what the funeral director gets. Traditional parlors must keep several models on hand. Traditional parlors have (often) large multi-room buildings to maintain (and they are usually well-maintained, not shabby,) decent looking office facilities for the bereaved to meet the director, at least a few special automobiles, investment in equipment and mortuary school education, a number of employees, and so on. In short, for a traditional funeral parlor, costs are high; therefore, so must the prices charged. Maybe the price doesn't have to be as high as it is, but it has to be high enough to cover costs plus a profit margin. Unlike Mandel, most parlors do not do a funeral a day, 365 days a year, and much of what they must support (building, etc.) is idle on any given day. Also, funeral directors usually take care of "everything" ... fees for the church, preacher, limos, etc. They say, often correctly, that a good part of their price goes for these things, not for themselves.

Mandel's is a cut-rate operation charging cut-rate prices. He has very little investment, rents out facilities as needed, and (in general) does things as cheaply as possible. His low price reflects this. Indeed, he could not have the low price unless he cut out all the extras.

An interesting assignment would be to have students do a bit of research to discover what a traditional funeral home's profit margin is and to estimate what a cut-rate operator (like Mandel) takes home out of his half-million in sales.

4.   *What additional marketing strategies would you suggest to marketers in the burial business?*

The number of additional strategies is limited only by the imagination (and nerve). Here are some possibilities.

Funeral directors are using price-cutting, new "products," and creative marketing. Driving this new promotional push are some basic economics. Increased longevity has held deaths steady at 2 million per year for the past decade. Meanwhile, profit margins are slipping, as families increasingly reject the costly pomp of traditional funerals. Cremation is at an all time high in the U.S. Some people see donating their bodies to medical schools as a way to avoid funeral costs. Faced with these sorts of developments, the industry is turning to marketing.

Starting at $125, for instance, Namsco Inc. of Spokane, Washington, compiles a
video "tribute" of the deceased's life, replete with nature scenes, fleecy images
of the deceased's face, and background music. A big favorite for the music
portion of the video is Namsco's version of the Frank Sinatra classic "My Way."
The videos are big sellers -- over $1 million in sales last year. One California
mortuary has even installed a 10-foot-by-10-foot screen to show Namsco's home
movies.

Niche marketing is in. Portland, Oregon's Little Chapel of the Chimes
enthusiastically pushes what it calls "life-centered" funerals. When Thomas
Jones, formerly part owner of the local Top-O-Scott golf course, died, the chapel
customized a $2,500 service for the onetime 2-handicap golfer. Displayed were
Jones' golf cart and clubs, along with old school report cards, his favorite salt
shaker -- he was a heavy user -- and the scorecards from his retirement golf
tourney. "Everybody got a big kick out of all that stuff," said his widow,
Nancy.

"What we're really doing now is event coordination -- just like wedding
planners," says Jacquie Taylor, president of the San Francisco College of
Mortuary Science.

Then there's Al Tacker, owner of Family Heritage Casket Gallery, an
entrepreneurial Memphis, Tennessee outfit. Tacker runs a kind of casket discount
house, selling 16 casket models from his storefront at substantially lower prices
than the local funeral home charges. For instance, Tacker's top-of-the-line
stainless steel model sells for $2,200, but costs up to $5,900 at a local funeral
home. A solid cherry casket with tufted velvet lining touchstones is sold
through two-dozen funeral homes across the country.

Another entrepreneur has applied for a patent on the process he uses to produce
cremation urns. He is negotiating with a large national funeral chain to offer
his line, which runs from about $100 for the touchstone to $450 for a larger
ceramic vase.

Marcel Hatch, who made porcelain enamel signs for zoos, is also trying to cash in
on the cremation craze by using a similar process for funerary urns. Hatch's
Vancouver-based IMI Urns saturates the 25,000 North American funeral homes on his
database with frequent mailings.

Funeral directors receive copies of "Cremation Chronicles," a wry look at
funerary oddities. A tasteful example is the New York biker whose gang wanted
his motorcycle to go up in flames with him. Hatch also runs a monthly "Win an
Urn" contest, and his promotion material features a bare-breasted "Urn Lady."
Says Hatch, "We're as much a junk mail outlet as we are a manufacturer."

That's extreme, but even conventional funeral homes are getting more promotion-
minded. Vanderlyn R. Pine took over his family's funeral business in New Paltz,
N.Y., and also runs an industry consulting business. When Pine's great-
grandfather ran the family business, he knew everyone in town and everyone knew
him. Pine concedes that same familiarity isn't possible today with a local
population that is constantly changing. Thus funeral directors simply have to
hustle more to make their names known.

The Mattox-Wood Funeral Home in Terre Haute, Indiana, for instance, runs public
service commercials on local television stations. On Memorial Day the ads
eulogize the local war dead, making sure that Mattox-Wood's name is featured
prominently.

One funeral home in Akron, Ohio, operates a 24-hour call-in service so locals can
check on funeral arrangements -- an obituary service via the phone. In smaller
towns, radio stations frequently list local deaths, as organ music softly plays
in the background. The minute-or-two listing, usually titled something like
"Lest We Forget" is, of course sponsored by a funeral parlor. TV stations in
Pittsburgh, Pennsylvania began carrying obituary listings during a prolonged
newspaper strike in the city during 1992. They were so well received by viewers
that station managers considered keeping them on after the strike. If that
occurred, no doubt a funeral parlor's name will somehow become associated with
the service.

On a grander scale, giant ($643 million sales) Houston-based Service Corp. International built a replica of the Vietnam Veterans Memorial, which it is exhibiting around the country, sponsored by local funeral homes and cemeteries. But there are limits. "We can't very well run an ad that says, 'Big Sale,'" says Robert L. Waltrip, SCI's chairman.

Funeral directors are also promoting themselves as so-called grief specialists, following up with comforting calls to bereaved family members after the burial and on holidays. Accord, Inc. of Louisville provides "bereavement services" for 1,200 funeral homes through "grief resource persons" trained at Accord's American Grief Academy and paid out of the local home's marketing budget.

At the San Francisco College of Mortuary Science, they're still trying to grapple with these changes as they turn out a new breed of undertaker. Students now sit through courses on marketing, management, and psychology, along with Embalming 101. "For a long time the funeral industry was stuck doing what it had always done," says President Jacquie Taylor. "But the public is giving us a message: 'We don't want what we're being told we have to have.' Now we have to figure out what it is they do want."

CASE 20-2   LITTLE GOLDEN BOOKS

SUBJECT MATTER: Pricing, Relationship of Price to Rest of the Marketing Mix, Pricing and Distribution, Consumer Sensitivity to Price (Price Elasticity)

AT-A-GLANCE OVERVIEW

This case involves the familiar-to-all Little Golden Books published by Western Publishing Company. Since 1942, the company has sold tens of millions of these books. Titles such as "The Poky Little Puppy" (new ones are added, but favorites are retained) have been read to generations of kids. The books once sold for 25 cents, but prices now hover around $1. They are sold in 100,000 retail outlets. Compared to "real books," they are a convenience product. There are some 900 titles in the Golden Book catalogue, but only about 200 are available at any given time.

1.   *What are the company's pricing objectives?*

The main pricing objectives of Little Golden Books are to maintain the dominant market share in the children's books market and undercut the competition. The company has been successfully following these objectives by charging the lowest prices for its products and making them readily available at a variety of stores. This strategy has generated a high sales volume while keeping the costs low.

Little Golden Books are a "tradition" that can be "ridden" for a long time. Low prices are part of the effort to maintain this tradition ... a tradition that's cheap beats a tradition that's expensive anytime. The pricing objective of keeping price down fits in with the overall objective of remaining a major seller of children's books.

2.   *How important is price to the market?*

Price is a very important consideration in the children's book market. Western Publishing Company uses mass production and mass distribution strategy to keep prices low so that it cannot be matched by the competition. Customers (parents) consider these books as a good value for their children because of their low prices and name recognition. The low price allows the books to be a convenience good.

As was indicated above, Little Golden Books are a tradition, something like candy bars. Like candy bars they are marketed like a convenience good. This product is probably familiar to every student and provides a good example of how the pieces of a marketing mix should fit together. The product is an inexpensive-to-make product, sold at a low price, widely distributed, and effectively (if not expensively) promoted.

3.   *Outline the channel of distribution used by Little Golden Books. How does it influence pricing strategy?*

For a manufacturer to reach its consumers via 100,000 outlets, it is almost mandatory that wholesalers of some type be used. It would be extremely difficult to perform this Herculean task any other way. Also, it would be very expensive, a fact that flies in the face of Western's pricing structure (cheap). Thus the channel of distribution for Little Golden Books looks like this:

```
         WESTERN
         PUBLISHING --> WHOLESALER --> RETAILER --> CONSUMER
         COMPANY
```

A question then arises. What sort of wholesaler is a member of the channel of distribution for Little Golden Books? Book dealers of some sort? No. Since the books are sold in supermarkets and food stores, as well as in airport locations, the retailers are served by the same wholesalers who serve those outlets.

In the case of the supermarkets, for example, the wholesalers employed are food brokers ("The same people who sell Birdseye vegetables to the supermarkets," reports the publisher of Golden Books.). In fact, like vegetables, the books are commodities, not "real books." The wholesalers offer selections of books for display, e.g., a collection of Christmas season stories. The retailers have no choice as to the titles they stock.

In short, the channel of distribution operates in a mechanical way, selling massive quantities of books "by the pound." This very successful publishing venture is quite removed from the trade publishers -- the people whose books sell in "real" book stores.

The company's basic strategy is one of placing its books in virtually any reasonable location. They are found in airports for last-minute, just-got-off-the-plane gift giving, for last-minute on-the-ride-let's-read-this use, in supermarkets, and in 7-Elevens. They are sold in discount stores like Kmart. They are, in short, sold "everywhere."

The strategy might be described as "seeking to obtain maximum product exposure at the retail level." This is the phrase used in the text to describe the intensive distribution strategy.

Students may feel that distribution coverage described in the case is not as totally intense as that found in cigarette marketing. However, intensity of distribution is measured in terms of competing products. Trade books are distributed selectively, even occasionally, exclusively. More than 100,000 outlets signifies intensive distribution in the book business. Note that other aspects of the marketing mix, especially price (e.g., 99 cents), is consistent with this strategy. Little Golden Books are the convenience goods of the book business; thus they are, like other convenience goods, distributed intensively.

Thus, Little Golden Books utilize a vast distribution network to reach as many customers as possible. These books are sold through discount stores, food stores, variety stores, convenience stores, supermarkets and airports. In this way, the firm can easily follow the strategy of mass production and mass marketing. This strategy enables the firm to charge a lower price than the competition and still earn considerable profits.

There are potential sources of channel conflict inherent in the distribution methods used by Western Publishing. In a limited way, Little Golden's inexpensive books compete with more expensive, and admittedly better quality, children's books. The better (higher priced) books carry higher margins for wholesaler and retailer. It is for this reason that traditional book dealers eschew the Little Golden Books. They can make more money carrying better-quality books.

Thus, price enters into Western's distribution strategy in another way. The low price means low margins. This is also part and parcel of why Little Golden Books are sold the way they are. Even if traditional bookstore owners and other higher-margin retailers were willing to carry the books, they would not sell them aggressively.   They would naturally try to sell the $13 book rather than the $1 book.

In short, the channel used by Western Publishing for its Little Golden Books is ideal for the type of goods these books are.   There should be little channel conflict, as the situation is described in the case, because the channels employed differ from those used for other sorts of books.   However, to the degree that some traditional bookstores carry other Western products, potential for genuine channel conflict exists.   The case notes that Western dominates the kids-book field, including coloring books and the like.   Selling through regular book dealers, and to supermarkets operating on a much smaller margin, would certainly encourage animosity between the two types of retailers.

4.   *Are Little Golden Books price elastic?*

Due to current low prices, good brand recognition (giving them a somewhat differentiated product look), lack of competition in their market segment and customer loyalty, Little Golden Books are not price-elastic within certain low-price limits.   That is, a price change (up or down) of small amount, will not affect sales.   However, a greater increase in their prices beyond the $2.00 price threshold would change this and they are highly price-elastic.

It can be noted that demand could be less price elastic even if the books' prices were raised significantly when other elements of the marketing mix are altered.   For example, a parent might not pay more than $2 at a grocery store or other location where alternatives are nearby, but a harried parent at an airport, where alternatives are few and no other dealers available, might pay (though grudgingly) quite a bit more.

21 PRICING STRATEGIES AND TACTICS

CHAPTER SCAN

This chapter focuses on the aspects of pricing in which the marketer's managerial judgment plays a major role. It identifies the target market and competitive considerations that pricing-decision makers must evaluate and shows the range of pricing strategies and discount policies faced by the marketer.

The chapter concludes with a brief review of the major legal influences on pricing.

SUGGESTED LEARNING OBJECTIVES

The student who studies this chapter will be exposed to a discussion of pricing as an often judgmental activity and will be able to:

1. Identify the various pricing strategies.

2. Discuss the nature of differential pricing strategies.

3. Describe skimming and penetration pricing.

4. Show how competition affects pricing activity.

5. Discuss the effects of inflation on pricing.

6. Discuss the nature of product line pricing strategies.

7. Explain some of the psychological aspects of price.

8. Show how time and geography influence pricing decisions.

9. Discuss such pricing tools as list price, and cash, trade, quantity, and other discounts.

10. Describe the major legal restrictions on pricing freedom.

11.   Identify some ethical issues dealing with price.

CHAPTER OUTLINE

I.   INTRODUCTION

II.   **AN OVERVIEW OF PRICING STRATEGIES**

III. **DIFFERENTIAL PRICING STRATEGIES**

    A.   One-Price Versus Variable Pricing
    B.   Skimming
    C.   Other Price-Reduction Strategies

IV.   **COMPETITIVE PRICING STRATEGIES**

    A.   Meeting-the-Competition
    B.   Undercutting-the-Competition
    C.   Price Leaders and Followers
    D.   Penetration Pricing
    E.   Traditional Pricing
    F.   Inflationary Pricing

V.   **PRODUCT-LINE PRICING STRATEGIES**

    A.   Captive Pricing
    B.   Leader Pricing and Bait Pricing
    C.   Price Lining
    D.   Price Bundling and Multiple-Unit Pricing

VI.   **PSYCHOLOGICAL AND IMAGE PRICING STRATEGIES**

    A.   Reference Pricing
    B.   Odd Versus Even Pricing
    C.   Prestige Pricing

VII. **DISTRIBUTION-BASED PRICE STRATEGIES AND TACTICS**

    A.   F.O.B.
    B.   Delivered Pricing
    C.   Basing Point Pricing

VIII. SOME ADDITIONAL PRICING STRATEGIES

IX.   ESTABLISHING THE EXACT PRICE

    A.   Markup on Selling Price and Markup on Costs
    B.   The Cost-Plus Method
    C.   The Average-Cost Method
    D.   Target Return Pricing
    E.   Break-Even Analysis

        1.   Price and Break-Even Analysis
        2.   Demand and Break-Even Analysis

X.   PRICE ADJUSTMENTS

    A.   Cash Discounts

        1.   Trade Discounts
        2.   Quantity Discounts
        3.   Seasonal Discounts
        4.   Chain Discounts
        5.   Promotional Allowances

XI.   PRICING AND THE LAW

        A.   Robinson-Patman Act
        B.   The Repeal of Fair Trade Acts
        C.   Other State and Local Laws
        D.   Unfair Sales Practices Acts
        E.   Additional Government Influences

XII.   ADDITIONAL ETHICAL ISSUES

XIII. SUMMARY

XIV.   KEY TERMS

XV.   QUESTIONS FOR DISCUSSION (14)

XVI.   ETHICS IN PRACTICE

XVII. CASE

        The following key terms are introduced and used in Chapter 21.   They are
defined in the text's Glossary.

Differential pricing strategy, or variable pricing
One-price strategy
Second market discounting
Skimming price
Periodic discounting
Random discounting
Meeting-the-competition strategy
Undercutting-the-competition strategy
Price leadership strategy
Follow-the-leader strategy
Penetration price
Predatory pricing strategy
Captive pricing
Loss leader
Bait pricing
Price-lining strategy
Price-bundling strategy
Multiple-unit pricing
Reference pricing strategy
Isolation effect
Prestige price
F.O.B.
Delivered pricing, or freight-allowed pricing
Zone pricing
Uniform delivered pricing
Basing-point pricing
Close-out price
Markup on selling price
Markup on cost
Keystoning
Total cost
Fixed cost
Variable cost
Target return pricing
Break-even point
Rebate
Discount
Cash discount
Anticipation discount
Trade discount, or functional discount
Noncumulative quantity discounts
Cumulative quantity discounts
Seasonal discount
Robinson-Patman Act
Unfair sales practices acts

THE CHAPTER SUMMARIZED

I.   INTRODUCTION

The chapter begins with a description of how American Airlines (and other
airlines) tries to squeeze as much money from each seat as they can. How
many seats of each fare type should be assigned to each flight to maximize
revenue? Too many discounts on popular flights that probably would have
filled up anyhow means lost revenue, but unpopular times and days need lots
of discounted seats to fill the planes. This differential pricing
strategy, and other pricing strategies, are discussed in this chapter.

II.   AN OVERVIEW OF PRICING STRATEGIES

Exhibit 21-1 illustrates that there is a wide range of pricing strategies
available to marketing managers. In this chapter prices are categorized
into five groups. They are:

1)   Differential pricing strategies
2)   Competitive pricing strategies
3)   Product-line pricing strategies
4)   Psychological and image pricing strategies
5)   Distribution-based pricing strategies

III. DIFFERENTIAL PRICING STRATEGIES

Prices may be varied to distinguish among products, to appeal to different
customer groups, or to attain specific marketing goals.

A.   One-Price Versus Variable Pricing

A basic decision is whether to charge one price to all customers or
to vary price with customer type, that is, whether to have a
differential pricing strategy or **variable pricing strategy**, or to
hold to a single price with a **one-price strategy**.

Though the Robinson-Patman Act prohibits using variable prices that
are discriminatory, there is room for "give and take" between buyer
and seller, especially when it can be shown that the various buyers
are not competing buyers.

The one-price policy is simple to use, and cheaper in that price need
not be debated at every sale. This is one reason why the supermarket
check-out clerk is paid less than an auto salesman. The variable-
price policy requires salespeople who "know what they are doing."

A one-price strategy is followed by most U.S. retailers. (Exceptions
can be found, e.g., car dealers.) Many defend the one-price approach
as fair and democratic. Some retailers and many other types of
marketers do allow "haggling" or "bargaining." This is a variable-
price policy.

Second market discounting involves selling at one price to a core
target market and at a lower price to a second market segment (i.e.,
matinee prices at the movies, off-hour plane tickets, senior citizen
prices). This is permissible under the Robinson-Patman Act since the
buyers do not compete with one another.

B.   Skimming

A **skimming price** is a high price intended to "skim the cream off the
market."

A skimming price assumes strong and relatively price inelastic
demand. The high price permits quicker recoupment of R&D costs.
Examples of products that were very high priced when new but are now
"cheap" include personal computers and VCRs. The same strategy may
be found in organizational marketing, too. G.D. Searle priced its

patented NutraSweet very high at the start, reduced the price as its production abilities improved, then reduced it greatly when the patent was about to run out to build up brand loyalty among buyers before competitors arrived on the scene.

C.   Other Price-Reduction Strategies

Periodic discounting reduces prices predictably from time to time, as when spring fashion items are reduced for sale in summer and fall. The original price was a short-term skimming price.

Random discounting involves lowering price unpredictably to attract new customers. Regular customers may buy at "regular" prices, but price-conscious buyers can be attracted by sales, coupons, etc.

IV.   COMPETITIVE PRICING STRATEGIES

These strategies involve basing pricing decisions on competitive strengths and weaknesses. Strong companies may exploit their positions of leadership while weak companies may elect to play the role of follower, setting their prices at or near the leaders.

A.   Meeting-the-Competition

Companies meeting competition's prices set prices equal to those of their competitors ... the "going rate." This is a **meeting-the-competition** strategy. Many U.S. companies follow the lead of their competitors to avoid setting off "price wars" and to focus competition on non-price areas.

In organizational buying, price competition may be more intense than in the consumer market. Here competitive bids and independent price quotations permit buyers to obtain the lowest prices available.

B.   Undercutting-the-Competition

The **undercutting-the-competition** strategy emphasizes the best price among the available choices. Price becomes the focal point of the entire marketing effort. Situations encouraging low price competition are: discounting, where low prices are used to raise the volume of merchandise sold; instances where comparative costs are low (e.g., lower labor costs overseas); and, the "experience curve" which permits experienced producers to develop economies of scale.

C.   Price Leaders and Followers

Price leadership strategies are used by organizations with large market shares and/or shares of the industry's production capacity. Other firms in these industries are likely to pursue a **follow-the-leader strategy**.

D.   Penetration Pricing

A **penetration price** is a low price, even a loss price, used to gain a foothold in the market. The policy makes particular sense when:

.   demand is thought to be price-sensitive (elastic).

.   economies of scale are attractive.

.   there is a strong competitive threat.

.   there is a mass market, thus cautious market segmentation using nonprice variables seems unattractive.

Examples of products that were priced to "penetrate" markets include Texas Instrument's semi-conductor computer chips, priced low in anticipation that high sales would lead to economies of scale and establishment of a strong market position before competitors could act.

Some businesspeople practice a **predatory pricing strategy,** pricing low to eliminate competitors, then pricing high after competitors have been wiped out. This is illegal under the Sherman Act and Robinson-Patman Act.

E.   Traditional Pricing

Certain prices are traditional or customary prices that are, for a period of time at least, considered as established or "given." For some 60 years, candy bars were 5 cents. Graphically, demand for a product that falls in such a category is shown to be price inelastic below the traditional price and price elastic above it. That is, a higher price will reduce demand significantly while a lower price will not increase it significantly.

This demand curve, called the "kinked" demand curve, also describes the oligopolistic situation where a few producers, sensitive to price changes, respond in kind to price shifts. There is thus no advantage to moving away from the "established" price. (Exhibit 21-2 shows this demand situation.)

F.   Inflationary Pricing

During periods of high inflation, consumers and executives become particularly sensitive to price. Buying power declines and price awareness rises. No-frills products may be offered successfully. Existing products may be altered (e.g., raise prices but make the product bigger or more attractive).

V.   PRODUCT LINE PRICING STRATEGIES

Pricing strategists may consider the entire product line rather than the product item, attempting to maximize profits for the total product line rather than for the individual products.

A.   Captive Pricing

A camera maker or manufacturer of razors may price the camera or razor quite low in hopes of selling film that fits the camera or blades for the razor at high prices. This is **captive pricing.** The buyer is "a captive" in that he/she needs to buy supplies from the marketer to keep the original product operating. Newspapers do something like this, selling papers at a low price to maintain or boost circulation, then profiting from resultant high advertising rates.

B.   Leader Pricing and Bait Pricing

Most are familiar with the **loss leader,** where a product is sold at a loss to attract customers who might buy other goods. There are also cost leaders (sold at cost) and low-profit leaders. Goods priced this way are usually popular, frequently purchased and familiar items so customers will be able to recognize the bargain being offered.

Bait pricing is also the offering of low-priced products to attract customers. However, some sellers do this with the intention that the products not be sold. Rather, the customer is to be "switched" to more expensive models of the product (bait and switch). The bait is called the "nailed down model," so unlikely is it to be sold. Bait and switch has an unsavory reputation and is frequently in the attention of the legal authorities.

C.   Price Lining

A **price lining** strategy is based on the belief that some price levels are more important to customers than are others. Men's suits are usually grouped around particular prices called "price points," thought by the marketer to be "strong price points." The belief is that these prices will attract customers and that cuts in these

prices will not attract many more purchasers until the next strong
price point is reached. Thus the assumed demand curve resembles a
flight of stairs. (See Exhibit 31-3.)

Sticking firmly to price points usually means:

- leaving oneself open to price competition from others using
  lower price points.

- leaving oneself open to a "profit squeeze" as expenses and
  costs rise (as they usually do).

D.   Price Bundling and Multiple-Unit Pricing

Selecting a car with an "options package" is reacting to **price
bundling** (offering a set of different products for a lower price than
the individual items would have cost, e.g., season's tickets or
options on a car). **Multiple-unit pricing** (e.g., two-for-one sales or
"six packs") can result in more sales and more consumption (if you
have six sodas or beers, you drink six sodas or beers). However, a
risk is that some customers will stock up on the product, and
replenish supplies only when "special prices" are offered.

VI.   PSYCHOLOGICAL AND IMAGE PRICING STRATEGIES

Price signals product attributes, as when a high price suggests quality.
Other types of prices also send "messages" to buyers.

A.   Reference Pricing

Retailers often use a **reference pricing strategy**, where high and
lower-priced models are placed together to suggest a bargain. This
is based on the **isolation effect**, which suggests that a choice looks
more attractive next to a high-price alternative than in isolation.

B.   Odd Versus Even Pricing

Prices seem never to be set at $2, $5, or $10, but at $1.99, $4.98,
or $9.99 (odd prices). Supposedly, these have psychological effects
on buyers, making them think that the $1.98 price is "less than" (at
a meaningful level) $2, or that the seller shaved expenses to get
that price down a few pennies. The assumed demand curve suggests
that a small drop in price will result in a reasonably large increase
in sales. (It resembles a bolt of lightening.)

There are obviously some occasions, such as when making change would
be a bother, that even prices would "sell more" than odd prices.

- A Coke machine would sell more cans of soda at 50 cents than at
  48 cents.

- Raffle tickets would sell better at $1 than at 93 cents.

Furthermore, some "even prices" suggest quality or an absence of
"money grubbing." Thus a doctor may charge $150 for a full annual
check up, or a jeweler $1,000 for a sapphire ring.

C.   Prestige Pricing

Customers seem to use price as a guide to product quality, especially
when quality is difficult to determine by inspection or due to lack
of knowledge. Thus, products ranging from gasoline to perfumes and
furs are usually believed to be "better" if they are priced higher
than competing products. Thus the name **prestige price**. Some of
these products could be called status goods.

VII.   DISTRIBUTION-BASED PRICE STRATEGIES

Many prices are based in part on the geographic distance separating buyer from seller. Prices are not always higher as distance grows but usually reflect the seller's effort to recover some portion of the shipping cost.

A.   F.O.B.

F.O.B. can be read "free on board" or "freight on board," and is usually followed by a designation of place: a city, factory, pier, etc. This tells at what point the buyer becomes responsible for shipping costs. At the same point, title changes from seller to buyer.

B.   Delivered Pricing

Delivered pricing, or freight allowed pricing, is reflected in such comments as "delivered free in our area" or "$1,000 delivered." Delivery charges are built into the price. Ill will may develop if a customer has to pay an additional charge if he/she lived just beyond the delivery area.

A variation is zone pricing, where charges increase as geographic zone lines are crossed. The Parcel Post System uses zone pricing. The phrase "slightly higher west of the Rockies" suggests zone pricing.

Uniform delivered pricing, or "postage stamp pricing" (so called because, as with stamps, the price is the same everywhere), treats the entire area served as a single zone. For example, candy bars are (usually) the same price whether bought in Maine or California.

C.   Basing Point Pricing

Under a basing point pricing plan, customers are charged as though a purchased product were shipped from a set location (the basing point) regardless of the actual location from which it was sent.

Because this system charges the customer an essentially false freight charge, it has been ruled to be illegal when "phantom freight" is charged. Nonetheless, cases involving the system are still encountered. Bulky and relatively cheap products like cement or lumber are typically involved.

Example:

- Basing point in Salt Lake City
- Seller is in Los Angeles
- Buyer is in San Diego
- Cost to ship from basing point

    - (Salt Lake) to San Diego
      (charged amount) -------------->$1,000

    - Cost to ship from Los Angeles
      to San Diego (true amount) ---->$ 100

    - "Phantom Freight" collected
      by shipper -------------------->$ 900

VIII. SOME ADDITIONAL PRICING STRATEGIES

Pricing strategies are responses to market conditions; thus, "any" pricing strategy may be used depending on circumstances.

- Professional pricing applies to doctors and lawyers, e.g., $500 for a divorce, $1,000 for a gall bladder removal.

. Ethical prices apply to situations where humanitarian reasons may suggest a lower price than might have been charged.

. Special prices apply where a "special deal" is involved, e.g., "two-fer" sales, or 15-minute only "blue-light specials."

. Guarantee against price-decline prices apply where price uncertainty makes customers reluctant to buy unless assured they will be paid back if prices do fall within a given period. A magazine "charter subscriber" deal may promise that the buyer's subscription cost will never rise or, at least, "always be our lowest price."

IX.   ESTABLISHING THE EXACT PRICE

A.   Markup on Selling Price and Markup on Costs

Many sellers, especially retailers and wholesalers, use a simple markup, a percentage added to the cost of a good, to arrive at a price.

Users of the method almost always express the mark-up in terms of the selling price rather than the cost, i.e., **markup on selling price**. This is mainly because the most important figures that sellers employ (gross sales, revenues, etc.) are sales, not cost, figures.

Example contrasting the two methods:

If an item costs a retailer $50 and was sold for $100, what was the mark-up?

1) $50 added to cost / $50 cost = 100%
2) $50 added to cost / $100 selling cost = 50%

Exhibit 21-5 shows a series of markups applied as a product moves through a channel of distribution.

Keystoning is a term for a retailer policy of doubling the wholesale price to derive the regular retail price. During Christmas an extra 15% may be added, the "sale price" being the original keystone price. Consumers who understand this may wait for the price to be dropped to the keystone price (the "real" price) before purchasing.

B.   The Cost-Plus Method

Cost-plus is commonly used by manufacturers. Costs involved in producing an item are added up and an amount added to that to arrive at the selling price. Once that added amount has been set, this method, like markup, is very easy to use. It is commonly used in government contract work.

C.   The Average-Cost Method

If all costs associated with offering a product can be identified, it is possible to determine what the average cost of a single unit might be.

If a margin for profit were added to the total cost figure, a likely price for a unit of product could be calculated.

Example:

All costs	$ 80,000
Margin for profit	$ 20,000
	$ 100,000

If it is judged that sales of 100 units would be made:

$ 100,000 / 100 = $ 1,000 as a likely price.

This price might be adjusted by management. It is only "something to look at," a "place to start."

It is important to note that the price of $1,000, while "logical," will be way off the mark if the demand estimate of 100 units is wrong. If true demand is 50 units, the firm will lose money at a price of $1,000 per unit.

D.   Target Return Pricing

Using this method, the marketing manager first calculates a total **fixed cost** figure, including salaries, rents, etc.

A target return, probably some percentage of investment, is added to that fixed cost total.

If the target return plus the fixed cost was $500,000 / 1,000 units = $500, a figure that shows fixed costs plus target return per unit.

Variable costs have not yet been included. If these are thought to be $75 per unit, then an estimated price for the product would be: $500 + $75 = $575 per unit.

As with the average cost method, if demand estimates are off, so is the suggested price. If, in this case, demand was not 1,000 units but 500, each item sold at $575 would ultimately mean a loss of $500 per sale.

E.   Break-Even Analysis

All marketers face costs, be they fixed costs or variable costs which are incurred as items are produced and/or sold. Fixed costs added to variable costs can be charted on a graph as total cost. As sales are (hopefully) made, revenues will rise and can be charted as total revenue. With careful planning, and some luck, it can be expected that total revenues (TR) will eventually exceed total cost (TC). Before this **break-even point** is reached, loss occurs. But once the firm has broken even, profit is made. (See Exhibit 21-6, and Appendix A.)

1.   Price and Break-Even Analysis

If we examine the break-even chart, we can see that price changes affect the break-even point ... everything else being equal.

- A higher price raises revenue more quickly so the break-even point falls.

- Cutting prices reduces total revenue so the break-even point rises.

2.   Demand and Break-Even Analysis

Simple manipulation of price or other figures to "raise" or "lower" the break-even point is not realistic despite the examples in accounting and finance books. Break-even analysis must be demand oriented. What change, it must be asked, will this change of price have on demand?

A raised price may not be accepted by the market. Thus, a higher price may not "lower the break-even point." The accounting and finance book examples always "assume" that the product will be bought at the new price. Marketers look at demand, not cost, and know that even a price cut may lose customers.

X.   PRICE ADJUSTMENTS

In many industries, list prices are adjusted with discounts. Rebates reduce price by returning part of an amount paid. A discount is a reduction from a list price typically for performing some act or function, e.g., making rapid payment.

A.   Cash Discounts

The purpose of a **cash discount**, e.g., 2/10 net 30, is to encourage prompt payment. All forms and sizes of discounts are legal if offered equally to all similar buyers. Discounts are usually large enough to encourage borrowing money from a bank in order to take advantage of the discount.

An **anticipation discount** is an additional discount, say 2/10 net 30 with an "anticipation" permitting a 5% discount if payment is made within three days. The purpose, of course, is to encourage even faster payment.

1.   Trade Discounts

Trade discounts are given to buyers who are "in the trade." Electricians get discounts on wires and switches, plumbers on pipes, and retailers on goods they sell. These are also called **functional discounts** since they reward the receiver for performing a function, e.g., installation or selling.

2.   Quantity Discounts

Quantity discounts are given to buyers who purchase large amounts of a product. There are two types:

- The **non-cumulative quantity discount** treats each order separately. The larger the order, the larger the discount.

- The **cumulative quantity discount** allows the discount to get larger and larger as quantities are ordered over some period of time (like a year).

The purpose of the non-cumulative plan is to increase the size of each order while the purpose of the cumulative plan is to keep the buyer coming back (to get ever increasing discounts).

3.   Seasonal Discounts

Seasonal discounts are given to encourage "off-season" purchase of such products as resort hotel rooms, outdoor paint, and winter or summer clothing items.

4.   Chain Discounts

Chain discounts are an array of discounts showing how, if properly taken, a list price is reduced to a buyer.

Example:

List Price	$ 1,000	
Less trade discount of 40%	− 400	
	$ 600	Balance
Less seasonal discount of 10%	− 60	
	$ 540	Balance
Less cash discount of 5%	− 27	
(Price to be paid)	$ 513	Balance

This reflects a chain of discounts of 40/10/5 net 30.

Note: Each discount applies to the immediately previous price, not to the original price.

5.   Promotional Allowances

A manufacturer may partially reimburse wholesalers or retailers for promotional assistance at the local level with cash payments or "free" merchandise.

X.   PRICING AND THE LAW

Price is a marketing tool that could be used to injure competition, and price obviously affects consumers. State, federal and local laws reflect these concerns. The Sherman Antitrust Act of 1890 and Clayton Act of 1914 were early attempts to curb pricing abuses. Additional laws amend these.

A.   Robinson-Patman Act

The **Robinson-Patman Act** (1936) is a federal law making it illegal to give, induce, or receive a discriminatory price (a price that is lower to one customer than to a similar buyer). Its Congressional sponsors thought it would wipe out chain stores, therefore helping small merchants survive the Depression.

The law, in its "brokerage provision," also prohibits giving a wholesaler's discount to any organization that does not meet the criteria identifying true wholesalers.

There are two legal defenses of what might appear to be discriminatory prices that the law itself provides:

- The cost justification, that a savings in distribution, production, or other costs is simply being passed on to a customer.

- The competitive situation, e.g., a price war in progress, is such that what appears to be a discriminatory price must be given to "meet competition."

B.   The Repeal of Fair Trade Acts

Until 1975, individual states could pass fair trade acts or resale price maintenance acts. These allowed manufacturers to set the prices of their products (vertically) in channels of distribution, thus prohibiting wholesalers or retailers from discounting those goods. It was argued that these laws would help small distributors and retailers by forcing all sellers to charge the same prices. Eventually the true effect of the laws, to keep prices high and stable, became widely appreciated and the federal government repealed the acts that permitted these "price fixing" state laws via the Consumer Goods Pricing Act of 1975.

C.   Other State and Local Laws

Many states and localities have laws and ordinances affecting prices. These must be familiar to marketers. Examples:

- In some places, a going-out-of-business sale must actually be followed by cessation of business.

- In some places, one cannot have a fire sale unless there was a fire.

A service industry has grown up to supply companies with the latest information on legislation and court cases that may affect their pricing and other marketing plans and actions.

D.   Unfair Sales Practices Acts

Unfair sales practices acts are state laws that specify that certain items must be sold at minimum markups ranging from zero (i.e., no loss leaders permitted) to high percentages. This guarantees that prices charged even by discounters would have to be of a certain level, a level closer to that charged by small dealers. These are also, and more accurately, called minimum mark-up laws.

E.   Additional Government Influences

The threat of legislation is often enough to influence business behavior even if that threat is very subtle. The effect may be almost the same as that of an actual law.

- Prices may be kept down by government demands, guidelines, or public statements that increases are not in the public interest.

- Prices may be kept stable, as with price support programs for agriculture products.

- Prices may be kept high by taxes or a laissez-faire approach, as when oil prices have been allowed to rise to encourage conservation.

In short, prices are subject to government influences not spelled out in the law.

XII.   ADDITIONAL ETHICAL ISSUES

Our society deems the right to make a profit important, but also cares about the consumer's right to fair pricing. Laws define certain aspects of pricing, but ethical questions, even about "legal" prices, remain. For example, should zoos or parks or libraries charge admission? If so, should some people, such as the poor or disabled, be allowed not to pay? Some marketing efforts, like advertising, may lead to higher prices, though some would argue that the purpose of business is to make money, not "sweet music."

Further, some ethical/environmental goals may raise prices for the "good guys" but not the "bad guys." Would a construction company want to buy a quieter jack-hammer if the price were fifty percent more than the noisier one?

XIII. SUMMARY

Pricing is one of the most logical parts of marketing in that most situations addressed by an organization actually suggest the pricing course to be taken. However, price and discount decisions rest mostly on the decision maker's informed good judgment.

Prices must be used to appeal to buyers and offer them satisfaction. Costs and profit considerations are important, but prices that do not appeal to customers are of no use, no matter how they are determined. Effective marketers employ a combination of pricing strategies to arrive at prices that appeal to buyers first and, almost coincidentally, meet other organizational goals.

<u>Learning Objective 1</u>: **Identify the various pricing strategies.**

Broadly stated, there are five categories of pricing strategies: (1) differential pricing; (2) competitive pricing; (3) psychological and image pricing; (4) product line pricing; and (5) distribution-based pricing.

Learning Objective 2:   Discuss the nature of differential pricing strategies.

Maintaining a single fixed price for all buyers is a one-price strategy. Organizations that sell the same product at different prices to different buyers use a differential pricing strategy. Second-market discounting, skimming, periodic discounting, and random discounting are differential pricing strategies.

Learning Objective 3: Describe skimming and penetration pricing.

Skimming and penetration pricing consider both competitive conditions and demand. The skimming strategy involves charging a high price to "skim" the market. It is most appropriate when demand for a product is strong and there is little competitive pressure to lower price. The penetration strategy is employed by an organization seeking to enter an established market; by charging a low price, the organization can quickly carve a niche in the market.

Learning Objective 4:   Show how competition affects pricing activity.

Several types of prices are the direct result of the competitive structure of the marketplace. Charging the going rate, or pricing above or below that rate, are clearly responses to competition. Similarly, charging a traditional price or following the lead of the industry's leading firms are competition-influenced policies. Competition, though one of many variables affecting prices, is among the most powerful influences on pricing activity.

Learning Objective 5:   Discuss the effects of inflation on pricing.

When inflation rates are high, the costs of doing business rise, typically necessitating raising prices. Buyers, however, become increasingly price-conscious during these periods. Effective marketers can meet this challenge by attempting to maintain their prices or control their upward spiral. They can also alter their products, tighten distribution, and use promotional methods to help allay buyer concern over rising prices. The total marketing mix, not just price, can be adjusted to respond to high inflation rates.

Learning Objective 6:   Discuss the nature of product line pricing strategies.

Many pricing strategies consider the product line as the unit of analysis rather than an individual item in the line. Captive pricing, loss leader pricing, bait pricing, price bundling, and multiple-unit pricing are product-line pricing strategies.

Learning Objective 7:   Explain some of the psychological aspects of price.

Price influences buyers psychologically, sometimes in ways that have little to do with the product or marketing mix. For example, to most buyers, a high price implies high quality, and a low price, lower quality. Odd prices and reference pricing suggest bargains. Prestige prices are used for high-status items.

Learning Objective 8:   Show how time and geography influence pricing decisions.

Timing is not everything, but it is important in making price decisions. Among the more familiar pricing practices associated with time are seasonal discounts, sale prices and such planned changes in price as rebates and coupon distribution. Prices influenced by geography include the various forms of F.O.B. price, basing-point pricing, and uniform delivered pricing. In most, but not all, cases, the greater distance a product must travel to its buyer, the higher the product's price will be.

Learning Objective 9: Discuss such pricing tools as list price, and cash, trade, quantity, and other discounts.

List price is the "official" or published price assigned by an organization to its products. The list price may be discounted in various ways to appeal to particular markets and to achieve certain marketing goals. The cash discount is used to encourage rapid payment by customers. The trade discount is used to reward channel intermediaries or members of specific trades by providing them with a margin of profit. Quantity discounts can be used to encourage large orders or to keep customers returning to a seller. Many other discounts, each with a specific purpose, are used by effective marketers.

Learning Objective 10: Describe the major legal restrictions on pricing freedom.

National, state, and local laws restrict the marketer's freedom to set price. The Robinson-Patman Act limits the size of discounts a seller may offer a buyer. In most cases, such discounts must be proportional to the discounts offered to other similar buyers. Unfair sales acts establish minimum markups that sellers must charge, or in other ways restrict pricing freedom. The now-defunct fair trade acts permitted manufacturers to set and enforce prices throughout their channels of distribution. Pricing agreements among competitors is strictly forbidden. In part because price is a visible element of the marketing mix and one that strongly affects buyers, it has been a frequent target of regulation at all levels of government.

Learning Objective 11: Identify some ethical issues dealing with price.

Price, as the economy's mechanism for allocating resources to individuals, has an ethical dimension. Pricing decisions, by their very nature, determine who will (and will not) be able to consume goods and services. Marketers must consider what impact socially responsible decisions will have on profits.

XIV.   KEY TERMS

XV.   QUESTIONS FOR DISCUSSION (14)

XVI.   ETHICS IN PRACTICE

XVII. CASE

ANSWER GUIDELINES FOR CHAPTER 21 QUESTIONS FOR DISCUSSION

1.   *What are the relative advantages and disadvantages of variable pricing and the one price strategy?*

ANSWER:

At first glance, it would appear that U.S. businesses have, for the most part, adopted a one-price strategy, especially at the retail level. Some noticeable exceptions include the variable prices encountered:

.   when dealing with car salespeople.

.   when dealing with real estate purchases or, occasionally, rentals.

.   when buying expensive furs, jewelry, and even some appliances where some "dickering" is to be expected.

.   when dealing with some retailers who offer reductions in price to those who will "buy by the case," pay with cash, or do without "free delivery."

.   at garage sales and auctions.

Advantages of the one-price strategy include these:

- It's simple.

- It's "democratic." Old time retailers used to say "Rockefeller or ribbon-girl, both pay the same price here."

- It reduces need for personnel to discuss price (it's "as marked").

- It lowers personnel costs in that a clerk can charge the fixed price but it takes some skill to negotiate the variable price. Skill earns more pay.

We have seen that the variable price approach can be found at the retail level. It is far more common at the organizational level where quantities bought vary widely, reciprocity may come into play, and where buyers and sellers can be expected to bargain more skillfully.

Advantages of the variable price strategy include:

- the opportunity to adjust price in the face of buyer resistance.

- the chance to tie price changes to other marketing mix variables (delivery, special promotions, etc.).

- the ability to use price to appeal to particular market segments.

- the ability to "dicker" when customers want to play that game. E.g., at the height of Volkswagen's popularity in the U.S., many dealers offered a take-it-or-leave-it price even though customers expected to, and wanted to, bargain. More recently, the most popular Toyota automobiles have had very "sticky" prices, as does the popular Miata.

The disadvantages of the one-price policy are the reverse of the above advantages of the variable price strategy, e.g., prices are not variable to fit particular market segments.

The major disadvantage of the variable price strategy is the need to have (relatively expensive) personnel to administer the policy and deal with the customer. Two lesser points may be mentioned here:

- Everything else being equal, it would appear that variable prices are more likely than fixed to run afoul of discriminatory price laws.

- A variable price strategy might anger customers who are less adept at bargaining, e.g., customer A finds that B got a "better deal."

2.   *In what competitive situations would you recommend a penetration price? A skimming price?*

ANSWER:

Price is the most variable variable in the marketing mix. It can be changed quickly to adjust to market or competitive conditions. There are many situations in which either price mentioned might be used. Therefore, we offer a "generic" situation for each which could be modified, as appropriate, to match student answers.

Penetration Price

A penetration price is a low price, possibly even a loss price or at-cost price. Its purpose is to "penetrate" a market quickly either because the market is established and a low price is needed to compete against established products or because it is expected that the market could quickly become competitive and the firm using a penetration price wishes to become firmly established before competitors enter the market.

An example of penetrating an established market is the Yugo automobile. This was priced at a penetrion level since it had to compete with a vast array of established cars. Lines of recorded classical music, recorded in countries with orchestras not familiar to American audiences, are offered for sale in the U.S. at bargain prices.

A "soon to be established" market might be found where a new product would be relatively easy to copy. If McDonald's were to decide that a smaller and cheaper hamburger could be sold to children or "by the bag" to adults, Burger King could quickly follow suit. Thus, McDonald's might price their mini-burgers at the lowest possible price so as to become established in that market quickly.

Skimming Price

A skimming price is a high price intended to "skim the cream" off the market. Such a price suits a situation where demand is high and relatively inelastic because of a real need for a product (a breakthrough industrial product, for example) or because of status value ("Be the first on your block to have one."). Such a situation allows a high price and a chance to recoup product-development costs quickly. This was the case with TVs, calculators, home computers and video games, and many more products.

A risk is that as prices fall, customers may come to think they were taken advantage of for buying early.

A skimming price might also be used to appeal to a segment of an established market. Curtis Mathes has done this for years with TVs and other appliances, stressing a "high price," but one that's well worth it because of high quality and good guarantees. BMW and Mercedes, and especially Rolls Royce, do the same thing.

3.   *What is the difference between periodic discounting and random discounting? How, if at all, do they differ in their purposes?*

ANSWER:

Periodic discounting employs discounts that occur from time to time but in predictable patterns. The basic idea is to set prices high (the "regular" price), then drop prices significantly at times when demand is low. A good example is long-distance telephone rates. The "regular price" is high during the hours of 8 a.m. to 5 or 7 p.m., but lower during the evening hours, and very low during the night (11 p.m. to 8 a.m.). Note that this pricing pattern reflects demand (numbers of calls) and price elasticity of demand (if you must call a customer or supplier during "business hours," you will make the call even though the rates are at their highest.).

Certain other pricing policies might be said to be periodic. We expect that a new product will be priced high when it first comes out, and that the price will decline (predictably) as time passes. Seasonal discounts are, in effect, periodic discounts, as are airline fares when these are lower if booked well in advance, but high if the traveler wants to travel today or tomorrow.

Random discounting also involves lowering of price to attract customers. The price cuts are made, if not truly "randomly," then in ways and patterns that customers are not supposed to anticipate. The issuance of a dollar-off coupon for Corn Flakes is not anticipated by the average consumer, nor is the announcement of a fifteen-minute only, "blue-light special" at a discount store.

The purposes of the two forms of discount vary somewhat. The periodic discount is used to help smooth out demand and/or use up "excess supply." This is what the varied long-distance rates are doing. The seasonal discount, a form of periodic discount, is used to accomplish the same goals. Overall, the purpose is to make highly profitable sales to those who can and will pay full freight (business travelers on air lines) and less profitable sales to those who cannot or will not pay full freight (tourists willing to fly on weekends or late-night flights).

The purpose of the random discount is somewhat similar in that some customers (e.g., the supermarket customer who "can't be bothered with coupons") pay full price while other, price-conscious customers are attracted by the reduced price. The basic difference between the two discounts is that one is predictable, the other is not. The unpredictability of the random discount means that people cannot, in the main, easily anticipate the discount and postpone the purchase until the price comes down.

The random discount, like the "blue-light special" deal at Kmart, has a secondary purpose of creating excitement or anticipation among shoppers, many of whom get so "into" the program that they buy the special, at its very low price, whether they need it or not. Kmart is able to "unload" a good deal of slow moving items in this way.

4.   *How might competitors influence a firm's pricing activities?*

ANSWER:

Few, if any, pricing decisions can be made in an environment free of competitive influences. If there are "no" competitors, there might soon be. If there is a patent involved, the product design might be copied but not so closely as to infringe on the patent. If there is a very strong patent, the government might require that it be broken or the production techniques "licensed out" to competitors. This last happens frequently in the interest of increasing or maintaining "competition."

Examples:

.   Western Electric developed the talking movie (note on TV someday that Western Electric's symbol and name appears in the credits of old movies) but was forced to surrender the patent.

.   Bell Labs developed the electronic speaking aid used by persons whose "voice box" has been removed due to cancer. Bell used to give these away until, in the interest of competitors, exclusive rights to the gizmo were taken away.

.   RCA once owned virtually "everything" connected with color TV broadcasting but was forced to license their inventions to other producers.

Prices may be low due to competitive influences or threat of them. This is, of course, the theory behind free enterprise, and it usually works.

Prices may be stable due to competitive influences. This is typical among retailers and other businesses where price leadership or some other type of price-war-avoiding behavior is the rule. Prices may be high because of competitive influences, not only because of price leadership but also because competitors keep their prices low, allowing some companies to have high prices that appeal to certain market segments.

5.   *How does inflation affect consumer perception of prices? How can marketers adjust their efforts to counter any negative perceptions of price?*

ANSWER:

Studies have shown, as if it were necessary to prove this point, that periods of inflation make consumers more price-conscious, more interested in bargains, and, in general, simply more aware of, and attentive to, price. Indeed, when inflation is quite high, as it was in the latter half of the 1970s, it is impossible not to become more price-aware (if only because of daily news stories on the subject). Marketers in general should be aware of these changes in consumer perception. Retailers in particular, since they are the marketers closest to the consumer and since the retailer "takes the money," should be especially aware of consumer perceptions of price.

In general, marketers follow several paths in trying to counter consumer negative perception of price. They might take some advantage of heightened awareness of price by running more sales. Sale prices are more attractive in such times, though the risk of the sale being seen as somehow "phony" must be considered. Marketers can also give more to the customer since the prices are seemingly ever-higher. Making the product bigger, including "2 extra ounces in this box," raising the quality, improving the guarantee, throwing in some "free options," and many similar efforts, have been used to enhance the product offered, thereby somewhat justifying the price.

Some marketers have been successful in using promotion to justify or explain the higher prices charged. Having an "honest" celebrity, like Bill Cosby or James Stewart, explain to the public why the prices for product X have been driven up is one approach that has been used many times. There have even been cases where marketers have sold their products at cost or even a loss to avoid the perception that they are "ripping off" the consumer.

6.   *Give three examples of a sacrifice of item profit for the sake of total profit.*

ANSWER:

Many examples of this common practice might be found. Some possibilities include:

.   Polaroid is famous for charging a low price for cameras and a high profit price for the appropriate film.

.   Newspapers charge 25 cents for a paper it cost 75 cents to deliver so that higher circulation will bring more ad money.

.   To a degree, this same approach applies to "free" radio and TV.

.   Many retailers use low-profit, at cost, or loss leaders to build traffic. Note: These are often called "door busters" since people are expected to trample the doors to get at them.

.   Gillette sells razors cheaply in the hope of selling many blades.

.   Free samples of anything would fit this pricing model.

.   Dry-cell battery companies frequently sell the flashlight at low-cost while the appropriate batteries remain high-margin items.

7.   *Why are some prices based in part on the geographic distances the products must travel to reach the customer? Are prices always greater if the distance traveled is greater and lower if the distance is less?*

ANSWER:

Even the casual consumer knows that "somebody" must pay for the transportation of products. When such a consumer thinks about it, he or she realizes that the Three Musketeers candy bar buyer who lives near the candy factory is paying for part of the cost of transporting candy bars across the country to more distant consumers since the candy costs the same in both places. The near-the-factory buyer is paying a form of "phantom freight." However, on a 35-cent item, this is not particularly annoying to the more local buyer. Yet here is a case where the distance traveled does not increase the price.

Similarly, "free delivery" by department stores (though it "punishes" those who do not take advantage of it), is not particularly vexing. But people living close to the seller get "free" delivery, as do the buyers living far away -- another case where distance does not raise price.

For some products. transportation becomes expensive on a per-unit basis. Thus, automobile buyers in New York pay more transportation costs for Japanese cars than do buyers living near West Coast ports-of-entry. Industrial buyers of steel, boilers, and shipments of raw materials also expect to pay some form of shipping charges if these products are sent over great distances.

When these are bought from a local dealer, the shipping to the dealer might be paid for by the buyer without complaint, while shipment from dealer to buyer would be expected to be "free."

There are many plans for setting prices in terms of geography, and many sellers "hide" the costs of delivery in the price of the product then offer "free delivery." For these reasons, it has been frequently pointed out that the most "fair" geographic pricing method is F.O.B. factory. Then, if the buyer is far

from the factory, he or she pays more than the one who is close. There would be
no phantom freight and no gimmicks if such an approach were used honestly.

8.   *If the manufacturing cost of an item is $250, the selling expenses*
        associated with the item $75, and the required return is 25%, what would
        the selling price of the item be?

ANSWER:

This is an ROI pricing problem. The text accents ROI as a percent of selling
price in calculating ROI prices. Some students may have been told in other
classes that the ROI can be expressed as a percent of the investment rather than
as a percent of selling price. Most marketers use the selling price approach.

As a percent of investment, the problem would work as follows:

   $250 cost + $75 expenses = $325 "invested in the product"

   $325 x .25 = $81.25 $325 + $81.25 = $406.25 (price)

When the ROI is expressed as a percentage of the selling price, the problem is as
follows:

   $250 cost + $75 expenses = $325

   $325 + .25x = x Where x = selling price

   $325 = .75x $325 ÷ .75 = x $433.33 = x   (price)

Many marketers prefer to express "everything" in terms of selling price, but both
methods are appropriate depending on the professor's preference.

For those who claim that only the cost of goods is an investment and that selling
expense is not an "investment," the problem looks like this:

   $250 cost x .25 = $62.50 $250 + $62.50 = $312.50   (price)

or:

   $250 cost + .25x = x Where x = selling price

   $250 = x - .25x $250 = .75x $250 ÷ .75 = x

   $333.33 = x Price

9.   *Describe the concept behind break-even analysis. Briefly explain the*
        limitations of break-even analysis.

ANSWER:

The logic of break-even analysis is discussed in Chapter 21. The gist of it is
this:

.   Organizations face fixed costs (FC).

.   Organizations face variable costs (VC) that are linked to levels of
       production (e.g., the raw materials used or the wage of the hourly worker).

.   FC + VC = total cost (TC).

.   At any given time or level of production, a firm faces a certain level of
       total cost (TC) and is making a certain level of total revenues (TR), that
       is price per unit x units sold = TR.

.   If TC > TR, a loss is incurred. If TR > TC, a profit is made.

.   Typically, as the graph shows, TR < TC at low, "beginning," levels of
       production.

. Sooner or later (we hope) TR > TC and a profit is made.

. Where the switch from loss to profit is made (TR = TC) is called the break-even point.

. This is shown graphically in the text by Exhibit 21-6.

The limitations of break-even analysis involve two oversimplifications that are unrealistic even for a textbook discussion.

. The first and least significant of these is the way the standard break-even graph is drawn. The use of straight lines is unrealistic. For example, even "fixed costs" are not permanent. They do not go on at a certain level forever. Further, the straight and on-going TR and TC lines suggest that profit will grow larger and larger "forever" as units sold grows larger. "Infinite profit" seems to be foreseeable.

. A far more important point to be mentioned is the typical textbook's assumption that prices, quantities, etc., can all be manipulated to move the break-even point. In finance texts, a higher price lowers the break-even point while a lower price raises it. In a marketing text, where we discuss customer demand, we recognize that such an approach assumes that the stuff is going to sell at the higher price. In fact, a lower price could even lead to lower sales. Thus, the simple changes of price/quantity problems of the finance texts are unrealistic and, in a sense, inaccurate.

10. *From time to time, automobile makers offer sizeable rebates to consumers. Why not simply lower the price?*

ANSWER:

Rebates, though they do alter the price charged, are a form of sales promotion. They are supposed to be temporary. A price change is not necessarily temporary. Rebates do not, therefore, create a low price which might then be difficult to raise. "Everyone" understands that the price will -- not really rise, but simply "go back to normal -- when the rebate program ends. Rebates are intended to create "excitement" and a feeling of "getting something special if I buy now." Also, as the text notes, by sending out rebates the manufacturer assures that the price cut actually gets to the buyer and is not skimmed off somehow by the dealer.

Rebates are also aimed at dealers in these ways.

. The program gives the dealer something to advertise and use in a sales presentation.

. The dealer is not lowering his or her price, the manufacturer is lowering its price. The rebate lowers the price the retailer charges, but costs the retailer nothing.

. Any payments to dealers, sales quotas, etc., remain unaffected. That is, a buyer gets a $15,000 car for $14,000 "after rebate," but on the dealer's books, the price paid is $15,000.

11. *What is a trade discount? Why is it sometimes called a functional discount?*

ANSWER:

A trade discount is given to someone who is "in the trade." Examples include:

. The carpenter gets a discount on tools and materials.
. The cement contractor doesn't "pay retail" for cement.
. The house painter gets a discount on paint.
. The electrician pays less for wire and switches, the plumber for pipes and sinks.
. The retailer and wholesaler get their appropriate discounts.

These discounts to professionals who are "in the trade" (in fact, some call these professional discounts) are also called functional discounts because they reward the receiver for a function performed. The contractor or repairman gets a discount for performing the installation function, the wholesaler performs the wholesaling function, the retailer the retailing function, etc.

Students may be interested to know that professors can usually get an educator's professional discount on books. What function are we expected to perform?

12.   *Name three products for which seasonal discounts are commonly offered. How do sellers use these discounts to sell products?*

ANSWER:

Seasonal discounts are almost inevitably used when the product, any product, is a seasonal one. Therefore, such products as the following are likely to be sold using seasonal discounts: paint, building supplies, resort vacations, seasonal clothing, holiday-related merchandise, many toys (since Christmas accounts for the major part of that business), seasonal sporting goods (skis), certain tools and machines (lawn mowers), and services (moving services since far more people move in the spring and summer than in the fall and winter).

Other products are, in effect, reduced in price "seasonally" though we may not put them totally in the "seasonal discount" realm. Houses usually sell more cheaply in the winter than in the spring; cars sell more cheaply at the end of the model year than at the beginning, regardless of what season it is. These pricing patterns point out that the "seasonal discount," while related to the season of the year, actually reflects the demand during different times of the year.

The point might be made that seasonal discounts used within the channel of distribution might be "one season off" from the seasonal discounts used to attract consumers since intermediaries have to coordinate their efforts before the actual sale to consumers. The toy industry gives us an example. The big "Toy Shows," where toy wholesalers, retailers, and manufacturers get together, are held in the spring. Christmas-related merchandise is displayed and ordered. By fall, toy makers whose products are not moving well are offering discounts to wholesalers and retailers. Retailers will not be offering discounts to consumers until several months later.

Sellers employ seasonal discounts to sell products "out of season" when demand is low. They realize that buyers, especially wholesalers and retailers, do not want to buy and stock, say, house paint, out of season because they will incur the costs of storage and the risk of loss due to fires, freezing, etc. Though the cost to consumers is less obvious, they too incur similar costs and risks when buying house paint in the late fall or winter months. The seasonal discount may be viewed as a way to move products not immediately in demand, but it is also a way to "pay" buyers back for incurring storage and related costs. Of course, in doing so the seller is relieved of the cost of storing the product himself. He also spreads out his distribution over a longer period of time, lessening the need to deliver the seasonal product "all at once" at the start of the appropriate season.

The point is made many times in the text that all four Ps of the marketing mix must fit together and work together. Note that the seasonal price is closely related to the nature of the product -- the desire to move products that would otherwise have to be stored and to spread distribution work out over more months in the year -- and promotion in that the attractive price gives the seller something to offer and to talk about besides the product.

13.   *Using the average cost method, what price would you recommend for a product if the costs associated with its production and marketing were $150,000, the margin for profit $50,000, and the anticipated sales were 5,000 units?*

ANSWER:

This is a straight-forward problem in which the average cost method of pricing described in the text is to be used. Besides working the problem, students should be asked to:

- Explain the logic of the method. (E.g., Are all the costs and profit variables in there?)

- Discuss the weaknesses of the approach. (E.g., It is cost-based mainly. It can easily go wrong if data, particularly demand estimates, are wrong.)

Costs associated with marketing and production = $150,000

Margin for profit = $50,000

Total of costs and profit margin = $200,000

Total costs and margin ÷ units demanded = $200,000 ÷ 5,000 units = $40 (price)

Remember, this or any other quantitative method yields only a likely or reasonable price, a "place to start." Managerial judgment takes over to decide if this is to be the price.

14. *A marketer using the target return method made a mistake in predicting demand; the actual demand turned out to be half the expected demand. What would be the resulting loss per unit if the marketer used the following data to calculate price?*

Expected Demand	2,000 units
Fixed Cost and Target Return	$200,000
Variable Cost Per Unit	$100

ANSWER:

The target return method is discussed in the text.

Using the figures offered in the question, we have:

$$\frac{\text{FIXED COST AND TARGET RETURN}}{\text{UNITS TO BE SOLD}} = \frac{\$200,000}{2,000} = \$100$$

$100 = Fixed Cost and Target Return Per Unit

FIXED COST AND TARGET RETURN PER UNIT + VARIABLE COST PER UNIT = SUGGESTED PRICE
(or) $100 + 100 = $200 Price

If we cut the expected demand in half, we get:

$$\frac{\$200,000}{1,000} = \$200 \text{ Fixed Cost and Target Return Per Unit}$$

$200 + $100 (variable cost per unit) = $300 (price)

With demand at 2,000 units, price = $200

But, with "true" demand at 1,000 units, price = $300

So, $300 - $200 = $100 loss per sale if firm charges $200 rather than the $300 the price "should have been."

ETHICS EXERCISE 21

CHAPTER 21 ETHICS IN PRACTICE

Overview

For more than 30 years, StarKist Seafood packaged 6 1/2 ounces of tuna in its regular-sized can. During a period of inflation, the can's weight was reduced by 3/8 ounce, but the price remained the same. Detecting this subtle change, which resulted in a 5.8% price increase, was a challenge for most consumers. The weight was clearly marked on the package but the size of the can did not change. Was this ethical?

This scenario entails a practice known variously as "downsizing" and "package shorting." It is a fairly common practice among packaged foods manufacturers. For example, a box of Luvs used to contain 88 diapers; now it holds 80. A can of Brim used to contain 13 ounces of coffee; now it holds 11.5. The number of sheets on a roll of both toilet tissue and paper towels has been reduced, and potato chip manufacturers have been known to decrease net weight while holding bag size constant.

Downsizing is done for a variety of reasons, usually economic, such as trying to offset rising raw material costs or the need to fatten profit margins by lowering unit costs. Also, the purpose is often to keep prices from rising above psychological barriers for particular products, so-called "fair" or "reference" prices, which are the prices people expect to pay in given categories. For example, candy bar manufacturers are subject to constantly fluctuating ingredients prices, and because there are expected prices for candy bars, package sizes are frequently adjusted without informing consumers. (Though, of course, content information is, or should be, on the packages.)

From a consumer behavior perspective, downsizing is based on a psychological concept known as the "just noticeable difference" (JND). This says that relatively small changes in a stimulus (such as a price hike or content shrinkage) go unnoticed by consumers; the amount of change which is just detectable is known as the JND. Generally, people are more sensitive to price changes (they have a lower JND) than to size and weight changes, so that size and weight are more frequently adjusted than price when a manufacturer attempts to maintain margins in the face of rising costs. Quite simply, price is easier to notice than small changes in the product.

According to critics, downsizing is sneaky and misleading, since consumers pay more without knowing it. It would seem that consumers who are in the habit of buying a particular product size generally don't scrutinize the net weight label on subsequent purchases. Critics like New York State attorney general Robert Abrams believe that this practice is deceptive and are calling for legislation to require manufacturers to announce such changes, either very noticeably on the package or by posting a sign where the item is displayed.

Manufacturers say that there is no deception since marketers have been aboveboard in labeling products accurately as to weight, serving size, price, and quantity, as required by law. They argue that it's the consumer's responsibility to read the label. Furthermore, the Food and Drug Administration has no laws against the practice. Other defenses are that smaller packages are better for the environment (less solid waste), changes are designed to bring a product more in line with competitive products, or the product has been reformulated so that a smaller amount has the same yield (e.g., the same number of cups of coffee per package).

Is it ethical to reduce the weight of a can of tuna fish by 3/8 of an ounce, clearly marking the weight on the package, while keeping price constant during a period of inflation?

The reason for the package downsizing in this instance was that StarKist was trying to offset rising raw materials costs due to inflation. It would appear that consumers don't generally check the net weight label (even though it is clearly marked) on subsequent purchases, since the weight has been constant for 30 years. Is this ethical? There are several ethical issues involved:

.   Are consumers deceived, i.e., misled, by downsizing? This would occur if there was a difference between perception and reality created by the downsizing.

.   What is the marketer's duty to inform customers about price and size changes?

.   Should it be the buyer's responsibility to check weight, price, quantity, and serving size? If they don't, is it true that "What they don't know won't hurt them?" If they don't check the package information every time they buy, is it "just too bad for them?"

- How can a marketer compete if downsizing becomes common practice within an industry, i.e., if most or all of the competitors downsize their products?

- How can a manager achieve an acceptable balance between the need to make a profit for the company and himself/herself and to maintain the trust and fair treatment of customers?

- What constitutes fair treatment of customers regarding significant price hikes? For instance, should price hikes just keep pace with inflation?

What would be StarKist's possible alternatives? Prices are rising and there is a need to maintain margins.

- Raise prices to cover the increased costs.

- Downsize the product so as to maintain margins.

- Maintain the price and incur a short-run loss.

- Accept a smaller than traditional margin by either slightly raising the price and/or slightly downsizing the product.

- Flag the product with "reduced size" or similar wording, for a certain time following the downsizing. (Another question arises, i.e., how to word this information. For example, is "new size can" enough, or should it say "new smaller sized can?")

- Voluntarily use a sign where the item is displayed for a certain time.

CHAPTER 21 TAKE A STAND QUESTIONS

1. *A retailer uses a 150% markup on cost for an item with a cost of $10. When the item is put on sale, the retailer advertises 50% off (markdown on selling price) and sells the item for $12.50. Is this deceptive?*

This is ethically within bounds:

Markup % on cost = $ amount added to cost/$ cost   (or)   1.5 = x/$10

Solving for x:

x = $10 x 1.5   x = $15 (dollar markup)

To arrive at the selling price:

Cost + markup = $10 + $15 = $25.

This ($25) is the only figure known to the buyer. So, a 50% off sale would be viewed by the buyer as a 50% markdown on this selling price, i.e., $12.50.

2. *A salesperson is allowed to vary the price a customer is charged by 10%. The salesperson sells 100 units to one wholesaler for $3,500. The next day, another wholesaler says he will buy 100 units only if the price is $3,000. The salesperson writes up the order and says "I hope this clears the order-processing department." Did the salesperson do the right thing?*

The salesperson writes up the order and says, "I hope this clears the order processing department."

At first glance it may appear that the salesperson has broken the employer's rules. If the first purchase is viewed as the "true" price ($3,500 for 100 units) then the second buyer could not get a discount bigger than $350 and have the deal remain in bounds. That is, the second buyer would have to pay at least $3,150, not $3,000.

However, whether what the salesperson did is ethical depends on how you interpret the phrase "vary the price by 10%." If you mean you can add plus or minus 10% to a given price, the salesperson is okay. The reasoning is as follows:

Let $3,500 be the upper end on the range: Price (P) plus or minus 10%.

To find the price (P) in the middle of the range: P + .10P = $3,5000

Solving for P:

P(1 + .10) = $3,500   P = $3,500/1.1   P = $3,181

The question is whether or not $3,000 can be obtained by lopping 10% or less off
of $3,181. It can. The markdown of $181 as a percentage of $3,181 is
$181/$3,181 = 5.6%.

However, if you interpret the phrase "vary the price by 10%" as meaning adding
plus or minus 5% to a given price, then the salesperson has gone against his
manager's wishes:

P + .05P = $3,500

Solving for P:

P(1 + .05) = $3,500   P = $3,500/1.05   P = $3,333

A 5% markdown from this would be .05 x $3.333 = $166.

$3,333 - $166 = $3167. The lowest price he'd be allowed to charge would be
$3167.

Incidentally, this policy of varying the price charged to different wholesalers
probably runs afoul of the Robinson-Patman Act. There are justifications for
varying price acceptable by the Robinson-Patman Act, but we do not have enough
information here to decide if they might apply.

3.   *A retailer's advertisement for fine china compares "our everyday price"
      with the "manufacturer's suggested retail price." A statement in small
      print at the bottom of the page says: "Manufacturer's suggested retail
      price is not a price at which our store offered or sold this merchandise
      and may not be a trade area price." Is this ethical?*

This is an example of a merchant-supplied reference pricing strategy. The
merchant establishes an external reference price, i.e., a posted price which
serves as a point of comparison for the on-sale price ("Was $... Now $...";
"Theirs $... Ours $..."; "List price $... Sale price $...."). The reference
price signals a deal, and the larger the difference (in both absolute and
percentage terms) between the reference price and the sale price, the better the
perceived deal. Consumers also have expectations for what are considered good
deals, and if the difference between the two prices is too small, they will be
disappointed. That is, if they expect at least a 10% markdown and are offered
only a 5% markdown, they will think it is a crumby deal.

In this example, it could be argued that the merchant is, in a sense, being
honest, but is also (in a sense) being dishonest. He is being honest by (in
effect) admitting that the manufacturer's retail price is really bogus, at least
for this trade area. If this merchant were unscrupulous, he wouldn't admit this,
although state law or local ordinances might have forced him to do it. However,
he is being dishonest by: (1) using very fine print in the qualifying statement
which will likely go unseen by many, and (2) using what is really a meaningless
reference price. As in the case of pre-ticketing, the question arises as to what
is the real price to which the sale price is compared. It is arguable that a
price never charged in this store or in this area is not a real price.

4.   *An airline arranges with a national association to offer a special discount
      fare to association members who are attending a convention. A travel agent
      uses these group fares for regular clients, who are not association
      members, so they can get the lowest possible air fares. Is this good
      business?*

This might help the travel agent build more loyalty among clients by offering
them a special reward, but it is not fair to the airline. In effect, the airline
is subsidizing the goodwill the travel agent has built (although some of the

goodwill could rub off on the airline, too.) The airline probably estimated the number of discounted fares it would end up offering. If, due to the agent's fudging, the actual number is significantly larger, the airline might be sacrificing seats that could have sold at full fare, thereby losing revenue. The travel agent might end up in hot water if the airline asks why there were so many discounted fares.

The agent has deliberately violated the request of the airline. A better option would be to ask the airline in advance if it would be willing to extend the discount to some of the best customers, giving the airline full credit for offering the deal as an incentive.

5.   *A mail order marketer in California sends its catalog to Connecticut but does not maintain a legal physical presence in Connecticut. It does not charge Connecticut state taxes on the goods it sends to Connecticut. Is this right? Should it be legal?*

By the time you are reading this, a decision will have probably been made on whether a state can require an out-of-state direct marketer to collect sales tax on sales to in-state purchasers. Currently, the 45 or so states that levy sales taxes can't require an out-of-state direct marketer to collect and turn taxes over to the states. A 1967 Supreme Court decision confirmed that the federal government, and not individual states, may regulate interstate commerce. This ruling requires a "physical presence" (i.e., a store or employees) in a state for a direct marketer to levy that state's tax. Otherwise, the High Court said, it is unconstitutional for a state or local government to require a vendor to collect a sales tax. Needless to say, this is the position mail order marketers prefer.

As direct marketing has boomed in recent years, a debate has arisen over whether it is legal and fair for direct marketers to avoid charging state and local sales taxes. The current system benefits direct marketers and their customers. The proposed changes would be to the advantage of retail stores and state and local governments.

Arguments in favor of legislation requiring direct marketers to collect sales taxes include:

.   State treasuries are losing over $1.5 billion in revenues per year from unpaid legally owned taxes. (Byron L. Dorgan, "States Need This Law to Collect Sales Taxes, *USA Today*, July 20, 1987, p. 10A.) As direct marketing continues to grow, states will lose more revenue. It is unfair for states to have to forfeit legally owed taxes which could be easily collected by out-of-state retailers. If state and local governments lose tax revenues, all citizens lose because the shortfall must be made up by raising sales tax rates even higher, boosting property taxes, or increasing or instituting other levies.

.   The current system is also unfair to in-state retailers, who are placed at a competitive disadvantage with out-of-state firms. They must charge sales taxes ranging from 2% to 7%.

.   The current system is obsolete. In the past 25 years direct marketing has mushroomed due to a high-tech explosion. Customers are bombarded by mail-order catalogs, national sellers with 800 telephone numbers and overnight delivery, and in-home shopping via TV.

Arguments against a new direct marketing sales tax law include:

.   It would place an undue and costly burden on direct marketers. A retail store has only one sales-tax law to administer, whereas direct marketers would be faced with the huge burden of tracking complex sales-tax rates, exemptions, and filing requirements; there are 6,700 state and local taxes, with as many variations. ("Shoppers Don't Need This Sales-tax Law," *USA Today*, July 20, 1987, p. 10A.)

.   Direct marketing customers would suffer. Unlike retail customers, people ordering directly would have to know the frequently complex sales tax structure in their state and which items are taxable. Much or most of the

high costs of collection would ultimately be passed on to consumers. This
could hurt the elderly, handicapped, rural, and ghetto residents who have
to buy by mail or phone.

.   Currently, many mail order advertisements include notes such as "N.Y.
        residents must add x% sales tax to order total." New ads, apparently,
        would have to list all states and all percentages.

.   The proposed system is unconstitutional. States would be literally
        drafting out-of-state companies to collect their taxes and send the
        proceeds back to them, yet the companies would get nothing in return.
        Direct marketers don't, for instance, use the streets or fire and police
        protection they'd be supporting, and they'd lack a voice in local politics
        or state governance.

.   The current system isn't unfair to retail stores, because sales taxes are
        usually less than postage and handling charges. Thus, people don't
        patronize direct marketers to stiff the states and localities on sales
        taxes.

.   The proposed system would be a windfall to governors and legislators, who
        could raise funds without voting for new taxes.

.   The proposed system would lessen competition, protecting merchants from
        out-of-state competitors.

.   Taxes should be paid to the state in which a sale was made. For instance,
        if you travel to another state to make a purchase, you pay that state's
        sales tax, not your home state's tax (although some large-ticket purchases
        made in tax-free states require charging the buyer his home-state tax).

On May 26, 1992, the Supreme Court ruled that states could require direct
marketers to collect sales taxes but only if Congress passed enabling
legislation. Direct marketers and the states hoped to reach some sort of an
agreement by Fall 1992 or Winter 1993. A threshold number of states and direct
marketers would then have to ratify or reject the mutually negotiated agreement.

GUIDE TO CASES

CASE 21-1   OUTFITTERS U.S.A.

SUBJECT MATTER: Pricing Alternatives, Costs, Break-Even, Estimation of Demand
                        and Profit, Skimming and Penetration Pricing

AT-A-GLANCE OVERVIEW

Outfitters U.S.A. is attempting to decide whether or not to proceed with a plan
to sell a certain shoe to be made by another firm for Outfitters. The questions
it faces are several, but among them are what prices to consider charging, the
effect of the price selected on demand, assignment of costs, break-even
estimates, and whether or not to proceed with the program. Outfitters has the
help of a marketing research company which has estimated demand under skimming
price and penetration price conditions.

This case presents the student with a perplexing pricing strategy problem. While
some knowledge of break-even analysis is required, most of the emphasis in the
case is on heuristic problem solving.

The case is a very challenging exercise in strategic marketing decision making.
The student must demonstrate proficiency in cost analysis and allocation, pricing
strategy, and break-even analysis. In addition, the case will require the
student to draw on knowledge on retail merchandising, channel strategy, and
marketing research analysis.

Variable Cost Analysis

All variable costs per unit are given except direct labor and transportation. The per unit cost must be calculated for these variable costs.

In determining the direct labor component, the total direct labor cost for last year is divided by the total number of hours worked (5,000,000 / 1,000,000 hours = $5.00). The new pair of canvas shoes requires 15 minutes of direct labor time per shoe. This results in a direct labor variable cost per pair of shoes of $1.25 (1/4 hour @ $5.00 per hour).

Estimation of the transportation component is more complicated. First, the average cost per mile is calculated by dividing the transportation cost for last year by the number of miles for last year ($900,000 / 1,500,000 miles). The average cost per mile, $.60, should be multiplied by the average number of miles per shipment (200). This results in an average transportation cost of $120 ($.60 x 200 miles). With an average order size of 600 pounds last year, the average cost per pound is $.20 ($120 / 600 pounds). This was calculated by dividing the $120 average transportation cost per order by the 600 pound order size. Since each packaged pair weighs 1 pound, the cost to deliver the shoes to the retailer would be $.20 (average cost per pound .20 / 1 pound weight of each pair).

Variable Cost Summary

Material	$1.75 per pair
Soles	$2.75 per pair
Thread	$ .05 per pair
Direct labor	$1.25 per pair
Transportation	$ .20 per pair
TOTAL VARIABLE COST	$6.00 per pair

Fixed Cost Analysis

In order to perform break-even analysis, an assessment of fixed cost for the new line of canvas shoes is necessary. One way of doing this is to determine the total company fixed costs and allocate a percentage of this amount to the line of shoes. The fixed cost allocation can be based on sales or labor hours. Labor hours may be a more accurate basis, as selling price of the shoes does not influence fixed cost allocation.

Total Company Fixed Costs

Managerial salaries	$1,600,000
Rent & utilities	$1,300,000
Depreciation	$1,400,000
Other overhead	$2,225,000
TOTAL COMPANY FIXED COST	$6,525,000

The new line of shoes will require 15 minutes (or 1/4 of an hour) of direct labor time for each pair of shoes produced. Central Marketing Research Company estimated sales at 120,000 to 150,000 pairs of shoes if a skimming pricing policy is employed. If 135,000 is used as the most likely estimate (135,000 pairs x 1/4 hours), 33,750 labor hours will be required. The new line of shoes will account for 3.25% of the company's direct labor hours (33,750 / 1,040,000).

If production for the company's other products continues next year at last year's rate, 1,033,750 hours of direct labor time will be required for production of the company's products (1,000,000 + 33,750). The new line of shoes will account for 3.26% of the company's total direct labor hours (33,750 / 1,033,750).

If a penetration pricing policy is used, Central Marketing Research Company estimates sales at 150,000 to 170,000 pair of shoes. If 160,000 is used as the most likely estimate, 40,000 labor hours will be required (160,000 / 1/4 hour). The new line of shoes will account for 3.84% of the company's direct labor hours (40,000 / 1,040,000).

Total company fixed costs were determined to be $6,525,000.   If 3.26% is used to allocate the $6,525,000 of the company's fixed costs when a skimming pricing policy is used, Outfitters' fixed cost allocation would be $212,715 ($6,525,000 x 3.26%).   If 3.84% is used to allocate the $6,525,000 when a penetration pricing policy is used, the fixed cost allocation would be $250,560 ($6,525,000 x 3.84%).

The total fixed cost for the new line of shoes must also include an analysis for the incremental Basic Marketing Cost incurred in the introduction of the new line.   For a skimming pricing policy, the incremental Basic Marketing Cost would be $475,000.   Therefore, the total fixed cost for the line would be $687,715 ($212,715 + 475,000).   For a penetration pricing policy, the incremental Basic Marketing Cost would be $350,000.   Therefore, the total fixed costs for the line would be $600,560 ($250,560 + $350,000).

Total Unit Cost Analysis

For a skimming pricing policy:

TC /pair = FC /pair + VC /pair

$$TC \text{ /pair} = \frac{\$687,715}{135,000} + \$6.00$$

TC /pair = $5.0941 + $6.00

TC /pair = $11.09

For a penetration pricing policy:

TC /pair = FC /pair + VC /pair

$$TC \text{ /pair} = \frac{\$600,560}{160,000} + \$6.00$$

TC /pair = $3.7535 + $6.00

TC /pair = $9.75

Price Determination

There are two basic pricing alternatives that Outfitters can employ: skimming or penetration pricing policy.   According to the data presented in the case, the average retail selling price for similar lines of shoes is approximately $21.00.

Assume $24.00 is selected as the desired retail selling price for a skimming pricing policy and $18.00 is selected as the desired retail selling price for a penetration pricing policy.   If a skimming pricing policy is employed, the retail selling price would be above the average -- $21.00.   If a penetration pricing policy is employed, the retail selling price would be below the average.

Since the retailer applies a 40% markup on the retail selling price, SCSC would establish $14.30 as their selling price to the retailer (Outfitters) for a skimming pricing policy and $12.90 for a penetration pricing policy.   This can result in a retail selling price of $24.00 if a skimming pricing policy were desired and $18.00 as the retail selling price if a penetration pricing policy were desired.

Break Even Analysis

For a skimming pricing policy:

$$BE \text{ units (pairs)} = \frac{FC}{SP \text{ /pair} - VC \text{ /pair}}$$

$$BE \text{ units (pairs)} = \frac{\$687,715}{\$14.30 - \$6.00}$$

BE units (pairs) = 82,857.22 units (pairs)

BE $ =   BE pairs x SP /pair

BE $ =   82,857.22 x $14.30

BE $ = $1,184,855.10

For a penetration pricing policy:

$$\text{BE units (pairs)} = \frac{FC}{SP \text{ /pair} - VC \text{ /pair}}$$

$$\text{BE units (pairs)} = \frac{\$600,560}{\$12.90 - \$6.00}$$

BE units (pairs) = 87,037.68 units (pairs)

BE $ =   BE pairs x SP /pair

BE $ =   87,037.68 x $12.90

BE $ = $1,122,786.00

Profit Analysis

For a skimming pricing policy:

Profit = Total Revenue - Total Cost

Profit = (SP /pair x units) - (TFC + TVC)

Profit = ($14.30 x 135,000) - [$687,715 + ($6.00 x 135,000)]

Profit = $1,930,500 - $1,497,715

Profit = $432,785

For a penetration pricing policy:

Profit = Total Revenue - Total Cost

Profit = (SP /pair x units) - (TFC + TVC)

Profit = ($12.90 x 160,000) = [$600,560 + ($6.00 x 160,000)]

Profit = $2.064,000 - $1,560,560

Profit = $503,440

Summary of Proposed Solution

Skimming
Penetration

Skimming		Penetration
$6.00	VC / pair	$6.00
$5.09	FC / pair	$3.75
$11.09	TC / pair	$9.75
$14.30	SCSC SP / pair	$12.90
3.26%	% of Company FC allocated to line	3.84%
$212,715	Company FC allocated to line	$250,560

$475,000	Basic Marketing Cost	$350,000
$687,715	Total FC for line	$600,560
82,857	BE pairs	87,038
135,000	Expected unit (pair) sales	160,000
$1,184,855.10	BE $	$1,122,786.00
$632,785	Expected Profit	$503,440

The student should provide a complete analysis of his/her findings.

Source: This case solution, "Proposed Solution To The Outfitters USA Case," was prepared by and used with permission of Jon M. Hawes, The University of Akron, and Cynthia Santucci, Ohio Edison.

22

IMPLEMENTING AND CONTROLLING THE MARKETING PROGRAM

CHAPTER SCAN

This chapter describes the integrated marketing program. It includes discussions of the importance of good implementation of marketing strategy, the functional activities involved in implementation, and the organizational forms used to achieve goals.

This chapter also includes a presentation of strategic control of marketing programs, and explains these tools: the marketing audit and the social audit.

SUGGESTED LEARNING OBJECTIVES

The student who studiesd this chapter will be exposed to a general discussion of the need to integrate the elements of a marketing mix so that they function as a complete program, and will have read about marketing control, the marketing audit, and the social audit. Students will, among other things, be able to:

1. Understand the nature of a marketing program, and describe the importance of the implementation of a marketing strategy.

2. Identify the functional areas involved in the implementation of a marketing strategy.

3. Describe the major forms of organizations used by marketing managers to achieve their goals.

4. Understand why marketing control is necessary.

5. Describe what is included in a marketing audit.

6. Understand how the social audit helps marketing managers evaluate the organizations' impact on society.

CHAPTER OUTLINE

I.   INTRODUCTION

II. THE MARKETING PROGRAM

III. ORGANIZING

    A.   The Marketing Era Organization
    B.   The Functional Organization
    C.   Decentralized and Specialized Organizations
    D.   Organizing by Product Type

IV. LEADERSHIP AND INTERACTION

V.   RESOURCE ACQUISITION AND ALLOCATION

VI. COORDINATION AND TIMING OF ACTIVITIES

VII. INFORMATION MANAGEMENT

VIII. CONTROL: ANALYZING MARKETING PERFORMANCE

    A.   Sales, Cost, and Profit

        1.   Sales Analysis
        2.   Sales Analysis: United Way of Mountain County
        3.   Cost Analysis
        4.   Cost Analysis: United Way of Mountain County
        5.   Profit Analysis
        6.   Profit Analysis: United Way of Mountain County

    B.   Striking an Analytical Balance
    C.   Yardsticks of Performance

IX. WHAT IS A MARKETING AUDIT?

    A.   The Costs of Auditing
    B.   An Audit Outline
    C.   The Audit Team
    D.   The Need for Marketing Audits

X.   TO WHOM IS MARKETING RESPONSIBLE?

XI. A CLOSING NOTE

XII. SUMMARY

XIII. KEY TERMS

XIV. QUESTIONS FOR DISCUSSION (9)

XV. ETHICS IN PRACTICE

XVI. CASES

    The following key terms are introduced and used in Chapter 22. They are defined in the text's Glossary.

Marketing program
Organizing
Marketing organization
Functional organization
Geography-based organization
Customer-based organization
Product-based organization
Combination organization
Internal marketing
Human resources

Financial resources
Sales analysis
Cost analysis
Direct cost
Indirect cost
Profit analysis
Social audit

THE CHAPTER SUMMARIZED

I.   INTRODUCTION

In Chapter 2, marketing was defined as the establishment of marketing goals and the design of marketing plans that are expected to be implemented in the future. Important marketing tools and concepts have been discussed throughout the book. This chapter "puts them all together" as a marketing manager would, implementing and evaluating entire marketing programs. The steps followed are:

.   identify and evaluate marketing opportunities.

.   analyze market segments and select target markets.

.   plan and develop the marketing mix to reach and satisfy consumers.

This introduction is built around the story of Holly Farms Corp. The company thought it had created the "Cadillac of poultry" with its roasted chicken, a convenient alternative to raw chicken that had scored big in a year of test marketing. But when phased into national distribution, the product flopped. The testing had shown high consumer acceptance, intention to re-buy, and that the taste was great.

Yet supermarkets bought far less of the product than had been expected. Grocers believed the chicken didn't last long enough on the shelf. In other words, Holly Farms hadn't considered the "front-line customer" ... that is, the grocer. The product had a shelf life of 18 days, but to play it safe was dated for sale within 14 days of roasting. But sometimes delivery to the stores took as long as nine days from the North Carolina plant Holly had built to produce the product (investment: $20 million). That didn't give the grocers much time to sell the product. To avoid being stuck with unsold inventory they began re-ordering only when they were sold out. This had not been a problem with raw chicken because it had high turnover and the grocers were experienced in selling it and therefore knew how much to stock.

In sum, Holly Farms' great product and plan was ruined by poor implementation. Planning is not enough. Plans must be implemented and carefully controlled.

II.   THE MARKETING PROGRAM

A formal marketing plan is a written statement of specific courses of action to be taken when, or if, future events occur. It outlines responsibilities for activities and tells when those activities are to be performed. Once a marketing plan has been executed, or is being executed, it is referred to as the **marketing program**. No element of the program stands alone, the parts of the program are tightly interrelated. A change in any one area almost certainly affects all others. Yet, the unified plan, the integrated marketing program, remains the goal. As with a puzzle, all the pieces must fit or the job isn't done.

Exhibit 22-1 shows that the appropriate strategy, properly executed, stands the greatest chance of success, and that chances for failure are greatest when an inappropriate strategy is poorly executed. Exhibit 22-2 outlines the basic functional activities required to implement a marketing plan.

III.   ORGANIZING

Implementing a strategy requires the organization of human and material resources.

Organizing for marketing consists of the assignment of tasks, the grouping of tasks into organizational units, and the allocation of resources to organizational units. This activity determines the structure of marketing organizations and assigns responsibilities.

There are many organizational designs, each with advantages and disadvantages but each assigning authority and responsibility to individuals or divisions within the organization.

A.   The Marketing Era Organization

The marketing concept suggests these two features for a **marketing organization:**

.   That some person (within a division, company or SBU) be clearly identified as responsible for managing all marketing activities.

.   That all marketing subfunctions be concentrated under the direction of the primary marketing official.

Ordinarily, refinement beyond these two precepts, to fit the organization to particular situations, is needed.

B.   The Functional Organization

Exhibit 22-3 portrays a **functional organization.** In such a model the various subfunctions of marketing are recognized and the organization constructed around them. Among the possible functions employed are advertising, pricing, and so on. Such an organization makes sense in that it permits a high level of specialization. Experts can concentrate their efforts where these can best be employed. All functional managers then report to a top-level marketing executive responsible for coordination.

This form of organization is thought to be best suited to small organizations, or to larger organizations if their marketing operations are not complex, rather than to large, decentralized organizations.

C.   Decentralized and Specialized Organizations

As marketing organizations grow, activities tend to become decentralized or specialized. Variables such as geography may be used as bases for such specialization, as might type of customer, e.g., large firms and small firms.

Geography-based organizations are common and make the most sense when customer needs vary from region to region.

Some have argued that **customer-based organizations** best meet the "spirit of the marketing concept" and its emphasis on customer orientation. (Exhibit 22-4 illustrates such an organization.) Yet other forms might be just as satisfactory and might result in savings to the customer.

D.   Organizing by Product Type

Some firms offer a variety of products and organize around those products. They are **product-based organizations.** Tire companies do this, accenting auto tires in one division, giant off-the-road tires in another, and specialty items in another. This is the product-based organization and may include product (or) brand managers who concern themselves with one brand or a small number of brands. (See Exhibit 22-5 for an example of this form of organization.)

Because this involves specialization by product type, it is commonly used when technical expertise is important. Marketers are able to specialize in a limited number of products under this arrangement.

Despite the several organization types mentioned here, it is easy to see that many organizations employ a **combination organization**, incorporating aspects of the various models.

For example: is the salesperson who specializes in industrial tools actually specializing in tools? Or is he or she specializing in customer types who buy the tools? (See Exhibit 22-6.)

Once again we see that marketing's complex environment is such that there are few (if any) "simple choices" to be made.

IV. LEADERSHIP AND INTERACTION

Leadership requires the skill to direct the actions of others in carrying out the marketing plan at various levels of authority. It entails interacting with others, influencing them to perform certain activities. It involves communication, motivation, and other actions that influence organizational values and behaviors. Marketing managers must undertake these activities, interacting with persons inside and outside of the organization.

The term **internal marketing** is often used by marketers, especially those in service businesses, when referring to marketing efforts aimed at their own employees who have a direct effect on the ultimate consumer's satisfaction with the product. These employees need to understand that what they do on the job helps create customer satisfaction, and that the (high) quality of the service they provide is essential to the firm's existence.

V. RESOURCE ACQUISITION AND ALLOCATION

Implementation of the marketing strategy requires the allocation of people, dollars, technology, and other resources to marketing tasks. Employees (their number and quality) are the organization's **human resources**. Inadequate **financial resources** can be a major problem. The "trick" is to allocate resources of both types to where they will be the most effective.

VI. COORDINATION AND TIMING OF ACTIVITIES

Effective marketing managers must assure that various marketing activities occur in the proper sequence and at the appropriate times. E.g.: a firm with multiple products whose sales rely on shared resources, such as a common sales force, must coordinate many elements of its marketing mix. Timing is so important because markets are dynamic, not static.

A marketing program must be both stable and dynamic (seemingly contradictory terms). But McDonald's illustrates that this can be done offering "quality, service, cleanliness, and value" as its stable program, but showing its flexibility in such tactical matters as advertising, product selection, and so on. The program, again, must be a unified whole, not a jumble of parts.

VII. INFORMATION MANAGEMENT

The importance of adequate information for decision making has been stressed throughout the book. To make sound decisions managers need sound information. This is provided by the marketing control system, the topic of the following sections of the text.

VIII. CONTROL: ANALYZING MARKETING PERFORMANCE

Analysis of marketing performance requires careful comparison of pre-established performance standards or results planned for a specific period

of time with the results actually achieved. Even when the predicted
results are achieved, analysis may show ways to refine efforts to gain even
greater success. Identification of the most profitable customers might
suggest concentrating efforts on those customers.

A.   Sales, Cost, and Profit

The following are the three major types of analysis:

.   Sales analysis, which focuses on performance shown by sales
     data,

.   Cost analysis, which yields measures of efficiency by
     concentrating on cost figures, and

.   Profit analysis, which compares sales achievements with
     marketing costs.

1.   Sales Analysis

Sales analysis is a detailed study of sales records or the
aggregation and breaking down of sales information in a way
that reveals patterns which can be used to evaluate the
effectiveness and efficiency of marketing efforts.

Sales analysis serves several purposes. Among them are:
providing a picture of recent successes and failures in the
marketplace; permitting managers to concentrate attention on
particular products, markets, or sales efforts; and, following
managers to see if their plans are being realized in the
market. Four types of sales analysis are shown in Exhibit 22-
7.

Salespeople and some managers disdain sales analysis on the
grounds that they "already know what's going on." It may be
necessary to educate individuals on the importance of this
matter. A bright spot is that much of the "paperwork" in this
effort can be handled by computer.

2.   Sales Analysis: United Way of Mountain County

Exhibit 22-8 shows the revenues of United Way of Mountain
County for 1991 and 1992. Analysis of these figures yields
this sort of information:

.   Revenues for 1992 were up 5.7% over 1991.
.   Pledges were up by 5.8%.
.   Out-of-county pledges were up 26.7%.
.   Uncollected pledges were up 9.2%.
.   Investment income is up.

Further analysis shows:

.   income by region served.
.   income by type of donor.
.   income by payment plan chosen by donor type.

While these figures are important, it is management's
interpretation of them that helps the organization. Questions
such as, "Why were pledges down in one area served and up in
others?" or "Are 'bad debts' and changes in payment plans a
sign of an aging population in the region?" can be asked by
management.

3.   Cost Analysis

Marketing costs can generally be associated with particular
SBUs, products, individual customers, etc. **Cost analysis**
summarizes and arranges accounting information to be useful for

marketing decision making. Some costs (**direct costs**) are
directly associated with a marketing effort (such as phone
calls to a client). Others are more **indirect costs** or common
costs (as is the rent on the building that houses the sales
offices). Thus, marketing costs can be direct costs or
indirect costs. A general approach to these costs involves
breaking down costs into customer-based accounts as illustrated
in Exhibit 22-9.

4.   Cost Analysis: United Way of Mountain County

Exhibit 22-10 shows United Way's costs for 1991 and 1992.
"Costs" in the form of money passed through the organization to
member charities are not shown but would also be monitored in
the "real world."

Costs may be grouped into natural accounts (rent, salaries,
benefits, etc.). More useful may be the functional accounts,
the costs associated with particular clients, products, etc.).
Exhibit 22-10 shows some natural accounts for United Way.
Exhibit 22-11 shows cost data broken down into functional
accounts (annual campaign costs, planning costs, administrative
costs, research costs).

Another approach would be to divide costs among types of
donors. This would show the costs associated with making
"sales" to the different customer groups.

5.   Profit Analysis

Analysis of sales and costs leads to comparison of the two
elements to yield profitability totals. Thus, **profit analysis**
develops profit totals for particular segments of the marketing
operation in order to evaluate them. This is often a simple
matter of subtracting costs from income. A complication arises
if costs are shared in such a way as to make their assignment
to one SBU or other element very arbitrary or essentially
impossible, such as when several products share the same
channel of distribution. In these cases a contribution to
profit approach may be used. Here only the direct costs
traceable to a particular SBU or product are subtracted from
the revenues associated with it.

6.   Profit Analysis: United Way of Mountain County

Exhibit 22-12 shows the profit or loss associated with each
type of donor in United Way's market. Again, the figures are
but a starting place for management which must now decide "what
to do." The unprofitable customer may be "dropped," or it may
be showing signs of improving profitability, or it may be
necessary to sustain a loss because of the customer group's
importance to the general reputation of United Way. These
matters are not decided by the analysis. Management must use
the analysis to judge alternate courses of action.

B.   Striking an Analytical Balance

In a sense, profit analysis addresses the "bottom line" while the
others do not. Yet it remains true that sales and cost analysis may
pinpoint areas of concern or success. The answer to the question of
which to use must be to "use them all."

C.   Yardsticks of Performance

Data is not of use unless it is put to work. Sales, costs, and
profit data are control instruments, ways of discovering whether or
not agreed upon performance standards have been met, whether or not
sales quotas or call quotas were met, whether or not a product meets
the required return on investment level, etc. Analysis of sales,

cost, and profit figures makes measuring performance by hunch and guesswork unnecessary and unacceptable.

IX.   WHAT IS A MARKETING AUDIT?

Auditors are supposed to be orderly and careful in their approach to information. Applying this same care to marketing performance is the basis of the marketing audit.

A marketing audit is a comprehensive appraisal of the organization's marketing activities and involves a systematic assessment of marketing plans, objectives, strategies, programs, organizational structure, and personnel. A commonly cited definition is:

> The marketing audit is a searching inquiry into the character and validity of the functional premises underlying a company's marketing operations.

A good marketing audit is:

. Systematic -- following logical, predetermined framework.

. Comprehensive -- all factors, not just trouble spots, are considered.

. Independent -- the auditor should be independent from the day-to-day marketing operation. Often this means employing an outside consultant.

. Periodic -- marketing operates in a dynamic environment so it makes sense that the audit should occur on a regular, periodic basis.

A.   The Costs of Auditing

The audit puts an organization and its people under scrutiny. Evaluations are made, people are "upset." Plus, the work involved is costly. One reason why audits should be periodic is to avoid the impression that the audit is aimed at making people "look bad."

B.   An Audit Outline

Audits usually begin with an organizational meeting and the setting of procedures, time frames, etc. The audit itself typically includes several sub-audits such as the following:

. Marketing environment audit, focusing on trends and forces in the environment.

. Marketing strategy audit, reviewing objectives and strategies and their compatibility with the environment.

. Marketing organization audit, determining the organization's ability to implement the strategies needed to operate in the environment.

. Marketing systems audit, investigating the quality of the organization's analysis, planning, and control systems.

. Marketing productivity audit, investigating the profitability of the marketing operation.

. Marketing function audit, evaluating the organization's marketing mix components.

Exhibit 22-13 lists questions (items) from a marketing audit "Request for Information Form." These show the areas of concern an audit is likely to address. Many similar checklists are available. None of them is complete, nor usable in all circumstances.

When the audit is completed and the last meeting is held, the real purpose of the audit is made manifest. The audit is not a goal in itself ... what is important is what management does with information in the audit and the debate and possible changes that information engenders.

The steps in the marketing audit are summarized in Exhibit 22-14.

C.   The Audit Team

There are similarities between the ways organizations handle audits and the way they handle new products. Here are several ways in which audits can be conducted:

.   By an outside firm or consultant.

.   By an internal department that regularly conducts audits.

.   By audit teams which "stay on" to manage the area of the organization they have monitored.

.   Organizing a "consulting division" within the firm that provides audits and other services.

Audit teams are likely to include such people as a marketing manager from some part of the organization not being audited, a non-marketing manager from another division, a marketing manager with a specialized technical background (if appropriate), someone totally unfamiliar with the marketing effort being studied, plus a few other individuals familiar with the problems faced by the unit to be audited.

D.   The Need for Marketing Audits

Marketing managers are often too busy "putting out fires" to pay close attention to things like marketing audits. Still, marketing operates in a dynamic environment and this is reason enough to scrutinize marketing activities to make sure they are as effective as they can be. In good times they can identify problems before they become big, in bad times they are even more necessary.

X.   TO WHOM IS MARKETING RESPONSIBLE?

There are many answers to this question; among them are the officers or owners of the business (and this is not far off the mark since it is they who are punishable for the organization's mistakes). But businesses face many publics as shown in Exhibit 22-15. These publics overlap.

We have just discussed the marketing audit. Similar is the **social audit,** where management reviews how its strategies and tactics affect society. The social audit investigates the firm's place in the macro marketing environment.

XI.   A CLOSING NOTE

At the start of the book, the authors stated that marketing is a fascinating subject, and hope the students agree with this. They hope they have answered some questions about marketing, though they admit there are many areas of gray in the field, and that today's answers may not fit tomorrow's questions. If the book helped instill the desire to ask more questions about marketing, it has done its job. The authors hope the reader is a satisfied customer.

XII.   SUMMARY

This chapter discussed implementation and control. It explained that all the elements of a marketing plan must come together as a synchronized, integrated marketing program. Strategic control, especially a marketing audit and a social, will help marketing managers evaluate their organization's marketing programs.

Learning Objective 1: Understand the nature of a marketing program, and describe the importance of implementation of a marketing strategy.

Effective marketing requires putting all the elements together into an integrated marketing program. This requires the proper implementation of new strategies, effective execution of continuing strategies, and control of the individual elements of the marketing mix. Marketing success depends on both strategy and implementation.

Learning Objective 2: Identify the functional activities involved in the implementation of a marketing strategy.

Organizing, leadership and interaction, resource acquisition and allocation, coordination and timing of activities, and information management are activities involved in implementing marketing strategies and tactics.

Learning Objective 3: Describe the major forms of organizations used by marketing managers to achieve their goals.

The effective marketing program cannot be implemented without assigning tasks and responsibilities. Responsibilities and authority are reflected in the organizational structure. There are several organizational types: the functional model, the geography-based model, the customer-based model, and the product-based model. Permeating all of these are the general organizational guidelines suggested by the marketing concept.

Learning Objective 4: Understand why marketing control is necessary.

Marketing managers can assess marketing performance through sales analysis, cost analysis, and profit analysis. By using all three methods, managers can gain several perspectives on marketing performance.

Learning Objective 5: Describe what is included in a marketing audit.

Organizations should periodically carry out the comprehensive appraisal of their marketing operations known as the marketing audit. Although a thorough investigation can be costly, the information it uncovers can be of inestimable value.

Learning Objective 6: Understand how the social audit helps marketing managers evaluate the organizations' impact on society.

The social audit is a means for reviewing whether an organization is accomplishing its mission in society, whether it is responsible not only to its customers, but also to competitors, government, and the general public. The social audit investigates the firm's place in the macromarketing environment.

XIII. KEY TERMS

XIV. QUESTIONS FOR DISCUSSION (9)

XV.   ETHICS IN PRACTICE

XVI. CASES

ANSWER GUIDELINES FOR CHAPTER 22 QUESTIONS FOR DISCUSSION

1.   *What are the characteristics of a good marketing program?*

ANSWER:

While the chapter does provide a list of characteristics of a good marketing program merely listing these is not enough. This question is truly a "discussion" question in that the characteristics should be mentioned and their often seemingly self-contradictory aspects discussed. Too, listing the characteristics of a good program is quite different from putting a good program together. This question can lead to lengthy class discussion as a result.

The characteristics of a good marketing program listed in the text are these:

- Integrated -- no element of the program stands alone. The elements are tightly interrelated.

- Strategically driven -- the organization possess a well developed strategy or plan and the marketing program is reflective of it.

- Internally consistent -- the parts work together and do not cancel one another out in any way.

- Coordinated -- the elements of the plan occur in the proper planned sequence.

- Stable -- the program must possess consistency over time. Product and/or company "image" is a factor that suggests this characteristic.

- Flexible -- the program must permit enough leeway to allow making adjustments needed in a dynamic environment.

2. *Consider a nonprofit organization with which you are familiar. Describe its marketing program.*

ANSWER:

Some likely candidates for this discussion are the local church, the YMCA, the symphony, a hospital, a private school, a zoo, and the United Way.

Because nonprofit organizations vary greatly in their marketing efforts (some seem to do nothing at all, others like United Way, are very well organized), this question might best be attacked by first listing the organizations chosen, outlining what is known of their marketing programs, then rating them on scales of complexity, effectiveness, and other variables, including the characteristics of a "good marketing plan" mentioned just above in A. 1.

3. *Describe the major features of the marketing organization. If a firm's organization chart incorporates these features, is that firm following the marketing concept in its activities?*

ANSWER:

The organization chart associated with the marketing concept incorporates two major features, whether it is a functional, geographic, customer-based, or other kind of chart. These two features are:

- There is a person responsible for marketing activities within the organization (or SBU, or other organizational division). This person is likely to have some title such as "Vice-President for Marketing."

- The person identified as the chief marketing officer has "under" him or her the various marketing subfunctions such as advertising, sales, etc.

The basic concept underlying these features is that the firm is expected to be customer-oriented and to have a customer-oriented, coordinated marketing program in place. The feeling is that this cannot be done unless there is someone in charge of organizing and coordinating this effort and that this person has the requisite "tools" (functions) to do the job.

A secondary point is that if the organization has a marketing officer equal to other corporate officers, e.g., a vice-president for marketing, the firm has acknowledged marketing's importance as a business function equal to the others (manufacturing, finance, etc.).

However, it should be noted that the fact that a firm can point to an organization chart that incorporates these features does not mean that the firm is practicing the marketing concept. No characteristic (high profits, letters of praise from customers, etc.) can prove the marketing concept is being followed. The concept is "mental," it is a philosophy of business. Organization charts may be outward signs that the company is trying to follow this philosophy of business but it does not prove it.

4.   *Choose any organization with which you are familiar and draw an organization chart for it. Now reorganize the firm by redesigning its organizational chart to reflect each of these major organization types: customer-based, product-based, and geography-based.*

ANSWER:

This question can be supplemented by a library assignment such as "Find out what the organization chart of XYZ Company is and then adjust it as the question suggests."

We think it is difficult to decide that a given chart is wholly customer-, geography-, or anything-else-based. Thus, students should be asked to defend the charts they draw. If a firm is organized into 12 territories within the U.S., is that geography-based? Or are there differences among the customers in those areas? Or ... further ... do they buy different products?

5.   *It has been suggested that it may be difficult to determine exactly what form of organization has provided the model for a particular firm's organization. Why is this the case?*

ANSWER:

The reason "this is the case" is complex. For one thing, most organizations are ... though perhaps not by design ... "combination organizations." Consider this: A car dealer has salespeople who sell used cars and salespeople who sell new cars. Also, the dealer has people who sell parts and some who sell repair services. How is this dealer organized?

By product? Maybe, since each type of salesperson sells a different product. By customer-type? Maybe, since a new car buyer is likely to differ from a used car buyer, a parts buyer or a buyer who needs repair work done. By function? In a way, since the function of repairing cars differs from the other functions mentioned. By geography? Well, at least a little bit since the used cars are out on a lot, the new cars inside, the repair garage across the street and the parts desk is in a wing of the repair garage.

6.   *Consider the examples of sales, cost, and profit data shown in this chapter's discussion of United Way of Mountain County. What other breakdowns of data not shown in the chapter would be of use to a marketing consultant working with United Way?*

ANSWER:

Many possible answers can be given to this question. One is mentioned in the text (costs by types of donors). However, this analysis is a form of research, thus the student should be able to defend the data he or she would like to see in terms of what "good" it might be; that is, what do we expect to be able to do with this information?

Among the additional breakdowns a consultant might like to see are:

.   More narrow geographic breakdowns than Metro I-IV.
.   Revenue by business broken down by specific company.
.   Revenue by workplace donor by individual company.
.   Revenue from foundations by specific foundation.
.   Revenue from non-workplace donor by location.
.   Breakdown of "other" donors in more detail.
.   Salaries and benefits by employee or employee type.
.   Expenses assigned to "annual campaign" broken down by specific donor groups and individual companies and foundations.

.   All of the above would mean that "profit" figures could be recalculated
        making Exhibit 22-12 far more detailed.

7.   *Describe the basic approach to information that underlies the marketing
        audit.*

ANSWER:

The basic approach is exemplified by the old image of the bank auditor who was
feared by all for his attention to detail, careful, methodical ways, and flinty-
eye stare. While the marketing audit is not intended to "scare" anyone as the
old bank auditor did, this careful and methodical approach to information is what
the marketing audit should reflect.

This is one reason that most articles and books on the marketing audit are heavy
on checklists and light on prose. The lists serve the purpose of helping an
auditor to remember "everything," and thus increase thoroughness.

It is our opinion that the reason the prose portion of the marketing audit
literature is awfully skimpy (for an idea that's been around for thirty years or
more) is that the audit, like marketing itself, is as much a state of mind or
philosophy as it is anything else. The marketing auditor tries, at a reasonable
level, to adopt the "other kind" of auditor's frame of mind and thus do a good
job. That being said, there is not much else to say ... that's why the "how to
conduct a marketing audit" literature is so rife with checklists and suggested
forms to use.

8.   *What sort of people should conduct a marketing audit? Should they be
        employees of the firm that is the subject of the audit?*

ANSWER:

In a sense, anyone whose services can be of use should be considered as a
potential auditor or member of an auditing team. The book notes that a "typical"
team might include a marketing manager familiar with the problems of the entity
being audited, a person with necessary technical background if this is
appropriate, a person unfamiliar with the problems at hand (to lend fresh
insight,) and so forth. These are the sorts of people commonly involved in the
auditing process and clearly many of them are employees of the firm. Note,
however, that a unit of the firm, not the firm as a whole, might be the subject
of the audit. Thus, these employees might be quite removed from the subject of
the audit.

Many authors suggest that the audit is best carried out by an experienced
consultant. This view makes sense in that such a person would ideally know what
he or she is doing but would also be enough removed from the process so as to be
totally candid.

In general, auditors should not be people whose "jobs are on the line" as a
result of the audit. If a consultant is not used, one of many forms of audit
team organizations might be used (as shown in the text). Reasons for not using
an outsider include expense, need for secrecy, need for a level of familiarity
with the firm or its products, and the availability within the firm of qualified
people.

9.   *What are some important questions you would like to have answered by a
        social audit?*

ANSWER:

As the text emphasizes, organizations are responsible to the individual who run
them and those people are responsible for the acts of their organizations. A
social audit allows management to review how the organization and its strategies
and tactics affect society. It serves as a means for reviewing whether an
organization is accomplishing its mission in society and is responsible not only
to its customers but also to its other publics in the macromarketing environment.

While students may generate additional questions, some typical issues addressed
in a social audit include:

- Are our products safe?
- How much nutritional information do consumers use and how much do they need?
- Is our distribution system without waste?
- Is our packaging environmentally friendly?
- Is our promotion fair and accurate?
- Have we engaged in any industrial espionage?
- Are all of our employees treated fairly and with respect?
- Are the counties and communities where we conduct business better or worse because of our presence?
- Are the directions for product usage clear and include all precautionary statements?

As students think of questions, each one should be defended against the counter-question, "What do you expect to learn from that?" or "What will you do if you get (or can't get) that information?" and "How will you approach obtaining that information?"

ETHICS EXERCISE 22

CHAPTER 22 ETHICS IN PRACTICE

Overview

In 1988, a Black and Decker Spacemaker Plus coffee maker caught fire apparently because the consumer who owned it did not correctly insert the water reservoir drawer. The incident led to testing which produced some evidence that a design flaw had made the product dangerous under normal usage conditions.

The case poses these questions.

- If you were the decision-maker at Black and Decker, would you recall the product?

- Should the recall effort be strongly pursued or would you conduct half-heartedly?

- Whatever you decide, what tactics would be needed to implement the decision?

A key here is the phrase "normal usage." Most consumer products of the type mentioned, manufactured in recent years, are virtually "idiot proof." Plugs can be inserted only the "right way," battery compartments are marked to show which way the batteries are to be installed or designed so that the only way they fit is the proper way, and so on. In this case it appears that a normal consumer, behaving in a normal manner, did not properly insert the water reservoir, a part that must be removed, filled, and inserted every time the product is used. Given that water and electricity don't mix, this part, probably above all others, should have been idiot-proofed.

The case does not tell us who did the testing, but says that testing provided some evidence that a design flaw could make the product hazardous. There are several qualifiers in that sentence, but it remains that there is at least some reason to think the product is flawed. Unless there is reason to believe that the consumer misused the product, and there is no suggestion of this here, some credence must be given to the possible seriousness of the situation.

Should there be a recall? The Black and Decker Company at first resisted a recall, saying that the coffee maker was perfectly safe. From a business and public relations perspective, this is a dangerous game. It is often easier and "safer" to withdraw the product from the market rather than risk law suits, bad press, or worse.

If there is a recall, Black and Decker could conduct it in a half-hearted way, hoping that most buyers were satisfied with the coffee makers, and/or never heard about the recall. The company could then claim it "tried" but relatively few appliances were turned in (as is often the case). This would be an unethical practice because, for one thing, some risk to personal safety is involved. On another level, the half-hearted approach would be wrong because a recall is supposed to be a recall, not a pretend recall. Thus, faking a recall would be unethical.

What in fact happened was that Black and Decker, at first resistant to a recall, tested the product further, and found other flaws. In a move that attests to both the honesty and the savvy of its managers, a recall was undertaken. The product is now off the market.

If a recall is undertaken, all reasonable steps to locate the affected consumers must be taken. The guarantee cards consumers (some of them) mail in after buying a product provide some record of ownership. However, consumers who returned the cards may have moved. A reasonable effort to locate them would include mailing them first class, i.e., forwardable letters, or calling the phone numbers the consumers provided. Of course, not everyone returns the guarantee cards when they buy appliances, and addresses and phone numbers change. Therefore, other measures to publicize the recall are appropriate, though not always effective. Releasing news of the recall to the media, and paying for radio and other announcements, are appropriate. If Black and Decker could show that it made a sincere effort to collect the names of purchasers, as by means of cards enclosed with the appliances (if the cards were postage-paid, so much the better), and if it made a reasonable effort to use the media to reach its buyers, the company would not be guaranteeing itself victory if sued by a consumer who was subsequently hurt by the product ... but such efforts would be very handy things to point to in a court case.

CHAPTER 22 TAKE A STAND QUESTIONS

1.   *An executive says "Our purpose is to make money for our stockholders. A social audit is a waste of time." Do you agree?*

The difficulty with this statement is that it says two things. One is that the organization's purpose is to make money for its stockholders. This is true, but it is not true that the organization's only purpose must be to make money for its stockholders. This is a primary duty, but others include obeying the law, keeping proper records, paying taxes, and many others.

The second part of the statement is that a social audit is a waste of time. Social audits can be defended from a selfish business perspective as being helpful in increasing profits, e.g., by avoiding the steely eyes and grasp of consumerists, government, protestors, and so on. All of these can end up costing many dollars (lawsuits, environmental clean-up fees, fines, assessments) and diminish the shareholders' profits, which this executive claims to want to augment.

From an ethical perspective, the social audit cannot be considered a waste of time, at least not dismissed out of hand as always being a waste of time (as the executive seems to suggest). Corporations are legal persons and cannot be permitted to do whatever they want to do in pursuit of profit, just as an individual cannot be permitted to do anything at all in pursuit of money. Dumping wastes in a river robs other citizens of the benefit of having clean water and, in effect, endangers them. People are realizing that such dumping is really not so different as robbing fellow citizens with a weapon.

Even the most ardent defenders of business, Theodore Levitt or Paul Harvey or Rush Limbaugh, would not agree that the social audit is a waste of time. They might disagree with conservationists on how much pollution is acceptable, but they would not state that the social consequences of business activities should be totally ignored, if only because they know that when businesses do "whatever they want," controlling legislation is sure to follow.

2.   *A Japanese company with manufacturing facilities in the United States, contributes to a local United Way campaign. Is this merely public relations?*

There is no way to answer this (absolutely) unless one can see into the mind of the executive(s) who decided to put the firm behind the United Way effort. Interestingly, even if the executive(s) cold-heartedly plotted the contribution strictly as a public relations gimmick, the contribution still did some good for the community.   And, if the executive kind-heartedly decided on the donation to repay and support the community strictly as an eleemosynary act it still garners publicity for the company.   A company manager would be shown in the newspaper presenting a check, or the firm would get a plaque to be displayed in the waiting room.   Even if the donation were given "in secret," at least some people in the community would find out about it, mention it to friends, etc.

If there were no contribution, or if the contribution given were very small, the company would still receive publicity ... bad publicity.   By giving a reasonable donation, the company cannot help but benefit public relations-wise.

Again, we cannot see into the mind of the executive(s) making this decision, but anyway you look at it, public relations sneaks in.

This is similar to the old question of whether or not there is such a thing as a selfish act.   (The professor might ask this question of the class.)   Many say that there is -- not because if I do a good deed and others find out about it, I am praised or otherwise rewarded, making the act not really unselfish.   If my good deed is not found out, even if I can keep myself from telling anyone, might I not, in my own mind, reflect on what a fine fellow I am?   Thus, again the act is not fully unselfish.

3.   *A national corporation operated a retail store in South Central Los Angeles.   The store was looted and severely damaged during the riots following the "Rodney King" verdict.   The company decided not to rebuild. Is this the right thing to do?*

Many would argue that the store owner paid dearly during the riots and, should he or she decide not to rebuild, well, who could blame them?   It is easy to say "They worked hard and look what they got for it."

Some would say that the store must have been "ripping off the people" and that's why it was looted.   While this is possible, the fact is that all kinds of businesses, owned by all kinds of people, were ruined in these riots.

Some would say that the store owner should rebuild because of one or more of the following reasons.   The students can think of others.

.   The community supported the business, at least until the riot.

.   The community needs the services provided by the store.

.   The store owner is a part of the community as are the people who live there.

.   If the store doesn't re-open, the neighborhood will decline further.

All of these are mostly "ethical" reasons, not business reasons.   Therefore they are very debatable.

A complicating variable could be added to the equation.   Suppose the store was fully insured and could be rebuilt at little or no direct cost to the owner. Would that obligate the owner to return?   It would not, but it would make it possible to return, an option not open to the merchant who was totally wiped out. The latter faces no question at all.

GUIDE TO CASES

VIDEO CASE 22-1 SEITZ CORPORATION[1]

FOCUS ON SMALL BUSINESS

SUBJECT MATTER: Total Quality Management, Relation of Manufacturing and Marketing, Internal Marketing, Measuring Success

Please see the Guide to Video Cases for video length and other information.

AT-A-GLANCE OVERVIEW

The Seitz Corporation, located in Torrington, Connecticut, manufactures thermoplastic mechanical drives, such as gears and pulleys, and perforated form "pin feed" tractors for printers. Family-owned and founded in 1949, Seitz's two plants employ 200 workers.

Seitz began as a small tool-making business and slowly grew. In the late 1960s, the company expanded its services to include custom injection molding. As the customer base grew to include leading printer manufacturers, Seitz developed and patented a proprietary line of perforated form-handling tractors. Utilizing its injection molding technology, the company engineered an all-plastic tractor, Data Motion, which replaced the costly metal version. By the late 1970s, business was booming, and Data Motion had become the world wide industry leader.

The 1980s, however, brought foreign competition to the business equipment market, and many of Seitz's customers relocated or closed shop altogether. Seitz started to feel the pinch as sales declined rapidly and profits eroded. Employment dropped from a high of 313 in 1985 to 125 workers in 1987. In order to restore growth and health to the company, drastic changes needed to be made.

In 1987, Seitz made a crucial decision to change the way it did business by implementing a formal five-year plan with measurable goals called "World-Class Excellence Through Total Quality." Senior management devoted countless hours to improving employee training and involvement. New concepts were explored and integrated into the business plan. Teams and programs were put into place to immediately correct deficiencies in Seitz's systems that were revealed in customer satisfaction surveys. All employees, whether they be machine operators or accountants, were taught that quality means understanding customers' needs and fulfilling them correctly the first time.

QUESTIONS

1. *What is the relationship between manufacturing operations and marketing in a total quality management program?*

Implementation of a total quality management program requires the allocation of people, dollars, technology and other resources to the marketing and production task. The number and quality of employees are an organization's human resources. Many strategies are improperly executed because the organization does not have an adequate number of experienced employees with the required skills. If the production people do not have resources to implement a quality program, the job will not be done.

If marketing people promise quality and production does not implement a total quality program, the strategy is sure to fail. In addition, since marketers are not simply "delivery boys" for the goods manufacturing produces, the efforts of marketers are part of the total quality management program. In short, both groups must work hard to bring about customer satisfaction.

2. *How important is internal marketing in Seitz's total quality management*

---

[1] Excerpts reprinted from *Strengthening America's Competitiveness* pp. 98-99, copyright 1991 by Connecticut Mutual Life Insurance Company.

program?

The term internal marketing is often used by marketers, especially service businesses and manufacturing operations, when referring to marketing efforts aimed at their own employees who have contact with the ultimate consumer or a consumer down the line in the manufacturing process. The objective of this marketing effort may be to have employees recognize their role in the organization's attempt to create customer satisfaction, and to fully understand that the quality of the work which the employee provides is essential to the firm's existence.

The Seitz Corporation created and implemented the "World-Class Excellence Through Total Quality" program to turn around a drastic decline in sales caused by foreign competition. By promoting and encouraging employee involvement in the success of the company, this program helped sales reach $19 million in 1990.

3.   *How can the effectiveness and efficiency of a total quality management program be measured?*

Traditionally defects, cost reductions, customer satisfaction, loss of goodwill, and other measures, both objective and subjective, indicate quality.

Although measuring the success of such a program can be difficult, especially in the subjective arena, thousands of dollars in cost-savings and two new products generating almost $1 million in sales have resulted since the program was implemented. The second goal, to restore the company's market share and sales revenue, can be more easily measured. Annual sales have grown from $10.8 million in 1987 to $19 million for 1990. Seitz's customer base has expanded from 312 in 1987 to 550 at the end of 1990. In 1989, Seitz International Japan (SIJ) was formed as a division of Seitz Corporation in order to recapture some of the market and technology lost to foreign competition. Starting from scratch, SIJ had sales over $3 million in 1989 and hopes to enjoy projected sales of $6.5 million in 1991.

VIDEO CASE 22-2   STEAM WAY INTERNATIONAL INCORPORATED[2]
FOCUS ON SMALL BUSINESS

SUBJECT MATTER: Market and Environmental Challenges, Cooperation in Channels, Adjusting to Marketing's Environment

Please see the Guide to Video Cases for video length and other information.

AT-A-GLANCE OVERVIEW

Founded in 1966 as one of the original manufacturers of the "steam" carpet cleaner, Steam Way quickly became a leader in the professional carpet and upholstery cleaning industry. By 1981, however, the founder had focused his attention on other enterprises and talked of liquidating Steam Way. Then vice-president, Ralph Bloss, purchased both the equipment and chemical divisions of the company and chose to try to restore its much depleted market share and regain Steam Way's name recognition.

As these decisions and changes were being made, several major obstacles developed. Steam Way relied mainly upon independent professional cleaning contractors, rather than franchises, as its customers. In 1986, DuPont, the largest manufacturer of carpet fiber in the world (65 percent market share), chose a national franchise as its recommended carpet cleaner for warranty work. This represented a legitimate threat to Steam Way and its customers. Also, environmental issues such as chemical safety, "right-to-know" laws, and waste water disposal were having an impact on the industry and needed to be addressed.

---

[2]Excerpts reprinted from *Strengthening America's Competitiveness*, pp. 22-23, copyright 1991 by Connecticut Mutual Life Insurance Company.

QUESTIONS

1.   *What changes, if any, should Steam Way make in its marketing program?*

Steam Way International, Inc., made a dynamic comeback when Ralph Bloss purchased the company and effectively merged a sound business plan with a genuine concern for the environment.

The company had to address both market-related and environment-related problems. This it did. Steam Way began holding important meetings with DuPont, exchanging useful information and agreeing to work together. Rather than wait for environmental problems to occur, Steam Way worked closely with representatives of the Environmental Protection Agency to avoid them. The company implemented recycling programs in its own operations and now sells only environmentally-safe products.

Steam Way has worked diligently to prove that a company with concern for the environment can work with regulatory agencies to establish techniques and products which are both economically sound and profitable. This aggressive approach to challenges was not without cost to Steam Way, but the results indicate significant progress. The Steam Way Power-Matic truck-mount is the single largest selling truck-mounted unit in the world. Steam Way's chemical line now ranks third in industry market share. In January of 1991, DuPont's Flooring System Division presented its Special Recognition Award to Steam Way for outstanding contribution to the entire carpet industry.

A policy was established to make all sales of Steam Way products through a network of independent, international distributors, thereby firmly establishing a vital link to the industry.

2.   *How will implementation of its plan influence Steam Way's success?*

This case shows that sometimes hard work and implementation of a strategy are the most important factors in success.

Bloss overcame the company challenges with the help of his two sons, R. Doyle Bloss, Vice President of Corporate Development, and Gregory Bloss, Vice President of Sales. In conjunction with Steam Way's loyal work force, they implemented an intense marketing plan using trade magazine advertising, association trade convention exhibition, direct mail and quarterly newsletters. Members of Steam Way's technical staff wrote articles that were published in industry trade publications. Steam Way's goal was to double its market share and sales in the first three years.

APPENDIX A

ARITHMETIC FOR BUSINESS ANALYSIS

Appendix A notes that the marketing concept stresses profitability as well as consumer orientation. Marketers thus need to know how to evaluate the organization's financial success.

The following financial/accounting tools are briefly explained. Arithmetic examples of how each is used are provided.

1)   The Profit and Loss Statement

The **profit and loss** or **operating statement** is explained using a retail operation as an example. Beginning with **gross sales,** and passing through **returns** and **allowances** to **net sales. Cost of goods sold, gross margin, operating expenses** are explained, and **net profit** calculated. This process is illustrated numerically in Exhibit A-1.

2)   Marketing Analysis and Performance Ratios

The purpose of **pro forma profit and loss statements** is discussed.   Then such ratios as **gross margin percentage, net profit percentage, returns and allowances percentage,** and **stock turnover ratio** (or **inventory turnover ratio**) are explained. How the organization might make use of these ratios is illustrated.

3)   Return on Investment

Return on investment was explained in Chapter 20 as the ratio of net profit to assets (or net worth.) Numerical information is taken from the profit and loss statement shown in Exhibit A-1 (also obtainable from the organization's **balance sheet**) and used to calculate the firm's return on investment (ROI) percentage.

4)   Break-Even Calculations

The break-even concept was discussed in Chapter 21. Here an organization's break-even point is calculated using simple selling price, variable cost, and fixed cost figures.

5)   Price Elasticity

Price elasticity was defined in Chapter 20 as the effect of a change of price on the quantity of a product demanded. A brief explanation of the price elasticity of demand formula is illustrated.

APPENDIX B

CAREER OPPORTUNITIES IN MARKETING

Appendix B presents brief explanations of the nature of several marketing careers, and some suggestions of additional marketing courses that would be useful to the marketing student interested in one of those career areas.

The following career positions are described.

1)   The Executive Level

The career of Beth Culligan, a 39-year old vice president at Sterling Drug, Incorporated, is described. The role of her college work is accented, as is the need for hard work to get to the level at which this executive operates.

Noting that few marketing students will start out at that level, the following career paths are outlined.

2)   Product and Brand Management

The job of brand managers/product managers is discussed, as is that of assistant brand manager or brand assistant and "what it takes" to work in these positions.

3)   Retail Management

The positions of buyer, department manager, and store manager are portrayed. There is frank discussion of the fact that "you either love retailing or you hate it." Fast-track positions offered by some retailers to recent graduates are described, as are the pride and pitfalls involved in owning your own retail business. The fact that retailing demands that one start out at lower than might be desired pay rates is noted, as is the other side of this ... that if one likes the work and perseveres, the monetary rewards can be high.

4)   Advertising

This often "glamorous" career is discussed frankly, not only in terms of what it takes to fill the various positions available in the field, but in terms of the hard work, rather than "glamour," that it entails. Advertising positions within agencies and within client firms are characterized.

5)   Public Relations

The nature of jobs in this field is described, as well as the various publics with which people in this profession must deal.

6)   Sales and Sales Management

That this is usually the logical starting point for a career in marketing is made clear in this section, as are the reasons why this is so often the case. Special skills, such as engineering or scientific abilities, are shown to be important in some sales positions. The difficulties associated with many sales careers cannot be denied, but the potential for "big money" is very real in various sales positions, especially for the self-motivated, hard worker.

7)   Distribution/Traffic Manager

The importance of this often forgotten area is stressed. The jobs of traffic manager/distribution manager and logistic manager and materials manager are described.

8)   Marketing Research

This, like advertising, is a field that may be misunderstood by students. The tasks of marketing researchers, whether in the firm's marketing research department or in the marketing research company, are discussed briefly.

9)   Your Second Course in Marketing

Completion of the introductory course suggests selecting subsequent courses. The advantages of particular courses are described, and a chart suggesting appropriate courses by career interest is offered. However, discussion with professors and other advisors is the major recommendation.